The Trademark Paradox

Schriften zum Medien-, Urheber- und Wirtschaftsrecht

Herausgegeben von Prof. Dr. Georgios Gounalakis

Band 20

PL ACADEMIC RESEARCH

Catherine M. Manley

The Trademark Paradox

Trademarks and Their Conflicting Legal and Commercial Boundaries

PL ACADEMIC RESEARCH

Bibliographic Information published by the Deutsche Nationalbibliothek
The Deutsche Nationalbibliothek lists this publication in the Deutsche Nationalbibliografie; detailed bibliographic data is available in the internet at http://dnb.d-nb.de.

Zugl.: Marburg, Univ., Diss., 2014

Library of Congress Cataloging-in-Publication Data
Manley, Catherine M., 1969- author.
The trademark paradox : trademarks and their conflicting legal and commercial boundaries / Catherine M. Manley.
pages cm
Dr. iur. Philipps-Universität Marburg 2014.
Includes bibliographical references.
ISBN 978-3-631-65643-3
1. Trademarks–Law and legislation–United States. 2. Trademarks–Law and legislation–European Union countries. I. Title.
K1555.M365 2015
346.2404'88–dc23
2014045965

D 4
ISSN 1867-1012
ISBN 978-3-631-65643-3 (Print)
E-ISBN 978-3-653-04912-1 (E-Book)
DOI 10.3726/978-3-653-04912-1

PL Academic Research is an Imprint of Peter Lang GmbH.

Peter Lang – Frankfurt am Main · Bern · Bruxelles · New York · Oxford · Warszawa · Wien

This publication has been peer reviewed.

www.peterlang.com

Table of Contents

Acknowledgements

This paper was accepted for submission in June 2014 by the Faculty of Law at Phillips-Universität Marburg and forms part of the requirements necessary to fulfill the degree of Doctor of Jurisprudence (*Dr. iur.*).

Without the assistance and support of Professor Dr. Georgios Gounalakis, this paper would not have been possible. His passionate interest in and deep knowledge of intellectual property law, coupled with his engaging and pragmatic approach, make working with him both intellectually rewarding and professionally enjoyable. I am further grateful for his efforts to help me navigate the administrative requirements for submitting this paper in such a timely fashion.

I further owe sincere thanks to Professor Dr. Florian Möslein, for so promptly reviewing, preparing, and submitting his evaluation.

I am deeply indebted to Dr. Nadine Herrmann, for encouraging me to follow this course of study in the first place, for giving me the time and space to write this paper, and for convincing me that I could complete it long before it otherwise would have been finished. I am grateful for her support and, more important, her friendship.

Very special thanks go to Dr. Klaus Winker. His balanced insights as to how this paper needed to change helped make it good, and his impressive talent as a journalist and an editor helped make it better. Alongside his professional advice, I am fortunate to have had his company and support.

I could not have completed this without the extraordinary friendship of my sister, Audrey Mina Manley. Without her unending support, patience, humor, and conviction in me, I could not have done this, or much else, in the past few years.

Finally, I dedicate this work to my parents, Maya and Edward Manley, whose never-ending support and love have guided me through this as well as every chapter of my life, and who continue to inspire me with their unwavering dedication to "do good work".

Frankfurt am Main, November 2014 Catherine M. Manley

"...the creation or recognition by courts of a new private right may work serious injury to the general public, unless the boundaries of the right are definitely established and wisely guarded."[1]

Justice Brandeis[2]

0. Introduction

0.1 The Trademark Paradox

It would be almost impossible to imagine a world without trademarks. From the moment we wake up (turning off the Sony alarm clock, showering under the Hansgrohe shower head, getting into our BMW to drive to work, stopping for a Starbucks coffee, turning on our Dell computer, opening up our Microsoft office programs, searching for something on Google, making a call on our Samsung smartphone, checking emails on our Blackberry, quenching our thirst with a Coca-Cola, or buying a book on Amazon) until the end of the day (when we can finally enjoy a glass of Veuve Cliquot with friends), we interact – whether consciously or unconsciously – with a constant parade of trademarks, each vying for our attention and selection.

Trademarks play a fundamental role in our everyday lives as consumers as well as in the market in general. They help us distinguish the products we like and avoid those that we don't, acting as a short-hand signal to give us certainty of what product we have chosen. They give us information about the source, manufacturer, or quality of the products we are purchasing, allowing us to make such choices quickly and efficiently. They allow companies to differentiate their products from those of their competitors, and to invest in and build brand (i.e., customer) loyalty, without fear of free-riding by competitors.

This paper examines the legal and commercial paradox we face with respect to trademarks. Trademarks are the essence of competition – in fact, they signal competition – since without competition there would be no need to distinguish

---

1 *International News Service v. Associated Press*, 248 U.S. 215, 262–63 (1918) (Brandeis, J., dissenting).

2 Associate Justice Louis Dembitz Brandeis was appointed to the U.S. Supreme Court by President Wilson. He took his judicial oath on 5 June 1916 and retired on 13 February 1939. *U.S. Supreme Court*: Members of the Supreme Court.

between the goods of one company from those of another. Robust trademark laws prevent unfairness between (or free riding by) competitors, ensuring protection of the business goodwill represented by a mark. They diminish customer confusion and deception. They make "communication" between seller and buyer simple. Trademarks are "an essential element in the system of undistorted competition",[3] acting as "aids to the exchange of commodities … considered … vitally important to the protection of commerce".[4]

However, the significant legal expansions in trademark protection coupled with the aggressive commercial strategies used by trademark owners – although made within the framework of *promoting* competition by combating free rider problems – have served to *restrict* competition by erecting overly-protectionist and often insurmountable barriers to market entry. The paradox lies in how we have dealt with this conflict: in our insatiable quest to promote competition, we have granted, and continue to grant, trademark owners new private rights and expanded claims without ensuring adequate boundaries of such rights, which has resulted, paradoxically, in a stifling of competition. We have failed to balance the private interests (increased protection of the investments made in the business goodwill of a trademark) with the public interests (ensuring robust market competition without restraints or barriers to trade).

In this regard, Justice Brandeis' admonition, made almost a century ago in *International News Service v. Associated Press*, is well worth remembering:

> "… with the increasing complexity of society, the public interest tends to become omnipresent; and the problems presented by new demands for justice cease to be simple. Then the creation or recognition by courts of a new private right may work serious injury to the general public, *unless the boundaries of the right are definitely established and wisely guarded*."[5]

---

3 Case C-10/89, *SA CNL-SUCAL NV v HAG GF AG*, 17 October 1990 [1990] ECR I-3711 (*HAG II*), para. 13.

4 In the *Trade-Mark Cases*, the Supreme Court noted that the use of trademarks "as aids to the exchange of commodities in the great markets of the world is so generally recognized, and they are considered … vitally important to the protection of commerce". *United States v. Steffens, United States v. Wittemann*, and *United States v. Johnson* (collectively, the *Trade-Mark Cases*) 100 U.S. 82 (17 November 1879).

5 *International News Service v. Associated Press*, 248 U.S. 215, 262–263 (1918) (Brandeis, J., dissenting) (emphasis mine). In this landmark case, the U.S. Supreme Court upheld an injunction prohibiting the International News Service from publishing news gathered and published by the Associated Press. In the case, the Court struggled to distinguish between interference with business practices versus interference with intellectual property rights. Although the Court upheld the common law rule that there

(a) The Problem: Where are we?

Long before they were defined or protected as trademarks, trade names, service marks, logos, or brands, identifying marks were put on a variety of items – including pottery, bricks, tiles, swords, cloth, books, wine, bread, medicines, gold, silver, and pewter – in order to signal ownership, source, or quality.[6]

In today's modern and global marketplace, however, trademarks no longer function as mere ownership marks, source identifiers, or assurances of quality. Trademarks today are classified among the most important competitive business assets a company may own.[7] They are big business, high value, aggressively protected, commercial assets. They are used to communicate the persona of a business to consumers worldwide and deemed an essential part of a comprehensive global business strategy.[8] In essence, they are bearers of information, signals of investment, and tools of influence, identity, and trust. Where rhetoric has been called the "art of persuasion", trademarks could be called the "symbols of persuasion" to gain customer loyalty and thus secure market share.

---

is no copyright in facts, they instead found a limited "quasi-property" right in the economic value of the news when it was first published. The Court found the actions by International News Services as a misappropriation of such right, thus expanding the common law doctrine of misappropriation through the tort of unfair competition (weaving property and unfair competition principles together). In Justice Brandeis' famously vigorous and long dissent – the dissent runs 19 pages, whereas the majority opinion is only 8 pages long – Brandeis objected primarily to two aspects of the majority position. First, he seriously questioned the Court's recognition of a property right in news, finding it unbounded and giving rights in almost endeavour. Second, Brandeis found the Court had ignored the public's interest in the dissemination of news, an omission he found deeply disturbing. For a review of the majority opinion, as well as Justice Holmes' separate opinion and Justice Brandeis' dissent (that both raise serious questions as to the necessity and wisdom of recognizing property rights in news), see *Samuelson*: Information as Property, pp. 391–395.

6 Many scholars have traced the use of distinguishing marks from antiquity to present day. See, for example, *Rogers*: Some Historical Matter Concerning Trade-Marks; *Schechter*: Historical Foundations; *Ruston*: On the Origin of Trademarks; *Paster*: Trademarks – Their Early History; *Diamond*: The Historical Development of Trademarks; *McClure*: Trademarks and Unfair Competition; *Port*: The Illegitimacy of Trademark Incontestability; *McKenna*: The Normative Foundations of Trademark Law; *Fezer*: Markenrecht, Geschichte des Markenrechts, paras. 2–17; and *Cornish/Llewelyn/Aplin*: Intellectual Property.

7 They have been called "essential business assets". *Klieger*: Trademark Dilution, p. 790. See also *Drescher*: The Transformation and Evolution of Trademarks.

8 *Klett/Sonntag/Wilske*: Intellectual Property Law in Germany, p. xxviii.

As the commercial significance and financial value of trademarks have increased, so too the instances for abuse. There is the traditional abuse by competitors wanting to "free ride" on the success of a well-known trademark – i.e., to ride on the coat-tails of a well-known trademark in order to benefit from the power of attraction, the reputation, and the prestige of such mark, without paying the requisite financial compensation – by passing off their goods as those of the famous mark. There is also related "copycat confusion" or "ambush marketing".[9] Solving the "free rider", passing-off, and ambushing problem has prompted much of the expansion in modern trademark law.

As trademarks' power to persuade has grown (to increase product sales and gain market share), so too have the efforts by trademark owners to aggressively seek and claim expanded legal protection to keep such market value, whether in the courts or through effective bullying tactics outside of the courtroom. This too can be a form of abuse, resulting in expansive, and arguably excessive, rights. Dominant trademark owners today have broad rights that ensure their trademarks – along with an expansive swath of goodwill associated with those trademarks and the business enterprise – are not sullied (tarnished), imitated, or even tangentially referenced.

This expansive increase in legal rights and commercial power has occurred without corresponding limitations – or defined boundaries – either within the trademark laws themselves or through consistently applied competition or unfair trade practice principles. As a result, instead of functioning as origin, source, or quality identifiers intended *to protect consumers* and thereby ensure a fair and efficient market, trademarks are strategically used by owners *to erect barriers to trade* – against competitors, against foreign market participants, and against other intellectual property owners. Trademark laws have not effectively dealt

---

9 Ambush marketing is an attempt by a third party to associate itself directly or indirectly with a major event (through association with the event's trademark or logo) to benefit from the goodwill or prestige of that event without having to pay for that privilege as an official sponsor would do. The effect is that consumers associate the event with non-sponsors, rather than with the official sponsors. There have been many examples of the ambushing of high profile events, in particular of sporting events. Ambushing can take place at the actual event, or months before it, in different locations, media etc. See generally, *Louw*: Ambush Marketing & the Mega-Event Monopoly. For an overview of many well-known cases of ambush marketing, including Michael Jordan at the 1992 Barcelona Olympics, Dutch fans at the 2006 FIFA World Cup in Germany, and Ling Ning at the 2008 Beijing Olympics, see *Sports Career Consulting*: Lesson 8.4 – Ambush Marketing.

with the consequences of having granted expanded rights – they have allowed trademark rights to become "untethered" from their "traditional moorings".[10] Although competition laws are suitable to address specific practices or prohibit illegal, unfair, or deceptive business practices, they have side-stepped the problems of powerful trademarks stifling competition. In the end, competition laws may not be the most suitable mechanism to align or "fix" the trademark paradox.

(b) The Reasons: How did we get here?

This configuration – of new but improvidently granted rights – is similar to the issues the justices faced in *International News Service*.[11] There, the majority held the position that courts can treat "any civil right of a pecuniary nature as a property right" and that "the right to acquire property by honest labor or the conduct of a lawful business is as much entitled to protection as the right to guard property already acquired."[12]

In his separate opinion,[13] Justice Holmes[14] began by observing that property rights are creations of law: they do *not* arise automatically from value, even if that value is exchangeable. Instead, they depend on a legal judgment that recognizing a right to exclude is *needed* to protect against unwarranted interferences. Justice Holmes suggested that the majority was wrong in creating a new right to protect interests. Where protection can be afforded *without* granting a right to exclude – *in particular when unfair competition principles can be applied to resolve the dispute* – Holmes felt it unnecessary to create new property rights to resolve the problem.[15]

The same can be said of trademarks. In allowing trademark protection to expand – including the introduction of "new" rights to resolve free rider and ambush marketing concerns – we have developed quasi-property rights in the "business persona" imbued in the trademark. We have done so without adequately considering the rationales for such expansion, whether principles already

---

10 *Travis*: The Battle for Mindshare, para. 7.

11 *International News Service v. Associated Press*, 248 U.S. 215 (1918).

12 *International News Service v. Associated Press*, 248 U.S. 215, 236 (1918). See also *Samuelson*: Information as Property, p. 389.

13 *International News Service v. Associated Press*, 248 U.S. 215, 246 (1918) (Holmes, J., separate opinion, with McKenna, J., concurring).

14 Associate Justice Oliver Wendell Holmes, Jr. was appointed to the U.S. Supreme Court by President Roosevelt. He took his judicial oath on 8 December 1902 and retired on 12 January 1932. *U.S. Supreme Court*: Members of the Supreme Court.

15 *Samuelson*: Information as Property, p. 392.

exist to resolve these problems, or the effects of such expansion on competition and the market.

From a legal rationale perspective, trademark protection was never intended to reward *owners* for an invention or artistic work,[16] which is traditionally the reason justifying the exclusive rights granted to patent and copyright owners. Instead, trademark law was – and still fundamentally is – based on principles of unfair competition[17] – i.e., it was developed in order to protect *consumers* from confusion. Patents and copyrights protect inventions and writings, allowing owners to prevent others from making, selling, using, or exploiting that invention or writing. A trademark merely allows to owner to bar others from use of that mark, but does not allow an owner to bar others from making a similar product. The relevant analysis in any trademark infringement (or unfair competition) action is whether the defendant's mark is likely to cause consumer confusion, mistake, or deception.[18] Initially, the scope of such consumer confusion was narrow: the laws and the courts only permitted trademark infringement between direct competitors in an industry.[19] Today, the standards for infringement are far broader, covering not only "actual" confusion, but a likelihood of confusion, whether in a competing market or *even markets not yet entered into*.

Furthermore, since trademarks can, in theory, be protected indefinitely, the traditional trade-off underlying patent and copyright protection – the short-term grant of exclusive rights in exchange for the long-term contributions to the public domain – does not apply to trademarks. The expanded rights granted to trademarks thus have a far more appreciable, and lasting, effect.

---

16 Although the rights granted trademark owners do in essence "reward" owners who have invested in producing a quality product, the protection is fundamentally intended to protect against consumer confusion by guaranteeing the origin of the goods and their quality.

17 "The law of trade-marks is but a part of the broader law of unfair competition." *United Drug Co. v. Theodore Rectanus Co.*, 248 U.S. 90, 97 (1918).

18 The Lanham Act defines infringement as any "use in commerce … likely to cause confusion, or to cause mistake, or to deceive." 15 U.S.C. § 1114(1)(a). The basic inquiry is the same whether an action is brought as a trademark infringement or unfair competition action. "Both the traditional common law and statutory regimes view the issue of consumer confusion as the *sine qua non* of infringement." *Denicola*: Trademarks as Speech, p. 162.

19 *Klieger*: Trademark Dilution, fn 29, citing *Schechter*: The Rational Basis of Trademark Protection, pp. 820–822.

Finally, trademark rights – similar to other intellectual property rights – are inherently territorial and national by nature.[20] Given the expanding uses of trademarks worldwide, crossing territorial boundaries where the laws may be different has added yet another layer to the complexity. Today, the top global brands are just that: global. They are known worldwide by name or by logo. They act as international "ambassadors" across languages, cultures and laws. Divergent national legal rights are coming more and more into conflict, testing both national laws' and businesses' ability to deal with conflicting laws, policies and trends. Particularly in the EU, trademarks' inherently exclusive and territorial nature have been seen as impediments to the creation of a single market.

Because of these fundamental differences in rationale, scope, and duration, as well as the tension between territorial protection and international use and reputation, it has been difficult to apply general intellectual property rationales (which were developed primarily with patents and copyrights in mind) or competition law principles and restrictions to trademark use.[21] These differences highlight the different interests (from the perspective of trademark owners) and challenges (from the perspective of law makers) that we face with respect to trademarks.

(c) The Consequences: Where are we headed?

Although courts today understand and recognize the value of trademarks,[22] there is no systematic or consistent application of legal restrictions dealing with them.

---

20 Although a number of international treaties and European directives and regulations have sought to harmonize the various national laws relevant to the protection of intellectual property, with harmonization of trademark rights being the most successful to date, "the protection of intellectual property remains to a large extent characterized by national idiosyncrasies". *Klett/Sonntag/Wilske*: Intellectual Property Law in Germany, p. xxviii. See infra, § 3.3(b) for a discussion of the EU trademark harmonization efforts.

21 For example, it would be very awkward to apply the compulsory license requirements under EU competition law on a dominant trademark owner. How would trademark "A" be licensed for use by the owner of trademark "B" who is having difficulty entering the market? Furthermore, how is dominance calculated for the trademark "market"? Is it the single trademarked product or the enterprise value of the trademark owner (which led to its dominance)?

22 "Trade mark rights are, it should be noted, an essential element in the system of undistorted competition which the Treaty seeks to establish and maintain. Under such a system, an undertaking must be in a position to keep its customers by virtue of the quality of its products and services, something which is possible only if there are

To date, neither intellectual property laws nor competition rules have developed a mature or coherent legal regime to manage the ways in which trademarks are used in our modern, global market place. Depending on the current political situation, the economic marketplace, and even the country registering the trademarks, the laws and policies applied to trademark use and protection have experienced pendulum swings of either unabated rights or micro-managing.

Currently, the competition rules and legal guidance either ignore trademarks from discussions of intellectual property (e.g., they are specifically excluded from both the U.S. and the EU competition guidelines on the licensing intellectual property) or approach them from an irrelevant or impractical point of view (e.g., the EU guidelines refer to their "ancillary" relationship to other intellectual property rights). Trademark owners – and in particular dominant trademark owners – have taken advantage of this imbalance and have, through aggressive litigation and bullying business tactics, incrementally pushed out the contours of trademark protection, in some cases created *new* rights, to expand the scope of trademark rights. What we have failed to do with such increased private right, in Justice Brandeis' words, is "prescribe limitations and rules for its enjoyment; and also to provide administrative machinery for enforcing the rules."[23]

(d) The Future: What alternatives do we have?

This paper will first highlight some of the legal and commercial conflicts we face with respect to trademarks and their modern system of protection. It will then conclude by suggesting principles and guidelines to resolve the imbalance.

Trademarks are a vital part of our lives – for businesses, for consumers, and for competitors. The fundamental principles underlying trademark protection still apply today, adapted and augmented as needed in our modern society. Although courts and policy makers have allowed imprudent expansion of private trademark rights, there are sufficient public interest principles and guidelines available to rebalance such imprudent expansion. The principles underlying trademark laws are good; they simply need some good "gardening" – i.e., pruning of the

---

distinctive marks which enable customers to identify those products and services. For the trade mark to be able to fulfil this role, it must offer a guarantee that all goods bearing it have been produced under the control of a single undertaking which is accountable for their quality." Case C-10/89, *SA CNL-SUCAL NV v HAG GF AG*, 17 October 1990 [1990] ECR I-3711, para. 13 (*HAG II*).

23 *International News Service v. Associated Press*, 248 U.S. 215, 262–263 (1918) (Brandeis, J., dissenting).

excess and establishment of well-defined borders – when being applied by courts and national authorities. Furthermore, in the spirit of Justice Holmes' suggestion, there are existing unfair competition laws in place which can be applied to resolve the dispute. By pruning the trademark expansion and re-applying unfair competition principles, we could abate the pendulum swings of over- and under-exuberance, resulting in a more measured and consistent approach to trademark use, protection, and exploitation, benefiting businesses, consumers, and the market.

0.2 Scope & Overview

(a) Trademarks & Society

Chapter 1 begins with a review of the historical functions and foundations of trademarks, and examines the contours of trademark law which continue to be revised in response to business and social demands. Chapters 2 and 3 look at the legal frameworks in which trademark rights were developed in the U.S. (Chapter 2) and the EU (Chapter 3), reviewing the fundamentals which govern their rights today.

These three chapters demonstrate that the function of trademarks in our society today has evolved significantly from an original means of source identification intended to prevent consumer confusion and minimize consumer search costs to a profitable and commercially powerful means by which companies communicate a wealth of information regarding their business as an enterprise (and not just the product they are selling). Trademarks today are big money, big business, competitive assets.

(b) Trademarks & Competition

With any exercise (and certainly with any expansion) of rights, concerns regarding the anti-competitive effects of such rights are raised. Even if additional rights are granted under the rationale of *promoting* competition, such expanded rights can serve to *restrict* competition. As a result, although trademarks act as important aids to competition (by prohibiting free-riding) and benefit consumers (by decreasing confusion and preventing fraudulent trade practices), their commercial dominance in the global market today, coupled with the expanding legal protections afforded under current laws, can have the effect of restraining free and fair trade.

Competition laws seek to minimize or prohibit anti-competitive effects which arise from the acquisition, exploitation, or enforcement of power in the market.

The exercise of intellectual property rights – including trademarks – are certainly not immune from the scrutiny of competition laws. Chapters 4 – 6 thus explore the collision of intellectual property and competition laws in order to review how the granting of exclusive rights under intellectual property laws directly or indirectly conflicts with the restrictions on monopoly and monopolistic behaviour underlying competition rules.

Chapter 4 sets out the overall issues and challenges of the collision. Chapter 5 (for the U.S.) and Chapter 6 (for the EU) analyze how competition laws have been applied to the obtainment, grant, acquisition, and exercise of intellectual property rights – in particular with respect to trademarks – to determine whether the application of competition laws to the exercise of trademark rights has been successful to combat the anti-competitive effects of trademark use and protection. Chapters 5 and 6 also acknowledge the political and social frameworks which shaped the development of antitrust and competition laws, and looked at how such laws have been and are applied to promote and maintain "fair" market competition by regulating anti-competitive conduct.

(c) Conflicting Commercial & Legal Boundaries

With this background of trademarks, competition, and the collision of intellectual property rights and competition restrictions, Chapters 7 and 8 highlight the commercial and legal challenges courts, legislatures, and regulatory authorities are faced with when analyzing the competitive and anti-competitive effects of trademark use, protection, and exploitation. Trademarks are pro-competitive, essential to fair and efficient competition. Chapters 7 and 8 make the observation, however, that the expanding legal protection afforded trademarks coupled with the aggressive commercial strategies used by trademark owners – made under the guise of *promoting* competition – has served to *restrict* competition.

Chapter 8 takes the position that neither the trademark rules nor the competition rules adequately address these issues. Although developments and changes in law are *vital* to adapt our laws to a mature and modern society, what is problematic is our failure to establish (and "wisely" guard, in Justice Brandeis' words) the boundaries of such developments or to address the anti-competitive effects of such changes. Chapter 8 posits that both intellectual property law and competition laws need to recognize the position of trademarks and address these issues accordingly, but that neither can do the work intended of the other. In fact, there are other well-established mechanisms available which might be better suited than competition rules to regulate the anti-competitive effects of trademark. This observation will lay the groundwork for Chapter 9 – "Striking a Balance".

(d) Striking a Balance

Recognizing the growing anti-competitive effects of trademarks (through the strong brand personalities they exude) and trademark law (through the expanded legal protection trademarks have been afforded) is one thing; determining what, if anything, can be done about such effects is quite another. Any solution needs to *balance* the pro-competitive functions of trademarks with the anti-competitive effects of their protection in order to achieve some reasonable measure of "workable competition".[24]

A balanced approach – in the words of Samuelson – "is not a decision between … extremes". Instead, solutions can be found in "the degree to which public policy should do less or more to modify the operation of particular private economic activities." Chapter 9 identifies two pragmatic principles which can be applied to "do less or more". These relate to (i) the nature and functions of trademark and trademark laws, and (ii) the legislative and judicial framework which informs and protects the same. These principles are based on well-developed (but now somewhat marginalized) doctrines and balance competing private and public interests (from the perspectives of trademarks owners, competitors, competition authorities, legislatures) to ensure efficient working of our modern, competitive economy.

The Conclusion summarizes the issues and the key lessons learned in 10 theses.

0.3 Sources, Citations & Legal Framework

(a) Sources & Citations

Primary source material comes from U.S., German, and EU founding documents (e.g., the U.S. Constitution, the German Basic Law – the *Grundgesetz*, and the EU treaties), along with material from U.S., English, German, and EU courts, legislative authorities, and other regulatory bodies. Secondary literature comes primarily from sources in the U.S., England, and Germany.

As has been sagely observed: "There are two golden rules for the citation of legal authorities. One is consistency. The other is consideration for the reader."[25] I have adopted somewhat of a hybrid style of legal citation to enable both a U.S.

---

24 *Samuelson*: Problems of Economic Organization, p. 74.

25 *Meredith/Nolan*: Oxford University Standard for the Citation of Legal Authorities (OSCOLA).

and an EU-trained professional to understand the references and thereby locate the materials as easily as possible. I have tried to be consistent yet considerate.

For U.S. materials, I have both followed and deviated from the standard conventions as set out in the BlueBook and the ALWD Manual,[26] with a generous nod to Richard Posner.[27] For EU materials (including individual Member State materials), I have adopted key aspects of the citation method suggested by Oxford University and Oxford University Press.[28]

---

26 In the US, there are myriad styles and conventions for legal citation. The two most widely used set of citation rules for law students are those found in The BlueBook and the ALWD Manual. The BlueBook is compiled and edited by The Columbia Law Review Association, Inc., The Harvard Law Review Association, the University of Pennsylvania Law Review, and The Yale Law Journal Company, Inc. It is so named because its cover is blue. It is currently in its 19th edition. *The Bluebook*: A Uniform System of Citation. The ALWD Manual is compiled by the Association of Legal Writing Directors. It is currently in its 5th edition. *ALWD Citation Manual*: A Professional System of Citation. Competing with these two is the University of Chicago Manual of Legal Citation, known as the "Maroonbook", which is used by journals published at the University of Chicago Law School. *University of Chicago Law Review*: The MaroonBook. Many state courts require citations to conform to The Bluebook, the ALWD, or their own state citation rules. For example, New York, California, Texas, and Michigan all have their own state court citation rules. Attorneys in those states must know which citation style is required and adapt accordingly, depending on whether their documents are being filed in federal or state court. For a list of court-specific citation requirements, see Appendix 2 of the ALWD Manual. Finally, the U.S. Supreme Court has it own citation requirements and uses it own style in its opinions. *Shapiro/Geller/Bishop/Hartnett/Himmelfarb*: Supreme Court Practice. For a review of some of the peculiarities of the Supreme Court style, see *Hopwood*: Matters of Practice: Citations and Quotations in U.S. Supreme Court Briefs. Finally, outside of university law journals, most professional legal publishers have their own styles. Finally, for a thoughtful review of the history of U.S. legal citation and the "undesirable effects of this devotion to citation form", including "the unintended, but real, effect the present citation system has in impeding free and open access to the law", see *Gallacher*: Cite Unseen.

27 In 2011, Richard Posner, currently a judge on the United States Court of Appeals for the Seventh Circuit in Chicago, wrote an article questioning the art of U.S. legal citation and offering his own short manual of citation forms. His idea: have a clear system, but not something that impedes reading. *Posner*: The BlueBook Blues, p. 855. As a point of interest, in 1986, 25 years earlier, Posner welcomed the introduction of the Maroonbook, noting that it "mounted a bold challenge to the Bluebook's hegemony", was "a refreshing contrast to the Bluebook", and corrected most of the "particular faults of the Bluebook". *Posner*: Goodbye to the Bluebook, p. 1343.

28 *Oxford University*: Legal Research & Mooting Skills Programme; and *Oxford University Press*: Citing of Legal Materials (Including Legal Tables).

(b) U.S. Federal Laws, Courts & Precedence

For a reader not knowledgeable about the U.S. legal system, understanding the U.S. legal framework and court system – and in particular its division between state and federal laws, and state and federal court systems – can be perplexing. The following is a high-level overview of some key aspects to keep in mind.

(i) Constitution: Federal Government

The U.S. Constitution – written in 1787, ratified in 1788, and in operation since 1789[29] – is the supreme law of the land in the United States. It creates the federal system of government in which power is shared between the U.S. federal government and the individual state governments.[30] The federal government is supreme

29 The United States Constitution is deemed the world's longest surviving written charter of government. *Office of the Secretary of the Senate*: Constitution of the United States. For a transcript of the Constitution, see *U.S. National Archives and Records Administration*: U.S. Constitution. The Declaration of Independence (4 July 1776) announced to the world the separation of the thirteen colonies from Great Britain and the establishment of the United States of America. The document, however, did not establish or give authority to a national government. It was only on 1 March 1781, that the Articles of Confederation – the first attempt at a constitution for the United States– went into force. *U.S. National Archives and Records Administration*: The First Constitution – The Articles of Confederation. The first draft of the U.S. Constitution was presented to the delegates of the Constitutional Convention in Philadelphia on 6 August 1787; a revised version was presented on 12 September 1787 and signed by the delegates on 17 September 1787. *U.S. National Archives and Records Administration*: A More Perfect Union. On 21 June 1788, the requisite number of nine (from the 13 founding) states ratified the Constitution. In *Owings v. Speed*, 18 U.S. 420 (1820), the Supreme Court held that the Constitution did not formally replace the Articles of Confederation until 4 March 1789, since there was a need for a transitional period following the ratification. *Rodgers*: United States Constitutional Law: An Introduction.

30 *U.S. Administrative Office of the U.S. Courts*: Comparing Federal and State Courts. The Tenth Amendment (part of the Bill of Rights) provides that any powers that are not enumerated in the Constitution are reserved for the states: "The powers not delegated to the United States by the Constitution, nor prohibited by it to the states, are reserved to the states respectively, or to the people." U.S. Constitution, Amendment X (1791). See also *U.S. National Archives and Records Administration*: The Charters of Freedom: Bill of Rights.

with regard to those powers expressly or implicitly delegated to it,[31] but states remain supreme in matters reserved to them.[32]

Article I of the U.S. Constitution establishes the legislative branch of the federal government, consisting of a Senate and a House of Representatives.[33] Article I, Section 8, lists the enumerated powers delegated to Congress.[34] These powers

---

31 Article VI, clause 2 (known as the "Supremacy Clause") provides that the federal laws are the highest form of law in the U.S. legal system, and mandates that the Constitution and federal law will take precedence over state law when a conflict arises between federal law and either the state constitution or state law of any state: "This Constitution, and the Laws of the United States which shall be made in Pursuance thereof; and all Treaties made, or which shall be made, under the Authority of the United States, shall be the supreme Law of the Land; and the Judges in every State shall be bound thereby, any Thing in the Constitution or Laws of any state to the Contrary notwithstanding". For a review of the background of the Supremacy Clause, including its discussion in the Federalist Papers, see *McAffee*: The Dilemma of American Federalism, p. 383 and fn. 95 and 96. In *McCulloch v. Maryland*, 17 U.S. (4 Wheat.) 316, 4 L. Ed. 579 (1819), Chief Justice John Marshall, who led the Supreme Court from 1801 to 1835, expressly invoked the supremacy clause, referring to the invalidity of state action incompatible with federal laws. *Currie*: The Constitution in the Supreme Court, pp. 934–935. Today, the U.S. Senate deems the Supremacy Clause "the most important guarantor of national union. It assures that the Constitution and federal laws and treaties take precedence over state law and binds all judges to adhere to that principle in their courts." *Office of the Secretary of the Senate*: Constitution of the United States.

32 Today, the U.S. is comprised of the 50 states (Hawaii joined as the 50th state in August 1959; *U.S. National Archives and Records Administration*: Hawaii Statehood), the District of Columbia, and numerous territories (American Samoa, Federated States of Micronesia, Guam, Midway Islands, Northern Mariana Islands, Puerto Rico, Republic of Palau, Republic of the Marshall Islands, and the U.S. Virgin Islands. *USA.gov*: State Government. The Law Library of Congress has a guide for finding the laws and regulations for each state and territory. *The Library of Congress*: U.S. States and Territories.

33 The positioning of Congress at the beginning of the Constitution is deemed significant, in that it both affirms that the government of the United States exists to serve its citizens (through their elected representatives in Congress) and that Congress is deemed the "First Branch" of the federal government. *Office of the Secretary of the Senate*: Constitution of the United States.

34 These enumerated powers set forth the authoritative capacity of Congress to collect and spend taxes, borrow money, regulate commerce, establish rules on naturalization and bankruptcy, coin money, set punishments for counterfeiting, establish post offices, protect writings and discoveries, establish tribunals, punish maritime crimes, declare war, raise armies, maintain a navy, establish the military, call forth the militia

include Congress' authority (i) to regulate commerce – the so-called "Commerce Clause",[35] which forms the basis for both trademark[36] and antitrust laws,[37] and (ii) to protect writings and discoveries – the so-called "Patent and Copyright Clause",[38] which provides the basis for patent and copyright protection.[39]

(ii) Federal Courts & Jurisdiction

Article III of the U.S. Constitution establishes the judicial branch of the federal government.[40] Section 1 establishes the Supreme Court but leaves to Congress

---

to enforce the laws and suppress insurrections, organize and discipline a militia, exercise exclusive legislation, and to make such laws as necessary and proper to carry out the foregoing. U.S. Constitution, Article I, Section 8. Transcript available from *U.S. National Archives and Records Administration*: U.S. Constitution.

35 "The Congress shall have Power ... To regulate Commerce with foreign Nations, and among the several States, and with the Indian Tribes", U.S. Constitution, Article I, Section 8, clause 3. The Commerce Clause represents one of the most fundamental powers delegated to Congress by the founders. In the Supreme Court's 1942 opinion in *Wickard v. Filburn*, the Court noted that, with the enactment of the Interstate Commerce Act in 1887 (24 Stat. 379) and the Sherman Antitrust Act in 1890 (25 Stat. 209), "interstate commerce power began to exert positive influence in American law and life." *Wickard v. Filburn*, 317 U.S. 111, 121 (1942). In the Supreme Court's 1995 opinion in *Lopez*, the Court echoed the sentiment that the Interstate Commerce Act and the 1890 Sherman Antitrust Act "ushered in a new era of federal regulation under the commerce power". *United States v. Lopez*, 514 U.S. 549, 554 (1995).

36 The current U.S. trademark act is codified at title 15 U.S.C. §§ 1051–1127 (the Lanham Trade-Mark Act). For a list of U.S. trademark laws, see *Vogl*: US Intellectual Property Law: Trademarks.

37 The Sherman Antitrust Act of 1890 and related antitrust laws are codified at 15 U.S.C. §§ 1–7 (Sherman Antitrust Act); 15 U.S.C. § 18a (Hart-Scott-Rodino Act); 15 U.S.C. §§ 12–27, 29, 52–53 (Clayton Antitrust Act); and 15 U.S.C. §§ 41–58 (Federal Trade Commission Act). For a list of U.S. antitrust laws, see *Vogl*: US Antitrust Law.

38 "The Congress shall have Power ... To promote the Progress of Science and useful Arts, by securing for limited Times to Authors and Inventors the exclusive Right to their respective Writings and Discoveries". U.S. Constitution, Article I, Section 8, clause 8.

39 The current patent act is codified at 35 U.S.C. §§ 1–376 (Patent Act); the current copyright act is codified at 17 U.S.C. §§ 101–810. Although many states had some form of state copyright, trademark, and trade secret law, today federal laws govern rights and protections for patents, copyrights, and trademarks. Trade secrets are still governed by state law.

40 In addition, Article I, Section 8, clause 9, grants Congress the power to establish tribunal courts. Such Article I (or "legislative") courts include magistrate courts, bankruptcy courts, the U.S. Court of Military Appeals, the U.S. Tax Court, and the U.S.

the authority to create lower federal courts as needed: "The judicial Power of the United States shall be vested in one supreme Court, and in such inferior Courts as the Congress may from time to time ordain and establish." These Article III courts – which hear most of the federal cases – include the U.S. District Courts, the U.S. Circuit Courts of Appeal, and the U.S. Supreme Court.[41]

Article III, Section 2, of the U.S. Constitution holds that federal courts have jurisdiction to hear cases "arising under" the Constitution.[42] Already by 1824, the Supreme Court interpreted this clause broadly, finding that it allows federal courts to hear any case in which there is a federal ingredient.[43] Alongside the constitutional basis, federal courts have the right to hear certain cases as set out in the statutory requirements of 28 U.S.C. § 1331[44] (which gives district courts original jurisdiction to cases "arising under" federal law)[45] and § 1338 (which gives district courts original exclusive jurisdiction over patent, copyright, and trademark claims).[46]

Court of Veterans' Appeals. *U.S. Administrative Office of the U.S. Courts*: Understanding Federal and State Courts.

41 Article III courts also include two special courts: the U.S. Court of Claims and the U.S. Court of International Trade. These courts are special because, unlike the other courts, they are not courts of general jurisdiction (which can hear almost any case). The U.S. Court of Claims sits in Washington, D.C., and handles cases involving suits against the government. The U.S. Court of International Trade sits in New York and handles cases involving tariffs and international trade disputes. *U.S. Administrative Office of the U.S. Courts*: Understanding Federal and State Courts.

42 "The judicial Power shall extend to all Cases, in Law and Equity, arising under this Constitution, the Laws of the United States, and Treaties made, or which shall be made, under their Authority". U.S. Constitution, Article III, Section 2.

43 *Osborn v. Bank of the United States*, 9 Wheat. (22 U.S.) 738 (1824). *Cornell University Law School*: Federal Question Jurisdiction.

44 28 USC § 1331 – Federal question: "The district courts shall have original jurisdiction of all civil actions arising under the Constitution, laws, or treaties of the United States."

45 The statutory "arising under" requirement has been found to be slighter narrower than the constitutional "arising under" requirement. For example, the Supreme Court found that a "suit arises under the law that creates the cause of action," *American Well Works v. Layne*, 241 US 257 (1916); therefore, only suits based on federal law, not state law suits likely to provoke a federal law defense, create federal question jurisdiction. *Louisville & Nashville R. Co. v. Mottley*, 211 U.S. 149 (1908). *Cornell University Law School*: Federal Question Jurisdiction.

46 28 USC § 1338 – Patents, plant variety protection, copyrights, mask works, designs, trademarks, and unfair competition: "The district courts shall have original

During Congress' first Session in 1789,[47] the Judiciary Act was passed by the Senate and thereafter by the House of Representatives.[48] It was signed into law by President George Washington on 24 September 1789.[49]

(A) U.S. District Courts

The district courts are the trial courts (or courts of first instance) of the U.S. federal court system. Most federal cases begin here. Within limits set by Congress and the Constitution, the district courts have jurisdiction to hear nearly all categories of federal cases, including both civil and criminal matters.[50] In many cases, the judge determines issues of law, while the jury (or judge sitting without a jury) determines findings of fact.[51]

---

jurisdiction of any civil action arising under any Act of Congress relating to patents, plant variety protection, copyrights and trademarks."

47 The 1st Congress met from 4 March 1789 until 4 March 1791; the 1st Session of Congress met from 4 March 1789 until 29 September 1789 in New York, which was the then-capital of the United States, thereafter moving first to Philadelphia (in 1790) and finally to Washington (in 1800). *The Library of Congress*: A Century of Lawmaking for a New Nation. At present (April 2014), the U.S. is in the 113th Congress, 2nd Session. A new Congress begins at noon January 3 of each odd-numbered year following a general election, unless it designates a different day by law. A Congress lasts for two years, with each year constituting a separate session. The 113th Congress first met in Washington, D.C., on 3 January 2013 and is scheduled to end on 3 January 2015. *U.S. House of Representatives*: Legislative Activity.

48 The Judiciary Act of 1789, September 24, 1789, 1 Stat. 73, Chapter 20. The Act was officially titled "An Act to Establish the Judicial Courts of the United States". The Senate passed the Act by a vote of 14-to-6. The House debated the bill on August 24, August 29, August 31, September 1, September 9, September 12, and September 14, before passing the Judiciary Act without a roll call vote on 17 September 1789. Principally authored by Senator Oliver Ellsworth of Connecticut, the Judiciary Act of 1789 established the structure and jurisdiction of the federal court system and created the position of attorney general. Although amended throughout the years by Congress, the basic outline of the federal court system established by the First Congress remains largely intact today. *The Library of Congress*: Primary Documents in American History: Judiciary Act of 1789.

49 *The Library of Congress*: Primary Documents in American History: Judiciary Act of 1789.

50 *Federal Bar Association*: About U.S. Federal Courts.

51 *U.S. Administrative Office of the U.S. Courts*: Understanding Federal and State Courts.

The Judiciary Act of 1789 originally created 13 judicial districts within the 11 states that had at that point ratified the Constitution.[52] In each judicial district, the Act established a district (trial) court to serve as the federal trial court for admiralty and maritime cases as well as for some minor civil and criminal cases, as well as circuit (appeals) courts.[53] As new states entered the union, Congress created additional district courts that in their geographical outline remained within state boundaries.[54]

Today, there are 94 federal judicial districts. Every state, the District of Columbia, and Puerto Rico have at least one district court.[55] Some large states, such as California, have as many as four.[56] Each district court has between two and 28 judges.[57]

(B) U.S. Circuit Courts of Appeal

Each district court falls under the jurisdiction of an appellate court (U.S. Circuit Court of Appeal).[58] There are currently 13 U.S. Circuit Courts of Appeal: 11 regional circuits (located in various cities throughout the country),[59] the D.C. Circuit,[60] and the U.S. Court of Appeals for the Federal Circuit (CAFC).

---

52 In order of ratification: Delaware (7 December 1787), Pennsylvania (12 December 1787), New Jersey (18 December 1787), Georgia (2 January 1788), Connecticut (9 January 1788), Massachusetts (6 February 1788), Maryland (28 April 1788), South Carolina (23 May 1788), New Hampshire (21 June 1788), Virginia (24 June 1788), and New York (26 July 1788). The two remaining states – North Carolina and Rhode Island – did not ratify the Constitution until 21 November 1789 (North Carolina) and 29 May 1790 (Rhode Island). *Rodgers*: United States Constitutional Law, pp. 108–109.

53 The Act also created the Office of Attorney General, whose primary responsibility was to represent the United States before the Supreme Court, and created a United States Attorney and a United States Marshal for each judicial district.

54 *Federal Judicial Center*: The U.S. District Courts and the Federal Judiciary.

55 In addition, three territories of the United States – the Virgin Islands, Guam, and the Northern Mariana Islands – have district courts that hear federal cases, including bankruptcy cases. *U.S. Administrative Office of the U.S. Courts*: Understanding Federal and State Courts.

56 *Federal Bar Association*: About U.S. Federal Courts.

57 *U.S. Administrative Office of the U.S. Courts*: Understanding Federal and State Courts.

58 *University of Washington*: United States Federal Government Resources.

59 See Schedule 2 for a listing and map of the circuits. The U.S. Administrative Office of the U.S. Courts offers a court locator. *U.S. Administrative Office of the U.S. Courts*: Understanding Federal and State Courts.

60 The U.S. Court of Appeals for the District of Columbia Circuit ("D.C. Cir." in U.S. case citations) is known informally as "the D.C. Circuit". It should not be confused

The CAFC is limited in jurisdiction by *subject matter* rather than geography: it has nationwide jurisdiction to hear appeals in specialized cases, in particular those involving patent laws and cases decided by the Court of International Trade and the Court of Federal Claims.[61] The CAFC was established on 1 October 1982 (pursuant to Article III of the Constitution) through the merger of the United States Court of Customs and Patent Appeals and the appellate division of the United States Court of Claims.[62] The CAFC sits in Washington, D.C.[63]

The federal appellate courts will examine the trial record for only mistakes of law; facts will have been determined by the relevant district court. Therefore, the court usually will neither review the facts of the case nor take any additional evidence. When hearing cases, these courts usually sit in panels of three judges.[64]

(C) U.S. Supreme Court

The Supreme Court of the United States was founded on 2 February 1790 and sits in Washington, D.C.[65] The Court consists of nine judges: the Chief Justice of the United States and eight Associate Justices.[66]

---

with the District of Columbia Court of Appeals, which is roughly equivalent to a state supreme court in the District of Columbia, established in 1970 to relieve the D.C. Circuit from having to take appeals from the local D.C. trial court. While it has the smallest geographic jurisdiction of any of the United States court of appeals, the D.C. Circuit, with eleven active judgeships, is arguably the most important appellate court. The court is given the responsibility of directly reviewing the decisions and rulemaking of many federal independent agencies of the United States government based in the nation's capital, often without prior hearing by a district court (e.g., some federal agencies statutes explicitly stipulate review by the D.C. Circuit). Given the broad areas over which federal agencies have power, this often gives the judges of the D.C. Circuit a central role in affecting national U.S. policy and law. The D.C. Circuit has a "unique character" and is "a court with special responsibility to review legal challenges to the conduct of the national government". *Roberts*: What Makes the D.C. Circuit Different? A Historical View, pp. 377 and 389. The official website of the D.C. Circuit is a helpful resource. *United States Court of Appeals*: District of Columbia Circuit.

61 *Federal Bar Association*: About U.S. Federal Courts.

62 *U.S. Court of Appeals for the Federal Circuit*: Jurisdiction.

63 *U.S. Administrative Office of the U.S. Courts*: Understanding Federal and State Courts.

64 *Id.*

65 *U.S. Supreme Court*: A Brief Overview of the Supreme Court. For a review of the U.S. Supreme Court and its struggle for judicial independence, see *Lepore*: Benched.

66 Supreme Court justices are appointed by the President, and are appointed for life. John G. Roberts, Jr., is the current Chief Justice of the United States. President George W. Bush nominated him as Chief Justice and he took his seat on 29 September

Parties who are not satisfied with a decision of a U.S. Circuit Court of Appeal (or, in rare cases, of a U.S. District Court) or a state supreme court can petition the U.S. Supreme Court to hear their case for a Writ of Certiorari (*cert.*).[67] At its discretion, and within certain guidelines established by Congress,[68] the Supreme Court hears a limited number cases.[69] Such cases usually involve interpretations of the U.S. Constitution or important questions about federal law.[70] The Court has complete control over the cases that it chooses to review.

(iii) Principle of Precedence

U.S. law is based on the principle of precedent.[71] In essence, if a court has already ruled on a given legal issue and another case arises with the same legal issue, the holding in the previous case will be applied to the new case: "judicial precedent

---

2005. The Associate Justices are (including the President who nominated them and the date they took their seat): Antonin Scalia (President Ronald Reagan; 26 September 1986); Anthony M. Kennedy (President Ronald Reagan; 18 February 1988); Clarence Thomas (President George H.W. Bush; 23 October 1991); Ruth Bader Ginsburg (President Bill Clinton; 10 August 1993); Stephen G. Breyer (President Bill Clinton 3 August 1994); Samuel Anthony Alito, Jr. (President George W. Bush; 31 January 2006); Sonia Sotomayor (President Barack Obama; 8 August 2009); and Elena Kagan (President Barack Obama; 7 August 2010). The three retired Associate Justices are Sandra Day O'Connor (President Ronald Reagan; 25 September 1981; retired 31 January 2006; O'Connor was the first woman appointed to the U.S. Supreme Court); David H. Souter (President H.W. Bush; 9 October 1990; retired 29 June 2009); and John Paul Stevens (President Gerald Ford; 19 December 1975; retired 29 June 2010). *U.S. Supreme Court*: Biographies of Current Justices.

67 *U.S. Administrative Office of the U.S. Courts*: Understanding Federal and State Courts.

68 The basic statute in conferring and controlling jurisdiction of the Supreme Court is found in 28 U. S. C. § 1251 et seq., and various special statutes. *U.S. Supreme Court*: A Brief Overview of the Supreme Court.

69 A case selected for argument (where *cert* has been granted) means that at least four Justices have selected the case as being of such importance that the Supreme Court must resolve the legal issues. The Justices grant review in approximately 100 of the more than 10,000 petitions filed with the Court each term. *U.S. Supreme Court*: Visitor's Guide to Oral Argument.

70 *Federal Bar Association*: About U.S. Federal Courts. The Court also has original jurisdiction over cases involving ambassadors and two or more states. *U.S. Administrative Office of the U.S. Courts*: Understanding Federal and State Courts.

71 See *Alexander*: Constrained by Precedent; and *Stinson*: Why Dicta Becomes Holding and Why it Matters. For discussions regarding the distinction between holdings and dicta, see *Abramowicz/Stearn*: Defining Dicta.

attaches a specific legal consequence to a detailed set of facts in an adjudged case or judicial decision, which is then considered as furnishing the rule for the determination of a subsequent case involving identical or similar material facts and arising in the same court or a lower court in the judicial hierarchy."[72] The use of precedent "helps to promote stability in the legal system, as all parties are given notice as to the current state of the law".[73] Adhering to the use of precedent is known as the doctrine of *stare decisis*, an abbreviation of *stare decisis et non quieta movere* (to stand by or adhere to decisions and not disturb that which is settled).[74]

(iv) U.S. Code

The United States Code (abbreviated as U.S. Code or U.S.C.) is a compilation and codification by subject matter of all general and permanent laws of the United States.[75] The U.S. Code, however, does *not* include regulations issued by executive branch agencies, decisions of the Federal courts, treaties, or laws enacted by state or local governments.[76]

The U.S.C. is published by the Office of the Law Revision Counsel of the U.S. House of Representatives.[77] It was first published in 1926, with another edition published in 1934; subsequent main editions have been published every six years since. In between editions, supplements are published during each interim year until the next comprehensive volume is published in order to present the most current information.[78]

The U.S. Code is arranged broadly by subject matter. It shows the present status of laws with amendments already incorporated in the text that have been

---

72 *Allegheny County Gen. Hosp. v. NLRB*, 608 F.2d 965, 969–70 (3d Cir. 1979) (footnote omitted).

73 See *U.S. Administrative Office of the U.S. Courts*: Precedents. For a comparative review of German, U.S., and UK statutory interpretation as well as comparative legal methodology, see *Fleischer*: Comparative Approaches to the Use of Legislative History in Statutory Interpretation.

74 *Aldisert*: Precedent: What it is and What it Isn't.

75 *U.S. Government Printing Office*: About United States Code.

76 *U.S. House of Representatives*: About the Office and the United States Code.

77 The Office of the Law Revision Counsel of the U.S. House of Representatives prepares and publishes the United States Code pursuant to 2 U.S.C. § 285b. *U.S. House of Representatives*: About the Office and the United States Code.

78 *U.S. Government Printing Office*: About United States Code.

amended on one or more occasions. Many statutes have "Short Titles" or "Popular Names" (e.g., the "Hart-Scott-Rodino Act" which is codified at 15 U.S.C. § 18).[79]

(c) EU Treaties, Courts & Legislation

In 1951, six countries founded the European Coal and Steel Community.[80] As of October 2014, 28 countries – each a Member State – make up the European Union.[81]

The European Union is *not*, however, a federal state. In fact, its structure does not fall into any traditional legal category. It is historically unique, and its decision-making system has been constantly evolving for the past 60+ years.[82] Unlike the U.S., whose law is founded on a single, constitutional document, EU law is founded on multi-lateral treaties, which have been adopted, modified, and replaced as the structure of the EU has changed.

For a reader not knowledgeable about the EU framework, understanding the EU legal framework – and in particular its division between national (Member State) and EU-level laws and courts – can be perplexing. The below gives a high-level overview of some key aspects to keep in mind.

(i) Primary Legislation: The Treaties

Unlike the U.S., whose law is founded on a single, constitutional document, EU law is founded on multilateral treaties, which have been adopted, modified and

79 The U.S. House of Representatives makes a "Popular Name Table" available. *U.S. House of Representatives*: United States Code: Popular Names.

80 The six founding members are Belgium, France, Germany, Italy, Luxembourg, and the Netherlands. *Europa.eu*: European Union, The history of the European Union, 1945–1959.

81 As of October 2014, the following 28 countries (including year of entry) form the EU: Germany (1951), France (1951), Italy (1951), the Netherlands (1951), Belgium (1951), Luxembourg (1951), Denmark (1973), Ireland (1973), United Kingdom (1973), Greece (1981), Spain (1986), Portugal (1986), Austria (1995), Finland (1995), Sweden (1995), Czech Republic (2004), Cyprus (2004), Estonia (2004), Latvia (2004), Lithuania (2004), Hungary (2004), Malta (2004), Poland (2004), Slovenia (2004), Slovakia (2004), Bulgaria (2007), Romania (2007), and Croatia (2013). See *Europa.eu*: European Union, Countries. For a map depicting the founding ECSC member countries, see *Europa.eu*: European Union, The history of the European Union, 1945 – 1959. For a map showing the current EU Member States, see *European Organisation for the Safety of Air Navigation*: Member States.

82 *Fontaine*: Europe in 12 Lessons, p. 21.

replaced as the structure of the EU has changed. All EU treaties are binding legal instruments, voluntarily and democratically created and approved directly by the Member States.[83] Under the treaties (deemed primary legislation), Member States cede part of their sovereignty by empowering the EU institutions to adopt laws (secondary legislation).[84]

The primary treaties (and the instruments amending and supplementing them[85]) contain the basic objectives and organization of the EU and set out the constitutional framework for the EU.[86] They set out how decisions are made and the relationship between the EU and its Member States. Today, four treaties – the EEC Treaty of 1957 (renamed the EC Treaty, now named the TFEU[87]), the 1957 Euratom Treaty,[88] the 1992 TEU,[89] and the 2007 Treaty of Lisbon,[90] along with the Charter of Fundamental Rights of the European Union[91] – are currently in force in the EU.[92]

The Treaty of Lisbon – the most recent of the amendments to the EEC – entered into force on 1 December 2009.[93] It made some sweeping reforms, bringing an end to the "European Community" as such and abolishing much of the former Community architecture. It emphasized the "European Union" and clarified the allocation of power between the EU and the Member States.[94]

---

83 *European Commission*: Application of EU Law.

84 *Id.*

85 For a complete list of the treaties – including all founding, current, accession and other treaties, in chronological order with links to the full texts, see *EUR-Lex*: Treaties.

86 For an excellent overview of European Law, see *Borchardt*: The ABC of European Union law.

87 Treaty on the Functioning of the European Union (TFEU), OJ C 115, 9.5.2008; consolidated version 2010, OJ C 83, 30.3.2010; consolidated version 2012, OJ C 326, 26.10.2012.

88 Treaty establishing the European Atomic Energy Community (Euratom); consolidated version 2010, OJ C 84, 30.3.2010; consolidated version 2012, OJ C 327, 26.10.2012.

89 Treaty on European Union (TEU), signed in Maastricht on 7 February 1992. OJ C 191, 29 July 1992; consolidated version 2012, OJ C 326, 26.10.2012.

90 Treaty of Lisbon amending the Treaty on European Union and the Treaty establishing the European Community, signed at Lisbon, 13 December 2007, OJ C 306, 17.12.2007.

91 OJ C 303/1, 14.12.2007; consolidated version 2010, OJ C 83, 30.3.2010; consolidated version 2012, OJ C 326, 26.10.2012, p. 391–407.

92 *EUR-Lex*: Treaties.

93 The Treaty of Lisbon, OJ C 306, 17.12.2007.

94 For a list of relevant TFEU terminology changes and renumbering, see Schedule 4.

(ii) Secondary Legislation

There are three types of EU secondary legislation: (i) regulations (which are directly applicable in that they do not require national implementing legislation by the Member States); (ii) directives (which must be implemented in the national legislation of Member States within a certain period of time); and (iii) decisions (which also require national implementing legislation but, unlike Directives which have general application, are addressed to particular Member States or particular persons or bodies). These laws (regulations, directives, and decisions) take precedence over national law and are binding on national authorities. The EU also issues non-binding instruments, in the form of recommendations and opinions, but these are a form of quasi-legislation, as well as rules governing how EU institutions and programmes work.

(iii) Court of Justice of the European Union

The judicial branch of the European Union is represented by the Court of Justice of the European Union, which consists of three courts: the Court of Justice (originally established in 1952, previously referred to as the ECJ); the General Court (created in 1988, previously called the Court of First Instance); and the Civil Service Tribunal.[95] All three courts sit in Luxembourg.

Since its establishment in 1952, the mission of the Court of Justice of the European Union – not to be confused with the Court of Justice with the European Court of Human Rights[96] or the International Court of Justice[97] – has been to ensure that "the law is observed" in the interpretation and application" of the

95 Articles 251–257 TFEU. See also *Curia*: General Presentation; and *Davies*: Understanding European Union Law, p. 43.

96 The European Court of Human Rights (ECHR) is *not* an EU court, but instead an international court set up in 1959 based in Strasbourg, France. The ECHR rules on individual or Member State applications alleging violations of the civil and political rights set out in the European Convention on Human Rights. *European Court of Human Rights*: The Court in Brief.

97 The International Court of Justice (ICJ) is the principal judicial organ of the United Nations. It was established in June 1945 by the Charter of the United Nations and began work in April 1946. The ICJ sits at the Peace Palace in The Hague, the Netherlands. Of the six principal organs of the UN, it is the only one not located in New York. The Court's role is to settle, in accordance with international law, legal disputes submitted to it by States and to give advisory opinions on legal questions referred to it by authorized UN organs and specialized agencies. *International Court of Justice*: The Court.

Treaties.[98] As part of that mission, the CJEU reviews the legality of the acts of the institutions of the European Union, ensures that the Member States comply with their obligations under the Treaties, and interprets European Union law at the request of national courts and tribunals[99] to ensure the uniform application and interpretation of European Union law.

(A) Court of Justice & Advocate Generals

The Court of Justice is the supreme or constitutional court. Prior to the Treaty of Lisbon (which entered into force in 2009), it was known as the European Court of Justice (or the ECJ). Today, most legal scholars and journalists refer to a judgment of the Court of Justice as a judgment of the Court of Justice of the European Union (or CJEU).

The primary task of the Court of Justice is to examine the legality of acts of the European Union institutions and to ensure, in particular by examining references for a preliminary ruling, that European Union law is interpreted and applied uniformly.[100] It also applies European Union law and resolves disputes between the European Union institutions, between those institutions and the Member States, or even between Member States.[101]

The Court of Justice is composed of 28 judges (one judge per EU country), appointed by the governments of the Member States after consultation by a panel responsible for giving an opinion on the suitability of candidates to perform the duties in question. The judges are appointed for a renewable term of six years. The judges elect one of their number as President for a term of three years.[102]

The Court of Justice also has nine Advocates General (or AGs).[103] While the judges of the Court act as decision makes, AGs assist the judges by delivering non-binding written "opinions" on cases, providing advice to the Court prior to the Court's deliberations.[104] The opinions are reasoned proposals as to how the

---

98 *Curia*: General Presentation.

99 *Id.*

100 For an excellent overview of the Court, see *Curia*: Composition, jurisdiction and procedures.

101 *Curia*: Your Questions on the Court of Justice of the European Union.

102 *Id.*

103 Article 252 TFEU.

104 "It shall be the duty of the Advocate-General, acting with complete impartiality and independence, to make, in open court, reasoned submissions on cases which, in accordance with the Statute of the Court of Justice of the European Union, require his involvement." Article 252 TFEU. Although Advocate-General's opinions are non-binding, they can have great analytical value, providing an independent, historical

Court should decide the case. The Court of Justice is not, however, bound to follow these opinions.[105]

(B) The General Court

The General Court was established in 1988 as a means of relieving the excessive workload of the Court of Justice under the Single European Act (the SEA).[106] Prior to the Treaty of Lisbon, it was known as the Court of First Instance (or CFI).

The General Court deals with actions brought by the Member States against the Commission and against certain acts of the Council, as well as actions brought before it by natural or legal persons against decisions of the European Union institutions, bodies, offices or agencies (for example, an action brought by a company against a decision of the European Commission to impose a fine on it) which are addressed to them or which are of direct and individual concern to them and against regulatory acts (which are of direct concern to them and which do not entail implementing measures).[107]

The General Court is composed of at least one judge per Member State. The judges are appointed by the Member States' governments after consultation by a panel responsible for giving an opinion on the suitability of candidates to perform the duties in question. They are appointed for a renewable term of six years. The judges elect one of their number as President, also for a term of three years.[108]

(C) Civil Service Tribunal

The Civil Service Tribunal was established in 2004.[109] It resolves disputes between the European Union institutions and their staff.[110] The Civil Service Tribunal is

---

analysis of the case law framing the case at hand, as well as suggesting guidelines and standards as to how a particular case should be decided. *Weatherill/Beaumont*: EU Law, pp. 178–181, cited by *Ryan*: DoubleMint: Case C-191/01, p. 395, n. 20.

105 *Curia*: Your Questions on the Court of Justice of the European Union.

106 The SEA, signed in Luxembourg on 17 February 1986 by the nine Member States and on 28 February 1986 by Denmark, Italy and Greece, was the first major amendment of the Treaty establishing the European Economic Community (EEC). It entered into force on 1 July 1987. OJ L 169, 29.6.1987. *Europa.eu*: Summaries of EU Legislation, Single European Act.

107 *Curia*: General Court. See also *Curia*: Your Questions on the Court of Justice of the European Union.

108 *Curia*: Your Questions on the Court of Justice of the European Union.

109 Articles 251–257 TFEU. See also *Curia*: General Presentation; and *Davies*: Understanding European Union Law, p. 43.

110 *Curia*: Civil Service Tribunal.

composed of seven judges appointed by the Council, for a renewable term of six years, after a call for applications and the opinion of a panel of seven persons chosen from among former Members of the Court of Justice and the General Court and lawyers of recognised competence.[111]

(iv) EU Decision Making

EU decision-making involves three main institutions: (i) the European Commission, which represents the interests of the EU as a whole; (ii) the Council of the European Union, which represents the individual member countries, and (iii) the European Parliament, which represents EU citizens and is directly elected by them. In principle, the European Commission proposes new laws, but it is the Council together with the Parliament that adopts them. This is the EU's standard decision-making procedure (known as the "ordinary legislative procedure" or "codecision").[112]

(v) European Commission

The Commission – as "guardian of the Treaties" and the "*acquis communautaire*" (i.e., guardian of all EU law)[113] – oversees and implements EU policies, enforces EU law (together with the Court of Justice), manages the EU's budget and allocating funding, and represents the EU internationally (for example, by negotiating agreements between the EU and other countries).[114]

While individual EU governments are responsible for applying EU law within their own countries, the Commission monitors that this is correctly done. Furthermore, pursuant to EC Regulation No 1/2003,[115] the Commission may apply Article 101 TFEU (prohibiting anti-competitive agreements between companies which prevent, restrict, or distort competition in the EU and which may affect trade between Member States) and Article 102 TFEU (prohibiting the abuse of a dominant position which may affect trade and prevent or restrict competition).[116]

---

111 *Curia*: Your Questions on the Court of Justice of the European Union.

112 *European Commission*: European Commission at Work: Decision Making.

113 *Europa.eu*: European Commission; and *Europa.eu*: Community acquis.

114 *Europan.eu*: European Union, Institutions and Bodies, European Commission.

115 Council Regulation (EC) No 1/2003 of 16 December 2002 on the implementation of the rules on competition laid down in Articles 81 and 82 of the Treaty (OJ L 1, 4.1.2003).

116 For a full listing of EU competition rules, see *European Commission*: EU Competition Law: Rules Applicable to Antitrust Enforcement, Volume I.

Commission cases can originate in a complaint, the opening of a Commission-initiated investigation, or a leniency application (e.g., from one of the participants in a cartel). At the end of any initial investigative phase, the Commission can take the decision to pursue the case as a matter of priority and to conduct an in-depth investigation, or to close it. If the in-depth investigation confirms the Commission's competition concerns, a statement of objections (SO) detailing the Commission's concerns is sent to the companies concerned. An SO is a formal step in Commission investigations. The Commission informs the parties concerned in writing of the objections raised against them and the parties can reply in writing and request an oral hearing to present comments.[117] Commission decisions can be challenged in the General Court in Luxembourg pursuant to Article 263 TFEU. General Court judgments can in turn be appealed on points of law to the CJEU.[118]

The Commission is composed of the College of Commissioners of 28 members. The Commissioners, one from each EU country, provide the Commission's political leadership during their 5-year term. Each Commissioner is assigned responsibility for specific policy areas by the President. The Commission is divided into several departments and services. The departments are known as Directorates-General (DGs), classified according to the policy it deals with.[119] The Commission services deal with more general administrative issues or have a specific mandate, for example fighting fraud or creating statistics.

(vi) The Official Journal

The authorized text of the treaties and secondary legislation are printed in the Official Journal of the European Union (OJ). The OJ is the official, authoritative source for European Union law.[120] The Publications Office of the European Union (*L'Office des publications de l'Union européenne*, or OPOCE) is responsible for the production of the OJ.[121]

---

117 Commission Regulation No 773/2004 of 7 April 2004 relating to the conduct of proceedings by the Commission pursuant to Articles 81 and 82 of the EC Treaty (OJ L 123/18, 27.04.2004). See also *European Commission*: Antitrust Manual of Procedures, in particular Chapter 11 (Statement of Objections), § 1 (Purpose of a Statement of Objections), p. 3/15.

118 Article 263 TFEU.

119 *European Commission*: About the European Commission: Departments.

120 For the rules governing authenticity of the Official Journal, see Council Regulation (EU) No. 216/2013 of 7 March 2013. *Europa.eu*: Publications Office, Official Journal of the European Union.

121 *Official Journal of the European Union*: what is the OJEC.

The OJ was first published on 30 December 1952 as the Official Journal of the European Coal and Steel Community,[122] then renamed as the Official Journal of the European Communities with the establishment of the European Community.[123] On 1 February 2003, the current title was adopted when the Treaty of Nice entered into force.[124]

The OJ is divided and published in different parts – the L (Legislation) series,[125] the C (Information and Notices) series,[126] and the S (Supplementary) series.[127] Except for the S series, the OJ is published every day from Tuesday to Saturday in 23 of the 24 official working languages[128] of the Member States from

---

122 This version was published as a single series (A) from 1952–1958. *EUR-Lex*: Official Journal of the European Union.

123 In April 1958, the A series was replaced by the P series. The P series existed from 1958 until 1967. *EUR-Lex*: Official Journal of the European Union.

124 Treaty of Nice amending the Treaty on the European Union, the Treaties Establishing the European Communities and Certain Related Acts, [2001] OJ C 80/1.

125 The L series contains EU legislation, including regulations, directives, decisions, recommendations, and opinions, as well as other binding acts adopted by the Commission and Council. See *EUR-Lex*: Official Journal of the European Union; and *Official Journal of the European Union*: what is the OJEC.

126 The "C" is derived from the French sub-title "Communications et Informations". *Swift*, European Union. The C series contains EU information and notices, including summaries of judgments of the Court of Justice and the General Court; minutes of European Parliament meetings; reports of the Court of Auditors; parliamentary written questions and answers from the Council or Commission; statements from the European Economic and Social Committee and the Committee of the Regions; competition notices for recruitment by the EU institutions; calls for expressions of interest for EU programmes and projects; other documents published pursuant to EU legislation; public contracts for food aid; and the table of contents of the OJ CE series (which contains the preparatory acts in the legislative process and is only available in the EUR-Lex database or in the monthly CD-ROM edition). *EUR-Lex*: Official Journal of the European Union.

127 The S series contains invitations to tender and other documents relating to public procurement under the EU Procurement Directives. The S series is the only series that is not issued in every working language of the Union. *EUR-Lex*: Official Journal of the European Union.

128 *European Commission*: Official Languages. The OJ is not published in Irish (*Gaeilge*). Until 31 December 2006, Irish was not included in the working languages of the EU institutions. Pursuant to an Agreement made in 1971 between Ireland and the Community, Irish was considered an official Community language, it being understood, however, that only primary legislation was drawn up in that language. On 1 January 2007, Irish became an official EU language. However, "the institutions

the date of their accession to the EU.[129] Only legal acts published in the OJ are binding.

Since 1998, an electronic version of the OJ has been made available online via EUR-Lex, the document portal service. In March 2013, the Council of the European Union adopted Council Regulation No 216/2013,[130] holding that the electronic (online) edition of the OJ is the authentic and legally binding one (whereas previously only the printed version had been binding).[131] The print version is nonetheless still printed.

(vii) European Court Reports

The European Court Reports (ECR) are the most authoritative law report series of the European Union. With respect to case-law, only the versions published in the ECR are deemed official sources. They are published in all the official languages of the EU. All language versions have the same page references.

Since 1990 the ECR has included cases heard by the General Court (previously the Court of First Instance). Often the ECR will contain both the Advocate-General's Opinion as well as the judgment.

Cases are numbered sequentially throughout the year; the second number in a case number is the year the case entered the court system. Since 1989, cases have had a letter included in the case number to indicate the court: CJEU case numbers are preceded by a "C", General Court (previously the Court of First Instance) case numbers are preceded by a "T", and Civil Service Tribunal case numbers are preceded by an "F.[132]

---

of the European Union shall not be bound by the obligation to draft all acts in Irish and to publish them in that language in the Official Journal of the European Union", except for regulations adopted jointly by the European Parliament and the Council. This derogation (which expires 31 December 2016) was initially set out in Council Regulation (EC) No 920/2005 of 13 June 2005 (OJ L 156, 18.6.2005, p. 3) and extended in Council Regulation (EU) No 1257/2010 (OJ L 343, 29.12.2010, p. 5). *European Union*: EU-28 and candidate countries.

129 *EUR-Lex*: Official Journal of the European Union. The English edition began in 1973, when the UK and Ireland joined.

130 Council Regulation (EU) No 216/2013 on the electronic publication of the Official Journal of the European Union, OJ L 69/1, 07.03.2013.

131 Art. 1(2), Council Regulation (EU) No 216/2013 on the electronic publication of the Official Journal of the European Union, OJ L 69/1, 07.03.2013.

132 *Meredith/Nolan*: Oxford University Standard for the Citation of Legal Authorities (OSCOLA).

Each part and volume of the ECR is now printed in two sequences distinguished by a roman numeral I or II: ECR I covers the CJEU (C-cases) and ECR II covers the General Court (T-cases). Each sequence has separate pagination. The first page of the report is attached to the volume number by a hyphen.[133]

(viii) Member State v. EU laws

The interplay between Member State laws and EU laws are of particular interest with respect to intellectual property and competition laws. Intellectual property rights – including patents, copyrights, and trademarks – are (notwithstanding some harmonization) created, protected, and maintained under national Member State law.[134]

Article 36 TFEU permits Member States to derogate from their obligations to ensure the free movement of goods as set out in Articles 34 and 35 TFEU "on grounds of ... the protection of industrial and commercial property".[135] Article 345 TFEU notes that the EU treaties "shall in no way prejudice the rules in Member States governing the system of property ownership." The *existence* of the exclusive rights granted by a Member State to the holder of an intellectual property right is *not* affected by the limitations of Articles 34 or 35 TFEU or the prohibitions of Articles 101 or 102 TFEU.[136]

However, the Court has noted that Articles 36 and 345 are not blanket exemptions for all conduct involving intellectual property.[137] In those cases where the

---

133 *Oxford University Press*: Citing of Legal Materials (Including Legal Tables).

134 In Germany, for example, trademarks are regulated by the Act on the Protection of Trade Marks and other Symbols (*Markengesetz* or *MarkenG*) along with the Trademark Ordinance (*Markenverordnung* or *MarkenV*).

135 Article 36 TFEU permits Member States to derogate from their obligations to ensure the free movement of goods "on grounds of public morality, public policy or public security; the protection of health and life of humans, animals or plants; the protection of national treasures possessing artistic, historic or archaeological value; or the protection of industrial and commercial property." The list is *exhaustive* and Article 36 nonetheless warns that: "Such prohibitions or restrictions shall not, however, constitute a means of arbitrary discrimination or a disguised restriction on trade between Member States."

136 Case 24/67, *Parke, Davis and Co. v Probel, Reese, Beintema-Interpharm and Centrafarm*, 29 February 1968, ECR 55, p. 72.

137 "Articles [36], [345] and [267] of the Treaty ... *do not exclude any influence* whatever of community law on the exercise of national industrial property rights. ... Article [345 TFEU] *confines itself* to stating that the 'Treaty shall in no way prejudice the rules in Member States governing the system of property ownership'." Joined

exercise of intellectual property rights conflict with EU competition laws, the Commission has the authority to limit the exercise of those intellectual property rights in order to harmonize them with EU law.[138]

Although each Member State has its own competition laws, such laws must conform to those set out in the TFEU, in particular Articles 101 and 102 TFEU, to ensure "that competition is not distorted".[139] In Germany, the national competition rules are contained in the Act Against Restraints of Competition (*Gesetz gegen Wettbewerbsbeschränkungen* or GWB) and the Act Against Unfair Competition (*Gesetz gegen den unlauteren Wettbewerb* or UWG).[140]

Cases 56 and 58/64, *Établissements Consten S.à.R.L. and Grundig-Verkaufs-GmbH v Commission*, 13 July 1966 [1966] ECR 299, p. 345 (emphasis mine).

138 As the Court noted in *Consten and Grundig*, "to refrain from using rights under national trade-mark law in order to set an obstacle in the way of parallel imports does not affect the grant of those rights but only limits their exercise to the extent necessary to give effect to the prohibition under Article 85 (1). The power of the Commission to issue such an injunction for which provision is made in Article 3 of Regulation No 17/62 of the Council is in harmony with the nature of the Community rules on competition which have immediate effect and are directly binding on individuals. Such a body of rules, by reason of its nature described above and its function, *does not allow the improper use of rights under any national trade-mark law in order to frustrate the Community's law* on cartels." Joined Cases 56 and 58/64, *Établissements Consten S.à.R.L. and Grundig-Verkaufs-GmbH v Commission*, 13 July 1966 [1966] ECR 299, pp. 345–346 (emphasis mine).

139 Protocol (No 27) on the internal market and competition, Consolidated version of the Treaty on European Union – PROTOCOLS, OJ C 115, 9.5.2008.

140 *Bundesministerium für Wirtschaft und Energie, Nationales Kartell- und Wettbewerbsrecht*: Wettbewerbsrecht.

1. Trademarks & Business: The Protection of Brand Assets

1.1 Overview: Trademarks in Transition

This chapter reviews the historical functions and foundations of trademarks, and examines the contours of trademark law which continue to be revised in response to business and social demands. This chapter begins with a review of trademarks in our modern society, including a few examples of recent trademark "turf wars", to highlight the presence – and commercial significance – of trademarks in our society today.

Chapter 1 concludes with the position that the function of trademarks in our society today has changed significantly: what began as an original means of ownership, source, or quality information intended to protect both producers (from free riding by competitors) and consumers (from confusion or fraudulent trade practices) has developed into a profitable and commercially powerful means by which companies communicate a wealth of information regarding their business as an enterprise – i.e., its social personality and commercial character – sometimes completely separate from (and at times irrelevant to) the underlying products that are being sold. This fundamental change in the function of trademarks, in response to business, political, and social demands, has consequently expanded the contours of modern trademark law far beyond its narrower, more practical, origins. Trademarks today are big money, big business, competitive assets.

Chapters 2 and 3 look at the legal frameworks in which trademark rights were developed in the U.S. (Chapter 2) and the EU (Chapter 3), reviewing the fundamentals which govern their rights today and highlighting some of the key differences between the U.S. and the EU legal regimes.

1.2 Trademarks Today

(a) Competitive Business Assets

Trademarks today are big money, big business, competitive assets. In 2014, the value of the top global *brand* – not the value of the company – was listed at

$118.86 billion.[141] Since global brand rankings began in 2000,[142] the top global *brand*, without interruption, had been Coca-Cola. In 2013, Coca-Cola lost its top position, dropping two places to 3rd, ceding its lead to Apple (in 1st place) and Google (in 2nd place). Displacing Coca-Cola's pole position (and, more generally, the seemingly impenetrable triad of Coca-Cola, IBM, and Microsoft), Apple's move to 1st place was deemed a "historic"[143] event, "reflecting the rising importance of ... consumer consciousness".[144]

This astounding – deemed "meteoric" – rise in Apple's brand value, increasing almost 15 times in value over a period of 13 years,[145] reflects how powerful

---

141 The value of the Apple brand – the 2014 top global brand – increased by 21% during 2014 (its brand value was $98.316 million in 2013). Google's brand sits in second place with a value of $107.43 billion, up 15% from its brand value in 2013. This is significant: two brands have a value that is upwards of $100 billion each. In third place is Coca-Cola, with a 2014 value of $81.563 billion. *Interbrand*: Best Global Brands 2014.

142 All brand rankings in this paper are based on Interbrand's annual reports. Interbrand is one of the oldest and largest brand consultancy companies. Founded in 1974, it has released an annual ranking of the best global brands, valuing each brand's financial performance, role, and strength, since 2000. It is headquartered in New York and has 35 offices worldwide. For more information, see *Interbrand*: About Us and *Funding Universe*: Interbrand Corporation History. In 2010, the Interbrand valuation methodology was the first to be certified as compliant with the requirements of the ISO 10668 international standard for monetary requirements for brand valuation. *Interbrand*: Interbrand's Methodology Becomes the World's First ISO Certified Approach for Valuing Brands, Press Release, dated 1 December 2010. Other brand calculation companies exist, notably Brand Finance Plc, based in the United Kingdom. It too conducts valuations of brands, intangible assets, and intellectual property for accounting, tax, corporate finance, and marketing purposes. See *Brand Finance Plc*: About Us. Brand Finance has been ranking the 500 top global brands since 2007. Brand Finance ranking reports, from 2007–2014, are available. *Brand Finance Plc*: League Tables.

143 "Apple has made history by unseating Coca-Cola and becoming Interbrand's most valuable global brand of 2013." *Interbrand*: Interbrand Released 14th Annual Best Global Brands Report.

144 *Shankland*: Apple bumps Coca-Cola to become world's top brand.

145 Apple's brand value does not necessarily track the success of its products; instead it tracks the social perception of the Apple brand and the personality of that brand. In 2000, Apple was in 36th place (with a value of $6.6 billion); in 2001, even though it had launched the new iPod device, it dropped to 49th place (with a value of $5.5 billion); in 2002, it dropped again, to 50th place (with a value of $5.3 billion); in 2003, it remained at 50th place (with a value of $5.5 billion); in 2004, after the successful

brands can, relatively quickly, infiltrate our society and have a *social association* value alongside any traditional corporate financial valuation made by shareholders or corporate advisors.[146] Today, corporate takeover battles often focus on the value of the *brands* at stake – not other physical assets or real property – thereby highlighting the importance of a trademark's commercial value. Brands can, in some cases, even account for a *majority* of a company's assets.

(b) Brand: *n.* A living business asset.[147]

In its *first* sentence describing what a trademark is, the United States Patent & Trademark Office (the USPTO) states the following: "A trademark is a brand name."[148] This definition is significant: the meaning and connotations of a *brand* have supplemented the understanding of a *trade* name or mark designation. Brands have been called "the agents of change" with "the power ... and the potential ... to change the world."[149] Big words for something that began with far

---

launch of the iTunes store in April 2003, it rose to 43rd place (with a value of $6.9 billion); in 2005, it rose to 41st place (with a value of $8 billion); in 2006, it rose to 39th place (with a value of $9.1 billion); in 2007, with the launch of the first generation of iPhones, it rose to 33rd place (with a value of $11 billion); in 2008, it rose to 24th place (with a value of $13.7 billion); in 2009, based primarily on its iPhone 4 sales, it rose to 20th place (with a value of $15.4 billion); in 2010, with its launch of the iPad, it rose to 17th place (with a value of $21.1 billion); in 2011, it rose to 8th place (with a value of $33.5 billion); in 2012, it rose an astounding 129% in value, jumping to 2nd place (with a value of $76.6 billion). In comparison, Coca-Cola, IBM and Microsoft's brand value have only changed insignificantly over the past decade. *Interbrand*: Best Global Brands – Previous Years.

146 Jez Frampton, Interbrand's Global Chief Executive Officer elaborated: "Every so often, a company changes our lives—not just with its products, but with its ethos. This is why, following Coca-Cola's 13-year run at the top of Best Global Brands, Apple now ranks #1." *Interbrand*: Interbrand Released 14th Annual Best Global Brands Report.

147 *Interbrand*: Best Global Brands 2011, p. 3. In later reports, Interbrand has expanded on this definition, noting that brands are "living business assets, brought to life across all touchpoints, which, if properly managed, create identification, differentiation and value". *Interbrand*: Branding in the Post-digital World. With somewhat exaggerated hyperbole, the authors of the Best Global Brands 2011 report state: "Each year as we value the world's top 100 brands, a few emerge as clear standouts. Brands that have used creativity and innovation to enable us to do things we never thought possible, and cause us to feel a spark of excitement and joy. These brands have, very literally, changed the world." *Interbrand*: Best Global Brands 2011, p. 4.

148 *USPTO*: What is a trademark or service mark?

149 *Interbrand*, Best Global Brands 2013, p. 81.

humbler origins – a simple mark on pottery to identify its source or a mark on cattle to identify its owner.[150]

Today, the top brands are global. These brands are known worldwide by name or by logo. They act as international "ambassadors" across languages, cultures, and laws. In 2014, the total value of the 100 top global brands was estimated at § 1.6 trillion.[151] In 2013, the total value was estimated at US$ 1.5 trillion – which itself was an 8.4% record increase over the total value of the 100 top global brands in 2012.[152]

In 2014, the top 10 global brands – representing a total brand value of US$ 610.3 billion – came from seven U.S. companies (Apple, Google, Coca-Cola, IBM, Microsoft, GE, and McDonald's), one South Korean company (Samsung), one Japanese company (Toyota), and one German company (Mercedes-Benz).[153] Of the top 100 brands worldwide, the U.S. (with 53)[154] and Germany (with 11)[155] are the world's two front-runners as the largest producers of and markets for

---

150 *McKenna*: The Normative Foundations of Trademark Law, p. 1849.

151 *Interbrand*: Best Global Brands 2014.

152 *Interbrand*: Interbrand Released 14th Annual Best Global Brands Report. To qualify as a "global" brand for the Interbrand annual report, the following must be met: (i) brands must have a presence in at least three major continents, as well as broad geographic coverage in emerging markets; (ii) at least 30% of revenues must come from outside the brand's home region; and (iii) there must be sufficient publicly available data on the brand's financial performance (hence, privately held companies such as the Mars and BBC brands, for example, are not included since they do not have publicly available financial data). For further methodology criteria, see *Interbrand*: Best Global Brands: Our Methodology.

153 Top 10 brands (by 2014 ranking and value, in $ million): 1. Apple ($118,863); 2. Google ($107,439); 3. Coca-Cola ($81,563); 4. IBM ($72,244); 5. Microsoft ($61,154); 6. GE ($45,480); 7. Samsung ($45,462); 8. Toyota ($42,392); 9. McDonald's ($42,254); and 10. Mercedes-Benz ($34,338). *Interbrand*: Best Global Brands 2014. For a complete list of Interbrand's top 100 "Best Global Brands 2014", see Schedule 1.

154 Remaining top US brands (by 2014 global ranking): 12. Intel, 13. Walt Disney, 14. Cisco, 15. Amazon, 16. Oracle, 17. HP, 18. Gillette, 22. Nike, 23. American Express, 24. Pepsi, 27. UPS, 28. eBay, 29. Facebook, 30. Pampers, 32. Kellogg's, 34. Budweiser, 35. J.P. Morgan, 39. Ford, 44. Accenture, 47. Goldman Sachs, 48. Citi, 50. Colgate, 61. Caterpillar, 62. Xerox, 63. Morgan Stanley, 66. 3M, 67. Discovery, 68. Kentucky Fried Chicken, 69. Visa, 71. Tiffany & Co., 72. Sprite, 76. Starbucks, 77. Adobe, 78. Johnson & Johnson, 79. John Deere, 80. MTV, 82. Chevrolet, 83. Ralph Lauren, 84. Duracell, 85. Jack Daniel's, 87. Harley-Davidson, 88. MasterCard, 89. Kleenex, 92. FedEx, 96. Pizza Hut, and 99. Gap. *Interbrand*: Brand Value by Region/Country.

155 Top 2014 German brands: 10. Mercedes-Benz, 11. BMW, 25. SAP, 31. Volkswagen, 45. Audi, 49. Siemens, 55. Allianz, 59. Adidas, 60. Porsche, 81. DHL, and 97. Hugo Boss. *Interbrand*: Brand Value by Region/Country.

top global brands.[156] Further augmenting the North American dominance, one of the top 100 brands came from Canada,[157] and one came from Mexico.[158] After Germany, the next closest contenders were Japan (with seven)[159] and France (with six)[160] of the top 100 brands.

Taking a quick look at the top 15 global brands (of 2014 and 2013) is an easy game of name and logo recognition.

	Brand	**Logo**[161]	**2014 Value**[162]	**2013 Value**[163]
1	Apple		$ 118.86 billion	$ 98.32 billion
2	Google		$ 107.44 billion	$ 93.29 billion
3	Coca-Cola		$ 81.56 billion	$ 79.21 billion
4	IBM		$ 72.24 billion	$ 78.81 billion

156 *Interbrand*: Best Global Brands 2011.

157 Top Canadian brands: 57. Thomas Reuters. *Interbrand*: Brand Value by Region/Country.

158 Top Mexican brands: 93. Corona. *Interbrand*: Brand Value by Region/Country.

159 Top Japanese brands: 8. Toyota, 20. Honda, 37. Canon, 52. Sony, 56. Nissan, 64. Panasonic, and 100. Nintendo. *Interbrand*: Brand Value by Region/Country.

160 Top French brands: 19. Louis Vuitton, 43. L'Oréal, 46. Hermès, 51. Danone, 53. AXA, and 58. Cartier. *Interbrand*: Brand Value by Region/Country.

161 All logos are registered trademarks of the applicable company and are used here for illustrative purposes only. All rights, title, and interest in and to such trademarks and any goodwill related thereto remain the sole and exclusive property of the applicable company.

162 These values are taken from *Interbrand*: Best Global Brands 2014. Interbrand discusses its value calculation methodology, noting that there "are three key aspects that contribute to the assessment: the financial performance of the branded products or services, the role of brand in the purchase decision process, and the strength of the brand." See Interbrand: Best Global Brands: Our Methodology.

163 *Interbrand*: Best Global Brands 2013.

	Brand	Logo[161]	2014 Value[162]	2013 Value[163]
5	Microsoft		$ 61.15 billion	$ 59.55 billion
6	GE		$ 45.48 billion	$ 46.95 billion
7	Samsung		$ 45.46 billion	$ 39.61 billion
8	Toyota		$ 42.39 billion	$ 35.35 billion
9	McDonald's		$ 42.25 billion	$ 41.99 billion
10	Mercedes-Benz		$ 34.34 billion	$ 31.90 billion
11	BMW		$ 34.21 billion	$ 31.84 billion
12	Intel		$ 34.15 billion	$ 37.26 billion
13	Disney		$ 32.22 billion	$ 28.15 billion
14	Cisco		$ 30.94 billion	$ 29.05 billion
15	Amazon		$ 29.48 billion	$ 23.62 billion

The EU Commission has noted that the value of the top ten brands in EU countries amounted to almost 9% of GDP on average in 2009.[164] In 2010, recognizing the importance of a trademark as a financial asset, the International Organization for Standardization (the ISO) issued a new standard: ISO 10668:2010, which sets out a framework for consistent and transparent brand valuation, including approaches to valuation and requirements for the procedures and methods of monetary brand measurement.[165]

Trademarks today embody far more than an efficient mechanism to differentiate goods, indicate origin or source, or guarantee quality. Today "trademarks" are more sophisticated both in form (encapsulating branding, advertising, logos, labels, slogans, and packaging) and in the information they communicate. A trademark (or brand) provides the consumer not only with reassurance about the origin of a product, but also about other features, such as quality, luxury, economy, and lifestyle.[166] Consumers associate their own person with the brand: "Transformational advertising transforms the use experience making the brand user feel (for example) more elegant, adventuresome, or warm, thereby potentially adding value to the customer."[167]

For companies, trademarks facilitate the development of brand persona – they are the "bridge" over which advertising, marketing, and persuasive brand imagery can flow.[168] For consumers, trademarks become the "agent" through

---

164 *European Commission*: Press Release IP/11/630.

165 *International Organization for Standardization*: ISO 10668:2010 (Brand valuation – Requirements for monetary brand valuation).

166 Thomas Drescher noted that "meaning can be created and manipulated by context" and "symbols, given their multi-layered, or harmonic meanings, can evoke associations perceived as attributes of a product". *Drescher*: The Transformation and Evolution of Trademarks, p. 305.

167 *Aaker*: Managing Brand Equity, p. 163. See also *Bannon*: The Growing Risk of Self-Dilution, p. 588. "Merchandising creates a market for an item. In merchandising, the owner of a well-known trademark licenses a trademark to someone else for application to goods of a different kind, probably a different trade. The practice utilizes a marks' commercial magnetism, building and retaining the market." *Bannon*: Revisiting "The Rational Basis of Trademark Protection", p. 88.

168 "[A trademark] is a narrow bridge over which all the traffic powered by product advertising must pass... With time, the symbol comes to be more than a conduit through which the persuasive power of advertising is transmitted, and acquires a potency, a "commercial magnetism," of its own." *Brown*: Advertising and the Public Interest, p. 1187.

which all this brand imagery is communicated: trademarks are a short cut for advertising, inducing the purchaser to select what she wants or what she has been led to believe she wants.[169]

The diminishing differences between products in terms of quality and ingenuity have also accentuated the importance of brands and, in particular, brand loyalty, to manufacturers and retailers alike. In a climate of rapidly developing technology and seemingly unlimited means of communication, no product is "new" for long. Therefore, consumers look to brands to give them reassurance as to their primary concern when deciding whether or not to buy, whether that concern is about the quality, the price, or the novelty of the product. The stakes are high: brand loyalty ensures product sales; product sales ensure market share.

(c) The iPad Trademark Saga in China

The trademark dispute between Apple and Proview regarding use (and ownership) of the iPad name in China – a US $2 billion showdown for *one* trademark in *one* country – shows how high the stakes can be.

In 2000, Proview Electronics (Taiwan) Company Ltd (hereafter "Proview Taiwan"), located in Yung Ho City, Taipei, registered the trademark "IPAD" in many countries throughout the world.[170] In 2001, Proview Technology (Shenzhen) Company Ltd (hereafter "Proview Shenzhen"), located in Guangdong province in southeastern China, filed trademark applications for "IPAD" and related logos in mainland China in class 9, covering, amongst other goods, "computers".[171]

---

169 As Justice Felix Frankfurter in *Mishawaka Rubber* noted: "The protection of trademarks is the law's recognition of the psychological function of symbols. If it is true that we live by symbols, it is no less true that we purchase goods by them. A trademark is a merchandising short-cut which induces a purchaser to select what he wants, or what he has been led to believe he wants. The owner of a mark exploits this human propensity by making every effort to impregnate the atmosphere of the market with the drawing power of a congenial symbol. Whatever the means employed, the aim is the same – to convey through the mark, in the minds of potential customers, the desirability of the commodity upon which it appears. Once this is attained, the trade-mark owner has something of value." *Mishawaka Rubber & Woolen Mfg. Co. v. S. S. Kresge Co.*, 316 U.S. 203, 205 (1942).

170 *Agile IP*: ipad trade mark settlement in china.

171 *Chiu/Wong*: iPads Being Taken off Shelves in China. See *Chiu/Wong* for an image of the logo Proview Shenzhen filed in its IPAD trademark registrations.

Proview Shenzhen claimed that IPAD stands for "Internet Personal Access Device".[172]

Proview Taiwan and Proview Shenzhen are both 100% owned by the same parent company, Proview International Holdings Ltd (hereafter "Proview International"). The Proview group of companies produce display devices including LCD monitors, CRT monitors, and flat panel digital products.[173]

It should be noted that both Proview Taiwan and Proview Shenzhen IPAD trademark registrations were made long before Apple's iPad were released in 2010[174] – and even before some of Apple's "i" devices were on the market.[175] Prior to the iPad launch, Apple's trademark searches revealed that the Proview group of companies owned the IPAD registrations.[176] According to testimony in the legal fight, Apple retained British lawyers and set up a UK-based proxy company, named IP Application Development Limited ("IPADL"), to buy up rights to the iPad name around the world.[177] In late 2009, just before the launch of the iPad, IPADL and Proview Taiwan entered into a trademark assignment under which Proview Taiwan assigned all of its "IPAD" global trademark registrations to IPADL for £35,000.[178] Shortly thereafter, in February 2010, IPADL sold and assigned all such trademark rights to Apple for £10.[179]

In October 2010, after Apple's launch of the iPad, Proview Shenzhen filed a trademark infringement case against Apple in the Guangdong provincial court

172 *Wong*: The IPAD Saga Continues and Rolls Bigger.

173 *Agile IP*: ipad trade mark settlement in china.

174 Apple announced its new tablet computer branded "iPad" in January 2010, launching it first in the U.S. in April of that year (*Apple*: Apple Sells Over 300,000 iPads First Day) and in other countries a month later (*Apple*: iPad Available in Nine More Countries). Apple purchased the iPad trademark rights in the U.S. from Fujitsu, prior to the 2010 launch. *Purcher*: Fujitsu Assigns their Entire Interest in iPad to Apple. For the assignment notice, see *USPTO*: serial nr. 76497338. For images of the various Apple iPad logos, see *Trends Gadget*: Apple iPad Logo.

175 Apple launched iMac in 1998 (*Sanford*: Apple History – iMac), iBook in 1999 (*Apple*: PC Data Ranks iBook Number One), iTunes in 2001 (*Apple*: Apple Introduces iTunes), iPod in 2001 (*Apple*: Apple Introduces iTunes), iPhone in 2007 (*Apple*: Apple Reinvents the Phone with iPhone) and iPad in January 2010 (*Apple*: Apple Launches iPad).

176 *Chiu/Wong*: iPads Being Taken off Shelves in China.

177 *Bradsher*: Apple Settles an iPad Dispute in China.

178 *Campbell*: Apple accuses Proview of 'misleading Chinese courts' over iPad name.

179 *Chiu/Wong*: iPads Being Taken off Shelves in China.

in China.[180] From the trademark registrations, the actual owner of the *Chinese* IPAD marks was not Proview Taiwan (from whom IPADL had acquired the assigned rights), but the sister company, Proview Shenzhen, which refused to assign its marks to Apple, arguing that the assignment was from Proview Taiwan and hence Proview Shenzhen was under no obligation to transfer the marks.[181] Proview Shenzhen went on to pursue litigation against Apple in multiple courts, including a suit in California,[182] claiming that it still owned the name. Making the matter more confusing were the fraud and unfair competition allegations by Proview Taiwan claiming that Apple misled Proview Taiwan in buying the trademark through the proxy company IPADL,[183] without explaining the true purpose behind the acquisition.

The story then became even more complicated: it was suggested that Proview Shenzhen, with deep debts and financial troubles (it was, in fact, insolvent), was using every available legal tool to force a large settlement from Apple.[184] The creditors of Proview Shenzhen mounted an additional challenge against Apple in its efforts to gain control of the trademark: the president of He Jun Vanguard Group (the consultancy group that represents the eight creditor banks who hold the assets of the insolvent Proview Shenzhen) held several rounds of negotiations with Apple over a potential additional payment for the China trademark; what shocked observers was when he suggested Apple should pay up to $2 billion for such right.[185] Finally, on 2 July 2012, a Chinese provincial court said that Apple and Proview had settled the lawsuit, under which Apple agreed to pay $60 million for the legal rights to use the iPad trademark in China.[186]

In 2012, Apple's brand was valued at $76,568 million.[187] In comparison to the initial $2 billion offer, the $60 million settlement amount seems almost modest. There is little to comment on the chain of title dispute: this is basic intellectual property ownership law. There is also little to comment on the drama of Proview Shenzhen's insolvency or Apple's cloaked "IP Application Development Limited" company guise. The issue is the financial significance of a name: $60 million for

---

180 *Agile IP*: ipad trade mark settlement in china.
181 *Agile IP*: ipad trade mark settlement in china.
182 *Byford*: California judge dismisses Proview's iPad trademark case.
183 *Campbell*: Apple accuses Proview of 'misleading Chinese courts' over iPad name.
184 *Sottek*: Proview sues Apple in US over iPad trademark.
185 *Hille*: Apple faces new fight in China IP dispute; and *Hille*: Proview drags Apple through a legal hailstorm.
186 *Bradsher*: Apple Settles an iPad Dispute in China.
187 *Interbrand*: Best Global Brands 2012 – Apple.

one name in one country. The iPad saga demonstrates how valuable trademarks have become to companies big and small.

How did trademarks become such valuable assets, "untethered" from their "traditional moorings"[188] and often more valuable than the underlying physical assets of a company? A look back at the historical functions of trademarks, the underlying principles justifying their protection, and the development of trademark laws in the U.S. and the EU gives some perspective on why trademarks today play such a significant role in the global market today.

1.3 Historical Overview

The importance of protecting patents[189] and copyrights[190] has been recognized for centuries. Trademarks, however, are deemed the earliest form of intellectual property used and protected.

(a) Practical Beginnings: Ownership, Origin & Quality

The practice of putting marks on goods has existed for thousands of years. Since at least as early as 1500 BC, potters made distinctive marks on the bottom of their creations to identify the source of their products.[191] Long before they

188 *Travis*: The Battle for Mindshare, para. 7.

189 For a review of the English common law system of protecting patents, see *Walterscheid*: Defining the Patent & Copyright Term, p. 321 and fn. 20, citing *Hulme*: The History of the Patent System, A Sequel, p. 52; and *MacLeod*: Inventing the Industrial Revolution: The English Patent System, p. 11.

190 For a review of early copyright protections, see *Seifert*: Über Bücher, Verleger und Autoren, pp. 1270–1276; *Geller*: Toward an Overriding Norm in Copyright, § 4; *Geller*: Must Copyright Be For Ever Caught, p. 159; *Dallon*: The Problem with Congress and Copyright Law, pp. 372–373; *Foster*: Invitation to a Discourse, pp. 175–182; *Potere*: Who Will Watch the Watchmen?, p. 302, fn. 224 (citations omitted); *Klett/Sonntag/Wilske*: Intellectual Property Law in Germany, p. 59; and *Bundeszentrale für politische Bildung*: Geschichte des Urheberrechts. For a detailed source of German writings on the granting of privileges in Germany, see *Loewenheim*: Handbuch des Urheberrechts, § I. Das Zeitalter der Privilegien, paras. 2–3 and accompanying notes.

191 *Port*: The Illegitimacy of Trademark Incontestability, p. 522 (citations omitted). For additional reviews of uses in antiquity and after, see *Rogers*: Some Historical Matter Concerning Trade-Marks; *Schechter*: Historical Foundations; *Ruston*: On the Origin of Trademarks; *Paster*: Trademarks – Their Early History; *Diamond*: The

were defined as trade, name, or service marks,[192] distinguishing marks have appeared on items such as porcelain, jars, stones, bricks and tiles, oil lamps, eye ointments and other medicines, shop sign boards, swords, weapons, tapestries, cloth/textiles, bells, paper, books, cheese, loaves of bread, wine, gold, silver, metal work, crossbows, pewter, knives and other steel or iron articles, pictures, trade cards, playing cards, cattle, timber logs, harpoons, gun barrels, and kegs of salt fish.[193]

These marks were primarily used to signal three types of information. First, to identify ownership: for example, merchants could demonstrate ownership of their goods (this was particularly useful when goods were recovered at sea), or farmers could identify their cattle when they roamed over hillsides.[194] Second, to indicate the source of goods: primarily this was to allow consumers to distinguish among products or for those who wished to purchase goods from a particular trader or a particular region.[195] Third, to establish quality: marks were important in medieval Europe for the guilds, which developed reputations for the quality of their products. To maintain that reputation, guilds needed to be able to restrict membership and identify and punish members who produced defective products. Guilds therefore required their members to affix distinguishing marks to their products so they could police their ranks effectively.[196] In sum, the reasons for marking goods initially served three primary *information* functions:

- **Ownership (identification) function:** the mark permitted the owner to reclaim her property if lost or stolen (e.g., cattle having been stolen by "rustlers",

Historical Development of Trademarks; *McClure*: Trademarks and Unfair Competition; and *Fezer*: Markenrecht, Geschichte des Markenrechts, paras. 2–12.

192 Trademarks are source identifiers used in connection with goods; service marks are source identifiers used in connection with services. In this paper, I use "trademarks" to collectively include trademarks, trade names, and service marks.

193 *Diamond*: The Historical Development of Trademarks, pp. 223–242; *Ruston*: On the Origin of Trademarks, pp. 127–129. Ruston notes the interesting observation that wall paintings of ancient Egypt show cattle being branded by field workers and cave paintings in southwestern Europe (dating from the late Stone Age or early Bronze Age) show cattle branded on their flanks.

194 *McKenna*: The Normative Foundations of Trademark Law, p. 1849.

195 *Cornish/Llewelyn/Aplin*: Intellectual Property.

196 *McKenna*: The Normative Foundations of Trademark Law, p. 1850.

wares recovered after a shipwreck, or logs being transported down a river).[197] This has also been classified as a "possessor's" or "personal" mark.[198]

- **Origin (source) function:** the mark identified the trade source of the goods (either the manufacturer or geographical origin) giving consumers information regarding the manufacturer or place or origin.[199]
- **Quality (guarantee) function:** the mark symbolized the qualities associated by con-sumers with the goods or services,[200] or at a minimum guaranteed a consistent level of quality.[201] This included the compulsory marks used to mark precious metals,[202] the principal purpose of which was to fix the responsibility (i.e., blame) for poor quality of merchandise.[203]

(b) The Trademark (R)Evolution: Goodwill & Advertising

Scholars point to the industrial revolution – and the growth of advertising – as the major turning point in the evolution of trademarks. At that time, manufacturers and wholesalers searched for a means by which to distinguish their otherwise indistinguishable goods (e.g., soap or flour) from those of other manufacturers.[204] In doing so, they substantially developed the fourth function of trademarks – that of the goodwill or advertising function:

- **Goodwill (through investment or advertising) function:** the mark permits the manufacturer to use the sign as a symbolic device, representing some sort of "good will", often acquired after conscientious investment by the manufacturer in the promotion of the product.[205] The use of the mark is a recognition (even an advertisement) of goodwill of the company – through a brand name – as

197 *Ruston*: On the Origin of Trademarks, p. 128; and *Diamond*: The Historical Development of Trademarks, p. 242.
198 *Ruston*: On the Origin of Trademarks, p. 127.
199 *Diamond*: The Historical Development of Trademarks, p. 246.
200 *Cornish/Llewelyn/Aplin*: Intellectual Property.
201 *Diamond*: The Historical Development of Trademarks, p. 246. The trademark does not necessarily guarantee "good" quality; it merely guarantees consistency for the quality of the goods purchased.
202 *Ruston*: On the Origin of Trademarks, pp. 141–144.
203 *Diamond*: The Historical Development of Trademarks, pp. 234 and 237.
204 *Drescher*: The Transformation and Evolution of Trademarks, p. 327.
205 *Cornish/Llewelyn/Aplin*: Intellectual Property.

a separate stand-alone function from the product such trademark may be identifying.[206]

By the turn of the 20th century, aggressive advertising campaigns introduced the idea of a "branded identity", which inexorably led to the value of trademarks as commercial symbols.[207] Manufacturers could develop trademarks as symbols "imbued with powerful, complex, highly charged and immediate symbolism aimed at a specific marketplace."[208]

By the middle of the 20th century, alongside the growing importance of intellectual property in an industrial and then an information economy, the value of trademarks as commercial symbols again advanced dramatically, used now to distinguish relatively identical products on the basis not of substance but of *mythical* appeal.[209] This goodwill function permitted producers to create a distinct product *identity* for the relatively anonymous commodities which they replaced.[210]

Today, goodwill lies at the heart of trademark protection (and trademark infringement claims). Goodwill is that "intangible asset that provides added value to the owner's worth".[211] Robert Bone has analyzed the development of "goodwill" in trademark law, and distinguishes between three kinds of goodwill: brand goodwill, firm goodwill, and inherent goodwill.[212] Brand goodwill is the most limited of the three. It refers to the positive information consumers have about a specific brand, such as its reliability, high quality, and the like. Firm goodwill is broader: this type of goodwill extends beyond associations with a brand to

---

206 *Diamond*: The Historical Development of Trademarks, p. 247.

207 *Fezer*: Markenrecht, § 1 Geschützte Marken, para. 13. Fezer observes that trademarks can identify and communicate in the market: "Schlagwortartig formuliert: Die Marke *identifiziert* und *kommuniziert* auf dem Markt." (emphasis in the original).

208 *Olins*: Corporate Identity, p. 115, cited by *Drescher*: The Transformation and Evolution of Trademarks, p. 327, fn. 93.

209 *Drescher*: The Transformation and Evolution of Trademarks, p. 330.

210 *Drescher*: The Transformation and Evolution of Trademarks, pp. 321–328. Drescher reviews the historical development of trademarks from ancient to modern times, focusing on the rise of advertising, branding and identities, concluding that trademarks today create symbolic associations through "obsessing techniques" (the range of advertising techniques applied to the marketing of a trademarked product).

211 *INTA*: Fact Sheets: Assignments, Licenses and Valuation.

212 *Bone*: Hunting Goodwill, pp. 550–552.

include positive impressions of the firm that sells the brand. When consumers like a particular brand, they sometimes generalize their good feelings to the firm that sells the brand and then to all other products that the firm markets. Finally, inherent goodwill is the broadest category of all: it nothing to do with the specific information being transmitted by the trademarks; instead it has to with the persona of the seller. Bone argues that the expanded protection of goodwill – from original brand goodwill to the broad inherent goodwill – has fundamentally changed the contours and the principles underlying trademark protection.

(c) Modern Significance and Function

Whereas marks initially may have functioned primarily as signs – of identification, origin, or quality – they have since become far more than that. In today's society, whether from a social and cultural point of view or from an economic point of view, trademarks have taken a more symbolic character, reflecting a set of social values and relationships. Inherent in every product are certain cultural association or mythical attachments. Trademarks are the symbols of those characteristics (or have become so through the strategic work of advertisers, who go to great lengths to assure that a product name or the trademark behind the name is highly impregnated with the desired associations).[213] These social values are impregnated back into the trademarks and the trademarks tend to function as omnipresent symbols of a persona.

Advertising around trademarks functions as the modern myth which "mediates between the abstract and the concrete, as well as between social values, cultural symbols and ordinary consumption behaviour. Further, it is a communication process and an intersection of at least two major types of communication: that of signs and that of values."[214] This is reflected in the value assigned to brands – Coca-Cola alone is valued at more than $7 billion – far more than any of its physical manufacturing plants. Roberto Goizueta,[215] the late CEO of Coca-Cola, has been quoted as follows: "All our factories and facilities could burn down tomorrow but you'd hardly touch the value of the company; all that actually lies in the goodwill of our brand franchise and the collective knowledge

213 *Drescher*: The Transformation and Evolution of Trademarks, pp. 306–307.

214 *Leymore*: Hidden Myth, p. 329.

215 Roberto Críspulo Goizueta was Chairman, Director, and Chief Executive Officer of The Coca-Cola Company from August 1980 until his death in October 1997. *CNN*: Coke CEO Roberto C. Goizueta dies at 65.

in the company."[216] A similar position is noted in a company booklet by Johnson & Johnson: "Our company's name and trademark are by far our most valuable assets."[217]

1.4 Chapter Observations

The function of trademarks in our society has evolved significantly. Originally, trademarks were used primarily as either origin/source identifiers to prevent consumer confusion or guarantees of quality to minimize consumer search costs. Today, trademarks are big business, big money, competitive commercial assets. Their value lies in the strength of their "commercial magnetism" and power to persuade.[218]

The laws protecting trademarks have played a role in this trajectory. As will be noted, the legal protection of trademarks – in both the U.S. (Chapter 2) and Europe (Chapter 3) – was originally based on public interest principles of fair competition and the deterrence of consumer confusion and fraudulent practices.[219] Trademarks were the short-hand signal through which consumers could identify a particular product with a specific source. Protection of trademarks has expanded beyond this function and beyond principles of unfair competition, however, as commercial transactions and our global economy have grown increasingly complex. Today, trademark law is characterized by a private entitlement – quasi-property right – perspective.

216 *Kotler*: Marketing Insights from A to Z, p. 8.

217 *Kotler*: Marketing Insights from A to Z, p. 8. For a case study of Johnson & Johnson's strategies regarding its brand, see *Global Intellectual Property Center*: Intellectual Property Protection and Enforcement Manual, pp. 31–32.

218 *Mishawaka Rubber & Woolen Mfg. Co. v. S. S. Kresge Co.*, 316 U.S. 203, at 205, coining the term "commercial magnetism." See *Klieger*: Trademark Dilution, p. 793.

219 *United Drug Co. V. Theodore Rectanus Co.*, 248 U.S. 90, 97 (1918): "There is no such thing as property in a trade-mark except as a right appurtenant to an established business or trade in connection with which the mark is employed. The law of trademarks is but a part of the broader law of unfair competition; the right to a particular mark grows out of its use, not its mere adoption; its function is simply to designate the goods as the product of a particular trader and to protect his good will against the sale of another's product as his; and it is not the subject of property except in connection with an existing business."

2. U.S. Trademark Protection: Common Law Roots & Commerce

2.1 Overview

Although trademarks played an important commercial role in the United States even prior to the nation's founding in 1776, they were the last type of intellectual property to be protected by federal statute in 1870,[220] and infringement cases were very rare until the late 19th century.[221] Originally, state common law provided the main source of protection for trademarks. However, in 1870, the U.S. Congress enacted the first federal trademark law. Since then, federal trademark law has consistently expanded, taking over much of the ground initially covered by state common law. Today, federal law provides the main, and by and large the most extensive, source of trademark protection, although state common law actions are still available.[222]

One interesting point to note is that protection in the United States today (alongside a few other common law countries) is unique in that it requires actual *use* of (or a showing of a bona fide *intent to use*)[223] the trademark *prior* to

---

220 Congress enacted the first federal patent law on 10 April 1790 and the first federal copyright law on 31 May 1790. *FTC*: To Promote Innovation, p. 34, n. 25. The first federal trademark statute was not enacted until 1870 (although this statute was then struck down by the Supreme Court in 1879). Although trade secret law is regulated primarily under state, not federal, law, the first trade secret case in the United States was in 1837 in *Vickery v. Welch*, 36 Mass. (19 Pick.) 523, 527 (1837). *Lemley*: The Surprising Virtues of Treating Trade Secrets as IP Rights, p. 315 and fn. 6.

221 See *Lindberg*: Intellectual Property and Open Source, p. 5. Edward Rogers reports that only sixty-two trademark cases were reported up until 1870, with which were included five others about newspaper names, four about hotel names, and others about names of stores and the like. *Rogers*: Some Historical Matter Concerning Trade-Marks, p. 253, fn. 36 (citations omitted).

222 The current federal trademark statute is the Lanham Act of 1946, codified in Title 15 of the United States Code. See below, §§ 2.3(a) and 2.4 for further discussion.

223 Section 1(a) of the Lanham Act (15 U.S.C. § 1051) requires that an application verifies that the mark is "in use in commerce" on or in connection with the goods or services listed in the application. Section 45 (§ 1127) clarifies further: "The term "use in commerce" means the bona fide use of a mark in the ordinary course

registration,[224] and gives some priority of rights based solely on use (as do other common law countries). Other countries (e.g., in the EU, under the Trademark Directive[225] and the Community Trade Mark Regulation[226]) only require "genuine use in the Community" within a period of five years *following* registration.[227] The principle of use *prior* to registration thus remains a unique aspect of U.S. law even today and differs from protection in most countries, where rights are typically secured first by registration and thereafter maintained by use in the country.

---

of trade ... a mark shall be deemed to be in use in commerce ... on goods when ... it is placed in any manner on the goods or their containers or the displays ... and the goods are sold or transported in commerce." For an "intent-to-use" application under Section 1(b) (§ 1051) (for national applications) or Section 44 (§ 1126) (for foreign applicants), the applicant is required to verify that it has a bona fide intention to use the mark in commerce on or in connection with the goods or services listed in the application, and actual use of the mark *must* occur before the registration is issued. See *USPTO*: Rules of Practice & Federal Statutes, pp. 25–27.

224 This is also the case in Canada, where the Trademarks Act (RS 1985, cT-13) and Trademarks Regulations (1996) (SOR/96-195) govern registered trademarks. Protection for unregistered marks (which begins essentially from the moment that they are put into commercial use) can be found in the common law action to restrain a competitor from passing off its goods, business or services as those of another. The Trademarks Act has also codified the common law cause of action in relation to unregistered marks in Section 7. See *Zimmerman/Zimmerman*: Canada, p. 28. See also *Fenwick & West LLP*: 2004 Update: International Legal Protection, p. 6.

225 First Council Directive 89/104/EEC of 21 December 1988 to approximate the laws of the Member States relating to trade marks (OJ L 040/1, 11.02.1989); codified as Directive 2008/95/EC (OJ L 299/25, 8.11.2008). See discussion below, at section § 3.3(c) et seq.

226 Council Regulation (EC) No 40/94 of 20 December 1993 on the Community trade mark; codified as Council Regulation (EC) No 207/2009/EC (OJ L 78/1, 24.3.2009). See discussion below, at section § 3.3(d) et seq.

227 Council Regulation (EC) No 207/2009/EC, OJ L 78/1, 24.3.2009, Art. 15. Directive 2008/95/EC, OJ L 299/25, 8.11.2008, Articles 10 (use of trademarks), 11 (sanctions for non-use of a trademark in legal or administrative proceedings) and 12 (grounds for revocation for non-use).

2.2 Early Protection

(a) 1772–1825: Early Beginnings

The history of trademarks and trademark law in the United States is long[228] and full of lore.[229] The first written reference to a *state* trademark registration in the U.S. appears in 1772 in the court records of Fairfax County, Virginia. It is filed by George Washington (at that time only a farmer and businessman, but later to become the first U.S. President), who went to court to get a trademark for his brand of flour, which he proposed would simply carry the name "G. Washington."[230] The court granted the mark.[231]

In 1791, just two years after the U.S. Constitution had been in operation, a Boston sail maker named George Breck petitioned to be allowed to register his trademark with the new federal government, and the matter was sent to the then-Secretary of State Thomas Jefferson.[232] Jefferson wrote:

> "That it would … contribute to fidelity in the execution of manufacturers, to secure to every manufactory an exclusive right to some mark on its wares, proper to itself.
> That it will, therefore, be reasonable for the General Government to provide in this behalf by law for those cases of manufacture generally, and those only which relate to commerce with foreign nations, and among the several States, and with the Indian Tribes."[233]

---

228 For an excellent review of the U.S. legislative and judicial background, see *Pattishall*: Two Hundred Years. See also *Rogers*: Good Will, Trade-Marks and Unfair Trading, pp. 34–39; *Greenberg*: The Ancient Lineage of Trade-Marks; *Ruston*: On the Origin of Trademarks; *Paster*: Trademarks – Their Early History; *Rogers*: Some Historical Matter Concerning Trade-Marks, and *Rosen*: In Search of the Trade-Mark Cases.

229 See *About.com – Inventors*: Points To Ponder – Trademarks; *University of Texas Libraries*: U.S. Trademark History Timeline; and *Invention Geek*: Beginning of US Trademark Laws.

230 *Preserving History*: Trademark Timeline, p. 1025. See also *Pattishall*: Two Hundred Years.

231 *Pattishall*: Two Hundred Years, p. 121 and n. 3, citing *Grubisich*: Washington's Flour, 46, col 1.

232 *Rosen*: In Search of the Trade-Mark Cases, pp. 830–31.

233 *Jefferson*: Report on the policy of securing particular marks, pp. 156–57, cited by *Rosen*: In Search of the Trade-Mark Cases, fn. 11. See also *Rogers*: Some Historical Matter Concerning Trade-Marks, pp. 251–252 and fn. 32. Jefferson's "commerce" language tracks the "Commerce Clause" language of the Constitution, which grants Congress the power "to regulate commerce with foreign nations, and among the several states, and with the Indian tribes." U.S. Constitution, Article 1, Section 8, Clause 3.

Although Jefferson advocated that a trademark law be passed by the federal government – based on Congress' enumerated powers – no laws were passed at the time, and a trademark law would not be contemplated by the federal government for nearly 70 years.[234]

Early cases revolving around trade identity or trade markings did not appear to acknowledge any inherent rights in a name or any concern that consumers might be confused. For example, in the 1825 trade identity case *Snowden v. Noah*,[235] the purchaser of a New York newspaper, *The National Advocate*, sought to enjoin the seller from publishing in New York another paper entitled *The New York National Advocate*. The court decided that the names were *sufficiently distinct* to prevent deception[236] – demonstrating how narrowly the courts viewed any rights in a name (if at all recognizing a right) and how easily they denied relief.

The first reported state *trademark* (as opposed to trade identity) case is *Thomson v. Winchester*, heard in the Massachusetts state courts in 1837[237] Here, the action was brought by a plaintiff who sold medicines of his own preparation under the name "Thomsonian Medicines." The defendant began to sell *inferior* medicines under the *same* name and suit was brought as an action on the case.[238] Here, again, no relief was granted against the use of an identical mark on similar goods. The judge noted: "The right to make and to sell is common to all, if no deceit is practiced by one, in falsely assuming the name and credit of another."[239]

Taylor v. Carpenter, decided in 1844, was the first reported case heard in the federal courts.[240] The plaintiff claimed that its name and other distinguishing devices on its spools of thread had been copied. Judge Story held that the case was "one of unmitigated and designed infringement of the rights of the plaintiffs for the purpose of defrauding the public and taking from the plaintiffs the fair

---

234 *Rosen*: In Search of the Trade-Mark Cases, pp. 830–31.

235 *Snowden v. Noah*, Hopkins, Ch R 347 (New York Chancery Court, 1825) as cited in *Preserving History*: Trademark Timeline, p. 1025; and by *Pattishall*: Two Hundred Years, pp. 123–124, fn. 10, citing *Cox*: A Manual of Trade-Mark Cases, p. 1. This case is categorized as the first reported decision of a U.S. *trade identity* case.

236 *Preserving History*: Trademark Timeline, p. 1025. See also *Pattishall*: Two Hundred Years, pp. 123–124, fn. 12, citing *Cox*: A Manual of Trade-Mark Cases, p. 5.

237 36 Mass (19 Pick) 214 (Sup Ct Mass 1837), cited by *Pattishall*: Two Hundred Years, pp. 123–124, fn. 5, citing *Cox*: A Manual of Trade-Mark Cases, pp. 27–28.

238 *Pattishall*: Two Hundred Years, pp. 123–124, fn. 5, citing *Cox*: A Manual of Trade-Mark Cases, pp. 27–28.

239 *Id.*

240 3 Story 458 (CC D Mass 1844), cited by *Pattishall*: Two Hundred Years, pp. 123–124, fn. 6, citing *Cox*: American Trade Mark Cases, p. 14.

earnings of their skill, labor, and enterprise."[241] Here the court found reason to protect the interests and investments of the plaintiffs against infringement.

(b) 1845–1860: New York State Trademark Statute

Until the 1840s, the inspection of traded goods in New York cities, which involved inspectors and weighers, was "treated as a monopoly" of the state government.[242] Business leaders, along with local politicians, complained that the inspection process "led to grotesque patronage and remained akin to imposing a commercial surcharge on goods and services" and lobbied for marks that would signal acceptable products, requiring no review or inspection.[243] In 1845 (or 1860),[244] New York became the first state to legislate state trademark protection for a variety of goods and services and became the epicentre of trademark registrations.[245]

In 1860, Francis H. Upton published the first American treatise on trademark law,[246] entitled *A Treatise on the Law of Trade Marks*.[247] Upton introduced his book and the importance of trademarks in commerce as follows:

> "The subject of this Treatise has assumed an interest and importance, within the past quarter of a century, not inferior to that attached to any branch of the law connection with the affairs of trade and commerce.
> The instruments by which the manufacturer or the merchant, is enabled to designate the merchandise that he makes, or sells, so that its identity in the marts of commerce shall be faithfully preserved, are often valuable beyond estimation, for the reason that the merchandise itself, without these, would become comparatively valueless."[248]

Upton understood the uniqueness of trademarks, noting that "the peculiar phraseology of the Patent Laws of the United States" "which grant to the inventor or producer of a new and original *design* the exclusive right of multiplying copes of the same, have, to some extent, let to the practice, of availing of its provisions to

---

241 *Pattishall*: Two Hundred Years, pp. 123–124, fn. 7, citing *Cox*: American Trade Mark Cases, p. 19.

242 *Clark*: The American Economy, pp. 683–684.

243 *Id.*, p. 684.

244 The date is disputed. *Clark*: The American Economy, p. 684, cites 1845; in *Preserving History*: Trademark Timeline, p. 1025, the date is 1860.

245 *Clark*: The American Economy, p. 683.

246 *Pattishall*: Two Hundred Years, fn. 43; *Preserving History*: Trademark Timeline, p. 1025.

247 *Upton*: A treatise on the law of trade marks.

248 *Id.*, Preface.

secure what is supposed to be an equivalent to trade mark property."[249] Upton also asserted that: "The right of property in trade marks does not partake in any degree of the nature and character of a patent or copyright, to which it has sometimes been referred – nor is it safe to reason from any supposed analogies existing between them."[250]

(c) 1870–1880: Federal Trademark Laws, Registration & Unconstitutionality

On 8 July 1870, Congress enacted the first federal trademark legislation,[251] which provided for the registration of trademarks in addition to civil remedies for their infringement.[252] Trade was growing rapidly during the Reconstruction Period after the Civil War and manufacturers needed a way to establish their identity and protect against infringement.[253] In 1876, a second federal trademark statute was enacted.[254] Congress did not, however, base the federal statutes on the Commerce Clause (as Jefferson had suggested in 1791). Instead, Congress based the statutes on the so-called "Patent and Copyright Clause" which reads: "The Congress shall have Power … To promote the Progress of Science and useful Arts, by securing for limited Times to Authors and Inventors the exclusive Right to their respective Writings and Discoveries."[255] Congress had already used this Clause 8

---

249 *Upton*: A treatise on the law of trade marks, p. 17. Although Upton specifically refers to and quotes from the "act of 1842", there was no 1842 patent act. Congress has enacted: (i) the Patent Act of 1790; (ii) the Patent Act of 1793; (iii) the Patent Act of 1836; (iv) the Patent Act of 1870; (v) and the Patent Act of 1952, codified as amended at 35 U.S.C. §§ 1–376, which is still in effect today. See *Rose/Jessup*: Whose Rules Rule?, p. 578, fn. 29; *Davis/Caltrider*: Timing (of Invention) Is Everything; and *Walterscheid*: Novelty & the Hotchkiss Standard.

250 *Upton*: A treatise on the law of trade marks, p. 14.

251 Act of July 8, 1870, 16 Stat. 198, cited by *Klieger*: Trademark Dilution, p. 798, fn. 43.

252 See *Trade-Mark Cases*, 100 U.S. 82 (1879) at 85.

253 *Spiegel & Utrera*: A Brief History.

254 Act of Aug. 14, 1876, 19 Stat. 141. *Trade-Mark Cases*, 100 U.S. 82 (1879).

255 U.S. Constitution, Article I, Section 8, Clause 8. The clause confers two distinct powers: the power to secure for limited times to authors the exclusive right to their writings (the basis for U.S. copyright law), and the power to secure for limited times to inventors the exclusive rights to their discoveries (the basis for U.S. patent law). For further information regarding the clause, see *Justia*: Copyrights and Patents. For the official transcript of the U.S. Constitution, see *U.S. National Archives and Records Administration*: U.S. Constitution. The U.S. Constitution is housed at the National Archives and Records Administration (NARA) and can be viewed in the

enumerated power to enact the first patent act on 10 April 1790[256] and the first copyright act on 31 May 1790.[257]

Common lore has it that Damon R. Averill registered the first trademark under the 1870 law, thereby receiving protection for a logo dominated by an eagle.[258] This logo was used to identify a brand of ready-mixed painted made of linseed oil and zinc oxide produced by the Averill paint company for which Averill had obtained a patent in 1867.[259]

Rotunda for the Charters of Freedom. *U.S. National Archives and Records Administration*: Visitor Information. For a fascinating review of the historical precedents of the Patent and Copyright Clause in state constitutions as well as the debates surrounding its inclusion in the U.S. Constitution, see *Walterscheid*: Defining the Patent & Copyright Term, pp. 347–356.

256 Patent Act of 1790, Ch. 7; 1 Stat. 109 (April 10, 1790). See *FTC*: To Promote Innovation, p. 34, n. 25, which cites *Mergers/Duffy*: Patent Law & Policy (reviewing history of patent law); and *Schechter/Thomas*: Intellectual Property, § 13.2 at 283–87(2003) (also reviewing the history of patent law).

257 Copyright Act, 1 Cong. Ch. 15; 1 Stat. 124 (1790). For a review of copyright law as it was conceived and developed in the United States, including the historical roots of copyright (with early "glimmers of copyright emanating from the Roman Empire") and the influence of England's Statute of Anne, enacted in 1710, see *Dallon*: The Problem with Congress and Copyright Law. For an overview of the development of copyright privileges in England, see *Walterscheid*: Defining the Patent & Copyright Term, pp. 331–346.

258 *Demand Media*: Who was the first U.S. citizen to have a trademark.

259 Averill was a paint manufacturer with a plant in Newburgh, Ohio, just south of Cleveland. In 1867, Averill was granted the first patent for ready-mixed paint in 1867 ("patent No. 7,031, dated April 4, 1876, and granted to Damon R. Averill, assignee, for an improvement in paints, the claim being for a mixed liquid paint composed of certain ingredients"). *Bragdon/Renfrew*: Paint, Varnish, and Plastics Chemistry; and *Funding Universe*: The Sherwin-Williams Company. Averill hoped the patent would help him dominate the ready-mixed paint business. The patent specified a mixture of linseed oil and zinc oxide, with smaller amounts of lead acetate, zinc sulfate, water, sodium silicate, lime water, and benzine. Although the patent set forth a long and precise recipe, Averill sued virtually every maker of zinc oxide paint as an infringer until his patent was declared excessively broad, and thus invalid, in 1881. *Funderburg*: Paint Without Pain. *Averill Chemical Paint Co. v. National Mixed Paint Co. and Others*, Federal Reporter, Vol. 9 (Circuit Court, S.D. New York, 29 October 1881). For access to the opinion, see *American Law*: Averill Chemical Paint Co.

In 1879, the Supreme Court declared both the 1870 and 1876 trademark statutes invalid and unconstitutional in *The Trade-Mark Cases*.[260] The Court found the initial trademark laws were unconstitutional, having been based improperly on and exceeding the powers granted by the Patent and Copyright Clause of the Constitution. The Court noted that, although the Patent & Copyright Clause "may be a judicious aid to the common law on the subject of trademarks, and may be within the competency of legislatures whose general powers embrace that class of subjects, we are unable to see any such power in the constitutional provision concerning authors and inventors, and their writings and discoveries."[261]

The Court suggested that Congress did have the power to regulate trademarks, but that any such law would need to be passed under Congress' power under the Commerce Clause.[262] Justice Miller went on further to say: "Congress having power to legislate upon the subject of trade-marks as a general interest of commerce, it is submitted that the legislation of Congress, the purpose of which is to give them uniform protection throughout the country, is constitutional."[263]

---

260 *Trade-Mark Cases*, 100 U.S. 82 (1879). The *Trade-Mark Cases* were a set of three cases consolidated into a single appeal before the United States Supreme Court. The Court found that the Patent and Copyright Clause of the Constitution gave Congress no power to protect or regulate trademarks. The combined cases were *United States v. Steffens*, *United States v. Wittemann*, and *United States v. Johnson*. The first two cases dealt with alleged counterfeiting of marks associated with champagne. The third dealt with alleged counterfeiting of a mark associated with whiskey. The opinion was written by Justice Samuel Freeman Miller. Thereafter, Congress passed the Trade Mark Act of 1881, which was based on the Commerce Clause power, and therefore passed constitutional muster: "The argument drawn from the likeness which property in the use of trade-marks bears to that in patents and copyrights, and from the fact that Congress, in legislating upon these three matters, has, both in the original act and in the Revised Statutes, classed them together, demands careful consideration." *Trade-Mark Cases*, 100 U.S. at 86.

261 *Id.* at 94.

262 "I maintain the constitutionality of the statute upon which the indictments and the information are found, upon the ground that it regulates commerce within the power given to Congress by clause 3 of section 8 of article 1 of the Constitution, which provides that the Congress shall have power 'to regulate commerce with foreign nations, and among the several States, and with the Indian tribes.'" *Trade-Mark Cases*, 100 U.S. 82, 86 (1879).

263 *Trade-Mark Cases*, 100 U.S. 82, 91 (1879).

(d) United States Trademark Association (INTA)

In November 1878, a group of merchants and manufacturers founded the United States Trademark Association (USTA) in New York, seeing the need for an organization "to protect and promote the rights of trademark owners, to secure useful legislation and to give aid and encouragement to all efforts for the advancement and observance of trademark rights."[264] In 1993, USTA changed its name to INTA (International Trademark Association) to reflect its international diversity. Today, more than 6,300 members from 190+ countries participate in INTA's global trademark research, policy development, education, and training activities.[265]

(e) 1881–1920: New Federal Trademark Laws

Congress interpreted *The Trade-mark Cases* decision very strictly: in 1881, Congress adopted a new federal registration statute that, unlike its predecessor, limited registration and regulation only to trademarks used in commerce with foreign nations and with the Indian tribes, areas specified under the Commerce Clause.[266] USTA (now INTA) lobbied for enactment of the 1881 Act, arguing that manufacturers should be able to protect their brands as a necessity of commerce when engaging in foreign trade.[267]

As the American – and international – economy changed, the 1881 U.S. federal trademark law quickly became outdated. In 1898, the then-President of USTA, Mr. Francis Forbes, was appointed by President William McKinley to head a commission to revise the U.S. statutes relating to patents and trademarks.[268] This commission's report to Congress in 1900 made recommendations that formed the basis of the Trade-Mark Act of 1905,[269] which adopted the principle of prior

264 *INTA*: About; *INTA*: History.

265 *Id.*

266 Act of March 3, 1881, ch. 138, 21 Stat. 502, entitled "An Act to authorize the registration of trade-marks and protect the same". It was not until 1905 that Congress would again enact a trademark law generally governing marks in use in the U.S., though the 1905 act was also carefully worded to fall within the Commerce Clause. For further information and history regarding the Commerce Clause and the authority it grants Congress, see *Cornell University Law School*: Commerce Clause.

267 *INTA*: History; and *Clark*: The American Economy, p. 685.

268 *Clark*: The American Economy, p. 685.

269 *INTA*: History. Act of February 20, 1905, ch. 592, 33 Stat. 724. The 1905 statue was given a major overhaul and then also saw additional changes in the years after. Primarily, the "intention to deceive" the consumer through trademark misappropriation

ownership and use. The new law triggered 16,224 applications that year – nearly a sevenfold increase from 1904.[270]

The Inter-American Convention of 1910 for the Protection of Industrial Property led to further changes implemented by the Trade-Mark Act of 1920. This third attempt at federal registration, which did reach marks used in interstate commerce, remained in force until the enactment of the Lanham Act.[271]

(f) Concurrent International Developments: Paris Convention & Madrid Agreement

As trade expanded, use of and reliance on commercial symbols grew. By the mid-nineteenth century, concerns and questions regarding trademarks were being posed by judges and regulators throughout Europe and the world.[272]

In 1883, the Paris Convention for the Protection of Industrial Property,[273] considered the *Magna Carta* of international trademark law[274] and one of the oldest intellectual property treaties in the world, was enacted. The Convention was designed to help people of one country obtain protection in other countries for their intellectual creations in the form of industrial property rights, including inventions (patents), trademarks and industrial designs[275] (but excluding copyright).

Specifically, the Convention requires its signatories to recognise applications made for patents, designs, and trademarks from other signatory countries in the same way as it recognises applications from its own nationals.[276] Furthermore, the Convention stipulates that, once the applicant indeed becomes the owner

---

was substituted with "the likelihood of consumer confusion". See *Feng*: Trademark: Its history, influence and issues.

270 *Clark*: The American Economy, p. 685.

271 *Klieger*: Trademark Dilution, p. 798.

272 See below, EU Legal Framework, § 3.1.

273 The Paris Convention for the Protection of Industrial Property was enacted on 20 March 1883, and revised in Brussels on 14 December 1900; in Washington on 2 June 1911; in The Hague on 6 November 1925; in London on 2 June 1934; in Lisbon on 31 October 1958; and in Stockholm on 14 July 1967 (hereinafter, the "Paris Convention of 1883"). It was further amended on 28 September 1979. See *WIPO*: Paris Convention, Summary. For a description of the revisions and amendments, see *Blakeney*: The International Protection of Industrial Property, pp. 4–9.

274 *Preserving History*: Trademark Timeline, p. 1027.

275 See *WIPO*: WIPO Treaties – General Information.

276 *European Commission*: Intellectual Property Strategy, MEMO/11/332.

of a patent, design, or trademark, the owner will have the same protection and the same remedies against an infringement as a national owner. The Convention is administered by the World Intellectual Property Organisation (WIPO). The Convention currently has 175 signatory countries, including all EU Member States and the United States.[277]

In 1891, the Madrid Agreement Concerning the International Registration of Marks was created within the Paris Convention.[278] To date, the United States has never become a contracting party to the Madrid Agreement, but it has enacted the Madrid Protocol.[279]

2.3 The Lanham Act and the Beginning of the Modern Phase

(a) The Lanham Trademark Act

On 5 July 1946, the U.S. Congress passed the Lanham Trademark Act.[280] The act modernized the trademark law in the United States and had as its goal: "To provide for the registration and protection of trade-marks used in commerce, to carry out the provisions of certain international conventions, and for other purposes." The Lanham Act is found in Title 15 of the U.S. Code and contains the federal statutes governing trademark law in the United States. However, this act is not the exclusive law governing U.S. trademark law, since both common law and state statutes also control some aspects of trademark protection.[281]

The Act was named for Democratic Congressman Fritz G. Lanham of Texas. On 22 January 1945, Congressman Lanham introduced a bill intended to encourage registration and protect marks from unfair competition. The bill defined

---

277 *WIPO*: Contracting Parties (Paris). The United States became a contracting party to the Paris Convention in 1887.

278 The Madrid Agreement Concerning the International Registration of Marks of 14 April 1891; revised in Brussels on 14 December 1900; in Washington on 2 June 1911; in The Hague on 6 November 1925; in London on 2 June 1934; in Nice on 15 June 1957; and in Stockholm on 14 July 1967; and amended on 28 September 1979 (hereinafter, the "Madrid Agreement of 1891"). See *Preserving History*: Trademark Timeline, p. 1028.

279 *WIPO*: Madrid Agreement (Marks) (1891) and Madrid Protocol (1989). *WIPO*. State member status (Madrid). The United States signed the Madrid Protocol on 2 November 2003.

280 15 U.S.C. § 1127.

281 *USPTO*: Trademark Basics. *INTA*: Trademark Basics: A Guide for Business. See also *Boston University School of Law*: Trademark Law Research Guide, which provides statutory research, legislative histories, agency decisions, and more.

a trademark as "any word, name, symbol, device or any combination thereof adopted by a manufacturer or merchant to identify his goods and distinguish them from those manufactured or sold by others." The bill also introduced a separate prohibition against unfair methods of competition, expanded the concept of infringement, allowed for registration of service marks, provided incontestability for marks in continuous use for five years, and made federal registration of a trademark constructive notice of the registrant's claim of ownership. These provisions form the basic structure of the law today.[282]

The bill was passed on 5 July 1946, signed into law by Democratic President Harry S. Truman and became known as the Lanham Act.[283] Later that year the Republicans regained control of both the U.S. Senate and U.S. House of Representatives, but the Lanham Act took effect in 1947, unimpeded by this shift.[284]

(b) Trademark Trial and Appeal Board

Almost a decade later, given the increase in the amount of trademark applications at the Patent Office and a backlog of appeals at the Patent Office, the Trademark Trial and Appeal Board (TTAB) was established in 1958.[285] The TTAB is an administrative tribunal of the United States Patent and Trademark Office (USPTO),[286] empowered to determine only the right to *register*.[287] In essence, it is the judicial arm of the USPTO and its proceedings are somewhat similar to a civil action in court.[288] TTAB panels hear hundreds of claims each year relating to trademarks.

---

282 See generally *Horwitz/Levi*: Fifty Years of the Lanham Act.

283 Trademark Act of 1946, 15 U.S.C. §§ 1051–1127. The Act took effect on 5 July 1947. See *Spiegel & Utrera*: A Brief History.

284 Ann Bartow argues that Congressional opposition to changes in the trademark laws haves not been particularly fractious, nor was it noticeably divided along party lines. Both political parties seem to have reached a rough consensus that strengthening the powers and privileges of trademark holders was beneficial for the nation. *Bartow*: When Bias is Bipartisan, p. 728.

285 1958 – Pub. L. 85-609, 15 U.S.C. § 1070. See *Spiegel & Utrera*: A Brief History.

286 *USPTO*: TTAB Manual of Procedure, § 102.01.

287 "In every case of interference, opposition to registration, application to register as a lawful concurrent user, or application to cancel the registration of a mark, the Director shall give notice to all parties and shall direct a Trademark Trial and Appeal Board to determine and decide the respective rights of registration." 15 U.S.C. § 1067 (a).

288 *Finnegan, Henderson*: Overview of TTAB Oppositions.

(c) Modern Amendments: Enhanced Protection

In more recent years, amendments and supplementary acts to the Lanham Act have been adopted. The effects of these amendments have been substantial, granting trademark holders enhanced rights and privileges with respect to the scope of their trademark protection. For example:

- In 1962, a number of minor changes were made to the Lanham Act, primarily correcting and clarifying various language difficulties and errors.[289] However, a more substantive amendment broadened the "likelihood of confusion" test by deleting from the remedial section the limitation to "purchasers" of those likely to be confused, mistaken or deceived.[290]
- In 1975, Congress amended the Act to allow for attorneys' fees to prevailing parties in exceptional cases.[291] That same year, the Patent Office was renamed the Patent and Trademark Office, which is an agency within the Department of Commerce.[292]
- In 1984, after an enormous growth in trademark counterfeiting, Congress passed the Trademark Counterfeiting Act of 1984.[293] Remedies included new

---

289 Act of 9 October 1962, Pub. L 87-772, 76 Stat 769. The revisions included insertion of provisions regarding the likelihood of use causing confusion, mistake, or deception, and deleted the limitation on recovery to acts committed with knowledge that such acts would deceive purchasers. See legislative notes to 15 USC § 1114 – Remedies; infringement; innocent infringement by printers and publishers.

290 Act of 9 October 1962, PL 87-772, 76 Stat 773. See *Pattishall*: Two Hundred Years, fn. 123–124.

291 15 USC § 1117 – Recovery for violation of rights, 1975 – Pub. L. 93-600. The amendments included insertion of provisions awarding of attorney fees in exceptional cases. Beverly Pattishall noted this amendment was in response to the Supreme Court's 1967 decision in *Fleischmann Distilling Corp. v. Maier* Brewing Co., 386 US 714 (1967), which barred attorney's fee awards as inappropriate under the Lanham Act. *Pattishall*: Two Hundred Years, p. 142.

292 15 USC § 1117 – Recovery for violation of rights, 1975 – Pub. L. 93-596 substituted "Patent and Trademark Office" for "Patent Office".

293 Act of 12 October 1984, Pub. L. No. 98-473, 98 Stat. 2178, codified at 18 U.S.C. § 2320. The Act created an offense which provides that: "Whoever intentionally traffics or attempts to traffic in goods and services and knowingly uses a counterfeit mark on or in connection with such goods or services" shall be guilty of a felony. 18 U.S.C. § 2320(a). Section 2320(b) enables the United States to obtain an order for the destruction of articles in the possession of a defendant in a prosecution upon a determination by the preponderance of the evidence that such articles bear counterfeit marks. The Act also amended 15 U.S.C. § 1501 et seq. to create stronger

civil actions with virtually mandatory awards of *treble* damages and attorneys' fees.

- In 1984, Congress passed the Trademark Clarification Act[294] in direct response to the Ninth Circuit's decision in *Anti-Monopoly, Inc. v. General Mills Fun Group, Inc.*,[295] which had held that purchaser *motivation* in buying a product was the crucial test in determining if a trademark was generic.[296]
- In 1988, Congress passed the Trademark Law Revision Act,[297] amending the strict use-based system prevalent in the US by including an intent-to-use registration system as well. With the 1988 amendments, a *bona fide* intention to use a mark protects it from infringing use if the mark is timely used.[298] This brought U.S. trademark law more in line with the global market, but the focus of the legal protection was no longer predicated upon consumer perception.[299]

---

remedies in civil cases involving the intentional use of a counterfeit trademark. The amendments provided mechanisms for obtaining statutory damages, treble damages, and attorney's fees. 15 U.S.C. § 1117. *DOJ*: Criminal Resource Manual, Section 1701.

294 Act of 8 November 1984, Pub. L. 98-620, title I, 98 Stat. 3335, codified at 15 U.S.C. § 1051, amending §§ 1064 and 1127.

295 684 F.2d 1316 (9th Cir. 1982), cert. denied, 459 U.S. 1227 (1983).

296 In contrast, § 1064(3) provides that "a registered mark shall not be deemed to be the common descriptive name of goods or services solely because such mark is also used as a name of or to identify a unique product or service, and that *the primary significance of the registered mark* to the relevant public *rather than* purchaser motivation shall be the test for determining whether the registered mark has become the common descriptive name of goods or services in connection with which it has been used." 15 U.S.C. § 1064(3) (emphasis mine).

297 Act of 16 November 1988, Pub. L. No. 100-667, 102 Stat. 3935, amending 15 U.S.C. §§ 1051–1127. See *Thill*: The 1988 Trademark Law Revision Act; and *Pierce*: The Trademark Law Revision Act.

298 The Lanham Act had originally required a mark to be used in interstate commerce *before* application for registration. This was not required in most countries and had led to "token use" or mock shipments across state lines to meet the requirement. Under the Revision Act, applicants had the choice of applying on the basis of use in commerce or on the basis of a *bona fide* intention to use the mark in commerce in the future. Duration and renewal periods were also reduced from twenty years to ten years and filing of an application would now be considered "constructive use", subject to the mark being registered. *Spiegel & Utrera*: A Brief History.

299 *Beebe*: Search and Persuasion in Trademark Law, p. 2069, citing generally *Carter*: The Trouble with Trademark, and *Port*: The Congressional Expansion of American Trademark Law.

The Act significantly expanded the subject matter and scope of protection under § 43(a).[300]

- In 1992, Congress passed the Trademark Remedy Clarification Act in 1992[301] pursuant to which states and state employees could be held liable in infringement suits to the same extent as private businesses.
- The Federal Trademark Dilution Act (FTDA) of 1996[302] provided owners of famous trademarks with a federal cause of action to: (i) protect famous marks from unauthorized use; (ii) prevent others from trading upon the goodwill and established renown of such marks; and (iii) prevent dilution of the distinctive quality of such marks. The FTDA sought to enable owners of famous marks to claim against those who lessen the distinctiveness of such famous marks by the use of the same or similar trademarks on similar or dissimilar products or services. The FTDA intended to prevent both actual dilution and likely dilution, without requiring that there be a likelihood of consumer confusion. The FTDA permitted owners of a famous mark to enjoin another party's "commercial use in commerce of a mark or trade name, if such use begins after the mark has become famous and causes dilution of the distinctive quality of the famous mark", thus giving them a course of against potential dilution of their mark's distinctiveness by similar marks.[303]
- The Anti-Counterfeiting Consumer Protection Act of 1996[304] allows greater involvement of law enforcement at all levels and provides stronger penalties, including civil fines based on the value of the genuine goods and statutory damage awards of up to one million dollars per mark.[305]
- The Anticybersquatting Consumer Protection Act of 1999 granted trademark protec-tion to domain names.[306] In order to establish liability, the mark owner

---

300 *Beebe*: Search and Persuasion in Trademark Law, p. 2069, citing generally *McCarthy*: The Sleeping Giant is Now Wide Awake.

301 Pub. L. No. 102-542, codified at 15 U.S.C. § 1122, amending §§ 1114, 1125 and 1127. See legislative note at 15 U.S.C. § 1114.

302 Pub. L. No. 104-98, 109 Stat. 985 (16 January 1996), codified at 15 U.S.C. §§ 1125(c), 1127).

303 15 U.S.C. § 1125(c)(1).

304 Pub. L. No. 104-153, 110 Stat. 1386 (2 July 1996) (18 U.S.C. § 1961(1)(B)). Codified at 15 U.S.C. § 1125(c).

305 15 U.S.C. § 117(b). See *Lane*: The Anticounterfeiting Consumer Protection Act of 1995.

306 Title III of the Intellectual Property and Communications Omnibus Reform Act of 1999, Pub. L. 106-113, 113 Stat. 1501, app. I 1501A-521 (29 November 1999), codified at 15 U.S.C. § 1125(d), 15 U.S.C. § 1129, and 15 U.S.C. § 1114(d).

must show that the alleged cybersquatter has "a bad faith intent to profit from the mark"[307] and has registered or used a domain name that is "(A) identical or confusingly similar to a distinctive mark; [or] identical, confusingly similar, or dilutive of a famous mark".[308]

- The Trademark Dilution Revision Act of 2006[309] significantly augmented the FTDA. Under the revised Act, the owner of a famous trademark may pursue two causes of action. The first is the infringement cause of action (which typically results in "a messy, multifactored, and unpredictable inquiry into whether consumers are confused").[310] The second is the dilution cause of action (which is a largely formal inquiry, looking at whether a defendant's mark is sufficiently similar to the plaintiff's as to be likely to create an "association" between the two marks in the consumer's mind). The Act lists six factors that courts should consider in determining dilution.[311]

(d) Further International Developments: TRIPs

The 1994 Agreement on Trade Related Aspects of Intellectual Property Rights (TRIPs)[312] was enacted to promote uniformity among member nations by introducing minimum protection standards for intellectual property protection worldwide, including patents, copyrights, geographical indications, and trademarks. TRIPs combined provisions of the 1883 Paris Convention[313] (which

307 15 U.S.C. § 1125(d)(1)(A)(i). The provision sets forth both a lengthy list of factors that may be considered bad faith along with a list of behaviour that is excluded. See *Hovenkamp/Janis/Lemley/Leslie*: IP and Antitrust, § 2.4c2, n. 349, pp. 2–71 (2011 Supplement).

308 15 U.S.C. § 1125(d)(1)(A)(ii).

309 Pub. L. No. 109-312, 120 Stat. 1730 (6 October 2006), H.R. 683, 109th Congress.

310 *Beebe*: Search and Persuasion in Trademark Law, p. 2069.

311 Beebe notes that the most important of the six factors will be the first, "the degree of similarity between the designation of source and the famous mark", but that the sixth factor, which asks the court to consider "any actual association between the designation of source," will invite anecdotal and survey evidence on the issue of "association." *Beebe*: Search and Persuasion in Trademark Law, p. 2071 and fn. 210.

312 TRIPS: Agreement on Trade-Related Aspects of Intellectual Property Rights, 15 April 1994, Marrakesh Agreement Establishing the World Trade Organization, Annex 1C, The Legal Texts: The Results of the Uruguay Round of Multilateral Trade Negotiations (1999). See *World Trade Organization*: TRIPS.

313 The Paris Convention of 1883. See above, § 2.2(f).

covered patents, designs, and trademarks) and the 1886 Berne Convention[314] (for copyright and related rights).[315]

The TRIPS Agreement sets down certain general principles applicable to all intellectual property rights enforcement procedures and contains provisions on civil and administrative procedures, remedies, and provisional measures. It contains special requirements related to border measures and criminal procedures, which specify, in a certain amount of detail, the procedures and remedies that must be available so that right holders can effectively enforce their rights. The Agreement also makes disputes between signatories of the TRIPS obligations subject to the WTO's dispute settlement procedures.

TRIPs is administered by the World Trade Organisation (WTO). Currently, all 159 WTO members are members of the TRIPS agreement, including all EU Member States and the United States. The U.S. has been a member of the WTO since 1 January 1995.[316]

---

314 The Berne Convention for the Protection of Literary and Artistic Works, dated 9 September 1886, completed in Paris on 4 May 1896; revised in Berlin on 13 November 1908; completed in Berne on 20 March 1914; revised in Rome on 2 June 1928; in Brussels on 26 June 1948; in Stockholm on 14 July 1967; and in Paris on 24 July 1971; and amended on 28 September 1979 (hereinafter, the "Berne Convention of 1886"). *WIPO*: Berne Convention. See generally *WIPO*: WIPO Treaties – General Information. The U.S. became a Berne Convention member effective as of 1 March 1989. *U.S. Copyright Office*: International Copyright Relations, p. 2.

315 The Berne Convention of 1886 requires its signatories to automatically recognise the copyright of works of authors from other signatory countries in the same way as it recognises the copyright of its own nationals. In addition, the Berne Convention requires the signatories to provide strong minimum standards for copyright law, including on the duration of protection. The Berne Convention is administered by the WIPO and currently has 167 signatory countries, including all EU Member States and the United States. *WIPO*: Berne Convention, Contracting Parties. Further worldwide copyright rights were promulgated in the Rome Convention for the Protection of Performers, Producers of Phonograms and Broadcasting Organisations of 1961, and the 2002 WIPO Copyright Treaty, which provides additional protection for copyright as it covers in particular on-demand, interactive communication through the Internet. It forms a special agreement under the Berne Convention and ensures that computer programmes are protected as literary works as well as the arrangement and selection of databases. See *European Commission*: Intellectual Property Strategy, MEMO/11/332.

316 *WTO*: Members & Observers.

2.4 Modern U.S. Trademark Law

(a) Scope & Duration of Protection

In the United States today, the term "trademark" is used to refer to any classification of mark that is protected under the Lanham Act (15 U.S.C. § 1127), including trademarks, service marks, collective marks, certification marks and geographic indications of source, trade names, trade dress, and product configurations.[317]

The Lanham Act states that the term trademark "includes any word, name, symbol, or device, or any combination thereof ... used by a person ... to identify and distinguish his or her goods ... from those manufactured or sold by others and to indicate the source of the goods, even if that source is unknown".[318]

As the definition suggests, a trademark may consist of a word ("Starbucks"), a name ("Hewlett Packard"), a symbol or device (the Nike "Swoosh"). Furthermore, shapes (the Coca-Cola bottle), sounds (the Intel "A♭ D♭ G♭ D♭ A♭" jingle), fragrances, and colors may also be registered as trademarks.[319] The term "trademark" therefore incorporates both verbal and non-verbal source indicators. Almost any word, name, phrase, symbol or design, or a combination thereof, *capable of distinguishing the source of goods*, may be used as a trademark subject to few limitations.[320]

At common law, trademark rights can endure for as long as the trademark in question continues to serve as a distinctive source indicator for the underlying goods or services.[321] Under the Lanham Act, a registration remains in force for ten years, but thereafter registrations can be renewed and endure indefinitely,

317 The different types of trademark classes cover different aspects and functions of trademarks, some with different protection levels. See *Cornell University Law School*: Trademark; *USPTO*: U.S. Trademark Law: Rules of Practice and Federal Statutes; and *USPTO*: Geographical Indications (GI) Protection.

318 15 U.S.C. § 1127 – Construction and definitions.

319 "Since human beings might use as a 'symbol' or 'device' almost anything at all that is capable of carrying meaning, this language, read literally, is not restrictive. The courts and the Patent and Trademark Office have authorized for use as a mark a particular shape (of a Coca-Cola bottle), a particular sound (of NBC's three chimes), and even a particular scent (of plumeria blossoms on sewing thread)." *Qualitex Co. v. Jacobsen Products Co., Inc.*, 514 U.S. 159, 253 (1995).

320 See *Cornell University Law School*: Trademark.

321 *Hovenkamp/Janis/Lemley/Leslie*: IP and Antitrust, § 2.4a2, pp. 2–64.

assuming that the registrant complies with the formal requirements for evidencing continued use and renewal.[322]

The Lanham Act remains the statutory authority for the federal trademark system, including registration of trademarks, protection and federal suits. The Lanham Act does not preempt state trademark regimes: each of the fifty U.S. states has its own state trademark statutes, including laws regarding state registration.[323] The Lanham Act, however, provides the main, and by and large the most extensive, source of protection, whereas the state statutes generally offer overlapping protection to the federal laws.

(b) Jurisdiction & Responsibilities

The U.S. Patent & Trademark Office takes initial jurisdiction over filings for federal trademark registration.[324] USPTO trademark examiners review applications and make registrability determinations.[325]

The TTAB has jurisdiction for hearing and deciding: (i) appeals from decisions by USPTO examiners refusing registration of a mark;[326] (ii) opposition proceedings filed against trademark applications;[327] (iii) four types of *inter partes* proceedings, namely, oppositions to registration, cancellation proceedings

---

322 15 U.S.C. § 1058(a) requires the registrant to filing a continued-use affidavit six years after registration and for each successive ten-year period after registration; 15 U.S.C. § 1059(a) requires the registrant to file renewal filings for each successive ten-year period after registration.

323 Owners of federally registered marks make use the registration ® symbol, whereas state or unregistered trademark users may only use the ™ symbol. 15 U.S.C. § 1111. State registrations are generally used for in-state commerce. Federal registration does not necessarily have rights over a state trademark; the time of registration and the actual use of the mark are all taken into consideration. *Segall*: United States, p. 304.

324 The United States Patent and Trademark Office (USPTO) is the Federal agency for granting U.S. patents and registering trademarks. *USPTO*: The USPTO: Who We Are.

325 The Trademark Office of the USPTO employs approximately 400 attorneys as trademark examiners. The Trademark Office receives more than 232,000 trademark applications every year. See *USPTO*: Career pages.

326 15 USC § 1070 – Appeals to Trademark Trial and Appeal Board from decisions of examiners. An appeal is typically based upon a substantive finding of a likelihood of confusion (§ 2(f)) or mere descriptiveness (§ 2(e)(1)). Once an appeal is filed, the applicant must argue, based on the record, why the USPTO examining attorney was wrong and why the applied for trademark or service mark should be registered. *USPTO*: TTAB Manual of Procedure, § 102.02.

327 15 U.S.C. §§ 1067 and 1068.

against registered marks, interferences, and concurrent use proceedings where one or more parties alleges its mark is entitled to concurrent registration, typically restricting the geographic territory held by a registered mark;[328] and (iv) claims asserting that trademarks should not be registered because they are generic, disparaging, or confusingly similar to existing marks.[329] Such challenges to registration are initially considered by trademark examining attorneys, whose judgment may be appealed to the TTAB. Practices and procedures for litigating before the TTAB are published in the Trademark Trial and Appeal Board Manual of Procedure, commonly known as the "TBMP".[330]

Once the TTAB issues a final decision (on motion or after trial), the losing party has the right to file a request for reconsideration within one month of the Board's decision. The losing party also has the right to file an appeal of the Board's decision to either the U.S. Court of Appeals for the Federal Circuit (for a "traditional" appeal)[331] or to a U.S. District Court (in the form of a civil action against the USPTO, for a *de novo* review in which the parties can introduce new evidence and assert claims and counterclaims for infringement, dilution, etc.).[332]

(c) Registration Application & Process

If the USPTO trademark examiner approves the application – i.e., determines that an application meets registrability requirements[333] – the application will be published in the Official Gazette of the USPTO for opposition.[334]

Any person who believes that he or she would be damaged by the registration of a mark, including damage caused by dilution, may initiate an opposition proceeding before the USPTO to challenge registrability.[335] Potential opponents have 30 days from the publication date to file an opposition or request an extension of

---

328 *USPTO*: TTAB Manual of Procedure, § 102.02.

329 15 U.S.C. §§ 1067, 1068, 1070, and 1092. See also *USPTO*: TTAB Manual of Procedure, § 102.01, fn. 1.

330 *USPTO*: TTAB Manual of Procedure.

331 15 U.S.C. § 1071(a) – Appeal to courts.

332 15 USC § 1071(b). See also *Finnegan, Henderson*: Overview of TTAB Oppositions. See also *USPTO*: TTAB Manual of Procedure.

333 Applications can be made under § 1 or § 44 of the Trademark Act, 15 U.S.C. §§ 1051 or 1126. Applications that fail to meet the prerequisites for Principal Register registration may be registrable on the Supplemental Registers. 15 U.S.C. §§ 1091–1096.

334 15 U.S.C. § 1062; 37 C.F.R. § 2.80 (Code of Federal Regulations).

335 15 U.S.C. § 1063 – Opposition to registration; 37 C.F.R. §§ 2.101–2.106.

time to do so.[336] Opponents must plead and prove that: (1) they are likely to be damaged by registration of the applicant's mark; and (2) that there are valid legal grounds why the applicant is not entitled to register the claimed mark. Unless registration is successfully opposed, all applications will proceed to registration upon expiration of the opposition period.[337] Furthermore, within five years after a trademark has been registered, any person may challenge an issued registration in a "cancellation" proceeding, based on the ground that she believes that she is or will be damaged.[338]

An application may be rejected on a number of grounds, including (i) generic marks or descriptive marks that have not attained secondary meaning,[339] (ii) marks that are "immoral, deceptive, or scandalous",[340] (iii) marks that are primarily surnames,[341] and (iv) marks that are confusingly similar to a prior registered mark.[342] The rejection of the application does *not* necessarily mean that it is not entitled to trademark protection; it only means that the mark is not entitled to the additional benefits of federal registrations as noted below.[343]

(i) Benefits of Registration

Although registration is not required to enjoy federal trademark protection, registration does confer a number of benefits to the registering party. Subject to various statutory requirements and exceptions, a registered mark may achieve an "incontestable" status after five years of continuous use.[344] An "incontestable"

336 Extensions of up to 90 days are possible without the consent of the applicant. One further 60-day extension is possible, but only with the consent of the applicant. No further extensions are possible, such that the total opposition period cannot exceed 180 days from publication. *Segall*: United States, p. 306.

337 Once registered in the PTO, a certificate of registration is issued, and notice of the registration is published in the Official Gazette. 15 U.S.C. § 1063.

338 5 USC § 1064 – Cancellation of registration.

339 Some of these designations may be registrable on the Supplemental Register (e.g., descriptive terms and surnames). Others may not be registered at all (e.g., generic terms, deceptively misdescriptive terms and geographically misdescriptive terms). *Segall*: United States, pp. 305–06.

340 15 U.S.C. § 1052(a).

341 15 U.S.C. § 1052(e).

342 15 U.S.C. § 1052(d).

343 *USPTO*: Frequently Asked Questions about Trademarks. *Liu*: Overview of Trademark Law.

344 15 U.S.C. § 1065.

registration stands as conclusive evidence of validity,[345] ownership,[346] and the owner's exclusive right to use, enhancing the owner's rights by eliminating a number of defenses to claims of infringement.

However, in accordance with 15 U.S.C. § 1115(b), incontestable status is expressly subject to a list of nine enumerated defences, including fraudulent procurement of a registration,[347] functionality,[348] and (of particular significance to the intellectual property/antitrust interface) if "the mark has been or is being used to violate the antitrust laws of the United States".[349]

Registered marks enjoy additional advantages over unregistered marks:

- Registered marks are afforded nationwide protection, dating back to the filing date of the underlying application,[350] even if actual sales are limited to a specific geographic area.[351]
- Owners of federally registered marks make use the registration ® symbol, whereas state or unregistered trademarks may only use the ™ symbol.[352]
- Registration is necessary in order to record a registration with the U.S. Customs Services so that infringing merchandise can be seized at the borders.[353]

---

345 15 U.S.C. § 1057(b) and 15 U.S.C. § 1115(a). Registered marks are considered presumptively valid, such that proof of secondary meaning is not required. See also *Segall*: United States, p. 304. Once a registration has become "incontestable", challenges to registration validity based on a mark's alleged descriptiveness are foreclosed. See *Park 'N Fly v. Dollar Park and Fly*, 469 U.S. 189 (1985) (confirming that the incontestability provision precludes descriptiveness challenges).

346 15 U.S.C. § 1115(a). Given the presumption of ownership for registered marks, the burden of proof in ownership disputes is shifted. *Segall*: United States, p. 304. Furthermore, registration serves as nationwide constructive notice of ownership and use of the mark under 15 U.S.C. § 1072.

347 15 U.S.C. § 1115(b)(1).

348 15 U.S.C. § 1115(b)(8).

349 15 U.S.C. § 1115(b)(7).

350 *Segall*: United States, p. 304. In contrast, protection for unregistered marks is limited to the geographic area in which such products are sold, along with any areas in which the producer would be expected to expand into or any areas where the reputation of the mark has been established. *Liu*: Overview of Trademark Law.

351 This right is limited, however, to the extent that the mark is already being used by others within a specific geographic area. If that is the case, then the prior user of the mark retains the right to use that mark within that geographic area; the party registering the mark gets the right to use it everywhere else. *Liu*: Overview of Trademark Law.

352 15 U.S.C. § 1111.

353 19 U.S.C. § 1526(b).

- Registration enables a party to bring an infringement suit in federal court.[354] Registration allows a party to potentially recover treble damages, attorneys fees, and other remedies.[355]

(ii) Unregistered Marks

The Lanham Act provides federal protection for distinctive marks that are used in commerce.[356] Federal protection for *unregistered* marks is generally available under 15 U.S.C. § 1125(a), which creates a civil cause of action for claims of false designation of origin and false advertising (i.e., as an unfair competition claim).[357]

Unregistered marks receive a great deal of protection at the state level by statute and/or common law. Under state common law, trademarks are protected as part of the law of unfair competition. State statutes vary, but most states have either adopted a version of the Model Trademark Bill (MTB), which provides for trademark registration, or the Uniform Deceptive Trade Practices Act (UDTPA), which does not.[358] Finally, because of the use requirement under U.S. trademark law, unregistered marks are essentially protected from the moment that they are put into commercial use.[359]

(d) Requirements for Protection

There are three basic requirements for trademark protection: (i) the mark must be distinctive; (ii) the protected mark cannot be functional, and (iii) the mark must be used (or intended to be used) in commerce.

---

354 15 U.S.C. § 1121(a).

355 15. U.S.C. § 1117(a).

356 15 U.S.C. §§ 1051 et seq.

357 15 U.S.C. § 1125(a) sets out the "likelihood of confusion" standard for infringement of an unregistered trademark or trade dress. Courts still frequently refer to this as "Section 43(a)", as this was the original Lanham Act numbering, before codification at 15 U.S.C. § 1125. The language refers to: "any false designation of origin, false or misleading description of fact, or false or misleading representation of fact, which (A) is likely to cause confusion, or to cause mistake, or to deceive as to the affiliation, connection, or association of such person with another person, or as to the origin, sponsorship, or approval of his or her goods, services, or commercial activities by another person". 15 U.S.C. § 1125(a)(1)(A).

358 *Cornell University Law School*: Trademark.

359 *Segall*: United States, p. 304.

(i) Distinctiveness Requirement

The first requirement, that a mark be distinctive, turns on whether a mark is capable of identifying the source of a particular good and distinguishing such good from the goods of another producer. In determining whether a mark is distinctive, the courts group marks into four categories, based on the relationship between the mark and the underlying product: (1) arbitrary or fanciful, (2) suggestive, (3) descriptive, or (4) generic.[360]

The primary purpose underlying the requirement that the subject matter is not functional is "to police the boundary between trademark and patent protection."[361] In the absence of this requirement, a registrant could assert trademark protection (which can last indefinitely) as a surrogate for patent protection (which endures for only a limited term).[362] As the Supreme Court held in *TrafFix*: "The Lanham Act does not exist to reward manufacturers for their innovation in creating a particular device; that is the purpose of the patent law and its period of exclusivity."[363]

(ii) Functionality Prohibition

Although the Lanham Act does not define functionality, it refuses registration for any mark that "comprises any matter that, as a whole, is functional"[364] and deems functionality a basis for cancellation of a registered mark.[365] Furthermore, in civil actions to enforce rights in unregistered trade dress, "the person who asserts trade dress protection has the burden of proving that the matter sought to be protected is not functional."[366]

Under case law, the Supreme Court established the test for functionality in *Inwood Laboratories, Inc. v. Ives Laboratories, Inc.*: "In general terms, a product feature is functional and cannot serve as a trademark, if it is essential to the use or purpose of the article or if it affects the cost or quality of the article."[367] Subsequently, in *Qualitex Co. v. Jacobson Prods. Co.*, the Supreme Court added

---

360 *Zatarain's, Inc. v. Oak Grove Smokehouse, Inc. and Visko's Fish Fry, Inc.*, 698 F.2d 786 (5th Cir. 1983).

361 *Hovenkamp/Janis/Lemley/Leslie*: IP and Antitrust, § 2.4b2, pp. 2–66.

362 *Id.*

363 *TrafFix Devices, Inc. v. Marketing Displays, Inc.*, 532 U.S. 23, 34 (2001).

364 15 U.S.C. § 1052(e).

365 15 U.S.C. § 1064(3).

366 15 U.S.C. § 1125(a)(3). See also *Cone*: Evaluating Trade Dress Functionality.

367 *Inwood Laboratories, Inc. v. Ives Laboratories, Inc.*, 456 U.S. 844, 850-51 n. 10 (1982).

to the *Inwood* test, explaining in the context of a single-color trade dress, that a functional feature is one "the exclusive use of [which] would put competitors at a significant non-reputation-related disadvantage."[368] A valid mark, as well as being source identifying, must be non-functional. The idea is to prohibit a trademark owner from "inhibiting legitimate competition by allowing a producer to control a useful product feature."[369]

(iii) Use (or Intent to Use) in Commerce

The Trademark Law Revision Act of 1988, which was implemented on 16 November 1989, contained "the most significant amendments to the Lanham Act since its enactment in 1947."[370] Prior to November 1989, U.S. applicants could not file an application for federal trademark registration until they had actually *used* a trademark in commerce. In order to comply with its obligations under the Madrid Protocol,[371] however, the USPTO extended potential protection to applicants that wished to file an application before they commenced use of a mark with goods or services in interstate commerce,[372] much like the majority of international trademark systems in civil law countries.

The Lanham Act defines a trademark as a mark *used* in commerce, or registered with a *bona fide* intent to use in commerce.[373] If a mark is not in use in commerce at the time the application for registration is filed, registration may

368 *Qualitex Co. v. Jacobson Prods. Co.*, 514 U.S. 159, 165 (1995).

369 *Id.*, at 164-65.

370 *USPTO*: Nr. 157, Questions and Answers.

371 These changes were implemented pursuant to the Madrid Protocol Implementation Act of 2002, Pub. L. 107-273, 116 Stat. 1758, 1913-1921 ("MPIA"). Effective 2 November 2003, the MPIA provides that: (1) the owner of a U.S. application or registration may seek protection of its mark in any of the countries party to the Protocol Relating to the Madrid Agreement Concerning the International Registration of Marks ("Madrid Protocol") by submitting a single international application to the International Bureau of the World Intellectual Property Organization ("IB") through the USPTO; and (2) the owner of an application or registration in a country party to the Madrid Protocol may obtain an international registration from the IB and request an extension of protection of the international registration to the United States.

372 For the owner of an application or registration in a country party to the Madrid Protocol seeking protection in the United States: "Use in commerce prior to registration is not required." *USPTO*: Examination Guide 2-03, as codified in 15 U.S.C. § 1141h(a)(3).

373 15 U.S.C. § 1127.

still be permitted if the applicant establishes, in writing, a good faith intent to use the mark in commerce at a future date.[374] The applicant has a six-month period (which can be extended for an additional, single 6-month period) to show evidence of actual use in commerce; if such evidence does not satisfy the Director of the USPTO, such application can be abandoned.[375] Furthermore, registration obtained through reliance on the Paris Convention or the Madrid Protocol (both of which do not require use) will not provide protection from infringement.[376]

The use of a mark generally means the actual sale of a product to the public with the mark attached. Both at common law and under traditional Lanham Act registration procedures, exclusive rights to a trademark are awarded to the first to use it in commerce.[377] At common law, the use requirement had a distinct geographic dimension: priority for protection was acquired for such use, but limited to the geographic area in which such products were sold, without giving rights sufficient to preclude use by a geographically remote user who adopted the same or similar mark in good faith.[378] In contrast, a Lanham Act registrant enjoys nation-wide constructive notice, eliminating the opportunity for geographically remote users to claim good faith adoption after the registrant's date of application.[379] Furthermore, prior to registration, priority is acquired for use in the geographic are in which the products are sold, along with any areas in which the producer would be expected to expand into or any areas where the reputation of the mark has been established.[380]

(e) Loss of Rights: Genericness

Trademark rights can be lost through genericity. Sometimes, trademarks that are originally distinctive can become generic over time, thereby losing their trademark protection.[381] A word will be considered generic when, in the minds of a substantial majority of the public, the word denotes a broad genus or type of product and not a specific source or manufacturer.[382] In deciding whether a term

---

374 15 U.S.C. § 1051(b)(1).
375 15 U.S.C. § 1051(d)(1)-(4).
376 *Segall*: United States, p. 304.
377 *Cornell University Law School*: Trademark.
378 *United Drug Co. v. Theodore Rectanus Co.*, 248 U.S. 90 (1918).
379 *Dawn Donut Co. v. Hart's Food Stores*, 267 F.2d 358 (2d Cir. 1959).
380 *Liu*: Overview of Trademark Law.
381 *Kellogg Co. v. National Biscuit Co.*, 305 U.S. 111 (1938).
382 *Liu*: Overview of Trademark Law.

is generic, courts will often look to dictionary definitions, the use of the term in newspapers and magazines, and any evidence of attempts by the trademark owner to police its mark.

However, trademark rights vary country by country, so trademarks deemed generic in one country (e.g., aspirin, cellophane, and thermos in the U.S.) still maintain protection as registered trademarks in other jurisdictions (e.g., Aspirin and Thermos in Germany; Cellophane in the U.K.[383] Similarly, Canada still regards YO-YO as a trademark for a brand of the popular spinner-on-a-string, even though a U.S. court declared it a generic term for such toys over 40 years ago.[384]

The chart below considers the trademark history of aspirin, cellophane, and thermos: originally these all had trademark protection in the U.S., but have subsequently lost legal protection in the U.S. by becoming the common name of the relevant product or service.[385] In some countries, they still enjoy trademark protection.

Aspirin	In the U.S., "aspirin" was declared generic in 1921.[386] In Germany (where it was first registered in 1899 by Bayer Aktiengesellschaft[387]) and many countries in the EU, "Aspirin" is still a protected trademark.
Cellophane	"Cellophane" was originally a trademark of DuPont. In 1936, it was declared generic in the U.S.[388] The court held that "The fact that [Dupont] had registered 'cellophane' as a trademark would give it no right to monopolize a term useful to designate a commercial article."[389] In Europe, it is still a registered trademark of Innovia Films Ltd, with a first filing date of 1 April 1912 in England.[390]

383 *Lockhart*: There's a Trademark Graveyard.

384 *Lockhart*: There's a Trademark Graveyard. *Meisenheimer*: Lucky's History of the Yo-Yo.

385 For additional examples of trademarks which have become generic in the U.S. (including Brassiere, Cola, Escalator, Linoleum, Murphy Bed, Yo-Yo, and Zipper), see Schedule 3.

386 *Bayer Co. v. United Drug Co.*, 272 F. 505 (S.D.N.Y. 1921).

387 *DPMA*: Registernummer 36433.

388 *Dupont Cellophane Co. v. Waxed Products Co.*, 85 F.2d 75 (2d Cir. N.Y. 1936).

389 *Id.*, at 80.

390 *U.K. Intellectual Property Office*: Trademark UK00000341636.

Thermos	Invented in 1892 by Sir James Dewar, a Scottish chemist and physicist, the "vacuum flask" was first manufactured for commercial use in 1904, when two German glass blowers formed Thermos-Gesellschaft M.B.H. (Thermos GmbH). They held a contest to name the "vacuum flask" and a resident of Munich submitted "Thermos", which came from the Greek word "Therme" meaning "heat".[391] The trademark is still protected in other countries, including Germany[392] and Japan.[393] On 20 March 1907, Thermos-Gesellschaft M.B.H applied to the U.S. patent office for registration of "Thermos" as a trademark. It was registered on 7 January 1908.[394] In 1907, Thermos GmbH sold the Thermos trademark rights to three independent companies, including The American Thermos Bottle Company in the U.S.[395] In the U.S., the trademark was declared generic in 1963. The Second Circuit found that, although a minority still considered the word trademarked, the substantial majority of the public perceived "thermos" as generic.[396]

(i) Xerox: Campaign Against Genericide

Xerox has become famous for its print campaign in order to save its trademark from becoming generic. Its trademark was threatened when people began to use the term 'xerox' in the place of 'photocopy'. Xerox took the position that an aggressive ad campaign could save Xerox from joining those trademarks – including aspirin, escalator, and yo-yo – lost to colloquial use.[397]

391 *Thermos*: Our History.

392 The German Patent and Trade Mark Office (*Deutsches Patent- und Markenamt* or DPMA) lists numerous "Thermos" trademarks, registered to Thermos LLC, Rolling Meadows, IL, in the U.S. and Thermos KK, Yoshida Niigata, in Japan.

393 The IPDL (Industrial Property Digital Library) of the Japanese Patent Office permits searching. *IPDL*: Trademarks. A basic search compiled 22 "Thermos" registered trademarks. *IPDL*: Thermos.

394 *American Thermos Products Co. v. Aladdin Industries, Inc.*, 207 F. Supp. 9, 12 (D. Conn. 1962).

395 *Thermos*: Our History.

396 *King-Seeley Thermos Co. v. Aladdin Indus., Inc.*, 321 F.2d 577, 579-80 (2d Cir. 1963) and *American Thermos Prods. Co. v. Aladdin Indus.*, 207 F. Supp. 9 (D. Conn. 1962), aff'd, 321 F.2d 577 (2d Cir. 1963), vacated, 418 F.2d 31 (2d Cir. 1969).

397 A famous Xerox ad depicts the "trademark graveyard". For an image of this ad, see *Banner*: U.S. Trademark Law, slide 25.

Xerox has thus spent millions taking out ads aimed at educating so-called "influencers" – lawyers, journalists, and entertainers[398] – about its brand name. A 2003 ad said: "When you use 'Xerox' the way you use 'aspirin', we get a headache."[399] More recently, a 2007 ad read: "If you use 'Xerox' the way you use 'zipper', our trademark could be left wide open."[400]

(f) Causes of Action

The Lanham Act offers a variety of theories by which trademark rights can be enforced, including infringement, anti-dilution, and unfair competition theories. The unfair competition causes of action (under Lanham Act § 43(a))[401] are used to combat reputational injuries arising from false or misleading statements or representations in commerce.[402]

(i) Trademark Infringement

If a party owns the rights to a particular trademark, that party can sue other parties for trademark infringement.[403] The infringement liability for trademarks, however, is markedly less robust than for patent or copyright infringement: for patent[404] or copyright[405] infringement, mere unauthorized use or reproduction will trigger infringement liability; under trademark law the standard is

---

398 *Randag*: Xerox Enlisting Hollywood in Fight Against "Genericide" with Ad.

399 For an example of the "aspirin" ad, see *Lizerbram*: Tiffany Setting – A Generic Term?

400 For examples from the "zipper" ad campaign, see *Atkins*: Are Anti-Genericism Ads Effective?, and *Anderson*: iPad prompts the question: What's in a brand name?

401 15 U.S.C. § 1125(a).

402 *Hovenkamp/Janis/Lemley/Leslie*: IP and Antitrust, § 2.4c, pp. 2–69 (2011 Supplement).

403 35 U.S.C. §§ 1114 and 1125.

404 35 U.S.C. § 271 – Infringement of patent: "(a) Except as otherwise provided in this title, whoever without authority makes, uses, offers to sell, or sells any patented invention, within the United States or imports into the United States any patented invention during the term of the patent therefor, infringes the patent."

405 17 USC § 501 – Infringement of copyright: "(a) Anyone who violates any of the exclusive rights of the copyright owner as provided by sections 106 through 122 or of the author as provided in section 106A (a), or who imports copies or phonorecords into the United States in violation of section 602, is an infringer of the copyright or right of the author, as the case may be." Under 17 USC § 106 – Exclusive rights in copyrighted works, the owner of copyright has the exclusive rights to do and to authorize specific acts.

"likelihood of confusion." More specifically, trademark law protects a trademark owner's exclusive right to use a trademark only in so far as use of the mark by another is likely to cause confusion as to the affiliation, connection or association of defendant with plaintiff, or as to the origin, sponsorship, or approval of defendant's goods, services, or commercial activities by plaintiff.[406]

To establish a violation of the Lanham Act for either a registered mark under 15 U.S.C. § 1114, or an unregistered mark under 15 U.S.C. § 1125(a), the plaintiff must demonstrate that: (i) it has a valid and legally protectable mark; (ii) it owns the mark; and (iii) the defendant's use of the mark to identify goods or services causes a likelihood of confusion.[407]

More specifically, the use of a trademark in connection with the sale of a good constitutes infringement if it is likely to cause consumer confusion as to the *source* of those goods or as to the *sponsorship* or *affiliation* of such goods.[408] Although a showing of actual confusion is not required,[409] claiming the mere "possibility" of confusion is not sufficient.[410]

In deciding whether consumers are likely to be confused, the courts will typically look to a number of factors, as enumerated in the *Polaroid* case,[411] including: the strength of the mark; the degree of similarity between the two marks at issue; the proximity of the products or services associated with the marks at issue; the likelihood that the prior owner will "bridge the gap" (i.e., expand offerings of goods and services in the future so as to come into direct competition with the alleged infringer); evidence of actual confusion; the alleged infringer's bad faith in adopting her mark; the quality of the alleged infringer's products or services; and the sophistication of the buyers of the products or services at issue.

---

406 *1-800 Contacts, Inc. v. WhenU.com, Inc.*, 414 F.3d 400 (2d Cir. 2005).

407 *A&H Sportswear, Inc. v. Victoria's Secret Stores, Inc.*, 237 F.3d 198 (3rd Cir. 2000).

408 15 U.S.C. § 1114(1).

409 Evidence of actual confusion is only required when a plaintiff seeks damages: "To insist on evidence might seem to be to commit the error of thinking that proof of actual confusion is required in a trademark-infringement case, and of course it is not unless damages are sought." *Libman Co v. Vining Indus.*, 69 F.3d 1360, 1363 (7th Cir. 1995) (citations omitted). In *Libman Co.*, the court found the absence of evidence on actual confusion important in concluding that there was no likelihood of confusion.

410 *A&H Sportswear v. Victoria's Secret Stores*, 166 F.3d 197 (3d Cir. 1999) (en banc).

411 *Polaroid Corp. v. Polarad Elect. Corp.*, 287 F.2d 492, 495 (2d Cir.), cert. denied, 368 U.S. 820 (1961). See also *AMF Inc. v. Sleekcraft Boats*, 599 F.2d 341 (9th Cir. 1979).

The *Polaroid* court noted that this catalogue of factors "does not exhaust the possibilities – the court may have to take still other variables into account."[412]

(ii) Trademark Dilution

Even if there is no likelihood of confusion – and therefore no trademark infringement – trademark owners can still bring an action for trademark dilution under either federal or state law, based on the theory that use of the mark at issue may blur or tarnish the prior owner's mark.[413] Under federal law, a dilution claim can only be brought if the mark is "famous".

Although anti-dilution remedies appeared in various state trademark regimes for several decades,[414] the Federal Trademark Dilution Act of 1996,[415] as substantially revised by the Trademark Dilution Revision act of 2006,[416] amended Section 43 of the Lanham Act to provide the cause of action for federal trademark dilution.[417] Under the Act, the owner of a "famous mark" is entitled to an injunction "against another person who, at any time after the owner's mark has become famous, commences use of a mark or trade name in commerce that is likely to cause dilution by blurring or dilution by tarnishment of the famous mark" *regardless* of the presence or absence of actual or likely confusion, of competition, or of actual economic injury.[418]

---

412 *Polaroid Corp. v. Polarad Elect. Corp.*, 287 F.2d 492, 495 (2d Cir.) (citations omitted).

413 "[T]he Act's legislative history further indicates that Congress understood that "dilution" might result either from "uses that blur the distinctiveness of [a famous] mark or [that] tarnish or disparage it." *Ringling Bros.-Barnum & Bailey Combined Shows, Inc. v. Utah Div. of Travel Dev.*, 170 F.3d 449, 452 (4th Cir. Va. 1999), citing H.R. Rep. No. 104-374, at 2 (1995).

414 *Hovenkamp/Janis/Lemley/Leslie*: IP and Antitrust, § 2.4c2, page 2-70 (2011 Supplement).

415 Pub. L. No. 104-98, 109 Stat. 985 (16 January 1996), codified at 15 U.S.C. §§ 1125(c), 1127).

416 Pub. L. No. 109-312, 120 Stat. 1730 (6 October 2006), codified at 15 U.S.C. §§ 1125(c)(1)-(2), 1117(a), 1118.

417 See *Ringling Bros.-Barnum & Bailey Combined Shows, Inc. v. Utah Div. of Travel Dev.*, 170 F.3d 449, 453-56 (4th Cir. Va. 1999) for a synopsis of the evolution of the dilution theory, beginning with Frank Schechter in 1925.

418 15 U.S.C. § 1125(c)(1). The 2006 legislation made the "likelihood of dilution" standard explicit, abolishing the Supreme Court's ruling under the prior legislation, which had imposed an "actual dilution" standard. In *Moseley v. V Secret Catalogue*, 537 U.S. 418, 433 (U.S. 2003), the Supreme Court had held that the 1996 FTDA "unambiguously requires a showing of actual dilution, rather than a likelihood of

A mark is considered famous if "if it is widely recognized by the general consuming public of the United States as a designation of source of the goods or services of the mark's owner."[419] Factors for determining whether a mark possesses the necessary degree of recognition include: the duration, extent, and geographic reach of advertising and publicity of the mark; the amount volume and geographic extent of sales of goods or services offered under the mark; and the extent of actual recognition of the mark.[420] To establish a claim of federal dilution, the mark must have become famous before use of the allegedly diluting mark or trade name began.[421] Under state law, however, a mark need not be famous in order to give rise to a dilution claim. Instead, dilution is available if: (i) the mark has "selling power" or, in other words, a distinctive quality; and (ii) the two marks are substantially similar.[422]

Dilution is comprised of two principal harms: "dilution by blurring" and "dilution by tarnishment".[423] Dilution by blurring occurs when the distinctiveness of a famous mark is weakened by its identification with another similar mark or trade name.[424] Dilution by tarnishment occurs when the reputation of a famous mark is harmed through identification or association with another similar mark or trade name (for example, Kodak brand bicycles or Xerox brand cigarettes).[425] Although neither example is likely to cause confusion among consumers, each dilutes the distinctive quality of the mark.[426]

The factors to be considered in determining whether a mark or trade name is likely to cause dilution by *blurring* include: the degree of similarity between the mark or trade name and the famous mark; the degree of the famous mark's inherent or acquired distinctiveness; the extent to which the owner of the famous mark is engaged in substantially exclusive use of the mark; the degree of recognition of the famous mark; whether the user of the mark or trade name intended to

---

dilution. This conclusion is fortified by the definition of the term "dilution" [in the 1996 legislation]."

419 15 U.S.C. § 1125(c)(2)(A).

420 15 U.S.C. § 1125(c)(2)(A).

421 *Cornell University Law School*: Dilution (Trademark).

422 *Mead Data Central, Inc. v. Toyota Motor Sales, U.S.A., Inc.*, 875 F.2d 1026 (2d Cir. 1989). *Liu*: Overview of Trademark Law, § 8.

423 See *Starbucks Corp. v. Wolfe's Borough Coffee, Inc.*, 588 F.3d 97 (2d Cir. N.Y. 2009), which analyzes claims of dilution by blurring (pp. 105–110) and dilution by tarnishment (pp. 110–111) under the 2006 legislation.

424 15 U.S.C. § 1125(c)(2)(B).

425 15 U.S.C. § 1125(c)(2)(C).

426 *Liu*: Overview of Trademark Law, § 8.

create an association with the famous mark; and any actual association between the mark or trade name and the famous mark.[427]

Dilution by *tarnishment* occurs when the mark is cast in an unflattering light, typically through its association with inferior or unseemly products or services.[428] As the court in *Starbucks* noted, a trademark "may be tarnished when it is linked to products of shoddy quality, or is portrayed in an unwholesome or unsavory context, with the result that the public will associate the lack of quality or lack of prestige in the defendant's goods with the plaintiff's unrelated goods."[429]

(iii) *Unfair Competition Theories*

In addition to the specific causes of action for infringement and dilution of registered marks, the Lanham Act offers another category that protects both registered and unregistered marks: claims of unfair competition under Lanham Act Section 43(a).[430] Section 43(a) is primarily invoked: (i) when the unauthorized use of an *unregistered* mark is likely to cause confusion as to source, sponsorship, or affiliation – analogous to the registered trademark infringement theory under

---

427 15 U.S.C. § 1125(c)(2)(B).

428 Dilution by tarnishment is "association arising from the similarity between a mark or trade name and a famous mark that harms the reputation of the famous mark." 15 U.S.C. § 1125(c)(2)(C). ToysRUs successfully brought a tarnishment claim against adultsrus.com, a pornographic web-site. *Toys "R" Us v. Akkaoui*, 40 U.S.P.Q.2d (BNA) 1836 (N.D. Cal. Oct. 29, 1996).

429 *Starbucks Corp. v. Wolfe's Borough Coffee, Inc.*, 588 F.3d 97, 110 (2d Cir. N.Y. 2009), citing *Hormel Foods Corp. v. Jim Henson Productions, Inc.*, 73 F.3d 497, 507 (2d Cir. 1996) (internal quotation marks omitted). The court listed a number of cases finding dilution by tarnishment: *Chemical Corp. v. Anheuser-Busch, Inc.*, 306 F.2d 433 (5th Cir. 1962) (finding that use of exterminator's slogan "where there's life, … there's Bugs" tarnished the use of beer company's slogan "where there's life, … there's Bud."); *Steinway & Sons v. Robert Demars & Friends*, 210 U.S.P.Q. 954 (C.D. Cal. 1981) (finding that use of "STEIN-WAY CO." to sell clip-on beverage handles tarnished high-end musical instrument company's use of its name of "STEINWAY & SONS"); *Eastman Kodak Co. v. Rakow*, 739 F. Supp. 116 (W.D.N.Y. 1989) (finding that comedian's stage name "Kodak" tarnished the mark of the Eastman Kodak Company because the comedian's act "includes humor that relates to bodily functions and sex … and … uses crude, off-color language repeatedly" (internal quotation marks omitted)); *Dallas Cowboys Cheerleaders, Inc. v. Pussycat Cinema, Ltd.*, 467 F. Supp. 366 (S.D.N.Y.) (finding that pornographic depiction of a Dallas Cowboys Cheerleader-style cheerleader in an adult film tarnished the professional mark of the Dallas Cowboys Cheerleaders), aff'd, 604 F.2d 200 (2d Cir. 1979).

430 15 U.S.C. § 1125(a).

§ 1114 and § 1125; and (ii) against false or misleading statements in commercial advertising.[431]

Furthermore, a number of additional state law causes of action exist, including passing off, contributory passing off, reverse passing off, and misappropriation.[432]

(g) Defenses

Defendants in a trademark infringement, dilution, or unfair competition claim can assert a number of affirmative defenses.

(i) Fair Use

The Lanham Act notes that "the use of the name, term, or device charged to be an infringement is a use, otherwise than as a mark, of the party's individual name in his own business, or of the individual name of anyone in privity with such party, or of a term or device which is *descriptive of* and *used fairly and in good faith* only to describe the goods or services of such party, or their geographic origin."[433] The fair use defense in trademark law, therefore, protects purely descriptive uses of marks, where the alleged use was undertaken in good faith.[434]

In *Car-Freshner Corp. v. S.C. Johnson & Son*, the Second Circuit noted that the fair use defense "is a fundamental principle marking an outer boundary of the trademark monopoly that, although trademark rights may be acquired in a word or image with descriptive qualities, the acquisition of such rights will not prevent others from using the word or image in good faith in its descriptive

431 15 U.S.C. § 1125(a)(1)(B).

432 "Passing off" occurs when the defendant tries to "pass off" its product as the plaintiff's product (for example, manufacturing computers and claiming that they are made by Apple Computer, Inc.). "Contributory passing off" occurs when the defendant assist or induces another (typically a retailer) to pass off its product as the plaintiff's product (for example, inducing a computer store to represent that the computers are made by Apple, when in fact they are not). "Reverse passing off" occurs when the defendant tries to pass off the plaintiff's product as its own (for example, taking a computer made by Apple, removing the label and putting on a different label). *Liu*: Overview of Trademark Law, § 9.

433 15 U.S.C. § 1115(b)(4) (emphasis mine).

434 *Hovenkamp/Janis/Lemley/Leslie*: IP and Antitrust, § 2.4d1, pp. 2–73 (2011 Supplement). In *Zatarain's, Inc. v. Oak Grove Smokehouse, Inc. and Visko's Fish Fry, Inc.*, 698 F.2d 786 (5th Cir. 1983), the court held that the defendant's use of "fish fry" to describe a batter coating for fish was fair use and did not infringe upon the plaintiff's mark "Fish-Fri" because defendant's use was purely descriptive.

sense, and not as a trademark." The court further noted that "[t]he principle is of great importance because it protects the right of society at large to use words or images in their primary descriptive sense, as against the claims of a trademark owner to exclusivity."[435]

In *Cairns v. Franklin Mint*, the Ninth Circuit distinguished between "classic fair use", in which the defendant uses the plaintiff's mark to describe the defendant's own product, and "nominative fair use", in which the defendant uses the plaintiff's mark to describe or refer to the plaintiff's product, usually for purposes of comparison to the defendant's product.[436]

Fair use includes use of the mark other than as a designation of source for the goods or services in connection with advertising or promotions, thereby permitting consumers to compare goods or services. It also permits identification, parody, criticism, and commentary regarding the owner of the mark or the goods or services connected with the mark.[437] Furthermore, use of a famous mark in any form of news commenting or news reporting, and any non-commercial use of the mark is also not actionable.[438]

(ii) Parody

Another affirmative defense available for trademark claims is parody. Certain parodic use of a trademark may be permissible if they are not too directly tied to commercial use. Similar to the doctrine under copyright law,[439] the theory is that

---

435 *Car-Freshner Corp. v. S.C. Johnson & Son*, 70 F.3d 267, 269 (2d Cir. N.Y. 1995) (citations omitted).

436 *Cairns v. Franklin Mint Co.*, 292 F.3d 1139, 1150 (9th Cir. Cal. 2002). In an earlier case, the newspaper USA Today had run a telephone poll, asking its readers to vote for their favorite member of the music group New Kids on the Block. The New Kids on the Block sued USA Today for trademark infringement. The court held that the use of the group's name was a privileged nominative use because: (i) the group was not readily identifiable without using the mark; (ii) USA Today used only so much of the mark as reasonably necessary to identify it; and (ii) there was no suggestion of endorsement or sponsorship by the group. The basic principle is that use of a trademark is sometimes necessary to identify and talk about another party's products and services. When such conditions are met, such a use will be privileged. *New Kids on the Block v. News America Publishing, Inc.*, 971 F.2d 302 (9th Cir. 1992). *Liu*: Overview of Trademark Law.

437 15 U.S.C. § 1125(c)(3)(A).

438 15 U.S.C. § 1125(c)(B) and (C).

439 17 U.S.C. § 107 contains a list of the various purposes for which the reproduction of a particular work may be considered fair, such as criticism, comment, news

artistic and editorial parodies of trademarks serve a valuable critical function, and that this critical function is entitled to some degree of First Amendment protection. The courts have adopted different ways of incorporating such First Amendment interests into the analysis. For example, some courts have applied the general "likelihood of confusion" analysis, using the First Amendment as a factor in the analysis. Other courts have expressly balanced First Amendment considerations against the degree of likely confusion. Still other courts have held that the First Amendment effectively trumps trademark law, under certain circumstances.[440] Thus, although the courts recognize a parody defense, the precise contours of such a defense are difficult to outline with any precision.

In general, U.S. courts appear to be more sympathetic to the defense when the parodies are less commercial in nature, and less sympathetic when the parodies involve commercial use of the mark.[441] However, some courts have found parodic use protected even when highly commercial.[442]

(iii) Trademark Misuse & Fraudulent Procurement

Generally speaking, intellectual property misuse – whether in the context of patent, copyright, or trademark misuse – is an affirmative, equitable defense to claims of intellectual property infringement, which recognizes that it is possible for an intellectual property owner to abuse her statutorily granted exclusive

---

reporting, teaching, scholarship, and research. In *Campbell v. Acuff-Rose Music Inc.*, the Supreme Court recognized parody as a potential fair use, even when done for profit.

440 See *Liu*: Overview of Trademark Law.

441 In *L.L. Bean, Inc. v. Drake Publishers, Inc.*, 811 F.2d 26, 28 (1st Cir. 1987), a risqué parody of an L.L. Bean magazine advertisement was found not to constitute infringement. Similarly, in *Hormel Foods Corp. v. Jim Henson Prods.*, 73 F.3d 497 (2d Cir. 1996), the use of a pig-like character named "Spa'am" in a Muppet movie was found not to violate Hormel's rights in the trademark "Spam." In contrast, in *Gucci Shops, Inc. v. R.H. Macy & Co.*, 446 F. Supp. 838 (S.D.N.Y. 1977), "Gucchie Goo" diaper bags were found not to be protected under the parody defense. Similarly, in *Coca-Cola Co. v. Gemini Rising, Inc.*, 346 F. Supp. 1183 (E.D.N.Y. 1972), posters bearing the logo "Enjoy Cocaine" were found to violate the rights of Coca-Cola in the slogan "Enjoy Coca-Cola".

442 In *Louis Vuitton Malletier S.A. v. Haute Diggity Dog, LLC*, 507 F.3d 252 (4th Cir. Va. 2007), the court found that Haute Diggity dog's "Chewy Vuiton" dog toys – which loosely resemble miniature handbags that are of similar shape, design, and color of plaintiff's luxury handbags – toys were successful parodies that were not likely to confuse consumers.

rights. Typically, it is invoked by an alleged infringer if and when a rights' owner seeks to enforce her rights with an anticompetitive effect that extends beyond the statutory grant of an intellectual property right.[443] If misuse is found, courts will withhold any remedy for infringement or breach, even against an infringer who is not harmed by the abusive practice.[444]

The doctrine of patent misuse is well established.[445] Although there is little case law on the subject, courts from time to time have intimated that the similarity of rationales underlying the law of patents and the law of copyrights argues for a defense to an infringement of copyright based on misuse of the copyright.[446]

Courts have recognized trademark misuse as a defense, but the doctrine is deemed considerably less robust than patent misuse. As the court noted in *Carl Zeiss Stiftung*:

> "Thus, although misuse of a patent almost inevitably is accompanied by unlawful restraints, *the opportunity for effective antitrust misuse of a trademark*, as distinguished from collateral anti-competitive activities on the part of the manufacturer or seller of the

---

443 In *Mallinckrodt, Inc. v. Medipart, Inc.*, 976 F.2d 700, 704 (Fed. Cir. 1992), the court noted that: "The concept of patent misuse arose to restrain practices that did not in themselves violate any law, but that draw anticompetitive strength from the patent right, and thus were deemed to be contrary to public policy."

444 Daryl Lim, *Misconduct in Standard Setting: The Case for Patent Misuse*, IDEA: The Intellectual Property Law Review, Franklin Pierce Law Center (2011). See also *Barron/Luk*: The Patent Misuse Defense after Princo.

445 In the U.S., the principle of intellectual property misuse as a doctrine was first developed with respect to patents in the 1917 Supreme Court decision, *Motion Picture Patents Co. v. Universal Film Mfg. Co.*, 243 U.S. 502 (1917). U.S. courts often treat patent misuse and antitrust interchangeably and most findings of patent misuse are, in fact, conditioned on conduct that would also violate the antitrust laws. However, there is a difference: the misuse doctrine is a defense grounded in intellectual property policy; the similar prohibitions developed under antitrust law came much later. In most patent misuses cases, however, there is a significant overlap and the laws co-exist. See *Hovenkamp/Janis/Lemley/Leslie*: IP and Antitrust, §§ 3.1, pp. 3–2 and 3–3 (2011 Supplement). See also *Hovenkamp*: Innovation and Competition Policy. As cited, see *United States Gypsum Co. v. National Gypsum Co.*, 352 U.S. 457, 465 (1957); see generally *Lipscomb:*, *Lipscomb's Walker on Patents* §§ 28:32–28:36; and *Calkins*: Patent Law.

446 See generally *Carr*: Copyright Misuse: An Overview; and *Hovenkamp*: Innovation and Competition Policy. For cases, see *United States v. Loew's, Inc.*, 371 U.S. 38, 44–51 (1962); *United States v. Paramount Pictures, Inc.*, 334 U.S. 131 (1948).

goods bearing the mark, *is so limited that it poses a far less serious threat to the economic health of the nation*."[447]

Although many courts and commentators have drawn a sharp distinction between the misuse defense in patent infringement suits, on the one hand, and its use in trademark suits, on the other, some scholars have argued for its revitalization.[448] Most, however, see it as a largely theoretical argument revolving on the boundaries of how a trademark holder can use its rights.[449]

The trademark misuse theory has been applied in only a few cases, primarily related to domain name registration issues. In 1997, Juno Online, an Internet online provider based in New York, claimed "trademark misuse" and violations of the Lanham Act, the Illinois Consumer Fraud and Deceptive Business Practice Act and the Illinois Deceptive Trade Practices Act against Juno Lighting, an Illinois lighting manufacturer and retailer.[450]

The Lanham Act specifically permits anyone to make a petition to cancel a registration of a registered mark at any time (even if the mark has been deemed "incontestable") if "its registration was obtained fraudulently or contrary to the provisions of this [Act]",[451] and expressly acknowledges fraudulent procurement

---

447 *Carl Zeiss Stiftung v. V.E.B. Carl Zeiss, Jena*, 298 F. Supp. 1309, 1314 (S.D.N.Y. 1969) (emphasis mine). In *Clorox Co. v. Sterling Winthrop, Inc.*, 117 F.3d 50, 56 (2d Cir. N.Y. 1997), the Second Circuit quoted from *Carl Zeiss* and cited *McCarthy*: McCarthy on Trademarks and Unfair Competition, 4, § 31:96, pp. 31–145: "Because the economic exclusivity of a trademark is far less than that of a patent, there is far less opportunity for a trademark to play and integral role in violations of the antitrust laws."

448 *Ridgway*: Revitalizing the Doctrine of Trademark Misuse.

449 *Chilling Effects Clearinghouse*: Frequently Asked Questions (and Answers) about Trademark. See also *Ridgway*: Revitalizing the Doctrine of Trademark Misuse. In *Microsoft Corp. v. Compusource Distributors, Inc.* 115 F. Supp. 2d 800 (E.D. Mich 2000), the majority noted that the Sixth Circuit had not addressed the issue of trademark misuse defense and that "courts in other circuits have questioned" its existence. In *Northwestern Corp. v. Gabriel Mfg. Co.*, 48 U.S.P.Q. 2d (BNA) 1902, 1909 (N.D. Ill. 1998), the court surmised that if a trademark misuse defense exists at all, it is likely meant only to cover instances where the trademark is not an effective identifier of source, but rather is misleading to potential purchasers. *ABA*: Antitrust Law Developments, fn. 514.

450 *Juno Online Services, L.P. v. Juno Lighting, Inc.*, 979 F. Supp. 684, (N.D. Ill. 29th September, 1997). The court did note, however, that a trademark misuse defense was deemed less justifiable than a patent misuse defense because "in trademark law, the mark holder usually does not have the ability to destroy competition."

451 15 U.S.C. § 1064(3). For a detailed review of the case law on trademark fraudulent procurement, see *Hovenkamp/Janis/Lemley/Leslie*: IP and Antitrust, § 2.4d2,

(either in the registration or the incontestable right to use) as a defense to a claim of infringement.[452] Furthermore, the Lanham Act allows awards of damages for injuries resulting from another's "false or fraudulent declaration or representation, oral or in writing, or by any false means" in the course of procuring a registration with the USPTO.[453]

(iv) Exhaustion ("First Sale") Doctrine

The so-called principle of "exhaustion" or "first sale" is considered "one of the most fundamental limitations on intellectual property rights".[454] In the U.S., the 1852 Supreme Court case of *Bloomer v. McQuewan*[455] is considered the earliest enunciation of the doctrine of patent exhaustion;[456] in England, the first reported case was in 1870.[457] The first-known U.S. trademark exhaustion case was in the 1886.[458]

The principle regulates when an intellectual property rights owner can and cannot act against a reseller of her protected products. In effect, the intellectual property rights are exhausted once the products have been sold by or with the consent of the rights' owner, and they cannot be used to control the secondary market for those products in that jurisdiction.[459]

Although the doctrine is applicable to all intellectual property rights,[460] there is little uniformity across the federal intellectual property laws.[461] There are two

---

pp. 2-73–75 (2011 Supplement). Hovenkamp et al. have noted that many fraudulent procurement allegations "center around misrepresentations regarding mark use, either on the part of the applicant or on the part of prior users."

452 15 U.S.C. § 1115(b)(1).

453 15 U.S.C. § 1120.

454 *Donnelly*: Parallel Trade and International Harmonization of the Exhaustion of Rights Doctrine, p. 447.

455 55 U.S. 539 (1852).

456 *Porcelli*: Bowman v. Monsanto, pp. 27–32.

457 *Betts v Wilmott* (1870–71) LR 6 Ch App 239, cited by *Stothers*: Patent Exhaustion: the UK Perspective, p. 1, fn. 2.

458 *Apollinaris v. Scherer*, 27 F. 18 (CCSD New York, 1886), cited by *Beier*: Territoriality of Trademark Law, p. 49, fn. 1.

459 *Stothers*: Patent Exhaustion: the UK Perspective, p. 1.

460 For a review of the doctrine as applied to U.S. patents, copyrights, and trademarks, see *Donnelly*: Parallel Trade and International Harmonization of the Exhaustion of Rights Doctrine. For a history of the doctrine with respect to patents, see *Porcelli*: Bowman v. Monsanto, pp. 27–32.

461 The patent exhaustion doctrine is not codified under 35 U.S.C.; instead, the doctrine has evolved in the courts, with two important and relatively recent cases

sources of law that address exhaustion of trademarks: § 42 of the Lanham Act (15 U.S.C. § 1124) and § 526 of the Tariff Act (19 U.S.C. § 1526).[462] Unlike exhaustion of patent rights, trademark law has developed a significant exception to the general rule that rights are exhausted by a lawful first sale: the exception is for genuine products containing material differences from those legitimately sold in the United States under the mark.[463]

(h) Remedies

In trademark infringement suits, successful plaintiffs are entitled to a wide range of remedies under federal law. Injunctive relief – prohibiting further infringing or diluting use of the trademark – is the preferred remedy.[464] Monetary relief may be available, including: (i) defendant's profits, (ii) damages sustained by the plaintiff, and (ii) the costs of the action.[465] Damages may be trebled upon showing of bad faith.[466] Generally speaking, damages are available only if the defendant willfully traded on the plaintiff's goodwill in using the mark; otherwise, plaintiffs in a dilution action are limited to injunctive relief.[467] If a willful violation is proved, the plaintiff may receive specific relief in the form of a destruction of offending articles.[468]

2.5 Chapter Observations

U.S. federal trademark law is designed to prevent consumer confusion in the marketplace by encouraging competitors to use distinctive marks to identify

---

setting precedent: the 2008 Supreme Court case *Quanta v. LG Electronics* (553 U.S. 617) and the 2013 Supreme Court case *Bowman v. Monsanto Co.* (134 S. Ct. 24). Copyright exhaustion was statutorily codified in 1976 at 17 U.S.C. § 109, and since limited by statutory exceptions in 1984 and 1990. For a review of copyrights exhaustion applied to digital distribution, see *Perzanowski/Schultz*: Digital Exhaustion.

462 See generally *Donnelly*: Parallel Trade and International Harmonization of the Exhaustion of Rights Doctrine, pp. 454–456.

463 See *Donnelly*: Parallel Trade and International Harmonization of the Exhaustion of Rights Doctrine, in particular note 74, p. 456, setting out the case law which has developed this exception.

464 15 U.S.C. § 1116(a).

465 The court can award treble damages and may, in exceptional cases, award reasonable attorney fees to the prevailing party. 15 U.S.C. § 1117(a).

466 15 U.S.C. § 1117(b).

467 15 U.S.C. § 1125(c).

468 15 U.S.C. § 1118.

their goods, which allows consumers to distinguish goods amongst competitors.[469] The basic understanding under U.S. trademark law is that protection of trademarks is justified only where marks serve the essential function of preventing customer confusion in the marketplace.[470]

With the implementation of, further revisions to, and interpretation of the Lanham Act, U.S. legislatures and courts have dramatically extended the scope of trademark protection. Some scholars have characterized this expansion – from public interest rationales to private entitlement protection – bleakly: "Trademark law, which was once limited to protecting against consumer confusion, has increasingly taken on the character of a property right, with the result that trademark "owners" now have the power to prevent various kinds of uses of their marks, regardless of whether consumers will be confused."[471]

Such expanded protection gives rise to restrictions on market efficiency and consumer welfare. In particular, the increasing use and scope of trademark dilution law in the U.S. has been deemed "a radical and imprudent alternative to the consumer protection model of trademark rights."[472]

469 *Lemley*: Beyond Preemption, pp. 134–35.

470 See *McCarthy*: McCarthy on Trademarks and Unfair Competition, § 2:14, stating that trademark infringement in the United States is based on the right of the buying public to be free of confusion.

471 See *Lemley*: The Modern Lanham Act (discussing ways in which trademark law has expanded).

472 *Klieger*: Trademark Dilution, p. 795.

3. EU Trademark Protection: Tension Between Competing Interests

The development of laws protecting trademarks in Europe highlights two important observations. First, trademarks were early recognized as important private, autonomous tools of commerce which needed regulation and protection.[473] Second, the network of national laws and registration systems that developed across Europe in the late nineteenth century were at tension with the principles of a united, single Europe that developed in the twentieth century.

3.1 Early Beginnings

The oldest recorded and known judicial trademark case – known as *Sandforth's Case* – was decided in England in circa 1584 and involved a dispute similar to modern trademark counterfeiting.[474] The relatively recent discovery of *Sandforth's Case* strengthens the conclusion that trademark infringement and unfair competition were recognized as a violation of English law as early as the mid-sixteenth century.[475] The *Sandforth* court recognized that the economic and commercial realities of the time required the expansion of the common law to

473 *Fezer*: Markenrecht, Geschichte des Markenrechts, paras. 18–19.

474 Throughout the twentieth century, commentators, academics and courts – on both sides of the Atlantic – cited the 1618 case of *Southern v. How* (Popham's Reports 143, 79 Eng. Rep. 1243) as the starting point of the Anglo-American common law recognition of trademark rights. In the late 1970s, a serendipitous discovery of unpublished legal reports debunked such analysis. For an excellent summary of the case, see *Stolte*: How Early Did Anglo-American Trademark Law Begin?, particular pp. 529–38; and *Thurmon*: Confusion Codified, pp. 258–260. Stolte notes the problem of conflicting dates for this case – either 1584 or 1585 (*Stolte*, p. 529, fn. 101) – as well as the discrepancy as to the name of the case (*Stolte*, p. 506, fn. 2).

475 The first published reference to the case occurred in 1979 in J.H. Baker's survey text, Introduction to English History (*Baker*: Introduction to English History, p. 385). Baker cited the case in a footnote (fn. 45), but provided no translation from the original Latin and only a short summary of the abstract, which Stolte surmises to have been in either Latin or French (*Stolte*: How Early Did Anglo-American Trademark Law Begin?, p. 536, fn. 134). There was no further reference to the case until seven years later, when Baker, together with S.F.C. Milsom, published Sources of English Legal History (*Baker/Milsom*: Sources of English Legal History, pp. 615–18). *Stolte*: How Early Did Anglo-American Trademark Law Begin?, pp. 509, 528 and 540.

protect merchants against trademark piracy and unfair methods of competition in the marketplace.

Trade expanded markets, economies, and commerce worldwide. As trade increased, use of and reliance on commercial symbols grew. By the mid-nineteenth century, concerns and questions regarding trademarks were being posed by judges and regulators throughout Europe.[476]

(a) France

In 1857, France implemented the Manufacture and Goods Mark Act of 1857, arguably the world's first comprehensive trademark system, which introduced the practice of upholding rights based on both a use-based and examination-based trademark system.[477] Criminal statutes for passing-off or fraudulently using geographic designations of origin were already in place earlier.[478] In 1964, the 1857 law was repealed and replaced with a registration-based system. The current law (in force since 1991) follows the lead of the European Union.[479]

(b) United Kingdom

By the mid-nineteenth century, concerns about intellectual property protection – including trademarks – were taking center stage in the UK Parliament and in the public opinion. In 1862, at a Select Committee hearing on trademarks, the Superintendent of Specifications in the Patent Office testified that trademark registration was already available in some European countries (including Austria, Bavaria, Belgium, France, Hanover, The Netherlands, Portugal, Prussia, Russia, Sardinia (Italy), Saxony, Spain, Sweden, Norway, Prussia, Wurttemberg

---

476 For references for scholarship on early trademark and branding practices in the UK and France, see *Desai/Waller*: Brands, Competition, and the Law, fn. 19, citing *Higgins*: The Making of Modern Trade Mark Law; *Duguid*: French Connections; and *Duguid*: Developing the Brand.

477 *Derambure*: The IP Guide to … France.

478 The Factory, Manufacture and Workplace Act of 20 April 1803 (Article 16) has been cited for establishing a system which made it a crime to pass off another's seal as one's own, and the Criminal Acts of 1810 (Article 142) and 1824 (Article 433) made it a punishable crime to abuse the name of others or wrongly use the names of production areas. *Qinghu*: Well-Known Marks.

479 Law No. 91-7 of January 4, 1991 on Trademarks and Service Marks (*Loi No. 91-7 du 4 Janvier 1991 relative aux marques de fabrique, de commerce ou de service*). *WIPO*: resources.

(Germany), and the United States).[480] It was hoped that granting similar rights in Britain would lead to reciprocal rights for British traders abroad.[481] Lawyers experienced in handling trademark piracy cases on behalf of British manufacturers also testified, holding that registration should involve a process of examination of the trademark and the registrar should have the authority to reject a claim on the ground of insufficient distinctness from any existing mark, as was already the case in Prussia.[482]

The scope of the proposed trademark law – including a system for the registration and examination of trademarks, for assignment and for a single trademark (registration) system applying to "all trade marks of all the various and very numerous manufactures of the United Kingdom" – supposedly troubled the Select Committee and it was not until 1875 (some thirteen years later) that such a law was finally put into place.[483] At the same time, another proposed law, which addressed more narrowly criminal remedies against fraudulent applications of trademarks and established criminal offences for uses of mis-descriptions in trade with intent to defraud, was enacted as the Merchandise Marks Act 1862.[484]

In 1875, the first comprehensive British trademark registration system, the Trade Marks Registration Act 1875, was passed which allowed formal registration of trademarks at the UK Patent Office for the first time.[485] In 1883, the new Patents, Designs and Trade Marks Act[486] was passed, followed by revisions in 1888 and 1905 (with statutory changes to the definition of registrable marks),[487] 1919 (which separated the trademark register into Parts A and B, each of which had different registration criteria) and 1938 (setting out infringement terms).[488]

---

480 *Richardson*: Trade Marks and Language, fn. 73 and 74 (2004), citing the Report of Select Committee on Trade Marks Bill (London: Parliament House of Commons, 1862) at 26.

481 *Richardson*: Trade Marks and Language, p. 203.

482 *Id.*, p. 203, fn. 74 and. 75.

483 *Id.*, fn. 74 and 77, citing the Report of Select Committee on Trade Marks Bill (London: Parliament House of Commons, 1862).

484 See *Bently*: The Making of Modern Trade Marks Law, for a detailed history of UK trademark law.

485 Trade Marks Registration Act 1875 (UK) 38 & 39 Vict, c91. See *Richardson*: Trade Marks and Language, fn. 77.

486 Patents, Designs and Trade Marks Act 1883 (UK) 46 and 47 Vict, c57 s64.

487 Trade Marks Act 1905 (UK) (Cth). See *Bently*: The Making of Modern Trade Marks Law, p. 15.

488 Previously, infringement terms were not specified in the early British Acts, but were left to courts, and were only codified in the 1938 Trade Marks Act to require the

The current law – the Trade Marks Act 1994 – implements the standards set down in the European Trade Marks Directive No 89/104/EEC.[489]

(c) Austria

In 1873, the need for international – and not just national – protection of intellectual property became evident when foreign exhibitors refused to attend the International Exhibition of Inventions in Vienna because they were afraid their ideas would be stolen and exploited commercially in other countries.[490] The exhibition was hosted by the government of the Empire of Austria-Hungary, who had invited other countries to participate in an international exhibition of inventions. Given the potential boycott, a special Austrian law was enacted to secure temporary protection to all foreign participants in the exhibition for their inventions, trademarks and industrial designs.[491]

Later that same year, the Congress of Vienna for Patent Reform was convened, elaborating a number of principles on which an effective and useful patent system should be based, and urged governments "to bring about an international understanding upon patent protection as soon as possible."

(d) Germany

German constitutional protection for intellectual property – including trademarks – existed even earlier than the first German trademark law of 1874. Both the 1867 Constitution of the North German Confederation (*Verfassung des Norddeutschen Bundes*)[492] and the 1871 Constitution of the German Empire

---

use of a trademark identical with the registered mark or one so nearly resembling it as to be likely to deceive or cause confusion (s4). *Richardson*: Trade Marks and Language, fn. 113.

489 Trade Marks Act 1994 (UK). See *Richardson*: Trade Marks and Language, fn. 59.

490 Participation "was hampered by the fact that many foreign visitors were not willing to exhibit their inventions at that exhibition in view of the inadequate legal protection offered to exhibited inventions." *WIPO*: Intellectual Property Handbook, Chapter 5, p. 241, § 5.3. See also *WIPO*: WIPO Treaties – General Information. See also *Blakeney*: The International Protection of Industrial Property, pp. 2–3.

491 See *WIPO*: Intellectual Property Handbook, Chapter 5, p. 241, §§ 5.3 and 5.4. See also *WIPO*: WIPO Treaties – General Information.

492 Constitution of the North German Confederation (*Verfassung des Norddeutschen Bundes*), dated 16 April 1867. *DocumentArchiv.de*: Verfassung des Norddeutschen Bundes. The original German text of the 1867 Constitution reads: "Der Beaufsichtigung Seitens des Bundes und der Gesetzgebung desselben unterliegen die

(*Verfassung des Deutschen Reiches*)[493] gave the government and its legislation authority to protect "intellectual property".[494] Unlike the U.S. Constitution, which distinguishes between the authority to protect patents ("discoveries") and copyright ("writings"), from the separate means to regulate trademarks (through the authority "to regulate commerce"), the first form of constitutional protection in Germany immediately referred to the broader concept of "intellectual property" without distinguishing any subcategories.

Interestingly, Art 73, Clause 1, paragraph 9, of the current German Basic Law (*Grundgesetz für die Bundesrepublik Deutschland*)[495] no longer uses the term "intellectual property". Instead, it follows the U.S. model to name the actual rights protected and states: "The Federation shall have exclusive legislative power with respect to: ... industrial property rights, copyrights and publishing."[496] The term "industrial property" includes both patents and trademarks,[497] and the

---

nachstehenden Angelegenheiten: ... 6) der Schutz des geistigen Eigenthums." *Verfassung des Norddeutschen Bundes*, Art. 4, Clause 4, 16 April 1867.

493 Act Concerning the Constitution of the German Empire (*Gesetz, betreffend die Verfassung des Deutschen Reichs*), dated 16 April 1871. Original copy of the Bundes-Gesetzblatt des Deutschen Bundes (RGBl. Nr. 16, 1871, pp. 63 et seq) available from *Landschaftsverband Westfalen-Lippe*: Westfälische Geschichte. *Huber*: Dokumente zur Deutschen Verfassungsgeschichte, Nr. 261. For a thorough review of the historical foundations of German constitutional law and the various forms of state organization in the German Confederation, the North German Confederation, and the German Empire through the Weimar Republic, see *Stern*: Das Staatsrecht der Bundesrepublik Deutschland. For the 1871 Constitution, see *Frotscher/Pieroth*: Verfassungsgeschichte, paras. 372 et seq.

494 "Der Beaufsichtigung Seitens des Reichs und der Gesetzgebung desselben unterliegen die nachstehenden Angelegenheiten:... 6) der Schutz des geistigen Eigenthums". *Verfassung des Deutschen Reichs*, Article 4, Clause 6, 16 April 1871.

495 The German Basic Law (*Grundgesetz*) was formally approved on 8 May 1949.

496 In the original: „Der Bund hat die ausschließliche Gesetzgebung über: ... den gewerblichen Rechtsschutz, das Urheberrecht und das Verlagsrecht."

497 „Der gewerbliche Rechtsschutz i. S. d. Art. 73 Abs. 1 Nr. 9 (1. Alt.) GG umfasst sämtliche Rechtssätze, die dem Schutz des geistigen Schaffens auf gewerblichem Gebiet dienen. [...] Ferner umfasst der gewerbliche Rechtsschutz das Markenrecht, so dass Art. 73 Abs. 1 Nr. 9 (1. Alt.) GG den Erlass diesbezüglicher Bestimmungen – etwa über den Markenbegriff, den Markenschutz u. ä. – ermöglicht. Art. 73 Abs. 1 Nr. 9 (1. Alt.) GG unterfällt zudem das Recht der Warenzeichen. Auf den Kompetenztitel können daher u. a. Bestimmungen über die Anmeldung von Warenzeichen, über ausschließliche Benutzungsrechte, über die Schutzdauer sowie über sog. Freizeichen gestützt werden." *Uhle*: in: *Maunz/Dürig*: Grundgesetz,

term "copyrights and publishing" covers the dual meaning of "author" rights (including moral or personal rights) and "copy" rights.[498] A 1979 German Federal Constitutional Court (*Bundesverfassungsgerichts*) decision reflected this Constitutional protection, holding that trademark rights – as protected under the then-current Trademark Act – were rights protected as property under the Constitution.[499]

The trademark law of 1874 – the *Gesetz über Markenschutz*[500] – is the first and oldest of the German intellectual property laws.[501] It provided a system for central registration without any prior examination and protected words and figurative elements,[502] classification of goods, and examination procedures. Furthermore, the use of a mark was not a prerequisite for registration; hence, the main goal of the law was to grant and guarantee a right – in and of itself – to the owner, without any requirement of use.[503] A second German law protecting trademarks – *Reichsgesetz zum Schutz der Warenbezeichnungen* – was enacted on 12 May 1894 (and effective 1 October 1894).[504] Under this statute, the Patent Office examined

---

Art. 73, paras. 194 et seq. See generally *Fromer*: Creativity and the Law; *Katyal*: Trademark Intersectionality; and *Bently/Bently*: The Making of Modern Intellectual Property Law, p. 168. Bently notes that there are a number of historical reasons for why trademarks were typically grouped with patents, principally given the "shared professional bodies (patents and trade mark agents), the nature and form of international treaties,... the logic of industrial property," and "similar subject matter". *Bently/Bently*: The Making of Modern Intellectual Property Law, p. 169 (citations omitted).

498 *Klett/Sonntag/Wilske*: Intellectual Property Law in Germany, p. 59. See also *Geller*: Toward an Overriding Norm in Copyright, p. 3; and *Bundeszentrale für politische Bildung*: Geschichte des Urheberrechts.

499 BVerfG 22.05.1979 1 BvL 9/75 "Weinbergsrolle", BVerfGE 51, 193 – Schloßberg (1979). The court held that: "The protectable trademark is legally protected by Article 14, para. 1, sentence 1." ("Das schutzfähig Warenzeichen ist eine durch Art. 14 Abs. 1 Satz 1 geschützte Rechtsposition.") Art. 14(1) of the German Basic Law (*Grundgesetz*) holds that: "Property and the right of inheritance shall be guaranteed. Their content and limits shall be defined by the laws." ("Das Eigentum und das Erbrecht werden gewährleistet. Inhalt und Schranken werden durch die Gesetze bestimmt.").

500 Das Gesetz über Markenschutz vom 30. November 1874 (RGBl. S. 143). The law was enacted on 30 November 1874, and became effective 1 May 1875.

501 *DPMA*: Jahresbericht 2008.

502 This was described as "figürlichen Warenbezeichnungen" (Bildmarken).

503 *Rayle*: The Trend Towards Enhancing Trademark Owners' Rights, p. 242.

504 Reichsgesetz zum Schutz der Warenbezeichnungen, v. 12.05.1894 (RGBl S. 441).

whether the particular mark was distinctive. Additionally, it informed owners of potentially conflicting marks with respect to filing an opposition.[505]

The current German Trademark Act of 1995[506] brought considerable changes to German trademark and competition law. While some of the changes were required by the 1989 EU Trademark Directive, others went beyond what was required therein.[507]

(e) International Protection

By the late 19th century, discussions about the importance of protecting of intellectual property were well under way throughout Europe[508] and laws – including legislation[509] – followed in quick succession.

---

505 *Rayle*: The Trend Towards Enhancing Trademark Owners' Rights, fn. 131, citing *Gamm*: Warenzeichengesetz.

506 Gesetz über den Schutz von Marken und sonstigen Kennzeichen, (Markengesetz) of 1995 § 3(1) v. 25.10.1994 (BGBl. I S. 3082), as amended.

507 Directive 2008/95/EC, OJ L 299/25, 8.11.2008. The Act of 1995 considerably widened the scope of protectable signs; under the old law only words, pictorial signs and combinations of words and pictorial signs were registrable. The new law allows the registration of all signs that are capable of distinguishing the goods or services of one undertaking from those of other undertakings. Furthermore, the new law permitted national persons to register trademark, deleting the prior requirement that only existing business establishments could register marks. See *Rayle*: The Trend Towards Enhancing Trademark Owners' Rights, fn. 10.

508 A quick search in Google Books, for example, shows references to "*geistigen Eigenthums*" as early as 1783 in Dresden, "*propriété intellectuelle*" in Paris in 1809, and "intellectual property" in London in 1813. In 1871, C. Schlickeysen (a machine manufacturer from Berlin), wrote a book lamenting the lack of German intellectual property laws and encouraging the adoption of good laws to protect ideas and inventions in order to ensure social development (*Schlickeysen*: Die Anerkennung des Geistigen Eigenthum). Although focusing more on patents, a succession of scholarly debate regarding the protection of intellectual property continued. In 1893, Josef Kohler wrote "Die Idee des geistigen Eigenthums" and in 1902, Max Vosberg-Rekow published "Der schutz des industriellen und geistigen eigenthums in den handelsverträgen".

509 *Der Schutz des geistigen Eigenthums*, relating to the copyright laws of January 1876 (granting copyright in works of art, photography, and designs); Vol. 6 of Rechtsbücher des Deutschen Reichs, Kortkampf, 1878.

(i) International Congress on Industrial Property & the Paris Convention

In 1878, the first International Congress on Industrial Property was held simultaneously with the International Exposition in Paris.[510] Its main result was a decision that one of the participating governments should be asked to convene an international diplomatic conference "with the task of determining the basis of uniform legislation" in the field of industrial property.[511]

As a direct consequence of the efforts of the International Congress in Paris, the Paris Convention for the Protection of Industrial Property of 1883 was enacted.[512] The Paris Convention was originally signed by 11 countries: Belgium, Brazil, El Salvador, France, Guatemala, Italy, the Netherlands, Portugal, Serbia, Spain, and Switzerland.[513] When it came into effect on 7 July 1884, Great Britain, Tunisia, and Ecuador adhered as well, bringing the initial number of participating member countries to 14.[514]

In 1897 and again resumed in 1900, the Brussels Revision Conferences revised the text of the Paris Convention.[515] Here, the principle of national treatment was extended to include protection against unfair competition:[516] a new Article 10*bis* was adopted,[517] wherein all members of the Convention "shall enjoy in all countries of the Union the protection afforded to nationals against unfair

510 *Preserving History*: Trademark Timeline, p. 1027.

511 See *WIPO*: Intellectual Property Handbook, Chapter 5, p. 241, § 5.5. *Blakeney*: The International Protection of Industrial Property, pp. 3–6.

512 The Paris Convention of 1883. See above, § 2.2(f) for further discussion.

513 El Salvador, Guatemala and Ecuador later denounced the Paris Convention of 1883 to join again in the 1990s. *WIPO*: Intellectual Property Handbook, Chapter 5, p. 241, § 5.7.

514 See *WIPO*: Intellectual Property Handbook, Chapter 5, p. 241, § 5.7.

515 *WIPO*: Intellectual Property Handbook, Chapter 5, p. 242, § 5.8; *Blakeney*: The International Protection of Industrial Property, pp. 4–9; and *Wadlow*: The Law of Passing-Off, p. 68, § 2-036.

516 The original text of the Paris Convention of 1883 did not contain any specific provision regarding the "repression of unfair competition." See *Bodenhausen*: Guide to the Application of the Paris Convention, p. 142.

517 Actes de Bruxelles, pp. 164 (proposal of France), 187/8, 310; 382/3 (discussions and adoption). *Bodenhausen*: Guide to the Application of the Paris Convention, p. 142, n. 1. Bodenhausen notes that the Revision Conference of Washington in 1911 went a step further, in introducing into Article 10*bis* the obligation for all member States to assure to nationals of the Union effective protection against unfair competition. Actes de Washington, pp. 53 (proposal), 105, 224 (observations), 305 (report of Committee), 310 (report to Plenary Committee), 255 (discussion and adoption in

competition."[518] Furthermore, the group of persons entitled to protection under the Convention was extended to include all persons domiciled or having an establishment in a Convention country.[519]

(ii) Madrid Agreement

In 1891, the Madrid Agreement Concerning the International Registration of Marks was created as an instrument under the Paris Convention.[520] The Arrangement of Madrid for the Repression of False or Deceptive Indications of Source on Goods was also adopted.

Almost 100 years later, the Protocol relating to the Madrid Agreement concerning the International Registration of Marks was established on 27 June 1989. The Protocol enables countries that are not parties to the Madrid Agreement – such as the United States,[521] England and Japan – to utilize the system of international registrations as created by the Agreement. In addition, the Protocol enabled the EU to become a Member and allows the use of a Community Trademark to be the basis for a request for international registration.

3.2 National Rights v. EU Common Market Principles

(a) Territorial Protection

By the mid-twentieth century, these developments to protect intellectual property rights – and specifically trademarks – established a strong network of national laws and registration systems throughout Europe.

The strength of these national territorial systems, however, conflicted on two levels with the principles which were slowly emerging to establish a common European market. First, these national, territorial rights were in conflict with common market principles – with respect to freedom of movement of goods and

---

Third Plenary Session). *Bodenhausen*: Guide to the Application of the Paris Convention, pp. 142–43.

518 *Wadlow*: The Law of Passing-Off, pp. 68–69, § 2-036. See the Paris Convention of 1883, Article 10*bis* (Unfair Competition).

519 *WIPO*: Intellectual Property Handbook, Chapter 5, p. 242, § 5.8.

520 The Madrid Agreement of 1891. See above, § 2.2(f). See also *Preserving History*: Trademark Timeline, p. 1028.

521 The United States has never becomes a contracting parts to the Madrid Agreement, but enacted the Madrid Protocol on 2 November 2003. *WIPO*: Madrid Agreement (Marks) and *WIPO*: State member status (Madrid).

competition laws. Second, there were discrepancies between the scope of protection afforded under national rights granted by individual counties.

(b) Free Movement: The Problem with Trademarks

Intellectual property rights in general – and trademarks in particular – present a particular challenge to the European Union's principle of free movement of goods and prohibitions on barriers to trade. Intellectual property rights are primarily based on national law.[522] This national, territorial nature means that an intellectual property owner's exercise of rights (including her ability to exclude others from using, making or selling her invention or product) can constitute a significant barrier to inter-state (i.e., European Union) trade. For example, problems arise when goods produced by companies which are legally and economically independent and which both register rather similar trademarks in their own countries. This can present a problem when one company imports its goods into another Member State.

(c) TFEU: Protection of Intellectual Property Rights

The Treaty on the Functioning of the European Union (TFEU)[523] explicitly addresses – and distinguishes – the protection of intellectual property rights.

Article 36 TFEU permits Member States, in certain defined cases, to derogate from their obligations to ensure the free movement of goods under Article 34 (prohibiting quantitative restrictions on imports and all measures having equivalent effect) and Article 35 (relating to exports). The "protection of industrial and commercial property" is such an express derogation. Article 36 nonetheless warns that "Such prohibitions or restrictions shall not, however, constitute a means of arbitrary discrimination or a disguised restriction on trade between Member States." Hence, Article 36 TFEU permits Member States to derogate from their "free movement of goods" obligations in limited circumstances.[524]

---

522 In Germany, for example, trademarks are regulated by the Act on the Protection of Trade Marks and other Symbols (*Markengesetz* or *MarkenG*) along with the Trademark Ordinance (*Markenverordnung* or *MarkenV*). For a list of German legislation, including implementation or regulations on procedures, applicable for trademarks, see *OHIM*: National Law Relating to the Community Trade Mark and the Community Design, pp. 18–19. See also *DPMA*: Trademarks.

523 Consolidated version 2012, OJ C 326, 26.10.2012.

524 Article 36 list of derogations is *exhaustive* and Article 36 nonetheless warns that: "Such prohibitions or restrictions shall not, however, constitute a means of arbitrary discrimination or a disguised restriction on trade between Member States."

Article 345 TFEU specifically promises that: "The Treaties shall in no way prejudice the rules in Member States governing the system of property ownership". Article 345 TFEU thus protects the *existence* of the exclusive rights granted by a Member State.[525]

In balancing the national (and inherently territorial) rights granted to intellectual property owners with fundamental EU principles on the free movement of goods and prohibitions on barriers to trade,[526] the CJEU has noted that Articles 36 and 345 TFEU are not blanket exemptions for all conduct involving intellectual property.[527] In those cases where the *exercise* of intellectual property rights conflict with EU competition laws, the Commission has the authority to limit the exercise of those intellectual property rights in order to harmonize them with EU law.[528]

---

525 Case 24/67, *Parke, Davis and Co. v Probel, Reese, Beintema-Interpharm and Centrafarm*, 29 February 1968 [1968] ECR 55, p. 72.

526 The CJEU stated clearly that "the determination of the conditions and procedures under which the protection of [EU intellectual property rights] is granted is a matter for the national rules of each Member State. It is for the national legislature to determine which products may benefit from protection, even where they form part of a unit which is already protected as such." Case 238/87, *Volvo AB v Erik Veng (UK) Ltd.*, 5 October 1988 [1988] ECR 6211, para. 7.

527 "Articles 36 [ ], 222 [345 TFEU] and 234 [ ] of the Treaty … *do not exclude any influence* whatever of community law on the exercise of national industrial property rights. … Article 222 [345 TFEU] *confines itself* to stating that the 'Treaty shall in no way prejudice the rules in Member States governing the system of property ownership'." Joined Cases 56 and 58/64, *Établissements Consten S.à.R.L. and Grundig-Verkaufs-GmbH v Commission*, 13 July 1966 [1966] ECR 299, p. 345 (emphasis mine).

528 As the Court noted in *Consten and Grundig*, "to refrain from using rights under national trade-mark law in order to set an obstacle in the way of parallel imports does not affect the grant of those rights but only limits their exercise to the extent necessary to give effect to the prohibition under Article 85 (1). The power of the Commission to issue such an injunction for which provision is made in Article 3 of Regulation No 17/62 of the Council is in harmony with the nature of the Community rules on competition which have immediate effect and are directly binding on individuals. Such a body of rules, by reason of its nature described above and its function, *does not allow the improper use of rights under any national trade-mark law in order to frustrate the Community's law* on cartels." Joined Cases 56 and 58/64, *Établissements Consten S.à.R.L. and Grundig-Verkaufs-GmbH v Commission*, 13 July 1966 [1966] ECR 299, pp. 345–346 (emphasis mine).

(d) Case Law: Priority of Intellectual Property Rights

The Court of Justice of the European Union has a long history of analyzing the interplay between the exclusive rights granted under intellectual property rights – and trademarks specifically – and other fundamental European Union principles or rights.

(i) Free movement of goods

In the 1976 case *Terrapin v. Terranova*, the CJEU was confronted with the conflict between free movement of goods and trademark protection.[529] Terranova, a German company, manufactured and marketed plaster for façades and other construction materials in Germany. It registered these products at the German patent office under the names 'terra', 'terra fabrikate', and 'terranova'. Terrapin, the British defendant, manufactured prefabricated houses which it sold under the name 'Terrapin' in both the UK and Germany. When Terranova objected to the use of the name Terrapin in Germany, the German Federal High Court (*Bundesgerichtshof*) found that there was some risk of confusion between the names used by the claimant and the defendant.

On request for a preliminary ruling, the CJEU said that, under the first sentence of Article 36 TFEU, industrial or commercial property rights "legally acquired in a Member State may legally be used to prevent … the import of products marketed under a name giving rise to confusion where the rights in question have been acquired by different and independent proprietors under different national laws."[530] The Court argued, that if the result were otherwise, the specific objective of industrial and commercial property rights would be undermined:

> "If in such a case the principle of the free movement of goods were to prevail over the protection given by the respective national laws, the specific objective of industrial and commercial property rights would be undermined. In the particular situation the requirements of the free movement of goods and the safeguarding of industrial and commercial property rights must be so reconciled that protection is ensured for the legitimate use of the rights conferred by national laws, coming within the prohibitions on imports "justified" within the meaning of Article [36] of the Treaty, but denied on the other hand in respect of any improper exercise of the same rights of such a nature as to maintain or effect artificial partitions within the Common Market."[531]

---

529 Case 119/75, *Terrapin (Overseas) Ltd. v Terranova Industrie CA Kapferer & Co*, 22 June 1976 [1976] ECR 1039.

530 *Id.*, para 7.

531 *Id.*

The Court concluded that:

> "[I]t is compatible with the provisions of the … Treaty relating to the free movement of goods for an undertaking established in a Member State, by virtue of a right to a trade-mark and a right to a commercial name which are protected by the legislation of that state, to prevent the importation of products of an undertaking established in another Member State and bearing by virtue of the legislation of that state a name giving rise to confusion with the trade-mark and commercial name of the first undertaking, provided that there are no agreements restricting competition and no legal or economic ties between the undertakings and that their respective rights have arisen independently of one another."[532]

(ii) Essential functions

In *HAG II*[533] the Court said that: "Trade mark rights are, it should be noted, an essential element in the system of undistorted competition which the Treaty seeks to establish and maintain."[534] The Court stressed that the essential function of a trademark would be jeopardized if the trademark holder could *not* invoke the trademark to oppose the import of similar goods bearing a designation which could be confused with its own trademark. In these circumstances consumers would not be able to identify the origin of the trademarked goods for certain and the trademark holder would not be responsible for quality.[535]

The Court extensively reiterated and paraphrased this reasoning in *Ideal Standard*:[536] "free movement of the goods would undermine the essential function of the trade mark: consumers would no longer be able to identify for certain the origin of the marked goods and the proprietor of the trade mark could be held responsible for the poor quality of goods for which he was in no way accountable."[537]

---

532 *Id.*, para 8.

533 Case C-10/89, *SA CNL-SUCAL NV v HAG GF AG*, 17 October 1990, 17 October 1990 [1990] ECR I-3711 (*HAG II*).

534 *Id.*, para 13.

535 *Id.*, para 16.

536 Case C-9/93, *IHT Internationale Heiztechnik GmbH and Uwe Danzinger v Ideal-Standard GmbH and Wabco Standard GmbH*, 22 June 1994, ECR 2789 [1994], paras. 37 and 45.

537 *Id.*, para 45.

(iii) Right of establishment

In *Pfeiffer Großhandel*,[538] the CJEU found that a restriction by one undertaking as to the right of establishment of another undertaking, where such restriction "is brought about by a provision of national law whose primary aim is to safeguard trade names against the risk of confusion … is justified by overriding requirements in the general interest pertaining to the protection of industrial and commercial property."[539]

In question in *Pfeiffer* was whether Löwa's use and re-naming of its products with the designation "Plus" and its stores with the name "Plus prima leben und sparen" would infringe (by risk of confusion) Pfeiffer's "Plus KAUF PARK" trademark, which had priority (1969 v. 1994). The Court found that "the protection granted by a national law against the risk of confusion" with respect to a trademark *pre-empted* the right of establishment, "since it corresponds to the specific subject-matter of a trade name, that is to say, protection of the proprietor of the trade name against that risk."[540]

(e) Differing National Rights within the EU

In his oft-cited opinion to the 1990 *HAG II* case,[541] Advocate General Jacobs first noted the general problem of trademark conflicts within the Union. In analyzing the "risk of confusion", he noted that the reliance on national laws to determine the "risk of confusion" question might create different results:

> "To make matters worse, the concept of confusingly similar marks must inevitably vary from one Member State to another and this can lead to a certain lack of reciprocity and to distortions of trade. For example, in *Terrapin v Terranova* the German courts found that there was a risk of confusion between the two marks. It is questionable whether an English court would take the same view. This could have the unfortunate consequence that the British manufacturer would be prevented from trading in Germany under his

---

538 Case C-255/97, *Pfeiffer Großhandel GmbH v Löwa Warenhandel GmbH*, 11 May 1999.

539 *Id.*, para. 21, citing Case 62/79, *Coditel and Others* [1980] ECR 881, para 15. See *Barnard*: The Substantive Law of the EU, p. 31, n. 178.

540 Case C-255/97, *Pfeiffer Großhandel GmbH v Löwa Warenhandel GmbH*, 11 May 1999, para. 21, citing Case 62/79, *Coditel and Others* [1980] ECR 881, para 16, citing Case C-317/91, *Deutsche Renault AG v AUDI AG*, 30 November 1993 [1993] ECR I-6227, para 37.

541 Case C-10/89, *SA CNL-SUCAL NV v HAG GF AG*, 17 October 1990 [1990] ECR I-3711 (*HAG II*).

usual mark, while the German manufacturer would have unrestricted access to the British market."[542]

He further noted that national courts may differ in how "narrowly" or "broadly" the scope of such confusion is applied:

> "In fact, it appears that the German courts take a particularly broad view of the concept of confusingly similar marks, as is well illustrated by the facts of the proceeding before the Commission reported as *Tanabe Seiyaku Company v Bayer* AG CMLR [1979], 2, p. 80. In one notorious case (BPatG, 28.3.1973, GRUR 1975, p. 74) the Bundespatentgericht held that the mark "LUCKY WHIP" was liable to be confused with the mark "Schoeller-Nucki", a decision that seems to postulate a body of consumers afflicted with an acute form of dyslexia."[543]

Regardless of the differing outcomes possible, Advocate General Jacobs felt there was no other effective alternative at present. A trademark owner was permitted to rely on his national rights against the owner of a parallel right in another Member State:[544]

> "I am convinced that the owner of a trade mark must be allowed to exclude from his territory goods on which an identical trade mark has been placed by another … who is the owner of the mark in another Member State. … Such a conclusion is justified from the point of view both of the trade mark owner and of the consumer."[545]
> "The conclusion reached above confirms my belief that the approach followed in *Terrapin v Terranova* (subject to my reservations about the genuineness of the risk of confusion and the possibility of eliminating it by means of additional information) was correct and that *HAG I* was wrongly decided."[546]

The problem of differing national perceptions of risk of confusion has remained an issue. In *Deutsche Renault*, the question was raised whether there was a risk of confusion between the names Audi "Quattro" and Renault "Quadra", both of which applied to four-wheel-drive vehicles.[547] The Court stated that:

> "the concept of actual risk of confusion must be strictly interpreted in order to avoid obstructing the free movement of goods further than is necessary for the protection of trade marks. As an exception to a basic principle of the common market Article [36]

542 Case C-10/89, *SA CNL-SUCAL NV v HAG GF AG*, [1990] ECR I-3711, Opinion of AG Jacobs, 13 March 1990.

543 *Id.*

544 *Id.*, § XII.

545 *Id.*, para. 46.

546 *Id.*, para. 47.

547 Case C-317/91, *Deutsche Renault AG v AUDI AG*, 30 November 1993 [1993] ECR I-6227.

> allows restrictions to the free movement of goods only in so far as they are justified by the protection of the rights which constitute the specific subject-matter of the industrial or commercial property at issue."[548]

The Court said that "[Union] law does not … lay down any strict interpretative criterion for the concept risk of confusion" and thus such analysis "must accordingly be governed by … national law."[549]

(f) Balancing Act: Exhaustion of IP Rights

The supremacy of the protection of intellectual property rights over fundamental European Union principles, however, goes only so far: although the TFEU safeguards national legislation protecting intellectual property rights, the exercise of their rights by holders of intellectual property rights are subject to limitations imposed by the TFEU in order to remove unjustified barriers to cross-border trade. One such limitation is application of the doctrine of exhaustion. Broadly speaking, the principle prohibits an intellectual property right being enforced to prevent the marketing of goods in an EU Member State if those goods have been previously marketed in another Member State by the intellectual property rights owner or with her consent.

(i) Overview of the Doctrine

In most jurisdictions, intellectual property rights cannot be used to prohibit genuine products (which have been legally released into the domestic market) from being resold within that jurisdiction. In effect, the rights are "*exhausted*" once the products have been sold by or with the consent of the intellectual property rights owner, and such rights cannot be used to control the secondary market for those products in that jurisdiction.[550] The doctrine holds that the exclusive rights of commercial exploitation for a given product end with the product's first sale or distribution. Unless otherwise specified by law, subsequent acts of resale, rental, lending or other forms of commercial use by third parties can no longer be controlled or opposed by the intellectual property owner.[551]

548 *Id.*, para. 29.
549 *Id.*, paras. 32 and 31, respectively.
550 *Stothers*: Patent Exhaustion: the UK Perspective, p. 1.
551 *WIPO*: International Exhaustion and Parallel Importation.

The doctrine is generally considered to be a creation of German law,[552] having been developed and influenced by the teachings of Josef Kohler, considered the "old master"[553] or intellectual father[554] of German intellectual and industrial property law.[555]

Kohler's Manual of German Patent Law (*Handbuch des Deutschen Patentrechts*),[556] published in 1900, and his Patent Law Textbook (*Lehrbuch des Patentrechts*),[557] published in 1908, originally framed the concept with respect to patent law. As he wrote in his *Textbook*:

> "The right can be exercised until its exhaustion, but no further. Any owner, who has put a product into circulation, has given up all his rights of ownership in the domestic market: he shall maintain no patent rights with respect to such material."[558]

---

552 *Beier*: Grenzen der Erschöpfungslehre im Markenrecht, p. 263, cited by *Keeling*: Intellectual Property Rights in EU Law, p. 75. See also the discussion of the issue by the European Council, in *European Council*: Records of the Luxembourg Conference, 40–1.

553 "… Joseph Kohler, dem Altmeister des deutschen gewerblichen Rechtsschutzes". *Beier*: Grenzen der Erschöpfungslehre im Markenrecht, p. 266, para. 13.

554 "Die Aufnahme des Erschöpfungsgrundsatzes in der Rechtsprechung wurde durch die von *Kohler* entwickelte Lehre vom "Zusammenhang der Benutzungsarten" vorbereitet." *Kraßer*: Patentrecht: Ein Lehr- und Handbuch, § 33v, p. 795.

555 A review of Kohler's writings related to intellectual property (ignoring his other civil law works), as available through digital library of the Max-Planck-Institut, gives an overview of his deep interest in the topic and his prolific nature: *Das Recht des Markenschutzes* (Würzburg, 1884); *Forschungen aus dem Patentrecht* (Mannheim, 1888); *Das literarische und artistische Kunstwerk und sein Autorschutz* (Mannheim, 1892); *Handbuch des deutschen Patentrechts in rechtsvergleichender Darstellung Band* [Hauptbd.] (Mannheim, 1900); *Das Eigenbild im Recht* (Berlin, 1903); *Handbuch des deutschen Patentrechts in rechtsvergleichender Darstellung Band Sach- und Schlagwortverzeichnis, in Buchstabenfolge* (Mannheim, 1904); *Kunstwerkrecht (Gesetz vom 9. Januar 1907)* (Stuttgart, 1908); *Lehrbuch des Patentrechts* (Mannheim and Leipzig, 1908); and *Musterrecht* (Stuttgart 1909). *Max-Planck-Institut für europäische Rechtsgeschichte*: Digitale Bibliothek Digitale Bibliothek.

556 *Kohler*: Handbuch des Deutschen Patentrechts.

557 *Kohler*: Lehrbuch des Patentrechts.

558 "Das Recht kann ausgeübt werden bis zur Erschöpfung, aber nicht weiter. … Wer ein Erzeugnis als Eigentum in den Verkehr setzt der übergibt es dem inländischen Verkehr für alles, wozu das Eigentum gut ist: er behält sich im Bezug auf den Stoff keine patentrechtlichen Befugnisse zurück." (English translation mine). Originally quoted in *Stieger*: "Kodak" – Eine Momentaufnahme, p. 2, fn. 2, citing *Kohler*: Lehrbuch des Patentrechts, p. 131, I.

Under Kohler's influence,[559] the German *Reichsgericht* applied the principle of exhaustion, as applicable to all industrial property rights, in a number of cases.[560] In their *Guajakol-Karbonat* judgment of 26 March 1902,[561] relating to patents, it was held that:

> "The effect of a patent (for a process) is that no-one, except the proprietor (or the persons whom he has authorized) may manufacture a product by the said process and put it on the domestic market. By this act, however, the effect of the protection conferred by the patent is exhausted. The proprietor who has manufactured the product and has put it on the market under this protection which excludes competition from other parties, has enjoyed advantages which the patent confers upon him and has thus exhausted his right."[562]

(ii) Trademark Exhaustion

The question of importation of genuine goods is an old one in the trademark law, with cases covering parallel import issues dating from 1886 (US), 1887 (England), and 1888 (Germany).[563] Although the protection of a trademark may be territorially limited, its subject matter and inherent function – e.g., the name of a merchant to distinguish goods – is not restricted by territorial boundaries, nor is

---

559 *Beier*: Grenzen der Erschöpfungslehre im Markenrecht, p. 266, para. 13; and *Beier*: Territoriality of Trademark Law, p. 56.

560 With respect to trademarks: *Kölnisch Wasser* (Reichsgericht, 28 February 1902, RGZ 50, 229) and *Mariani* (Reichsgericht, 2 May 1902, RGZ 51, 263); with respect to patents: *Guajakol-Karbonat* (Reichsgericht, 26 March 1902, RGZ 51, 139) (alternative case name: *Duotal*); and with respect to copyrights: *Konig's Kursbuch* (Reichsgericht, 16 June 1906, RGZ 63, 394) (alternatively written: *Koengis Kursbuch*). For *Kölnish Wasser* and *Mariani*, see *Beier*: Grenzen der Erschöpfungslehre im Markenrecht, p. 266, para. 13. For the additional cases (including their subject matter distinctions) see *Cook*: Exhaustion, pp. 354–366, p. 356, n. 11. The alternative case names come from *Riehle*: Immaterialgüterschutz in Sekundärmärkten, pp. 175–194, p. 177, n. 9. See also *Keeling*: Intellectual Property Rights in EU Law.

561 *Guajakol-Karbonat* (Reichsgericht, 26 March 1902) 51 RGZ 139, cited by *Stothers*: Patent Exhaustion: the UK Perspective, p. 1, n. 5.

562 For a reproduction of the case decision, see *European Council*: Records of the Luxembourg Conference, 40–1.

563 For these cases and an analysis of the case law developing the principle of parallel imports, see *Beier*: Territoriality of Trademark Law, p. 48. The cases are *Apollinaris v. Scherer*, 27 F. 18 (CCSD New York, 1886); *Apollinaris v. Herrfeldt*, 4 RPC 478 (Ch. D., 1887); and OLG Hamburg, April 13, 1898, 1899 Bl. F. PMZ – 115 – *Enterprise*. *Beier*: Territoriality of Trademark Law, p. 49.

the trade of products bearing such name necessarily limited to a certain national territory.[564] The three main concepts of exhaustion that have developed and been applied by courts around the world are: (i) national exhaustion; (ii) regional exhaustion; and (iii) international exhaustion.[565]

The exhaustion principle has been conscientiously included in EU trademark legislation[566] and extensively applied by EU courts for the main purpose of balancing the exclusive (national) rights of a trademark owner with the principle of the common market – in effect, the exhaustion principle is applied to prevent segmentation of the European market into national territories.[567] If the owner of a national trademark – or any other intellectual property right – were allowed to rely on her national intellectual property rights to prevent parallel imports from other Member States, the theory of the "common market" would be divided.[568]

The CJEU has held that – once the protected good or service had been sold or put on the market by or with the consent of the intellectual property owner – the right is exhausted and cannot be used to keep the product out of other Member States.[569] In other words, the national and territorial exclusivity of intellectual property rights cannot be used to discriminate against customers in other Member States.[570] Thus, in the EU *national exhaustion* has been replaced by the concept of *regional exhaustion*, where the European Union represents the region at stake.[571]

---

564 *Beier*: Territoriality of Trademark Law, p. 56.

565 *WIPO*: International Exhaustion and Parallel Importation.

566 Both the Trademark Directive (Directive 2008/95/EC, OJ L 299/25, 8.11.2008) and Community Trade Mark Regulation (Council Regulation (EC) No 207/2009/EC, OJ L 78/1, 24.3.2009) specifically address the exhaustion of rights conferred by a trademark within the European Community. Trademark Directive, Article 7(1); CTM Regulation, Article 13. For a detailed analysis of the legislative history of the Trademark Directive and the drafting process of Article 7 on the exhaustion of trademark rights, see *Calboli*: Trademark Exhaustion in the European Union.

567 *WIPO*: Interface Between Exhaustion of Intellectual Property Rights and Competition Law, p. 17, para. 44.

568 *Korah*: Intellectual Property Rights and the EC Competition Rules, § 2.1, p. 6.

569 Case C-173/98, *Sebago Inc. and Ancienne Maison Dubois et Fils SA v G-B Unic SA*, 1 July 1999 [1999] ECR I-4103, para. 2.

570 *Korah*: Intellectual Property Rights and the EC Competition Rules, § 2.1, p. 6.

571 *WIPO*: Interface Between Exhaustion of Intellectual Property Rights and Competition Law, p. 17, para. 45.

3.3 Modern EU Trademark Law

(a) Goals & Challenges

As the European Commission has noted, the promotion, creation, granting, enforcement, and protection of intellectual property rights within Europe and at its borders remain imperfect.[572] The Preamble to the TFEU makes clear that "[s]uch differences amongst the national laws can constitute barriers to intra-state trade and distort competition. This result is in direct conflict with the European Union's goal of creating a single, common market characterized by the removal and prohibition of any obstacles to the free movement of goods in order to "guarantee ... balanced trade and fair competition".[573]

In May 2011, the European Commission published the "Single Market IP Strategy" – a "blueprint" for a new European intellectual property rights strategy – to keep pace with a modern economy, "rewarding creative and inventive efforts ... in an open and competitive market."[574] The report acknowledged both the fragmentation of the intellectual property rights landscape and the imperfect enforcement of those rights in the European Union and set out the Commission's overall strategic vision for a harmonization and modernization of intellectual property rights.[575]

Trademarks represent a particular challenge: given their exclusive national character, the inherently territorial (or geographical) use and enforcement of trademarks directly contradicts with the principles of free movement of goods and adds complexity to the harmonization efforts within the EU.

(b) Trademark Harmonization

The idea of adopting a European-wide trademark was already in place in 1958, soon after the adoption of the Treaty of Rome in 1957.[576] The then-six EEC countries[577] acknowledged that an EEC-wide trademark protection regime would both ensure that the free movement of goods within the market would not be obstructed by nationally protective laws and result in a consistent, EEC-wide

572 *European Commission*: A Single Market for Intellectual Property Rights, p. 6.
573 TFEU, Preamble.
574 *European Commission*: A Single Market for Intellectual Property Rights, p. 3.
575 *Id.*, p. 6.
576 *Beier*: Ziele und Leitgedanken, p. 363, para. 3 and fn. 3.
577 The six European Economic Community members were Belgium, France, Italy, Luxembourg, the Netherlands and Germany.

protection that would be attractive to businesses.[578] Discussions and proposals were shared by experts, primarily under the direction of the German Association for the Protection of Intellectual Property (*Deutsche Vereinigung für gewerblichen Rechtsschutz und Urheberrecht* or GRUR), resulting in the 1960 publication of "Principles for the Creation of an EEC Trademark."[579]

A working group, formed under the aegis of the Common Market, was established in 1961, chaired by C.J. de Haan, the President of the Dutch Patent Office.[580] The group submitted a first draft of a "Convention on European Trademark Law" in 1962.[581] The work was again resumed nine years later, in 1973.[582] Although two subsequent drafts appeared in 1976 and 1978, the first concrete proposal for a regulation on a Community Trademark did not appear until 1980.[583] The 1980 proposal, presented by the Commission to the Council on 25 November 1980, contained the language both for a "Directive" to approximate the laws and language for a "Regulation" on a Community trademark.[584] The recitals in the proposed Directive noted that the current trademark rules applicable in the Member States "contain disparities which may … distort competition within the common market".[585] It emphasized that the intent was not to deprive the Member State of "the right to continue to protect trade-marks", but rather "to ensure that henceforth trade-marks enjoy uniform protection under the legal systems of all the Member States."[586]

In the years following, two official "Opinions" on the proposal were issued,[587] and the Council working party on intellectual property was requested to examine

578 *Beier*: Ziele und Leitgedanken, p. 363, para. 3 and fn. 3.

579 *Grunsätze für die Schaffung einer EWG-Marke*, GRUR Int. 1960, 359, cited by *Beier*: Ziele und Leitgedanken, p. 363, para. 4, and fn. 4.

580 *Beier*: Ziele und Leitgedanken, p. 363, para. 4, and fn. 4. See also *Ladas*: Patents, Trademarks, and Related Rights, p. 180 and fn. 65.

581 *Ladas*: Patents, Trademarks, and Related Rights, p. 180 and fn. 65. See also *Gambrell*: Patents and Antitrust.

582 *Beier*: Industrial Property and the Free Movement of Goods, p. 135.

583 *Id.*

584 *Commission of the European Communities*: New trade-mark system for the Community: Proposed Directive and Regulation.

585 *Id.*, p. 8.

586 *Id.*

587 The Economic and Social Committee delivered an Opinion in September 1981 (OJ C 310/22, 30.11.1981); the European Parliament discussed the proposal in October 1983 and adopted its own Opinion (OJ C 307/45, 14.11.1983), as cited in

the proposal from a technical point of view.[588] The discussions and negotiations centered primarily around the discrimination among applicants and owners of trademarks in the Member States due to differences in the national trademark laws.[589] In 1984, the Commission presented a revised proposal, taking into account the various opinions and proposed amendments, as well as the deliberations of the Council working party on intellectual property (trademarks).[590] Although the substantive issues were almost unanimously agreed to, two main points were still be discussed at this point: the location of the European Trademark Office[591] and the choice of official languages.[592]

Commission of the European Communities: Amended proposal for a Council Regulation on the Community trade mark, Introduction, p. (iii), n. 2 and 3.

588 *Commission of the European Communities*: Amended proposal for a Council Regulation on the Community trade mark, Introduction, p. (iii), n. 4.

589 *Ladas*: Patents, Trademarks, and Related Rights.

590 *Commission of the European Communities*: Amended proposal for a Council Regulation on the Community trade mark.

591 The debate centered on four of the original 12 locations for the Trademark Office: The Hague (the Netherlands), London (UK), Madrid (Spain) and Munich (Germany). As Munich was already home to the European Patent Office, the German Patent Office and the Federal Patent Court, many believed it unlikely (from a political point of view) that Munich would be selected as the location for the EU trademark office. See *Beier*: Industrial Property and the Free Movement of Goods, p. 135. Beier surmised that Madrid (although "not exactly in the center of Europe") was likely to have the best chance, since it was the capital of a relatively new Member State (having joined in 1986) and, unlike The Netherlands, the UK, and Germany, did not have any European institutions. *Beier*: Industrial Property and the Free Movement of Goods, pp. 135–36. In the end, Spain was chosen to host the Office for Harmonization in the Internal Market (Trade Marks and Designs) (the OHIM). See *European Council*: Presidency Conclusions, Article 1(h), p. 15. The Spanish government then decided to locate the OHIM in the city of Alicante.

592 The language regime ultimately agreed upon was a complex one. Community trademark applicants can file in all the official languages of the EU, but the OHIM would have only five working languages (Spanish, German, English, French, and Italian). "1. The application for a Community trade mark shall be filed in one of the official languages of the European Community. 2. The languages of the Office shall be English, French, German, Italian and Spanish." Regulation 207/209, Art. 119. See *Maier*: OHIM's Role in European Trademark Harmonization. Since 2005, Maier has been President of the Boards of Appeal of OHIM; in January 2013 he was appointed Director of the European Observatory on Infringements of Intellectual Property Rights.

Finally, with the trademark harmonization Directive of 1989 and the establishment of a European Union "Community Trade Mark" under the Regulation, a system to ensure uniform application was successfully implemented. As the Directive noted, recalling the language set out in the 1980 proposal,[593] the trademark laws applicable "before the entry into force of Directive 89/104/EEC contained disparities which may have impeded the free movement of goods and freedom to provide services and may have distorted competition within the common market. It was therefore necessary to approximate the laws of the Member States in order to ensure the proper functioning of the internal market."[594]

The Trademark Directive[595] and the Community Trade Mark Regulation[596] were developed specifically to achieve an "approximation" of the trademark laws of the Member States and harmonize those differences between national laws that most directly restricted (or impacted) the functioning of the internal market.[597] They represent a "supra-national" set of trademark rights and policies providing harmonized registered trademark protection throughout the European Union, to exist *alongside* existing national, Member State trademark rights.[598] The goal was two-fold: on the one hand, to ensure *equal* protection under the various legal systems;[599] on the other hand, to remove any obstacles to the free

---

593 *Commission of the European Communities*: New trade-mark system for the Community.

594 Directive 2008/95/EC, Recital 2. See also *Larkin*: Harmony in Disarray, for a review of the situation leading up to the adoption of the Directive.

595 Directive 2008/95/EC, OJ L 299/25, 8.11.2008. See *OHIM*: Regulations and related texts.

596 Council Regulation (EC) No 207/2009/EC, OJ L 78/1, 24.3.2009. See also the related Commission Regulation (EC) No 2869/95 of 13 December 1995 on the fees payable to the Office for Harmonization in the Internal Market (Trade Marks and Designs), OJ L 303/33, 15.12.1995.

597 Other than Belgium, the Netherlands, and Luxembourg (whose national trademark laws were replaced by one uniform Benelux Trademark Act in 1971), each EU Member State has its own national laws relating to trademarks. For a comprehensive list of the most important national laws, regulations and decrees concerning EU trademark laws, see *OHIM*: National Law Relating to the Community Trade Mark and the Community Design, p. 7.

598 For a list of EU trademark regulations, see *Fina*: European Union Intellectual Property Law – Trademarks. Prior to the harmonization, trademark rights existed only by way of the national laws of individual Member States. *Shaw*: Likelihood of Coexistence, p. 57. See also *Stone/Domingo/Groebl/duSorbier*: European Union, p. 64.

599 Directive 2008/95/EC, Recital 10.

movement of goods. To date, the internal laws of the Member States have all been conformed to the Directive.[600]

(c) The Trademark Directive

The first harmonization Directive (89/104/EEC) set out the procedure for the approximation of trademark laws throughout the EU. A codified harmonization Directive (2008/95/EC) in November 2008 replaced the 1989 Directive, without making any substantive legislative changes.[601] The Trademark Directive explicitly stipulates that no full-scale approximation of the trademark laws of the Member States was contemplated; it did, however, envisage an approximation of those national provisions of law that most directly affected the functioning of the internal market.[602]

The Directive applies to all registered national trademarks with respect to goods and services, but requires EU Member States to develop their own procedures for registration and maintenance of national trademarks. The Directive establishes common use requirements,[603] a single exhaustion doctrine,[604] as well as rules governing licensing and acquiescence by trademark owners in use by third parties.[605] Significantly, the Directive also sets forth a common definition of a trademark[606] and establishes absolute and relative grounds for refusal of registration and for cancellation of national trademark registrations.[607]

---

600 *Hildebrandt*: Harmonised Trade Mark Law in Europe, p. v.

601 Directive 2008/95/EC. The Directive came into force on 28 November 2008 (20 days after its publication in the Official Journal, as set forth under Article 18). All the substantive articles of the new 2008 Directive have the same numbering as the 1989 Directive.

602 *Id.*, Recital 4.

603 *Id.*, Art. 10 (use of trademarks), Art. 11 (sanctions for non-use of a trademark in legal or administrative proceedings), and Art. 12 (grounds for revocation for non-use).

604 *Id.*, Art. 7 (exhaustion of the rights conferred by a trademark).

605 *Id.*, Art. 8 (licensing) and Art. 9 (limitation in consequence of acquiescence).

606 "A trade mark may consist of any signs capable of being represented graphically, particularly words, including personal names, designs, letters, numerals, the shape of goods or of their packaging, provided that such signs are capable of distinguishing the goods or services of one undertaking from those of other undertakings." *Id.*, Art. 2.

607 *Id.*, Art. 3 (grounds for refusal or invalidity), 4 (further grounds for refusal or invalidity concerning conflicts with earlier rights), 13 (grounds for refusal or revocation

(d) The Community Trade Mark Regulation

Council Regulation (EC) No. 40/94 established the Community Trade Mark (or CTM).[608] Under the CTM Regulation, a single application submitted to a central office will result in a registration valid in all Member States of the European Union.[609] The CTM Regulation does not abolish national trademark protection but creates a process that co-exists with (and respects the rights granted by) national trademarks.[610]

A CTM has a unitary character and has unitary effect throughout the European Union. It is registered and administered by the Office for Harmonization in the Internal Market (Trade Marks and Designs) (referred to as OHIM) based in Alicante, Spain.[611] The OHIM began accepting applications as of 1 January 1996

---

or invalidity relating to only some of the goods or services) and 14 (establishment *a posteriori* of invalidity or revocation of a trademark).

608 Council Regulation (EC) No 40/94 of 20 December 1993 on the Community trade mark; codified as Regulation (EC) No 207/2009/EC, OJ L 78/1, 24.3.2009. See also the related Commission Regulation (EC) No 2869/95 of 13 December 1995 on the fees payable to the Office for Harmonization in the Internal Market (Trade Marks and Designs), OJ L 303/33, 15.12.1995. See generally, *OHIM*: National Law Relating to the Community Trade Mark and the Community Design.

609 A CTM is valid in the European Union as a whole. It is not possible to limit the geographic scope of protection to certain Member States. See *OHIM*: What is a Community Trade Mark?

610 For example, existing national trademarks may provide grounds that bar registration of a CTM. Council Regulation (EC) No 207/2009, Article 8.

611 According to an OHIM press release of 2011, the "OHIM is the EU agency responsible for the registration of trade marks and designs in the 27 Member States of the European Union, and has had its seat in Alicante since 1994, pursuant to the decision of the Council of Ministers, in the Agreement of 5 November 1993." *OHIM*: Seat Agreement between the Kingdom of Spain and the Office for Harmonization. Such 5 November 1993 regulation was not located. As Beier has noted, there was debate as to the location and language of the court. *Beier*: Industrial Property and the Free Movement of Goods, p. 135. See also *Maier*: OHIM's Role in European Trademark Harmonization. Some argue that Alicante was chosen by Spanish politicians with political debts to pay to appease local party officials, not for convenience (since access to Alicante is rather difficult: there are no direct flights there, for example, from any major non-European cities, or, for that matter, from any European city, save Madrid). Remoteness makes hearings before the Office burdensome, and makes the OHIM's desire to discourage hearing practice less a point of contention. *Ladas*: The Community Trademark. The "political vote" decision was also noted by trademark attorney Metzler on his *Visae Patentes* blog: "An example of such a

and all applications filed between that date and 1 April 1996 received a filing date of 1 April 1996.[612]

(e) Interaction with National Trademark Laws

Neither the CTM system, nor the OHIM office in Alicante, exist in isolation from the national law and the national industrial property offices of the Member States of the European Union.

Firstly, each applicant for a Community Trade Mark has the choice of filing his application either directly at OHIM in Alicante, Spain, or through the intermediary of a national office,[613] which then has to forward the application to Alicante.[614]

Secondly, the CTM Regulation at times abstains from governing all questions and expressly refers to national law. For example, infringement of a CTM "shall be governed by the national law relating to infringement of a national trade mark",[615] as administered by the EU trademark courts competent for infringement actions[616] (i.e., the EU trademark courts as designated by the Member States[617]). Similarly, sanctions for infringement of a CTM (e.g., damages, seizure,

---

decision on where to locate may be seen in the purely political decision in the 1990s that the new Office for Harmonisation in the Internal Market (OHIM) should reside in Alicante, Spain – instead of the the [*sic*] much better prepared London – since it simply was Spain's turn to receive a major EU institution." *Metzler*: Will the Unified EU Patent Court be Situated in Munich, or rather Warsaw?

612 *OHIM*: Examination Guidelines, § 5.1.

613 For example in Germany, an applicant could file an application with the German Patent and Trade Mark Office (*Deutsches Patent- und Markenamt*, or DPMA), headquartered in Munich and with supplemental locations in Jena and Berlin. The DPMA is the central, national authority in the field of industrial property protection in Germany. *DPMA*: The German Patent and Trade mark Office.

614 Council Regulation (EC) No 207/2009, Article 25(1).

615 *Id.*, Article 14.

616 *Id.*, Article 96.

617 In Germany, the Trademark Act gives each of the 16 German state governments the right to have certain district courts (*Landgerichte*) operate exclusively as specialized trademark courts. *Gesetz über den Schutz von Marken und sonstigen Kennzeichen (Markengesetz-MarkenG)*) § 140(2). Currently, 21 such specialized district courts are competent to hear trademark matters in Germany. See *Klett/Sonntag/Wilske*: Intellectual Property Law in Germany, pp. 111. The district courts have exclusive jurisdiction as the courts of first instance for any trademark dispute. *MarkenG* § 140(1). If the infringing good or service is distributed or offered nationwide or

destruction, or claims for information) are governed by the law of the relevant Member State, including its private international law.[618]

Thirdly, and even more significantly, the express aim of the CTM Regulation was not to abandon the national trademark systems, but ensure their continued existence alongside and parallel to the CTM system. The recitals of the CTM Regulation expressly state that the "Community law relating to trade marks nevertheless does not replace the laws of the Member States on trade marks. It would not in fact appear to be justified to require undertakings to apply for registration of their trade marks as Community trade marks. National trade marks continue to be necessary for those undertakings which do not want protection of their trade marks at Community level."[619]

This parallel existence necessitated a number of legal rules on the coexistence of the CTM and national trademarks which the CTM Regulation addressed.[620]

(f) Scope of Protection

A Community Trade Mark is a trademark valid across the whole European Union, registered with the OHIM in accordance with the provisions of the CTM Regulations. Once granted, a CTM is valid in all Member States of the European Union as a whole. It is not possible to limit the geographic scope of protection to

---

on the internet, the plaintiff may select the forum. Appeals against first instance decisions are heard by the competent higher regional courts (*Oberlandesgerichte*). If leave to appeal is granted, these decisions may be further appealed to the Federal High Court (*Bundesgerichtshof*). *Klett/Sonntag/Wilske*: Intellectual Property Law in Germany, pp. 111–112.

618 Council Regulation (EC) No 207/2009, Articles 98(2), 14(1) and 102. Where rights have been infringed, the CTMR provides a claim for injunction (Article 98(1)) as the only sanction. The CTMR is silent on criminal sanctions for the use of a CTM. See *OHIM*: National Law Relating to the Community Trade Mark and the Community Design, p. 135.

619 Council Regulation (EC) No 207/2009, Recital 6.

620 *Id*. National trademarks already existing and registered in a Member State are presumed valid (Art. 99); national courts dealing with CTMs are presumed valid (Art. 107); a CTM or CTM application which has failed may be converted into a national trademark application (Arts. 112–114); a CTM may benefit from the seniority of an earlier national trademark registered in or for a Member State (Arts. 34–35); and both national trademarks and CTMs must be taken into account against each other as earlier rights and relative grounds for refusal (for example, CTMs will constitute prior rights in relation to all subsequent trademarks and other conflicting rights in all Member States and vice versa) (Arts. 8, 34–35).

certain Member States. In the event of any future enlargement of the European Union, any CTM registered or applied for will be automatically extended to the new Member States without formality or fee.[621]

A CTM is valid for ten years from the date of application and may be renewed (*indefinitely*) for further 10-year periods.[622] In effect, it can last forever (provided the renewal fees are paid and no other oppositions arise).

The rights conferred by a CTM will be exhausted once goods bearing the mark have been put on the market in the European Union by the owner of the mark or with her consent.[623] This does not apply, however, if there are legitimate reasons for the trademark owner to oppose further commercialization of the goods, in particular in those cases where the condition of the goods is changed or impaired after they have been put on the market.[624]

(i) Registration

The CTM system provides for one single registration procedure, consisting of: (i) a single application; (ii) a single language of procedure; (iii) a single administrative centre; and (iv) a single file to be managed.[625]

---

621 *OHIM*: What is a Community Trade Mark?

622 Council Regulation (EC) No 207/2009, Art. 46. This mirrors many national trademark laws. For example, German trademarks will be protected for a period of ten years from the date of the trademark application. *Markengesetz*, § 47.

623 The CJEU has developed a large body of case law on exhaustion of rights, interpreting the provisions in both the Trademark Directive (Arts. 5 and 7) and the CTM Regulation (Art. 13). See for example, Case C-427/93, *Bristol-Myers Squibb et al v Paranova A/S*, 11 July 1996 [1996] ECR 1-3457 (the well-known repackaging case); Case C-355/96, *Silhouette International Schmied GmbH & Co. KG v Hartlauer Handelsgesellschaft mbH*, 16 July 1998 [1998] ECR I-4799; Case C-173/98, *Sebago Inc. and Ancienne Maison Dubois & Fils SA v G-B Unic SA*, 1 July 1999 [1999] ECR I-4103; and C-416/99, *Zino Davidoff SA v A & G Imports Ltd and Levi Strauss & Co. and Others v Tesco Stores Ltd and Others*, 20 November 2001 [2001] ECR I-8691. For example, for German trademarks, the rights will be exhausted once goods have been put on the market in the European Union or the European Economic Area. *Klett/Sonntag/Wilske*: Intellectual Property Law in Germany, p. 107. As of 1 January 1994, Iceland, Liechtenstein, and Norway, together with all EU Member States, make up the EEA. Agreement on the European Economic Area (OJ L 1, 3.1.1994).

624 CTM Regulation, Article 13. *Klett/Sonntag/Wilske*: Intellectual Property Law in Germany, p. 107.

625 *OHIM*: What is a Community Trade Mark?

The CTM grants the trademark owner an exclusive right to use the trademark and to prevent third parties from using, without consent, the same or a similar mark for identical or similar goods and/or services as those protected by the CTM. If an unauthorised third party engages in any prohibited practices, it is guilty of infringing the exclusive right of the proprietor. The proprietor of a CTM can act against infringements by taking measures expressly provided for under the CTM Regulation in relation to disputes concerning the infringement and validity of CTMs, and in particular by initiating proceedings at the Community trademark courts established under the CTM Regulation or filing requests for action with EU customs authorities. This administrative procedure permits proprietors of a CTM to request the EU customs authorities to retain suspected counterfeit goods while under their control.

(ii) Requirements of "Genuine Use"

CTMs must put to genuine use in the European Union within a period of five years following registration.[626] Genuine use may be found when the mark has been used in only one part of the EU, such as in a single Member State or in a part thereof. Any person (legal or natural) can protect their registered CTM against revocation on the grounds of lack of use – provided it is put to genuine use in the EU after the initial five-year post-registration grace period or if there are proper reasons for such non-use.

If a CTM is not genuinely used for a consecutive period of five years from the registration date, it may be revoked for non-use,[627] either based on absolute grounds[628] or based on relative grounds (i.e., earlier rights owned by the party requesting cancelation of the mark).[629]

Furthermore, an opponent may request proof that the CTM has been put to genuine use in the European Union (for such consecutive five-year period) in connection with the goods and services for which it was registered, provided the mark has been registered for more than five years from the date of publication of

---

626 Council Regulation (EC) No 207/2009, Art. 15. See also Directive 2008/95/EC, Art. 10 (use of trademarks), Art. 11 (sanctions for non-use of a trademark in legal or administrative proceedings), and Art. 12 (grounds for revocation for non-use).

627 Council Regulation (EC) No 207/2009, Articles 15 and 50.

628 *Id.*, Article 52.

629 *Id.*, Article 9.

the CTM application.[630] In *Kabushiki Kaisha Fernandes v OHIM*,[631] the General Court (then known as the CFI) clarified that when an opponent is challenged to show genuine use of its trademark, the burden on the opponent is to establish the mark is present in a substantial part of the territory where it is protected and that it functions properly in such territory as to identify the origin of the goods or services.[632] Minimal or any artificial use for the purpose of maintaining a mark on the register will not be sufficient.[633]

In *Ansul BV v Ajax Brandbeveiliging BV*, the CJEU provided some guidance on what is considered "genuine use".[634] First, it set out that for use to be "genuine", the trademark had to be used in accordance with its essential function, which is to guarantee the identity of the origin of the goods or services for which it is registered." Furthermore, such use had to be "warranted in the economic sector

---

630 *Id.*, Article 43. See also *OHIM*: National Law Relating to the Community Trade Mark and the Community Design, p. 177; and *Stone/Domingo/Groebl/duSorbier*: European Union, p. 68.

631 Case T-39/01, *Kabushiki Kaisha Fernandes v OHIM*, 12 December 2002 [2002] ECR II-5233.

632 "Accordingly, not only does genuine use of a trade mark exclude artificial use for the purpose of maintaining the mark on the register; genuine use means that the mark must be present in a substantial part of the territory where it is protected, inter alia exercising its essential function, which is to identify the commercial origin of the goods or services". Case T-39/01, *Kabushiki Kaisha Fernandes v OHIM*, 12 December 2002 [2002] ECR II-5233, para. 36, citing Case T-79/00, *Rewe Zentral AG v OHIM*, 27 February 2002 [2002] ECR II-704 (regarding registration of the term "LITE").

633 "It must be noted first of all that genuine use implies real use of the mark on the market concerned for the purpose of identifying the goods or services. Genuine use is therefore to be regarded as excluding minimal or insufficient use when determining that a mark is being put to real, effective use on a particular market. In that regard, even if it is the owner's intention to make real use of his trade mark, if the trade mark is not objectively present on the market in a manner that is effective, consistent over time and stable in terms of the configuration of the sign, so that it cannot be perceived by consumers as an indication of the origin of the goods or services in question, there is no genuine use of the trade mark." Case T-39/01, *Kabushiki Kaisha Fernandes v OHIM*, 12 December 2002 [2002] ECR II-5233, para. 36.

634 Case C-40/01, *Ansul BV v Ajax Brandbeveiliging BV*, 1 March 2003 [2003] ECR I-2439. The court further developed its position in *Sunrider* (*The Sunrider Corp. v OHIM*, 11 May 2006 [2006] ECR I-04237; Appeal Case before the General Court T-203/02); as well as in *La Mer Technology* (C-259/02, *La Mer Technology Inc. v Laboratoires Goemar SA*, 27 January 2004 [2004] ECR I-1159).

concerned to maintain or create a share in the market for the goods or services protected by the mark".[635] Consideration must be given to the nature of the goods or services at issue, the characteristics of the market concerned, and the scale and frequency of use of the trademark.[636]

Another factor is the territorial scope of the trademark's use. From prior CJEU case law, it seemed that it was sufficient that the trademark was used in a single Member State.[637] More recently, however, in the *Onel/Omel* case,[638] the CJEU held that the territorial borders of a Member State should be disregarded in the assessment of whether a trademark has been put to "genuine use in the Community". The CJEU clarified that the earlier case law was only applicable to the interpretation of the provisions regarding the protection of well-known Community trademarks, but not to the requirement of genuine use in the sense of Article 15, paragraph 1, of the CTM Regulation.[639]

(g) Jurisdiction: National Courts, OHIM & EU Courts

(i) National Trademark Courts

Pursuant to Article 91 of the CTM Regulation, each Member State designates certain national courts and tribunals of first and second instance as their "Community trade mark courts".[640] The Community trademark courts are specialised national courts, entrusted with EU-wide jurisdiction on Community trademarks.[641] The aim is to have, for each Member State, a number of such courts as

---

635 Case C-40/01, *Ansul BV v Ajax Brandbeveiliging BV*, 1 March 2003 [2003] ECR I-2439, paras. 36 and 38.

636 *Id.*, para. 43.

637 Case C-375/97, *General Motors Corporation v Yplon SA*, 14 September 1999 [1999] ECR I-05421; Case C-328/06, *Alfredo Nieto Nuño v Leonci Monlleó Franquet*, 2 November 2007 [2007] ECR I-10093; C-301-07, *PAGO International GmbH v Tirolmilch registrierte Genossenschaft mbH*, 6 October 2009 [2009] ECR I-09429.

638 Case C-149/11, *Leno Merken BV v Hagelkruis Beheer BV*, 19 December 2012 [16.2.2013 OJ C 46/3]. For a review of the case, see *Sosnitza*: Auslegung des Begriffs "ernsthafte Benutzung"; as well as *Bogatz*: EuGH: Rechtserhaltende Benutzung einer Marke in der EU unabhängig von Ländergrenzen. See also *Ruess/Obex*: Rechtserhaltende Benutzung einer Gemeinschaftsmarke.

639 *Klett/Schlüter*: ONEL/OMEL-decision of the CJEU regarding genuine use.

640 The list of designated national CTM courts is available from the OHIM. *OHIM*: List of Community trade mark courts.

641 In Germany, for example, there are 18 designated 1st instance regional court (*Landgericht*) forums: Landgericht Mannheim, Stuttgart, Nürnberg-Fürth, München I,

limited as possible.[642] Pursuant to Article 92 of the CTM Regulation, the CTM courts have exclusive jurisdiction for a variety or cases, including all infringement actions or threatened infringement, and all counterclaims for revocation or for a declaration of invalidity of a CTM pursuant to Article 96 of the CTM Regulation.

(ii) OHIM: Applications & Appeals

Once an application has been made for a CTM, it is possible for the OHIM to refuse registration on absolute grounds. Applications may also be opposed, after publication, by a third party holding relevant earlier rights. After the CTM has been registered, a third party can apply for its cancellation. The OHIM will then decide on the cancellation.[643]

Any final decision by the examiners and the various divisions of the OHIM (i.e., refusals by a trademark examiner, oppositions lodged with the opposition division, or cancellations made by the cancellation division), in so far as it adversely affects one party, is subject to appeal on the initiative of that party. The appeal is brought before OHIM's Boards of Appeal.[644] Each party can file an appeal against the decision at the Office within two months of the date of the notification of the decision.[645]

Berlin, Bremen, Hamburg, Frankfurt am Main, Rostock, Braunschweig, Düsseldorf, Koblenz, Frankenthal (Pfalz), Saarbrücken, Leipzig, Magdeburg, Kiel, Erfurt; and 18 designated 2nd instance, higher regional court (*Oberlandesgericht*) forums: Oberlandesgericht Karlsruhe, Oberlandesgericht Stuttgart, Oberlandesgericht Nürnberg, Oberlandesgericht München, Kammergericht Berlin, Hanseatisches Oberlandesgericht Bremen, Hanseatisches Oberlandesgericht Hamburg, Oberlandesgericht Frankfurt am Main, Oberlandesgericht Rostock, Oberlandesgericht Braunschweig, Oberlandesgericht Düsseldorf, Oberlandesgericht Koblenz, Pfälzisches Oberlandesgericht Zweibrücken, Saarländisches Oberlandesgericht Saarbrücken, Oberlandesgericht Dresden, Oberlandesgericht Naumburg, Schleswig-Holsteinisches Oberlandesgericht, Thüringer Oberlandesgericht. See *OHIM*: Gemeinschaftsmarkengerichte.

642 *OHIM*: National Law Relating to the Community Trade Mark and the Community Design, p. 159.

643 *OHIM*: Decisions of the Office.

644 Council Regulation (EC) No 207/2009, Preamble para. 13 and Title VII (Appeals), paras. 58–65.

645 *OHIM*: Decisions of the Office.

(iii) *General Court*

An OHIM Board of Appeal decision may in turn be subject to appeal before the Community trademark courts on the initiative of the aggrieved party. The appeal procedure consists in a party making a first appeal against OHIM before the General Court.[646] This appeal is subject to the General Court's own procedural rules which may differ in significant aspects from the rules applied by the OHIM.

The General Court may confirm, annul, or alter the Board of Appeal's decision. A final appeal on the points of law of the decision of the General Court can only be filed before the Court of Justice, which has sole jurisdiction to annul or to alter the contested decision.[647]

(iv) *Court of Justice*

The Court of Justice of the European Union has jurisdiction to hear appeals of decisions rendered by the General Court as well as any national court.[648] The CJEU has rendered significant numbers of decisions in trademark matters in appellate proceedings against decisions by the General Court subsequent to opposition proceedings against CTM applications.[649]

In accordance with Article 267 TFEU, any national court may submit a request for a *preliminary ruling* concerning the interpretation of EU law which is material to the outcome of a pending case.[650] This would include issues involving CTMs, trademarks and other distinctive signs, geographical indications of origin, design, and free movements of goods. The decisions of the CJEU are binding

---

646 Council Regulation (EC) No 207/2009, Preamble para. 14 and Title VII (Appeals), paras. 58–65, note that the jurisdiction of the Court of Justice to cancel and alter decisions of the OHIM Boards of Appeal should accordingly be exercised at *first instance* by the General Court. Under Article 256 TFEU, the General Court has jurisdiction to hear and determine at first instance actions or proceedings – in particular those referred to in Article 263 TFEU (which include reviewing the legality of acts of bodies, offices or agencies of the Union intended to produce legal effects vis-à-vis third parties).

647 Council Regulation (EC) No 207/2009, Preamble para. 13 and Title VII (Appeals), paras. 58–65.

648 Art. 263 TFEU.

649 *Klett/Sonntag/Wilske*: Intellectual Property Law in Germany, pp. 112.

650 The CJEU has jurisdiction to give preliminary rulings concerning the interpretation of EU law pursuant to TFEU, Art. 267.

on the national courts. Such referrals by domestic courts seem to be particularly frequent in trademark cases.[651]

(h) Categories of Protectable Subject Matter

(i) Article 4: Definition of a Community Trademark

Under the CTM Regulation, any sign which can be *represented graphically* and which is capable of *distinguishing the goods or services* of one undertaking from those of another is prima facie registrable as a trademark,[652] subject to the "absolute" and "relative" grounds for refusal as laid out in Articles 7 and 8 of the CTM Regulation.

Non-exhaustive examples of signs which may constitute trademarks include "any signs capable of being represented graphically, particularly words, including personal names, designs, letters, numerals, the shape of goods or of their packaging".[653] Further case law has shown that slogans, internet domain names, smells, sounds, colors, gestures, and moving digital images *may be* granted protection, so long as they can be *graphically represented.*[654]

(ii) Graphical Representation

The CJEU's decision in *Sieckmann v Deutsches Patent-und Markenamt* provides guidance on and establishes the test for determining whether smells, sounds, tastes, and colors meet the graphical representation requirement.[655] In *Sieckmann*, the applicant applied to the German Patent Office to register a smell as a trademark. The description was of an olfactory mark of the pure chemical substance methyl cinnamate. The applicant gave a further verbal description of the scent as "balsamically fruity with a slight hint of cinnamon" and submitted a sample in a container. In its decision, the CJEU held that a non-visual trademark *can* be registered, provided that it can be represented graphically, "particularly by means of images, lines or characters", and that the representation is

---

651 *Klett/Sonntag/Wilske*: Intellectual Property Law in Germany, pp. 112.

652 Trademarks may consist of "any signs capable of being represented graphically ... provided that such signs are capable of distinguishing the goods or services of one undertaking from those of other undertakings." Council Regulation (EC) No 207/2009, Article 4.

653 Council Regulation (EC) No 207/2009, Article 4.

654 Case C-273/00, *Ralf Sieckmann v Deutsches Patent- und Markenamt*, 12 December 2002 [2002] ECR I-11754.

655 *Id.*

"clear, precise, self-contained, easily accessible, intelligible, durable and objective." However, these requirements were *not* satisfied by a chemical formula, a written description, the deposit of an odour sample or any combination of these elements. Hence, the applicant in *Sieckmann* was not awarded a trademark for the smell mark. Practically speaking, *Sieckmann* ruled out the valid registration of smells as trademarks until technology provides a precise method for recording smells.[656]

The CJEU later re-affirmed the *Sieckmann* criteria as they apply to sound marks. A sound mark may be registered if: (i) it is capable of distinguishing the goods or services of one undertaking from those of other undertakings; (ii) it can be represented graphically (particularly by means of images, lines or characters); and (iii) its representation is clear, precise, self-contained, easily accessible, intelligible, durable and objective. In *Shield Mark BV v Joost Kist*, the CJEU ruled against the description of "a cock crow" and its onomatopoeic representation "kukelekuuuuu".[657] According to the CJEU, a tune represented on a musical stave may meet the *Sieckmann* representation of a sign. However, the description of the sound in a foreign language, including onomatopoeia, or a description of the successive pattern of the musical notes making up the work, would generally be insufficient for registration.[658]

Similarly, taste marks have not met the *Sieckmann* requirements for graphical representation: In *Eli Lilly and Company*, the OHIM Board of Appeal rejected the application for "The Taste of Artificial Strawberry Flavour".[659]

Single colors that have the required distinctiveness may be registered as trademarks.[660] A sample of the colour, however, is not enough for the purposes of registration.[661] Best practices is to refer to the relevant color code of an internationally recognised color identification system (e.g., Pantone or RAL).[662]

The CJEU has also held that a graphic representation consisting of two or more colours (i.e., a combinations of colors) are registrable, provided they are "systematically arranged by associating the colours in a pre-determined and uniform

656 *Stone/Domingo/Groebl/duSorbier*: European Union, p. 64.

657 *Shield Mark BV v Joost Kist*, C-283/01 (27 November 2003).

658 *Practical Law Company*: Trade marks: Registration and portfolio management.

659 OHIM Case R-120/2001-2, *Eli Lilly and Company*, 4 August 2003, Second Board of Appeal.

660 Case C-104/01, *Libertel Groep BV v Benelux-Merkenbureau*, 6 May 2003 [2003] ECR I-03793.

661 *Id.*

662 *Stone/Domingo/Groebl/duSorbier*: European Union, p. 65.

way".[663] Without such strict limitations, the applicant would gain a monopoly which would protect him against the use by others of any of the colours in any combination. The CJEU provided no guidance on the "systematic arrangement" requirement, but this decision presumably means that trademark protection is unlikely to be able to extend to any combination of two or more colours (in this case, the applicant had applied to register two colours "in every conceivable form"), but will be limited to the way they are combined in the graphical representation in the application (for example, in alternating stripes or checks).[664]

(iii) *Article 7: Refusal on Absolute Grounds*

Article 7(1) of the CTM Regulation sets out the categories of marks which are not registrable as CTMs (the so-called "refusal on absolute grounds" instances). Article 7(2) notes that a CTM application will be rejected even if the disqualifying factor applies only *in part* of the European Union. Article 7(3) notes that the certain grounds for absolute refusal can be rebutted by evidence of distinctiveness acquired through use. Practitioners have noted that this can be a difficult criteria to achieve for non-traditional trademarks (such as sounds, shapes, or colors), as consumer may need to be educated to understand that these types of signs can function separately and independently as a designation of origin (since such non-traditional signs are generally used together with a word or other more traditional trademark).[665]

In *Nestlé v. Mars*,[666] the CJEU held that a word sequence (in this case, the slogan "HAVE A BREAK") used in conjunction with a registered trademark (in this case, KIT KAT) as part of a composite mark (in this case, the full slogan "HAVE A BREAK … HAVE A KIT KAT") could acquire a distinctive character on its own: "In order to prove that distinctive character has been acquired through use as an element of a composite mark the relevant consumer groups must be

---

663 See Case C-49/02, *Heidelberger Bauchemie GmbH*, 24 June 2004 [2004] ECR I-6129. In practical terms, the *Heidelberger* decision limits the scope of protection accorded to registrations consisting of colour combinations (as opposed to single colours), since businesses which use certain colours in a variety of different ways may not always be able to pin down in an application how those colours will be used consistently.

664 This is how the OHIM Board of Appeal applied the decision in Case no R799/2004-1, *Inter IKEA Systems BV v OHIM First Board of Appeal*, 1 July 2005; and in Case no R1004/2006-2, *Mars Incorporated v OHIM*, 13 December 2006.

665 *Stone/Domingo/Groebl/duSorbier*: European Union, p. 65.

666 Case C-353/03 *Société des produits Nestlé SA v Mars UK Ltd*, 7 July 2005 [2005] ECR I-6135.

shown to understand that the element in question, if used separately, designates a product as originating from a specific undertaking, thus distinguishing it from products of other undertakings."[667]

(iv) Article 8: Refusal on Relative Grounds

Article 8 of the CTM Regulation sets out the relative grounds for refusal and states what kind of trademarks and other rights are relevant.[668] The OHIM examines CTM applications on absolute grounds only; it does not examine applications on relative grounds. However, following publication of the application by OHIM, prior rights owners may file opposition proceedings during a non-extendible three-month period.[669] Under Article 8, owners of earlier trademarks may rely on prior:

- CTMs (Article 8.2(a)(i));
- trademarks registered in an EU Member State or at the Benelux Trademark Office (Article 8.2(a)(ii));
- international trademarks under the Madrid Union having effect in a Member State, the Benelux territory or the European Union (Article 8.2(a)(iii));
- marks that are well-known in a Member State (within the meaning of Article 6bis of the Paris Convention[670]) (Article 8.2(c)); and
- a trademark application that later matures into a relevant registration (Article 8.2(b)).

(v) Opposition Proceedings

At opposition, a CTM application will be refused if:

- it is identical to an earlier trademark and the goods or services for which registration is sought are identical to those for which the earlier trademark is registered (Article 8.1(a));
- due it its identity with, or similarity to, the earlier trademark and the identity or simi-larity of the goods or services covered by the trademarks, there exists a likelihood of confusion on the part of the public in the territory in which the

667 Case C-353/03 *Société des produits Nestlé SA v Mars UK Ltd*, [2005] ECR I-6135, Opinion of AG Kokott, 27 January 2005, para. 46.

668 *OHIM*: National Law Relating to the Community Trade Mark and the Community Design, pp. 53–54.

669 *Stone/Domingo/Groebl/duSorbier*: European Union, p. 67.

670 *WIPO*: Article 6*bis*.

earlier trademark is protected (which includes the likelihood of association with the earlier trademark) (Article 8.1(b)); or

- it is identical with, or similar to, the earlier trademark which has a reputation within the European Union and, and where use without due cause of the applied-for trademark would take unfair advantage of, or be detrimental to, the distinctive character or the repute of the earlier trademark (Article 8.5).

A sign is deemed "identical" to an earlier trademark "where it reproduces, without any modification or addition, all the elements constituting the trade mark or where, viewed as a whole, it contains differences so insignificant that they may go unnoticed by an average consumer."[671]

The assessment of similarity between two *trademarks* "must be based on the overall impression given by the marks, bearing in mind, in particular, their distinctive and dominant components."[672] Courts must take into account "the visual, aural or conceptual similarity of the marks in question."[673]

The assessment of similarity between the *goods or services* "must be appreciated globally, taking into account all factors relevant to the circumstances of the case",[674] including: (i) the nature of the goods or services; (ii) their intended purpose (including their end users) and method of use; and (iii) whether they are competing or complementary.[675]

(i) Infringement & Causes of Action

(i) Likelihood of Confusion

The vast majority of oppositions fall under Article 8.1(b) of the CTM Regulation[676] and require an assessment of the likelihood of confusion.[677] The "likelihood

---

671 Case C-291/00, *LTJ Diffusion SA v Sadas Vertbaudet SA*, 20 March 2003 [2003] ECR I-2799, para 54.

672 Case C-251/95, *SABEL BV v Puma AG, Rudolf Dassler Sport*, 11 November 1997 [1997] ECR I-6191, para 23.

673 Case C-342/97, *Lloyd Schuhfabrik Meyer & Co. GmbH v Klijsen Handel BV*, 22 June 1999 [1999] ECR I-3819, para 25.

674 Case C-251/95, *SABEL BV v Puma AG, Rudolf Dassler Sport*, 11 November 1997 [1997] ECR I-6191, para 22.

675 Case C-39/97, *Canon Kabushiki Kaisha v Metro-Goldwyn-Mayer Inc., formerly Pathe Communications Corporation*, 29 September 1998 [1998] ECR I-5507, para. 17. See also *Stone/Domingo/Groebl/duSorbier*: European Union, p. 67.

676 Council Regulation (EC) No 207/2009, 8(1).

677 *Stone/Domingo/Groebl/duSorbier*: European Union, p. 67.

of confusion must be assessed globally, taking into account all relevant factors",[678] including: (i) the degree of similarity between the goods or services; (ii) the degree of similarity between the relevant marks; and (iii) the distinctive character of the earlier mark.[679] As the court in both *Canon Kaubshiki Kaisha* and *Lloyd Schuhfabrik* held, "a lesser degree of similarity between those goods or services may be offset by a greater degree of similarity between the marks, and vice versa."[680]

The wording of Article 4(1)(b) of the Directive – "... there exists a likelihood of confusion on the part of the public ..." – shows that the perception of marks in the mind of the average consumer of the type of goods or services in question "plays a decisive role in the global appreciation of the likelihood of confusion. The average consumer normally perceives a mark as a whole and does not proceed to analyse its various details."[681] The more distinctive the earlier mark, the greater will be the likelihood of confusion.[682] Therefore "marks with a highly distinctive character, either *per se* or because of the reputation they possess on the market, enjoy broader protection than marks with a less distinctive character."[683]

(ii) Well-Known Marks

Article 5(2) of the Directive (setting out a trademark owner's rights to prevent unauthorized use of her trademark)[684] allows stronger protection to be given to

---

678 Case C-39/97, *Canon Kabushiki Kaisha v Metro-Goldwyn-Mayer Inc., formerly Pathe Communications Corporation*, 29 September 1998 [1998] ECR I-5507, para. 1.

679 Case C-342/97, *Lloyd Schuhfabrik Meyer & Co. GmbH v Klijsen Handel BV*, 22 June 1999 [1999] ECR I-3819, paras. 19 and 22.

680 Case C-39/97, *Canon Kabushiki Kaisha v Metro-Goldwyn-Mayer Inc., formerly Pathe Communications Corporation*, 29 September 1998 [1998] ECR I-5507, para. 17; and Case C-342/97, *Lloyd Schuhfabrik Meyer & Co. GmbH v Klijsen Handel BV*, 22 June 1999 [1999] ECR I-3819, para. 19.

681 Case C-251/95, *SABEL BV v Puma AG, Rudolf Dassler Sport*, 11 November 1997 [1997] ECR I-6191, para 23.

682 *Id.*, para 24.

683 Case C-39/97, *Canon Kabushiki Kaisha v Metro-Goldwyn-Mayer Inc., formerly Pathe Communications Corporation*, 29 September 1998 [1998] ECR I-5507, para 18.

684 Directive 2008/95/EC, Art. 5(2): "Any Member State may also provide that the proprietor shall be entitled to prevent all third parties not having his consent from using in the course of trade any sign which is identical with, or similar to, the trade mark in relation to goods or services which are not similar to those for which the trade mark is registered, where the latter has a reputation in the Member State and where use of that sign without due cause takes unfair advantage of, or is detrimental to, the distinctive character or the repute of the trade mark."

marks with a reputation[685] than that conferred under Article 5(1) (setting out the exclusive rights of a trademark owner and her rights to prevent general unauthorized use).[686] Oppositions under Article 8(5) of the CTM Regulation (setting out the higher level of protection for marks having gained a reputation)[687] can be difficult to prove, at times requiring substantial evidence of reputation to be deemed "well-known".[688]

Originally Article 8(5) applied only if the goods and services specified in the CTM application were *different* from those for which the earlier trademark had reputation. In *Davidoff & Cie SA v Gofkid*,[689] the CJEU expanded the scope of protection given to well-known marks to include *all* goods and services. The court did so by *not* adopting a literal interpretation of Article 5(2) of the Directive: Article 5(2) allows Member States to give trademark owners the right to prevent third parties using an identical or similar mark in relation to goods or services which are not similar to those for which the mark is registered, where the mark has a reputation in the Member State and where use of the mark takes unfair advantage of, or is detrimental to, the distinctive character or reputation of the registered mark. There is no need to prove confusion. Notwithstanding the wording of Article 5(2), the CJEU concluded that Article 5(2) needed to apply in cases where an identical or similar mark is used for goods or services which are identical or similar to those covered by the registration, *as well as* non-similar goods or services. The Court noted that the Directive "cannot be given an interpretation which would lead to marks with a reputation having less protection where a sign is used for identical or similar goods or services than where a sign is used for non-similar goods or services."[690]

In order for Article 8(5) to apply:

- nominal use of the CTM applied for must be without due cause and must take unfair advantage of the earlier right (the so-called "piggy-back" effect or be detrimental to its distinctive character (the classic "dilution" argument) or damage its reputation (through the principle of "tarnishment");[691] and

685 *Hildebrandt*: Harmonised Trade Mark Law in Europe, p. 70, § 401–407.

686 Directive 2008/95/EC, Art. 5(1).

687 Council Regulation (EC) No 207/2009, 8(5).

688 *Stone/Domingo/Groebl/duSorbier*: European Union, p. 67.

689 Case C-292/00, *Davidoff & Cie SA and Zino Davidoff SA v Gofkid Ltd*, 9 January 2003 [2003] ECR I-389.

690 *Id.*, para. 25.

691 *Stone/Domingo/Groebl/duSorbier*: European Union, p. 68.

- the relevant consumers must establish a link between the two trademarks – merely finding a degree of similarity between the mark with a reputation and the other mark is not sufficient for protection.[692]

(iii) Likelihood of Confusion v. Existence of Confusion

In *Marca Mode v Adidas*,[693] the Court found that Article 9(1)(b) of the Trademark Directive *cannot* be interpreted as meaning that where:

> "– a trade mark has a particularly distinctive character, either *per se* or because of the reputation it enjoys with the public, and
> – a third party, without the consent of the proprietor of the mark, uses, in the course of trade in goods or services which are identical with, or similar to, those for which the trade mark is registered, a sign which so closely corresponds to the mark as to give rise to the possibility of its being associated with that mark,
> the exclusive right enjoyed by the proprietor entitles him to prevent the use of the sign by that third party if the distinctive character of the mark is such that the possibility of such association giving rise to confusion cannot be ruled out."[694]

The reputation of a mark does not give grounds for presuming the existence of a likelihood of confusion simply because of the *existence of a likelihood of association* in the strict sense. A positive finding of the existence of a likelihood of confusion, which constitutes the matter to be proved, is necessary.[695]

(iv) National Reviews Different

In determining whether there is a likelihood of confusion, the court must focus on the overall impression made by the respective signs. It is not permissible to isolate one element out of a graphic ensemble and to restrict examination of the likelihood of confusion to that element alone. However, an individual component may be recognized as having a particularly distinctive character which characterizes the sign as a whole, and, consequently, a likelihood of confusion

---

692 Case C-408/01, *Adidas-Salomon AG and Adidas Benelux BV v Fitnessworld Trading Ltd.*, 23 October 2003 [2003] ECR I-12537, paras. 2 and 40.

693 Case C-425/98, *Marca Mode CV v Adidas AG and Adidas Benelux BV*, 22 June 2000 [2000] ECR I-4861.

694 *Id.*, para. 42.

695 *Id.*, paras. 39 and 41.

may be found to exist if another party's sign resembles the whole of the sign so characterized. Even in such a case, however, the two signs must be compared in their entirety and the comparison must not be confined to their individual (characterizing) elements.[696]

A sign may have a particularly distinctive character either *per se* or because of the reputation the mark enjoys with the public. The more distinctive its character, the greater the risk of confusion.[697]

Advocate General Jacobs, in his Opinion regarding *HAG II*, noted that "there are very many cases in which a trade mark protected in one Member State is found to be confusingly similar to a trade mark owned by someone else in another Member State (as in *Terrapin v Terranova*). ... [T]he owner of the trade mark may rely on [the holding of Terrapin] to prevent other persons from purveying goods under an identical or confusingly similar mark."

Commentators have noted that courts have grappled with such issues and that the case law has "continued to perplex".[698] In *Sabel BV v Puma AG*, the Court went through a long discussion of how to address the "risk of confusion" analysis and noted that different countries interpret the meaning of the Directive in different ways.[699]

3.4 Chapter Observations

(a) From *Sirena* to *HAG II*

It is worth remembering how the perception of trademarks in the European Union has changed. Trademarks were for a time regarded as significantly inferior to other intellectual property rights, in particular in comparison to patents. In

---

696 Case C-251/95, *SABEL BV v Puma AG, Rudolf Dassler Sport*, 11 November 1997 [1997] ECR I-6191, para 6.

697 *Id.*

698 *Barnard*: The Substantive Law of the EU, p. 32, n. 184, citing *Seville*: Intellectual Property.

699 "The Belgian, Luxembourg and Netherlands Governments claimed that the term 'likelihood of association' was included in those provisions of the Directive at their request, in order that they should be construed in the same manner as Article 13a of the Uniform Benelux Law on Trade Marks which adopts the concept of resemblance between marks, rather than that of likelihood of confusion, in defining the scope of the exclusive right conferred by a trade mark.... Such an interpretation of the Directive is contested by both the United Kingdom Government and by the Commission." Case C-251/95, *SABEL BV v Puma AG, Rudolf Dassler Sport*, 11 November 1997 [1997] ECR I-6191, paras. 14 and 17, respectively.

his Opinion in *Sirena Srl v Eda Srl* in 1971,[700] Advocate General Dutheillet de Lamothe noted that:

> "Both from the economic and from the human point of view the interests protected by patent legislation merit greater respect than those protected by trade marks."[701]

He continued:

> "From the human point of view, the debt which society owes to the 'inventor' of the name 'Prep Good Morning' [a brand of shaving cream] is certainly not of the same nature, to say the least, as that which humanity owes to the discoverer of penicillin."

The Court echoed those remarks in their decision:

> "The exercise of a trade-mark right is particularly apt to lead to a partitioning of markets, and thus to impair the free movement of goods between States which is essential to the Common Market. Moreover, a trade-mark right is distinguishable in this context from other rights of industrial and commercial property, inasmuch as the interests protected by the latter are *usually more important*, and merit a *higher degree of protection*, than the interests protected by an *ordinary* trade-mark."[702]

By 1990, the situation had changed and trademarks were recognized as important means to aid commerce. In his influential opinion in *HAG II*, Advocate General Jacobs was highly critical of the earlier, disparaging views.[703] He argued that trademarks reward the manufacturer who consistently produces high-quality goods and this stimulates economic progress. Without trademark protection, he said, there would be little incentive for manufacturers to develop new products or to maintain the quality of existing ones. He continued:

> "Trade marks are able to achieve that effect because they act as a guarantee, to the consumer, that all goods bearing a particular mark have been produced by, or under the control of, the same manufacturer and are therefore likely to be of similar quality. The guarantee of quality offered by a trade mark is not of course absolute, for the manufacturer is at liberty to vary the quality; however, he does so at his own risk and he – not his competitors – will suffer the consequences if he allows the quality to decline. Thus, although trade marks do not provide any form of legal guarantee of quality – the

700 Case 40/70, *Sirena S.r.l. v Eda S.r.l. and others*, 18 February 1971 [1971] ECR 69.

701 Case 40/70, *Sirena S.r.l. v Eda S.r.l. and others*, [1971] ECR 69, Opinion of AG Lamothe, 21 January 1971, p. 87.

702 Case 40/70, *Sirena S.r.l. v Eda S.r.l. and others*, 18 February 1971 [1971] ECR 69, para 7.

703 Case C-10/89, *SA CNL-SUCAL NV v HAG GF AG*, 17 October 1990 [1990] ECR I-3711 (*HAG II*), para. 18.

absence of which may have misled some to underestimate their significance – they do in economic terms provide such a guarantee, which is acted upon daily by consumers."

In its judgment in *HAG II*, the Court agreed with Advocate General Jacobs, recognizing the value of trademarks:

> "Trade mark rights are, it should be noted, an essential element in the system of undistorted competition which the Treaty seeks to establish and maintain. Under such a system, an undertaking must be in a position to keep its customers by virtue of the quality of its products and services, something which is possible only if there are distinctive marks which enable customers to identify those products and services. For the trade mark to be able to fulfil this role, it must offer a guarantee that all goods bearing it have been produced under the control of a single undertaking which is accountable for their quality."[704]

(b) The EU Perspective

Unlike the U.S. (with an integrated, federal trademark law), the EU continues to seek ways to harmonize the individual national trademark laws that exist in the Member States. Intellectual property rights in general – and trademarks in particular – present a particular challenge to the European Union's principle of free movement of goods and prohibitions on barriers to trade. With respect to trademarks, two issues are of particular relevance: (i) national and territorial rights are in conflict with common market principles, and (ii) there are discrepancies between the scope of protection afforded under national rights granted by individual counties.[705]

The EU has done much to modernize the national trademark laws in order to ensure a more effective and efficient trademark protection regime across the EU, at both at EU and at national level. This includes making trademark systems all over the EU more accessible and efficient, lowering costs and complexity,

---

704 *Id.*, para. 13.

705 For a review of some noteworthy recent case law (since 2012) from the CJEU and the German Federal Supreme Court related to trademarks, see *Rohnke/Thiering*: Die Rechtsprechung des EuGH und des BGH zum Markenrecht. For a review of some differences regarding recognition of famous marks in Germany (as compared to the EU), and proposals for harmonization, see *Heise/Ebert-Weidenfeller/Nordemann-Schiffel/Kefferpütz/Hackbarth*: Relevant public for determining the degree of recognition of famous marks. For an analysis of differences between German court and CJEU interpretations of "confusion", see *Sack*: Die abstrakte Verwechslungsgefahr im Markenrecht. See also *Fezer*: Markenrecht, § VI. Abstraktheit der Verwechslungsgefahr, paras. 279–80.

and increasing speed and legal security.[706] As the Commission has noted, the Trademark Directive and the CTM Regulation have been remarkably successful in achieving this harmonization:

> "National trademark registration in the EU Member States has been harmonised for 20 years and the unitary Community trademark was created more than 15 years ago. Since then, almost 1 million Community trademarks have been registered, compared to the 9 million "national" trademarks currently registered at Member States' industrial property offices since the beginning of trademark registrations there, demonstrating the popularity of the Community trademark. Community trademarks now represent around a quarter of all trademarks filed in the EU each year: in 2011, there were 105 000 applications for Community trade marks, against 435 000 applications for national trademarks."[707]

(c) Differences between U.S. & EU Laws

Although there has been substantial convergence in trademark laws, differences between U.S. and EU trademark laws certainly exist.[708] Such differences can have a commercial effect and need to be kept in mind by a global company wishing to register it rights in the jurisdictions where it does business (as well as those jurisdictions where it may want to do business).

---

706 *ECTA*: Position Paper on the revision of the OHIM Manual of the Trade Mark Practice.

707 *European Commission*: Press Release AGENDA/13/10. For more information on EU trademark legislation and policy, see *European Commission*: Internal Market, Trade Marks including Community Trade Mark.

708 For some broad conclusions on where EU law stands compared to U.S. law, see *Dubois*: Trademark Law Evolves in Europe's Highest Courts.

"Trademarks, patents, and advertising are often responsible for ... market imperfections. It would be humanly impossible, therefore, to attempt to create perfect competition by law. The problem is one of achieving reasonable effective 'workable competition.'"[709]

Paul Samuelson[710]

4. Trademarks & Competition: Competition's Role in Resolving the Tension between Proprietary Rights & Market Competition

4.1 Chapter Overview

(a) Interim Summary

As Chapters 1-3 demonstrated, the function of trademarks in our society today has evolved significantly from their practical identification, source, and quality

709 *Samuelson*: Problems of Economic Organization, p. 70 (emphasis in the original).

710 Paul Anthony Samuelson (15 May 1915 – 13 December 2009) was an American economist and the first American Nobel laureate winner of the Sveriges Riksbank Prize in Economic Sciences in Memory of Alfred Nobel in 1970. *Nobel Foundation*: Paul A. Samuelson; *Lindbeck*: Nobel Lectures, Economics 1969–1980. *The New York Times* considered him to be the "foremost academic economist of the 20th century." *Weinstein*: Paul A. Samuelson, p. A1. Though regarded as America's leading standard-bearer for Keynesian economics, he called himself a "cafeteria Keynesian", just picking the bits he liked. His combination of Keynesian and classical economic ideas became known as the "neoclassical synthesis". *The Economist*: Economics focus – Paul Samuelson. His textbook, "Economics: An Introductory Analysis", first published in 1948 and updated every three years thereafter, became the best-selling economics textbook of all time: "Paul Samuelson's Economics ranks with the most successful textbooks ever published in the field, including the works of Adam Smith, David Ricardo, John Stuart Mill and Alfred Marshall." *Skousen*: The Perseverance of Paul Samuelson's Economics. For further analysis of the Keynesian views set forth in Samuelson's textbook, see *Pearce/Hoover*: After the Revolution: Paul Samuelson. Finally, for Samuelson's review of his own textbook, see *Samuelson*: "Economics" at Fifty, pp. 352–363. As a point of interest, Mr. Samuelson's nephew, Lawrence (Larry) H. Summers, was President Obama's chief economic adviser (Director of National Economic Council, 2009–2010), former secretary of the Treasury under President Clinton, and former President of Harvard.

origins. Trademarks today are big money, big business, competitive assets, representing a profitable and commercially powerful means by which companies communicate a wealth of information regarding their business as an enterprise – i.e., its social personality and commercial character – sometimes completely divorced from the underlying products being sold.[711]

On the one hand, trademark protection promotes competition by preventing unfairness and facilitating quality competition (prohibiting competitors from free riding) and benefits consumers (diminishing confusion, lowering search costs, and prohibiting unfair trade practices). On the other hand, trademark protection can restrict competition by maintaining substantial barriers to entry, permitting trademark owners to carve out niche markets through "artificial" product differentiation (i.e., based on brand loyalty and advertising, not on quality).[712] As the commercial significance of and protection afforded to trademarks has expanded, so too the concerns that such expansive (and expanding) rights have significant anti-competitive effects on the market.

(b) Basic Considerations

Competition laws seek to minimize or prohibit anti-competitive effects which arise from the acquisition, exploitation, or enforcement of power in the market. The exercise of intellectual property rights – including trademarks – are certainly not immune from the scrutiny of competition laws. Since trademarks can have the effect of restraining trade, and competition laws in general are applied to ensure trade is not restrained, Chapters 4–6 will explore the interface – or collision – of intellectual property and competition laws.

Chapter 4 sets out the overall issues and challenges of the collision. Chapter 5 (for the U.S.) and Chapter 6 (for the EU) analyze how competition laws have been applied to the obtainment, grant, acquisition, and exercise of intellectual property rights – in particular with respect to trademarks – to determine whether the application of competition laws to the exercise of trademark rights

---

711 "Some trademarks occupy such a prominent place in the public mind that they have come to symbolize not only particular products and firms but broader social themes as well." *Shaughnessy*: Trademark Parody, p. 1079.

712 "Trademark promotion may in some markets be the sole cause of high barriers to entry which preserve the monopoly power of one maker. New brands of equal or higher quality may be unable to compete solely because of the strength of the established trademark whose power is sustained by persuasive advertising. Consumers end up paying higher prices for a better-known but lower-quality brand." *McClure*: Trademarks and Unfair Competition, p. 351.

has been successful to combat the anti-competitive effects of trademark use and protection. Chapters 5 and 6 also acknowledge the political and social frameworks which have influenced the development of antitrust and competition laws, and look at how such laws have been and are applied to promote and maintain "fair" market competition by regulating anti-competitive conduct.

4.2 Areas of Conflict Between Trademark Laws and Competition Principles

(a) Competition Law: Key Objectives

Competition laws seek to promote, protect, and maintain fair and effective competition within markets and reduce barriers to trade. They do so by prohibiting most aspects of exclusivity, dominant actions, and private restraints to trade, as well as thwarting monopolies that engage in anti-competitive activities.[713] Broadly speaking, competition laws seek to make businesses compete "fairly". "Fair" competition can only function if certain rules are in place which all competitors have to comply with. Since market mechanisms are not always sufficient to curb unfair practices, both the U.S. and the EU have systems and rules in place to ensure that dominant companies do not pre-empt the competitive process. Such policies are intended to protect consumers, encourage enterprise and efficiency, create a wider choice for consumers, help reduce prices, and improve quality.[714]

First, competition laws seek to prevent practices which restrain trade. To do so, competition laws regulate commercial practices that pose an arguable threat to competition, prevent concerted restraints on trade, and, more specifically and directly in the EU, prohibit businesses with significant market shares from unfairly exploiting their strong market positions (the so-called "abuse of a dominant market position").[715]

Second, competition laws generally forbid the wrongful acquisition or preservation of monopoly power. Concentrations of economic power in the hands of a few – as epitomized by trusts, cartels, and monopolies – are generally believed

713 *Peritz*: Competition policy and its implications for intellectual property rights, p. 171. *Giocoli*: Competition Versus Property Rights, Part VI.

714 *European Commission*: Competition: Making Markets Work Better, p. 3.

715 "Any abuse by one or more undertakings of a dominant position within the internal market or in a substantial part of it shall be prohibited as incompatible with the internal market in so far as it may affect trade between Member States." Article 102 TFEU.

to harm consumers, as such power leads to anti-competitive practices, such as price-fixing, unlawful restraints, and limited supplies, causing markets to stagnate and depressing economic growth.[716]

(b) Intellectual Property Rights: Key Objectives

Patent and copyright laws seek to encourage innovation and enterprise by rewarding inventors or authors for their efforts through the grant of certain exclusive rights. Ownership of intellectual property confers owners certain exclusive rights (sometimes called "legal monopolies"[717]) to prevent others (i.e., to exclude others) from exploiting the relevant patent, copyright, design right, or other intellectual (or industrial) property right. The limited "reward" enhances overall consumer welfare, as it provides an incentive to innovators to seek intellectual property protection and therefore brings into the public domain innovative information that might otherwise remain a trade secret.[718]

Trademark laws encourage enterprise by protecting business goodwill created through investment and quality; they stimulate market efficiency by preventing unfair business practices through free riding by competitors); and they diminish customer confusion and deception by allowing distinction between competitive goods.[719] They make "communication" between seller and buyer simple. Trademarks are "an essential element in the system of undistorted competition",[720] acting as "aids to the exchange of commodities … considered … vitally important to the protection of commerce".[721] Trademarks thus balance fair trade (for producers and consumers) with free trade.

(c) Legal Collision

It has long been recognized that both competition and intellectual property laws share the *common purpose* of enhancing consumer welfare, ensuring an efficient allocation of resources, and encouraging and promoting innovation.[722] Sharing

716 *Cornell University Law School*: Antitrust.

717 *Bartenbach*: Patentlizenz- und Know-how-Vertrag, p. 194.

718 *Peritz*: Competition policy and its implications for intellectual property rights, p. 171.

719 *Taggart*: Trade-Marks: Monopoly or Competition?, p. 668.

720 Case C-10/89, *SA CNL-SUCAL NV v HAG GF AG*, 17 October 1990 [1990] ECR I-3711 (*HAG II*), para 13.

721 *Trade-Mark Cases*, 100 U.S. 82 (1879).

722 *Taladay/Carlin*: Compulsory Licensing of Intellectual Property.

common objectives, however, does not necessarily mean that the laws interact without conflict. As described by Commissioner Ohlhausen of the Federal Trade Commission, the intersection of intellectual property and antitrust laws might be best described as a "collision".[723] When they collide, complex questions arise – regarding fundamental rights to intellectual property protection, the relative scope and jurisdiction of competition laws, and, from a policy perspective, how best to balance the short and long-run trade-offs between favoring one set of laws over the other – making the application of any legal or policy principles challenging.[724]

In simplest terms, intellectual property laws grant certain exclusive rights to restrain – i.e., *exclude* – others, while competition laws prohibit restraints to trade and anti-competitive practices.[725] In most cases, the methods of achieving the common goals of promoting innovation and enhancing consumer welfare are harmonious, permitting intellectual property holders to exclude others from using their inventions and thereby encouraging the further development of innovation and maintenance of quality investments. As a general matter, conduct that is authorized by the relevant intellectual property laws does not give rise to liability under the competition laws. However, intellectual property are not immune from competition scrutiny and can come into conflict with the principles underlying competition law.[726]

723 *Ohlhausen*: A Pragmatist's Approach to Navigating the Intersection of IP and Antitrust, p. 1.

724 As Commission Ohlhausen noted, "Reasonable minds can, and do, disagree on each of these subjects." *Ohlhausen*: A Pragmatist's Approach to Navigating the Intersection of IP and Antitrust, p. 2.

725 *Peritz*: Competition policy and its implications for intellectual property rights, p. 188.

726 As noted by the U.S. Court of Appeals for the Federal Circuit: "intellectual property rights do not confer a privilege to violate the antitrust laws". *CSU, LLC v. Xerox Corp.*, 203 F.3d 1322, 1325-30 (Fed. Cir. 2000). The U.S. Supreme Court found "frivolous" Microsoft's argument that "if intellectual property rights have been lawfully acquired... their subsequent exercise cannot give rise to antitrust liability". *Microsoft Corp. v. United States*, 253 F.3d 34, 63 (D.C. Cir. 2001) (en banc), cert. denied, 534 U.S. 952 (2001) EU courts have been even freer with applying competition laws to the exercise of patent and copyright rights: Case 238/87, *Volvo AB v Erik Veng (UK) Ltd.*, 5 October 1988 [1988] ECR 6211; Joined cases C-241/91 P and C-242/91 P, *Radio Telefis Eireann (RTE) and Independent Television Publications Ltd (ITP) v Commission* (Magill), 6 April 1995 [1995] ECR I-743; Case C-418/01, *IMS Health GmbH & Co. OHG v NDC Health GmbH & Co. KG.*, 29 April 2004 [2004] ECR

Application of competition principles to intellectual property rights presents no conflict when it *enforces* the boundaries of statutorily granted rights. For example, competition laws can step in to ensure there is no misuse of the intellectual property system, finding antitrust liability when rights are obtained by fraud or misrepresentation.[727]

However, competition rules may also challenge the boundaries of intellectual property right and may unduly restrain practices which are reserved (and permitted) under intellectual property rights but which are counter to competition legislation in abstract or general terms.[728] Current authorities presume that the licensing of intellectual property rights is generally pro-competitive in effect.[729] However, when a rights owner exerts too much control over her property, it can have anti-competitive effects that result in a violation of the competition laws.[730] Thus, competition laws will act to prevent the excesses of private property owners in order to maintain effective competition on, and access to, markets.[731] Practically speaking, this becomes a balancing act – for both the owners of intellectual

---

I-5039; and Commission, COMP/C—3/37.792—Microsoft, March 2004, Decision of 24 May 2007, OJ L 32/23; upheld by Case T-201/04, *Microsoft Corp. v Commission*, 17 September 2007 [2007] ECR II-3601.

727 In the U.S., fraudulent acquisition of a patent by knowingly making false representations to the USPTO may lead to a violation of § 2 of the Sherman Act. *Walker Process Equipment, Inc. V Food Machinery & Chemical Corp.*, 382 U.S. 172 (1965). In the EU, the CJEU has found that (i) a pattern of misleading representations before national patent offices and courts, and (ii) abuse of regulatory procedures could be deemed abuse of a dominant position and a violation of Article 102 TFEU. Case T-321/05, *AstraZeneca AB and AstraZeneca plc v Commission* 1 July 2010 [2010] ECR II-2805.

728 See in particular *Ohly*: Geistiges Eigentum und Wettbewerbsrecht, pp. 47–67.

729 "Licensing is vital for economic development and consumer welfare. ... However, licensing agreements can also have a stifling effect on competition. ... How intellectual property right holders license their rights to other market participants is crucial for achieving the right balance between stimulating innovation and preserving a level playing field in the internal market." *European Commission*: Press Release MEMO/13/120.

730 "The question ... is whether ... restrictions are justified ... or whether they are ... entered into with intent or effect of unduly restricting or preventing competition." *Ladas*: Trademark Licensing and the Antitrust Law, pp. 254, 257–59.

731 *Anderman*: The competition law/IP 'interface', pp. 6–7. "The fact that intellectual property laws grant exclusive rights of exploitation does not imply that intellectual property rights are immune from competition law intervention." Communication from the Commission – Guidelines on the application of Article 101 of the Treaty

property who want to license their assets and the competition authorities who want to oversee such licensing practices.

The courts face a difficult choice when drawing an appropriate dividing line between the general aims of ensuring free competition and encouraging the development of intellectual property.[732] An approach that is too interventionist will lessen the value of intellectual property rights and will reduce the financial incentive to innovate and invest.[733] However, if the courts ignore the effects that the unrestrained exercise of intellectual property rights may have on competition, a broad area of commercial activity would effectively be rendered immune from competition law.[734]

Furthermore, in the EU, the territorial nature of intellectual property rights (and the lack of a harmonized system of rights) presents yet further challenges. Intellectual property rights granted and exercised on a *national* level can have the effect of partitioning the EU common market by erecting barriers to cross-border trade, thereby contradicting the general principles of the free movement of goods and market competition with the Union.[735]

---

on the Functioning of the European Union to technology transfer agreements (OJ C 89/3, 28.03.2014), para. 7.

732 *Flynn*: Antitrust and the Suppression of the Technology, fn. 56. Flynn notes that the classic article discussing this balancing process is *Kaplow*: The Patent Antitrust Intersection.

733 Justice Oliver Wendall Holmes routinely dissented from court decisions that limited the sale or licensing of items protected by intellectual property laws. In cases dealing with the intersection between intellectual property and antitrust law, Holmes consistently voted to protect the value and enforceability of intellectual property rights regardless of the nature of the vertical restrictions imposed. He regarded such restrictions as an "ordinary incident of ownership" and as having "become a rule of property that law and justice require to be retained." *Motion Picture Patents Co. v. Universal Film Mfg. Co.*, 243 U.S. 502, 519 (1917). See *Waller*: Oliver Wendell Holmes, Jr., pp. 299–300.

734 *Peritz*: Competition policy and its implications for intellectual property rights, p. 171. The litigation between Microsoft and the U.S. DOJ demonstrated how difficult it is for antitrust regulators to intervene in intellectual property matters and has generated suggestions that the enforcement of antitrust policy is inappropriate for rapidly changing high-technology markets. *Bank*: Why Software and Antitrust make an Uneasy Mix, at B1.

735 See generally, *Kaczorowska*: European Union Law, pp. 608–627.

(d) Anti-Competitive Behaviors

In both the U.S. and the EU, competition laws primarily prevent: (i) unilateral conduct (i.e., monopolization by a single entity); and (ii) collusive conduct (i.e., agreements between entities that may restrain trade).[736]

With respect to unilateral conduct, it is not illegal to posses a monopoly (such a prohibition could deter legitimate business conduct).[737] However, it is illegal to actively acquire or maintain a monopoly through anticompetitive conduct.[738] Both U.S. and EU competition authorities do not regard market dominance or

---

736 Both the U.S. and EU competition laws also regulate mergers and acquisitions that are sufficiently large to constitute a threat to competition. This paper will not analyze competition laws with respect to mergers. For further information, the framework legislation in the EU is Council Regulation (EC) No 139/2004 of 20 January 2004 on the control of concentrations between undertakings (the EC Merger Regulation), OJ L 24/1, 29.01.2004. For a full list of the core TFEU provisions, implementing regulation, annexes, notices and guidelines, international co-operation (e.g., between the EU and the U.S.), best practice guidelines and practical information related to mergers, see *European Commission*: EU Competition Law: Rules Applicable to Merger Control. In the US, most merger enforcement actions are based on Section 7 of the Clayton Act, including the Hart-Scott-Rodino Act. Mergers may also be challenged as unreasonable restraints of trade, monopolization, or attempted monopolization under §§ 1 or 2 of the Sherman Act, or the FTC may challenge a merger as a violation of § 5 of the Federal Trade Commission Act, which prohibits "unfair methods of competition". Finally, the 1992 Merger Guidelines issued by the U.S. Department of Justice and the Federal Trade Commission are the most recent comprehensive statement outlining the agencies' analysis of *horizontal* mergers. The Department's 1984 Merger Guidelines are the agencies' most recent comprehensive statement on evaluating *vertical* mergers, but they should be "read in the context of" the 1992 Guidelines. *DOJ/FTC*: Statement Accompanying Release of Revised Merger Guidelines. *Blumenthal*: Merger Analysis under the U.S. Antitrust Laws. *Valentine*: The Evolution of U.S. Merger Law.

737 It As Judge Hand put it: "A single producer may be the survivor out of a group of active competitors, merely by virtue of his superior skill, foresight and industry.... The successful competitor, having been urged to compete, must not be turned upon when he wins." *United States v. Aluminum Company of America*, 148 F.2d 416, 430 (2d Cir. 1945). A similar point has been made in the EU: "The fact that a dominant trader has, by virtue of his dominance, a competitive advantage over competitors is not an abuse." Mr. Justice Laddie, in *Getmapping v. Ordnance Survey*, 31 May 2002, High Court, England, HC 02C 00521 [2002] EWHC 1089 (Ch).

738 The U.S. Supreme Court has noted that: "the law directs itself not against conduct which is competitive, even severely so, but against conduct which unfairly tends to destroy competition itself. It does so not out of solicitude for private concerns but

monopoly in and of itself to be unlawful; rather, the concern arise when market dominant firms engage in abusive or anticompetitive conduct.[739] Differences, however, exist between the United States and the EU, as to how much market power is required,[740] what types of conduct are considered anticompetitive, and the analytical frameworks used to determine if there is a violation. In the U.S., monopolists and firms acquiring monopoly power are subject to greater scrutiny of their behavior.[741] In the EU, Article 102 TFEU similarly focuses on the

---

out of concern for the public interest." *Spectrum Sports, Inc. v. McQuillan*, 506 U.S. 447, 458, (1993).

739 The Unilateral Conduct Working Group, in a study regarding dominance and market power, has found that: "All jurisdictions agree that unilateral conduct laws address specific conduct and its anticompetitive effects, rather than the mere possession of dominance/substantial market power or its creation through competition on the merits." *Unilateral Conduct Working Group*: Int'l Competition Network, Dominance/Substantial Market Power Analysis.

740 In the U.S., a court has found a 90% market share to be "enough to constitute a monopoly" but noted that "it is doubtful whether sixty or sixty-four percent would be enough; and certainly thirty-three percent is not." *United States v. Aluminum Company of America*, 148 F.2d 416, 424 (2nd Cir. 1945). The EU requirement is lower: market shares exceeding 70% raise a strong presumption of dominance, while market shares in the 50-70% range may in themselves raise a similar presumption under certain circumstances. *European Commission*: DG Competition Discussion Paper on the Application of Article 82 of the Treaty to Exclusionary Abuses (citing Case 85/76, *Hoffmann-La Roche & Co. AG v Commission*, 13 February 1979 [1979] ECR 461, para 41; Case C-62/86, *AKZO Chemie BV v Commission*, 3 July 1991 [1991] ECR I-3359, para. 60; and Case T-395/94, *Atlantic Container Line AB and others v. Commission*, 28 February 2002 [2002] ECR II-875, para 328). *Rill*: Remarks presented to Federal Trade Commission and Department of Justice, p 9. See also *DOJ*: Competition and Monopoly: Single Firm Conduct, fn. 7. The DOJ eventually withdrew the report, noting that it "raised too many hurdles to government antitrust enforcement and favored extreme caution and the development of safe harbors for certain conduct within reach of Section 2". *DOJ*: Press Release 09-459.

741 In *Kodak*, Justice Scalia (in dissent) conceded that: "Where a defendant maintains substantial market power, his activities are examined through a special lens: Behavior that might otherwise not be of concern to the antitrust laws – or that might even be viewed as procompetitive – can take on exclusionary connotations when practiced by a monopolist." *Eastman Kodak Company v. Image Technical Services, Inc.*, 504 U.S. 451 (1992), J. Scalia (dissenting), at p. 488.

conduct of dominant firms, but emphasizes the heightened scrutiny applied to dominant firms.[742]

With respect to collusive conduct, agreements might be among competitors (i.e., horizontal agreements)[743] or agreements between buyers and sellers (i.e., vertical agreements).[744] Vertical restraints are generally less threatening to competition than horizontal restraints. With the exception of vertical minimum price fixing (or "resale price maintenance"), courts typically evaluate vertical restraints under the rule of reason. Under the rule of reason, courts balance the anticompetitive harms of a restraint against its pro-competitive benefits. Only those restraints which produce harms in excess of benefits to competition are deemed unreasonable. Horizontal restraints are more troubling because they may allow the participants to create a cartel, which can then behave anti-competitively, much as a monopolist would. Historically, most agreements between competitors were deemed illegal *per se*, without any necessity for a weighing of harms and benefits to competition. Today, U.S. and EU courts have retreated from that position, recognizing that certain agreements among competitors may be efficient and pro-competitive. Most horizontal restraints are now judged under the rule of reason. Only certain forms of "naked" agreements to fix prices or divide territories remain illegal *per se*.

---

742 As the Court of Justice noted in *Michelin v. Commission*, the dominant firm "has a special responsibility not to allow its conduct to impair undistorted competition on the common market." Case 322/81, *NV Nederlandsche Baden-Industrie Michelin v Commission* [1983] ECR 3461, para. 57. See also Commission Notice: Guidance on the Commission's enforcement priorities in applying Article 82 of the EC Treaty to abusive exclusionary conduct by dominant undertakings (OJ C 45/7, 24.2.2009), paras. 1 and 6.

743 Horizontal agreements are those among competitors at the same level of the market structure (e.g., between two producers, two manufacturers, two distributors, or two retailers). *Business Elecs. Corp. v. Sharp Elecs. Corp.*, 485 U.S. 717, 730 and fn. 4 (1988). Horizontal agreements are typically looked upon with care since they are the most harmful to competition: instead of competing against one other to benefit the market, these agreements allow competitors to collude.

744 Vertical agreements are those among persons at different levels of the market structure (e.g., between a manufacturer and its distributors, or between a wholesaler and retailer), which may also affect the availability of goods and services and the terms on which they are supplied. *Business Elecs. Corp. v. Sharp Elecs. Corp.*, 485 U.S. 717, 730 and fn. 4 (1988).

(e) Ongoing Efforts

Historically, the relationship between competition principles and intellectual property rights has been seen either in bleak[745] or more positive[746] terms. Some find the conundrum "to a large extent illusory."[747]

Today, both the U.S. Federal Circuit and the European Commission find the two bodies of law "complementary." In *Atari Games Corp. v. Nintendo of North America, Inc.*, the Federal Circuit said that:

> "the aims and objectives of patent and antitrust laws may seem, at first glance, wholly at odds. However, the two bodies of law are actually *complementary*, as both are aimed at encouraging innovation, industry and competition."[748]

Reporting on a Round Table on competition policy and the exercise of intellectual property rights, the European Commission stated that:

---

745 Some examples include: *Bartenbach*: Patentlizenz- und Know-how-Vertrag, p. 194: "ein Spannungsverhältnis" (a charged relationship); *Bretthauer*: Die Beurteilung von Markenlizenzverträgen, p. 20: "ein kartellrechtliches Grundproblem" (a fundamental antitrust problem); *Bork*: The Antitrust Paradox: p. 81: "a paradox"; *Carrier*: Unravelling the Patent-Antitrust Paradox, p. 762: "a formidable paradox"; *Feil*: Lizenzkartellrecht, p. VII: "ein sachlicher Widerspruch" (a factual contradiction); *Giocoli*: Competition Versus Property Rights, pp. 747 and 748: a "dichotomy" and a "perennial antagonism; *Kreutzman*: Neues Kartellrecht und geistiges Eigentum, p. 453: "diese Spannungsfelds" (an area of tension); *Peritz*: Frontiers of Legal Thought, pp. 278 and 271: called it a "conflict", noted its "tension", and acknowledged its "battles". See also *Image Technical Servs. V. Eastman Kodak Co.*, 125 F.3d 1195, 1217 (9th Cir. 1997): "At the border of intellectual property monopolies and antitrust markets lies a field of dissonance yet to be harmonized by statute or the Supreme Court."

746 *Anderman*: The competition law/IP 'interface', p. 1: sees a "considerable overlap" and finds the conflict not as dramatic as most believe; *Katarzyna*: Intellectual Property and the Limits of Antitrust, p.vii: calls the relationship "perplexing," but deems the conflict to be "only illusory"; *Hamilton*: Software Tying Arrangement under the Antitrust Laws, p. 607: finds the notion of a conflict "erroneous"; Turner: Basic Principles in Formulating Antitrust and Misuse: believes that "harmonization" is possible; *Ward*: Patent and Antitrust Law, pp. Ix and 1: finds the conflict "illusory" and sees instead a "compatibility" of goals.

747 *Bowman*: Patent and Antitrust Law, p. ix.

748 *Atari Games Corp. v. Nintendo of North America, Inc.*, 897 F. 2d 1572, 1576 (Fed. Cir. 1990).

> "At the highest level of analysis IP and competition law are *complementary* because they both aim at promoting consumer welfare."[749]

Since the 1990s, the competition authorities in both the U.S. and the EU have developed core competition regulations, guidelines, and other communications regarding their policies with respect to the licensing of intellectual property rights and recommendations on how to navigate the intersection. The primary guidelines are as follows:

- In 1992, the EU Commission adopted Commission Regulation (EEC) No 151/93 of 23 December 1992 amending Regulations (EEC) No 417/85, (EEC) No 2349/84 and (EEC) No 556/89 on the application of Article 85(3) of the Treaty to certain categories of specialization agreements, research and development agreements, patent licensing agreements and know-how licensing agreements.[750]
- In 1995, the EU Commission adopted Commission Regulation (EC) No 70/95 of 17 January 1995, amending Regulation (EEC) No 2349/84 on the application of Article 85(3) of the Treaty to certain categories of patent licensing[751] and Commission Regulation (EC) No 2131/95 of 7 September 1995 (amending the same).[752]
- In 1995, the DOJ and FTC jointly published the "Antitrust Guidelines for the Licensing of Intellectual Property"[753] outlining the agencies' analyses with respect to intellectual property licensing, including agreements among competitors.
- In 1996, the Federal Trade Commission published a Staff Report, "Anticipating the 21st Century: Competition Policy in the New, High-Tech, Global Marketplace",[754] which looked at the development of high-tech technologies (specifically the telephone, television, and computer), identified significant consumer protection issues associated with the new technologies; and considered how best to address those emerging issues. The report analyzed and

749 *European Commission*: Competition policy and the exercise of intellectual property rights, p. 6.

750 OJ L 021/8, 29.01.1993. This regulation has since been replaced.

751 OJ L 012/13, 18.01.1995.

752 OJ L 214/6, 08.09.1995.

753 *DOJ/FTC*: 1995 IP Licensing Guidelines. See also *ABA*: The Federal Antitrust Guidelines for the Licensing of Intellectual Property.

754 *FTC*: Anticipating the 21st Century.

made recommendations on how to continue the FTC's missions in light of increased global and innovation based competition.

- Also in 1996, the EU Commission adopted Commission Regulation (EC) No 240/96 of 31 January 1996 on the application of Article 85(3) of the Treaty to certain categories of technology transfer agreements.[755] This regulation was replaced by Regulation 774/2004 (see below).
- In 1997, the EU Commission adopted Commission Regulation (EC) No 1582/97 of 30 July 1997 amending Regulations (EEC) No 1983/83 and (EEC) No 1984/83 on the application of Article 85(3) of the Treaty to categories of, respectively, exclusive distribution agreements and exclusive purchasing agreements.[756] Later that year, the Commission adopted Commission Regulation (EC) No 2236/97 of 10 November 1997 amending Regulations (EEC) No 417/85 and (EEC) No 418/85 on the application of Article 85(3) of the Treaty to categories of, respectively, specialization agreement and research and development agreements.[757]
- In 1999, the EU Commission adopted Commission Regulation (EC) No 2790/1999 of 22 December 1999 on the application of Article 81(3) of the Treaty to categories of vertical agreements and concerted practices.[758]
- In 2000, the DOJ and FTC jointly published the "Antitrust Guidelines for Collaborations Among Competitors", outlining how the Agencies analyze certain antitrust issues raised by collaborations among competitors.[759] Also in 2000, the DOJ and FTC issue the revised "Horizontal Merger Guidelines" which outline the agencies' approach to horizontal mergers and acquisitions, as well as certain competitor collaborations.[760]
- During 2002, the DOJ and FTC held a series of public hearings on "Competition and Intellectual Property Law and Policy in the Knowledge-Based Economy," to help the agencies address evolving IP and antitrust issues and their interface.[761]

---

755 OJ L 031/2, 09.02.1996.

756 OJ L 214/2, 06.08.1997.

757 OJ L 306/12, 11.11.1997.

758 OJ L 336/21, 29.12.999,.

759 *DOJ/FTC*: Collaboration Guidelines. See also *Lampert*: Antitrust in IP Licensing, p. 4.

760 *DOJ/FTC*: Horizontal Merger Guidelines. The 2000 Horizontal Merger Guidelines replace the Horizontal Merger Guidelines issued in 1992, revised in 1997.

761 Transcripts, prepared remarks, and some papers from the hearings are available from the FTC. *FTC*: Competition and IP Law and Policy in the Knowledge-Based Economy Hearings.

- In October 2003, the Federal Trade Commission Staff published a report, "To Promote Innovation: The Proper Balance of Competition and Patent Law and Policy".[762]
- In 2004, the European Commission adopted Commission Regulation (EC) No 772/2004 of 7 April 2004 on the application of Article 81(3) of the Treaty to categories of technology transfer agreements (the so-called Technology Transfer Block Exemption or TTBE Regulation),[763] replacing Regulation (EC) No 240/96 of 31 January 1996, which expired on 30 April 2004. The TTBE Regulation created a safe harbor for technology transfer agreements under EU competition law.
- In 2004, the European Commission also published the Guidelines accompanying the TTBE Regulation (the TTBE Guidelines).[764] The TTBE Guidelines gave guidance on the application of the TTBE Regulation as well as on the application of EU competition law to technology transfer agreements that fall outside the safe harbor of the TTBE Regulation. The competition rules aim to strengthen the incentives for initial R&D, facilitate diffusion of intellectual property and generate market competition.
- In June 2005 and June 2006, respectively, the European Commission published its 2004 and 2005 Annual Report on Competition Policy.[765] For the 2005 Report, then Competition Commissioner Neelie Kroes stated that "The competition policy pursued by the European Commission is fundamental in

762 *FTC*: To Promote Innovation.

763 Commission Regulation (EC) No 772/2004 of 27 April 2004 on the application of Article 81(3) of the Treaty to categories of technology transfer agreements (OJ L 123/11, 27.04.2004). The 2004 TTBE Regulation expired on 27 April 2014. In March 2014, the European Commission adopted new competition rules for the assessment of technology transfer agreements. See Commission Regulation (EU) No 316/2014 of 21 March 2014 on the application of Article 101(3) of the Treaty on the Functioning of the European Union to categories of technology transfer agreements (OJ L 93/17, 28.3.2014). The 2014 TTBE Regulation replaced the 2004 TTBE Regulation on 1 May 2014.

764 Commission Notice: Guidelines on the application of Article 81 of the EC Treaty to technology transfer agreements (OJ C 101/2, 27.04.2004). On 1 May 2014, the 2004 TTBE Guidelines were replaced with the new 2014 TTBE Guidelines. Communication from the Commission – Guidelines on the application of Article 101 of the Treaty on the Functioning of the European Union to technology transfer agreements (OJ C 89/3, 28.03.2014).

765 See *European Commission*: Report on Competition Policy 2004; and *European Commission*: Report on Competition Policy 2005.

shaping competitive European markets, and promoting growth and jobs. This report gives an overview of our recent decisions and policy initiatives, and will help stimulate debate and ensure compliance with the EU rules on cartels, abuses of dominant position, merger control and state subsidies".[766] With respect to rules on restrictive business practices and abuse of dominance, the 2005 Report reviewed the publication of a Green Paper on damages actions for breach of such rules,[767] as well as a Discussion Paper on exclusionary abuses of dominance,[768] both of which are part of a drive to develop antitrust policy on a sound economic footing.

- In 2007, the DOJ and FTC issued a joint report, "Antitrust Enforcement and Intellectual Property Rights. Promoting Innovation and Competition,"[769] to inform consumers, business and intellectual property rights holders about the agencies' competition view with respect to a wide range of activities, including refusals to license, collaborative standard setting, patent pooling, licensing, and the tying and bundling of intellectual property rights, and methods of extending market power conferred by a patent beyond the patent's expiration.[770]
- In 2008, the Justice Department issued a report "Competition and Monopoly: Single Firm Conduct Under Section 2 of the Sherman Act", finding that the combination of complementary factors of production by intellectual property licensing is "generally procompetitive," but that a unilateral, unconditional refusal to license to a rival is generally *per se* legal.[771]
- In March 2011, the FTC issued a report entitled "The Evolving IP Marketplace, Aligning Patent Notice and Remedies With Competition", recommending improvements to policies affecting patent notice and remedies for patent infringement.[772]

---

766 *European Commission*: Press Release IP/06/804.

767 *European Commission*: Press Release IP/05/1634. The texts of the Green Paper and an accompanying Staff Working Paper are available from the Commission. *European Commission*: Actions for Damages – Key documents.

768 *European Commission*: Press Release IP/05/1626.

769 *DOJ/FTC*: Promoting Innovation and Competition.

770 *FTC*: Federal Trade Commission and Department of Justice Issue Report on Antitrust and Intellectual Property, Press Release.

771 *DOJ*: Competition and Monopoly: Single Firm Conduct. This report was disavowed by the FTC in 2008 and withdrawn by the Department of Justice in 2009. *DOJ*: Press Release 09-459.

772 *FTC*: The Evolving IP Marketplace. The report continues the Commission's policy with respect to the patent system, begun with its 2003 report (*FTC*: To Promote Innovation). The 2011 report is based on the hearings, public comments, and selected

- In November 2011, the European Commission published an external report on the interface between competition policy and intellectual property rights, in particular providing an economic assessment of intellectual property licensing agreements that may have significant anti-competitive effects.[773]
- In December 2011, the European Commission announced that it had begun a review of the EU competition rules with respect to technology transfer agreements[774] and in February 2013, the European Commission published a draft of a new technology transfer block exemption regulation and revised guidelines on the application of Article 101 TFEU to technology transfer agreements.[775]
- In 2013, the DOJ and USPTO issued a "Policy Statement on Remedies for Standards-Essential Patents Subject to Voluntary F/RAND Commitments" outlining the DOJ's and USPTO's perspective on whether injunctive relief in judicial proceedings or exclusion orders in investigations under section 337 of the Tariff Act of 1930 are properly issued when a patent holder seeking such a remedy asserts standards-essential patents that are encumbered by a RAND or FRAND licensing commitment.[776]
- In March 2014, the European Commission adopted a new set of competition rules and guidelines for the assessment of technology transfer agreements. The revised TTBE Regulation[777] and TTBE Guidelines[778] replaced the existing TTBE Regulation and TTBE Guidelines as of 1 May 2014.[779]

---

panels of a conference held in May 2010. *FTC*: The Evolving IP Marketplace, Conference.

773 *Regibeau/Rockett*: European Commission, Assessment of Potential Anticompetitive Conduct in the Field of Intellectual Property Rights.

774 *European Commission*: Commission consults on review of current regime for technology transfer agreements.

775 *European Commission*: Draft Commission Regulation EU; *European Commission*: Draft Communication, Guidelines on the application of Article 101; *European Commission*: Draft proposal for a revised block exemption; *European Commission*: Press Release MEMO/13/120.

776 *DOJ/USPTO*: Policy Statement on Remedies for Standards-Essential Patents.

777 Commission Regulation (EU) No 316/2014 of 21 March 2014 on the application of Article 101(3) of the Treaty on the Functioning of the European Union to categories of technology transfer agreements (OJ L 93/17, 28.3.2014).

778 Communication from the Commission – Guidelines on the application of Article 101 of the Treaty on the Functioning of the European Union to technology transfer agreements (OJ C 89/3, 28.03.2014).

779 *European Commission*: Press Release IP/14/299.

However, despite the plethora of guidelines and communications, the conflicts remain and the formulation of a coherent and mature competition policy with respect to intellectual property rights remains an ongoing, frustratingly difficult process.[780]

(f) The Trouble with Trademarks

Although the U.S. and the EU have sought to clarify the intersection between intellectual property rights and competition laws, neither the U.S. nor the EU have provided much guidance with respect to the anti-competitive effects of *trademarks* or *trademark licensing*, since trademarks are specifically excluded from the U.S.[781] and EU[782] intellectual property guidelines and instead relegated to a general antitrust analysis which does not address the anti-competitive barriers inherent in brand protection.

Furthermore, trademark protection been argued to create "market power". Measurement of such "legal" market power under competition rules, which is a crucial factor in competition liability analysis, is difficult. Furthermore, the

---

780 *Vogelaar*: Competition law in the EU and the Netherlands, pp. 138–140.

781 The 1995 Guidelines specifically exclude trademark licenses from their scope ("These Guidelines do not cover the antitrust treatment of trademarks. Although the same general antitrust principles that apply to other forms of intellectual property apply to trademarks as well, these Guidelines deal with technology transfer and innovation-related issues that typically arise with respect to patents, copyrights, trade secrets, and know-how agreements, rather than with product-differentiation issues that typically arise with respect to trademarks.") *DOJ/FTC*: 1995 IP Licensing Guidelines, fn. 2. The 2000 Guidelines do not once refer to "trademarks".

782 The TTBE Regulation does not apply to trademark licences, and the TTBE Guidelines make it clear that the Commission will not extend the principles developed in the technology transfer block exemption to trademark licensing (TTBE Guidelines, para. 50). The Guidelines state that trademark licensing often occurs in the context of distribution and resale of goods and services and is generally more akin to distribution agreements than technology licensing. Where a trademark licence is directly related to the use, sale, or resale of goods and services, and does not constitute the primary object of the agreement, the licence agreement is covered by Regulation (EC) 330/2010 (the vertical agreements block exemption, OJ L 102/1, 23.10.2010). However, the Commission Guidelines on vertical restraints (OJ C 130/1, 19.05.2010) that accompany the vertical agreements block exemption specifically state that the vertical agreements block exemption does not apply to the pure licence of a trade mark or sign for the purposes of merchandising (para. 33). Accordingly, the vertical agreements block exemption would not apply to any trademark licence granted as part of a character merchandising licence.

definition of the "relevant market" with respect to a product covered by an exclusive right (which by its very nature could be its own market for the period of exclusivity) is also problematic.

4.3 Chapter Observations

(a) Comparison of U.S. and EU Approaches

There is a broad consensus on both sides of the Atlantic that intellectual property rights do not create monopolies, that intellectual property rights and competition principles have the common objective of stimulating innovation and economic grow, and that intellectual property rights need to be treated with some level of deference so that competition enforcement does not undermine the objectives of intellectual property policy.[783]

As we shall see in Chapters 5 and 6, the approach of competition authorities when faced with intellectual property issues has differed from one side of the Atlantic to the other:[784] the U.S. authorities have a more "hands-off" approach to applying antitrust restrictions to intellectual property imperfections,[785] whereas the EU authorities are more willing to step in and establish competition approaches to apply to intellectual property issues:[786]

> "U.S. antitrust enforcers see little scope for antitrust policy to mitigate the consequences of imperfect IP policies. They are reluctant to intervene in what is perceived to be the sphere of IP policy and take the view that any competitive concerns are better remedied by changes in the IP policy. ... Exactly the opposite tendencies are present in

783 See *Czapracka*: Intellectual Property and the Limits of Antitrust, p. viii.

784 For a comparison of the U.S. IP Guidelines and the TTBE Regulation, see *Gilbert*: Antitrust Policy for the Licensing of Intellectual Property, pp. 206–223.

785 The current approach in the U.S. treats intellectual property rights "as having primacy within their established boundaries, and relegates antitrust to the role of policing departures from those boundaries". *Lemley*: A New Balance Between IP and Antitrust, p. 255.

786 *Giocoli*: Competition Versus Property Rights, p. 747. For an obvious example, consider the Microsoft cases. The U.S. found Microsoft had not infringed the antitrust laws by refusing to license. *United States v. Microsoft Corp.*, 147 F.3d 935, 949-50 (D.C. Cir. 1998). The CJEU found an abuse of dominance because of the foreclosures and the violation of the principle of openness. COMP/C—3/37.792—Microsoft, March 2004, Decision of 24 May 2007, OJ L 32/23; upheld by Case T-201/04, *Microsoft Corp. v Commission*, 17 September 2007 [2007] ECR II-3601. See also *Fox*: Monopolization and Dominance in the United States and the European Community, pp. 1014–15, for a description of U.S./EU clash in the IBM case.

EU competition law. Both the European Commission and the ECJ seem to see a role for competition law to correct improvidently defined IPRs, even if it entails adjusting competition principles. … Yet, there is an inherent danger in this approach. It may lead antitrust authorities to adopt analytically questionable approaches that undermine the coherence of antitrust law."[787]

(b) Reconciliation Challenges

Many of today's most exciting and challenging developments in law arise in cases involving the intersection of intellectual property rights and competition law. Given the ever-increasing globalization of business – particularly by businesses with innovative intellectual property assets who which to license their assets worldwide – the different legal policies in, and the varying approaches taken by, the U.S. and Germany (and, through application of the TFEU, Europe), makes the intersection of antitrust and intellectual property law more challenging than ever.

The reasons making the task of reconciling IP and antitrust laws difficult can be broadly summarized as follows:

- IP Laws are changing: the contours of IP rights – in number, type and scope – keeps expanding,[788] making it difficult for courts to apply a unitary approach and requiring courts to re-examine and re-apply the new laws to old situations.[789]
- Jurisdictional Conflicts: In the US, different courts have jurisdiction over intellectual property claims, without binding precedence,[790] often following

787 *Czapracka*: Where Antitrust Ends and IP Begins, p. 45.

788 See generally below § 8.2.

789 *Dratler*: Intellectual Property Law.

790 At the trial level, the patent and copyright laws are federal statues, and each of the 93 district courts have original, exclusive jurisdiction (*Christianson v. Colt Indus. Operating Corp.*, 486 U.S. 80 (1988)). However, no district judge binds any other – even if they are located in the same district. Furthermore, questions under IP licenses may wind up in state court. At the appellate level, the Federal Circuit Court of Appeals has exclusive jurisdiction over appeals from district courts for actions relating to patents (28 U.S.C. § 1295(a)(1)). If the case arose under state unfair competition law, however, the Federal Circuit may lack subject matter jurisdiction (*The Holmes Group, Inc. v Vornado Air Circulation System, Inc.*, 535 U.S. § 826 (2002)). Copyrights, on the other hand, are allocated to the several geographic Courts of Appeal, none of which binds any other (28 U.S.C. § 1295(a)(1)). See *Lampert*: Antitrust in IP Licensing, pp. 2–3.

different approaches, and ultimately leading to different results.[791] Antitrust claims may be separated from an IP claim, so separate courts may actually adjudicate claims arising from the same transaction.[792] Finally, the variety of enforcement mechanisms regarding antitrust claims (private civil suits, government civil suits by both the Federal Trade Commission and the DOJ, and in some cases criminal prosecution by the DOJ) is yet another impediment to the consistent and coherent reconciliation of intellectual property and antitrust laws.[793] In the EU, although the European Commission and the national competition authorities in all EU Member States cooperate with each other through the European Competition Network (the ECN), various national competition authorities have come up with differ-ent (and controversial) interpretations of cases based on similar claims.[794]

---

791 See *Carrier*: Unraveling the Patent-Antitrust Paradox. Carrier reviews in depth four cases all involving a refusal to license that highlight the diversity of approaches that courts have applied to similar cases: (i) the Federal Circuit's decision in *In re Independent Service Organizations Antitrust Litigation* ("Xerox"), 203 F.3d 1322 (Fed. Cir. 2000), whose approach favored patentees by emphasizing the centrality of the right to exclude in the patent system; (ii) *Image Technical Services, Inc. v. Eastman Kodak Co.* ("Kodak II"), 125 F.3d 1195 (9th Cir. 1997), whose approach favored competitors, since "presumptively valid business justifications" (such as a refusal to license) could be rebutted by evidence; (iii) *Intergraph Corp. v. Intel Corp.*, 3 F. Supp. 2d 1255 (N.D. Ala. 1998), vacated, 195 F.3d 1346, 1357-58 (Fed. Cir. 1999), whose approach relied on the "essential facilities" doctrine when it found that Intel's refusal to supply likely violates Section 2 of the Sherman Act; and (iv) *United States v. Microsoft Corp.*, 84 F. Supp. 2d 9, 61 (D.D.C. 1999) (findings of fact), 87 F. Supp. 2d 30 (D.D.C.) (conclusions of law), aff'd in part and rev'd in part, 253 F.3d 34 (D.C. Cir. 2000) (en banc), cert. denied, 122 S. Ct. 350 (2001), whose approach ignored the fundamental nature underlying intellectual property laws, which – by definition – promote welfare through exclusion.

792 When a case involves both antitrust and patent claims, the case is frequently bifurcated for separate discovery or trial. Antitrust issues are often postponed until rights are determined. *ABA*: Antitrust Law Developments, p. 1161. Where the antitrust and patent claims are severed in the district court under Rule 42 of the Federal Rules of Civil Procedure, appellate jurisdiction over the antitrust claims normally will remain in the Federal Circuit. However, where the patents claims are voluntarily dismissed, the Federal Circuit does not have jurisdiction over the remaining non-patent issues. *ABA*: Antitrust Law Developments, at 1159.

793 See *Lampert*: Antitrust in IP Licensing, p. 3.

794 Compare the 2009 German Federal High Court (*Bundesgerichtshof*) Orange Book decision (BGH 6.5.2009 – KZR 39/06 – Orange Book Standard), with the 2010 Dutch District Court *Philips v. SK Kassetten* case (*Koninklijke Philips Electronics N.V.*

- Legal blurring: In spite of the differences between intellectual property rights, courts have sometimes defaulted to relying on the conflict of patent-competition decisions when resolving asserted conflicts between other intellectual property rights and competition laws.[795]
- Supremacy of Market Integration: in the EU, an increased emphasis on the goals of market competition takes precedence over both national and private rights. Competition laws are seen as an instrument to attain a wider objective – i.e., market integration – thereby justifying a wider scope for active competition law intervention.[796]

---

v. SK Kassetten GmbH & Co. KG, District Court The Hague, The Netherlands, 17 March 2010, Joint Cases No. 316533/HA ZA 08-2522 and 316535/HA ZA 08-2524. The German BGH affirmed the option for a defendant to raise a competition law defense in infringement cases of an (alleged) "essential" patent, provided that the defendant acts like a *bona fide* licensee, by: (i) making an irrevocable offer to take a license under FRAND terms (which can not be objected by the patentee without breaching Article 102 TFEU), and (ii) paying the reasonable royalty fees to the patentee or deposits the fees in escrow. The Dutch court found the German Orange-Book ruling could not be applied in The Netherlands, as it contravened Dutch patent law (paras 6.19–6.20), created legal uncertainty (para 6.21), and was unnecessary to protect the defendant's interests (paras 6.22 and 6.23). *European Patent Lawyers Association*: NL – Philips v. SK Kasetten / FRAND. Furthermore, the European Commission has recently stepped in and expressed that the seeking of an injunction based on standard essential patent may constitute an abuse of a dominant position in terms of Art. 102 TFEU if an SEP holder has given a commitment to license its SEPs on FRAND-terms and where the company against which an injunction is sought is willing to enter into a license agreement on FRAND terms. See *European Commission*: Press Release IP/13/971; and *European Commission*: Press Release IP/12/345.

795 This has been the case in the U.S., when the Supreme Court has addressed copyright-antitrust conflicts. *ABA*: Antitrust Law Developments, p. 1080.

796 Philip Lowe, Director General of DG Competition at the European Commission, stated that the goal of Regulation 1/2003 and the revised TTBE Regulation (i.e., the position of the EU Competition Rules as applied to Intellectual property) were "reforms which aim at improving the effectiveness of our competition policy and at enhancing its real impact in opening and maintaining competitive markets. This is a goal that we must achieve to ensure that the European Union is able to cope with two major and immediate challenges, namely to guarantee that business and authorities are able to operate under the same competition policy constraints in the enlarged European Union and to make European markets more open and competitive in order to foster sustainable growth.". *Lowe*: Current Issues of EU Competition Law, pp. 583–84.

The globalization of the economy makes the interplay between intellectual property rights and competition rules even more significant.[797] Currently, we are in a market where both competition concerns and intellectual property rights are competing at the highest standards – intellectual property rights (e.g., patents protecting wireless communications underlying our mobile phones) are omnipresent in the news and being litigating in countries around the world; while competition authorities are investigating business practices and beginning to co-operate globally (e.g., the European Commission, along with the Federal Trade Commission in the U.S., are investigating the practices of standard essential patent holders – including Apple, Google, Motorola, and Samsung).

(c) Chapters 5 and 6

Chapter 5 (for the U.S.) and Chapter 6 (for the EU) evaluate the statutory regimes that govern the application of competition rules to intellectual property transactions in general, review how courts and competition authorities have applied competition law principles to the exercise of intellectual property rights, and consider what practices by an trademark holder would be deemed to run afoul of the antitrust laws of the U.S. and the competition rules of the EU.

797 "[C]ompetition enforcement agencies are also "going global"." *Lowe*: How different is EU anti-trust?, p. 2.

5. Application of U.S. Antitrust Laws to Intellectual Property Rights: Deference to Proprietary Rights

5.1 Legal Framework

(a) The Sherman Antitrust Act

The Sherman Antitrust Act of 1890 remains the bedrock legislation for all U.S. antitrust law.[798] Congress passed the Sherman Act as a "comprehensive charter of economic liberty" aimed at preserving free and fair competition.[799] The law was drafted primarily in response to fears during the late 1800s that monopolies dominated America's free market economy.[800] The Act was intended to combat anticompetitive practices, reduce market domination by individual corporations, and preserve "free and unfettered competition as the rule of trade".[801]

Although several states had enacted antitrust laws *prior* to the 1890 federal law,[802] most modern state antitrust statutes today are modelled on the Sherman Act.[803] Generally, these are modelled after the federal antitrust laws, although there are some differences.[804]

---

798 15 U.S.C. § 1 et seq. For an excellent overview of the Sherman Act, see *ABA*: Antitrust Law Developments, Chapter 1 (Restraints of Trade), pp. 1–224.

799 *FTC*: Competition Guidance: The Antitrust Laws.

800 *Cornell University Law School*: Antitrust.

801 *Northern Pacific Railway v. United States*, 356 U.S. 1, 4 (1958).

802 *ABA*: Antitrust Federalism: the Role of State Law. By the time the Sherman Act was passed in 1890, at least twenty-six states already had some form of antitrust prohibition. *ABA*: Antitrust Law Developments, p. 623. Senator Sherman noted that his bill was designed (among other things) to "supplement the enforcement" of existing state laws. 21 Cong. Rec. 2457 (1890), cited in *ABA*: Antitrust Law Developments, p. 634, fn. 6.

803 Since Congressional jurisdiction does not reach purely intra-state commerce, most states have laws that parallel the Sherman and FTC Acts to prevent anticompetitive behavior within local commerce. *Cornell University Law School*: Antitrust. Today, all fifty states have some type of antitrust statute. For a list of antitrust laws by state, see 6 Trade Reg. Rep. (CCH) 30,000 et seq. (Trade Regulation Report). See also *American Bar Association*: State Antitrust Enforcement Handbook.

804 State antitrust laws increasingly add to the claims that can be asserted under federal antitrust laws. The most significant divergence between state and federal antitrust

The Sherman Act is divided into three sections. Section 1 defines and prohibits specific means of anticompetitive conduct (e.g., those practices that restrain trade).[805] Section 2 deals with end results that are anticompetitive in nature (e.g., monopolies or attempted monopolization).[806] Finally, Section 3 simply extends the provisions of § 1 to U.S. territories and the District of Columbia.

Although § 1 would – if read literally – prohibit all concerted activity in restraint of trade, the Supreme Court soon recognized that the "legality of an agreement or regulation cannot be determined by so simple a test, as whether it restrains competition. Every agreement concerning trade, every regulation of trade, restrains."[807] Consequently, the Court decided that § 1 of the Sherman Act does not prohibit every restraint of trade, but rather only those that are "*unreasonably* restrictive."[808]

A variety of practices may be challenged under § 1, including: horizontal and vertical arrangements[809] affecting prices, territorial and customer allocations, refusals to deal, reciprocal dealing, tying or exclusive dealing, and mergers,

---

schemes is that many states have rejected the federal prohibition on damages recoveries by indirect purchasers as established in *Illinois BrickCo v. Illinois*, 431 U.S. 720 (1977). *ABA*: Antitrust Law Developments, Chapter 7 (State Antitrust Laws), p. 623.

805 "Every contract, combination in the form of trust or otherwise, or conspiracy, in restraint of trade or commerce among the several States, or with foreign nations, is declared to be illegal." 15 U.S.C. § 1.

806 "Every person who shall monopolize, or attempt to monopolize, or combine or conspire with any other person or persons, to monopolize any part of the trade or commerce among the several States, or with foreign nations, shall be deemed guilty of a felony..." 15 U.S.C. § 2.

807 *Chicago Board of Trade v. United States*, 246 U.S. 231, 238 (1918). See generally *ABA*: Antitrust Law Developments, Chapter 1 (Restraints of Trade), pp. 1–224.

808 *Standard Oil Co. v. United States*, 221 U.S. 1, 58 (1911) (emphasis mine). In *Standard Oil*, the Court concluded that Congress did not intend to prohibit contracts that caused insignificant or attenuated restraints of trade but only those agreements "which were unreasonably restrictive of competitive conditions." See *ABA*: Antitrust Law Developments, p. 2, fn. 6. More recently, the Supreme Court has reaffirmed the principle that § 1 prohibits only *unreasonable* restraints of trade. See, e.g., *NCAA v. Board of Regents*, 468 U.S. 85, 98 (1984); *National Soc'y of Prof'l Eng'rs v. United States*, 435 U.S. 679, 687-91 (1978); and *Continental T.V., Inc. v. GTE Sylvania Inc.* 433 U.S. 36, 49 (1977).

809 Horizontal agreements are those among competitors at the same level of the market structure (e.g., between two manufacturers). Vertical agreements are those among persons at different levels of the market structure (e.g., between a manufacturer and

acquisitions, and joint ventures. Regardless of the nature of the practice challenged, three elements must be established to prove a violation of § 1: (i) the existence of a contract (or any combination or conspiracy among two or more separate entities); (ii) which unreasonably restrains trade; and (iii) affects interstate or foreign commerce. In addition, a private plaintiff seeking damages or injunctive relief must prove, respectively, that she has suffered or is likely to suffer antitrust injury.[810]

Whereas § 1 of the Sherman Act applies to concerted action (i.e., contracts, combinations, and conspiracies in restraint of trade), § 2 applies to *unilateral* activity. It prohibits monopolization and attempted monopolization by a single firm, as well as monopolization by combination or conspiracy.[811] The two offenses prohibited by § 2 – monopolization or attempted monopolization – have similar, but slightly different, elements. *Monopolization* requires proof that the defendant: (i) possesses monopoly power in the relevant market, and (ii) has acquired, enhanced, or maintained that power by the use of exclusionary conduct (as opposed from growth or development as a consequence of a superior product, business acumen or historic accident).[812] *Attempted monopolization* requires proof that the defendant: (i) engaged in exclusionary conduct, (ii) with a specific intent to monopolize, and (iii) with a "dangerous probability" of achieving monopoly power.[813] Monopoly power under § 2 traditionally has been defined as "the power to control prices or exclude competition."[814]

(b) The Clayton & FTC Acts

Relatively soon after its adoption, however, courts found certain anti-competitive activities to fall *outside* the scope of the Sherman Act. Hence, two additional

---

its distributors). *Business Elecs. Corp. v. Sharp Elecs. Corp.*, 485 U.S. 717, 730 and n. 4 (1988).

810 See, e.g., *American Ad Mgmt. v. GTE Corp.*, 92 F.3d 781, 788 (9th Cir. 1996); *Maric v. St. Agnes Hosp. Corp.*, 65 F.3d 310, 313 (2d Cir. 1995); and *Tunis Bros. Co. v. Ford Motor Co.*, 952 F.2d 715, 722 (3d Cir. 1992).

811 See generally *ABA*: Antitrust Law Developments, Chapter 2 (Monopolization and Related Offenses), pp. 225–324.

812 *Verizon Communs. v. Law Offices of Curtis v. Trinko, LLP*, 540 U.S. 398, 407 (2004).

813 *Spectrum Sports v. McQuillan*, 506 U.S. 447, 456 (1993).

814 *United States v. E.I. DuPont de Nemours & Co.*, 351 U.S. 377, 391 (1956). The Tenth Circuit, however, requires proof of the ability both to control prices *and* exclude competition. *Rural Tel. Serv. Co. v. Feist Publ'ns*, 957 F.2d 765, 768 n. 2 (10th Cir. 1992).

federal laws were passed in 1914 to address these weaknesses: the Clayton Antitrust Act[815] and the Federal Trade Commission Act (the FTC Act).[816]

The Clayton Antitrust Act prohibits: (i) price discrimination between different purchasers, if such discrimination tends to create a monopoly; (ii) exclusive dealing agreements; (iii) tying arrangements; and (iv) mergers and acquisitions that substantially reduce market competition.

The FTC Act created the Federal Trade Commission (the FTC) – a regulatory agency empowered to administer and enforce laws. The FTC has jurisdiction over anticompetitive practices, including but not limited to violations of the Sherman and Clayton Acts and broad powers to cope with new threats to the competitive free market.[817] Section 5 of the FTC Act declares "unfair methods of competition … unlawful."[818] In 1938, the Wheeler-Lea Amendments expanded the language to include "unfair or deceptive acts or practices."[819] The language is left undefined – some say deliberately to allow a broad interpretation and application to a variety of business practices.[820]

The FTC has emphasized that "[u]njustified consumer injury is the primary focus of the FTC Act" Although consumer injury "by itself" cannot "be sufficient to warrant a finding of unfairness", a finding of unfairness will be found if three tests are satisfied: the unfairness must be substantial; it must not be outweighed by any countervailing benefits to consumers or competition that the practice produces; and it must be an injury that consumers themselves could not reasonably have avoided.[821] In practice, this means that practices that violate the

815 15 U.S.C. § 12 et seq.

816 15 U.S.C. §§ 41–58.

817 Act of September 26, 1914, ch. 311, § 5, 38 Stat. 717, 719 (codified as amended at 15 U.S.C. §§ 41–58. See generally *ABA*: Antitrust Law Developments, Chapter 8 (Civil Government Enforcement), pp. 643–732.

818 15 U.S.C. § 45.

819 15. U.S.C. § 45(a)(1). As noted by Senator Wheeler in his remarks to Congress, the intent of the amendments was to "[make] the consumer who may be injured by an unfair trade practice of equal concern before the law with the merchant injured by the unfair methods of a dishonest competitor." 83 Cong. Rec. 3255 (1938).

820 In 1994, however, Congress clarified that an "unfair" act or practice over which the FTC has authority is one that "causes or is likely to cause substantial injury to consumers which is not reasonably avoidable by consumers themselves and not outweighed by countervailing benefits to consumers or to competitors." FTC Act Amendments of 1994, 15 U.S.C. § 45(n). See *ABA*: Antitrust Law Developments, p. 643.

821 *FTC*: FTC Policy Statement on Unfairness. See also 15 U.S.C. § 45(n).

Sherman or Clayton Acts may also be deemed a violation of the FTC Act. As a result, the FTC Act reaches practices that harm competition, but that may not fit neatly into categories of conduct formally prohibited by the Sherman Act.

Although there have been amendments to these three federal laws – most importantly, the 1936 Robinson-Patman Act,[822] the 1938 Wheeler-Lea Amendments,[823] and the 1976 Hart-Scott-Rodino Act[824] – the basic framework has not changed significantly since 1914[825] and the Sherman Act of 1890, the Federal Trade Commission Act of 1914, and the Clayton Act of 1914 remain the core antitrust laws in the U.S.[826] Antitrust matters are heard, except in certain cases, by federal courts.[827]

(c) The *Per se* Rule vs. the *Rule of Reason*

Violations under either §§ 1 or 2 of the Sherman Act take one of two forms – either as a *per se* violation or as a violation subject to the *rule of reason*.

The *per se* rule declares certain types of agreements illegal as a matter of law and requires no further inquiry into the intentions of those engaged in the practice, the actual effect of such practice, or any market consequences of the restraint (nor the need to define the relevant market). The standard was established in the Supreme Court's 1958 *Northern Pacific Railway* decision.[828] Such

---

822 15 U.S.C. § 13 et seq. The amendment aimed to outlaw certain practices in which manufacturers discriminated in price between equally-situated distributers to decrease competition.

823 15. U.S.C. § 45(a)(1).

824 The HSR Act is named after Senators Philip A. Hart and Hugh D. Scott, Jr. and Representative Peter W. Rodino. HSR is now § 7A of the Clayton Act, 15 U.S.C. § 18(a). The amendment requires companies planning large mergers or acquisitions to notify the government in advance. The amendments also authorize private parties to sue for triple damages when they have been harmed by conduct that violates either the Sherman or Clayton Act and to obtain a court order prohibiting the anticompetitive practice in the future.

825 *Foer*: United States of America.

826 The Sherman Antitrust Act of 1890 and related antitrust laws are codified at 15 U.S.C. §§ 1–7 (Sherman Antitrust Act); 15 U.S.C. §§ 12–27, 29, 52–53 (Clayton Antitrust Act); and 15 U.S.C. §§ 41–58 (Federal Trade Commission Act). For a list of U.S. antitrust laws, see *Vogl*: US Antitrust Law.

827 U.S. Constitution, Article III, Section 2, as codified under 28 U.S.C. *Cornell University Law School*: Federal Question Jurisdiction.

828 *Northern Pacific Railway v. United States*, 356 U.S. 1, 5 (1958): "[T]here are certain agreements or practices which because of their pernicious effect on competition

per se conduct "would always or almost always tend to restrict competition and decrease output"[829] instead of being designed to "increase economic efficiency and render markets more, rather than less, competitive."[830] Section 1 of the Sherman Act characterizes certain business practices as a *per se* violation. These are restraints of trade (such as horizontal price fixing, bid-rigging, or the division of customers or markets) that are considered so unreasonable that there is no need to undertake an elaborate inquiry about the factual context, actual effect on the market or the intentions of those individuals who engaged in the practice. When the *per se* rule is applied, a violation of the antitrust laws is found merely by proving that the conduct occurred (or that the restraint falls within a *per* se category).[831]

Some business practices, however, are not inherently antithetical to competition. At times they may constitute anticompetitive behavior while at other times they may encourage competition within the market. For these cases, a *rule of reason* analysis is applied. Here it is necessary to weigh the various circumstances and to decide whether the conduct is on the whole pro-competitive or anti-competitive. Courts apply a totality of the circumstances test and asks whether the challenged practice promotes or suppresses market competition. The tests require a detailed examination of a restraint's actual competitive impact in a properly defined relevant market.[832] Under a *rule of reason* analysis, a practice will be

---

and lack of any redeeming virtue are conclusively presumed to be unreasonable and therefore illegal without elaborate inquiry as to the precise harm they have caused or the business excuse for their use." This standard was confirmed (and quoted in full) by the Court in their 1977 *GTE* decision. *Continental T.V. Inc. v. GTE Sylvania Inc.*, 433 U.S. 36, 50 (1977).

829 *Broadcast Music, Inc. v. CBS*, 441 U.S. 1, 19-20 (1979).

830 *Id.*, at 20, citing *United States v. United States Gypsum Co.*, 438 U.S. 422, 441 n. 16 (1978).

831 In *White Motor*, the Court distinguished the following *per se* violations: "[T]he sale of an unpatented product … tied to a patented article... is a *per se* violation…. […] Group boycotts are another examples of a *per se* violation. Price-fixing arrangements, both vertical and horizontal, have also been held to be *per se* violations of the antitrust laws; and a trial to show their nature, extent, and degree is no longer necessary." *White Motor Co. v. United States*, 372 U.S. 253, 259-60 (1963) (internal citations omitted).

832 In *Standard Oil Co. v. United States*, 221 U.S. 1, 62 (1911), the Court held that "it becomes obvious that the criteria to be resorted to in any given case for the purpose of ascertaining whether violations of the section have been committed, is the rule of reason guided by the established law."

prohibited only if a comprehensive analysis of the its purpose and effect indicates that, on balance, the practice unreasonably restrains competition.[833] In recent years, the *rule of reason* has been applied in an increasingly large proportion of cases. It is often uncertain where the line between *per se* and *rule of reason* lies.[834] A presumption exists in favor of the *rule of reason* for ambiguous cases.

5.2 Historical Overview

Since the passing of the Sherman Act in 1890, the power and impact of U.S. antitrust law has ebbed and flowed in accordance with the economics and politics of the time.[835] Judicial views on the nature of the relationship between antitrust and intellectual property rights have similarly varied significantly over time and from court to court,[836] depending on the political administration and the economic policies in place at the time.[837] As antitrust scholars have noted, "The role that courts have played in developing antitrust law through the past century has been a versatile one, exhibiting 'tremendous flexibility and … responsiveness to changes in economic thinking and social policy.'"[838]

(a) Early Decisions: IP Rights Paramount

Decisions in the early days of the Sherman Act endorsed "absolute freedom in the use or sale of rights under the patent laws of the United States" because the

---

833 See *Broadcast Music, Inc. v. Columbia Broadcasting Sys., Inc.*, 441 U.S. 1, 24 (1979); and *Board of Trade v. United States*, 246 U.S. 231, 238 (1918).

834 *Foer*: United States of America.

835 Peritz reviews the early history of the Sherman Act and the contending streams of argument that permeate current antitrust discourse (*Peritz*: The "Rule of Reason" in Antitrust Law). Giocoli reviews the influence from the origins of the Sherman Act to present day enforcement (*Giocoli*: Competition Versus Property Rights). Waller reviews the explicit assumptions behind U.S. antitrust law, and tries to identify the values and governance norms underlying the current position (*Waller*: Neo-Realism and the International Harmonization of Law, pp. 574–75).

836 See generally *ABA*: Antitrust Law Developments, Chapter 12 (Antitrust Issues Involving Intellectual Property), pp. 1080–83.

837 *Giocoli*: Competition Versus Property Rights, p. 750. Giocoli provides a detailed chronological breakdown and analysis of the enforcement of the antitrust laws in the U.S., which she analyzes as having swung between aggressive pursuit of antitrust violators to a relative neglect of antitrust's underlying principles.

838 *Hammer*: Antitrust Beyond Competition, p. 913, cited by *Carrier*: Unravelling the Patent-Antitrust Paradox, p. 810 and n. 217.

"very object of these laws is monopoly."[839] Based on this principle, the Supreme Court permitted even the most egregious of antitrust violations – such as horizontal price fixing and minimum resale price maintenance that would have been illegal *per se* had it involved tangible property.[840]

(b) The *Nine No-No's*: Stringent Scrutiny – IP Rights Narrowly Construed

The policies swung sharply in the opposite direction from the 1930s through the 1970s.[841] While the courts continued to view intellectual property – and particularly patents – as conferring a "monopoly",[842] court decisions tended to focus on whether the conduct of intellectual property owners was "within their statutory exclusive rights."[843] The rights granted by the Patent Act and Copyright Act were "narrowly construed."[844] Courts found certain licensing provisions to warrant as *per se* violations: this policy was embodied in the Justice Department's now abandoned "Nine No-No's".[845]

Broadly speaking, the Nine No-No's covered attempts by patent holder to extend their patent "monopolies" to unpatented supplies, to gain control over improvements of innovations, to determine prices for the resale of patented

---

839 *E. Bement & Sons v. National Harrow Co.*, 186 U.S. 70, 92 (1902). See *Pate*: Antitrust and Intellectual Property, § II (Historical Period).

840 *ABA*: Antitrust Law Developments, pp. 1080–81. See also *Pate*: Antitrust and Intellectual Property, § II (Historical Period).

841 *ABA*: Antitrust Law Developments, p. 1081.

842 A "patent is an exception to the general rule against monopolies and to the right to access to a free and open market". *Precision Instrument Mfg. Co v. Automotive Maint. Mach. Co.*, 324 U.S. 806, 816 (1945).

843 "As long as the inventors kept within their statutory exclusive rights, they were not engaging in unreasonable restraints of trade violating the Sherman Act." *United States v. Line Material Co.*, 333 U.S. 287, 341 (1948).

844 "Once the patent issues, it is strictly construed, it cannot be used to secure any monopoly beyond that contained in the patent, the patentee's control over the product when it leaves his hands is sharply limited, and the patent monopoly may not be used in disregard of the antitrust laws". *Sears, Roebuck & Co. v. Stiffel Co.*, 376 U.S. 225, 230 (1964).

845 The list of nine potentially offending technology licensing practices was first outlined in a speech by Bruce Wilson on "Patent and Know-How License Arrangements", held in Boston on 6 November 1970. *Gilbert/Shapiro*: Antitrust Issues in the Licensing of Intellectual Property, p. 284, n. 6.

products or to engage in market allocations.[846] However, the application of these "no-no" policies were formalistic *without* regard to the actual competitive effects of such conduct.[847]

(c) Modern Economic Focus: Encourage Innovation and Competition

Beginning in the 1980s, however, the Department of Justice began to question the theory underlying the Nine No-No's. The introduction of economic rigor into antitrust analysis in the late 1970s and 1980s finally led to the final abandonment of almost all of these *per se* rules and to a more consistent inquiry into the likely competitive effects of certain conduct or business arrangements.[848] During the same period, patent law itself afforded more valuable rights to holders of intellectual property, as reflected in the decisions of the newly-created Federal Circuit.[849]

---

846 The Nine No-No's consisted of *per se* prohibitions against: (1) mandatory package licensing; (2) tying of unpatented supplies to the licensing of patented products ("tie-ins"); (3) compulsory assignment of grantbacks; (4) vertical distribution restraints, such as post-sale restraints on resale by purchasers; (5) compulsory payment of royalties of amounts not reasonably related to the sales of the patented product; (6) restrictions on the licensee's freedom to deal in products or services outside the scope of the patent ("tie-outs"); (7) licensee veto power over licensor's grant of further licenses; (8) restraints on sales of unpatented products made with a patented process; and (9) minimum price maintenance. For a review of the prohibitions, see *Gilbert/Shapiro*: Antitrust Issues in the Licensing of Intellectual Property, p. 285. See also *Rule*: The Antitrust Implications of International Licensing; *Lipsky*: Current Antitrust Division Views on Patent Licensing Practices; and *Griffin*: The Demise of the "Nine No-No's".

847 *Pate*: Antitrust and Intellectual Property, § II (Historical Period), citing *Wilson*: Patent and Know-How License Agreements (providing also a recent statement by the current Assistant Attorney General for Antitrust explaining that the DOJ is far more willing to consider the pro-competitive aspects of various licensing arrangements than it was thirty years ago). See also *Gilbert/Shapiro*: Antitrust Issues in the Licensing of Intellectual Property (discussing how much the 1995 DOJ/FTC Guidelines for the Licensing of Intellectual Property differ from the earlier enforcement approach).

848 *Lind/Kleymenova/Miauton/Muysert*: Report on Multiparty Licensing, pp. 33–34. The work of four economists, Joseph Farrell, Richard Gilbert, Michael Katz, and Carl Shapiro – all of whom served as Deputy Assistant Attorney General for Economics in the Antitrust Division of the US DOJ – stands today as the "accepted intellectual framework" for competition analysis of intellectual property practices. *Id.*, p. 34.

849 In 1982, in an effort to promote greater uniformity in certain areas of federal jurisdiction and relieve the pressure on the dockets of the Supreme Court and the courts

In 1988, in its "Antitrust Enforcement Guidelines for International Operations,"[850] the DOJ formalized its view that patent licensing increases the value of patents and encourages licensing and innovation. The Guidelines noted that, while some patents may indeed confer market power and a few may even create a monopoly, "intellectual property ... does not necessarily confer a monopoly or market power in any relevant market."[851] The 1988 Guidelines adopted a *rule of reason* approach to patent licensing that balanced the pro-competitive effects of licensing against the possible anti-competitive effects in related markets.[852]

By the 1990s, enforcement agencies and courts were de-emphasizing any apparent conflict between intellectual property and antitrust and instead characterizing them as "two bodies of law [that] are actually complementary, as both are aimed at encouraging innovation, industry and competition."[853]

(d) 1995 Guidelines: Three Principles

In 1995, the Department of Justice and the Federal Trade Commission issued their "Antitrust Guidelines for the Licensing of Intellectual Property" (the 1995

---

of appeals for the regional circuits, the U.S. Congress passed the Federal Circuit Act of 1982 (96 Stat. 25, 2 April 1982), establishing the U.S. Court of Appeals for the Federal Circuit (CAFC). The CAFC is the only U.S. court of appeals defined exclusively by its *jurisdiction* rather than geographical boundaries. The CAFC has appellate jurisdiction over any final decision of the district courts of the United States, if the jurisdiction of that court was based, in whole or in part, *relating to patents*, over the U.S. Court of Customs and Patent Appeals and the U.S. Court of Claims, as well as authorization to hear appeals from several federal administrative boards as well. See *U.S. Court of Appeals for the Federal Circuit*: An Act To establish a United States Court of Appeals; and *Federal Circuit Historical Society*: History of the United States Court of Appeals for the Federal Circuit. In 1998, the Federal Circuit held that all appeals of antitrust cases involving patents should be heard by the Federal Circuit. *Nobelpharma AB v. Implant Innovations, Inc.*, 141 F.3d 1059, 1067-68 (Fed. Cir. 1998), cited by *Pate*: Antitrust and Intellectual Property, § II (Historical Period).

850 *DOJ/FTC*: Antitrust Enforcement Guidelines for International Operations.

851 *Id.*, § 3.6 (1988), Part II, Case 12.

852 See *Gilbert/Shapiro*: Antitrust Issues in the Licensing of Intellectual Property, p. 286.

853 *Atari Games Corp. v. Nintendo of North America, Inc.*, 897 F. 2d 1572, 1576 (Fed. Cir. 1990). The "aims and objectives of patent and antitrust laws may seem, at first glance, wholly at odds. However, the two bodies of law are actually complementary, as both are aimed at encouraging innovation, industry and competition."

Guidelines)[854] The 1995 Guidelines are the basis for reviewing technology licensing and exemplify the "common purpose" approach to the relationship: "The intellectual property laws and the antitrust laws share the common purpose of promoting innovation and enhancing consumer welfare."[855]

The 1995 Guidelines articulate three core principles underlying the agencies' antitrust analysis of intellectual property licensing transactions:[856]

- An endorsement of the validity of applying the same general antitrust approach to the analysis of conduct involving intellectual property that the agencies apply to conduct involving other forms of tangible or intangible property: "for the purpose of antitrust analysis, the Agencies regard intellectual property as being essentially com-parable to any other form of property."[857]
- A clear rejection of any presumption that intellectual property necessarily creates market power in the antitrust context: "the Agencies do not presume that intellectual property creates market power in the antitrust context."[858] More recently, in its 2003 report on the proper balance between competition and patent law and policy, the FTC explained that "[e]ven when a patent does confer monopoly power, that alone does not create an antitrust violation. Antitrust law recognizes that a patent's creation of monopoly power can be necessary to achieve a greater gain for consumers."[859]
- An explicit recognition by the agencies that intellectual property licensing allows firms to combine complementary factors of production and is generally a precompet-itive activity: "the Agencies recognize that intellectual property licensing allows firms to combine complementary factors of production and is generally procompetitive."[860]

---

854 *DOJ/FTC*: 1995 IP Licensing Guidelines.

855 *Id.*, § 1.0. See also *ABA*: Antitrust Law Developments, pp. 1082–83.

856 *Rosch*: Some Thoughts on the Role of Intellectual Property in Innovation Market Cases. See also *Gilbert/Shapiro*: Antitrust Issues in the Licensing of Intellectual Property, p. 287.

857 *DOJ/FTC*: 1995 IP Licensing Guidelines, § 2.0.

858 *Id.* In its 2006 holding in *Illinois Tool Works v. Independent Ink, Inc.*, the Supreme Court formally abandoned the presumption that intellectual property confers market or monopoly power, rejecting the idea that tying arrangements involving intellectual property should be treated more harshly than tying involving tangible goods: "a patent does not necessarily confer market power upon the patentee". *Illinois Tool Works v. Independent Ink, Inc.*, 126 S. Ct. 1281, 1293 (2006).

859 *FTC*: To Promote Innovation.

860 *DOJ/FTC*: 1995 IP Licensing Guidelines, § 2.0.

The articulation of these principles – which recognized the many benefits of intellectual property licensing and rejected the presumption that intellectual property necessarily creates market power – represented a significant shift in the agencies' attitude, which some scholars find demonstrated a new, unified, and more coherent antitrust policy in treating agreements pertaining to intellectual property.[861]

(e) 2000 Guidelines: Collaboration

In 2000, the FTC and the DOJ jointly issued the "Antitrust Guidelines for Collaborations Among Competitors" (the 2000 Guidelines).[862] These guidelines outlined how the agencies analyze certain antitrust issues raised by collaborations among competitors, addressing a broad range of horizontal agreements among competitors, including joint ventures, strategic alliances, and other competitor collaborations. The guidelines describe an analytical framework to assist businesses in assessing the likelihood of an antitrust challenge to a collaboration with one or more competitors.

The 2000 Guidelines, like the 1995 Guidelines, begin by recognizing pro-competitive opportunities, in this case the opportunities are seen as stemming from collaboration among competitors, which represented a significant change in tone from the earlier attitudes. They note that:

> "In order to compete in modern markets, competitors sometimes need to collaborate. Competitive forces are driving firms towards complex collaborations to achieve goals such as expanding into foreign markets, funding expensive innovation efforts, and lowering production and other costs. Such collaborations often are not only benign but *pro-competitive*."[863]

(f) Modern Application of the Guiding Principles

Intellectual property rights give owners the right to exclude others from making, using, selling, or exploiting their intellectual property. In the US, the bare exercise of this right to exclude as granted by the applicable law does *not* violate the antitrust laws.[864] However, the terms under which an intellectual property

---

861 *Lind/Kleymenova/Miauton/Muysert*: Report on Multiparty Licensing, p. 36.

862 *DOJ/FTC*: Collaboration Guidelines.

863 *Id.*, p. 2 (emphasis mine).

864 The "patent laws which give a 17-year monopoly on 'making, using, or selling the invention' are *in pari materia* with the antitrust laws and modify them *pro tanto*." *Simpson v. Union Oil Co.*, 377 U.S. 13, 24 (1964). "The owner of a copyright, if he

owner commercializes its invention or work by licensing it to others *may* raise antitrust issues if such terms unreasonably restrain competition, particularly if they restrain competition that would have occurred absent the license.[865]

(i) Principle 1: General Antitrust Analysis Applies

As set out in the 1995 Guidelines, U.S. antitrust law generally applies the same principles to cases involving intellectual property rights as to cases involving any other property rights. Hence, the analysis begins with the Sherman Act.

Section 1 of the Sherman Act prohibits an agreement between two or more economically independent entities that unreasonably restrains competition. For intellectual property licensing arrangements, the antitrust examines whether the relationship among the parties to the arrangement is primarily horizontal or vertical in nature, or whether it has substantial aspects of both. The following general observations can be made:

- Agreements between horizontal competitors which fix minimum prices or divide markets into exclusive territories are classic examples that are so inherently anticompetitive that they are treated as illegal *per se*.[866] The mere presence of intellectual property rights does not immunize such conspiracies from liability.
- Vertical agreements are generally treated under the *rule of reason*.[867] Hence, in analyzing a restraint in an intellectual property license where there is no express or implied agreement between actual or potential horizontal competitors, the decisive question is "whether the restraint is likely to have anticompetitive effects and, if so, whether the restraint is reasonably necessary to achieve procompetitive benefits that outweigh those anticompetitive effects."[868] However, an intellectual property license that incorporates a tying

---

pleases, may refrain from vending or licensing and content himself with simply exercising the right to exclude others from using his property." *Fox Film Corp. v. Doyal*, 286 U.S. 123, 127 (1932). See generally *ABA*: Antitrust Law Developments, p. 1101 and fn. 163.

865 "It is in any event well settled that concerted and contractual behaviour that threatens competition is not immune from antitrust inquiry simply because it involves the exercise of copyright privileges." *Data Gen. Corp. v. Grumman Sys. Support Corp.*, 36 F.3d 1147, 1185 and n. 63 (1st Cir. 1994). *ABA*: Antitrust Law Developments, p. 1101 and fn. 164.

866 *DOJ/FTC*: 1995 IP Licensing Guidelines, §§ 3.4 and 5.2.

867 *Valentine*: Abuse of Dominance in Relation to Intellectual Property.

868 *DOJ/FTC*: 1995 IP Licensing Guidelines, § 3.4.

provision[869] may be illegal if (i) "the seller has 'appreciable economic power' in the tying product market" (which is not necessarily implicit in the fact of ownership of a relevant intellectual property right), and (ii) "the arrangement affects a substantial volume of commerce in the tied market."[870]

- Cases involving <u>unilateral abuse</u> of intellectual property power often arise under Sec-tion 2 of the Sherman Act.[871] Section 2 does not require an agreement, but instead requires either actual or likely monopoly power.[872] It prohibits monopolization, defined as "(i) the possession of monopoly power in the relevant market and (ii) the willful acquisition or maintenance of that power as distinguished from growth or development as a consequence of a superior product, business acumen, or historic accident."[873] It also prohibits attempted monopolization, which requires exclusionary conduct with "specific intent to monopolize" which creates a "dangerous probability" of monopolization of a relevant antitrust market.[874] Under these standards, merely having monopoly power by virtue of a patent is no problem in and of itself, but exclusionary practices with the purpose of extending the scope or likely duration of such power are subject to rule of reason antitrust scrutiny.[875]

---

869 The Supreme Court has stated the applicable rule as follows: "A tying arrangement is 'an agreement by a party to sell one product but only on the condition that the buyer also purchases a different (or tied) product, or at least agrees that he will not purchase that product from any other supplier.' Such an arrangement violates § 1 of the Sherman Act if the seller has 'appreciable economic power' in the tying product market and if the arrangement affects a substantial volume of commerce in the tied market." *Eastman Kodak Co. v. Image Tech. Servs.*, 504 U.S. 451, 461-62 (1992) (citations omitted). For an example of such an unlawful agreement, see *Systemcare, Inc. v. Wang Corp.*, 117 F.3d 1137, 1143 (10th Cir. 1997) (en banc). For the approach taken by the enforcement agencies, see *DOJ/FTC*: 1995 IP Licensing Guidelines, § 5.3, and *Valentine*: Abuse of Dominance in Relation to Intellectual Property, fn. 22.

870 "Congress authorized Sherman Act scrutiny of single firms only when they pose a danger of monopolization. Judging unilateral conduct in this manner reduces the risk that the antitrust laws will dampen the competitive zeal of a single aggressive entrepreneur." *Copperweld Corp. v. Independence Tube Corp.*, 467 U.S. 752, 768 (1984).

871 *Valentine*: Abuse of Dominance in Relation to Intellectual Property.

872 *Aspen Skiing Co. v. Aspen Highlands Skiing Corp.*, 472 U.S. 585, 596, n. 19 (1985), cited by *Valentine*: Abuse of Dominance in Relation to Intellectual Property, fn. 24.

873 *Spectrum Sports, Inc. v. McQuillan*, 506 U.S. 447, 456 (1993), cited by *Valentine*: Abuse of Dominance in Relation to Intellectual Property, fn. 25.

874 *Valentine*: Abuse of Dominance in Relation to Intellectual Property, text at fn. 26.

875 See *DOJ/FTC*: 1995 IP Licensing Guidelines, § 2.2; *Abbott Labs. v. Brennan*, 952 F.2d 1346, 1354-55 (Fed. Cir. 1991). In *Jefferson Parish Hosp. Dist. No. 2 v. Hyde*, 466 U.S.

(ii) Principle 2: No Presumption of Market Power

The Federal Circuit and the Supreme Court have repeatedly held that the acquisition or procurement of patents – even if such patents convey monopoly power in a relevant economic market[876] – is not deemed illegal *per se*: "mere accumulation of patents, no matter how many, is not in and of itself illegal."[877] Principle 2 of the 1995 Guidelines confirms this point of view: "The Agencies will not presume that a patent, copyright, or trade secret necessarily confers market power upon its owner."[878] An assignment or acquisition of a patent may, however, violate the Sherman Act where the assignment constitutes unlawful monopolization or is part of an agreement by competitors to restrain trade.[879] Furthermore, the acquisition of an intellectual property right through inequitable conduct – i.e., fraud – will render all of the claims of the patent unenforceable in an infringement action and may expose the patentee to liability for the defendant's attorneys' fees under the Patent Act.[880]

It is also important to take care in defining the relevant market.[881] For example, an intellectual property right or licensing agreement may have a competitive

2, 16 (1984), dicta suggested that patent rights raise a presumption of market power (in particular in a tying agreement involving intellectual property rights), but Justice O'Connor (in a concurring opinion) argued that it was "a common misconception" to find that "a patent or copyright ... suffices to demonstrate market power ... [as] it is also possible that a seller in these situations will have no market power", since "a patent holder has no market power in any relevant sense if there are close substitutes for the patented product". *Id.*, at 37, n. 7 (O'Connor, J., concurring. The U.S. concept of market power and the European law concept of dominant position appear to be in harmony on this point. See, e.g., Case 78-70, *Deutsche Grammophon Gesellschaft mbH v Metro-SB-Großmärkte GmbH & Co. KG*, 8 June 1971 [1971] ECR 487, para. 16, as cited by *Valentine*: Abuse of Dominance in Relation to Intellectual Property, fn. 27.

876 See *SCM Corp. v Xerox Corp.*, 645 F.2d 1195, 1206 (2d Cir. 1981): "the procurement of a patent ... will not violate § 2 even where it is likely that the patent monopoly will evolve into an economic monopoly".

877 *Automatic Radio Mfg. Co. v Hazeltine Research*, 339 U.S. 827, 834 (1950).

878 *DOJ/FTC*: 1995 IP Licensing Guidelines, § 2.2.

879 *ABA*: Antitrust Law Developments, p. 1084–85.

880 *Id.*, p. 1087. Furthermore, fraud in procuring a patent from the PTO may form the basis for liability under Sections 1 and 2 of the Sherman Act and may also support an action for cancellation of the patent at the request of the U.S. *ABA*: Antitrust Law Developments, p. 1087–88, and fn. 73–75.

881 *Valentine*: Abuse of Dominance in Relation to Intellectual Property, text at fn. 28-30.

effect in a products market, for final or intermediate goods made using that intellectual property; in a technology market, if the IP right is marketed separately from the products in which it is used; or in an innovation market, i.e., on competition in research and development to develop new or improved goods or processes.[882] As set forth in the Guidelines, the agencies will analyze the competitive effects of the arrangement within the relevant market(s) for the goods affected – whether in a "goods" market (i.e., for the final or intermediate goods made using that intellectual property), a "technology" market (if the intellectual property is marketed separately from the products in which it is used), or an "innovation" market (i.e., on competition in research and development to develop new or improved goods or processes).[883]

(iii) *Principle 3: Intellectual Property Licensing is Pro-Competitive*

Principle 3 of the 1995 Guidelines holds that intellectual property licensing agreements are generally deemed pro-competitive, since they facilitate the integration of intellectual property rights with complementary factors of production.[884] This is particularly true of cross-licenses of blocking or complementary patents, i.e., cases in which it is either impracticable or inefficient to practice one invention without another.

Both the 1995 Guidelines and the 2000 Guidelines make very clear that there are two modes of analysis: that of a *rule of reason*, which applies to the majority of cases involving intellectual property, and that of *per se* violations, which are considered so plainly anticompetitive that they are concluded to be anticompetitive, and therefore illegal, without any enquiry into the restraint's likely competitive effect.[885]

Because of the pro-competitive potential of the license, licenses containing ancillary restraints, including exclusive licenses, are – in the vast majority of cases – analyzed under a *rule of reason* approach.[886] The Agencies' general approach in

882 *DOJ/FTC*: 1995 IP Licensing Guidelines, §§ 2.3, 3.1, 3.4.

883 See the *DOJ/FTC*: Horizontal Merger Guidelines for definition of product and geographic markets. For further definitions of the relevant markets, see *DOJ/FTC*: 1995 IP Licensing Guidelines, §§ 2.3, 3.1, 3.2, and 3.4.

884 *DOJ/FTC*: 1995 IP Licensing Guidelines, § 4.1.2, and *Valentine*: Abuse of Dominance in Relation to Intellectual Property, fn. 31.

885 *DOJ/FTC*: 1995 IP Licensing Guidelines, § 3.4, pp. 11, 12; and *DOJ/FTC*: Collaboration Guidelines, §§ 3.2, 3.3, pp. 6–8.

886 *DOJ/FTC*: 1995 IP Licensing Guidelines, § 4.3; and *Valentine*: Abuse of Dominance in Relation to Intellectual Property, fn. 32.

analyzing a licensing restraint under the *rule of reason* is to inquire whether the restraint is likely to have anticompetitive effects and, if so, whether the restraint is reasonably necessary to achieve pro-competitive benefits that outweigh those anticompetitive effects.[887]

In some cases, however, the courts conclude that a restraint's "nature and necessary effect are so plainly anticompetitive" that it should be treated as unlawful *per se*, without an elaborate inquiry into the restraint's likely competitive effect. Among the restraints that have been held *per se* unlawful are naked price-fixing, output restraints, and market division among horizontal competitors, as well as certain group boycotts and resale price maintenance.[888] In the case of *per se* violations, the analysis focuses upon whether the illegal act occurred. There is no in-depth analysis of the facts surrounding the alleged conduct or of the effects of that conduct upon competition and consumer welfare. Under *per se* treatment, the alleged conduct is presumed to harm competition and is therefore prohibited. Accordingly, there is no need to analyse the competitive effects or to weigh competitive benefits against costs.[889]

By contrast, in *rule of reason* analysis there is generally an in-depth analysis of the competitive consequence of the conduct in question. This analysis may find that there are no anticompetitive effects, given the facts of the case, or that there are. In cases where there are both, *rule of reason* analysis will typically weigh the competitive benefits against the anticompetitive costs. Thus, *rule of reason* analysis involves, first, an in-depth analysis of the competitive consequences of the conduct in question, and the factual setting and, second, an analysis of the trade-off between pro-competitive and anticompetitive effects, when both are present.[890] Given the uncertainty inherent in the *rule of reason*, the 1995 Guidelines create a presumptive antitrust "safety zone" for restraints in intellectual property licensing arrangements if: (i) the restraints are not facially anticompetitive – i.e., illegal *per se*; and (ii) the licensor and licensees collectively account for no more than 20% of each relevant market significantly affected by the restraint."[891]

To determine whether a particular restraint in a licensing arrangement is given *per se* or *rule of reason* treatment, the Agencies will assess whether the restraint in question can be expected to contribute to an efficiency-enhancing

887 *DOJ/FTC*: 1995 IP Licensing Guidelines, § 3.4.
888 *Id.*
889 *Lind/Kleymenova/Miauton/Muysert*: Report on Multiparty Licensing, pp. 43–44.
890 *Id.*, pp. 43–44.
891 *DOJ/FTC*: 1995 IP Licensing Guidelines, § 4.3.

integration of economic activity. Application of the *rule of reason* generally requires a comprehensive inquiry into market conditions.

(g) The Trademark Analysis

Both the 1995 Guidelines and the 2000 Guidelines avoid addressing the anti-competitive effects of trademarks: the 1995 Guidelines specifically exclude trademark licenses from their scope,[892] and the 2000 Guidelines do not once refer to "trademarks".[893] Hence, any review of the anti-competitive effects of trademarks or trademark licensing would follow a standard review under U.S. antitrust analysis without the benefit of the 1995 Guidelines" antitrust safety zone (assuming there are no other intellectual property rights included in any licensing agreement which would bring the license under the 1995 Guidelines).

5.3 Chapter Observations

(a) Goal of Antitrust: Enhancing Consumer Welfare

As affirmed by the Supreme Court in 1904 in *Northern Securities*, free competition is the most desirable mechanism for resource allocation.[894] Section 1 of the Sherman Antitrust Act thus prohibits all agreements, combinations, and conspiracies that unreasonably restrain interstate and foreign trade. This includes agreements among competitors to fix prices, rig bids, and allocate customers, all of which are punishable as criminal felonies. Section 2 of the Sherman Antitrust Act makes it a crime to unlawfully monopolize any part of interstate commerce.

---

892 The 1995 Guidelines specifically exclude trademark licenses from their scope ("These Guidelines do not cover the antitrust treatment of trademarks. Although the same general antitrust principles that apply to other forms of intellectual property apply to trademarks as well, these Guidelines deal with technology transfer and innovation-related issues that typically arise with respect to patents, copyrights, trade secrets, and know-how agreements, rather than with product-differentiation issues that typically arise with respect to trademarks.") *DOJ/FTC*: 1995 IP Licensing Guidelines, fn. 2. The 2000 Guidelines do not once refer to "trademarks".

893 For disclosure, copyrights are also not mentioned and patents are only mentioned twice.

894 "Be all this as it may, Congress has, in effect, recognized the rule of free competition by declaring illegal every combination or conspiracy in restraint of interstate and international commerce." *Northern Securities Co. v. United States*, 193 U.S. 197 (1904).

In seeking to prevent conduct that undermines the competitive process, the U.S. antitrust laws do *not* aim to discourage aggressive competition, whether that aggressive competition stems from the dominant competitor itself (in the form of a monopolist) or from other competitors.[895] As the U.S. Supreme Court explained in *Spectrum Sports*:

> "The law directs itself not against conduct which is competitive, even severely so, but against conduct which unfairly tends to destroy competition itself. It does so not out of solicitude for private concerns but out of concern for the public interest."[896]

This public interest factor lies at the heart of any antitrust intervention. The Supreme Court has repeatedly clarified that the overriding legislative and judicial emphasis of the Sherman Act is a focus on consumer welfare: "The purpose of the [Sherman] Act is not to protect businesses from the working of the market; it is to protect the public from the failure of the market."[897] In its 1974 decision of *Reiter v. Sonotone Corp.*, the Court found the legislative histories of both the Sherman and the Clayton Acts to suggest that Congress designed the Sherman Act as a "consumer welfare prescription".[898]

The language of the Sherman Act prohibits business practices in general terms, leaving courts to decide which practices are illegal based on the facts of each case. As a result, varying courts, under different administrations and political influences, have applied the antitrust laws to changing markets with different results. Nonetheless, for over 100 years, the antitrust laws have had the same basic objective: to protect the process of competition for the benefit of consumers, making sure there are strong incentives for businesses to operate efficiently, keep prices down, and keep quality up.[899]

(b) Application of U.S. Antitrust Laws to Intellectual Property Licenses

Broadly speaking, antitrust authorities in the U.S. have been reluctant to intervene in what they see as the sphere of intellectual property rights and policy. U.S. courts and regulators begin their analysis from the point of view of the intellectual property laws: they look at the scope of legislative protection and consider whether those rights are abridged by the antitrust laws. The prevailing view in

895 *DOJ*: Single-Firm Conduct Under Section 2 of the Sherman Act, Executive Summary.

896 *Spectrum Sports, Inc. v. McQuillan*, 506 U.S. 447, 458 (1993).

897 *Id.*

898 *Reiter v. Sonotone Corp.*, 442 U.S. 330, 343 (1979).

899 *FTC*: Competition Guidance: The Antitrust Laws.

the U.S. is that antitrust laws act to prevent the *excesses* of private property owners in order to maintain effective competition on, and access to, markets.[900] The principles on which antitrust laws are based, however, should be flexible enough to accommodate the specific features and dynamics of intellectual property rights.[901] Hence, with limited exceptions, U.S. antitrust law generally applies the same principles to cases involving intellectual property rights – be they patents, copyrights, trade secrets, or trademarks – as to cases involving any other property rights: "[i]ntellectual property is … neither particularly free from scrutiny under the antitrust laws, nor particularly suspect under them."[902] As noted by an FTC Commissioner, "the Commission remains ready, willing, and able to challenge violations of the antitrust laws involving intellectual property."[903]

Nevertheless, Commissioner Rosch of the FTC has noted the inherent difficulties in applying antitrust policies to intellectual property rights as if they were another property right:

> "… intellectual property is *not* comparable to other forms of property for purposes of antitrust analysis. Patents, copyrights, trade secrets, know-how and trademarks, while they possess attributes of property in that they can be acquired and conveyed, do not always exhibit a clear and direct linkage to the goods markets that are the central focus of the antitrust laws. Consequently, the antitrust analysis may be even less clear and more tenuous …"[904]

In the U.S., there is no presumption that intellectual property rights necessarily create market power.[905] Furthermore, the 1995 and 2000 Guidelines advance the principle that a licensing arrangement may raise antitrust concerns if it harms competition that would have occurred *in the absence of the license.*[906] Licenses that have such an effect do not necessarily lower overall economic welfare. The

900 *Anderman*: The competition law/IP 'interface', pp. 6–7.

901 *Czapracka*: Intellectual Property and the Limits of Antitrust, pp. 82–83.

902 "Standard antitrust analysis applies to intellectual property". *DOJ/FTC*: 1995 IP Licensing Guidelines, § 2.1.

903 *Rosch*: Some Thoughts on the Role of Intellectual Property in Innovation Market Cases, p. 22.

904 *Id.*, p. 2.

905 See *Gilbert/Shapiro*: Antitrust Issues in the Licensing of Intellectual Property, p. 287.

906 "The key competitive issue raised by the licensing arrangement is whether it harms competition among entities that would have been actual or likely potential competitors in the absence of the arrangement." *DOJ/FTC*: 1995 IP Licensing Guidelines, Discussion of Example 1.

harm to competition should be compared to other pro-competitive effects of the arrangements.[907]

The common theme, therefore, in the literature dealing with the application of the antitrust rules to intellectual property rights is *caution* with respect to intervention. Furthermore, commentators warn that intellectual property and antitrust cases present daunting technical and economic questions which lay judges are not qualified to answer and that markets deal better with competitive issues than antitrust regulators.[908]

(c) Conclusion: IP Rights Dominate

The DOJ has clearly held that "antitrust enforcement policies must be carefully designed so they do not interfere with or discourage the legitimate exploitation of intellectual property rights through technology licensing. After all, the economic return from technology licensing is what encourages innovative firms to produce new products and feed the global economy."[909]

---

907 See *Gilbert/Shapiro*: Antitrust Issues in the Licensing of Intellectual Property, p. 287.

908 *Posner*: Antitrust in the new Economy, pp. 936–40; and *Czapracka*: Intellectual Property and the Limits of Antitrust, pp. 82–83.

909 *Delrahim*: The Long and Winding Road: Convergence.

6. Application of EU Principles to Intellectual Property Rights: Deference to Competition & The Internal Market

6.1 Historical Perspectives & Overview

(a) A Two-Dimensional Challenge

By the time it passed the Sherman Antitrust Act in 1890, the U.S. already benefited from an integrated economy and could rely on consistent application of the federal antitrust rules throughout the entire U.S.[910] In the EU, however, long before any "common" European market existed, most European countries had well-developed national rules in place regulating trade practices. Hence, the 20th century EU approach to anticompetitive behaviour has necessarily been two-dimensional: first, the principles regulating competition promote market competition; second, and perhaps even more importantly, they are applied to achieve a fully integrated and economically competitive community of diverse countries.[911]

To address this two-dimensional challenge, the European Union developed a mechanism to superimpose *supra-national* EU competition rules and policies upon the oft long-standing, national competition laws of the individual Member States.[912] The competition and reconstruction policies set out in the 1951

910 *Waller*: Antitrust and American Business Abroad 16-2, cited by *Hovenkamp/Janis/Lemley/Leslie*: IP and Antitrust, § 45.3(b) and n. 40, pp. 45–12 (2011 Supplement).

911 *Waller*: Neo-Realism and the International Harmonization of Law, pp. 584–585. *Fox*: US and EU Competition Law: A Comparison, pp. 339–54. For the use of law as the principle instrument of European integration, see *Cappelletti/Seccombe/Weiler*: Integration Through Law: Europe and the Federal American Experience; and *Dehousse/Weiler*: The Legal Dimension.

912 For historical reviews of the development of EU competition law, in particular the influence of the Freiburg school of law and economics and its Ordoliberalism principles on EU competition principles, see *Giocoli*: Competition Versus Property Rights, pp. 747 and 748; *Buxbaum*: German Legal Culture and the Globalization of Competition Law; and *Gerber*: Constitutionalizing the Economy, p. 64, *Gerber*: Law and Competition in Twentieth Century Europe, pp. 124–25; and *Maxeiner*: Policy and Methods in German and American Antitrust Law, p. 7. For an examination of German competition law in the decades preceding the war, see generally *Nörr*: Die Leiden des Privatrechts, pp. 31–100. For some relatively recent research

ECSC Treaty[913] and the 1957 EEC Treaty[914] demonstrate the early recognition of this policy: the 1957 EEC Treaty in particular focused on the creation of a general common market, aimed to achieve economic integration and cooperation via trade and the free movement of goods.[915] This "common" internal market, is – and was – characterized by the removal and prohibition of any obstacles to the free movement of goods, persons, services, and capital between Member States.

Upon implementation of the EEC Treaty in 1958, tariff barriers and border controls on goods were quickly removed between Member States. However, invisible barriers – in the shape of national measures – had the effect of discriminating between the goods of the various Member States, resulting in a "distortion of competition".[916] The elimination of these invisible barriers to the free movement of goods was – and continues to be – central to the creation and functioning of an internal market. With these principles in mind, the TFEU

---

articles on the Freiburg Ordoliberal school scholars and politicians, such as Walter Eucken, Wilhelm Roepke, Ludwig Erhard, and Franz Böhm, see *Backhaus*: Historische Schulen; and *Grossekettler*: Franz Böhm. See also *Mackaay*: Schools and Approaches,§ 3.4, p. 413.

913 Treaty Establishing the European Coal and Steel Community (ECSC Treaty) was signed in Paris in 1951 by France, Germany, Italy, Belgium, Luxembourg, and the Netherlands, with the aim of organising free movement of coal and steel and free access to sources of production.

914 Treaty establishing the European Economic Community (EEC Treaty) of 25 March 1957; renamed the Treaty establishing the European Community (TEC) in 1993; and renamed the Treaty on the Functioning of the European Union (TFEU) in 2009; consolidated version 2012, OJ C 326, 26.10.2012. *Europa.eu*: EU Treaties.

915 The focus on economic development and stability, rather than on defense, was likely one of the reasons its ratification in 1958 did not create problems. The earlier failure of the European Defence Community (EDC) in 1954 is deemed evidence that Member States were not ready to relinquish that part of their sovereignty related to defense. *Europa.eu*: EEC Treaty.

916 Article 113 TFEU notes that "The Council shall … adopt provisions for the harmonisation of legislation … to the extent that such harmonisation is necessary *to ensure the establishment and the functioning of the internal market* and *to avoid distortion of competition*." (emphasis mine). Article 173(1) TFEU states that both the activities of the EU and the Member States shall be "in accordance with a system of open and competitive markets".

addresses restrictions (distortions of competition) aimed at conduct by the Member States[917] as well as practices engaged in by undertakings.[918]

(b) EU Principles & Intellectual Property Rights

The overriding objective of the Treaty on the Functioning of the European Union (TFEU) remains the elimination of "barriers which divide Europe" "in order to guarantee steady expansion, balanced trade and fair competition" in an "internal market … without internal frontiers in which the free movement of goods, persons, services and capital is ensured".[919] To achieve this, the TFEU confirms that the European Union has exclusive jurisdiction "in establishing … the competition rules necessary for the functioning of the internal market"[920] and contains specific provisions that are designed to prohibit unjustified barriers to the free movement of goods and services to ensure that competition in such internal market is not restricted or distorted.

---

917 The following key provisions are aimed at regulating (and removing) trade restrictions and abusive practices that Member States may directly or indirectly impose: (i) Articles 28 and 30 TFEU (prohibiting customs duties on imports and exports and all charges having equivalent effect) in conjunction with Article 110 TFEU (prohibiting discriminatory or protectionist internal taxation) to prohibit Member States from imposing fiscal border charges or discriminatory internal taxes; (ii) Articles 34 and 35 TFEU (regulating quantitative restrictions and measures having an equivalent effect to quantitative restrictions) to prohibit Member States from adopting overt or covert protectionist policies on imports (Article 34) and exports (Article 35) from and to other Member States (or measures having the same effect), unless such restrictions can be justified under criteria laid down in Article 36 TFEU or in some cases under the *Cassis* formulation of the rule of reason; (ii) Article 37 TFEU and Articles 107 and 108 TFEU (regulating state monopolies of a commercial character and state aids to nationalized industries) to prevent Member States from favouring national entities, contractors or industries, unless such aid falls into one of the block exemptions for certain categories of state aid. For further analysis of these provisions, see *Fairhurst*: Law of the European Union, pp. 547–660.

918 Articles 101 and 102 TFEU form the basis of the EU's competition-focused efforts and are aimed at practices by undertakings which have the effect of excluding or restricting goods or services from or between Member States. Article 101 TFEU regulates agreements between undertakings; Article 102 TFEU regulates unilateral anti-competitive behaviour. For further analysis of these provisions, see *Fairhurst*: Law of the European Union, pp. 661–712.

919 Preamble (clauses 3 and 5) and Article 26(2) TFEU (respectively).

920 Article 3(1)(b) TFEU.

The grant and enforcement by Members States of national intellectual property rights,[921] and the terms under which such rights may be exercised or exploited, generate challenges: national rights can frustrate the creation of a single internal market (since, by permitting national exclusive rights to exist, integration is thwarted)[922] and can have anti-competitive effects (by restricting trade – i.e., excluding others – even within a Member State). Although the essential function of intellectual property rights is "to grant the holder the right to exclude others from exploiting its intellectual property without its consent",[923] this does not imply that intellectual property rights are immune from EU law intervention.[924]

When considering the applicability of EU principles to intellectual property rights, two sets of TFEU provisions are of particular importance.[925] First, the rules on the free movement of goods prohibiting any unjustified barriers or restrictions to intra-EU trade (Articles 34–36 TFEU).[926] Although these are not the principle articles forming the basis of EU competition law, these articles apply to practices which constitute a barrier to inter-state trade (or one of "equivalent effect").

Second, the competition rules (Articles 101 and 102 TFEU)[927] apply to any exercise of an intellectual property owner's exclusive rights, as they seek to secure fair competition by prohibiting or carefully regulating restraints on trade.

---

921 Each Member State has the authority to enact laws establishing intellectual property rights in its own country. Article 345 TFEU (ex Article 295 TEC) states that "The Treaties shall in no way prejudice the rules in Member States governing the system of property ownership." The term "property" includes intellectual property. *Colston/Galloway*: Modern Intellectual Property Law, § 1.4.2.1 at p. 14; § 3.10 (patents) at p. 91.

922 As the Court noted in *Deutsche Grammophon v Metro-SB-Großmärkte*, intellectual property rights which "legitimize the isolation of national markets, would be repugnant to the essential purpose of the Treaty, which is to unite national markets into a single market." Case 78-70, *Deutsche Grammophon Gesellschaft mbH v Metro-SB-Großmärkte GmbH & Co. KG*, 8 June 1971 [1971] ECR 487, para. 12.

923 Commission Notice: TTBE Guidelines (OJ C 89/3, 28.03.2014), para. 6.

924 *Id.*, para. 7.

925 For a full listing of EU competition rules, see *European Commission*: EU Competition Law: Rules Applicable to Antitrust Enforcement, Volume I.

926 Articles 34-36 TFEU form part of Title II TFEU (Free Movement of Goods).

927 Articles 101 and 102 TFEU form the first two provisions of Title VII TFEU (Common Rules on Competition, Taxation and Approximation of Laws), Chapter 1 (Rules on Competition), Section 1 (Rules Applying to Undertakings).

Article 101 (which deals with agreements between undertakings) may restrict the terms under which an intellectual property right can be licensed (e.g., by prohibiting certain restrictions or divisions of territory). Article 102 (which regulates unilateral anti-competitive behaviour) may be breached by an intellectual property owner's refusal to license, enforcement of tying requirements, or other anti-competitive practices.

6.2 Articles 34–36 TFEU

(a) Quantitative Restrictions

Article 34 TFEU states that: "Quantitative restrictions on imports and all measures having equivalent effect shall be prohibited between Member States." Article 35 contains an identical prohibition applicable to exports. The two articles seek to limit restrictive behavior generally. Because the prohibited types of behavior are not defined, the effect of the articles can be very broad: not only overtly restrictive behaviors – but also those having "equivalent effect" – will be caught.[928]

Intellectual property rights grant exclusive rights in the territory of the Member State. This national, territorial nature means that an intellectual property owner's exercise of rights – including her ability to exclude others from using, making or selling her invention or product – can constitute a significant barrier to inter-state (i.e., European Union) trade and thus run afoul of Articles 34 or 35 TFEU[929] For example, two legally and economically independent companies could technically each register rather similar trademarks for goods in their respective Member State. This presents a problem when one company imports its goods into the other company's Member State: the other company could rely on its national, intellectual property rights to prevent such import, but such national barrier breaches the principles underlying Article 34.[930]

In order to resolve this tension (between the principle of free movement of goods and national property rights), the case law around the application of Article 36 of the exercise of intellectual property rights has resulted in the development of two important principles, and the enforcement of a third. First, the

928 For a detailed review of Articles 34 and 35, see *European Commission*: Free movement of goods – Guide to the application of Treaty provisions.

929 *Barnard*: The Substantive Law of the EU, p. 1. See also *Hovenkamp/Janis/Lemley/Leslie*: IP and Antitrust, § 45-3, pp. 45-9 (2011 Supplement).

930 *Barnard*: The Substantive Law of the EU, p. 30, § 4 (Similarity of Trade Marks and Risk of Confusion).

CJEU developed an "*existence v. exercise*" distinction (or dichotomy).[931] Second, the CJEU established that the application of Article 36 (allowing exceptions to the principle of free movement of goods) in light of Article 345 TFEU (promising the protection of national intellectual property rights will only be permitted to the extent necessary to preserve the integrity of the "*specific subject matter*" of the intellectual property right at issue.[932] Finally, the Court has upheld and enforced the exhaustion principle in order to reduce the market partitioning effects of national intellectual property rules.[933]

(b) Principle 1: Existence v. Exercise of Intellectual Property Rights

In its landmark 1966 case, *Consten and Grundig v. Commission*,[934] the CJEU drew a distinction (albeit questionable)[935] between the *existence* of an intellectual property right and the *exercise* of such intellectual property right. This distinction enabled the CJEU to dismiss the argument that it lacked jurisdiction to restrict the assertion of a trademark right by virtue of Article 345 TFEU. The Court first clarified that Articles 36 and Articles 345 protect the *existence* of intellectual property rights. Article 36 TFEU permits Member States to derogate from their obligations to ensure the free movement of goods "on grounds of … the protection of industrial and commercial property".[936] Article 345 TFEU notes that the

---

931 Joined Cases 56 and 58/64, *Établissements Consten S.à.R.L. and Grundig-Verkaufs-GmbH v Commission*, 13 July 1966 [1966] ECR 299, p. 345.

932 *Hovenkamp/Janis/Lemley/Leslie*: IP and Antitrust, § 45.3a, p. 45–10 (2011 Supplement).

933 "Read together, the principles of specific subject matter and exhaustion of rights ensure some reward for the [intellectual property rights] holder while at the same time reducing the market partitioning effects of the national [intellectual property rights] rules." *Barnard*: The Substantive Law of the EU, p. 4 and fn. 20–22. For more analysis of the exhaustion principle applied to EU intellectual property rights, see above § 3.2(f).

934 Joined Cases 56 and 58/64, *Établissements Consten S.à.R.L. and Grundig-Verkaufs-GmbH v Commission*, 13 July 1966 [1966] ECR 299. See also Case 78-70, *Deutsche Grammophon Gesellschaft mbH v Metro-SB-Großmärkte GmbH & Co. KG*, 8 June 1971 [1971] ECR 487.

935 Beier finds this distinction "ambiguous" and find that it "contributes little to resolving the conflict between the principle of the free movement of goods and the protection of industrial property." *Beier*: Industrial Property and the Free Movement of Goods, p. 147.

936 The list of Article 36 TFEU derogations are *exhaustive* and Article 36 nonetheless warns that "Such prohibitions or restrictions shall not, however, constitute

EU treaties "shall in no way prejudice the rules in Member States governing the system of property ownership."[937] The *existence* of the exclusive rights granted by a Member State to the holder of an intellectual property right is *not* affected by the limitations of Articles 34 or 35 or the prohibitions of Articles 101 or 102 TFEU.[938] However, the Court then noted that Articles 36 and 345 TFEU are not blanket exemptions for all conduct involving intellectual property.[939] In those cases where the *exercise* of intellectual property rights conflict with EU competition laws, the Commission has the authority to limit the exercise of those intellectual property rights in order to harmonize them with EU law.[940] That is, although the *existence* of an intellectual property right is protected, the *exercise* of an intellectual property right is subject to all the other Treaty provisions, including the competition rules and the free movement of goods provisions.[941]

---

a means of arbitrary discrimination or a disguised restriction on trade between Member States." See *Reindl*: Intellectual Property and Intra-Community Trade; and *Somorjai*: The Evolution of a Common Market, who gives particular attention to Article 36 issues in intellectual property cases.

937 The term "property" includes intellectual property. *Colston/Galloway*: Modern Intellectual Property Law, p. 14 (§ 1.4.2.1) and p. 91 (§ 3.10) (specifically for patents).

938 *Parke, Davis and Co. v Probel, Reese, Beintema-Interpharm and Centrafarm*, Case 24/67, 29 February 1968, ECR 55, p. 72.

939 "Articles [36], [345] and [267] of the Treaty … do not exclude any influence whatever of community law on the exercise of national industrial property rights. … Article [345] confines itself to stating that the 'Treaty shall in no way prejudice the rules in Member States governing the system of property ownership'." Joined Cases 56 and 58/64, *Établissements Consten S.à.R.L. and Grundig-Verkaufs-GmbH v Commission*, 13 July 1966 [1966] ECR 299, p. 345.

940 As the Court noted in *Consten-Grundig*, "to refrain from using rights under national trade-mark law in order to set an obstacle in the way of parallel imports does not affect the grant of those rights but only limits their exercise to the extent necessary to give effect to the prohibition under Article [101](1). The power of the Commission to issue such an injunction for which provision is made in Article 3 of Regulation No 17/62 of the Council is in harmony with the nature of the Community rules on competition which have immediate effect and are directly binding on individuals. Such a body of rules, by reason of its nature described above and its function, does not allow the improper use of rights under any national trademark law in order to frustrate the Community's law on cartels." Joined Cases 56 and 58/64, *Établissements Consten S.à.R.L. and Grundig-Verkaufs-GmbH v Commission*, 13 July 1966 [1966] ECR 299, p. 345–46.

941 In its application of Articles 101 and 102 TFEU to intellectual property rights, the CJEU has repeatedly returned to this reasoning to emphasise that it is only concerned with policing the exercise of intellectual property rights and does not seek to

This existence-exercise distinction was further developed a few years later in *Deutsche Grammophon*,[942] which demonstrated the compromise made by the Court. It said that the *existence* of an intellectual property right is a matter for national law (as expressly permitted by Article 345 TFEU and, to a lesser extent, the first sentence of Article 36), but that the *exercise* of the intellectual property right is a matter for EU law.[943] In its grounds of judgement, the Court clarified that "although the Treaty does not affect the existence of rights recognized by the legislation of a Member State with regard to industrial and commercial property, the exercise of such rights may nevertheless fall within the prohibitions laid down by the Treaty."[944]

It should be noted that the European Commission has not necessarily respected this *existence v. exercise* distinction, and has investigated behaviour it considers a violation of Article 102 TFEU which falls close to the *existence* aspect, including investigations: (i) which concern misuse of the patent system to exclude potential competition;[945] (ii) which concern the use of vexatious litigation regarding the assertion of intellectual property rights;[946] and (iii) which

---

interfere with their very existence, which is fundamentally protected by both Articles 36 and 345 TFEU. For example, the *exercise* of an intellectual property right can lead to the finding of a concerted action that has the potential of infringing Article 101(1) TFEU, just as the *exercise* of an intellectual property right can lead to finding of abuse of a dominant position infringing Article 102 TFEU (Article 102 will not apply to the exercise of an intellectual property right if no dominant position exists). *Parke, Davis and Co. v Probel, Reese, Beintema-Interpharm and Centrafarm*, Case 24/67, 29 February 1968 [1968] ECR 55, p. 72.

942 Case 78-70, *Deutsche Grammophon Gesellschaft mbH v Metro-SB-Großmärkte GmbH & Co. KG*, 8 June 1971 [1971] ECR 487.

943 "The Treaty does not intend to prohibit restrictions on competition arising from the existence of industrial property rights or literary or artistic property rights but, in Article 36, it outlines the boundary between the existence of those rights, which is recognized by the Treaty, and the exercise of those rights in a way which is contrary to one of the fundamental objectives of the Treaty." *Id.*, p. 496.

944 *Id.*, para. 11, pp. 499–500.

945 Case COMP/39.246 *Boehringer*, initiated in 2007. For an analysis of the investigation, including questions whether the Commission's actions had any legal basis, see *Straus*: Patent Application: Obstacle for Innovation and Abuse. In July 2011, the Commission closed the case file in its *Boehringer/Almirall* investigation. It did so without a formal decision, without formal remedies, and without imposing a fine. For a review, see *Brankin*: European Commission Enforcement in the Pharmaceutical Sector.

946 Case T-111/96 *ITT Promedia v the Commission* [1998] ECR II-2937.

concern misrepresentations or deceptive practices with the patent office in order to extend the duration of protection or procurement of intellectual property rights and delay the arrival of competing products.[947]

(c) Principle 2: Specific Subject Matter

Furthermore, although Article 36 "permits prohibitions or restrictions on the free movement of products, which are justified for the purpose of protecting industrial and commercial property", Article 36 only admits derogations from that freedom to the extent to which they are justified for the purpose of safeguarding rights which constitute the *specific subject-matter* of such property.[948] A firm seeking to use or protect a right which constitutes the "specific subject matter" or "essential function" of its intellectual property rights will be regarded as protecting the *existence* of that right and therefore as not infringing the free movement or competition rules of the TFEU. If, on the other hand, a firm seeks to use or protect a right which does *not* constitute the specific subject matter or essential function of its intellectual property rights, this will be examined under the free movement and competition rules of the Treaty. The scope of the specific subject matter is different for each type of intellectual property right.

- The specific subject matter of a patent was described by the CJEU as "the guarantee that the patentee, to reward the creative effort of the inventor, has the exclusive right to use an invention with a view to manufacturing industrial products or putting them into circulation for the first time ... as well as the right to oppose infringements".[949]
- The specific subject matter of copyright may consist of a number of elements, including the rights to: (i) prevent reproduction of a work; (ii) first place a

947 Case T-321/05 *AstraZeneca v Commission* [2010] ECR II-2805. Ohly questions the actions taken by the Commission in the *AstraZeneca* case. *Ohly*: Geistiges Eigentum und Wettbewerbsrecht, pp. 47–67.

948 Case 78-70, *Deutsche Grammophon Gesellschaft mbH v Metro-SB-Großmärkte GmbH & Co. KG*, 8 June 1971 [1971] ECR 487, para. 11; as reiterated again in Case 16/74, *Centrafarm BV and Adriaan de Peijper v Winthrop BV*, 31 October 1974 [1974] ECR 1183, para. 7; and Case C-9/93, *IHT Internationale Heiztechnik GmbH and Uwe Danzinger v Ideal-Standard GmbH and Wabco Standard GmbH*, 22 June 1994 [1994] ECR I-2789, para. 33.

949 Case 15/74, *Centrafarm BV et Adriaan de Peijper v Sterling Drug Inc.*, 31 October 1974 [1974] ECR 1147.

work on the market; (iii) require payment for public performance or transmission; or (iv) rent out a work.[950]

- The specific subject matter of a trademark has been defined as the right, amongst other things, to ensure the holder the exclusive right to use the mark for the first marketing of a product, and so to protect him against competitors who would take advantage of the position and reputation of the mark by selling goods improperly bearing that mark.[951] The CJEU also found that "the basic function of the trade-mark is to guarantee to consumers that the product has the same origin",[952] "by enabling him without any possibility of confusion to distinguish that product from products which have another origin. This guarantee of origin means that the consumer or ultimate user can be certain that a trade-marked product which is sold to him has not been subject at a previous stage of marketing to interference by a third person, without the authorization of the proprietor of the trade-mark, such as to affect the original condition of the product. The right attributed to the proprietor of preventing any use of the trade-mark which is likely to impair the guarantee of origin so understood is therefore part of the specific subject-matter of the trade-mark

950 In *BBC v. Commission*, the General Court reviewed past case law and noted that: "It is common ground that in principle the protection of the specific subject-matter of a copyright entitles the copyright-holder to reserve the exclusive right to reproduce the protected work. The Court of Justice expressly recognized that in its judgment of 17 May 1988 in Case 158/86, *Warner Brothers v Christiansen*, … in which it held that "[t]he two essential rights of the author, namely the exclusive right of performance and the exclusive right of reproduction, are not called in question by the rules of the Treaty" (citations omitted). Case T-70/89, *British Broadcasting Corporation and BBC Enterprises Ltd v Commission*, 10 July 1991 [1991] ECR II-535, para. 57. In *Deutsche Grammaphon v Metro-SG-Grossmärkte*, for example, the licensor of copyright in records marketed in France could not rely on its copyright to prevent a third party from subsequently importing the records into Germany and selling them at a price which undercut the licensor's own distributors in Germany. The Court noted that "A manufacturer of sound recordings who holds a right related to copyright does not occupy a dominant position within the meaning of Article 86 of the Treaty merely by exercising his exclusive right to distribute the protected articles." Case 78-70, *Deutsche Grammophon Gesellschaft mbH v Metro-SB-Großmärkte GmbH & Co. KG*, 8 June 1971 [1971] ECR 487, para. 16, p. 501.

951 Case 16/74, *Centrafarm BV and Adriaan de Peijper v Winthrop BV*, 31 October 1974 [1974] ECR 1183, grounds para. 8.

952 Case 119/75, *Terrapin (Overseas) Ltd. v Terranova Industrie CA Kapferer & Co*, 22 June 1976 [1976] ECR 1039, para. 6.

right."[953] The owner of a mark may therefore enforce restrictions which prevent its mark being used in such a way that the origin of the products on which it is used may be brought into doubt, or the reputation of the trademark itself be damaged (by unauthorized interference).

Although the specific subject matter of each intellectual property right varies, in essence the specific subject matter is the exclusive right of the intellectual property owner to the first marketing of the product.

(d) Principle 3: Principle of Exhaustion

Once the owner of an intellectual property right has received the benefit of the specific subject matter of those rights, the right is said to be "exhausted".[954] This means that a holder of intellectual property rights in Member State A cannot prevent the import of goods into Member State A if the goods have been marketed in Member State B by the owner in Member State A or by another with the owner's consent.[955] The principle applies even if the rights' owner did not have the benefit of intellectual property protection in Member State B.[956] However, it should be noted that the relevant right is only exhausted with respect to the particular products that have been marketed: the intellectual property rights' holder can still control distribution of individual products which have not yet been placed on the market.[957]

(e) Application of Free Movement of Goods Rules to Trademarks

The landmark *Consten-Grundig* case (which established the existence v. exercise distinction) was one of the first truly important decisions addressing the

---

953 Case 102/77, *Hoffmann-La Roche & Co. AG v Centrafarm Vertriebsgesellschaft Pharmazeutischer Erzeugnisse mbH*, 23 May 1978 [1978] ECR 1139, para. 7.

954 For further discussion, see above, § 3.2(f).

955 *Korah*: Intellectual property law in the context of competition law.

956 In *Merck v Stephar*, the holder of intellectual property rights in the Netherlands used another member of the group to sell a pharmaceutical product in Italy, where the product was not patented. It was held that the firm could not invoke its Dutch patents to prevent the import of the products into the Netherlands from Italy, as it had exhausted its rights by selling the products in Italy even though the products were not protected by an Italian patent. Case 187/80, *Merck & Co. Inc. v Stephar BV and Petrus Stephanus Exler*, 14 July 1981 [1981] ECR 2063. See *Reindl*: Intellectual Property and Intra-Community Trade, pp. 822–825.

957 Case C-173/98, *Sebago Inc. and Ancienne Maison Dubois & Fils SA v G-B Unic SA*, 1 July 1999 [1999] ECR I-4103.

intersection of the national intellectual property rights with the principle of free movement of goods under the TFEU. It was, incidentally, about trademarks.

As noted above, the Court established the principle that trademarks (and other intellectual property rights) should never be used to circumvent competition law, even when a Member State's domestic law might allow it. In striking a balance between the opposing rights granted under national property legislation and principles of EU competition law, the Court gave *priority* to the needs of the EU. Faced with the difficult questions of how far the owner of a property right should be allowed to exercise such right, the Court ruled that the TFEU did not allow the improper use of rights under any national trademark law, defining improper as "such as to frustrate the Community's competition law."[958]

6.3 Articles 101 and 102 TFEU

(a) Competition Law Framework & Enforcement

Articles 101 and 102 TFEU form the basis of EU competition. Both seek to secure fair competition by prohibiting or carefully regulating restraints on trade: Article 101 regulates anti-competitive agreements between undertakings, holding that agreements that distort competition will be in breach of Article 101, but may escape liability if the practice falls under one of the Article 101(3) exemptions. Article 102 regulates abuse of market power by a single undertaking, holding that a dominant undertaking has a special responsibility "not to allow its conduct to impair genuine undistorted competition."[959] Both are concerned with the abuse – rather than the existence – of economic power. Both are applicable to the exercise of intellectual property rights.

---

958 See *Hay/Oldekop*: EMI/CBS and the Rest of the World, which reviews three closely related cases – Case 51/75 (*EMI Records Limited v. CBS United Kingdom Limited*), Case 86/75 (*EMI Records Limited v. CBS Records ApS*), and Case 96/75 (*EMI Records Limited v. CBS Schallplatten GmbH*) from 15 June 1976 – dealing with questions concerning the impacts of the (then) EEC-Treaty's antitrust provisions (Art. 85 and 86) on the exercise of trademark rights, in which the direct import, into one of the Member States, of goods produced outside the EU was sought to be prevented. They also looked back on the decisions rendered in the *Consten-Grundig* and *HAG* cases.

959 Commission Notice: Guidance on the Commission's enforcement priorities in applying Article 82 of the EC Treaty to abusive exclusionary conduct by dominant undertakings (OJ C 45/7, 24.2.2009), para. 1.

For example, Article 101 may place significant restrictions on intellectual property licensing practices and arrangements, whether between competitors or non-competitors. Generally speaking, it prohibits restrictive trading agreements and practices between otherwise independent business undertakings which may affect trade between Member States and thereby distort competition within the internal market. Although EU competition policy accepts that some contractual limitations on the parties are necessary to protect an owner's underlying intellectual property rights, other restrictions (including exclusive licenses which impose restrictions on how the licensee may or may not exploit the licensed intellectual property right) may raise competition concerns. If caught by Article 101(1), such restrictions may be unenforceable unless they can satisfy the criteria of Article 101(3), including falling into a "safe harbor" afforded by a block exemption.

Article 102 TFEU prohibits firms holding a dominant position in a relevant market from abusing that position. In exceptional cases, the way in which an intellectual property owner exploits her rights may raise Article 102 issues and be deemed an abuse (including refusals to license, imposition of unfair prices, limits to production, enforcement of bundling arrangements, or refusals to innovate to the prejudice of consumers).[960]

(b) Authority to Enforce Competition Rules: Regulation No 1/2003

In the EU, competition law is primarily enforced by the European Commission,[961] through its Directorate-General for Competition (DG Competition).[962] Commission decisions can be challenged in the General Court; General Court judgments can in turn be appealed on points of law to the Court of Justice of the European Union (CJEU).[963]

---

960 Article 102 TFEU has been used to tackle a variety of anti-competitive behaviour by dominant firms. For critical studies designed to offer some guidance on how application of Article 102 could be improved, see *Geradin/Petit/Walker/Hofer/ Louis*: The Concept of Dominance.

961 The Commission is the "guardian of the Treaties" and of the "*acquis communautaire*" (i.e., all EU legislation). *Europa.eu*: European Commission; and *Europa.eu*: Community acquis.

962 *European Commission*: Directorate-General for Competition, Competition Policy.

963 Article 263 TFEU. For an overview of the EU courts, see above, Introduction, § 0.3(c)(iii).

(i) Regulation No 17/62

In 1962, EC Regulation No 17/62[964] established a centralized "notice and authorization" system. Under this arrangement, any undertaking which entered into a restrictive agreement liable to restrict and affect trade between Member States had to make – in order to qualify for an exemption under TFEU 101(3) permitting certain – either a formal application to the European Commission pursuant to Regulation No 17/62 or draft its agreement to comply with one of the block or group exemption regulations which had been specifically drawn up by the Commission.[965] Hence, although Articles 101(1) and 102 TFEU had "direct effect" (that is, they were enforceable directly in national courts, regardless of and without the need for implementation of national law covering the same topic),[966] the authority to grant exemptions under Article 101(3) was reserved exclusively to the European Commission. In practice, this meant that a defendant before a national court in Germany could raise an Article 101(3) defense,[967] but the national tribunal lacked the power to grant Article 101(3) exemptions for activities caught by Article 101(1). The Commission's exclusive power to exempt agreements which restricted competition (but which met an exemption under Article 101(3)) led to a large number of applications being made to the Commission, "a fact which ... undermined efforts to promote a rigorous and decentralised application of the EU competition rules."[968]

---

964 EEC Council Regulation No 17: First Regulation implementing Articles 85 and 86 of the Treaty (OJ 013/204, 21.02.1962).

965 Regulation 3385/94 set out the procedures under which parties could apply for a formal decision that the agreement was not caught by Article 101(1). Commission Regulation (EC) No 3385/94 of 21 December 1994 on the form, content and other details of applications and notifications provided for in Council Regulation No 17 (OJ L 377/28, 31.12.1994).

966 "The competence of [national] courts to apply the provisions of Community law ... derives from the direct effect of those provisions." Case 127-73, *Belgische Radio en Televisie and société belge des auteurs, compositeurs et éditeurs v SV SABAM and NV Fonior* (BRT I), 30 January 1974 [1974] ECR 51, para. 15.

967 *Fairhurst*: Law of the European Union, p. 685. *Hovenkamp/Janis/Lemley/Leslie*: IP and Antitrust, § 45-3(c), pp. 45–13 (2011 Supplement).

968 *Europa.eu*: Application of Articles 101 and 102 TFEU.

(ii) Regulation No 1/2003: Direct Effect

In December 2002, the European Council adopted EC Regulation No 1/2003,[969] replacing (and repealing) Regulation No 17/62.[970] Regulation No 1/2003 dramatically changed the way Articles 101 and 102 TFEU were applied. The Commission called its enactment "a landmark reform, the most far-reaching overhaul of EC antitrust procedures in more than 40 years".[971]

Prior to the implementation of Regulation No 1/2003, the enforcement of Articles 101 and 102 TFEU was the sole responsibility of the Commission. Pursuant to Regulation No 1/2003, Member States, along with national competition authorities (NCAs)[972] and Members State courts, are entitled – and empowered – to apply and enforce EU competition law directly, alongside domestic competition laws.[973] Regulation No 1/2003 made it compulsory for NCAs and national courts to apply Articles 101 and 102 TFEU *whenever* they apply national competition law to restraints of competition that fall within the scope of Articles 101 and 102, without being blocked or delayed by notifications to the Commission.[974]

The result is that cases having only a national scope are now judged by similar provisions as cases that have a European dimension.[975] National courts may also apply Articles 101 and 102 TFEU on a stand-alone basis.[976] In each case, national courts are under an obligation to avoid taking decisions which would contradict

---

969 Council Regulation (EC) No 1/2003 of 16 December 2002 on the implementation of the rules on competition laid down in Articles 81 and 82 of the Treaty (OJ L 1/1, 4.1.2003), as implemented by Commission Regulation (EC) No 773/2004 of 7 April 2004 relating to the conduct of proceedings by the Commission pursuant to Articles 81 and 82 of the EC Treaty (OJ L 123/18, 27.04.2004) (hereinafter Regulation No 1/2003 (OJ L 1/, 4.1.2003)).

970 Council Regulation No 17 (EEC): First Regulation implementing Articles 85 and 86 of the Treaty (at present Articles 81 and 82) (OJ 013, 21.02.1962).

971 See *European Commission*: Press Release IP/09/683.

972 The European Commission maintains a list of the national competition authorities. *European Commission*: National Competition Authorities. See generally *European Commission*: European Competition Network: Frequently Asked Questions.

973 See generally *Lowe*: Current Issues of EU Competition Law, pp. 568–69.

974 According to the Commission, this has eliminated unnecessary bureaucracy and "has allowed the Commission to focus its resources on serious competition problems." Furthermore, the system change under Regulation No 1/2003 does not seem to have given rise to particular difficulties. *European Commission*: Press Release IP/09/683.

975 See *Müller*: The New Council Regulation (EC) No. 1/2003.

976 *Lowe*: Current Issues of EU Competition Law, p. 569.

or be in conflict with decisions that might be taken by the Commission in the same case.[977] In order to guarantee a uniform and harmonized enforcement structure, their decisions are still subject to review by the Commission.[978] Finally, as the CJEU established in *Walt Wilhelm v Bundeskartellamt*, for conflicts between national and EU law, EU law takes precedence.[979]

Regulation No 1/2003 also laid the groundwork for the establishment of the European Network of Competition Authorities (ECN), within which the Commission and national competition authorities coordinate the application of the Treaty antitrust rules.[980] Regulation No 1/2003 thus modernized the procedural

---

977 Regulation No 1/2003 (OJ L 1/1, 4.1.2003), recitals (8) and Article 3. Article 3(2) provides that the application of national competition law may not lead to the prohibition of agreements, decisions, or concerted practices which may affect trade between Member States but which do not restrict competition within the meaning of Article 101(1) TFEU, or which fulfil the exemption conditions of Article 101(3) of the Treaty or which are covered by a block exemption.

978 Commission Notice on cooperation within the Network of Competition Authorities (OJ C 101/43, 27.4.2004); and Commission Notice on the co-operation between the Commission and the courts of the EU Member States in the application of Articles 81 and 82 EC (OJ C 101/54, 27.4.2004).

979 Case 14/68, *Walt Wilhelm v Bundeskartellamt*, 13 February 1969 [1969] ECR 1, para. 6: "The EEC Treaty has established its own system of law, integrated into the legal systems of the Member States, and which must be applied by their courts. It would be contrary to the nature of such a system to allow Member States to introduce or to retain measures capable of prejudicing the practical effectiveness of the Treaty. The binding force of the Treaty and of measures taken in application of it must not differ from one state to another as a result of internal measures, lest the functioning of the Community system should be impeded and the achievement of the aims of the Treaty placed in peril. Consequently, conflicts between the rules of the Community and national rules in the matter of the law on cartels must be resolved by applying the principle that Community law takes precedence."

980 Regulation No 1/2003 makes it compulsory for national competition authorities (NCAs) to apply Article 101 TFEU in cases when they apply national competition law to agreements or concerted practices which may affect trade between EU Member States, and to apply Article 102 TFEU in cases when they apply national competition law to any abuse prohibited by Article 102 TFEU. Furthermore, Regulation 1/2003 described mechanisms of close co-operation between all competition authorities in the European Union, which led to the establishment of the European Competition Network (ECN): "The Commission and the competition authorities of the Member States should form together a network of public authorities applying the Community competition rules in close cooperation. For that purpose it is necessary to set up arrangements for information and consultation." Regulation

rules which govern how the Treaty's antitrust rules are enforced. Furthermore, given the enlargement of the EU, it established a new enforcement system that could guarantee a continued and effective application of Articles 101 and 102 TFEU.[981] In order for this "joint enforcement" regime (enforcement of the EU competition rules by both the Commission and national authorities) to function efficiently, the Commission further produced a package of six accompanying notices and a Commission implementing regulation, the so-called "Modernization Package."[982]

(c) Legislative Tools: Block Exemptions & Guidelines

Regulation No 1/2003 was "designed to restore the focus on the primary task of effective enforcement of the competition rules," by creating "legal certainty" inasmuch as it provides that agreements which fall under Article [101](1) but fulfil the conditions in Article [101](3) are valid and fully enforceable *ab initio* without a prior decision by a competition authority.[983]

To ensure consistent application of the competition rules, the Commission further introduced a range of measures to assist national competition authorities, courts, and individual entities regarding such rules. These include a range of block exemption regulations and extensive guidance found in Commission guidelines, notices, and other communications to better understand and apply EU competition laws.

(i) Block Exemption Regulations

A block exemption is a standalone, legally binding, framework regulation. If an agreement strictly complies with every condition and term of a block exemption regulation, it will be automatically valid and enforceable, thereby automatically

---

No 1/2003 (OJ L 1/1, 4.1.2003), intro para 15 and Article 11. See *European Commission*: European Competition Network: Commission Authorities.

981 *Lowe*: Current Issues of EU Competition Law, p. 568.

982 *Id.*, p. 567. Lowe notes that "a goal that we must achieve [is] to ensure that the European Union is able to cope with two major and immediate challenges, namely to guarantee that business and authorities are able to operate under the same competition policy constraints in the enlarged European Union and to make European markets more open and competitive in order to foster sustainable growth." *Id.* at pp. 583–784.

983 Commission Notice on informal guidance relating to novel questions concerning Articles 81 and 82 of the EC Treaty that arise in individual cases (guidance letters) (OJ C 101/78, 27.4.2004), para. 2.

exempt from Article 101(1), *unless* it involves an abuse of dominance under Article 102. If exempt, however, it will enjoy the same protection as was previously given to an agreement exempted on an individual basis under Article 101(3) TFEU.[984]

The Commission has adopted a number of sector-specific block exemptions, notably applicable to vehicle agreements in the motor vehicle sector,[985] certain agreements in the insurance sector,[986] various agreements in the air transport sector,[987] and certain agreements relating to maritime transport,[988] as well as block exemptions covering state aid.[989] The main block exemptions relevant to intellectual property rights are:

- the Technology Transfer Block Exemption relating to the licensing of patens, proprietary know-how, software copyright, and/or certain design rights;[990]
- the Vertical Restraints Block Exemption;[991] and

---

984 *Kaczorowska*: European Union Law, p. 845.

985 Regulation 1400/2002 (OJ 2002 L 203/30), Regulation 461/2010 (OJ 2010 L 129/52), and Regulation 330/2010 (OJ 2010 L 102/1).

986 Regulation 267/2010 (OJ 2010 L 83/1).

987 Regulation 3976/87 (OJ 1987 L 374/9) and Regulation 411/2004 (OJ 2004 L 68/1).

988 Regulation 906/2009 (OJ 2009 L 256/31).

989 Regulation 800/2008 (OJ L 214/3) (covering "horizontal" State aid not specific to particular industry sectors); Regulation 1998/2006 (OJ L 379/5) (*de minimis* aid).

990 Regulation No 316/2014 of 21 March 2014 on the application of Article 101(3) of the Treaty on the Functioning of the European Union to categories of technology transfer agreements (OJ L 93/17, 28.3.2014). The TTBE Regulation provides a blanket exemption or "safe harbor" for all technology transfer agreements meeting certain criteria. The block exemption is not available if the parties' market shares exceed a 20% threshold (for agreements between competitors) or a 30% threshold (for agreements between non-competitors). An agreement will also fall outside the TTBE Regulation if it includes any "hardcore" restrictions, such as price-fixing restrictions, limitations on output, allocation of markets or customers, or restrictions on the exploitation of technology (for agreements between competitors). The accompanying Guidelines (Communication from the Commission – Guidelines – on the application of Article 101 of the Treaty on the Functioning of the European Union to technology transfer agreements, OJ C 89/3, 28.03.2014) provide guidance on the application of the TTBE Regulation as well as on the application of Article 101 to technology transfer agreements that fall outside the scope of the TTBE Regulation. The 2014 TTBE Regulation and accompanying TTBE Guidelines replaced the earlier 2004 versions on 1 May 2014. *European Commission*: Press Release IP/14/299.

991 Regulation No 330/2010 (OJ L 102/1, 23.04.2010). This block exemption regulation adopts an "effects-based" approach, focusing not so much on the form of

- the R&D[992] and Specialisation Block Exemptions.[993]

Agreements or practices which do *not* qualify for a block exemption will be subject to review under general Article 101 and 102 TFEU analysis.

(ii) Guidelines & Notices

Certain EU legislative instruments, including notices, guidelines, and communications, form part of so-called EU "soft law".[994] They are non-binding[995] and without prejudice to interpretation by both EU courts (from the General Court or the CJEU) as well as national competition authorities. However, although deprived of legally binding force, they tend to represent a strong political signal that they are priorities for the Union.[996] Although an increasing number of scholars find the use of "soft law" problematic, from both a legal and policy

---

the vertical agreement, but rather on whether it has appreciable negative effects on competition in the relevant market. The Commission's accompanying Vertical Guidelines (OJ C 130/1, 19.05.2010) set out principles for the assessment of vertical agreements under Article 101 TFEU.

992 Regulation No 1217/2010 (OJ L 335/36, 18.12.2010). The R&D block exemption encourages horizontal collaboration for the purposes of conducting R&D and paid for R&D. It also expressly permits cooperation extending to joint exploitation of the results of R&D and marketing, subject to a 25% market share threshold and other criteria.

993 Regulation 1218/2010 (OJ 2010 L 335/43, 18.12.2010). The specialisation agreements block exemption applies to agreements containing provisions which relate to the assignment or licensing of intellectual property rights, "provided that those provisions do not constitute the primary object of such agreements, but are directly related to and necessary for their implementation". It expressly permits certain types of cooperation in the field of production (which may extend to commercialisation), subject to a 20% market share threshold and other criteria.

994 "Soft law" is the term applied to EU measures, such as guidelines, declarations and opinions, which, in contrast to regulations, directives, and decisions, are not binding on those to whom they are addressed. However, soft law can produce some legal effects. See *Eurofound*: Soft law.

995 Under Article 288 TFEU, only regulations, directives, and decisions are legally binding.

996 See *Snyder*: The Effectiveness of European Community Law, p. 33: "Communications play a vital role in Commission efforts to secure the effectiveness of Community law. They identify what is settled and what is dispute, circumscribe the arena for debate, and define the agenda for negotiation and, if necessary, litigation."

perspective,[997] others – and primarily those within the EU institutions – find the combination of "soft law" and legally binding tools effective to address European policy priorities, including competition law.[998]

Key guidelines relevant to Article 101 and Article 102 TFEU analyses include: (i) the 2004 Guidelines on the effect of trade, which confines the scope of application of Articles 101 and 102 TFEU to agreements and practices that are capable of having a minimum level of cross-border effects within the EU;[999] and (ii) the 2001 *de minimis* notice,[1000] which defines what is *not* considered as an appreciable restriction of competition under Article 101 TFEU.[1001]

---

997 This trend – of using non-legal measures to address certain principles or priorities – has come under growing scrutiny: "The increasing use in the EU of soft law norms has created an extensive debate over the centrality of law as the principle instrument of European integration." *Dawson*: Soft Law and the Rule of Law in the European Union. "As experienced in international law contexts, the legal or practical effects that soft law can produce in the absence of legally binding force remain rather unclear, which makes the enforceability of such instruments problematic." *Stefan*: Relying on EU Soft Law Before National Competition Authorities.

998 "To a certain extent, competition guidelines and precedent setting case decisions can themselves effectively function as ex-ante safeguards on anticompetitive behaviour." *Ungerer*: The Current Competitive Issues. Herbert Ungerer was Head of Unit Telecommunications, Posts and Information Society Coordination, DG Competition, from September 1994–July 1999.

999 Commission Notice: Guidelines on the effect on trade concept contained in Articles 81 and 82 of the Treaty (OJ C 101/81, 27.4.2004). See also *Europa.eu*: Summaries of EU Legislation.

1000 Commission Notice: Commission Notice on agreements of minor importance which do not appreciably restrict competition under Article 81(1) of the Treaty establishing the European Community (*de minimis*) (OJ C 368/13, 22.12.2001).

1001 This negative formulation, however, does not imply that agreements between firms which exceed the thresholds will appreciably restrict competition; instead, the notice only creates a safe harbor. The safe harbor applies to agreements (i) between actual or potential competitors (i.e., horizontal agreements) as long as their aggregate market share does not exceed 10% (para. 7(a)); (ii) between non-competitors (i.e., vertical agreements) as long as the market share held by each of the parties does not exceed 15% (para. 7(b)); and (iii) in markets where there is a cumulative effect of parallel networks of similar agreements, market share thresholds are reduced to 5% (para. 8).

(d) Article 101 TFEU

Article 101(1) prohibits all agreements which have as their object or effect to restrict competition.[1002] Article 101(1) is applicable if: (i) there is an agreement between two or more *independent* undertakings;[1003] (ii) the agreement is capable of affecting trade between Member States to an appreciable extent;[1004] and

1002 Article 101(1) TFEU includes a non-exhaustive list of the types of conduct and practices which are prohibited.

1003 Article 101 "draws a distinction" between the concepts of "agreements between undertakings", "decisions by associations of undertakings" and "concerted practices." Case 48-69, *Imperial Chemical Industries Ltd. v Commission*, 14 July 1972 [1972] ECR 619, para 64. Given the broad language, the application of Article 101 also captures any understanding (written or oral, voluntary or involuntary) or loose arrangements (the so-called "gentlemen's agreement"). Case 41/69, *ACF Chemiefarma NV v Commission*, 15 July 1970 [1970] ECR 661, para 9. In Case C-277/87, *Sandoz prodotti farmaceutici SpA v Commission*, 11 January 1990 [1990] ECR I-45, para 1, the Court found that the "systematic dispatching" of invoices constituted an agreement. In Joined Cases 32/78 and 36/78 – 82/78, *BMW Belgium SA and others v Commission*, 12 July 1979 [1979] ECR 2435, the Court held that a company circular urging certain behaviour (i.e., urging BMW car dealers in Belgium not to sell BMW cars to other Member States) was an "agreement". In Case T-148/89, *Tréfilunion SA v Commission*, 6 April 1995 [1995] ECR II-1063, the General Court found it sufficient for the undertakings to have expressed their joint intention to conduct themselves in the market in a particular way. Article 101(1) is also applicable to undertakings, trade associations, and professional bodies. Case T-144/99, *Institute of Professional Representatives before the European Patent Office v Commission* (28 March 2001), [2001] ECR II-1087, summary para 1. Article 101(1) is not, however, concerned with agreements between undertakings belonging to the same concern, such as a parent company and its subsidiaries.

1004 If there is no appreciable effect on inter-state trade (i.e., the effect is purely domestic within one Member State), any competition issues will be a matter exclusively for domestic competition rules. An agreement will only be caught by Article 101(1) if the nature or terms of the agreement and the parties' positions on the relevant market are significant enough for its operation to have an appreciable effect on the market. Commission Notice: Commission Notice on agreements of minor importance which do not appreciably restrict competition under Article 81(1) of the Treaty establishing the European Community (*de minimis*) (OJ C 368/13, 22.12.2001). The Commission will not bring proceedings under Article 101(1) in respect of agreements between parties whose combined market share does not exceed 10% (in the case of horizontal agreements) or 15% (in the case of vertical agreements). Blatantly anti-competitive restrictions, however, such as price-fixing or market sharing restrictions, cannot benefit from the Notice.

(iii) the agreement prevents, restricts, or distorts competition[1005] to an appreciable extent in a relevant market within the European Economic Area (EEA).[1006]

An agreement that is caught by Article 101(1) TFEU is deemed automatically void (by virtue of Article 101(2)), but it may nevertheless escape prohibition (and therefore voidness) should it meet the criteria for exemption set out in Article 101(3). In essence, Article 101(3) provides for limited legal "exceptions" when the anti-competitive effects of an agreement are outweighed or equalled by the efficiency benefits of such agreement.[1007]

Since 1 May 2004, with entry into force of Regulation No 1/2003 and the abolishment of advance notification and approval of agreements, individual exemptions are no longer granted by the Commission. Instead, the parties "self-assess" (i.e., without involving the Commission or any national competition authority)[1008] whether their commercial conduct/agreements are compatible with the principles of Article 101 and, if not, have sufficient benefits satisfy either:

1005 Establishing whether an agreements has as its "object or effect" the restriction, prevention or distortion of competition in the EU is not necessarily straightforward. Relevant factors in assessing such include: (i) understanding the background to the agreements and the surrounding circumstances, including the market context; (ii) understanding the impact on the relevant market; and (iii) analyzing the types and effects of the restrictions (rather than solely their form). In Case 172/80, *Gerhard Züchner v Bayerische Vereinsbank AG*, 14 July 1981 [1981] ECR 02021, the Court set out the underlying principle of the two-part "object or effect" analysis. In Case 56-65, *Société Technique Minière v Maschinenbau Ulm GmbH*, 30 June 1966 [1966] ECR 235, the Court described the two stages, adopting a *rule of reason* refinement by applying the concept of the *de minimis* rule. *Fairhurst*: Law of the European Union, p. 680.

1006 Restrictions relating solely to the exploitation of technology in markets outside Europe will not be caught by the Article 101(1) prohibition unless they are capable of having an effect on trade within the EEA. Joined cases C-89/85, C-104/85, C-114/85, C-116/85, C-117/85, C-125/85, C-126/85, C-127/85, C-128/85 and C-129/85, *A. Ahlström Osakeyhtiö and others v Commission*, 31 March 1993 [1993] ECR I-1307.

1007 This balancing applies even to agreements that are by their nature anti-competitive or that contain hard-core restrictions. See *Office of Fair Trading*: Article 101(3) – A discussion of narrow versus broad definition of benefits.

1008 However, undertakings may still consult with the Commission on novel questions of competition law and secure an *informal* guidance letter. See Commission Notice on informal guidance relating to novel questions concerning Articles 81 and 82 of the EC Treaty that arise in individual cases (guidance letters) (OJ C 101/78, 27.4.2004). Para. 25 notes that "Guidance letters are not Commission decisions

(i) the individual conditions under Article 101(3); or (ii) benefit from a block exemption.

To qualify for an individual exemption, an agreement must satisfy *each* of the four conditions contained in Article 101(3), which are that:[1009]

- the agreement must offer efficiency gains, for example by contributing to improving the production and/or distribution of goods or to promoting technical or economic progress;
- the agreement must offer consumer benefits – i.e., consumers must be allowed to obtain a fair share of these efficiency gains;
- the agreement may not impose any restraints or restrictions on the parties concerned which are not indispensable to the achievement of these efficiency objectives; and
- the agreement may not afford the parties concerned the possibility of eliminating competition in respect of a substantial part of the market (or products) in question.

This four-step test is intended to ensure a full analysis of the agreement's *effects* on competition. The Commission has sought to facilitate the process of "self-assessment" by publishing Guidelines on the application of Article 101(3),[1010] which outline the (then-current) case law and set out the Commission's policy on a number of issues that may be subject to interpretation (e.g., they identify various potential positive efficiency effects).

(e) Article 102 TFEU

Article 102 TFEU regulates conduct by an undertaking: (i) which holds a *dominant position* in one or more relevant markets; (ii) there is an *abuse* of such position of dominance; and (iii) the abuse *affects trade* (or have the potential to affect trade) between EU Member states. Although the prohibition only applies to firms with a dominant position on a relevant market, the relevant product and geographic market for this purpose is often narrowly defined.

---

and do not bind Member States' competition authorities or courts that have the power to apply Articles 81 and 82."

1009 The Commission first set out the four cumulative conditions required under Article 101(3) in its 1973 *Prym-Werke* decision. Commission Decision 73/323/EEC of 8 October 1973 (IV/26.825 – PRYM-BEKA) (OJ L 296/24, 24.10.1973). Section III (paras. 1–4) sets out and analyse the four conditions.

1010 Commission Notice: Guidelines on the application of Article 81(3) of the Treaty (OJ C 101/97, 27.4.2004). See also *European Commission*: Antitrust Legislation.

Unlike Article 101, it is not possible to gain an exemption from Article 102. Since Article 101 and Article 102 apply independently, an arrangement which has been exempted from Article 101(1) may therefore *still* give rise to an infringement of Article 102.[1011] A firm which infringes Article 102 can be ordered by the Commission to cease the abusive conduct and may be fined up to 10% of its annual turnover.[1012] An infringement may also enable third parties to claim damages or injunctive relief in national courts.[1013]

(i) Establishing Dominance

Article 102 will only regulate the conduct of a firm if it is "dominant".[1014] In *United Brands v. Commission*, the Court stated that dominance is "a *position of economic strength* enjoyed by an undertaking which enable it to *prevent effective competition* being maintained on the relevant market by giving it the power to behave to an appreciable extent *independently* of its competitors, customers and ultimately of its consumers."[1015] In *Hoffmann-La Roche*, the Court noted further that dominance

---

1011 Case T-51/89, *Tetra Pak Rausing SA v. Commission*, 10 July 1990 [1990] ECR II–309, para. 25: "In these circumstances, this Court holds that in the scheme for the protection of competition established by the Treaty the grant of exemption, whether individual or block exemption, under Article [101](3) cannot be such as to render inapplicable the prohibition set out in Article [102]. This principle follows... from the general scheme of Articles [101 and 102] which... are independent and complementary provisions designed, in general, to regulate distinct situations by different rules.... Article 86... by reason of its very subject-matter (abuse), precludes any possible exception to the prohibition it lays down" (citations omitted).

1012 Regulation No 1/2003 (OJ L 1/1, 4.1.2003), Chapter VI (Penalties), Art. 23 (Fines), para. 2.

1013 *Id.*, Chapter II (Powers), Art. 5 (Powers of the competition authorities of the Member States).

1014 Such a position may be held by one undertaking (single dominance) or by two or more undertakings (collective or joint dominance) if they are sufficiently closely linked. Commission Notice: Guidance on the Commission's enforcement priorities in applying Article 82 of the EC Treaty to abusive exclusionary conduct by dominant undertakings (OJ C 45/7, 24.2.2009), para. 4, p. 7. For economic links based on alignment of conduct sufficient to meet this standard, see Commission Decision No 97/26/EC (24 April 1996), Case No IV/M.619 – *Gencor/Lonrho*, OJ 1997 L 11/30; as confirmed in Case T-102/96, *Gencor Ltd v Commission*, 25 March 1999 [1999] ECR II-753.

1015 Case 27/76, *United Brands Company and United Brands Continentaal BV v Commission* ("Chiquita Bananas"), 14 February 1978 [1978] ECR 207, para 65 (emphasis mine).

"enables the undertaking which profits by it, if not to determine, at least to have an appreciable influence on the conditions under which that competition will develop."[1016] In a Commission decision related to the *AKZO Chemie BV* case,[1017] the Commission added that "[t]he power to exclude effective competition is not however in all cases coterminous with independence from competitive factors but may also involve the ability to eliminate or seriously weaken existing competitors or to prevent potential competitors from entering the market."[1018]

More recently, however, the Commission has taken a more economic approach, taking into account the competitive structure of the market,[1019] including a careful look at the ability of the allegedly dominant firm to control prices in the face of pressure from competitors and to erect barriers to entry.[1020] In most cases, the mere finding of a large market share will not be sufficient to establish dominance. It is therefore necessary to consider other factors such as:

- barriers to entry to the market, such as *intellectual property rights*, product licences, the existence of established distribution networks, and the presence of brand or customer loyalty (high barriers to entry to a market make a finding of dominance more likely); and
- constraints on market power (for example, the strength of existing competitors or the extent of buyer power on the part of the firm's customers).

As part of determining dominance, the relevant market must be identified.[1021] The Commission's approach to defining the relevant market is laid down in

---

1016 Case C-85/76, *Hoffmann-La Roche & Co. AG v Commission*, 13 February 1979 [1979] ECR 461, paras. 38–39.

1017 Case C-62/86, *AKZO Chemie BV v Commission*, 3 July 1991 [1991] ECR I-3359.

1018 Commission Decision of 14 December 1985 relating to a proceeding under Article 86 of the EEC Treaty (IV/30.698 - ECS/AKZO, Case 85/609/EEC (OJ L 374, 31.12.1985).

1019 The Commission's guidance demonstrates that the Commission intends to follow an economic and effects-based approach to establish its enforcement priorities under Article 102 TFEU in relation to exclusionary conduct. Commission Notice: Guidance on the Commission's enforcement priorities in applying Article 82 of the EC Treaty to abusive exclusionary conduct by dominant undertakings (OJ C 45/7, 24.2.2009). See also *EAGCP*: An economic approach to Article 82; and *Kaczorowska*: European Union Law, pp. 854–859.

1020 *Hovenkamp/Janis/Lemley/Leslie*: IP and Antitrust, pp. 45–60, § 45.5(a)(1) (2011 Supplement).

1021 The importance of defining the relevant market cannot be overstated: in Case 6-72, *Europemballage Corporation and Continental Can Company Inc. v Commission*, 21

its market definition guidelines.[1022] The relevant market definition combines two primary components:[1023] the relevant product market[1024] and the relevant geographic market.[1025] There is no fixed geographical definition with respect to the territory of the relevant market. It could be a worldwide market or a narrowly localized market.

(ii) Abuse of a Dominant Position

A dominant undertaking violates Article 102 TFEU if it engages in "[a]ny abuse". The mere holding of a dominant position is not unlawful; it is the *abuse* of the dominant position that results in an infringement of Article 102. Abuse is not specifically defined in Article 102, which instead sets out a non-exhaustive list of specific conduct that may constitute abuse.[1026] The Commission's Guidelines

---

February 1973 [1973] ECR 215, the Commission's decision was annulled due to the inability of the Commission to define the relevant market.

1022 Commission Notice on the definition of relevant market for the purposes of Community competition law (OJ C 372/5, 9.12.1997). The Commission further addresses aspects of market definition that are of particular importance in the field of technology licensing in its Commission Notice: TTBE Guidelines (OJ C 89/3, 28.03.2014).

1023 In some cases, a third component – the relevant temporal market – is included in the analysis. See *Kaczorowska*: European Union Law, pp. 854 and 870.

1024 A relevant product market comprises all those products and/or services which are regarded as interchangeable or substitutable by the consumer by reason of the products' characteristics, their prices and their intended use. Commission Notice on the definition of relevant market for the purposes of Community competition law (OJ C 372/5, 9.12.1997), para. 7. See Case 27/76, *United Brands Company and United Brands Continentaal BV v Commission* (Chiquita Bananas), 14 February 1978 [1978] ECR 207, para 35, in which "the banana market is a market which is sufficiently distinct from the other fresh fruit markets." In *Tetra-Pak*, the CJEU included supply-side substitution in the definition of the relevant market. Case C-333/94 P, *Tetra Pak International SA v Commission*, 14 November 1996 [1996] ECR I-5951.

1025 A relevant geographic market comprises the area in which the firms concerned are involved in the supply and demand of products or services and in which the conditions of competition are sufficiently homogeneous. Commission Notice on the definition of relevant market for the purposes of Community competition law (OJ C 372/5, 9.12.1997), para. 8.

1026 As noted by the CJEU, the list "merely gives examples, not an exhaustive enumeration of the sort of abuses of a dominant position prohibited by the Treaty." Case 6-72, *Europemballage Corporation and Continental Can Company Inc. v Commission*,

suggest that it will reject any *per se* application of the prohibitions, instead relying on a *rule of reason* approach, where the *effects* of the abuse are analysed.[1027] Hence, the anti-competitive effect of the unilateral practice – rather than the exact type of practice – is the key factor and will be reviewed by the courts and competition authorities on a case-by-case basis.

Abuses are typically classified into one of four categories: (i) exploitative abuses, (ii) discriminatory abuses; (iii) exclusionary or predatory abuses; and (iv) reprisal abuses.[1028] In practice, most of the Article 102 cases have involved pricing abuses, refusals to supply, and tying.[1029] Hence, the abusive conduct may be expressed through the *terms of an agreement* with another entity (e.g.,

---

21 February 1973 [1973] ECR 215, para. 26, p. 245. See also Case C-333/94 P, *Tetra Pak International SA v Commission*, 14 November 1996 [1996] ECR I-5951, para. 37: "It must, moreover, be stressed that the list of abusive practices set out in the second paragraph of Article [102] of the Treaty is not exhaustive."

1027 Commission Notice: Guidance on the Commission's enforcement priorities in applying Article 82 of the EC Treaty to abusive exclusionary conduct by dominant undertakings (OJ C 45/7, 24.2.2009), para. 8: "In applying the general enforcement principles set out in this Communication, the Commission will take into account the specific facts and circumstances of each case. … The Commission may therefore adapt the approach set out in this Communication to the extent that this would appear to be reasonable and appropriate in a given case."

1028 See generally *Kaczorowska*: European Union Law, pp. 878 and 897; and *Anderman/ Schmidt*: EC competition policy and IPRs, pp. 46–51.

1029 Tying and bundling cases have led to some of the highest fines. In *Hilti AG v Commission*, the Commission imposed a heavy fine of EUR6 million in respect of Hilti's requirement that purchasers of its nail guns must also acquire nails from it. Case T-30/89, *Hilti AG v Commission*, 12 December 1991 [1991] ECR II-1439; and Case C-53/92P, *Hilti AG v Commission*, 2 March 1994 [1994] ECR I-667. The Commission's continued proceedings against Microsoft (most recently for alleged non-compliance with its Commitments) confirms this trend. For example, in March 2013, Microsoft was fined EUR 561 million for failing to comply with its commitments to promote a range of web browsers, rather than just Internet Explorer (i.e., tying Microsoft's web browser, Internet Explorer, to its dominant client PC operating system Windows) to users in the European Union. *European Commission*: Press Release IP/13/196. This case, and the fines imposed, were separate from the Commission's investigation of Microsoft which concluded in 2004 with a Decision finding that Microsoft had abused its dominant position and imposing fines (among other things) for the tying of Windows Media Player to Windows, for which the Commission imposed fines of EURO 497.2 million. *European Commission*: Press Release IP/04/382.

a license) or through a *purely unilateral act* (such as a decision to raise prices or refuse to license).

There is no exemption from Article 102 because as a matter of principle an abuse of market dominance cannot be beneficial to consumers. However, the courts and the Commission have developed a number of limited justifications for any such abusive conduct, including imperative considerations (such as health and safety) or substantial efficiencies. In this context, the Commission will assess whether the conduct in question is indispensable and proportionate to the goal allegedly pursued by the dominant undertaking.[1030]

Finally, in *Hoffmann-La Roche*, the Court noted that dominant firms are entitled to compete on their strength; they are simply prohibited from engaging in behavior that deviates from "normal competition" practices.[1031] In *Deutsche Telekom*, the Court reiterated that abuse by a dominant undertaking occurs when such undertaking, "through recourse to methods different from those governing normal competition", engages in conduct which "has the effect of hindering the maintenance of the degree of competition still existing in the market or the growth of that competition".[1032] Furthermore, the Court distinguished that Article 102 prohibits not only practices which may cause damage to consumers *directly*, but also to those which are detrimental through their *impact* on competition.[1033]

(iii) Effect on Trade (abuse inside the EU): Consten and Grundig v Commission

Both Articles 101 and 102 TFEU cover abuses having an effect on trade between the Member States.[1034] The analysis has received careful examination by

---

1030 Commission Notice: Guidance on the Commission's enforcement priorities in applying Article 82 of the EC Treaty to abusive exclusionary conduct by dominant undertakings (OJ C 45/7, 24.2.2009), paras. 28–31.

1031 Case C-85/76, *Hoffmann-La Roche & Co. AG v Commission*, 13 February 1979 [1979] ECR 461, para. 91, p. 451.

1032 Case C-280/08 P, *Deutsche Telekom AG European Commission*, 14 October 2010 [2010] ECR I-9555, para. 174 (appeal Case before the General Court T-271/03), para. 174; citing Case 322/81, *NV Nederlandsche Banden Industrie Michelin v Commission*, 9 November 1983 [1983] ECR 3461, paras. 12 and 70 (further citations omitted).

1033 Case C-280/08 P, *Deutsche Telekom AG European Commission*, 14 October 2010 [2010] ECR I-9555, para. 176.

1034 As a cautionary note for international undertakings, the Court has endorsed the extra-territorial application of Articles 101 and 102: anti-competitive actions

the Court. In the landmark case of *Consten and Grundig v Commission*,[1035] the Commission reviewed the effects on trade of abuses *within* the Member States. In *Consten-Grundig*, the Commission condemned an exclusive distribution agreement between Grundig (a German manufacturer of electrical equipment) and Consten (its French distributor), pursuant to Grundig appointed Consten as Grundig's sole representative in a given territory (France, Corsica, and the Saarland). The agreement authorized Consten to use Grundig's name and trademark, and further permitted Consten to register a second trademark of Grundig ("GINT" – a contraction of Grundig International)[1036] under Consten's name in France. This secured for Consten an "absolute territorial protection", sheltering it from all intra-brand competition, since it could use its rights as proprietor of the registered trademark to control and prevent parallel imports (that is, Grundig products legitimately sold in Germany). The Commission found that Consten was prohibited from asserting its trademark rights in order to prevent parallel imports, finding that the sole distribution agreement constituted an attempt to partition the market through territorial restrictions.[1037]

The applicants in *Consten-Grundig* argued that the agreement did not affect trade within the meaning of Article 101(1), as it actually increased the volume of trade between Member States. The Court of Justice (on appeal) rejected the argument and upheld the Commission decision. Even though territorial restrictions did not expressly appear on the Article 101(1) restricted practices list, the Court concluded that the practices by Grundig and Consten were "antithetical to the very notion of an integrated European market."[1038] The aim of Article 101

---

by undertakings established outside of the EU may still be subject to EU competition analysis when the effects of such actions "affect trade between Member States". Joined cases C-89/85, C-104/85, C-114/85, C-116/85, C-117/85, C-125/85, C-126/85, C-127/85, C-128/85 and C-129/85, *A. Ahlström Osakeyhtiö and others v Commission*, 31 March 1993 [1993] ECR I-1307, paras. 142–44. In *Ahlström Osakeyhtiö*, the Commission found that the coordinated transaction prices in the EU for wood pulp – even by undertakings established outside of the EU – affected trade between the Member States.

1035 Joined Cases 56 and 58/64, *Établissements Consten S.à.R.L. and Grundig-Verkaufs-GmbH v Commission*, 13 July 1966 [1966] ECR 299.

1036 *Keeling*: Intellectual Property Rights in EU Law, p. 51.

1037 *Hovenkamp/Janis/Lemley/Leslie*: IP and Antitrust, pp. 45–20, § 45.4a2 (2011 Supplement).

1038 The Commission has consistently applied this reasoning, including in its 2007 investigation into major record companies, including Apple, against alleged territorial restriction in on-line music sales. *European Commission*: Press Release

is not to increase the volume of trade between Member States *but rather* to ensure that competition in the common market is *not* distorted.[1039] The Court held that "whether the agreement is capable of constituting a threat, either direct or indirect, actual or potential, to freedom of trade between Member States "was the key factor.[1040]

The effect of *Consten-Grundig* is that Article 101 TFEU applies not only to competing undertakings at a horizontal level, but also to vertical agreements between companies which are not themselves competing with each other but which aim to exclude competitors from the market (through such "absolute territorial protection"), even if the agreements are not explicitly concerned with trade outside one Member State.[1041] The principle has been confirmed by later courts: citing *Consten-Grundig*, the Court in *Nungesser* held that the granting of "absolute territorial protection ... results in the artificial maintenance of separate national markets, contrary to the Treaty."[1042] Finally, the Commission has advised that the "effect on trade" is an autonomous criterion which must be assessed separately in each case.[1043]

6.4 EU Competition Rules Applicable to Trademarks

(a) Application of Article 101 to Trademark Licensing

The essential purpose of a trademark is to guarantee the origin of the goods. By using a trademark on a product, the producer associates it with the owner of the trademark. As the use of a trademark without the owner's consent is generally an infringement of the mark, any arrangement for the use of the trademark will require a license. The application of Article 101 to trademark licensing raises many

---

MEMO/07/126. *Tart*: Competition: Apple to Equalise iTunes Music Downloads, p. 1. 'Which?' claimed Apple was applying 20% higher prices to British users than for the other European users. *European Digital Rights*: European Commission Closes Enquiry On Apple. *European Commission*: Press Release IP/08/22.

1039 *Keeling*: Intellectual Property Rights in EU Law, p. 309.

1040 Joined Cases 56 and 58/64, *Établissements Consten S.à.R.L. and Grundig-Verkaufs-GmbH v Commission*, 13 July 1966 [1966] ECR 299, p. 341.

1041 *Fairhurst*: Law of the European Union, p. 675.

1042 Case 258/78, *L.C. Nungesser KG and Kurt Eisele v Commission* (Maize Seed), 8 June 1982 [1982] ECR 2015, para 61. See also Case 56/65, *Société Technique Minière v Maschinenbau Ulm GmbH*, 30 June 1966 [1966] ECR 235, p. 249.

1043 Commission Notice, Guidelines on the effect on trade concept contained in Articles 81 and 82 of the Treaty, OJ C 101/81, 27.04.2004, para. 13.

of the same issues as arise in relation to the licensing of other intellectual property rights. There is, however, less express guidance in this area than in the case of patent and know-how licensing, primarily because there is *no block exemption* dealing specifically with trademark licensing, and there are few decided cases dealing specifically with the application of Article 101 to trademark licences.[1044]

(i) Trademark Licensing Provisions likely to fall outside *Article 101(1)*

A provision in a trademark licence may well fall *outside* Article 101(1) altogether, on the ground that the maintenance of the link between the owner's trademark and the goods produced or marketed under his control or authority is necessary to protect an essential element of the mark's existence. Restrictions falling outside Article 101(1) on this basis would include, for example: (i) an obligation to affix the owner's trademark to all products manufactured to its specifications; (ii) quality control measures; or (iii) an obligation on the licensee to purchase special ingredients only from the licensor (provided that such ingredients really are essential and are not available from other sources); (iv) advertising and promotion obligations on the licensee (provided that these are objective and not excessive); and (v) restrictions on the sub-licensing of the trademark, or change of control provisions (if they reflect the legitimate need of the licensor to control the use of its trademark).

An obligation on the licensee not to challenge the licensor's *ownership* of the mark will not be viewed as a restriction of competition, because the question of whether the licensor or licensee owns the trademark will not affect the competitive position of third parties, who are in either case prevented from using the trademark. However, a clause preventing the licensee from challenging the *validity* of the mark may fall within Article 101(1).[1045]

(ii) Trademark Licensing Provisions likely to fall within *Article 101(1)*

The Commission takes a strict approach to exclusive trademark licences. Even though the granting of an exclusive right to exploit a trademark in a specific territory is present in most distribution agreements (which include a license to

1044 On the other hand, there is a substantial body of case law dealing with the effect of the TFEU's free movement of goods provisions on the enforcement of trademark rights.

1045 90/186/EEC: Commission Decision of 23 March 1990 relating to a proceeding under Article 85 of the EEC Treaty (IV/32.736 – *Moosehead/Whitbread*) (OJ L 100/32, 20.04.1990).

use the trademark), the Commission views restrictions that prevent a licensor from licensing its trademark to any other party within the licensee's appointed territory as a *de facto* restriction of competition, on the basis that it prevents intra-brand competition (i.e., competition from other companies in the provision of the same goods and services bearing the same mark). This will be the case whether or not the licensor itself is also prohibited from using the trademark in the appointed territory. An exclusive licence will therefore infringe Article 101(1) (assuming that the relevant restriction is appreciable and that there is an effect on trade between Member States), and will accordingly be unenforceable.

Further provisions likely to infringe Article 101(1) for which no exemption is likely include: (i) an obligation on a licensee not to sell any products which compete with those bearing the licensed trademark (on the basis that it reduces the scope for competition from such products);[1046] (ii) a prohibition on the licensee from actively marketing products bearing the licensed trademark in an EEA territory outside its own allocated territory (on the basis that it reduces the scope for competition in that other territory);[1047] (iii) a prohibition on passive sales (i.e., an obligation on the licensee not to supply anyone outside the appointed territory, even if she is approached by a potential customer); (iv) resale restrictions which distinguish permissible sales according to the type of customer; and (v) an outright prohibition on the licensee challenging the validity of the trademark.[1048]

(b) Application of Technology Transfer Block Exemption to Trademark Licensing

In assessing whether an agreement falls within the safe harbor provided by a block exemption, three aspects must be considered: (i) whether the parties to the agreement are *competitors* or *non-competitors*;[1049] (ii) the *market shares*

1046 *Heinisch/Woodgate*: EU Intellectual property transactions.

1047 *Practical Law Company*: Overview: EU competition law.

1048 90/186/EEC: Commission Decision of 23 March 1990 relating to a proceeding under Article 85 of the EEC Treaty (IV/32.736 – *Moosehead/Whitbread*) (OJ L 100/32, 20.04.1990).

1049 With respect to technology transfers, determining whether the parties are competitors involves a review of competition in the relevant *technology* market as well as in the relevant product and geographic markets. The relevant technology market is assessed by reference to actual competition and on a worldwide basis and takes into account all substitutable technologies. Commission Notice: TTBE Guidelines (OJ C 89/3, 28.03.2014), paras. 22-29. The parties are not considered to

attributable to each party;[1050] and (iii) whether the agreement contains any *problem clauses* (hardcore or excluded restrictions).[1051]

Unless there are hardcore restrictions, the TTBE Guidelines affirm that there is *no presumption of illegality* of agreements that fall outside the scope of the block exemption. Furthermore, there is *no presumption* that Article 101(1) applies merely because the market share thresholds are exceeded.[1052] Furthermore, they confirm that most exclusive agreements between non-competitors fall outside Article 101(1) or satisfy the exemption criteria of Article 101(3).[1053] Such agreements may exceptionally fall within Article 101 if either party enjoys an appreciable degree of market power.

The TTBE Guidelines note that certain obligations typically found in licensing agreements are generally *not restrictive*, including: confidentiality obligations; obligations on licensees not to sub-license; obligations not to use the licensed technology after the expiry of the agreement, provided that the licensed technology remains valid and in force; obligations to assist the licensor in enforcing the licensed intellectual property rights; obligations to pay minimum royalties or to

---

be competitors where they both hold intellectual property rights to a substitutable technology but one party does not license out the technology to third parties.

1050 For agreements concluded between *competing* undertakings, the combined market share of the parties may not exceed 20% of the relevant product and geographic market or the relevant technology market. For agreements concluded between *non-competing* undertakings, neither party may have a market share in excess of 30% of the relevant product and geographic market or the relevant technology market. TTBE Regulation (OJ L 93/17, 28.3.2014), Art. 3 (Market-share thresholds).

1051 TTBE Regulation (OJ L 93/17, 28.3.2014). There are two categories of prohibited clauses: "hardcore restrictions" (as set forth in Article 4) and "excluded restrictions" (set forth in Article 5). Hardcore restrictions (the earlier "blacklisted" clauses) are clauses that, if included, will void the entire agreement. Commission Notice: TTBE Guidelines (OJ C 89/3, 28.03.2014), paras. 94–95. Hardcore restrictions include such practices as a restriction on a party's ability to determine its prices when selling to a third party or an allocation of market. Article 5 of the TTBE Regulation lists types of restrictions that are not block exempted and which require individual assessment of their anti-competitive and pro-competitive effects under a *rule of reason* approach. If an excluded clause is deemed to violate Article 101(1), the excluded clause is void, but it is severable from the remainder of the agreement, so that the remaining provisions of the agreement may still be subject to the block exemption. Commission Notice: TTBE Guidelines (OJ C 89/3, 28.03.2014), para 128.

1052 Commission Notice: TTBE Guidelines (OJ C 89/3, 28.03.2014), para 156.

1053 *Id.*, para 194.

produce a minimum quantity of products incorporating the licensed technology; and obligations to use the licensor's trademark or indicate the name of the licensor on the product.[1054]

The 2004 TTBE Regulation did not once mention trademarks or include trademark licenses under the defined scope of a "technology transfer agreement".[1055] The 2014 TTBE Regulation only mentions trademarks once – in its definition of intellectual property rights[1056] (which is not the same as the definition of technology rights). By its language, however, a trademark license might fall under the scope of the TTBE Regulation "if, and to the extent that, those provisions are directly related to the production or sale of the contract products".[1057] Notable is that the 2014 TTBE Regulation drops the "primary object of the license" test of the 2004 TTBE Regulation to determine the application of the block exemption to such "ancillary agreements".[1058] The new test is the "direct link" between the technology transfer and the production of the contract products. The 2014 TTBE Guidelines confirm this approach.[1059] In such cases where the trademark license

---

1054 *Id.*, para. 183(f).

1055 Under the 2004 TTBE Regulation, a "technology transfer agreement" is "a patent licensing agreement, a know-how licensing agreement, a software copyright licensing agreement or a mixed patent, know-how or software copyright licensing agreement". TTBE Regulation (OJ L 123/11, 27.04.2004), Art. 1(1)(b).

1056 TTBE Regulation (OJ L 93/17, 28.3.2014), Art. 1(1)(h).

1057 TTBE Regulation (OJ L 93/17, 28.3.2014), Preamble 9. Furthermore, the definition of "technology rights" covers both "a technology rights licensing agreement entered into between two undertakings *for the purpose of the production of contract products* by the licensee and/or its sub-contractor(s)" or "an assignment of technology rights between two undertakings *for the purpose of the production of contract products* where part of the risk associated with the exploitation of the technology remains with the assignor". Art. 1(1)(c) (emphasis mine).

1058 The 2004 TTBE Regulation (as confirmed in the 2004 TTBE Guidelines) did not extend to trademark licensing unless such licences were only *ancillary* to a licence of rights covered by the TTBE Regulation (i.e., they were not the primary object of the agreement). TTBE Regulation (OJ L 123/11, 27.04.2004), Art. 1(1)(b) and TTBE Guidelines (OJ C 101/2, 27.04.2004), para. 49.

1059 The 2014 TTBE Guidelines state that trademark licenses will be covered "if, and to the extent that, they are directly related to the production or sale of the contract products. This condition ensures that provisions covering other types of intellectual property rights are block exempted to the extent that these other intellectual property rights serve to enable the licensee to better exploit the licensed technology rights." Commission Notice: 2014 TTBE Guidelines (OJ C 89/3, 28.03.2014), para. 47. The 2004 TTBE Regulation only covered the licensing of trademarks "to

is *not* "directly related to the production or sale of the contract products",[1060] the TTBE Guidelines specifically *exclude* trademark licenses from the scope of the TTBE Regulation, suggesting the Vertical Exemption to be more applicable.[1061]

Despite this, the TTBE Guidelines – in conjunction with the Commission's guidance on application of Article 101(3)[1062] – serve as an essential point of reference in assessing how the Commission would likely see restrictions contained in trademark licence agreements *not* meeting the criteria set out in the TTBE Regulation applies to the licensing of rights under Article 101 TFEU.[1063] In fact, the TTBE Guidelines commit more than 18 pages (from a total of 50 – the entire Section IV) to the application and analysis of factors for dealing with agreements that fall *outside* of the TTBE Regulation.

(c) Application of Vertical Restraints Block Exemption to Trademark Licensing

The Vertical Restraints Block Exemption (VRBE) Regulation[1064] applies to distribution, franchising, and sales agency agreements (among others). A vertical agreement is on in which two or more undertakings – each operating at different

---

the extent that they are directly related to the exploitation of the licensed technology and do not constitute the primary object of the agreement." Commission Notice: TTBE Guidelines (OJ C 101/2, 27.04.2004), para. 50.

1060 Commission Notice: TTBE Guidelines (OJ C 89/3, 28.03.2014), para. 47.

1061 "The Commission will also not extend the principles developed in the TTBER and these guidelines to trademark licensing. ... Where a trademark licence is directly related to the use, sale or resale of goods and services and does not constitute the primary object of the agreement, the licence agreement is covered by Commission Regulation (EU) No 330/2010." Commission Notice: TTBE Guidelines (OJ C 89/3, 28.03.2014), para. 50.

1062 Commission Notice: Guidelines on the application of Article 81(3) of the Treaty (OJ C 101/97, 27.4.2004).

1063 This is particularly important now that parties to an agreement can no longer seek an individual exemption under Article 101(3) from the Commission. *Lowe*: Current Issues of EU Competition Law, p. 682.

1064 Commission Regulation (EU) No 330/2010 of 20 April 2010 on the application of Article 101(3) of the Treaty on the Functioning of the European Union to categories of vertical agreements and concerted practices (OJ L 102/1, 23.4.2010) (hereinafter VRBE Regulation). The VRBE Regulation entered into force on 1 June 2010 and expires 31 May 2022. It replaced the earlier 1999 block exemptions for vertical agreements (Commission Regulation 2790/1999 on the application of Article 81(3) of the Treaty to categories of vertical agreements and concerted practices,

levels of the production/distribution chain, such as producers and retailers – enter into an agreement.[1065] These undertakings do not typically "compete" with one another, since they operate at different levels in the market.[1066] Under EU competition law, vertical agreements are treated less severely than horizontal agreements, as they are generally less obviously anti-competitive than horizontal agreements.[1067] Each party to such an agreement – producer and retailer, for example, or supplier and distributor – exercise their powers independently. If any such party is in a dominant position and abuses such position, the abuse would be analysed and dealt with under Article 102 TFEU.

The VRBE Regulation is accompanied by VRBE Guidelines[1068] which set out the Commission's substantive assessment criteria for assessment of vertical agreements under EU competition rules. Broadly, the block exemption excludes: (i) all vertical agreements between *non-competing* entities where the supplier and buyer's market does not exceed 30% of the relevant market[1069] (the so-called "market share test");[1070] and (ii) vertical agreements containing provisions relating to the *assignment* of intellectual property rights to or *use* of intellectual property rights by the buyer where five conditions are fulfilled.[1071]

OJ L 336, 29.12.1999), which in turn had replaced earlier block exemptions relating to exclusive distribution, purchasing and franchising agreements.

1065 Regulation 330/2010 defines vertical agreements as those "between two or more undertakings each operating, for the purposes of the agreement, at a different level of the production or distribution chain and relating to the conditions under which the parties may purchase, sell or resell certain goods or services". VRBE Regulation (OJ L 102/1, 23.4.2010).

1066 The only anti-competitive effects of such vertical agreements are usually found when there is not enough *intra-brand* competition – that is, insufficient competition between distributors of the same brand. See *Kaczorowska*: European Union Law, p. 801 and fn. 2002.

1067 *Kaczorowska*: European Union Law, pp. 800–801.

1068 VRBE Guidelines (OJ C 130/1, 19.05.2010), replacing the previous guidelines (OJ C 291/1, 13.10.2000).

1069 VRBE Regulation 330/2010 (OJ L 102/1, 23.4.2010), Art. 3, para. 1.

1070 In principle, the Commission finds vertical agreements do not have an adverse effect on competition. The market share test was introduced to make sure that when parties to a vertical agreement have market power, the agreement will not produce anti-competitive effects. *Kaczorowska*: European Union Law, p. 848.

1071 The five conditions are: (i) the intellectual property rights provisions must be part of a vertical agreement, under which the parties may purchase, sell or resell certain goods or services; (ii) the intellectual property rights must be assigned to, or licensed for use by, the buyer; (iii) the intellectual property rights provisions must

The VRBE Regulation does not mention trademarks in the definition of "intellectual property rights".[1072] The VRBE Regulation exempts provisions relating to the licensing or assignment of intellectual property rights if the licence or assignment of such intellectual property rights is *not* the primary object of the particular agreement, but is nonetheless directly related to the agreement.[1073] Examples of trademark-related provisions which generally *will* fall within the scope of the block exemption on this basis are:

- a provision in a distribution agreement permitting the distributor to use the manufacturer's trademark to sell goods (as the sale of goods is the primary object of the agreement); and
- a licence of know-how and trademarks from the franchisor under a franchise agreement to assist the franchisee in marketing goods or services under the franchise (as the franchise business is the primary object of the agreement).

Furthermore, the agreement may not contain any "hardcore" restrictions. Should any of the listed restrictions (for example, restrictions on the ability of the buyer to determine its sale price, or restrictions which confer absolute territorial protection through partitioning) be included in an agreement, the entire agreement will not be covered by the VRBE Regulation (and therefore will not benefit from the block exemption "safe harbor").

(d) Application of Article 102 to Trademark Ownership & Licensing

Article 102 will only regulate the conduct of a firm if it is dominant. A position of dominance (i.e., economic strength) may be derived from a variety of factors

not constitute the primary object of the agreement; (iv) the intellectual property rights provisions must be directly related to the use, sale or resale of goods or services by the buyer or its customers; and (v) the intellectual property rights provisions relating to goods or services must not contain restrictions of competition having the same object as vertical restraints which are not exempted under the Regulation. VRBE Guidelines (OJ C 130/1, 19.05.2010), paras. 31–34.

1072 Intellectual property rights are defined as "industrial property rights, know how, copyright and neighbouring rights". VRBE Regulation 330/2010 (OJ L 102/1, 23.4.2010), Art. 1(f).

1073 "Where the vertical agreement, in addition to the supply of the contract goods, also contains IPR provisions – such as a provision concerning the use of the supplier's trademark – which help the buyer to market the contract goods, the supplier's market share on the market where it sells the contract goods is relevant for the application of the Block Exemption Regulation." VRBE Guidelines (OJ C 130/1, 19.05.2010), para. 92.

including, but not limited to, market share. Many other factors are just as important as market share in establishing dominance, such as the strength of competitors, barriers to market entry, the regulatory environment, and customer preferences.[1074] Article 102 does not penalise dominance itself; it does, however, place a "special responsibility" on a dominant firm not to act in a manner which abuses its position.[1075] As a rule, there must be a link between the dominant position and the abusive conduct.[1076] This generally requires that the abuse must impede competition on the market in which a dominant position is held. In certain cases, however, it is possible for a firm to infringe Article 102 if it uses its dominant position on one market to impede competition on a separate, albeit closely related, market.[1077]

Assessment of abuse under Article 102 TFEU is complicated by the presence of intellectual property rights. It is important to note that although owners of intellectual property rights enjoy a legal monopoly over certain acts, ownership of an exclusive intellectual property right – whether through statutory grant of the right[1078] or through acquisition of an exclusive right[1079] – will not in itself

---

1074 Commission Notice: Guidance on the Commission's enforcement priorities in applying Article 82 of the EC Treaty to abusive exclusionary conduct by dominant undertakings (OJ C 45/7, 24.2.2009), paras. 9–15.

1075 "A finding that an undertaking has a dominant position is not in itself a recrimination but simply means that, irrespective of the reasons for which it has such a dominant position, the undertaking concerned has a special responsibility not to allow its conduct to impair genuine undistorted competition on the common market." Case 322/81, *NV Nederlandsche Baden-Industrie Michelin v Commission* [1983] ECR 3461, para. 57.

1076 The "application of Article 86 presupposes a link between the dominant position and the alleged abusive conduct". Case C-333/94 P, *Tetra Pak International SA v Commission*, 14 November 1996 [1996] ECR I-5951, para. 27.

1077 "In the case of distinct, but associated, markets... application of Article 86 to conduct found on the associated, non-dominated, market and having effects on that associated market can only be justified by special circumstances." *Id.*

1078 As the CJEU held in *Magill*, "So far as dominant position is concerned, it is to be remembered at the outset that mere ownership of an intellectual property right cannot confer such a position." Joined cases C-241/91 P and C-242/91 P, *Radio Telefis Eireann (RTE) and Independent Television Publications Ltd (ITP) v Commission* (Magill), 6 April 1995 [1995] ECR I-743, para. 46. See also Case 40/70, *Sirena S.r.l. v Eda S.r.l. and others*, 18 February 1971 [1971] ECR 69; Case 78-70, and *Deutsche Grammophon Gesellschaft mbH v Metro-SB-Großmärkte GmbH & Co. KG*, 8 June 1971 [1971] ECR 487.

1079 "This Court holds that the mere fact that an undertaking in a dominant position acquires an exclusive licence does not per se constitute abuse within the meaning

place the owner in a dominant position. It may, however, be an important factor in determining whether the owner can impede effective competition, and in certain circumstances the intellectual property rights concerned may be of such importance for competition on the market that their possession alone comes close to conferring dominance. Intellectual property-related conduct that has been found to fall foul of Article 102 typically falls into four categories:

- the acquisition of a licence by a firm in a dominant position which would strengthen that dominance;[1080]
- the application of abusive terms in granting a licence, including excessive or predatory pricing, tying ("bundling") one product or service to another so as to foreclose a market from competitors,[1081] discriminating between licensees

---

of Article 86. For the purpose of applying Article 86, the circumstances surrounding the acquisition, and in particular its effects on the structure of competition in the relevant market, must be taken into account." Case T-51/89, *Tetra Pak Rausing SA v. Commission*, 10 July 1990 [1990] ECR II-309, para. 23.

1080 In *Tetra Pak,* the General Court held that Tetra Pak had abused its dominant position on the market for aseptic milk cartons and filling machinery by acquiring its competitor and, with it, an exclusive licence to a patented new technology. It is important to note, however, that the mere fact of dominant firm acquiring a patent will not in itself infringe Article 102. The application of Article 102 must be looked at in the light of all the circumstances, particularly the effect on the structure of the market as a whole: in Tetra Pak, the firm held a 90% share of the market and the acquisition would have prevented a new competitor from entering the market. Case T-51/89, *Tetra Pak Rausing SA v. Commission*, 10 July 1990 [1990] ECR II-309. See also *Heinisch/Woodgate*: EU Intellectual property transactions.

1081 Both the 1984 IBM case and the Commission's January 2008 investigation (and 2009 decision) against Microsoft provide examples of the tying which the Commission finds contrary to Article 102. In the IBM case, the Commission objected, among other things, to IBM's practice of only selling mainframe processors (CPUs) with memory included, a practice known as "memory bundling" - thereby "tying" the purchase of one product to another product as part of an IP licence. 4/233/EEC: Commission Decision of 18 April 1984 relating to a proceeding under Article 85 of the EEC Treaty (IV/30.849 - *IBM personal computer*) (OJ L 118, 04.05.1984). In the Microsoft decision, the Commission found illegal tying of various software products (in particular, Microsoft's Internet Explorer) with its dominant Windows operating system. Summary of Commission Decision of 16 December 2009 relating to a proceeding under Article 102 of the Treaty on the Functioning of the European Union and Article 54 of the EEA Agreement (Case COMP/39.530 - *Microsoft (Tying)*) (OJ C 36, 13.2.2010).

without objective justification, or applying unreasonable license terms and conditions;
- discriminatory refusal to licence;[1082] and
- the misuse of a patent[1083] which was obtained in an anti-competitive way either by making misrepresentations to patent offices or by otherwise playing the rules.

6.5 Chapter Observations

(a) EU Principles & Goals: Competitive Market

Robust application and enforcement of the free movement of goods and competition principles in the EU are seen as an instrument to attain a wider objective

1082 Case 238/87, *Volvo AB v Erik Veng (UK) Ltd.*, 5 October 1988 [1988] ECR 6211. Although the Court held that held that the right to *prevent* third parties from manufacturing and importing products incorporating Volvo's intellectual property rights constituted the very subject matter of those rights, the following *could* constitute an abuse: (i) an arbitrary refusal to supply spare parts to independent repairers; (ii) the charging of unfair prices; or (iii) a decision no longer to produce spare parts for a particular model even though many cars of that model are still in circulation.

1083 Patent misuse is a known defense in the U.S., frequently used in patent litigation. Although a patent might be valid and infringed, the patent holder might be prevented from asserting its patent if the patent was obtained by breaching antitrust laws or by illegally extending the term of the patent. In the EU, the Commission and the CJEU have confirmed that a dominant undertaking may not use regulatory procedures in such a way as to prevent or make more difficult entry of competitors on the market, unless it can, as an undertaking engaged in competition on the merits, rely on grounds relating to the defense of legitimate interests or on objective justifications. In June 2005, the Commission announced that it had fined AstraZeneca EUR60 million for breach of Article 102 due to misuse of the patent system by blocking or delaying market access for generic versions of Losec, which at that time was the world's best-selling prescription medicine, and preventing parallel imports of Losec. The CJEU (Case C-457/10 P) confirmed that AstraZeneca had abused its dominant position by making misleading representations to patent offices. In 2009, the Commission identified the misuse of the patent and licensing systems as a potential issue of concern in its 2009 sector inquiry into the pharmaceuticals sector. The Commission found that originator drug companies were using a number of methods (including patent filing strategies) to extend the commercial life of their medicines and to prevent or delay the entry of generics. *European Commission*: Press Release IP/05/737.

– i.e., market integration.[1084] The goal of the laws is thus both to achieve the highest degree of competition as possible,[1085] while at the same time creating a fully integrated *union* of Member States,[1086] providing consumers with the benefits of a free market system.[1087]

Although the Commission has stated that consumer welfare is an important factor in its enforcement activities,[1088] it is the *not* the exclusive or overriding goal. Instead, a *competitive market process* is deemed the priority:[1089] Practices that distort competition or establish barriers between Member States are prohibited – even if they are reasonable:[1090] "exclusionary conduct which maintains, creates or strengthens a market position approaching that of a monopoly can normally not be justified on the grounds that it also creates efficiency gains."[1091] Hence, even though consumer welfare may be enhanced (e.g., through efficiency gains) or not at all affected, the Commission focuses on the "special responsibility" of a dominant undertaking "not to allow its conduct to impair genuine undistorted

---

1084 Spencer Weber Waller has noted that "In part, EC competition law must play the role that the commerce clause and the supremacy clause played in the United States in creating a true community-wide market in which to have competition at all." *Waller*: Understanding and Appreciating EC Competition Law, p. 55.

1085 *Bartenbach*: Patentlizenz- und Know-how-Vertrag, p. 194.

1086 *Waller*: Neo-Realism and the International Harmonization of Law, pp. 584-85.

1087 *European Commission*: Making Markets Work Better.

1088 "The aim of the Commission's enforcement activity … is to ensure that dominant undertakings do not impair effective competition by foreclosing their competitors in an anti-competitive way, thus having an adverse impact on consumer welfare". Commission Notice: Guidance on the Commission's enforcement priorities in applying Article 82 of the EC Treaty to abusive exclusionary conduct by dominant undertakings (OJ C 45/7, 24.2.2009), para. 19.

1089 "Articles 81 and 82 of the Treaty have as their objective the protection of competition on the market." Regulation No 1/2003 (OJ L 1/1, 4.1.2003) p. 1–25, para 9.

1090 "The objective of Article 101 is to ensure that undertakings do not use agreements – in this context, vertical agreements – to restrict competition on the market to the detriment of consumers. Assessing vertical restraints is also important in the context of the wider objective of achieving an integrated internal market. Market integration enhances competition in the European Union. Companies should not be allowed to re-establish private barriers between Member States where State barriers have been successfully abolished." VRBE Guidelines (OJ C 130/1, 19.05.2010), para. 7.

1091 Commission Notice: Guidance on the Commission's enforcement priorities in applying Article 82 of the EC Treaty to abusive exclusionary conduct by dominant undertakings (OJ C 45/7, 24.2.2009), para. 30.

competition"[1092] and emphasizes that "what really matters is protecting an effective competitive process."[1093]

(b) Intellectual Property Rights: Additional Challenges

Intellectual property rights present additional challenges in the EU, given its goal to achieve a single, integrated economy.[1094] EU courts have to balance the conflicting national (and inherently territorial nature of)[1095] intellectual property rights with the fundamental EU principles of an integrated market, as well as reconcile the various derogations and prohibitions of the Treaty provisions.[1096] The lack of harmonized national rules means that the exercise of intellectual property rights can constitute a significant barrier to inter-state trade, which fundamentally contradicts with the free movement of such goods and open competition within the internal EU market.[1097]

1092 *Id.*, para. 1.

1093 *Id.*, para. 6.

1094 Richard Gilbert, Deputy Assistant Attorney General in the Antitrust Division of the DOJ has observed that, unlike EU competition laws, "US antitrust laws apply to interstate commerce, but do not have the promotion of interstate trade as a specific objective." *Gilbert*: Converging Doctrines? US and EU Antitrust Policy, p. 13.

1095 In contrast to the U.S., territorial restrictions in the EU "are paid more attention to because of the additional market integration objective which EC competition policy has." *Lowe*: Current Issues of EU Competition Law, p. 583.

1096 For a recent example of this, see Case C-466/12, *Nils Svensson, Sten Sjögren, Madelaine Sahlman, Pia Gadd v Retreiver Sverige AB*, decision dated 13 February 2014, in which the CJEU held that the EU single market principle trumps the right by Member States to implement more restrictive copyright laws. The case, a request for a preliminary ruling from the Swedish court of appeal (*Svea hovrätt*) lodged on 18 October 2012, centered on whether links on a website to copyrighted content constitute an act of "communication to the public" that would require authorization from the rights holder. The CJEU answered the copyright issue in the negative: publically accessible weblinks should not require authorization. Although a Member State had the right to change its law to require authorization (i.e., by giving wider rights to copyright owners to prohibit a link), "the Member State must refrain from adopting" a measure "which appears to be contrary to Union law." (para. 39). In essence: "Any national protections that harm the bloc's internal market are illegal." *Franklin*: EU single market trumps treaty rights in copyright.

1097 "The national rules relating to the protection of industrial property have not yet been unified within the Community. In the absence of such unification, the national character of the protection of industrial property and the variations between the different legislative systems on this subject are capable of creating obstacles

Thus the U.S. and the EU face different challenges when confronted with situations where intellectual property and competition collide. Given its integrated economy, the U.S. has tended – or had the leisure – to adopt a more "hands-off" approach to situations where the existence or exercise of intellectual property rights restrict competition.[1098] In general, the U.S. tends to adopt a more *consumer welfare* perspective: its aim is "to protect the *public* from the failure of the market".[1099]

With its overarching goal of achieving a single, integrated economy, the EU has been quicker to intervene in situations where intellectual property and competition collide and see a wide scope for competition intervention and have been much more active in addressing the consequences of what they see as imperfect intellectual property laws.[1100] The inherently national rights protecting intellectual property can directly undermine the single market objective. Hence, a more interventionist approach in the face of any activity that is found to restrict competition is deemed necessary.[1101] The EU's competition policy has focused more

---

both to the free movement of the patented products and to competition within the Common Market." *Parke, Davis and Co. v Probel, Reese, Beintema-Interpharm and Centrafarm*, Case 24/67, 29 February 1968, ECR 55, p. 71. In *Deutsche Grammophon v. Metro*, the CJEU held that arbitrary discrimination would arise if states were able to partition the market on national lines through the use of intellectual property rights. Case 78-70, *Deutsche Grammophon Gesellschaft mbH v Metro-SB-Großmärkte GmbH & Co. KG*, 8 June 1971 [1971] ECR 487, para 12.

1098 The current approach in the U.S. treats intellectual property rights "as having primacy within their established boundaries, and relegates antitrust to the role of policing departures from those boundaries". *Lemley*: A New Balance Between IP and Antitrust, p. 255.

1099 *Spectrum Sports, Inc. v. McQuillan*, 506 U.S. 447, 458 (1993) (emphasis mine).

1100 For an obvious example, consider the Microsoft cases. The U.S. found Microsoft had not infringed the antitrust laws by refusing to license. See United States v. Microsoft Corp., 147 F.3d 935, 949-50 (D.C. Cir. 1998). The CJEU found an abuse of dominance because of the foreclosures and the violation of the principle of openness. CITE EU CASE. See also *Fox*: Monopolization and Dominance, pp. 1014–15 (1986) for a description of U.S./EU clash in the IBM case.

1101 EU competition law "prohibits agreements that limit trade between Member States" whereas "US antitrust laws apply to interstate commerce, but do not have the promotion of interstate trade as a specific objective." *Gilbert*: Converging Doctrines? US and EU Antitrust Policy, p. 13. Philip Lowe, Director General of DG Competition at the European Commission, has noted that the EU competition policy (in comparison to the US) has "the additional market integration objective". See *Lowe*: Current Issues of EU Competition Law, p. 583.

from the perspective of the *competitive market*, taking a more interventionist approach to monitor, protect, and influence the workings of the market to achieve and maintain an integrated economy.

Many recent cases, which have involved a direct conflict between intellectual property rights and competition laws, have included remedies which deprive the right holders of exclusivity either by imposing licensing obligations or by limiting their ability to enforce their rights.[1102] Some have argued that the Commission's position creates a serious risk of over-enforcement and the focus on open market access lacks some balance.[1103]

The EU's efforts to improve the effectiveness of its competition policy and at enhancing its real impact in opening and maintaining competitive markets is "a goal that we must achieve to ensure that the European Union is able to cope with two major and immediate challenges, namely to guarantee that business and authorities are able to operate under the same competition policy constraints in the enlarged European Union and to make European markets more open and competitive in order to foster sustainable growth."[1104]

1102 Commission Decision in COMP/37.507 – Generics/AstraZeneca (2005), Case T-201/04, *Microsoft Corp. v Commission*, 17 September 2007 [2007] ECR II-3601. See *Czapracka*: Intellectual Property and the Limits of Antitrust, pp. vii–viii.

1103 *Czapracka*: Intellectual Property and the Limits of Antitrust, pp. 87, 90–91.

1104 *Lowe*: Current Issues of EU Competition Law, pp. 583–84.

7. Commercial Boundaries: Significance & Strategies

7.1 Interim Summary

(a) Trademarks – Competition – Collision

Chapters 1–3 focused on trademarks. They looked at the historical uses and functions of trademarks, the principles of commerce and unfair competition underlying their protection, and the legal framework which developed in both the U.S. and the EU to ensure their protection. The function of trademarks in our society today has changed significantly: what began as an original means of source identification intended to protect both producers (from free riding by competitors) and consumers (from confusion or fraudulent trade practices) has expanded significantly. Today, trademarks represent a profitable and commercially powerful means by which companies communicate a wealth of information regarding their *business* as an *enterprise* – i.e., its social personality and commercial character – sometimes completely disassociated from the underlying *products* that are being sold. Trademarks today are big money, big business, competitive assets.

With any exercise (and certainly with any expansion) of rights, concerns regarding the anti-competitive effects of such rights are raised. Even if additional rights are granted under the rationale of *promoting* competition, such expanded rights can serve to *restrict* competition. As a result, although trademarks act as important aids to competition (by prohibiting free-riding) and benefit consumers (by decreasing confusion and preventing fraudulent trade practices), their commercial dominance in the global market today, coupled with the expanding legal protections afforded under current laws, can have the effect of restraining free and fair trade.

Competition laws seek to minimize or prohibit anti-competitive effects which arise from the acquisition, exploitation, or enforcement of power in the market. Chapters 4–6 thus explored the collision of intellectual property and competition laws in order to review how the granting of exclusive rights under intellectual property laws directly or indirectly conflicts with the restrictions on monopoly and monopolistic behaviour underlying competition rules. In particular, Chapter 5 (for the U.S.) and Chapter 6 (for the EU) analyzed how the antitrust rules in the U.S. and the competition rules in the EU have been applied to the obtainment, grant, acquisition, and exercise of intellectual property rights – in particular with respect to trademarks – to determine whether the application of competition laws to the exercise of trademark rights has been successful to combat the anti-competitive effects of trademark use and protection. These chapters also highlighted the political and social frameworks which shaped the development of antitrust and competition laws, and looked at how such laws have been and are applied to promote and maintain "fair" market competition by regulating anti-competitive conduct.

Chapters 5 and 6 made a few observations: first, that because the U.S. and the EU face different challenges, the U.S. has tended (or has had the leisure) to adopt a more "hands-off" approach to situations where the existence or exercise of intellectual property rights restrict competition. In contrast, the EU has been quicker to intervene in situations where intellectual property and competition collide. The difference in approach can be attributed to the political and social priorities that have shaped both the development and application of the laws: specifically, the U.S. has long enjoyed the benefits of an integrated economy, as a result of which, a more "hands-off" approach can be taken. The EU still strives to achieve a single, integrated economy. The inherently national rights protecting intellectual property can directly undermine the single market objective, and thus a more interventionist approach in the face of any activity that is found to restrict competition is deemed appropriate.

Chapters 5 and 6 further observed that the U.S. tends to adopt a more *consumer welfare* perspective: its aim is "to protect the *public* from the failure of the market". By comparison, the EU's competition policy has focused more from the perspective of the *competitive market*, taking a more interventionist approach to monitor, protect, and influence the workings of the market.

(b) Trademarks' Commercial and Legal Boundaries

With this background, Chapter 7 highlights the particular conundrum with respect to the anti-competitive effects of trademarks from the perspective of their expanding commercial boundaries. Chapter 8 will analyze trademarks' legal boundaries.

Trademarks act as "aids to the exchange of commodities … considered … vitally important to the protection of commerce"[1105] and "undistorted competition".[1106] Commerce – and the protection of competition – lies at the heart of trademark

1105 *Trade-Mark Cases*, 100 U.S. 82 (1879), Syllabus at 10.

1106 Case C-10/89, *SA CNL-SUCAL NV v HAG GF AG*, 17 October 1990 [1990] ECR I-3711 (*HAG II*), para. 13.

protection. As the commercial significance and economic value of trademarks have grown, so too the tactics by trademark owners to protect that value – as sovereign, absolute property. Trademarks are increasingly equated with property or with their intellectual property brethren – patents, copyrights, and trade secrets – when questions regarding protection arise. However, the laws protecting patents, copyrights, and trade secrets, as well as real property, are grounded in significantly different legal theories based on different rationales and policies. Furthermore, the laws protecting patents, copyrights, and trade secrets have different types of limits and restrictions built into their scope (e.g., limited duration), which trademark protection does not. Trademarks, and the history and development of trademark protection, therefore fit uneasily into the principles, rationales, and natural balance of interests underlying the granting of patents and copyrights.

Moreover, how trademarks are used today – and how trademark owners employ aggressive commercial and litigation strategies to protect their trademarks – have different consequences and different challenges for the legal systems to address. In fact, the rise of so-called "trademark bullies" is significantly changing the landscape of competition *outside* of the courts' or authorities' control. These factors are important to keep in mind, in particular in understanding how we have failed to address the anti-competitive effects of trademark ownership and use.

7.2 Intellectual Property Rights: Creativity v. Commerce

(a) The Intellectual Property Umbrella

Patents, copyrights, and trademarks – as well as an increasing list of other rights – are all referred to as "intellectual property". However, the umbrella term is deceiving, as trademarks stand apart from their intellectual property brethren in a number of ways.[1107] These differences – although potentially immaterial on

1107 For a contrary view, see *Barnes*: A New Economics of Trademarks. "According to conventional wisdom, trademark law has no theoretical or practical connection to copyright and patent law.... This article takes issue with the common assumptions that trademarks, unlike expressions and innovations, are private rather than public goods, that there is no market failure in the private provision of source-indicating devices, and that trademark law is fundamentally different from copyright and patent law. It argues that because trademark owners contribute to the store of information available for all people to use, their efforts are more similar to the efforts of authors and inventors than is generally recognized." *Id.* at 22 and 24.

some levels – are material when it comes to understanding trademarks, when discussing the pros and cons of "intellectual property" rights, when making generalizations about the principles underlying their rights or restrictions, and – most importantly – when attempting to develop legal and policy strategies applicable to their use. Specifically, generalizations or analyses applied to "intellectual property" rights are often not suited to trademarks.

The prevalent modern standardization of the term has been traced to the World Intellectual Property Organization (WIPO), whose founding Convention in 1967 defined the term "intellectual property" to include "rights resulting from intellectual activity in the industrial, scientific, literary or artistic fields."[1108] Since then, WIPO has provided a further nuance to this definition, explaining that intellectual property is actually divided into two categories: Industrial property, which includes inventions (patents), trademarks, industrial designs, and geographic indications of source; and Copyright, which includes literary and artistic works such as novels, poems and plays, films, musical works, artistic works such as drawings, paintings, photographs and sculptures, and architectural designs.[1109]

(b) Foundations of Legal Protection & Historical Perspectives

As noted in Chapter 2, the U.S. Constitution grants Congress the right to protect discoveries and writings pursuant to Article I, Section 8, Clause 8 (the Patent and Copyright Clause).[1110] The clause contains *no* specific language regarding trademarks. In declaring the first U.S. trademark statutes invalid for having been improperly based on this clause, the U.S. Supreme Court reasoned that trademarks – lacking creative and inventive qualities – were to be treated differently from patents and copyrights:

> "The ordinary trade-mark has no necessary relation to invention or discovery. ... It is often the result of accident rather than design. ... If we should endeavor to classify it

---

1108 Convention Establishing the World Intellectual Property Organization, July 14, 1967, art. 2(viii), 6 I.L.M. 782, 784. According to Mark Lemley, since WIPO's promulgation of the term, numerous groups such as the American Patent Law Association and the ABA Section on Patent, Trademark, and Copyright Law have changed their names (to the American Intellectual Property Law Association and the ABA Section on Intellectual Property Law, respectively). *Lemley*: Property, Intellectual Property, and Free Riding, fn. 4.

1109 *WIPO*: What is Intellectual Property?

1110 "Congress shall have Power... To promote the Progress of Science and useful Arts, by securing for limited Times to Authors and Inventors the exclusive Right to their respective Writings and Discoveries". U.S. Constitution, Article 1 § 8 cl. 8.

under the head of writings of authors, the objections are equally strong. In this, as in regard to inventions, originality is required. And while the word writings may be liberally construed, … it is only such as are original, and are founded in the creative powers of the mind. The writings which are to be protected are the fruits of intellectual labor, embodied in the form of books, prints, engravings and the like."[1111]

Constitutional authority to regulate trademarks was finally based on Article I, Section 8, Clause 3 (the Commerce Clause), which granted Congress the specific, enumerated right "To regulate Commerce".[1112] In sum, constitutional protection of trademarks in the U.S. is based on the regulation of *commerce*: a trademark, unlike a patent and copyright, does not "depend upon novelty, invention, discovery, or any work of the brain. It requires no fancy or imagination, no genius, no laborious thought. It is simply founded on *priority of appropriation*."[1113]

Similarly in the EU, trademarks were initially regarded as different from other intellectual property rights, in particular in comparison to patents. In his Opinion in *Sirena Srl v Eda Srl* in 1971,[1114] Advocate General Dutheillet de Lamothe noted that:

"Both from the economic and from the human point of view the interests protected by patent legislation merit greater respect than those protected by trade marks."[1115]

Although the situation changed – in his influential 1990 opinion in *HAG II*, Advocate General Jacobs was highly critical of these earlier, disparaging views[1116] – the U.S. and the EU both saw trademarks as inferior rights to patents and copyrights: trademark protection was based on principles of unfair competition – appropriation, false or misleading practices, etc. – whereas patent and copyright protection was based on the more lofty principles of encouraging contributions of inventions and writings to the public domain.

(c) Rationales for Protection

Patent and copyright law recognize *near absolute rights* in inventors and authors for a *limited term*. Such rights are justified by an *incentive* or *reward* rationale

1111 *Trade-Mark Cases*, 100 U.S. 82, 94 (1879).

1112 U.S. Constitution, Article 1 § 8 cl. 3.

1113 *Trade-Mark Cases*, 100 U.S. 82, 94 (1879) (emphasis mine).

1114 Case 40/70, *Sirena S.r.l. v Eda S.r.l. and others*, 18 February 1971 [1971] ECR 69.

1115 Case 40/70, *Sirena S.r.l. v Eda S.r.l. and others*, [1971] ECR 69, Opinion of AG Lamothe, 21 January 1971.

1116 Case C-10/89, *SA CNL-SUCAL NV v HAG GF AG*, [1990] ECR I-3711 (*HAG II*), Opinion of AG Jacobs, 13 March 1990, para. 18.

for the innovation and creativity which such protection promotes.[1117] The main purpose of patent and copyright protection is *to benefit and enrich the public* at large. Inventors and authors are granted exclusive rights for a specified period of time; thereafter such inventions and writings become part of the public domain, accessible by all. The exclusive rights are granted in the short term with the *expectation* that the public will be rewarded with the release of such inventive and creative works in the long term.

In contrast, the protection of trademarks concentrates on *commerce* rather than creativity. The main purpose of trademark law is *to protect consumers* by indicating source thereby *facilitating the smooth functioning of the marketplace.*[1118] In essence, "while the law of patents and copyright is largely concerned with incentivizing contributions to the marketplace of ideas, trademark law concerns itself exclusively with the marketplace."[1119] The result is protection of "the integrity of the marketplace by preventing deceptions".[1120] Understanding this difference – the stimulation of commerce rather than creativity – is important in understanding the difference in protection and the legal framework in which such rights have developed.

In the U.S., the primary purpose underlying patent and copyright protection has been about "generating *incentives* to create."[1121] As scholars have noted: "The principal basis for intellectual property protection in the United States is the utilitarian or economic incentive framework."[1122] As the U.S. Constitution sets forth, the rationale behind granting authors and inventors exclusive rights to their writings and discoveries is "to promote the progress of science and the useful arts".[1123] Although the provision was hotly debated by the founding fathers,[1124] it was included, with the primary goal to benefit the public once those writings and discoveries entered the public domain.[1125] Hence, the provision was drafted

1117 *McClure*: Trademarks and Unfair Competition, p. 307 and fn. 11, citing *Kaysen/Turner*: Antitrust Policy, pp. 160–68; and *Demsetz*: Industry Structure, Market Rivalry, and Public Policy, p. 3.

1118 *Barnes*: A New Economics of Trademarks, pp. 22–23. See also *Lastowka*: Trademark's Daemons, p. 781, fn. 8.

1119 *Katyal*: Trademark Intersectionality, p. 1614.

1120 *Lemley/McKenna*: Owning Mark(et)s, p. 143.

1121 *Lemley*: Property, Intellectual Property, and Free Riding.

1122 *Hovenkamp/Janis/Lemley/Leslie*: IP and Antitrust, § 1.1 at pp. 1–2.

1123 U.S. Constitution, Article 1 § 8 cl. 8.

1124 See *Walterscheid*: Defining the Patent & Copyright Term, pp. 347–356.

1125 "The sole interest of the United States and the primary object in conferring the [copyright] monopoly lie in the general benefits derived by the public from the

to include both an incentive for the inventor or author (by granting them exclusive rights), as well as an assurance that the public domain would benefit (by restricting the right to a limited period of time).[1126]

EU case law has similarly maintained that *rewarding* the inventor or author is an essential aspect under the patent and copyright laws. With respect to patent rights, the CJEU said that: "the substance of a patent right lies essentially in according the inventor an exclusive right of first placing the product on the market. That right of first placing a product on the market enable the inventor, by allowing him a monopoly in exploiting his product, to obtain the reward for his creative effort without, however, guaranteeing that he will obtain such a reward in all circumstances."[1127] With respect to copyright, the CJEU specified that the essential function of a copyright "is to protect the moral rights in the work and ensure a reward for the creative effort."[1128] In *Warner Brothers v. Chistriansen*, the

---

labors of authors." *Fox Film Corp. v. Doyal*, 286 U.S. 123, 127 (1932). "The ... privileges that Congress may authorize are neither unlimited nor primarily designed to provide a special private benefit. Rather, the limited grant is a means by which an important public purpose may be achieved. It is intended to motivate the creative activity of authors and inventors by the provision of a special reward, and to allow the public access to the products of their genius after the limited period of exclusive control has expired." *Sony Corporation of America v. Universal City Studios, Inc.*, 464 U.S. 417, 429 (1984). "The... goal of the Copyright Clause is to ensure that works enter the public domain after an author's rights, exclusive, but limited, have expired. ... The public is protected in two ways: the grant of a copyright encourages authors to create new works ... and the limitation ensures that the works will eventually enter the public domain, which protects the public's right of access and use. ... The primary objective of copyright is not to reward the labor of authors, but 'to promote the Progress of Science and useful Arts.'" *Suntrust Bank v. Houghton Mifflin Co.*, 268 F.3d 1257, 1262 (11th Cir. 2001).

1126 For an insightful analysis of the incentive-assurance concept applied to database protection, see *Blanke*: Vincent Van Gogh.

1127 Case 187/80, *Merck & Co. Inc. v Stephar BV and Petrus Stephanus Exler*, 14 July 1981 [1981] ECR 2063, paras. 9-10; re-iterated in Case 19/84, *Pharmon BV v Hoechst AG*, 9 July 1985 [1985] ECR 2281, para. 26: "As the Court held most recently in its judgement of 14 July 1981 (*Merck v. Stephar*), the substance of a patent right lies essentially in according the inventor an exclusive right of first placing the product on the market so as to allow him to obtain the reward for his creative effort."

1128 Case T-70/89, *British Broadcasting Corporation and BBC Enterprises Ltd v Commission*, 10 July 1991 [1991] ECR II-535, para. 58.

CJEU held that the grant of exclusive rights to an author are necessary in order to guarantee a satisfactory remuneration.[1129]

Trademark law, unlike copyright and patent law, however, was never intended to provide incentives or rewards to promote the sciences or creative contributions to the public domain.[1130] The dominant justification for trademark protection has continued to be the protection and stimulation of commerce either on behalf of the trademark owner (against free riding) or the consumer (to assist in identifying a single source, reducing search costs, and deterring being misled by fraudulent or deceptive trade practices).[1131]

Hence, whether defined as an *ex ante* incentive or *ex post* reward,[1132] patent and copyright laws (and even trade secret laws)[1133] in both the U.S. and the EU

1129 Case 158/86, *Warner Brothers Inc. and Metronome Video ApS v Erik Viuff Christiansen*, 17 May 1988 [1988] ECR 2605, paras. 13–16. In the *Warner Brothers* case, the Court found exclusive rights of performance and reproduction distinct to guarantee rights to makers of films in the rental market which was deemed distinct from the sales market and the size of which – owing to developments in technology – offered great potential as a source of revenue.

1130 Many have derided the creativity or inventiveness of "creating" a trademark. The U.S. Supreme Court noted a trademark does not "depend upon novelty, invention, discovery, or any work of the brain. It requires no fancy or imagination, no genius, no laborious thought." *Trade-Mark Cases*, 100 U.S. 82, 93–94 (1879).

1131 See *Landes/Posner*: Trademark Law: An Economic Perspective (discussing trademark law from an economic perspective). In *Dastar Corp. v. Twentieth Century Fox Film Corp.*, 539 U.S. 23, 32 (2003), the Supreme Court noted that trademark infringement "deceives consumers and impairs a producer's goodwill". In *Two Pesos, Inc. v. Taco Cabana, Inc.*, 505 U.S. 763, 773 (1992), the Supreme Court noted that the purpose of trademark protection is "preventing deception and unfair competition".

1132 Scholars have noted that the U.S. (and most common law countries) take an *ex ante* perspective (an incentive to encourage investment) whereas most civil law countries favour an *ex post* perspective (as a reward for creative effort). *Korah*: Intellectual Property Rights and the EC Competition Rules, p. 2. Both rationales lead to a similar policy (i.e., in the granting and protection of intellectual property rights), but the different view points give insight into the legislative undercurrents that apply with respect to intellectual property rights. For further discussion, see *Lemley*: Ex Ante Versus Ex Post Justifications.

1133 Broadly speaking, trade secret law protects certain types of information, provided that: (i) it is not generally known; (ii) such information has been reasonably protected to prevent disclosure; and (iii) the information was wrongfully acquired by another – i.e., that the information was misappropriated. Use of a trade secret belonging to another does not, however, always constitute misappropriation. Trade

consciously strike a *balance* between establishing an incentive/reward for inventors and authors with the expectation of later dissemination of such works into the public domain.[1134] Trademark laws instead balance society's interest in *free* competition against its interest in *fair* competition.[1135]

(d) Scope of Rights & Protectable Subject Matter

In order to obtain protection, patents, copyrights, and even trade secrets require a certain threshold of ingenuity (for patents), originality (for copyrights), and economic advantage (for trade secrets). Meeting this threshold is part of the public interest balancing equation: where such threshold is met, the limited exclusive rights are granted; where not met, no exclusive rights are granted or protected.

Under the patent laws in the U.S. and Germany (and mirrored in the standards promulgated by the EPC and WIPO), an invention must meet several strict criteria in order to be eligible for patent protection. These include, most significantly, that: (i) the invention must consist of patentable subject matter;[1136] (ii) it

---

secrets may be obtained by lawful (or "proper") means such as independent discovery, reverse engineering, and inadvertent disclosure resulting from the trade secret holder's failure to take reasonable protective measures. Trade secret law thus also balances protection with disclosure.

1134 *Denicola*: Institutional Publicity Rights, p. 627: "The patent and copyright statutes are elaborately crafted to balance the concern for incentive... with the interest in dissemination and efficiency."

1135 *Klieger*: Trademark Dilution, pp. 864–866. However, as will be noted later, the ongoing expansion of trademark rights – in the absence of any evidence of consumer confusion – has distorted the original balance inherent in trademark law.

1136 Under U.S. patent law, patentable subject matter is "any new and useful process, machine, manufacture, or composition of matter, or any new and useful improvement thereof". 35 U.S.C. § 101. As set out in the Supreme Court's 1980 decision, *Diamond v. Chakrabarty*, 447 U.S. 303 (1980), Chief Justice Warren E. Burger, writing for the majority, clarified the interpretation of this definition with his famous words that patentable subject matter covered "anything under the sun that is made by man." He found that Congress, in using the broad language of "any new... manufacture, or composition of matter", contemplated that the patent laws would be given wide scope, and cautioned that courts "should not read into the patent laws limitations and conditions which the legislature has not expressed", citing *United States v. Dubilier Condenser Corp*, 289 U.S. 178 (1933).
Under the German Patent Act (*Patentgesetz* or *PatG*), an invention is considered to be patentable it if comprises a technical teaching. PatG § 1(1). BGH 27 March 1969, X ZB 15/67, GRUR 1969, 672 – *Rote Taube*; EPO T 1173/97, ABl. 1999, 609 – Computerprogrammproduckt I. Unlike U.S. law, there is no defined list of what

must be industrially applicable (useful);[1137] (iii) it must be new (novel);[1138] (iv) it must exhibit a sufficient "inventive step" (be non-obvious);[1139] and (iv) the disclosure of the invention in the patent application must meet certain standards as to permit reproduction of the process or invention (enablement).[1140]

---

the invention might cover (e.g., that it be a "process, machine, manufacture, or composition of matter").
The European Patent Convention (EPC) does not provide any positive guidance on what should be considered an invention for the purposes of patent law. Article 52(1) EPC states that patents shall be granted "for any inventions, in all fields of technology." Article 52(2) EPC then provides a non-exhaustive list of what are *not* to be regarded as inventions, and therefore not patentable subject matter: "The following in particular shall not be regarded as inventions within the meaning of paragraph 1: (a) discoveries, scientific theories and mathematical methods; (b) aesthetic creations; (c) schemes, rules and methods for performing mental acts, playing games or doing business, and programs for computers; (d) presentations of information."

1137 Under U.S. law, the second requirement for patentability is that the patentable subject matter is useful (known as the "utility" requirement). 35 U.S.C. § 101). Under German law and the EPC, an invention is considered to be patentable it if comprises is susceptible of industrial application (PatG 5(1) and EPC Art. 57).

1138 Under U.S. law, novelty is set out in 35 U.S.C. § 102 (which distinguishes between "novelty" and "statutory bars to patentability"). In contrast to the U.S. system, under German law and in accordance with the EPC, there is a requirement of "absolute" novelty (PatG § 3, EPC Art. 54). In examining novelty, the claimed invention is deemed new if it differs from each respective piece of prior art in at least one feature. Scholars have noted that the standards for determining novelty applied by the German Patent Court (*Bundespatentgericht*) and the German Federal Constitutional Court (*Bundesverfassungsgerichts*) and those applied by the European Patent Office differ. See *Klett/Sonntag/Wilske*: Intellectual Property Law in Germany, p. 5.

1139 Under U.S. law, non-obviousness is set out in 35 U.S.C. § 103. Under German law (PatG § 1(1)) and the EPC (EPC Art. 52(1)), an invention is considered to be patentable it if involves an inventive activity (PatG § 4, EPC Art. 56). A German patent must be distinguished from a German utility model (*Gebrauchsmuster*). Utility models are deemed an intellectual property right that, in addition to but separate from patents, will provide protection for technical inventions that are new, involve an inventive *step* as opposed to an inventive activity (*Gebrauchsmustergesetz, GebrMG*, § 1), and have industrial application. Further formal requirements for patents include the "unity of invention" (PatG § 34(5) and EPC Art. 82). See also *Klett/Sonntag/Wilske*: Intellectual Property Law in Germany, p. 40.

1140 Under U.S. law, the fifth requirement is "enablement", i.e., the patent holder discloses the teaching of the patent in such a way as to "enable" others to use the patent (35 U.S.C. § 112). German patent law and the EPC also include formal

The hurdles are high: mere ideas, motifs, and scientific theories and discoveries are not protected.[1141] As the Supreme Court noted in 1989, "free exploitation of ideas will be the rule, to which the protection of a federal patent is the exception".[1142] Once granted, the period of coverage begins from the date of its issuance and normally expires twenty years from the day (or the day after) the application for the patent was filed.[1143]

Copyright law protects the form of expression of ideas – but not the ideas themselves or the subject matter of such expression.[1144] Like patents, the primary purpose of copyright law is to reward authors for the creation of original works (works where the author has expended independent effort to create the work). The subject matter of copyright protection includes any creation in the literary, scientific, and artistic domain, whatever the mode or form of expression.[1145] For

---

requirements regarding the "sufficiency of disclosure" (PatG § 34(4) and EPC Art. 83).

1141 *Klett/Sonntag/Wilske*: Intellectual Property Law in Germany, p. 60, at n. 8. See also *Schricker/Loewenheim*: Urheberrecht, § 2 n. 38.

1142 *Bonito Boats, Inc. v. Thunder Craft Boats Inc.*, 489 U.S. 141, 151, 156–60 (1989).

1143 35 U.S.C. § 154(a)(2). Previously, the patent term was 17 years from issue. Under German law, patent protection is for twenty years beginning on the day *following* the filing of the patent application. PatG § 16.

1144 "In no case does copyright protection for an original work of authorship extend to any idea, procedure, process, system, method of operation, concept, principle, or discovery." 17 U.S.C. § 102(b). "Copyright does not protect facts, ideas, systems, or methods of operation, although it may protect the way these things are expressed." *U.S. Copyright Office*: What does Copyright Protect? See also *Mazer v. Stein*, 347 U.S. 201, 217 (1954) ("protection is given only to the expression of the idea – not the idea itself").

1145 In the U.S., copyrights and mask works (semiconductors) are both protected under the Copyright Act. (17 U.S.C. § 901 et seq.) In Germany, the Act on Copyright and Related Rights (*Urheberrechtsgesetz* or *UrhG*) protects copyright and related author rights. According to *Klett/Sonntag/Wilske*, copyright law may be the most confusing area of German intellectual property law for foreign lawyers and legal academics, particularly those trained in the Anglo-American legal tradition. Under German law, copyright – and certain moral rights – cannot be transferred by the author like a piece of property; instead, the work remains with the author who can only grant certain rights of use and exploitation. Furthermore, there is no concept of a "work made for hire". *Klett/Sonntag/Wilske*: Intellectual Property Law in Germany, pp. 58–76. Semi-conductor rights are protected under the Act on the Protection of the Topographies of Microelectonric Semiconductor Products (*Halbleiterschutzgesetz* or *HalblSchG*). Protection can last for a period of nearly 11 years (the end date is always December 31 of the respective 10th year after the grant has

a work to enjoy copyright protection, however, it must be original. The ideas in the work do not need to be new but the form – be it literary or artistic – in which they are expressed must be an original creation of the author.[1146] Although copyright law is intended to prevent copying, it does not provide a true monopoly, since it does not matter if a similar or even *identical* work already exists or is later created.[1147] What is protected is the unjustified copying thereof. For this very reason, copyright laws require a lower threshold of originality than under patent laws.

Trade secrets are non-patented practical information, and can include a formula, pattern, compilation, program, device, method, technique or process. To meet the most common definition of a trade secret and be protected by law, the information must be used in business, must give an opportunity to obtain an *economic advantage* over competitors who do not know or use it, and must be confidential and only disclosed in circumstances requiring an obligation of confidence.[1148] The rights that this confers can be enforced against the recipient of such information, or any subsequent third-party recipient of such information.[1149]

---

issued) *HalbSchG* § 5(2). Furthermore, Germany – and Europe – protect databases either specifically as a copyright in the strict sense of the word if an inventive step is included (§ 4(2) UrhG) or under a *sui generis* rights ("neighboring rights" – *Verwandte Schutzrechte*) for compilation or collections of data (§ 87(a)-(e)). This separate protection was introduced in 1997 in order to implement the European Database Directive 96/9/EC of 11 March 1996 (OJ L 77/20, 27.03.1996). Protection lasts 15 years from publication of the database. *Klett/Sonntag/Wilske*: Intellectual Property Law in Germany, p. 69.

1146 See generally *WIPO*: Intellectual Property Handbook, Chapter 2, "Copyright and Related Rights".

1147 U.S. Copyright Law (17 U.S.C. § 102(a) (2006)). German Copyright Law (*Urheberrechtsgesetz* or *UrhG*) protects literary, scientific and artistic works (UrhG § 1) if they constitute personal intellectual creations (UrhG § 2(2)). Such creations do not need to be novel or unique (BGH, 9 May 1985 (I ZR 52/83), GRUR 1985, 1047 – Inkassoprogramm); they need to be creative and individual to the author.

1148 World Trade Organization (WTO) TRIPs, Art 39, § 2 requires member nations to provide a means for protecting information that is secret, commercially valuable because it is secret, and subject to reasonable steps to keep it secret. See also *USPTO*: Patent Trade Secrets.

1149 Mark Lemley has the following to say about trade secrets: "Trade secret law is a puzzle. Courts and scholars have struggled for over a century to figure out why we protect trade secrets. The puzzle is not in understanding what trade secret law covers; there seems to be widespread agreement on the basic contours of the law. Nor

Trademark law, by contrast, recognizes rights *only insofar as necessary* to prevent consumer confusion: "A 'trademark' is not that which is infringed. What is infringed is the right of the public to be free of confusion and the synonymous right of the trademark owner to control his product's reputation."[1150] Trademark laws do not protect the underlying product (what might be covered by a patent), nor any creative aspect of the trademark (protection is not given simply for the invention of an aesthetically superior mark, which design rights might protect). For a trademark to obtain protection it must be distinctive. Distinctive character is evaluated in relation to the goods to which the trademark is applied (e.g., the word "kodak" is not distinctive with respect to the sale of computers, but it is highly distinctive with respect to the sale of cameras). The distinctiveness of a sign is not an absolute and unchangeable factor. The test of whether a trademark is distinctive typically depends on the understanding of the consumers, or at least the persons to whom the sign is addressed. Depending on the steps taken by the user of the sign or third parties, distinctiveness can be acquired or increased or even lost.[1151]

(e) *Existence* versus *Use*

Patents and copyrights protect the inventor's and the author's right to the intellectual property they have created. There is no requirement (at least in the U.S.) that the inventor or author use the protected creation in any manner whatsoever: "the bare fact that the creator has brought the *res* into existence is the reason for its protection."[1152]

---

is the problem that people object to the effects of the law. ... Rather, the puzzle is a theoretical one: no one can seem to agree where trade secret law comes from or how to fit it into the broader framework of legal doctrine. Courts, lawyers, scholars, and treatise writers argue over whether trade secrets are a creature of contract, of tort, of property, or even of criminal law. None of these different justifications has proven entirely persuasive. Worse, they have contributed to inconsistent treatment of the basic elements of a trade secret cause of action and uncertainty as to the relationship between trade secret laws and other causes of action." *Lemley*: The Surprising Virtues of Treating Trade Secrets as IP Rights, p. 311 (citations omitted).

1150 *James Burrough Ltd. v. Sign of the Beefeater, Inc.*, 540 F.2d 266, 274 (7th Cir. 1976), cited by *Klieger*: Trademark Dilution, fn. 441.

1151 See generally *WIPO*: Intellectual Property Handbook, Chapter 2, "Trademarks".

1152 *Carter*: Does It Matter Whether Intellectual Property Is Property?, p. 720.

Trademarks cannot be obtained through discovery or invention alone. Some actual *use* of the trademark – e.g., affixing a label to a good which is sold in commerce – is necessary to establish rights (under common law) or maintain protections: "Neither conception of an idea for a mark, nor solicitation of advertising business constitute use of the trademark sufficient to acquire proprietary rights in the mark."[1153] Rights in a trademark flow from its use, not from its existence.

In essence, there is no "property" in a trademark "apart from the business or trade in connection with which it is employed."[1154] It is only the use of the trademark in conjunction with a good or service – in order to specifically identify the *source* of such goods or services – that is protected.[1155] Trademark laws protect the *function* of the trademark as a signifier; trademark laws do *not* protect the trademark as a stand-alone invention or the underlying trademarked product. As soon as an underlying trademark looses its function to distinguish goods (e.g., it is abandoned or it becomes generic), trademark protection is withdrawn.

7.3 Commercial Power: Predatory Practices (and the Rise of the Trademark Bully)

As the commercial value – and market power – of trademarks has increased, so too the efforts by trademark owners to protect and defend such value. This has resulted in aggressive behavior by trademark owners to enforce and expand the scope of their rights. These predatory, proprietary practices accomplish two things: first, by engaging in litigious and bullying tactics, owners can fully "reap

---

1153 *Gilberto Arvelo v. American International Insurance Company*, 875 F. Supp. 95, at 101 (U.S. District Court for the District of Puerto Rico) (8 February 1995). See also *Dinwoodie/Janis*: Confusion over Use, p 1610: "[A] firm must use a mark (not merely conceive of it) in order to assert rights", cited by *Fromer*: Creativity and the Law, fn. 77.

1154 *Am. Steel Foundries v. Robertson*, 269 U.S. 372, 380 (1926), cited by *Fromer*: Creativity and the Law, p. 1896, fn. 75.

1155 "Rights in a trademark... cannot be obtained through discovery or invention alone. Some actual use of the trademark, such as affixing a label to a good which is sold in commerce, is necessary to establish use. Neither conception of an idea for a mark, nor solicitation of advertising business constitute use of the trademark sufficient to acquire proprietary rights in the mark." (citation omitted). *Arvelo v. Am. Int'l Ins. Co.*, 875 F. Supp. 95, 101 (D.P.R. 1995), cited by *Fromer*: Creativity and the Law, p. 1896, fn. 77.

the benefits" of their legal rights.[1156] Second, such behaviors help carve out a market niche and prohibit competitors entry to that market (through expanded rights afforded to "famous" trademark owners).

Those trademark owners with greater financial resources benefit the most from these strategies.[1157] Aggressive legal bullying (whether inside or outside the court room) will stifle some market participants who lack the financial resources or business savvy to fight back; over-the-top advertising to encourage "famous" mark status encourages market entry barriers and closes off market segments (e.g., ancillary markets) from new competition.[1158]

(a) Aggressive Policing and Over-Enforcement of Rights

Although the increased commercial significance (and parallel increased legal protection) of trademarks does not, in and of itself, result in more or abusive litigation by trademark owners, the increased commercial value and parallel expansion of rights has certainly *incentivized* litigious tactics. An owner's trademark rights can be lost through failure to control how third parties are using the trademark (or even similar trademarks).[1159] Trademark owners thus have the burden of ensuring that their trademark does not lose its distinctive element through

---

1156 "An aggressive strategy of trademark enforcement is needed in order to reap the benefits of the legal expansions" available under trademark law. *Grinvald*: Shaming Trademark Bullies, fn. 37.

1157 "Expense, delay, and discovery abuse hurt plaintiffs as well as defendants. This abuse can negatively impact poorer clients even more than wealthier ones." *Subrin*: On Thinking About a Description of a County's Civil Procedure, p. 143. "The effectiveness of lawsuits to silence corporate critics derives in part from the disparity of resources between the plaintiff corporation and the defendant... artist. Corporate plaintiffs with famous marks will usually have large treasuries with which to mount protracted litigation... [and] can claim tax advantages for the legal expenses involved". *Schlosser*: The High Price of (Criticizing) Coffee, p. 948. "Lawsuits ... require enormous expenditures in legal fees, time, and energy, and particularly disadvantage those least able to afford the expense." *Greene*: Abusive Trademark Litigation, p. 613. "An aggressive strategy of trademark enforcement is needed ... larger businesses with the resources to undertake such a strategy are oftentimes the beneficiaries of such expansions." *Grinvald*: Shaming Trademark Bullies, p. 633, fn 38.

1158 See generally *Dreyfuss*: Expressive Genericity: Trademarks as Language in the Pepsi Generation.

1159 *Grinvald*: Shaming Trademark Bullies, p. 640. For an examination of over-enforcement under copyright laws, see *Cotter*: Fair Use and Copyright Overenforcement; and *Gallagher*: Trademark and Copyright Enforcement in the Shadow of IP Law.

third-party (junior) use. In order to do this, trademark owners need to be vigilant in policing the extent to which their trademarks are used in similar product categories, as well as in other categories: "We have an obligation to protect our trademark; otherwise we'd lose it."[1160] As one commentator has noted, "The fear that not bringing a suit now might foreclose or damage interests in bringing suit later may lead to unnecessary litigation."[1161]

The case of the Hard Rock Cafe in Germany demonstrates this trend. In the 1970s, the defendants – admittedly inspired by the Hard Rock Cafe which had opened up in London in June 1971[1162] – opened up a local café in Heidelberg, Germany, called the "Hard Rock Cafe Heidelberg". The defendants copied the well-known circular Hard Rock Cafe logo and, by 1978, were using it on menus, glasses, on the entrance door, and on the windows.[1163] Thereafter, they also started selling merchandise under the Hard Rock Cafe logo and registered domain names which included the words "hardrock-cafe". The plaintiffs (owners of the original Hard Rock Cafe) filed their first trademark for clothing in Germany in 1986 and opened their first German Hard Rock Cafe in Berlin in 1992.[1164] Shortly afterwards, they obtained a preliminary injunction against the defendants, which they withdrew, however, after the defendants appealed.[1165]

After losing their requests for injunction at the district and appeals level proceedings,[1166] the plaintiffs sought recourse with the German Federal High Court (*Bundesgerichtshof*). The BGH confirmed the lower courts' finding that the plaintiffs, in having remained inactive for over 14 years after first objecting to the defendants' use, had *forfeited* their rights with respect to defendants' use of the Hard Rock Cafe logo in the cafe and its operation. However, the BGH noted that the forfeiture only applied to those specific acts of infringement that were tolerated; the forfeiture did not cover *new* acts of infringement, even if similar in

1160 *Evangelista*: Monster Fiercely Protects Its Name, quoting Noel Lee, President, Monster Cable; cited by *Grinvald*: Shaming Trademark Bullies, p. 641 and fn. 94.

1161 *Greene*: Abusive Trademark Litigation, p. 640; cited by *Grinvald*: Shaming Trademark Bullies, p. 641 and fn. 98.

1162 *Hard Rock Cafe International*: London.

1163 See *Bundesgerichtshof*: Press Release Nr. 136/2013, regarding decision dated 15 August 2013, case nr. I ZR 188/11 – Hard Rock Café (decision not yet published).

1164 *Hard Rock Cafe International*: Berlin.

1165 *Ghalamkarizadeh*: Hard Fight for the Hard Rock Cafe – Germany.

1166 Regional Court Mannheim (*Landgericht Mannheim*), decision dated 7 May 2010, case nr. 7 O 275/09; Higher Regional Court Karlsruhe (*Oberlandesgericht Karlsruhe*), decision dated 14 September 2011, case nr. 6 U 94/10.

nature to the previously tolerated acts. Hence, each offer of merchandise, each new advertisement, and each new online presence thus would need to be examined individually. The BGH referred the matter back to the appeals court to review.[1167]

The lesson for "famous" trademark owners is to aggressively police (and enforce) their trademarks, since trademark rights may be forfeited through tolerance. Aggressive policing, however, can quite easily cross the line into bullying, since, "after all, one person's policing is another person's harassment, or worse, abusive trademark litigation."[1168]

(b) Non-Meritorious Litigation

Trademark law effectively protects a producer's investment in a mark's goodwill (by prohibiting free riding by competitors) and reduces consumer confusion and search costs. Unfortunately, both trademark law's widening scope and less-than-clear "likelihood of consumer confusion" infringement standard permit – and even promote – non-meritorious litigation. Owners of trademarks can successfully repress competition in the market by undertaking either or both opportunistic (i.e., weak) lawsuits and/or predatory (i.e., anti-competitive or abusive) lawsuits against more vulnerable entities. "Socially harmful IP litigation is common because the rights are easy to get and potentially apply quite broadly, and the problem is growing worse because of the expansion of the scope and strength of IP law."[1169]

Opportunistic lawsuits – i.e., those with weak or low probability of successfully proving infringement – are all too common, particularly in the U.S. Even if such lawsuits do not "succeed" in the courtroom, they invariably "succeed" outside the courtroom for three primary reasons. First, the probability of success is both vague and inconsistent: the liability standard for trademark infringement "is inherently noisy"; experts submit conflicting opinions about matters relevant to the scope of an intellectual property right; and judges make errors.[1170] Second, even a weak lawsuit may present a credible threat, in particular at the initial

1167 *Ghalamkarizadeh*: Hard Fight for the Hard Rock Cafe – Germany. See also *Hard Rock Cafe International*: Milestone Victory In Trademark And Unfair Competition Dispute.

1168 *Grinvald*: Shaming Trademark Bullies, p. 641, quoting *Desai/Rierson*: Confronting the Genericism Conundrum, p. 1834.

1169 *Meurer*: Controlling Opportunistic and Anti-Competitive Intellectual Property Litigation, p. 510.

1170 *Id.* at 513–514.

phases of a litigation where plaintiffs can more easily bluff a defendant, since the defendant likely does not have all the information it needs.[1171] Finally, a weak lawsuit may be credible because of the costs it may impose on the defendant. A defendant may settle an opportunistic lawsuit to avoid the nuisance of mounting a defense.[1172]

Trademark owners also engage in predatory litigation, primarily to serve several anticompetitive purposes: eliminating competitors, disciplining competitors, raising rivals' costs, or creating barriers to entry.[1173] The difference to opportunistic behaviour is that this type of behaviour is more insidious and abusive. This sort of behaviour could, in fact, be seen as willful maintenance of monopoly power (as distinguished from growth or development as a consequence of a superior product, business acumen, or historic accident) or evidence of anticompetitive, predatory, or unfair conduct designed to achieve monopolization (all prohibited by competition or unfair competition laws).

(c) Aggressive Bullying Tactics *Outside* of the Courtroom

While over-active legal strategies *inside* courtrooms have increased (through over-policing and non-meritorious litigation), much enforcement of trademark rights takes place not *inside* a courtroom, but in the everyday practices of intellectual property owners and their lawyers.[1174]

Trademark owners are increasingly using a number of "private enforcement" techniques to bully other trademark uses into submission and thus expand the power and control of their own trademarks. Such uses include sending cease and desist notices and aggressive demand letters over-stating rights or potential remedies.[1175] Others will use the treat of litigation (for example, by sending a *draft*

1171 See generally *Meurer*: The Settlement of Patent Litigation, in which Meurer examines models of patent litigation where plaintiffs with weak claims can essentially "bluff their way to a settlement payment".

1172 *Id.*

1173 *Myers*: Litigation as a Predatory Practice.

1174 *Gallagher*: Trademark and Copyright Enforcement in the Shadow of IP Law, p. 456. *Gibson*: Risk Aversion and Rights Accretion in Intellectual Property Law. *Nathenson*: Civil Procedures.

1175 *Port*: Trademark Extortion, p. 587. Kenneth Port investigates the use of cease-and-desist letters and trademark infringement filings, finding that the objective is primarily not to stop the conduct of the would-be-infringer, but with the objective "to raise the cost of market entrance or continuation for the competitor." *Id.*, p. 589. Port also notes that: "These cases are almost never prosecuted to a conclusion on

legal complaint, with the implied threat to file the same) to deter others. Such tactics "constitute the bulk of IP enforcement efforts in trademark ... practice."[1176] Furthermore, trademark owners have lawyers call an alleged infringer, take very aggressive and unyielding positions in any negotiations, and generally object to the registration of marks before the relevant trademark authorities, *regardless* of whether the goods in connection with the "disputed" marks are used in competition.[1177]

As a result of these tactics *outside of the courtroom*, many "settlements" are not published, the aggressive strategies by trademark owners are not reviewed or chastened, and the broad claims are not rested. This prohibits good law from being made.[1178] This out-of-court bullying also diminishes robust competition. Such bullying blocks off market access to many legitimate, competing and non-competing players, as well as raising costs of market entrance or market continuation.[1179] Generally, small businesses and individuals are more adversely affected, as these victims do not have the resources – financial, legal, staff – to fight legal battles. "While changing or ceasing to use the trademark at stake without a battle may seem to be the least expensive option, altering a trademark (especially if it is also the business' name) can be an expensive proposition."[1180]

---

their merits. In fact, if prosecuted to a trial on their merits, the trademark holder/plaintiff would likely lose because they are not very meritorious claims." *Id.*, p. 589. Port reports that trademark claimants prevailed only 51% of the time. *Id.*, p. 585.

1176 See *Gallagher*: Trademark and Copyright Enforcement in the Shadow of IP Law, pp. 466–481. Gallagher presents his findings based on interviews he conducted with experienced intellectual property attorneys who advise clients on how to enforce their rights.

1177 *Port*: Trademark Extortion, pp. 590–591. Port notes that "competition no longer is relevant. This is the holder's intended life cycle of trademarks."

1178 For a discussion of the effect of increased "out of court" settlements (in the form of alternative dispute resolution mechanisms or judicial settlements), see *Perschbacher/Bassett*: The End of Law, p. 8. The authors claim that the increased privatization of the legal process through alternative dispute resolution or other settlement mechanisms leaves law privately, not publicly, judged, and hinders society's ability to view the workings of the judicial system.

1179 *Port*: Trademark Extortion, p. 587.

1180 *Grinvald*: Shaming Trademark Bullies. Grinvald explains further: "In addition, it is not merely a change in trademark that the bully demands, but also a cessation of sales of goods bearing the trademark, along with any marketing materials, and, further, the delivery of the remaining products bearing the trademark to the bully (presumably for destruction), along with an accounting of past profits. For a small business, the destruction of inventory and the payment of a licensing fee may push

(d) Trademark Turf Wars

The so-called "trademark turf wars"[1181] between companies to protect – and expand – the boundaries of their brands is increasing.[1182] Some trademark owners cross the line from aggressive – but reasonable – trademark enforcement to abusive trademark enforcement.

Notwithstanding public statements that its intellectual property rights are less important than the skills of its employees,[1183] Apple has generated a reputation for "vigorously defending"[1184] its intellectual property. In particular, Apple is known as one of the most aggressive (and successful) trademark litigants – primarily against *any* third-party use of "apple" as a word mark or the use of an apple as an image – whether or not such use is competing and whether not such third-party rights may have existed prior to (and are thus senior to) Apple's trademarks. Apple's strategy in protecting its trademarks – which has even been called Apple's "Logo Lunacy"[1185] – could be considered an example of how dedicated policing can run towards illegitimate harassment.

(i) Apple Trademark Usage Guidelines

Apple's Trademark Usage Guidelines give an initial picture of its trademark strategies.[1186] First, with respect to word marks, Apple prohibits third parties from

---

the business into bankruptcy, which reduces the potential for competition for the bully. Even for individuals with no commercial interest at stake, complying with a cease-and-desist letter can still be expensive, as some letters demand payment of attorney's fees even if the recipient agrees to cease in its use of the trademark." *Id.* at 629-630 (citations omitted).

1181 *Behr*: Trademarks for the Cure, pp. 243–244.

1182 In 2010, trademark infringement cases increased by 8% over the previous year, according to FTI Consulting – the biggest percentage increase in the last 10 years. See *Kavilanz*: Trademark wars heat up.

1183 "The Company currently holds rights to patents and copyrights…[and]…has registered or has applied for trademarks and service marks in the U.S. and a number of foreign countries. Although the Company believes the ownership of such patents, copyrights, trademarks and service marks is an important factor in its business and that its success does depend in part on the ownership thereof, the Company relies primarily on the innovative skills, technical competence and marketing abilities of its personnel." *Apple Inc.*: Form 10-K, p. 7.

1184 *Apple Inc.*: Form 10-K, p. 13.

1185 *Raphael*: Apple's Logo Lunacy.

1186 *Apple Inc.*: Guidelines for Using Apple Trademarks.

using "a variation, phonetic equivalent, foreign language equivalent, takeoff, or abbreviation of an Apple trademark for any purpose." The guidelines state that the following are "not acceptable":[1187]

Appletree Jackintosh Apple Cart PodMart

There is no limitation (e.g., use on a competing product, in a competing market), just a simple prohibition. Although it may wish to be, Apple is not the owner of the word "apple", "tree", "jack", "cart", "pod", or "mart". The competent courts or authorities – not Apple – decide what combination of words or phonetic equivalent may be prohibited use. However, the aggressive statements in such "guidelines" serve to dissuade potential legitimate uses, thereby solidifying Apple's "ownership" interest in the word "apple". Of particular interest was the inclusion of "Jackintosh" as a prohibited word. The clothing manufacturer of the classic British Mackintosh coat (or jacket)[1188] would likely have more claims against infringing use of "Jackintosh" than Apple; the same would apply to the Jack-in-the-Box restaurant chain as well as the Macintosh restaurant (and in particular if they ever wanted form a joint partnership).[1189] Finally, the McIntosh apple (the cultivar) is still being grown and enjoyed.[1190] Such existing rights, or non-competing ones, however, are of little interest to Apple. It simply prohibits any third-party use.

1187 *Id.*

1188 The Mackintosh coat – a classic of British outerwear – was devised and patented by Charles Macintosh. It was first introduced in 1824 as the Mackintosh (with an additional "k"). *Science on the Streets*: Charles Macintosh.

1189 The American fast-food restaurant "Jack in the Box" was founded in 1951 by Robert O. Peterson in San Diego, California (long before the first Apple Macintosh computer was sold in 1984). There is a Macintosh restaurant in Charleston, South Carolina, that has nothing to do with Apple computers. For Jack in the Box, see *Jack In the Box*: History. For the Apple Macintosh, see *Williams*: The Apple Macintosh Computer, p. 30. For the Macintosh restaurant, see *The Macintosh*: Contact.

1190 The apple cultivar, the McIntosh or McIntosh Red (colloquially known as the Mac), was discovered by John McIntosh on his Dundela farm in Upper Canada in 1811. Once the most popular cultivar in Eastern Canada and New England, the McIntosh is well known for the pink apple sauce the unpeeled fruit make. It is also well-suited for cider and pies. *Canadian Geographic*: Canadian food firsts. Apple Inc. supposedly based the name of its Apple Macintosh computer on this variety. *Williams*: The Apple Macintosh Computer, p. 30.

In the Trademark Usage Guidelines (under the "unauthorized use" section), Apple further states that: "You *may not use an image of a real apple* or other variation of the Apple logo *for any purpose*."[1191] This sort of language – expressed in absolute terms, establishing Apple's turf and the rights to use the image of an apple as sovereign – is lunacy. It is also becoming standard and acceptable, prompted by silent acquiescence by the courts and competition authorities. By doing so, the public domain is being looted, striped of a rich variety of words and images. This does not protect or promote competition; this stifles robust, legitimate competition.

(ii) Apple's Trademark Wars: Individual Cases of Deterring Others

Apple's interest in trademarking its name and the apple silhouette logo began as soon as the company was formed. Established in 1977,[1192] the company immediately began filing applications at the USPTO for trademark protection. Its first series of USPTO applications – many of which remain active and form the foundations for the current logo – were as follows: (i) a March 1977 application for the word mark "Apple";[1193] (ii) a March 1978 application for a design "consisting of an apple with a bite removed" (in monochrome, the basis for the current logo);[1194] and (iii) a November 1978 application for multicolor version ("lined for the colors green, yellow, coral, red, violet and blue"[1195] – the rainbow-colored logo[1196]).

Both of Apple's 1981 registrations for a combined design and word mark (including the full "Apple Computer Inc." and "Apple" name) have since been abandoned and cancelled.[1197] Today, the silhouette of only the apple with a "bite"

1191 *Apple Inc.*: Guidelines for Using Apple Trademarks (emphasis mine).

1192 *Apple Inc.*: Form 10-K, p. 1.

1193 This appears to be Apple's first registered trademark application. The application was filed on 25 March 1977, for the word mark "Apple", used for computers and computer programs recorded on paper and tape. The application stated that it had first been used in commerce since April 1976. *USPTO*: serial nr. 73120444. The registration is still active.

1194 Application filed 20 March 1978, relating to the design for computers and computer programs recorded on paper and tape. *USPTO*: serial nr. 73162799.

1195 Application filed 20 November 1978. *USPTO*: serial nr. 73193803.

1196 For a background history of the rainbow-colored logo, see *Raszl*: Interview with Rob Janoff; *Kahney*: Apple Doin' the Logo-Motion; and *Rodbard*: I Invented … the Apple Logo.

1197 *USPTO*: serial nr. 73303406 and *USPTO*: serial nr. 73307818.

cut-out (and the stem definitively more detached) is the trademark logo we recognize so easily:

[1198] [1199] [1200]

As the apple silhouette with the bite has become more and more recognizable (even iconic), Apple has increasingly flexed its muscles more and more aggressively against any third-party use of an apple image in a trademark (whether or not Apple is the junior or senior user of such mark and whether or not there is any evidence of consumer confusion).

The table below highlights a few recent trademark cases that Apple has initiated based on uses of an apple image by third parties. There are most certainly many more, which never make it to court or to the press. Do these cases demonstrate legitimate policing in the name of trademark protection or bully-harassment?

1198 Image: *USPTO*: serial nr. 73303406. The trademark application containing the apple and the words "Apple Computer Inc." was filed with the USPTO on 30 March 1981, but was abandoned on 10 October 1982 and cancelled on 8 November 2003. It covered use for the categories "Computers, Computer Software and Computer Peripherals-Namely, Floppy Disk Drives, Printers, Electronic Graphics Tablets, and Video Monitors", claiming first use in commerce as of 1977. *USPTO*: serial nr. 73303406.

1199 Image. *USPTO*: serial nr. 73307818. The trademark application containing the apple and the word "Apple" was filed with the USPTO on 27 April 1981, registered on 9 March 1982, and then cancelled on 20 October 1988. *USPTO*: serial nr. 73307818.

1200 Image: *USPTO*: serial nr. 73162799.

	Case Highlights	Logos at Issue[1201]
Apple v. GreeNYC (2008)	**Apple v. The Big Apple** Apple sued New York City for its use of an apple in its GreeNYC environmental campaign. The GreeNYC logo, Apple alleged, could cause "consumer confusion resulting in damage and injury" to Apple, along with "dilution of the distinctiveness" of Apple's trademark.[1202] New York City has been known as "The Big Apple" since the beginning of the century – long before the 1977 founding of the computer company. Many landmark images or emblems of the City use an apple image.[1203] The GreeNYC symbol morphs the symbol for infinity with the outline of an apple, a stem and a single leaf. "We believe the 'infinity apple' design and its mission to create environmental awareness are unique and distinctive and do not infringe upon the Apple computer brand."[1204] **No Competitive Use & No Consumer Confusion:** NYC's use of the image in a marketing campaign promoting the environment had nothing to do with the sale of computer devices. No consumer confusion evidence was presented. **The Bully Wins**: NYC (the City!) wilts under Apple's pressure and agrees to change its logo.[1205]	

1201 All logos are registered trademarks of the applicable company and are used here for illustrative purposes only. All rights, title, and interest in and to such trademarks and any goodwill related thereto remain the sole and exclusive property of the applicable company.

1202 *Samson*: Apple fights NYC; and *Stone*: Logo Smackdown!

1203 Consider, for example, the iconic Tiffany & Co. glass apple paperweight, which has been a classic New York City gift for decades. *Tiffany & Co.*: Apple Paperweight.

1204 Kimberly Spell, spokeswoman of NYC & Company Inc.; quoted in *Larson*: Apple sues New York.

1205 In June 2008, NYC filed a motion to amend its application to delete the leaf element from its design, leaving the stem. USPTO, Trademark Trial and Appeal Board, *Apple Inc. v. NYC & Company, Inc.*, Opposition No. 91181984, July 22, 2008. For the updated logo, see *USPTO*: TSDR listing for serial nr. 77179942.

	Case Highlights	Logos at Issue[1201]
Apple v. Victoria School of Business and Technology (2008)	**Apple v. Higher Education** Apple sent Canada's Victoria School of Business and Technology (VSBT) – a small Vancouver Island college – a cease-and-desist letter demanding that VSBT drop the apple-shaped logo from its identity.[1206] The logo in question featured the outline of an apple (with three bumps instead of two, and no bite) and a leaf, and incorporated a mountain silhouette[1207] (which mirrors the mountain design on their website[1208]) and the initials of the school. Apple's letter to the institution reportedly noted that: "Your business logo … reproduces, without authority, our client's Apple design logo which it widely uses. By doing so, you are infringing Apple's rights, and further, falsely suggesting that Apple has authorized your activities".[1209] VSBT's president was incensed: "Are you suggesting that anyone using any variation of an apple for technology education is infringing on Apple's trademark?"[1210] **The Bully Wins:** In April 2011, the school reported it had settled its 3-year dispute with Apple, and launched a new logo under a new name, Q College.[1211]	

1206 For full coverage of the dispute, including copies of Apple's cease-and-desist letter, VSBT's response, links to various news articles and news clips, see *Q College*: Apples and Oranges.

1207 *CTV*: Will Apple's suit against B.C. school bear fruit?

1208 See lower banner image of the official website. *Q College*: Victoria's School for Business Technology.

1209 *Heibert*: Apple Sues Canadian School for Similar Logo.

1210 *CBC News*: No apple for Vancouver Island school.

1211 *Times Colonist*: Business school drops use of Apple's forbidden fruit.

	Case Highlights	Logos at Issue[1201]
Apple v. Woolworth (2009)	**Apple v. Apples** Apple sued the Australian supermarket chain Woolworths (not related to the retail chain) over a new logo the supermarket chain created for its fresh produce line. Woolworths changed its logo in 2008 as part of a rebranding to stress its commitment to fresh food.[1212] The logo shows a "W" stylized into an abstract apple-like shape, leading Apple to contend the look is too similar to its own apple-shaped symbol.[1213] Woolworths has insisted that the logo is meant to represent the letter "W" with connotations of freshness, rather than depicting an apple.[1214] The man who designed it, Hans Hulsbosch, said Apple was taking trademark protection "to the extreme": "Based on this logic, they would have to take action against every fruit seller."[1215] A trademark lawyer, Trevor Choy, said it was common for Apple to prevent anyone from using anything that resembled an apple in a logo or marketing, even though less than 5% cent of such claims actually make it to court: "This is often the prelude to settling [the matter]."[1216] **Restricted goods and services**: In April 2011, Woolworths amended its trademark application to remove various goods and services, such as "computer devices and computer peripheral devices, … electrical devices for personal and household use; … computer hardware and software"[1217] and Apple withdrew its opposition,[1218] allowing the trademark to proceed to registration.	↓ **Amended Registration** <u>**Not for**</u> "computer devices and computer peripheral devices, … electrical devices for personal and household use; … computer hardware and software"

1212 *Lee*: Apple bites over Woolworths logo.

1213 *Watt*: Apple Has No Monopoly on Fruit Trademark.

1214 *Moore*: Apple demands Woolworths drops new logo.

1215 *Lee*: Apple claims Woolies is getting fresh with new logo.

1216 *Id.*

1217 *IP Australia*: Trademark 1258288, 6 April 2011.

1218 *IP Australia*: Trademark 1258288, 18 April 2011.

	Case Highlights	Logos at Issue[1201]
Apple v. Sichuan (2011)	**Apple v. A Fruit (or a Bomb)** Apple accused Sichuan Fangguo Food Co., Ltd., a Sichuan-based company producing noodles and flour, of trademark infringement. Fangguo's logo depicts a circular apple, with a stem and right-facing leaf, with the bottom left quarter missing.[1219] Fangguo has been said to sound like "apple" in Mandarin.[1220] Apple's Chinese lawyers say that the logo of Sichuan Fangguo uses conceptual elements taken from the computer company's.[1221] Most commentators have reported that Sichuan Fangguo's logo more closely resembles LG Electronics' logo than Apple's.[1222] Fangguo CEO Zhao Yi commented: "There's a leaf so you can tell it's an apple, but it also contains two Chinese characters … The orientation is also different, and ours is a totally different shape … Besides, when I started Fangguo, I had never even heard of Apple."[1223] Apple sent a letter to Sichuan Fangguo to remove the "leaf" from the logo. To that CEO Zhao Yi replied: "I'm Fangguo, it's a fruit, if the leaf is removed, it'll just look like a bomb."[1224] **Unknown Ending**: CEO Zhao Yi has stated that "the law firm who sent the letter hasn't contacted me since they sent it."[1225]	?

1219 *Matyszczyk*: Apple objects to Chinese food maker's logo. *Chaffin*: Apple Objects to Chinese Food Company's Logo. *Jane*: Apple tells Chinese food company to change its logo.

1220 *GMA News*: Apple lawyers hit Chinese food maker over logo.

1221 *Jane*: Apple tells Chinese food company to change its logo.

1222 *Chan*: Why Is Apple Suing a Chinese Food Company for Stealing LG's Logo?

1223 *Id.*

1224 *Fahran*: Another Lawsuit? Sichuan Fangguo Infringes On Apple's Logo.

1225 *Ong*: iCloud Communications drops trademark suit.

	Case Highlights	Logos at Issue[1201]
Apple v. Apfelkind (2011)	**Apple v. Apple Child Café** Christine Römer opened a small German café, Apfelkind ("apple child") in Bonn on 30 April 2011.[1226] The café serves coffee and cake, and has a children's playroom.[1227] The logo is a red apple with a white silhouette of a child in a cap in the lower left-hand area of the apple. Apple sent a letter stating that the logos were too similar and people could become confused, thinking the cafe was somehow associated with the tech giant.[1228] Two years of litigation (including settlement talks) ensued. Römer held firm.[1229] **Bully backs down!** The café owner perseveres: "My trademark is free, I am happy."[1230] However, the fear is always present that the bully will return for another round.[1231]	

(iii) Apple Computer v. Apple Records

Apple's success as an *offensive* trademark bully is only one side of the story. Apple's litigation with Apple Records – where it was originally on the *defensive* side as "junior" user – demonstrates just how strategically savvy famous trademark owners have become. In brief: in 1981, Apple signed an agreement with Apple Records agreeing to stay out of the music business *so as not to infringe on the trademark rights* of Apple Records, who had an established, senior trademark. Within a decade, Apple was ignorning its promises, ultimately launching first the iPod and then iTunes, which are undeniably connected to the music industry.

1226 *Apfelkind*: die apfelkind idee.

1227 *Id.*

1228 *Jacob*: Apfelkind in der Südstadt. *Wilson*: Is Apfelkind's apple a ripped off Apple logo? *Floyd*: Apple threatens to sue small German cafe for logo. *Thornhill*: German cafe owner sued by Apple. *Cleaver*: Bonn café stands up to Apple over trademark.

1229 *Kutzim*: Markenrechtsstreit: Apple macht Zugeständnisse an Apfelkind.

1230 „Meine Marke ist frei, ich bin froh." (English translation mine), as reported in *Brinkmann*: Café Apfelkind besiegt Apple. See also *Oltermann*: Apfelkind cafe owner wins trademark battle with Apple.

1231 *Ivits*: Café Apfelkind gewinnt gegen Apple.

Apple Records is the record label division of Apple Corps Ltd, a management and distribution company established by the Beatles.[1232] Apple Records was launched in 1968, and from then onwards, new releases by The Beatles were issued by Apple Records.[1233]

In 1977, Apple Computer, Inc. (now Apple Inc.)[1234] was founded.[1235] Already in 1976, however, it had designed its first logo[1236] and applied for its first trademark application with the USPTO.[1237]

In the role of *defensive infringer*, Apple's dispute with Apple Records began in 1980, when George Harrison – former lead guitarist of the Beatles – saw a

---

1232 The Beatles first established a company called Beatles Ltd in 1963, primary as a way to invest the band's growing cash reserve. The name was first changed to Beatles and Co in 1967 and to Apple Corps Ltd in February 1968. Apple Corps (the name was an intended pun, as it is pronounced "apple core") was established as a vehicle for which The Beatles could sign other musicians and fund various creative projects. See *Lowe*: An Apple A Decade. Apple Corps had five divisions – including Apple Records, Apple Electronics, Apple Films, Apple Publishing, and Apple Retail.

1233 The copyrights, however, remained with EMI, and Parlophone/Capitol catalogue numbers continued to be used. See *The Beatles Wiki*: Apple Corps.

1234 On 9 January 2007, Apple amended Article I of its Restated Articles of Incorporation solely to change the corporate name from "Apple Computer, Inc." to "Apple Inc.", and filed a copy of the Company's Certificate of Ownership with the Secretary of State of the State of California, reflecting the new corporate name, on the same day. *Apple Inc.*; Form 8-K. Apple CEO Steve Jobs publically announced the name change on the same day, at the 2007 Macworld Expo. See *Honan*: Apple drops 'Computer' from name. See also *Ricker*: Apple drops "Computer" from name.

1235 *Apple Inc.*: Form 10-K.

1236 Apple's very first logo, dating back to 1976, was drawn by Ronald Wayne, an early (but often forgotten) co-founder of the company. The image featured Sir Isaac Newton sitting under the apple tree where he supposedly discovered gravity, by an apple falling on his head. Around the frame of the image, an excerpt from poet William Wordsworth, reading "Newton – A mind forever voyaging through strange seas of thought ... alone." The framed image is swathed in a cloth banner reading "Apple Computer Co.". See *Unisource Design*: The Apple Logo Story; and *Hughes*: Logos that became legends. For an image of the logo, see *Wikipedia*: Apple First Logo.

1237 The first – and still active – USPTO trademark application dates from 25 March 1977, for the word mark "Apple", used for computers and computer programs recorded on paper and tape. The application stated that it had first been used in commerce since April 1976. See *USPTO*, serial nr. 73120444.

magazine advertisement for a company called Apple Computer and saw potential for consumer confusion between it and the Apple Corps name.[1238] Legal proceedings began, resulting in an out-of-court trademark delimitation settlement agreement in November 1981. Under the settlement agreement, Apple Computer paid Apple Corps $80,000; furthermore, Apple Corps could continue to use the name for goods and services related to records, music, entertainment and sound (but would not enter the computer industry), while Apple Computer could use the name for goods and services related to computers, computer systems and computer peripheral equipment (but would not enter the music industry).[1239] Furthermore, the agreement contained a trademark "no challenge" clause.[1240]

By the end of the 1980s, Apple Computer equipment was regularly being used for high quality (digitized) sound generation, including popular music. When renegotiation of the agreement to cover such new digital uses failed, Apple Computer filed cancellation suits of the Apple Corps trademark for non-use[1241] and Apple Corps filed its own suit claiming breach of the 1981 agreement and the "no challenge" clause. After intense court arguments and negotiation, the parties entered into a second trademark delimination agreement in September 1991, pursuant to which Apple Computer paid US$26.5 million to Apple Corps and thereby obtained rights to use Apple Computer marks to play or deliver content falling within Apple Corps' field of use *provided* that this did not extend to use on or in connection with physical media delivering pre-recorded content.[1242]

Apple Computer's launch of the iTunes Music Store (which allows individuals to download songs over the internet and to store them on a computer with a view to playing them back over the computer or via portable players) and the offerings available through the iPod, re-ignited the dispute. Apple Corps filed a suit on 4 July 2003 in London, in the English High Court of Justice, Chancery Division, alleging that Apple breached the 1991 agreement. On 8 October 2003, Apple filed a lawsuit in the U.S. District Court for the Northern District of California

---

1238 *Lowe*: An Apple A Decade, cited by *Bernstein*: A Case for Mediating Trademark Disputes, p. 146, n. 37.

1239 *Bernstein*: A Case for Mediating Trademark Disputes, p. 146.

1240 See *Perkins*: The Apple Computer vs Apple Corps Trademark Litigation, slide 4.

1241 Apple filed cancellation suits in Germany, Sweden, the United Kingdom; Austria, Australia, Belgium, Canada, France, Hungary, Japan, Spain, New Zealand and the United States and oppositions to pending Apple Corps trademark applications in France, Germany and South Korea. See *Perkins*: The Apple Computer vs Apple Corps Trademark Litigation, slide 6.

1242 See *Perkins*: The Apple Computer vs Apple Corps Trademark Litigation, slide 8.

requesting a declaratory judgment that it did not breach the 1991 agreement. Apple Corps challenged jurisdiction and the California case was stayed during the pendency of the English action.[1243]

In 2006, the English High Court issued its decision, declaring Apple's use of "Apple" in its iTunes and iPod offering did *not* violate the parties 1991 agreement.[1244] In 2007, the long-running trademark dispute seems to have achieved a "final" settlement, with Apple purchasing *all* of the trademarks related to "Apple" and licensing certain of those trademarks back to Apple Corps for their continued use.[1245] The terms of the settlement were confidential, although reports suggest that Apple paid a total of US$500 million for the ownership rights.[1246]

This is Formula 1 Bullying: Apple – as the *junior* mark owner – used the power of its brand to expand its product lines, even in *direct breach* of agreements it had made. It did so without respect to the Apple Records trademarks and in direct breach of its own commitments.

(iv) Amazon and the Kindle AppStore

In November 2011, Apple filed a suit to enjoin Amazon from using the trademarked "Appstore" as part of the Kindle Fire (Amazon's tablet computer) hardware,[1247] claiming that Amazon's use of "Appstore" in connection with sales of applications ("apps") for Android devices and the Kindle Fire was likely to "dilute the distinctiveness of Apple's APP STORE mark, to tarnish the image of Apple's APP STORE mark, to misrepresent the nature, characteristics and qualities of Amazon's mobile download service and/or to deceive or have a tendency to deceive a substantial segment of consumers into believing that Amazon's service has the nature, characteristics, and/or qualities of Apple's APP STORE service."[1248] Although the USPTO approved Apple's 2008 application to register "App Store" as a trademark, many competitors (including Microsoft)[1249] have filed challenges to such trademark, claiming that the "combined term "app store"

1243 Apple dismissed the California lawsuit without prejudice. See *Apple Computer Inc.*: Form 10-K (2004), p. 18.

1244 Case No: HC03C02428, *Apple Corps, Ltd. and Apple Computer, Inc.*, May 8, 2006 [2006] EWHC 996 (Ch), High Court of Justice, Chancery Division, Royal Courts of Justice, Mr. Justice Mann.

1245 *Apple Inc.*: Apple Inc. and The Beatles' Apple Corps Ltd. Enter into New Agreement.

1246 *Purcher*: The Beatles' Apple Corps Logo is now a Registered TM of Apple.

1247 *Cheng*: Kindle Fire dragged into Apple's "app store" suit against Amazon.

1248 *Choney*: Kindle Fire added to Apple app store suit against Amazon.

1249 *Hutchens*: Apple and Microsoft Fight Over "APP STORE" Trademark App.

is commonly used in the trade, by the general press, by consumers, by Apple's competitors, and even by Apple's founder and CEO Steve Jobs as the generic name for online stores featuring apps.

In January 2013, the U.S. District Court for the Northern District of California rejected Apple's claim that Amazon's use of the term was false advertising. U.S. District Judge Phyllis Hamilton noted that although Apple's digital storefront for apps is called the "App Store" and Amazon's is called the "Appstore", Apple failed to provide any proof that Amazon ever tried to pass itself off as a place to get iPhone or iPad apps.

> "There is no evidence that a consumer who accesses the Amazon Appstore would expect that it would be identical to the Apple App Store, particularly given that the Apple App Store sells apps solely for Apple devices, while the Amazon Appstore sells apps solely for Android and Kindle devices," Hamilton wrote in her order to dismiss the claim. "Further, the integration of Apple devices has more to do with Apple's technology than it does with the nature, characteristics, or qualities of the App Store."[1250]

(e) Dilution Claims Run Amok

Apple is not the only company aggressively guarding its brand turf. The examples below demonstrate how famous trademark owners are using litigation strategies to expand their trademark rights beyond what seems reasonable – in particular in cases *where consumers are not confused.*

(i) Italicized Fonts: Walgreens v. Wegmans

Walgreen Co. (doing business as Walgreens, a publically-traded company) is the largest drug retailing chain in the United States, offering customers consumer goods and services, pharmacy, and health and wellness services.[1251] Walgreens was founded in Chicago, Illinois, in 1901 by Charles R. Walgreen Sr.[1252]

Wegmans Food Markets, Inc. is a privately-held, family-owned U.S. regional supermarket chain headquartered in Gates, New York, near Rochester.[1253] Wegmans – originally named the Rochester Fruit & Vegetable Company – was founded in 1916 by John Wegman.[1254]

1250 *Olivarez-Giles*: Judge Says No One Is Confusing Apple's App Store and Amazon's Appstore.

1251 See New York Stock Exchange (NYSE) profile entry for Walgreens (traded as WAG). *NYSE*: Walgreens (WAG).

1252 *Walgreens*: Company Information.

1253 *Wegmans*: Company Overview.

1254 *Wegmans*: History.

In 2010, Walgreens opposed a Wegmans USPTO trademark application, alleging that the script design of the Wegmans mark was likely to cause confusion with the script version of its own Walgreens mark. On the same day, Walgreens further filed a federal trademark infringement lawsuit against Wegmans,[1255] claiming that Wegmans' use of the italicized logo could mislead consumers into thinking the companies were connected and further alleging that Walgreens' "flying W" deserved protection having been used since 1951.[1256]

Walgreens[1257]

Wegmans[1258]

Wegmans contended, however, that the flying "W" they started using in 2008 (as a replacement of their upright, 1990s font) was a revival of a logo that they used in the 1930s.[1259] A spokesperson for Wegmans said that there was no confusion between the two logos. According to a report Southern Tier of New York, people that the news channel interviewed were apparently more confused about why the lawsuit was filed than about the "W"s alleged similarity at all.[1260] In March 2011, the parties settled their dispute, with Wegmans agreeing to stop using the "circle W" logo by 30 June 2012.[1261]

In court, the factual evidence that (i) Wegmans had used the italicized font and "flying W" in the 1930s, and (ii) consumer were not confused, might have resolved the issue so that both Walgreens and Wegmans could continue to use their logos. Instead, the out-of-court settlement demonstrates how famous trademark owners are successfully using "turf" war strategies to expand the exclusive contours of their trademarks.

1255 *Turek*: Ridiculous Trademark Opposition of the Week – Walgreens v. Wegmans.

1256 *Associated Press*: Wegmans, Walgreens Settle Suit Over 'W' logos.

1257 *Walgreens*: Company Information.

1258 *Wegmans*: History.

1259 Wegmans offers a superb historical image gallery of their logos, showing the progression of various typefaces from the 1930s onwards, including happy 1950s-style, psychedelic/space-age 1960s-style, and 1990s computer stylized fonts. See *Wegmans*: History, Wegmans Logos.

1260 *Ward*: Letter from AmeriKat.

1261 *Associated Press*: Wegmans, Walgreens Settle Suit Over 'W' logos.

(ii) From Alpha to Omega

The names of North American fraternities and sororities generally consist of two or three Greek letters, typically representing the initials of a Greek motto. The use of Greek letters is traced back to Phi Beta Kappa, which was a male social and literary fraternity founded in 1776 at the College of William and Mary and since 1898 an honor society in arts and sciences.[1262] Many fraternities and honor societies have names containing the Greek letter Omega,[1263] which have been used since their founding date, including Alpha Tau Omega (1865), Kappa Sigma Omega (1867), Alpha Chi Omega (1885), Chi Omega (1895), Alpha Omega Alpha (1901), Omega Psi Phi (1911), Pi Omega Pi (1923), Omega Chi Epsilon (1967), and Pi Omega Pi (1965).[1264]

Omega SA is a privately-held, Swiss watch company founded by Louis Brandt in 1848.[1265] Omega SA has a valid, registered U.S. trademark dating from July 1894.[1266]

In 2009, the Omega Psi Phi Fraternity (founded in 1911)[1267] filed an application to register a trademark containing its Greek letters for a variety of jewelry products, namely lapel pins, charms and rings.[1268] The Omega Psi Phi Fraternity already had a number of U.S. trademark registrations on file, some giving

---

1262 See *Warren*: Historical Information, Prelude to the New Millennium. The first Greek-lettered fraternity for *women* was Kappa Alpha Theta, formed at Indiana Asbury College (now DePauw University) on 27 January 1870. *Kappa Alpha Theta*: Theta Roots. In 1851, the first sorority (then a secret society) for women, named The Adelphean Society (in 1905 later renamed Alpha Delta Pi), was founded at Wesleyan Female College, the first college chartered to grant degrees to women in the world (since 1917, Wesleyan College), in Macon, Georgia. *Alpha Delta Pi*: Heritage.

1263 Omega (capital: Ω, lowercase: ω; Greek ō) is the 24th and last letter of the Greek alphabet.

1264 See *Warren*: Historical Information, Prelude to the New Millennium; and *Greek Pages*: History of College Fraternities.

1265 See *Omega*: Omega: A Journey Through Time.

1266 USPTO, for design and word mark "OMEGA" for watch movements and watch cases, first used 10 March 1894. *USPTO*: serial nr. 70025036. Omega holds other U.S. trademark registrations for the word "Omega" and the "Ω" symbol for use on timepieces and timepiece accessories. See, e.g., U.S. Trademark Registration No. 577,415 (14 July 1953); U.S. Trademark Registration No. 578,041 (28 July 1953); and U.S. Trademark Registration No. 660,541 (15 April 1958).

1267 See official website of the Omega Psi Phi fraternity. *Omega Psi Phi*: About Omega.

1268 *Turek*: Ridiculous Trademark Opposition of the Week – 12/06/09.

priority back to 1912.[1269] Omega SA opposed the 2009 trademark application, saying it was confusingly similar to its logo when used in connection with jewelry products.[1270]

Here, it is unlikely that any consumer confusion would arise. Customers purchasing Omega Psi Phi jewelry would likely be doing so in order to show affiliation with their fraternity, not because they believed they were buying the Swiss watch makers' products. As one trademark attorney noted:

> "I do not take issue with Omega SA challenging applications for legitimately confusingly similar marks that are used in connection with jewelry products. What I do have a problem with, however, is Omega SA bullying a fraternity with which it has coexisted for nearly 100 years, all because the fraternity uses OMEGA and Ω (along with two other Greek letters).... [U]nfortunately, the current opposition system allows such abuse without any consequences whatsoever. ... Omega SA and other wealthy companies will continue to make it more difficult and costly for smaller businesses and organizations to obtain the benefits and legal presumptions that stem from federal registration of their marks."[1271]

7.4 Chapter Observations

Trademark protection originally grew out of the principles of unfair competition and consumer confusion.[1272] The relevant analysis in any trademark infringement or unfair competition action was whether the defendant's mark was likely

---

1269 See, e.g., U.S. Trademark Registration No. 1692006 (9 June 1992) for the word mark "OMEGA PSI PHI FRATERNITY", first used in commerce 11 November 1914 (since cancelled); U.S. Trademark Registration No. 1720789 (29 September 1992) for the design mark of the fraternity coat of arms/emblem (since cancelled); U.S. Trademark Registration No. 3396832 (18 March 2008) for a word and design mark; and many more.

1270 Omega SA has filed other trademark oppositions against Omega Psi Phi, including for the marks OMEGA PSI PHI FRATERNITY GRAND CONCLAVE (Serial No. 77354572), OMEGA PSI PHI FRATERNITY (Serial No. 77354564), and a logo that displays the Ω with the other two Greek letters of the Fraternity's name (Serial No. 76593847). These oppositions are currently pending. Omega SA has also filed oppositions against other fraternities, including Omega Delta Phi's application for OMEGA DELTA PHI (Serial No. 78949191). Cited by *Turek*: Ridiculous Trademark Opposition of the Week – 12/06/09.

1271 *Turek*: Ridiculous Trademark Opposition of the Week – 12/06/09.

1272 "The law of trade-marks is but a part of the broader law of unfair competition." *United Drug Co. v. Theodore Rectanus Co.*, 248 U.S. 90, 97 (1918).

to cause consumer deception.[1273] Initially, the scope of such consumer confusion was narrow: the laws and the courts only permitted trademark infringement between direct competitors in an industry.[1274]

Today, under the guise of "dilution" of the goodwill of a company, trademark owners are engaging in aggressive tactics to protect the *commercial* (i.e., economic and financial) value of their trademarks as sovereign property against non-confusing, non-fraudulent, non-deceptive use. Such tactics – claiming quasi-property entitlement – restrict legitimate, robust competition.

1273 The Lanham Act defines infringement as any "use in commerce … likely to cause confusion, or to cause mistake, or to deceive." 15 U.S.C. § 1114(1)(a). The basic inquiry is the same whether an action is brought as a trademark infringement or unfair competition action. *Denicola*: Trademarks as Speech: Constitutional Implications, p. 162: "Both the traditional common law and statutory regimes view the issue of consumer confusion as the *sine qua non* of infringement."

1274 *Schechter*: The Rational Basis of Trademark Protection, pp. 820–22, cited by *Klieger*: Trademark Dilution, fn. 29.

8. Trademark's Legal Boundaries: Conflict Between Private Rights & Public Interests

8.1 Interim Summary

(a) Commercial Significance

The commercial significance and economic value of trademarks in our society continue to grow. Trademarks are useful in more expansive ways than in their earliest incarnations, representing a profitable and commercially powerful means by which companies communicate a wealth of information and establish customer – and brand – loyalty. Trademarks are the "bridge" over which advertising, marketing, and persuasive brand imagery flow.[1275] For these reasons, companies have invested headily in trademarks (through brand advertising) and in the development of goodwill. This goodwill has then been used to apply to an ever-increasing range of products and services – products that may not have anything to do with the original association of a particular trademark or source.

Given this commercial significance, economic value, and opportunity to secure market share (through brand loyalty), companies have actively sought protection of their investments. "Much of this behaviour is not troublesome. A company's interest in preventing confusion about its product generally aligns with trademarks law's underlying purpose to minimize consumer search costs."[1276] Moreover, protecting financial investments and rights through legal action is generally deemed part of good business practices. However, some of these prevention and protection activities have been one-sided (in the form of "trademark bullies"), to the detriment of consumers and market competition. Trademark owners have used their power to bend the contours of trademark law towards their interests and their advantage. The problem is that as such rights expand, there are no natural "checks and balances" – whether in trademark law or competition law – that adequately limit such expansion. As a result, trademark owners have taken advantage of trademark laws' expanding contours – and

1275 A trademark "is a narrow bridge over which all the traffic powered by product advertising must pass. ... With time, the symbol comes to be more than a conduit through which the persuasive power of advertising is transmitted, and acquires a potency, a "commercial magnetism,' of its own." *Brown*: Advertising and the Public Interest, p. 1187, cited by *Klieger*: Trademark Dilution, p. 793, n. 17.

1276 *Ridgway*: Revitalizing the Doctrine of Trademark Misuse, p. 1548.

courts' and legislatures' failure to intervene – to engage in tactics that result in significant competitive barriers to trade, unduly distorting the underlying "pro-competitive" nature of trademarks. What was once a means to ensure fair competition has evolved into a means to restrict competition.

(b) Legal Failures

Trademark protection has grown dramatically over time, from more narrowly protecting against fraudulent or competitive uses of a trademark owner's mark to shielding a host of non-competitive uses. Legally, the justifications for protection keep expanding, thus prompting further protection, the definition of what is (and can be) protected keeps increasing, and the standards of liability and causes of actions available to a trademark owner (i.e., the type of infringement claims that can be made) keep expanding. Although changes in law are *vital* to adapt our laws to a mature and modern society, these significant changes beg the question: what is the ultimate role of trademark protection? Do trademark laws serve primarily to protect consumers and producers from unfair trade practices or do they protect the business of individual trademark holders without regard to the best interests of consumers and the workings of a competitive market?

Trademark and competition laws have failed to implement requisite limits (or counter-balancing beneficial effects) to that expansion, and failed to address the anti-competitive effects of such expanding private protection on the competitive market. Intellectual property laws have existed alongside competition laws for decades. However, as competition laws have increasingly been applied to the exercise of patent and copyright rights, competition laws have either ignored trademarks (by explicitly removing them from regulations or guidelines addressing their appropriate spheres of conduct) or misunderstood their competitive aspects or licensing arrangements (e.g., addressing them only when they are "ancillary" to other intellectual property transactions).

8.2 Expanding Legal Rights

(a) Overview

Intellectual property laws were never designed to grant rights' owners "a timeless and absolute right to their inventions, expressive works, and identifying marks."[1277] Originally, intellectual property rights were understood to be "islands of protection in a sea of competition."[1278] As the boundaries of intellectual

---

1277 *Klieger*: Trademark Dilution, pp. 864–866.
1278 *Reichman*: Charting the Collapse of the Patent-Copyright Dichotomy, p. 517.

property rights – and in particular those relating to trademarks – have expanded, the result today is "a sea of protection in which intrepid entrepreneurs encounter remote islands of competition."[1279]

Specifically, the traditional understanding and boundaries of intellectual property rights have expanded dramatically over the past few decades:[1280] terms of protection are longer;[1281] the types of things that are protected has

---

1279 *Id.* Reichman was referring to the proliferation of hybrid legal regimes protecting patents and copyrights which have disrupted the historical balance between free competition and legal incentives to create. The statement is equally applicable to the expanding protection afforded trademarks.

1280 For a summary (and critique) of the expansion of the scope of patent law, see, e.g., *Beckerman-Rodau*: The Problem with Intellectual Property Rights, pp. 54–62. For discussions regarding the expanded scope of copyright, see *Samuelson*: The Uneasy Case for Software; *Bettig*: Copyrighting Culture; *Lessig*: Free Culture; and *Vaidhyanathan*: Copyrights and Copywrongs. For a summary of the expanded rights of publicity, see *Greene*: Intellectual Property Expansion; and *Madow*: Private Ownership of Public Image. For the expansion of trade secret protection in the U.S., see *Carrier*: Cabining Intellectual Property, p. 9, fn. 9–12. In the EU, all Member States had to implement European Database Directive 96/9/EC of 11 March 1996 (OJ L 77/20, 27.03.1996) to protect database rights. In the U.S., the copyright laws have been augmented by the Semiconductor Chip Protection Act, 17 U.S.C. §§ 901–914; the Digital Millennium Copyright Act, 17 U.S.C. §§ 1201–1205 (2000); the Vessel Hull Design Protection Act, 17 U.S.C. § 1301–1332; 17 U.S.C. § 1101 (creating an anti-bootlegging right); Federal Trademark Dilution Act, 15 U.S.C. § 1125(c); and the Anticybersquatting Consumer Protection Act, 15 U.S.C. § 1125(d).

1281 In 1995, in order to adhere to its obligations under the General Agreement on Tariffs and Trade, Congress changed the patent term from 17 years from issue to 20 years from filing – cf 35 U.S.C. § 154(a)(2)) – a change Mark Lemley has found adds length to the patent term for the majority of patentees. *Lemley*: An Empirical Study. The first copyright law in the U.S. (enacted in 1790) protected copyrighted works for 14 years, with the privilege of renewal for another 14 years, giving true meaning to the "limited times" contemplated by the Constitution (U.S. Constitution, Article I, Section 8, clause 8). *U.S. Copyright Office*: A Brief Introduction and History. Thereafter, the length of the copyright term was extended 11 times between 1963 and 1998. *Lessig*: Copyright's First Amendment, p. 1065. Today, the length of protection is a term lasting the author's life plus an additional 70 years after the author's death (or 70 years after the death of the last surviving author in case of a joint work) or for 95 years from publication or 120 years from creation (whichever expires first) for works-made-for-hire or anonymous or pseudonymous works. 17 U.S.C. § 302. *U.S. Copyright Office*: Circular 1. In general, see *Carrier*: Cabining Intellectual Property, who systematically looks at the extension of copyrights (pp. 13–16), patents (pp. 16–19), trademarks (pp. 19–22), and the rights of publicity (pp. 22–24).

increased;[1282] the rationales for protection have broadened (thereby justifying further protection); and the claims actionable have multiplied.

A particular problem is the expanding scope of trademark law,[1283] since – unlike its intellectual property brethren – trademark laws have far fewer statutory restrictions or boundaries than those built into patent and copyrights laws.[1284] Trademark law has expanded from a relatively narrow cause of action (intended to prevent deceptive practices, including the fraudulent sale of one merchant's good as those of a competitor by means of misleading the latter's trademark) into a broadly applicable tort against any sort of confusion or misappropriation – be it misappropriation of a color, of a shape, of good feelings, or even of a potential (but not yet tapped) market. Such broad rights in trademarks have the potential to diminish competition and variety in the market, as the ability to compete fairly, use common words, or engage in satire, parody, or even criticism, is severely restricted.[1285] As one scholar has lamented, trademark law has become "unthethered from its traditional moorings".[1286]

1282 For example, throughout its legislative history, the scope of copyright protections has expanded with changing times: the first copyright law, the Copyright Act of 1790, granted a copyright interest to authors of maps, charts, and books. In 1802, prints and engravings became eligible for protection. In 1831, musical compositions were added to the list. In 1856, the subject matter was extended to include the public performance of dramatic works, in 1865, photographs, and in 1870, paintings, drawings and statues. In 1909, the copyright law was completely revised: it provided copyright protection for "all the writings of an author". *Blanke*: Vincent Van Gogh, pp. 650–651.

1283 For further analyses of trademark laws' expansion, see *Lemley/McKenna*: Owning Mark(et)s; *Schlosser*: The High Price of (Criticizing) Coffee; *Gallagher*: Trademark and Copyright Enforcement in the Shadow of IP Law; *Hackbarth*: Weiter Schutzbereich berühmter Marken; and *Bogatz*: Sparkassen-Rot, Nivea-Blau, Langenscheid-Gelb.

1284 For example, unlike the limited terms of patent and copyright laws, trademarks can be protected indefinitely. Patent law recognizes only narrow rights by others to use or access a work, but the term of protection is very short (20 years from filing). Copyright protection is longer (it could exceed 100 years), but copyright laws do not preclude others from independently creating similar works and allows legal access to and the right to make limited use of the copyright owner's original work in certain circumstances (e.g., under the fair use doctrine) even for competing, commercial purposes. Trademarks are not limited in duration and have fewer built-in means to allow others legal access and competing use.

1285 *Travis*: The Battle for Mindshare, paras. 37 and 50.

1286 *Id.*, para. 7.

(b) Rationales for Protection

The rationales for protecting trademarks have broadened significantly, expanding as the functions of trademarks in our society have expanded. Such changes have justified – or helped instigate – expanded protection. As noted earlier, whereas patent and copyright law recognize *near absolute rights* in inventors and authors for a limited term, trademark law, by contrast, originally recognized rights *only insofar as necessary* to prevent unfair competition or consumer confusion,[1287] by making actionable the use of another's trademark in ways that lead to a "likelihood of confusion".[1288]

Early protection of trademarks was narrow and focused on ownership (identification), origin (source), and quality functions. Early U.S. court decisions repeatedly make clear that the purpose of trademark law was to target unfair or fraudulent business or trade practices.[1289] Trademark infringement was thus a form of unfair competition and nineteenth century commentators note that trademark infringement and unfair competition were aimed at the same wrong.[1290] In *Amoskeag Manufacturing Co. v. Spear*,[1291] for example, Justice Duer

1287 "A 'trademark' is not that which is infringed. What is infringed is the right of the public to be free of confusion and the synonymous right of the trademark owner to control his product's reputation." *James Burrough Ltd. v. Sign of the Beefeater, Inc.*, 540 F.2d 266, 274 (7th Cir. 1976), cited by *Klieger*: Trademark Dilution, fn. 441.

1288 Trademark law also protects owners of highly distinctive or well-known makers against dilution or a tarnishing of their image even *absent* a likelihood of confusion. *Ridgway*: Revitalizing the Doctrine of Trademark Misuse, quoting *Ginsburg/Goldberg/Greenbaum*: Trademark and Unfair Competition Law, pp. 45–47.

1289 *McKenna*: The Normative Foundations of Trademark Law, p. 1859. McKenna cites a New York case from 1845 (*Coats v. Holbrook*, 7 N.Y. Ch. Ann. 713), in which the court said a person is not allowed to imitate the product of another and "thereby attract to himself the patronage that without such deceptive use of such names... would have inured to the benefit of that other person."

1290 *McKenna*: The Normative Foundations of Trademark Law, p. 1863. McKenna notes that cases of trademark infringement and those of unfair competition differed primarily in terms of what the plaintiff had to prove. Use of another's technical trademark could be condemned categorically and thus trademark infringement plaintiffs did not have to prove intent. Use of another's trade name, on the other hand, may have had an innocent purpose, such as description of the product's characteristics or its geographic origin. As a result, in contrast to trademark infringement plaintiffs, unfair competition claimants had to prove that the defendant intended to pass off its products as those of the plaintiff. *McKenna*: The Normative Foundations of Trademark Law, p. 1862.

1291 2 Sand. 599 (N.Y. Super. Ct. 1849), cited by *McKenna*: The Normative Foundations of Trademark Law, fn. 107.

wrote, that "he who affixes to his own goods an imitation of an original trade-mark, by which those of another are distinguished and known, seeks, by deceiving the public, to divert and appropriate to his own use, the profits to which the superior skill and enterprise of the other had given him a prior and exclusive title. He endeavors, by a false representation, to effect a dishonest purpose; he commits a fraud upon the public and upon the true owner of the trade-mark."[1292]

Similarly, the case law of the CJEU consistently emphasizes that the essential function of a trademark is to guarantee the identity of origin of the trademarked goods or services.[1293] In *Kabushiki Kaisha v Metro-Goldwyn-Mayer*, the Court noted:

> "The essential function of the trade mark is to guarantee the identity of the origin of the marked product to the consumer or end user by enabling him, without any possibility of confusion, to distinguish the product or service from others which have another origin. Furthermore, for the trade mark to be able to fulfil its essential role in the system of undistorted competition which the Treaty seeks to establish, it must offer a guarantee that all the goods or services bearing it have originated under the control of a single undertaking which is responsible for their quality."[1294]

The function of a trademark is to enable the consumer, without any danger of confusion, to distinguish the goods and services from one producer from the goods and services of another.[1295] The eleventh recital in the Trademark Directive notes that: "The protection afforded by the registered trade mark, the function

---

1292 *Amoskeag Manufacturing Co. v. Spear*, 2 Sand. 599 (N.Y. Super. Ct. 1849).

1293 Case C-48/05, *Adam Opel AG v Autec AG*, 25 January 2007 [2007] ECR I-1017, para. 21: "the exclusive right under Article 5(1) of the directive was conferred in order to enable the trade mark proprietor to protect his specific interests as proprietor, that is, *to ensure that the trade mark can fulfil its functions* and that, therefore, the exercise of that right must be reserved to cases in which a third party's use of the sign affects or is liable to affect the functions of the trade mark, *in particular its essential function* of guaranteeing to consumers the origin of the goods".

1294 Case C-39/97, *Canon Kabushiki Kaisha v Metro-Goldwyn-Mayer Inc., formerly Pathe Communications Corporation*, 29 September 1998 [1998] ECR I-5507, para. 3.

1295 The "essential function of a trade mark is to guarantee the identity of origin of the marked goods or services to the consumer or end user by enabling him, without any possibility of confusion, to distinguish the goods or services from others which have another origin". "For that guarantee of origin, which constitutes the essential function of a trade mark, to be ensured, the proprietor must be protected against competitors wishing to take unfair advantage of the status and reputation of the trade mark by selling products illegally bearing". Case C-206/01, *Arsenal Football Club plc v Matthew Reed*, 12 November 2002, paras. 48 and 50.

of which is in particular to guarantee the trade mark as an indication of origin, should be absolute in the case of identity between the mark and the sign and goods or services."[1296]

The industrial revolution dramatically increased production capacity for goods: trademarks could be used to help the consumer easily distinguish between goods. As Jeanne Fromer has noted, this development led, invariably, to consumers knowing less and less about the *specific* source of particular goods, but gave them information which enabled them to distinguish *between* sources.[1297] The function of trademarks, therefore, expanded to capture the intangible "symbol" manifested in the brand name of a manufacturer – the "goodwill" of a trademark.[1298] This goodwill function of a trademark (also called the "advertising" function) is one of the most important functions of a trademark today: in today's world, a trademark is "charged" by the advertising messages in which the trademark plays a role – i.e., by the goodwill created for the trademark. Over time, a trademark increasingly becomes a symbol for consumers' experiences with the trademarked products or services. For the consuming public, the trademark becomes the summary of more than just a designation of origin, communicating the more complicated messages about the product than just a name.[1299] The protection of the trademark thereby protects the investment in the trademark itself as well as the quality of the product, the marketing and positioning of the product and the

1296 Directive 2008/95/EC, OJ L 299/25, 8.11.2008.

1297 "[A] trademark affixed to goods would help consumers know that those goods originated from the *same* source, whatever that source was." *Fromer*: Creativity and the Law, p. 1891, fn. 46 (emphasis mine), citing *Schechter*: The Rational Basis of Trademark Protection, pp. 814–15 and 817.

1298 "Goodwill is an intangible asset that provides added value to the owner's worth. A mark is a symbol of the owner's goodwill in the business *and the goods or services* associated with the mark." *INTA*: Fact Sheets: Assignments, Licenses and Valuation. Professor Bone argues that the protection of goodwill "has nothing directly to do with facilitating consumer choice or safeguarding the quality of market information. It has to do instead with protecting sellers from misappropriation." Bone distinguishes between three forms of goodwill – brand goodwill, firm goodwill, or the inherent goodwill associated with a mark's popularity – and argues that protection of the broadest category of "inherent goodwill" has resulted in "some rather broad, and ultimately ill-advised, doctrinal expansions. *Bone*: Hunting Goodwill.

1299 *Jehoram/van Nispen/Huydecoper*: European Trademark Law, p. 13.

general image,[1300] specifically recognized by the CJEU[1301] and the General Court.[1302]

In addition, there is an increasing tendency to discuss the "creative" aspects of trademarks, or the "creative" influence such trademark have in advertising and brand valuation.[1303] In so doing, the tendency is to "reward" creativity in trademarks, thereby justifying absolute protection closer to that found in patent and copyright law. As has already been noted, patent and copyright protection are strictly limited in duration; trademark protection can be indefinite. The balance (short-term grant of exclusive rights countered by the long-term contributions to the public domain) does not, therefore, exist with trademark protection.

(c) Protected Categories

Trademark law protects words, names, logos, devices, and a plethora of other distinctive symbols used in connection with goods and services to indicate the source of such goods and to distinguish them from the goods and services of others.[1304] What constitutes a "trademark" and the categories of features that can be protected has expanded. Protection can be obtained for:

1300 *Id.*, p. 14.

1301 "Dior ... argued in particular that the expression 'condition of the goods' used in Article 7(2) of the Directive also covers the 'mental' condition of the goods, by which it means the allure, prestigious image and aura of luxury surrounding the goods, resulting from the manner in which the trade mark owner has chosen to present and advertise the goods using his trade mark rights." Case C-337/95, *Parfums Christian Dior SA and Parfums Christian Dior BV v Evora BV*, 4 November 1997 [1997] ECR I-6013, para. 10.

1302 "The fact remains that a mark also acts as a *means of conveying other messages* concerning, inter alia, the qualities or particular characteristics of the goods or services which it covers or the images and feelings which it conveys, such as, for example, luxury, lifestyle, exclusivity, adventure, youth. To that effect the mark has an inherent economic value which is independent of and separate from that of the goods and services for which it is registered. The messages in question which are conveyed inter alia by a mark with a reputation or which are associated with it confer on that mark a significant value which deserves protection, particularly because, in most cases, the reputation of a mark is the result of considerable effort and investment on the part of its proprietor." Case T-215/03, *Sigla SA v OHIM*, 22 March 2007 [2007] ECR II-711, para. 35.

1303 *Fromer*: Creativity and the Law.

1304 Under the Lanham Act (15 U.S.C. § 1127), the "term 'trademark' includes any word, name, symbol, or device, or any combination thereof ... used ... to identify

- the shape of a product[1305] (e.g., the Coca-Cola bottle;[1306] the Lindt chocolate

---

and distinguish [one's] goods, including a unique product, from those manufactured or sold by others and to indicate the source of the goods, even if that source is unknown."
Under the Trademark Directive 2008/95/EC (OJ L 299/25, 8.11.2008), Article 2: a "trade mark may consist of any signs capable of being represented graphically, particularly words, including personal names, designs, letters, numerals, the shape of goods or of their packaging, provided that such signs are capable of distinguishing the goods or services of one undertaking from those of other undertakings".
Under the TRIPs Agreement (1994), Article 15, the definition is even broader: "Any sign, or any combination of signs, capable of distinguishing the goods or services of one undertaking from those of other undertakings, shall be capable of constituting a trademark. Such signs, in particular words including personal names, letters, numerals, figurative elements and combinations of colours as well as any combination of such signs, shall be eligible for registration as trademarks. Where signs are not inherently capable of distinguishing the relevant goods or services, Members may make registrability depend on distinctiveness acquired through use. Members may require, as a condition of registration, that signs be visually perceptible."

1305 Case C-299/99, *Koninklijke Philips Electronics NV v. Remington Consumer Products Ltd*, 18 June 2002 [2002] ECR I-5475, para. 1: "The criteria for assessing the distinctive character of three-dimensional trade marks are no different from those to be applied to other categories of trade mark and the shape in question must simply be capable of distinguishing the product of the proprietor of the trade mark from those of other undertakings and thus of *fulfilling its essential purpose* of guaranteeing the origin of the product. Case 102/77, *Hoffmann-La Roche & Co. AG v Centrafarm Vertriebsgesellschaft Pharmazeutischer Erzeugnisse mbH*, 23 May 1978 [1978] ECR 1139, summary para. 2 and grounds para. 7: "regard must be had to the essential function of the trade-mark, which is to guarantee the identity of the origin of the trade-marked product to the consumer or ultimate user, by enabling him without any possibility of confusion to distinguish that product from products which have another origin."

1306 The distinctive shape of the Coca-Cola bottle was originally protected under a design patent (granted on 25 December 1923 for the "hobble skirt" contour bottle, also known as "the Christmas bottles"). The second design patent for the contour bottle was granted to the Coca-Cola Company on 3 August 1937, preventing imitation of the bottle for another 14 years. On 12 April 1960, the Coca-Cola Company sought and obtained a federal trademark registration for its contour bottle shape, enabling the company to safeguard the bottle design indefinitely. *Purvis*: What Every Small and Medium Sized Business Should Know.

Easter bunny;[1307] the HARIBO *Goldbären* gummy bear;[1308] and (perhaps even)

1307 In June 2000, Swiss-based Lindt & Sprüngli applied to register as a three-dimensional Community trademark the form and presentation of its chocolate bunny – sold since the early 1950s – wrapped in gold-coloured foil, with red and brown markings, wearing a red ribbon and attached bell around its neck, and bearing on its haunch a design including the words 'Lindt Goldhase'. The mark was registered on 6 July 2001. Following registration, Lindt sued Austrian-based Franz Hauswirth GmbH for trademark infringement proceedings, alleging a likelihood of confusion with respect to Hauswirth's chocolate bunnies, which were usually decorated with a ribbon (but without a bell), and bore no identifying name. The Hauswirth label, affixed to the underside, was normally invisible when the rabbit was placed on its base. The Commercial Court of Vienna decided against Hauswirth, finding its chocolate bunnies confusingly similar to Lindt's bunnies. Hauswirth appealed the decision. In judgment C-529/07, *Chocoladefabriken Lindt & Sprüngli AG v Franz Hauswirth GmbH*, also known as the *Easter bunnies case*, the court discussed bad faith in trademark invalidity proceedings. In March 2012, the Austrian Supreme Court confirmed the Commercial Court's decision. See *Forstner*: Osterhase legt Hauswirth bittere Niederlage ins Nest. Unfortunately, Lindt has had problems defending this form in Germany. In 2010, the German Federal High Court (*Bundesgerichtshof*, case reference I ZR 72/12) refused to grant Lindt's final appeal (decision dated 15 July 2010 – I ZR 57/08) against a decision by the Higher Regional Court of Frankfurt (*Oberlandesgericht Frankfurt*, OLG Frankfurt am Main – decision dated 8 November 2007 – 6 U 10/03; LG Frankfurt am Main – decision dated 19 December 2002 – 2/3 O 443/02), which held that there was no likelihood of confusion between Lindt's famous chocolate bunny and Riegelein's slightly more bronze coloured bunny. The trademark dispute went on for 12 years (decision dated 26 October 2006 – I ZR 37/04, BGHZ 169, 295 – Goldhase I; press release Nr. 146/2006 from 27 October 2006). *Bundesgerichtshof*: Press Release, Nr. 150/2010. See also *Die Welt*: Goldhase von Lindt muss Konkurrenz dulden.

1308 The Cologne Regional Court banned Lindt from selling its chocolate bears wrapped in gold foil. According to the ruling, the Lindt golden teddy infringed the word trademark "Goldbären" (gold bear) registered by HARIBO, on the basis that the chocolate bear constituted a three-dimensional reproduction of the word. It was immaterial to the court that Lindt specifically chose to label its product "Lindt Teddy" – as opposed to "Goldbär" – which would have suggested a brand extension over Lindt's litigious "Goldhase". The court did not accept Lindt's point that there was no ground for confusion between a jelly bear and a chocolate bear. *IPKat*: Monday Miscellany. "The decision is noteworthy … because it constitutes the first German decision on a registered word trade mark being infringed by a three-dimensional product shape." *IPKat*: Monday Miscellany, quoting Thorsten Lauterbach. See *Wood*: Gummy bear wins court battle; and *Kölner Stadt-Anzeiger*: Lindt verliert im Teddy-Streit.

Kit Kat's breakable chocolate "fingers"[1309];

- the look and feel of a retail environment (e.g., the interior layout of a store[1310]; and

---

1309 The form of the Kit Kat bar is undergoing scrutiny. In a case from the United Kingdom's Trade Mark Registry, O-237-13 Société des Produits Nestlé SA, Nestlé's application to register the shape of its Kit Kat bar (a rectangular slab of chocolate with breaking grooves along the length of the bar which divide the bar into 'fingers') was opposed by competitor Cadbury UK Ltd. The court held the shape to be non-distinctive and opposed registration. Nestlé appealed. In *Société Des Produits Nestlé SA v Cadbury UK Ltd* [2014] EWHC 16 (Ch), Mr. Justice Arnold referred certain questions to the CJEU. The case is still pending.

1310 In May 2010, Apple submitted two trademark applications (US registrations numbers 4277913 and 4277914) to the U.S. Patent and Trademark Office. Both trademark applications were for a three-dimensional trademark consisting of the representation, by a design in color (in particular, metallic grey and light brown) of the interior features of Apple's flagship retail stores, specifically for "'retail store services featuring computers, computer software, computer peripherals, mobile phones, consumer electronics and related accessories and demonstrations of products relating thereto". The "description of the mark" of registration 4277913 reads as follows:

"The color(s) steel gray, light brown and black is/are claimed as a feature of the mark. The mark consists of the design and layout of a retail store. The store features a clear glass storefront surrounded by a paneled, steel gray facade consisting of large, rectangular horizontal panels over the top of the glass front, and two narrower panels stacked on either side of the storefront. Within the store, rectangular recessed lighting units traverse the length of the store's ceiling.

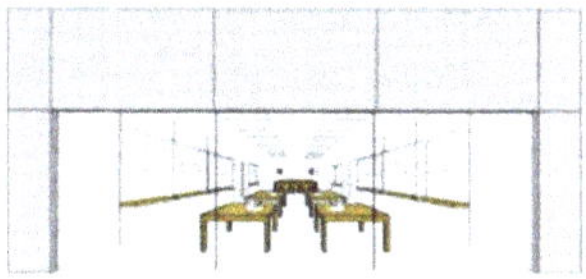

There are light brown cantilevered shelves below recessed display spaces along the side walls, and light brown rectangular tables arranged in a line in the middle of the store parallel to the walls and extending from the storefront to the back of the store. There is multi-tiered shelving along the side walls, and a light brown oblong table with black stools located at the back of the store, set below video screens flush mounted on the back wall."

Text and application image available from *USPTO*: serial nr. 85036986.

The USPTO granted the registrations on 22 Janaury 2013. Subsequently, Apple sought to extend this trademark internationally under the Madrid Agreement. On 24 January 2013, the German PTO (the *Deutsches Patent- und Markenamt* or DPMA) refused the extension of such three-dimensional international trademark (IR 1060321) in Germany on the ground that consumers would not regard the sign as a trademark in sense of indicating trade origin – the depiction of the space

- sounds, smells;[1311] and color[1312] (including colors in an environment to

devoted to the sale of Apple's products was nothing other than the representation of an essential aspect of Apple's business. The DPMA found that consumers would unlikely perceive the layout of a retail store as an indication of a product's commercial origin, in particular as the DPMA did not find the layout sufficiently distinguishable from the stores of other providers of electronic products. In 2013, Apple appealed to the German Federal Patent Court (the *Bundespatentgericht*) against the DPMA's refusal decision. Finding that the case raised fundamental questions concerning trademark law, the Bundespatentgericht elected to stay the proceedings and refer a number of questions to the CJEU. On 10 July 2014, the CJEU confirmed that the representation of the layout of a retail store, such as the one Apple sought to protect, may – subject to certain conditions – be registered as a trademark. Case C-421/13, *Apple Inc. v Deutsches Patent- und Markenamt*, 10 July 2014 (decision not yet published, EU:C:2014:2070).
Such registrations illustrate "the increasing importance of the visual effect of marketing and what is called 'trade dress'". *IPKat*: Get-up and go! Protecting interior features. In the U.S., protection of trade dress was established in the 1992 Supreme Court case, *Two Pesos, Inc. v Taco Cabana*, 505 U.S. 763 (1992), which held that inherently distinctive trade dress in the form of business décor – in this case a chain of Mexican restaurants, described as "a festive eating atmosphere having interior dining and patio areas decorated with artifacts, bright colors, paintings and murals" – could be protected from infringement. For more on the history and a review of the precedents leading up to the case, see *Cooley*: Trade Dress Protection.

1311 *Holah*: United Kingdom – Unconventional marks in Europe.

1312 "The elevation of color to stand-alone trademark status illustrates the unbounded nature of trademarks within the judicial consciousness. The availability of color-alone marks also facilitates the commoditization of color in ways that complicate the development and distribution of products and services that use color for multiple purposes co-terminously. The economic case for color-alone trademarks is severely undermined by careful observation of the ways that colors are actually deployed in commerce, which makes it clear that the trademarks of multiple goods and services can utilize the same color to telegraph the same message without confusing anyone or diluting the commercial power of textual or symbolic trademarks." *Bartow*: The True Colors of Trademark Law, p. 263. In the U.S., the Supreme Court case *Qualitex Co. v. Jacobson Products Co., Inc.*, 514 U.S. 159 (1995) established that a color could meet the legal requirements for trademark registration under the Lanham Act, provided that it has acquired secondary meaning in the market. In Germany (as confirmed by Case C-49/02, *Heidelberger Bauchemie GmbH*, 24 June 2004 [2004] ECR I-6129, reference from the *Bundespatentgericht*, relating to combinations of the colors blue and yellow for certain products used in the building trade) and the Netherlands (as confirmed by Case C-104/01, *Libertel Groep BV v Benelux-Merkenbureau*, 6 May 2003 [2003] ECR

express corporate identity[1313]).

so long as each of these aspects can be represented graphically.[1314]

This increasingly broad array of protected marks or symbols was not always the case. In the U.S., under traditional common law principles, the law distinguished between protection of a "trademark" versus a "trade name".[1315] The distinction was important: a trademark owner could proceed on an action for trademark infringement (which did not require the trademark owner to prove intent to infringe),[1316] whereas a trade-name owner could only proceed under an action for unfair competition (which did require the trade-name owner to

---

I-3793, reference from the *Hoge Raad der Nederlanden*, regarding the trademark of orange as a color), registration of colors as trademarks is certainly possible.

1313 Under UK and European Community law, trademark registrations for marks involving the use of color and design can be obtained for the use of particular color(s) as applied to retail environments; however, the level of distinctiveness required is quite high.

For example, in 1995 BP p.l.c. obtained registrations in UK retail petrol station services, the mark being a recently adopted shade of green disposed on surfaces in a particular way as shown in a representation of a petrol filling station (UK No. UK00001469513). The idea was to provide a uniform corporate identity that would allow a motorist to spot BP's filling stations from a distance. The mark "consists of the colour green as applied to the exterior surface of the premises used for the provision of the services". For text and registration image, see *UK Intellectual Property Office*: Trademark UK00001469513.

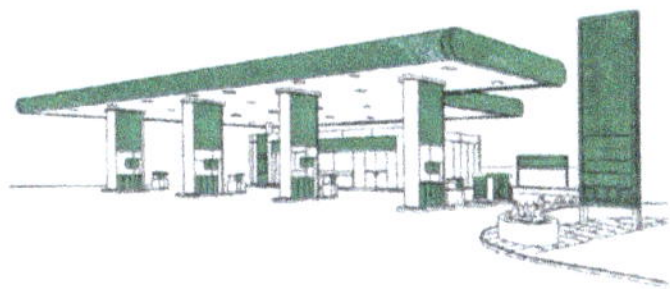

When another company claimed that the application of color to the stations was not distinctiveness, the Court of Appeal of Northern Ireland found that BP's color trademark - on its own - was not distinctive, but that it had acquired distinctiveness given the period of time (more than a decade of use) that had elapsed.

1314 Council Regulation (EC) No 207/2009 of 26 February 2009 on the Community trade mark: Article 2 states: "A trade mark may consist of any signs capable of being represented graphically".

1315 *Grinvald*: Shaming Trademark Bullies, pp. 633–35.

1316 *Handler/Pickett*: Trade-Marks and Trade Names, p. 169, cited by *Grinvald*: Shaming Trademark Bullies, p. 634, fn. 42.

prove such intent).[1317] Furthermore, the potential remedies in a trademark infringement action were broader than that those for unfair competition action (plaintiffs in a trademark infringement case had recourse to broad injunctive remedies; unfair competition plaintiffs did not).[1318]

By the turn of the twentieth century, this strict distinction began to blur and trade names began to be afforded protection similar to that of a technical trademark if the trade-name owner could prove "secondary meaning" – i.e., some association of the trade name by consumers with the source of the product, so that the trade name was deemed to have acquired *distinctiveness* similar to that of a trademark.[1319] With the passage of the Lanham Act in 1946,[1320] the distinction between the two categories and the use of the two terms was officially eliminated.[1321] The case law in the European Union shows a similar trend of expansion. In particular, there is a tendency to find a plethora of modern "functions" in trademark, each of which needs to be acknowledged (and valued).[1322] There is also increased inconsistency in the meaning (and thus the application) of the "specific subject matter" of trademarks.[1323]

The expansion in the types of source identifiers that may qualify for trademark protection is troubling "because it not only impacts the ability of businesses to compete, but it also impacts the free expression rights of all entities

1317 *Grinvald*: Shaming Trademark Bullies, p. 634, fn. 44, citing *Schechter*: Historical Foundations, p. 161. See also *McKenna*: Trademark Use and the Problem of Source, pp. 781–83.

1318 *Handler/Pickett*: Trade-Marks and Trade Names, p. 169, cited by *Grinvald*: Shaming Trademark Bullies, p. 634, fn. 45.

1319 *Grinvald*: Shaming Trademark Bullies, p. 634–35.

1320 15 U.S.C. § 1051 et seq.

1321 *Grinvald*: Shaming Trademark Bullies, p. 635.

1322 "... a use which the proprietor of the trade mark is entitled to prevent if use of that sign affects, or is likely to affect, the *functions* of the trade mark as a trade mark." Case C-48/05, *Adam Opel AG v Autec AG*, 25 January 2007 [2007] ECR I-1017, summary judgment para. 1. See also *Jehoram/van Nispen/Huydecoper*: European Trademark Law, p. 9. Fezer makes note of at least seventeen functions: coding function, guarantee function, origin function, guarantee of origin function, identification function, individualization function, information function, communication function, monopolization function, name function, quality function, type function, distinguishing function, consumer protection function, trust function, sales function, and advertising function. *Fezer*: Markengesetz.

1323 *Larkin*: Harmony in Disarray.

and individuals".[1324] Additionally, when combined with the increased rationales for trademark protection, along with the standards and claims for trademark infringement, these expansions are alarming, as "the breadth of potentially infringing uses balloons to unprecedented proportions".[1325]

(d) Infringement Standards & Causes of Action

Just as the scope of what is deemed a "trademark" has increased, so too the liability standards and causes of action available for a trademark owner: today, trademark owners have a broad range of infringement claims they can make.

(i) Likelihood of Confusion & Initial Interest Confusion

Trademark law protects a trademark owner's exclusive right to use a trademark when use of the mark by another would be *likely* to cause *consumer confusion* as to the source or origin of goods. As the Tenth Circuit court put it: "Likelihood of confusion forms the gravamen for a trademark infringement action."[1326] To establish a violation under the U.S. Lanham Act, the plaintiff must demonstrate that: (i) it has a valid and legally protectable mark; (ii) it owns the mark; and (iii) the defendant's use of the mark to identify goods or services causes a likelihood of confusion.[1327]

The likelihood of confusion test covers the probability (but not the actuality) that consumers will be confused by the same or similar trademarks.[1328] The "likelihood of confusion" test imposes liability if an "appreciable number of ordinarily prudent purchasers are likely to be misled, or indeed simply confused, as to the source of the good".[1329] The problem is that the case law has developed in an

1324 *Grinvald*: Shaming Trademark Bullies, p. 635–636 (citations omitted).

1325 *Id.*, p. 636 (citations omitted).

1326 *King of the Mountain Sports, Inc. v. Chrysler Corp.*, 185 F.3d 1084, 1089, 51 U.S.P.Q. 2d 1349, 1352 (10th Cir. 1999), citing 15 U.S.C. §§ 1114(1), 1125(a). Scholars – like courts – also hold likelihood of confusion as the hallmark of any trademark infringement. *McCarthy*: McCarthy on Trademarks and Unfair Competition, § 23:1.

1327 *A&H Sportswear, Inc. v. Victoria's Secret Stores, Inc.*, 237 F.3d 198 (3rd Cir. 2000). The protection applies both to registered marks (15 U.S.C. § 1114) and unregistered marks (15 U.S.C. § 1125(a)).

1328 *Grinvald*: Shaming Trademark Bullies, p. 636.

1329 *McGregor-Doniger Inc. v. Drizzle Inc.*, 599 F.2d 1126, 1130 (2d Cir. 1979), quoting *Mushroom Makers, Inc. v. R.G. Barry Corp.*, 580 F.2d 44, 47 (2d Cir. 1978), cert denied, 439 U.S. 1116 (1979). See *McKenna*: Trademark Use and the Problem of Source, p. 822, fn. 234, for a summary of cases citing this test. McKenna notes that

inconsistent fashion, with no definitive test and no clarity as to the factors a court should consider. In the U.S., each of the circuit court courts have each adopted their own test, setting out (similar) factors for determining the likelihood of confusion.[1330] Robert Bone described the test as follows:

> "The test is a mess. It produces bad results, is doctrinally incoherent, and lacks a sensible normative foundation. It chills socially valuable uses and facilitates excessively broad expansions of trademark law, and it includes factors that make no sense as predictors of likely confusion. Most importantly, the test erroneously assumes that consumer confusion is enough to warrant liability without regard to the harmful consequences or the moral wrongfulness of the defendant's conduct."[1331]

Mark McKenna has further noted the test's problems:

> "consumers are bombarded with marketing information designed to shape their understanding of commercial relationships;... dependence on consumer understanding creates particular instability in trademark law because courts are required to instantiate consumer understanding of "source" relationships.... "source" in modern trademark law is an extraordinarily broad concept capable of encompassing virtually any relationship between entities.... trademark law condemns confusion about sponsorship or affiliation without precisely defining those terms or attempting to determine whether, or in what circumstances, consumers care about such relationships.... And the modern marketplace abounds with licensing arrangements."[1332]

Moreover, the types of deception that the consumer confusion test reaches have also multiplied. Courts have refocused the underlying principle, replacing the

---

there is no absolute quantitative threshold for determining what level of confusion is "appreciable", but finds that courts have generally been persuaded by evidence of 15% confusion. McKenna notes that in *Grotrian, Helfferich, Schulz, Th. Steinweg Nachf. v. Steinway & Sons*, 365 F. Supp. 707, 716 (S.D.N.Y. 1973), modified on other grounds, 523 F.2d 1331 (2d Cir. 1975), the court called evidence of 8.5% confusion "strong evidence" of a likelihood of confusion.

1330 *Cody*: Initial Interest Confusion, pp. 652–654. At fn. 42, Cody lists each federal circuit courts of appeals' test for likelihood of confusion. The most comprehensive test – commonly referred to as the *Du Pont* test – was set forth by the United States Court of Customs and Patent Appeals, and is still used today by the Federal Circuit (*Interpace Corp. v. Lapp, Inc.*, 721 F.2d 460, 463 (3d Cir. 1983)). The Second Circuit employs the *Polaroid* test (*Polaroid Corp. v. Polarad Elecs. Corp.*, 287 F.2d 492, 495 (2d Cir. 1961)). The Ninth Circuit employs the Sleekcraft test (*AMF, Inc. v. Sleekcraft Boats*, 599 F.2d 341, 348–49 (9th Cir. 1979)).

1331 *Bone*: Taking the Confusion out of "Likelihood of Confusion".

1332 *McKenna*: Trademark Use and the Problem of Source, pp. 821–822. For a European perspective, see *Ohlgart*: Gebrauch der Marke eines Dritten.

"consumer" confusion theory with more liberal "owner identity" confusion theory (which has also been called "associational"[1333] or "subliminal"[1334] confusion). In the EU, a parallel expansion of the likelihood of confusion test has occurred. Here too "likelihood of confusion includes confusion as to sponsorship, affiliation, or connection."[1335] In sum, the boundaries of what constitutes "likelihood of confusion" is vague and has been applied even in the *absence* of actual or overt confusion.

As a derivative expansion of the "likelihood of confusion" test, the so-called "initial interest confusion" test, has crept into use.[1336] This doctrine allows for a finding of liability where a plaintiff can demonstrate that a consumer was confused by a defendant's conduct at the time of interest in a product or service, *even if* that initial confusion is *corrected* by the time of purchase.[1337] The doctrine

---

1333 *Klieger*: Trademark Dilution, p. 809, citing *Toys "R" Us, Inc. v. Canarsie Kiddie Shop, Inc.*, 559 F. Supp. 1189, 1200–01 (E.D.N.Y. 1983). Klieger notes that "A likelihood exists that even those purchasers who do not consciously assume that the plaintiff and defendants are related entities will be attracted to the defendant's store on the basis of the goodwill established by the plaintiff... creating a likelihood of associational confusion."

1334 *Ehrlich*: When Should Post-Sale Confusion Prevent Use or Registration of Marks?, p. 278. Ehrlich categorizes subliminal confusion as "part of a broader body of questionable trademark case law which introduces other unpredictable pro-plaintiff 'wild cards' into trademark law". See also *Hartman*: Subliminal Confusion: The Misappropriation of Advertising Value, pp. 508–10 (1988), who examines the unconscious "deception" that can lead a consumer to graft associations with the senior mark onto the junior mark despite the absence of overt confusion.

1335 *McCarthy*: Proving a Trademark Has Been Diluted, p. 723, interpreting Advocate General Jacobs' opinion in *Canon Kabushiki Kaisha*. Article 4(1)(b) of the Trademark Directive prohibits the registration of a trademark if "because of its identity with, or similarity to, [an] earlier trademark and the identity or similarity of the goods or services covered by the trademarks, there exists *a likelihood of confusion* on the part of the public, which includes the likelihood of association with the earlier trade mark." (emphasis mine). Advocate General Jacobs found that "if, despite recognising that the goods or services have different places of origin, the public is likely to believe that there is a link between the two concerns, there will be a likelihood of confusion within the meaning of the Directive." Case C-39/97, *Canon Kabushiki Kaisha v Metro-Goldwyn-Mayer Inc., formerly Pathe Communications Corporation*, [1998] ECR I-5507, Opinion of AG Jacobs, 2 April 1998, para. 30.

1336 See *Lastowka*: Google's Law, pp. 1367–71, for a description of how the doctrine of initial interest confusion has grown.

1337 For further criticism of the initial interest test – in particular how it has expanded by application to the internet – see *Grynberg*: The Road Not Taken; *Fritch*:

was developed by U.S. courts in the 1970s.[1338] Before then, "traditional" likelihood of confusion cases focused on confusion that occurred *at the point of sale or after*.[1339] European courts have adopted the concept[1340] and initial interest confusion is actionable under Article 5 of the EU Trade Marks Directive.[1341]

Like the "likelihood of confusion" test, the "initial interest confusion" infringement standard is problematic. There is no conformity on what elements must be shown to establish initial interest confusion. Many courts seem to be using the doctrine to find liability for perceived bad acts without engaging in any analysis – they merely conclude there is initial interest confusion and therefore infringement has occurred. This expanded understanding of – and automatic liability for – confusion, including liability in cases where the "confusion" does not affect a consumer's purchasing activity or where the consumer is no longer confused – is no longer protection grounded in the pragmatic rationales of protecting trademark owners from fraudulent use and consumers from confusion as to source. Today the law supports an open-ended concept of confusion, in which

---

Searching for Initial Interest Confusion; *Glazer/Dhamija*: Revisiting Initial Interest Confusion on the Internet; *Klein/Glazer*: Reconsidering Initial Interest Confusion on the Internet. See also *Cody*: Initial Interest Confusion.

1338 *INTA*: Request for Action by the INTA Board of Directors, p. 3. One of the earliest initial interest confusion cases was *Grotrian, Helfferich, Schulz, Th. Steinweg Nachf. v. Steinway & Sons*, 365 F.Supp. 707 (S.D.N.Y. 1973), aff'd, 523 F.2d 1331 (2d Cir. 1975). The court found a likelihood of confusion between STEINWEG and STEINWAY for pianos, holding that the harm to Steinway was that a potential customer, initially thinking there was a connection, would be attracted by the GROTIAN-STEINWEG name to consider that brand of piano, even though later investigation would reveal no connection with the makers of STEINWAY. *INTA*: Request for Action by the INTA Board of Directors, p. 3, fn. 2.

1339 "It again seems clear from this that there can be... confusion... at the point when a consumer views an advertisement, whether or not the advertisement leads to a sale and whether or not the consumer remains confused at the time of any such sale." *Arnold*: Initial Interest Confusion in European Trade Mark Law, slide 11.

1340 *Arnold*: Initial Interest Confusion in European Trade Mark Law, slide 2. Case C-278/08, *Die BergSpechte Outdoor Reisen under Alpinschule Edi Koblmüller GmbH v Guni*, 25 March 2010 [2010] ECR I-2517, para. 39.

1341 Article 5(1)(b) of Directive 2008/95/EC, OJ L 299/25, 8.11.2008, provides that a trademark owner may prohibit a third party from using "any sign where, because of its identity with, or similarity to, the trade mark and the identity or similarity of goods or services covered by the trade mark and the sign, *there exists a likelihood of confusion* on the part of the public, which includes *the likelihood of association* between the sign and the trade mark" (emphasis mine).

any kind of confusion – not only confusion as to the source of products, but also as to association, sponsorship, or affiliation – will be sufficient to support a claim for trademark infringement. INTA has tracked this development and has formally recommended that "courts should engage in traditional likelihood of confusion analysis in cases of initial interest confusion, rather than creating a new doctrine or treating initial interest confusion as a substitute for actual confusion in the likelihood of confusion analysis. To put it another way, the subcommittee believes that confusion is confusion is confusion, whether it is prior to or at the point of sale, and that the same likelihood of confusion factors should be used in all instances."[1342]

(ii) Dilution: Famous Trademarks

The expanded – and inconsistently applied – likelihood of confusion and initial interest confusion tests have an even greater impact when applied to famous trademarks. Pursuant to the theory of dilution, a famous trademark receives the benefits of an *expanded* likelihood-of-confusion liability standard in three ways. First, trademark strength is a key factor in any analysis: the stronger the trademark, the more likely it is that the court will determine that there is a likelihood of confusion and find infringement.[1343] Second, a strong trademark can claim confusion over the expanded category of products and the various types of confusion, as the ability to claim such protection depends on the strength of the trademark.[1344] Finally, famous trademarks are afforded an alternative form of protection against *potential* – even absent the presence of actual – dilution.[1345] In effect, anti-dilution laws allow famous trademark holders to guard

1342 *INTA*: Request for Action by the INTA Board of Directors.

1343 *Dinwoodie/Janis*: Trademarks and Unfair Competition, pp. 506–09, cited by *Grinvald*: Shaming Trademark Bullies, p. 638, fn. 76. As one court has observed, "The stronger the mark, the more likely it is that encroachment on it will produce confusion." *Little Caesar Enterprises, Inc. v. Pizza Caesar, Inc.*, 834 F.2d 568, 571 (6th Cir. 1987), cited by *Grinvald*: Shaming Trademark Bullies, p. 638, fn. 77.

1344 *Grinvald*: Shaming Trademark Bullies, p. 638.

1345 15 U.S.C. § 1125(c): "Subject to the principles of equity, the owner of a famous mark that is distinctive... shall be entitled to an injunction against another person who ... commences use of a mark or trade name in commerce that is *likely to cause dilution* by blurring or dilution by tarnishment of the famous mark, *regardless of the presence or absence of actual or likely confusion*, of competition, or of actual economic injury." (emphasis mine).

against use of their mark or a similar mark even when there is no consumer confusion.[1346]

The theory of dilution[1347] has been traced back to Frank Schechter's 1927 article *The Rational Basis of Trademark Protection*, in which he found that "the preservation of the uniqueness of a trademark should constitute the only rational basis for its protection."[1348] Schechter believed that a trademark's role "not merely as the symbol of good will but often as the most effective agent for the creation of good will"[1349] required absolute protection of a mark's uniqueness, and thus the recognition of trademark rights similar to real property.[1350] Some states began protecting against dilution beginning in the mid-twentieth century;[1351] in 1996,

---

1346 *Fromer*: Creativity and the Law, p. 1917. Generally, see also *Long*: Dilution, pp. 1030–31 (2006); and *Lastowka*: Google's Law, pp. 1367–71.

1347 The term "dilution" has been traced back to the German *Odol* case, decision dated 11 September 1924, Landgericht Elberfeld, 25 Juristische Wochenschrift 502, XXV Markenschutz und Wettbewerb 264). See *Schechter*: The Rational Basis of Trademark Protection, cited by *Klieger*: Trademark Dilution, p. 806, fn. 96. For a discussion of the *Odol* case (concerning Dresdner Chemisches Laboratorium Lingner's "Odol" mouthwash and the company's concerns regarding the use of "Odol" for steel railroad ties), see *Sanders*: Odol, pp. 51–61.

1348 *Schechter*: The Rational Basis of Trademark Protection. For an analysis of Schechter's article and its legal consequences, see *Klieger*: Trademark Dilution, pp. 801–810. Klieger warns of the expanding nature of the dilution doctrine, noting that it has not only supplemented, but – more dangerously – supplanted consumer protection principles. See generally *Port*: The "Unnatural" Expansion of Trademark Rights, who argues that federal dilution laws are incongruent with traditional trademark law; and *Magid/Cox/Cox*: Quantifying Brand Image. For contrasting views and defenses of the doctrine, see *Schwartz/Morfesi*: Dilution Comes of Age, p. 468, who note that the protection of trademarks under the dilution principle "has evolved independently worldwide, has reached a critical junction, and must be further nurtured if it is to mature to its full potential"; *Strasser*: The Rational Basis of Trademark Protection Revisited, who argues that trademarks cannot fulfill their intended function if not protected against dilution; *Beebe*: A Defense of the New Federal Trademark Antidilution Law, p. 1174, who argues that the federal law is – relatively – narrower than dilution theory; and *Long*: Dilution, pp. 1029–1033, who also finds that dilution is narrowly interpreted and not easily found.

1349 *Schechter*: The Rational Basis of Trademark Protection, p. 819.

1350 *Id.*, p. 830.

1351 Some 20 years after Schechter's 1927 article was published, Massachusetts enacted the first state statute protecting trademarks from dilution, expressly prohibiting both tarnishment and blurring. 1947 Mass. Acts, p. 300, ch. 307; as cited in *Moseley v. V Secret Catalogue*, 537 U.S. 418, 430 (U.S. 2003). At least 25 states passed similar

the U.S. Congress passed the first federal anti-dilution law.[1352] The federal law protects marks that are sufficiently famous against dilution by blurring and dilution by tarnishment.[1353]

Anti-dilution laws in the EU were in place even earlier.[1354] In some countries, such as the Benelux, the laws were part of trademark law;[1355] in other countries, such as Germany, they were part of unfair competition law.[1356] Article 5(2) of the 1989 Trademark Directive, loosely modeled on those in place in the Benelux and other European countries, contained a model anti-dilution provision – albeit not using the word "dilution" – which provided that a famous trademark owner could prevent another's use of a mark "where use of that sign without due cause takes unfair advantage of, or is detrimental to, the distinctive character or the repute of the trade mark."[1357]

---

laws in the decades before the Federal Dilution Trademark Act (FDTA), referring both to injury to business reputation (tarnishment) and to dilution of the distinctive quality of a trademark or trade name (blurring). For a discussion of the anti-dilution statutes and the history of the FDTA, see *Moseley v. V Secret Catalogue*, 537 U.S. 418 (U.S. 2003).

1352 Federal Trademark Dilution Act of 1995, codified at 15 U.S.C. § 1125(c); as revised by the Trademark Dilution Revision Act of 2006, codified as amended at 15 U.S.C.§§ 1052, 1063, 1064, 1092, 1125, 1127.

1353 Dilution by blurring is "association arising from the similarity between a mark or trade name and a famous mark that impairs the distinctiveness of the famous mark." 15 U.S.C. § 1125(c)(2)(B). Dilution by tarnishment is "association arising from the similarity between a mark or trade name and a famous mark that harms the reputation of the famous mark." 15 U.S.C. § 1125(c)(2)(C).

1354 *Strasser*: The Rational Basis of Trademark Protection Revisited.

1355 "Benelux cases [pre-EU Trademark Directive] have enjoined junior uses which arguably engendered an unmistaken awareness that the mark denoted a different product emanating from a different source". *McCarthy*: Proving a Trademark Has Been Diluted, p. 718, fn. 20, citing *Martino*: Trademark Dilution, p. 100.

1356 *McCarthy*: Proving a Trademark Has Been Diluted, p. 718, fn. 20.

1357 First Council Directive 89/104/EEC of 21 December 1988 to approximate the laws of the Member States relating to trade marks, OJ L 40/1 (1989). As Advocate General Jacobs noted, "The Commission points out that Article 5(2) did not appear in the initial proposal for the Directive put forward by the Commission which considered that such extensive protection was not justified for national trade marks, but should be restricted to a limited number of Community marks, namely marks of wide repute. However in the course of negotiations in the Council, a provision protecting marks 'with a reputation' was included at the request of the Benelux countries, and became Article 5(2) of the Directive." Case C-375/97, *General Motors Corporation v Yplon SA*, 14. September 1999 [1999] ECR I-05421, Opinion of

Implementation of Article 5(2) was optional: the Directive did not require Member States to provide such protection. However, as was later reported by Advocate General Jacobs, "the provisions of Article[]… 5(2)… have in fact been implemented by all the Member States."[1358] The Article 5(2) anti-dilution provision in the Trademark Directive of 2006 is identical.[1359]

Furthermore, both the initial Trademark Regulation of 1994[1360] as well as the CTM Regulation of 2004[1361] provide anti-dilution protection for Community trademarks. In Regulation 40/94, Article 9(1)(c) provides that the proprietor of a CTM may prevent third parties from non-consensual use, without due cause, in the course of trade of any sign identical or similar to their mark on non-similar goods, where their mark has a *reputation* in the EU, and such use takes unfair advantage of or is detrimental to the *distinctive character* or *repute* of their mark.[1362] A claim of dilution under the Regulation for a mark of "reputation" provides a basis for opposition at Article 8(5). Reputation is not defined. Article 8(2), which provides relative grounds for refusal of a trademark registration, refers to "well known" marks ("in the sense in which the words 'well known' are used in Article 6bis of the Paris Convention"). Since the same term is not used, there may be a distinction between having a "reputation" versus being "well known".

Regardless of its implementation, however, analysis of the scope and application of the doctrine seems to be "tentative and vague" and the CJEU seems reluctant – even adverse – to using the word "dilution".[1363] Even when attempts

---

AG Jacobs, 26 November 1998, para. 28. Advocate General Jacobs continued, noting: "While Article 5(2) is clearly based on Article 13A(2) of the former Uniform Benelux Law, there are none the less several important differences. First, protection is provided only for marks 'with a reputation'. Secondly, protection is provided only in relation to goods or services which are not similar. Thirdly, the Directive spells out the type of harm against which protection is provided. These are key features of Article 5(2)." *Id.*, para. 29.

1358 Case C-292/00, *Davidoff & Cie SA and Zino Davidoff SA v Gofkid Ltd*, [2003] ECR I-389, Opinion of AG Jacobs, 21 March 2002, para. 7.

1359 Directive 2008/95/EC, OJ L 299/25, 8.11.2008.

1360 Council Regulation (EC) No 40/94 of 20 December 1993 on the Community trade mark (OJ L 11, 1994).

1361 Council Regulation (EC) No 207/2009/EC (OJ L 78/1, 24.3.2009).

1362 *Id.*, Art. 9.

1363 *McCarthy*: Proving a Trademark Has Been Diluted, pp. 718–719. *McCarthy* cites the Adidas case as one of the rare cases where the Court uses the word "dilution". In the CJEU's judgment, the Court found as follows: "According to the Commission, Article 5(2) of the Directive concerns protection against the use of a sign which

are made to understand its scope and application, these remain someone abbreviated.[1364]

Finally, commentators have noted the error of applying anti-dilution in situations where parties are competitive or when they are selling their products in the same niche market: "Why the need to invoke the "super weapon" of the anti-dilution law to resolve a garden variety infringement case?"[1365]

---

is similar to the mark with a reputation to such an extent that the use in question involves a likelihood of dilution of or detriment to the mark's reputation." Case C-408/01, *Adidas-Salomon AG and Adidas Benelux BV v Fitnessworld Trading Ltd.*, 23 October 2003 [2003] ECR I-12537, para. 27.

1364 *McCarthy*: Proving a Trademark Has Been Diluted, pp. 718–719. *McCarthy* also cites Advocate General Jacobs' opinion in the Adidas case. Jacobs writes: "The concept of detriment to the distinctive character of a trade mark reflects what is generally referred to as dilution. That notion was first articulated by Schechter, who advocated protection against injury to a trade mark owner going beyond the injury caused by use of an identical or similar mark in relation to identical or similar goods or services causing confusion as to origin. Schechter described the type of injury with which he was concerned as the 'gradual whittling away or dispersion of the identity and hold upon the public mind' of certain marks. The courts in the United States, where owners of certain marks have been protected against dilution for some time, have added richly to the lexicon of dilution, describing it in terms of lessening, watering down, debilitating, weakening, undermining, blurring, eroding and insidious gnawing away at a trade mark. The essence of dilution in this classic sense is that the blurring of the distinctiveness of the mark means that it is no longer capable of arousing immediate association with the goods for which it is registered and used. Thus, to quote Schechter again, 'for instance, if you allow Rolls Royce restaurants and Rolls Royce cafeterias, and Rolls Royce pants, and Rolls Royce candy, in 10 years you will not have the Rolls Royce mark any more'." Case C-408/01, *Adidas-Salomon AG and Adidas Benelux BV v Fitnessworld Trading Ltd.*, [2003] ECR I-12537, Opinion of AG Jacobs, 10 July 2003, para. 37.

1365 *McCarthy*: Proving a Trademark Has Been Diluted, p. 731. *McCarthy* notes that the CJEU Justice has also "fallen into this error", citing the 2003 Davidoff decision, in which the CJEU (then the ECJ), rejecting the opinion of A.G. Jacobs and contrary to the wording of the EU Directive, decided that antidilution law is an overarching legal remedy applicable to any and all situations, whether the goods and services are competitive, similar, or non-similar. *McCarthy*: Proving a Trademark Has Been Diluted, pp. 731–732, referring to Case C-292/00, *Davidoff & Cie SA and Zino Davidoff SA v Gofkid Ltd*, 9 January 2003 [2003] ECR I-389.

(iii) *Infringement for Non-Competitive & Non-Competing Uses*

Trademark protection originally protected only *competitive* uses of a trademark owner's mark. Courts limited plaintiff recovery to situations of *direct* competition: the scope of protection focused primarily on protecting producers from competitors' illegitimate interference with their trade.[1366] Broadly speaking, courts conducting a likelihood of confusion analysis apply a different standard to directly competing, as opposed to non-competing, goods.[1367] When the alleged infringer and the trademark owner deal in *competing* goods or services, the court rarely needs to look beyond the mark itself; infringement will usually be found if the two marks at issue are sufficiently similar that consumer confusion can be expected. If the goods in question are completely *unrelated*, confusion is unlikely and infringement will generally not be found. If the goods in question are related but do not directly compete for sales, the likelihood of confusion analysis becomes more complex.[1368]

Early twentieth century trademark law clung to the view that trademarks – and thereby consumers – only demanded protection when marks were used on directly competing products.[1369] In the mid-twentieth century, however, courts, and eventually legislatures, eliminated the direct competition requirement. Slowly but certainly, the law changed to protect trademark owners against a host of *non*-competitive uses.[1370] As a result, trademark law today allows evidence of confusion even in areas where there is no direct competition and even when only a relatively small number of consumers are confused.[1371] With the potential for confusion to reach across unrelated product categories, trademark owners

1366 See *McKenna*: The Normative Foundations of Trademark Law, p. 1841; and *Fromer*: Creativity and the Law, p. 1891.

1367 *A&H Sportswear, Inc. v. Victoria's Secret Stores, Inc.*, 237 F.3d 198 (3rd Cir. 2000).

1368 *Interpace Corp. v. Lapp, Inc.*, 721 F.2d 460 (3d Cir. 1983).

1369 *Klieger*: Trademark Dilution, p. 802.

1370 *Id.*, p. 808, notes that by the second half of the twentieth century, "few could question the degree to which the consumer confusion test protected the source and quality identification functions of trademarks and, at least indirectly, safeguarded trademarks' advertising function as well."

1371 *McKenna*: Trademark Use and the Problem of Source, p. 822, fn. 234, notes that in *Grotrian, Helfferich, Schulz, Th. Steinweg Nachf. v. Steinway & Sons*, 365 F. Supp. 707, 716 (S.D.N.Y. 1973), modified on other grounds, 523 F.2d 1331 (2d Cir. 1975), the court called evidence of 8.5% confusion "strong evidence" of a likelihood of confusion.

have the ability to allege infringement over trademark use in increasingly larger swathes of life and "provide fodder" for unnecessary lawsuits.[1372]

As scholars have noted, the evidence does not show that consumers derive information about the quality of a product from the use of a mark associated with a *non-competitive* product.[1373] This would suggest that the protection of non-competitive use is unnecessary. Finally, an increasing number of scholars have analyzed the paralyzing effect of how trademark law has been applied to prohibit some forms of non-commercial speech (i.e., encroaching on freedom of speech principles), as well as commercial speech that is not misleading.[1374]

(iv) Future & Ancillary Market Preemption

Mark Lemley and Mark McKenna have reviewed – and expressed deep scepticism with – the trend of protecting the possibility of market expansion via trademark law: "This is a market preemption argument analogous to the derivative works right in copyright."[1375] Unlike copyright protection, however, which does (eventually) end, trademarks can be protected indefinitely.

The claim is that the trademark holder owns not just the right to use a particular sign or mark in connection with particular goods, but to the sign or mark itself, *wherever* it has value, i.e., even in a market or a class of goods or services in which the trademark holder is not currently engaged, on the basis that the holder might expand their market.[1376]

The argument that a senior user of a trademark ought to have superior rights to ancillary markets is troubling for the maintenance of a competitive, market economy because it presupposes the right to control use of a mark in a market

1372 *Grinvald*: Shaming Trademark Bullies, pp. 637–638, gives the example of the case of International House of Pancakes v. International House of Prayer, where the plaintiff alleged confusion between the use of "IHOP" for pancakes (plaintiff's use) and religion (defendant's use).

1373 *Fromer*: Creativity and the Law, p. 1916 and fn. 190.

1374 See principally *Ramsey*: Free Speech and International Obligations to Protect Trademarks.

1375 *Lemley/McKenna*: Owning Mark(et)s, pp. 143–144 and 170–172. Lemley and McKenna note that derivative rights are generally accepted and justified in copyright law by the same sort of incentive theory as copyright law, even though some have argued that any marginal incentive the derivative right provides is outweighed by the costs of impeding vigorous competition for works that build on an original work.

1376 *Id.*, pp. 167 and 179.

in which that mark owner does not compete.[1377] Such rights may *protect* a trademark owner's proprietary rights, but they have the effect of *reducing* vigorous market competition by raising significant – and at time unjustified – barriers to market entry.

(v) Composite Mark Confusion

Another type of legal expansion – also reminiscent of the derivative works argument in copyright – is the composite mark confusion doctrine. This doctrine is finding increased traction in European courts. The theory is that a junior trademark can infringe a senior trademark based not on the similarity of elements, but on a single, distinctive element that has been combined with other elements. It is the "overall impression" conveyed by the composite sign which will determine whether there is a similarity or likelihood of confusion.[1378]

In 2005, the CJEU, on a referral from the Düsseldorf Higher Regional Court (*Oberlandesgericht Düsseldorf*), issued their finding in the *Thomson Life* case.[1379] The *Thomson Life* case focused on a dispute over the trademark "LIFE" (for leisure electronic devices) and the composite name "THOMSON LIFE" (for the marketing of television sets, cassette players, and hi-fi products). The CJEU reviewed whether there was a likelihood of confusion behind the single trademark element "LIFE" and the composite mark "THOMSON LIFE". In coming to its decision, the CJEU considered the case law of the German Federal High Court (*Bundesgerichtshof*), and the theory known as the "*Prägetheorie*" (theory of the impression conveyed). That theory holds that "in order to appreciate the similarity of the sign at issue, it is necessary to consider the overall impression conveyed by each of the two signs and to ascertain whether the common component characterizes the composite mark to the extent that the other components are largely secondary to the overall impression. There will be no likelihood of confusion if the common component merely contributes to the overall impression of the sign. It will not matter whether the trade mark incorporated still has an independent distinctive role ('*kennzeichnende Stellung*') in the composite sign."[1380] The CJEU held that the mere juxtaposition of the word "LIFE" with

1377 *Id.*, pp. 170–171.

1378 For a thorough review of the legal framework of this doctrine, see *Fezer*: Die Kollision komplexer Kennzeichen.

1379 Case C-120/04, *Medion AG v Thomson multimedia Sales Germany & Austria GmbH*, 6 October 2005 [2005] ECR I-8551.

1380 *Id.*, para. 12.

the famous "THOMSON" trademark was not enough to distinguish itself. The earlier "LIFE" mark needed to be protected. The Court found that the "global appreciation of the likelihood of confusion, in relation to the visual, aural or conceptual similarity of the marks in question, must be based on the overall impression given by the marks, bearing in mind, in particular, their distinctive and dominant components."[1381]

Until recently, the German courts and the German Patent and Trademark Office (*Deutsches Patent- und Markenamt* or DPMA) applied the *Thomson Life* doctrine rarely, and if so only narrowly.[1382] However, in December 2013, the German Federal Patent Court (*Bundespatentgericht* or BPatG) overruled a decision by the DPMA, allowing an opposition from the owner of an earlier mark – "Protan" – against a new mark – "Triflex Pro Than Detail" – on the basis of the *Thomson Life* doctrine. The BPatG found that the separation of "Protan" into "pro than", juxtaposed with other words, was still too similar to the original mark and constituted a trademark violation.[1383]

The issue here – and the cause for concern[1384] – is that a small element of the senior trademark could be seen as distinctive, without necessarily constituting the dominant element of a junior trademark. As a result, the scope of words, marks, and signs available to be registered and used is further growing narrower – thereby limiting the creative library of trademarks.

(e) Priority of Rights

In the U.S. and other common law countries, trademark rights traditionally were defined by a party's *use*. One acquired rights in a mark through *use* of the mark *in connection with* particular goods or services; priority as between competing users was determined by first use. Registration of a trademark (e.g., with the USPTO) existed primarily for documentation and ease of enforcement.[1385] Even today, protection for trademark owners in the U.S., alongside other common law countries (including the United Kingdom, Australia, and Canada), is unique in

---

1381 *Id.*, para. 28.

1382 *Bhatti*: German Court Adopts Wide Application of ECJ Composite Mark Confusion Doctrine.

1383 BPatG, Docket Nr. 24 W (pat) 526/10, re trademark nr. 30 2008 055 415, decision dated 15 October 2013.

1384 *Bhatti*: German Court Adopts Wide Application of ECJ Composite Mark Confusion Doctrine, quoting trademark attorney Kai Jüdemann.

1385 *McDaniel*: Slammed! How Trademark Laws Hurt the Little Guy.

that it requires actual use of the trademark[1386] or, since 1989, a showing of a bona fide intent-to-use the trademark[1387] *prior* to registration[1388] and gives some priority of rights based *solely* on use.

The "use in commerce" requirement remains a unique aspect of U.S. law and differs from protection in most countries, where rights are typically secured first by registration and thereafter maintained by use in the country. Under common law principles, use of a trademark delineates the scope of rights afforded to such trademark. It underscores the rationale of protecting producers and consumers against unfair trade practices or confusion *in commerce*. Traditionally, one's rights in a mark extended only to the specific goods or services with which the mark was used.[1389] One result of the U.S. complying with its obligations under the Paris Convention and Madrid Protocol is that foreign trademark owners can register for trademark protection in the U.S. (and potentially elsewhere) without actual use of their mark.[1390] Such registration without use restricts competitive uses of names and symbols and changes the focus of trademark protection and

---

1386 Section 1(a) of the Lanham Act requires that an application verifies that the mark is in use in commerce on or in connection with the goods or services listed in the application. Actual use of the mark *must* occur before the registration is issued. See *USPTO*: Rules of Practice & Federal Statutes, pp. 25–27.

1387 In 1989, the U.S. adopted the additional "intent-to-use" process. For an "intent-to-use" application under Section 1(b) or Section 44 of the Act, the applicant is required to verify that it has a bona fide intention to use the mark in U.S. commerce on or in connection with the goods or services listed in the application, and actual use of the mark still *must* occur before the registration is issued. See *USPTO*: Rules of Practice & Federal Statutes, pp. 25–27.

1388 This is also the case in Canada and the Philippines. See *Fenwick & West LLP*: 2004 Update: International Legal Protection for Software – Trademarks, p. 6. In Canada, the Trademarks Act RS 1985, cT-13 and Trademarks Regulations (1996) SOR/96-195 govern registered trademarks. Protection for unregistered marks (which begins essentially from the moment that they are put into commercial use) can be found in the common law action to restrain a competitor from passing off its goods, business or services as those of another. The Trademarks Act has also codified the common law cause of action in relation to unregistered marks in Section 7. See *Zimmerman/Zimmerman*: Canada, p. 28.

1389 *McKenna*: The Normative Foundations of Trademark Law, p. 1888. Consequently, only uses by direct competitors were deemed infringing. As noted above, such "direct competitor" restrictions no longer apply. However, in common law countries, a senior party's use of its mark continues to play an anchoring role. *McKenna*: Trademark Use and the Problem of Source, p. 779.

1390 *McDaniel*: The Madrid Protocol/Section 44, p. 34.

rights away from the regulation of commerce to the preservation of creative expression – i.e., closer to the rationale underlying copyright and patent, but without copyright's restrictions.

8.3 The Legal System's Failure to Establish Limits

(a) Basic Observations

Courts, legislatures, and competition authorities have failed to address the expanding – and conflicting – legal and commercial boundaries of trademark law and use. Trademark law has expanded almost unabated, through the cumulative expansions of legal protection (in scope of protectable symbols, causes and claims of action available, the significance afforded famous marks, and the rationales underlying such protection), bolstered by bullying tactics and predatory legal strategies of trademark owners. The statutorily-endorsed expansion has gone on without appreciation of the impact such expansion has on the competitive market and without implementation of reasonable boundaries to clarify the scope of such expansion.

Competition laws regulate and prohibit anti-competitive restraints of trade. The problem with trademarks is that the rights granted and proprietarily guarded – in an of themselves – can be anti-competitive. Competition laws have, in general, failed to address the anti-competitive impact of trademarks today or understand the commercial power of trademarks. Most policies that address the application of competition restrictions to the exercise of intellectual property rights specifically *exclude* trademarks from the analysis or only address them when are "ancillary" to other intellectual property rights. There is good reason to single out trademarks and good reason to conclude that competition principles may be unsuited to combat the anti-competitive effects of trademark protection. However, simply ignoring such effects – thus signalling acceptance through acquiescence – will not solve the trademark paradox. Instead, it has allowed the protectionist scope of trademark ownership to go unabated.

(b) Protection of Trademarks as Property

Trademarks are integral to a competitive market and influence our consumer demands and decisions in fundamental ways. As the role of trademarks in commerce has evolved, so too the contours of the laws protecting them. However, the trend of expanding legal rights in modern trademark law has substantially veered away from the pragmatic rationales of trademark protection (to prohibit free riding and diminish confusion) based on principles of unfair competition to quasi-sovereign, property rights.

Trademarks are valuable corporate assets. In business transactions and on corporate balance sheets, they are listed as economic assets, often more highly valued than other intellectual property rights.[1391] Their strength represents brand loyalty, and brand loyalty represents market share. Numerous scholars have noted the "inexorable pressure" to treat as property anything having "substantial value" to anyone.[1392] The rhetoric of real property is "increasingly dominating the discourse and conclusions of the very different world of intellectual property."[1393] Such arguments have been the "driving force" behind many expansions of trademark rights.[1394]

When viewed as stand-alone property assets, trademarks are valued "entirely divorced from, and sometimes actually in conflict with, [the] mark's informational role".[1395] This creates a tension between the unfair competition principles underlying trademark protection and the competitive market ideal. Patent and copyrights are characterized and justified by their inherent balance: exclusionary rights for a limited time in return for contributions to the public domain. Trademarks do not have this balance. By propertizing trademarks – which can be indefinitely protected – robust competition is stifled as barriers to market entry are built and the public domain suffers, since common words, colors, or symbols are increasingly brought under the scope of trademark protection and enjoy near-absolute "property" rights.[1396]

The property analogy – or justification – is particularly troubling, since the rights and restrictions inherent in property laws are not mirrored in trademark

---

1391 *Jehoram/van Nispen/Huydecoper*: European Trademark Law, p. 7.

1392 *Litman*: Breakfast with Batman, p. 1725. See also Carrier, who summarizes the scholarly works lamenting the propertization of intellectual property (in particular, pp. 4–5 and 12, fn. 17), those scholars encouraging such analogies (in particular, p. 12, fn 16), as well as multiple examples of how courts have used the "property" analogy when discussing intellectual property (in particular, p. 10, fn. 14). *Carrier*: Cabining Intellectual Property Through a Property Paradigm.

1393 *Lemley*: Romantic Authorship, p. 895.

1394 *Travis*: The Battle for Mindshare, para. 47. See also *Fisher*: The Growth of Intellectual Property.

1395 *Lunney*: Trademark Monopolies, p. 419. Lunney notes that a trademark "has become its owner's property not merely in a formal and limited sense, but in an ordinary and increasingly absolute sense".

1396 Consider Apple's warning that: "You may not use an image of a real apple... for any purpose". *Apple Inc.*: Guidelines for Using Apple Trademarks. Apple has claimed as its "property" words which existed before Apple went into business, but which it has now appropriated as its quasi-sovereign property. See above, § 7.3(d)(i).

laws. In property law there are natural restrictions, statutory limits, and multiple defenses that "limit" (i.e., measurably balance) the absolute and exclusionary rights of property ownership and use.[1397] Trademark rights have expanded without such limits and defenses, thereby creating a dangerous imbalance largely to the benefit of trademark owners and correspondingly to the detriment of consumers and the public sphere.

(c) Protection of Trademarks' "Commercial Magnetism"

Today, trademarks act as complex symbols of both corporate *and* consumer identity, serving commercial, expressive, and communicative functions often more powerful than any means to identify or distinguish source or quality.[1398] Already in the 1942 *Mishawaka Rubber* case, Justice Felix Frankfurter noted the symbolic function – and psychological power – of trademarks:

> "The protection of trade-marks is the law's recognition of the psychological function of symbols. If it is true that we live by symbols, it is no less true that we purchase goods by them. A trade-mark is a merchandising short-cut which induces a purchaser to select what he wants, or what he has been led to believe he wants. The owner of a mark exploits this human propensity by making every effort to impregnate the atmosphere of the market with the drawing power of a congenial symbol. Whatever the means employed, the aim is the same – to convey through the mark, in the minds of potential customers, the desirability of the commodity upon which it appears. Once this is attained, the trademark owner has something of value. If another poaches upon the commercial magnetism of the symbol he has created, the owner can obtain legal redress."[1399]

In dissent, Justice Black, with Justices Douglas and Murphy concurring, warned of the expanding nature of trademark laws and the remedies which far exceeded any violation:

1397 Carrier reviews the limits inherent in real property doctrine, including (i) easements, encroachments, bona fide purchasers, imminent necessity, eminent domain, public trust, and public accommodation (as limitation to the absolute right to exclude); (ii) adverse possession, the rule against perpetuities, market inalienability, a tenant's right to transfer, recording statutes, notice requirements and fraud (as limitations to the absolute right to transfer); and (iii) zoning, nuisance, licenses, waste, and servitudes (as limitations to the absolute right to use). Carrier observes that "property rights are not absolute, but are cabined by several important limits." *Carrier*: Cabining Intellectual Property Through a Property Paradigm, p. 52.

1398 *Katyal*: Trademark Intersectionality.

1399 *Mishawaka Rubber & Woolen Mfg. Co. v. S. S. Kresge Co.*, 316 U.S. 203, 205 (1942).

"...under the circumstances of this case, I believe the effect of the decision handed down is to grant a windfall to the petitioner and to impose a penalty upon the respondent, neither of which is deserved."[1400]

Courts and authorities have shown a strong tendency to accepting a trademark as a broad "repository for value and meaning". This feeds the perception that *any* form of consumer confusion – and, equally, any form of mental association between marks – is a dilution of the property rights of a trademark. Trademark owners and special interest groups have aggressively lobbied for such a position, whereby any "possibility" (instead of "probability") of dilution is seen as an infringement of the trademark.[1401] The treatment of trademarks as exclusive properties (by trademark owners) rather than *informational* sources for *commerce*, means that trademark protection has expanded outward from the regulation of commerce and unfair competition to the more nebulous protection of business property.

A few courts in the U.S. and the EU have fought against this. For example, in the *Sabel* case, Advocate General Jacobs dismissed the argument that a trademark owner can oppose "the use of signs which 'bring to mind' his mark, even if there is *no risk* of the consumer thinking that the product bearing the competing sign is in any way connected with the trade-mark owner".[1402] This "mental association" was not in itself sufficient evidence to prove dilution. In the U.S., one court sagely commented that: "The very fact of calling to mind may indicate that the mind is *distinguishing*, rather than being *confused* by, two marks."[1403]

Barton Beebe, a trademark scholar, has noted the following: "Trademark law is arguably the most difficult of the intellectual property laws to contemplate, and its outcomes when applied to facts are the most difficult to predict."[1404] The reason, he argues, is that trademark (and the historical expansion of trademark rights) has developed the idea of a "sovereign trademark". Here, the rights of

1400 *Id.*, at 209 (Black, J., dissenting).

1401 See *McCarthy*: Dilution of a Trademark for summaries of U.S. and EU courts that have taken this position, as well as trademark interest groups (including INTA) who have lobbied for such broad protection of "likely" association.

1402 Case C-251/95, *SABEL BV v Puma AG, Rudolf Dassler Sport*, [1997] ECR I-6191, Opinion of AG Jacobs, 29 April 1997, para. 41.

1403 *In re Ferrero*, 479 F.2d 1395, 1397 (C.C.P.A. 1973) (emphasis mine), cited by *McCarthy*: Dilution of a Trademark, p. 1171, fn 32.

1404 *Beebe*: Search and Persuasion in Trademark Law, p. 2022.

trademarks (and their owners) have broader protection and power over the rights of consumers (who are deemed less and less sophisticated).[1405]

(d) Availability of Overlapping (and Supplementary) Protection

The undeserved "windfall" that Justice Black described in *Mishawaka-Rubber*,[1406] in particular for non-competing goods, is not the only imbalance resulting from expanded trademark protection. Additional claims of action – i.e., supplemental causes of action – are available to trademark owners both from (i) overlaps between various types of intellectual property rights and (ii) supplemental causes of action that are *cumulative*.

Legal interplays – and overlaps – in protection have long existed between intellectual property rights.[1407] With respect to trademarks, there is substantial – and unresolved – overlap between trademarks, design rights, and copyrights whether in registration, enforcement, or commercialization. For example, a pattern or a product design might be protected as a design patent, a registered design, an unregistered design, a work of applied art under copyright, or as a two- or three-dimensional trademark, if it is distinctive enough. An artistic work can be registered as a trademark, whether or not it is protected under copyright. There are also overlapping rights between trademarks and trade dress, trademarks and geographical indications, and trademarks and domain names.[1408]

There are several reasons for this increasing overlap. The primary reason is the expanded protection granted trademarks beyond their historical or traditional borders have the consequence of overlapping with other established rights. The next reason is the rampant creation of new intellectual property rights (e.g., *sui*

1405 *Id.*, pp. 2067 and 2069.

1406 *Mishawaka Rubber & Woolen Mfg. Co. v. S. S. Kresge Co.*, 316 U.S. 203, 209 (1942) (Black, J., dissenting).

1407 Overlaps exist between utility patents and copyright law, between patent and design protection, between patent and utility models, and between patent and trade secrets. See *Fabrica, Inc. v. El Dorado Corp.*, 697 F.2d 890, 892 (1983), noting historical evolution of expanding copyright protection for functional features that had previously been prohibited under patent law in order to prevent the monopolization of useful technical advances. See also *Reichman*: Charting the Collapse of the Patent-Copyright Dichotomy.

1408 For a comprehensive overview of these and other intellectual property overlaps from an international perspective, see *Wilkof/Basheer*: Overlapping Intellectual Property Rights. See also *Derclaye/Leistner*: Intellectual Property Overlaps.

generis rights)[1409] which has added to the variety of "species" protected.[1410] Third, the functions of some of the intellectual property rights are changing – particularly with respect to trademarks.[1411]

The effects of these overlaps, however, is to allow an intellectual property rights owner *yet further* claims of infringement or violation: if a trademark infringement claim proves inadequate, plaintiffs can rely on alternative causes of action – including passing-off or unfair competition claims.[1412] Use of a trademark may also be subject to comparative advertising statutes or consumer protection laws. This overlap poses problems, both at a practical and legal level. However, there is no general rule that forbids intellectual property overlaps under EU law; in fact, EU secondary law maintains that each intellectual property right is "without prejudice to any other and to unfair competition law."[1413]

With respect to trademarks, a key example can be seen in the two European directives relating to unfair competition law: the Misleading and Comparative Advertising Directive (MCAD)[1414] and the Unfair Commercial Practices Directive (UCPD).[1415] These two only partially harmonize unfair competition law

---

1409 This includes, for example, the separate rights in semi-conductor chips and databases, and recent considerations of whether mobile applications should have their own protection. *IPKat*: Apps: do we regard them as a protected species?

1410 *Derclaye/Leistner*: Intellectual Property Overlaps, p. 1.

1411 "For instance, the justification for protecting trademarks was originally only to safeguard the origin of goods/services, but now trademark law also protects the advertising function and, therefore, can also protect the investment in a trademark and consequently the interests of the seller/producer and no longer only those of the consumer/user." (citations omitted). *Id.*, p. 2.

1412 See *Fezer*: Markenrecht, § 3 MarkenG, paras. 57–58, discussing briefly the phenomena of the "Abgrenzung des legitimen Kennzeichenschutzes als Immaterialgüterrechtsschutz von den anderen Rechten des geistigen Eigentums".

1413 See generally, *Derclaye/Leistner*: Intellectual Property Overlaps, p. 113. As an example, Recital 9 of the UCPD allows cumulation between intellectual property rights. See *Derclaye/Leistner*: Intellectual Property Overlaps, p. 107.

1414 Directive 2006/114/EC of the European Parliament and of the Council of 12 December 2006 concerning misleading and comparative advertising, OJ L 376/12 (2006).

1415 Directive 2005/29/EC of the European Parliament and of the Council of 11 May 2005 concerning unfair business-to-consumer commercial practices in the internal market and amending Council Directive 84/450/EEC, Directives 97/7/EC, 2002/65/EC of the European Parliament and of the Council and Regulation (EC) 2006/2004 of the European Parliament and of the Council, OJ L 149/22 (2005). Although the Directive only regulates unfair B2C practices, recital 8 notes that it

and national laws still apply for situations not covered by the Directives.[1416] The UCPD, for example, allows the overlap between trademark law and passing off (or alternatively unfair competition) for risk of confusion at a national level.[1417] Hence, even with the Directive, national laws still apply and overlap can occur.[1418]

Cumulation appears to be the default norm. The Green Paper on the Legal Protection of Industrial Design ventures an explanation:[1419] for the Commission, cumulation between intellectual property rights and unfair competition rules is natural because intellectual property and unfair competition have a different nature: unfair competition laws "tend to protect the fairness in the behaviour of the operators in trade and … require, next to objective acts of misbehaviour, the existence of a subjective element of fault on conditions on the side of the offender."[1420]

The effect (and consequent implementation) of cumulative practices in the law can be seen in the recent (February 2014) German Federal High Court

---

also "indirectly protects legitimate businesses from their competitors who do not play by the rules in this Directive and thus guarantees fair competition in fields coordinated by it."

1416 See *Derclaye/Leistner*: Intellectual Property Overlaps, pp. 106–107. As Derclaye and Leistner note, this could include situations for famous marks (which get an expanded treatment under the MCAD beyond what is granted under the Trademark Directive) or when regimes conflict due to an overlap (e.g., if a trademark is also protected under copyright and/or design law).

1417 Article 6(1) UCPD covers "misleading" practices ("A commercial practice shall be regarded as misleading if it contains false information and is therefore untruthful or in any way, including overall presentation, deceives or is likely to deceive the average consumer, even if the information is factually correct, in relation to one or more of the following elements, and in either case causes or is likely to cause him to take a transactional decision that he would not have taken otherwise." Article 6(2) UCPD includes as a misleading practice any practice "which creates confusion with any products, trade marks, trade names or other distinguishing marks of a competitor".

1418 In Case 6/81, *BV Industrie Diensten Groep v J.A. Beele Handelmaatschappij BV*, 2 March 1982 [1982] ECR 707, para. 9ff, the CJEU confirmed that national unfair competition laws can prohibit imitation which causes confusion so long as they do not discriminate between domestic and imported EU goods.

1419 Commission of the European Communities, Green Paper on the Legal Protection of Industrial Design, III/F/5131191, June 1991, cited by *Derclaye/Leistner*: Intellectual Property Overlaps, p. 109 and n. 455.

1420 Commission of the European Communities, Green Paper on the Legal Protection of Industrial Design, III/F/5131191, June 1991, § 2.7.1, p. 24.

(*Bundesgerichtshof* or BGH) *Hard Rock Café* decision.[1421] In the *Hard Rock Café* case, the claimant brought – in addition to its trademark infringement claim – claims based on unfair competition law, in particular based on Article 5 (Misleading commercial practices) and Article 3 (Prohibition of unfair commercial practices) of the German Act Against Unfair Competition (*Gesetz gegen den unlauteren Wettbewerb* or UWG). These provisions were introduced in accordance with the UCPD.[1422] Prior to the *Hard Rock Café* decision, it was the BGH's established case law that wherever a conflict was covered by trademark laws, unfair competition law was not applicable in parallel.[1423] Expressly in light of the UCPD provisions, the BGH now allows concurrent application of both laws.

Trademark owners therefore have two bites at the apple: they can claim protection under trademarks law on the one hand (which offers exclusive rights with respect to the specific trademark) *and* claims against acts of unfair competition on the other (which prohibit acts contrary to honest business practice). Although the link between the two kinds of protection is clear, protection against unfair competition effectively *supplements* the protection afforded by the trademark laws.[1424]

(e) Lack of Guidance Under Competition Laws

Competition laws seeks to minimize or prohibit anti-competitive effect which arise from the acquisition, exploitation and enforcement of intellectual property rights – whether in the form of patents, copyrights, trademarks, trade secrets, and other rights created by statute or common law.[1425]

As stated in the 1995 U.S. Guidelines on Intellectual Property Licensing: "Intellectual property is … neither particularly free from scrutiny under the antitrust laws, nor particularly suspect under them."[1426] As further noted by an FTC

1421 BGH I ZR 188/11 – Hard Rock Café, 9 February 2014. For further discussion of this case, see above § 7.3(a).

1422 *IPKat*: Some additional thoughts on the BGH's landmark decision.

1423 *Id.*

1424 WIPO, chapter 2. For further discussions of this under U.S. law, see *Barrett*: Finding Trademark Use and *Reichman*: The TRIPS Component of the GATT's Uruguay Round, pp. 211–212.

1425 In the US, for a full analyses of the tensions between competition policy and common law property rights, including explanations of their doctrines and rationales, see *Peritz*: A Genealogy of Vertical Restraints Doctrine; and *Peritz*: The "Rule of Reason" in Antitrust Law.

1426 "Standard antitrust analysis applies to intellectual property". *DOJ/FTC*: 1995 IP Licensing Guidelines, § 2.1.

Commissioner, "the Commission remains ready, willing, and able to challenge violations of the antitrust laws involving intellectual property."[1427] Similarly, the European Commission Technology Transfer Block Exemption Guidelines state: "The fact that intellectual property laws grant exclusive rights of exploitation does not imply that intellectual property rights are immune from competition law intervention. Article 101 of the Treaty is in particular applicable to agreements whereby the holder licenses another undertaking to exploit its intellectual property rights."[1428]

The application of competition rules *specifically* to trademark licensing raises many of the same issues that arise in relation to the licensing of other intellectual property rights. There is, however, less express guidance in this area than in the case of patent (and know-how) licensing. As noted in Chapters 5 and 6, both the U.S. 1995 Guidelines[1429] and the European Commission Guidelines[1430] specifically exclude trademarks and trademark licensing from their scope. Second, there are few decided "competition" cases dealing specifically with the anti-competitive effects of trademark ownership separately from an underlying patented product.

(f) No Measurable Tools to Gauge Market Power or Abuse

Competition laws aim to prohibit conduct which negatively affects free and efficient competition. In most cases, competition laws do not condemn conduct automatically; instead they look at the relevant circumstances, including the presence or likelihood of *market power*. As the European Commission has noted, market power is "ability to profitably maintain prices above competitive levels for a period of time or to profitably maintain output in terms of product quantities, product quality and variety or innovation below competitive levels for a period of time."[1431] Market power is generally estimated by defining a relevant

---

1427 *Rosch*: Some Thoughts on the Role of Intellectual Property in Innovation Market Cases, p. 22.

1428 Commission Notice: TTBE Guidelines (OJ C 89/3, 28.03.2014), para. 7.

1429 *DOJ/FTC*: 1995 IP Licensing Guidelines, fn. 2.

1430 Commission Notice: TTBE Guidelines (OJ C 89/3, 28.03.2014), paras. 47 and 50.

1431 Case 27/76, *United Brands Company and United Brands Continentaal BV v Commission* (Chiquita Bananas), 14 February 1978 [1978] ECR 207, paras. 63–65. See also Commission Notice: Guidelines on the applicability of Article 101 of the Treaty on the Functioning of the European Union to horizontal co-operation agreements (OJ 2011/C 11/01, 14.01.2011), paras. 39, 40–47 for further explanations of market power.

product and geographical market and computing the defendant's share of that market.[1432] "The goal in defining the relevant market is to indentify market participants and competitive pressures that restrain an individual firm's ability to raise prices or restrict output."[1433]

In the EU, an assessment of market power is particularly useful under Article 101 TFEU in considering the appreciability test (i.e., the appreciability of the effect on competition); it is also central to the Article 102 prohibition in the identification of dominance.[1434] Although the concepts of appreciable effect and dominance are different, it is helpful in both cases to consider the competitive constraints that affect the undertaking (or undertakings).

(i) Trademarks: Relevant Product Markets

The first step in any competition analysis is defining the relevant market or markets:[1435] it is the cornerstone of competition policy.[1436] Most courts find the fact that a brand is protected by a trademark does *not* imply that the brand or

---

1432 The Commission Notice on the definition of relevant market for the purposes of Community competition law (OJ C 372/5, 9.12.1997) provides general guidance for assessing the relevant market and methodologies for estimating market power.

1433 *Geneva Pharmaceuticals Technology Corp. v. Barr Laboratories Inc.*, 386 F.3d 485 (2d. Cir. 2004) at 485.

1434 In the EU, dominant undertakings have a special responsibility to behave in a certain way – i.e., in a way which does not damage or hinder the development of competition.

1435 "Without defined relevant markets, there is no way for a court to determine whether a defendant has restrained trade... or to measure a defendant's ability to lessen or destroy competition in violation." *Adidas America, Inc. v. NCAA*, 64 F.Supp. 2d 1097, 1101 (D. Kan. 1999) (citations omitted). For a thorough overview of market share analysis under U.S. antitrust analysis, see *Werden*: Assigning Market Shares. For the European Commission perspective, see *European Commission*: Roundtable Discussion on Techniques and Evidentiary Issues in Proving Dominance/Monopoly Power.

1436 As Commissioner Mario Monti described it, "market definition is a cornerstone of competition policy, but not the entire building. Market definition is a tool for the competitive assessment, not a substitute for it." *Monti*: Market definition as a cornerstone of EU Competition Policy. "The definition of the relevant market is not an end in itself. However, it is a central tool and starting point to identify situations where there might be competition concerns. It is an important qualitative first step in a structured effects based investigation as it enables to scope the competitive landscape and identify the relevant (potential) competitors." *OECD*: Roundtable on Market Definition.

trademark constitutes a separate product market.[1437] In *Generac*, the Seventh Circuit held that: "Product markets are not defined in terms of one trademark or another; trademarks simply identify the origin of a product."[1438] In *Compare Digital*, the Seventh Circuit similarly rejected a product market consisting solely of one company's products.[1439] Many courts note that the parties have failed to adequately define the relevant market.[1440]

A few courts and scholars, however, have found that a powerful brand *could* constitute a separate product market,[1441] serve as goods in and of themselves,[1442] or define a unique set of products.[1443] In *Geneva Pharmaceuticals Technology Corp. v. Barr Laboratories Inc.*, the Second Circuit found a pioneering, branded

---

1437 *ABA*: Antitrust Law Developments, p. 1103, fn 506 (citations omitted).

1438 *Generac Corporation v. Caterpillar Inc.*, 172 F.3d 971, 977 (7th Cir. 1999).

1439 "One could hardly imagine a weaker case for the claim that DEC's computers are a market unto themselves." *Digital Equipment Corporation v. Uniq Digital Technologies, Inc.*, 73 F.3d 756, 763 (7th Cir. 1996).

1440 "In fact, "[c]ases in which dismissal on the pleading is appropriate frequently involve either (1) failed attempts to limit a product market to a single brand, franchise, institution, or comparable entity that competes with potential substitutes or (2) failure even to attempt a plausible explanation as to why a market should be limited in a particular way." *Bayer Schera Pharma AG v. Sandoz, Inc.*, 2010 U.S. Dist. LEXIS 33252, at 13 (S.D.N.Y., Mar. 29, 2010) (citations omitted); cited by *Hovenkamp/Janis/Lemley/Leslie*: IP and Antitrust, § 4.3a1, fn. 249, pp. 4–64 (2011 Supplement).

1441 "A single branded product may, in rare cases, constitute its own relevant market." *U.S. Anchor Mfg., Inc. v. Rule Industries, Inc.*, 7 F.3d 986, 998 (11th Cir. 1993) (citations omitted). Dreyfuss observes that, in recent years, trademarks have become "products in their own right, valued as indicators of the status, preferences, and aspirations of those who use them." *Dreyfuss*: Expressive Genericity: Trademarks as Language in the Pepsi Generation, p. 397.

1442 "A trademark may even become the product itself. To illustrate, assume that the insignia used by Mercedes-Benz to identify its cars has become so popular that consumers are willing to don the Mercedes emblem as earrings, key-holders, etc. Such use is a non-trademark use. The mark has become a good of its own. In its new incarnation, the mark is emancipated from the physical product to which it previously had been attached." *Dilbary*: Famous Trademarks and the Rational Basis, p. 620. The "theory of dilution has always treated trademarks as goods". *Barnes*: A New Economics of Trademarks, p. 33.

1443 The district court in American Needle, for example, found that the National Football League ("NFL") trademarks did define a unique set of products – in particular, for members of the public who want to be indentified with a particular football team. *American Needle, Inc. v. New Orleans Louisiana Saints*, 385 F. Supp. 2d 687,

drug and its chemically identical generic substitute were *not* the in same relevant market because so many consumers chose the drug on the basis of the branded name alone.[1444]

The research on branding and trademarks supports such finding. Famous trademarks – through extensive advertising – can result in product differentiation creating nearly insurmountable barriers to entry.[1445] Professor Rebecca Tushnet has reviewed the new marketing research tools available – cognitive research, neuromarketing, and behavioural science – to demonstrate that advertising, packaging, marketing, and the mere presence of a trademark can change a person's objective buying choices, including their "taste" preferences. For example, it is well known that people *prefer the taste* of Pepsi over Coke *until* they know what it is they are drinking, at which point preferences *shift* to Coke.[1446] "Part of what people are drinking is the trademark."[1447] "[P]eople choose Ben & Jerry's ice cream largely for reasons other than taste."[1448]

---

694 (N.D. Ill. 2005). For further analysis of the *American Needle* case, see *Werden*: Initial Thoughts on the American Needle Decision.

1444 *Geneva Pharmaceuticals Technology Corp. v. Barr Laboratories Inc.*, 386 F.3d 485 (2d. Cir. 2004), as cited by *Hovenkamp/Janis/Lemley/Leslie*: IP and Antitrust, p§ 4.3a1, fn. 249, p. 4–64 (2011 Supplement). But see *American Sales Company, Inc. v. AstraZeneca AB, Aktiekolaget Hassle, AstraZeneca LP, KBI, Inc., KBI-E, Inc. and The Procter & Gamble Company*, 10 Civ. 6062 (PKC), 2011 U.S. Dist. LEXIS 41182; 2011-1 Trade Cas. (CCH) P77, 486 (S.D.N.Y. 2011) dismissing the case for failure to adequately plead a relevant product market: "These allegations do not plausibly allege a relevant product market consisting solely of [the branded drug] and its generic counterpart. The plaintiff has failed to allege any product characteristics or evidence of consumer buying patterns that limit [the branded drug's] interchangeability of use or the cross-elasticity of demand"; at 10-12 (citations omitted).

1445 *McClure*: Trademarks and Unfair Competition, p. 307 and fn. 15, citing *Areeda*: Antitrust Analysis, p. 117.

1446 "In a blind taste test, Diet Pepsi was preferred by 51 per cent of the subjects while Diet Coke was preferred by 44 per cent. In contrast, a branded taste test resulted in Diet Pepsi being preferred by 23 per cent with Diet Coke being preferred by 65 per cent." *Sanjoy/Lowengart*: Taste Tests, p. 30, cited by *Tushnet*: Gone in Sixty Milliseconds, pp. 513–514, fn. 20. See also *Lemley/McKenna*: Is Pepsi Really a Substitute for Coke?

1447 *Tushnet*: Gone in Sixty Milliseconds, p. 510 (citations omitted). See also *McClure*: Neural Correlates of Behavioral Preference, pp. 385, 383–85, noting the "wealth of cultural meaning" the Coke and Pepsi brands possess.

1448 *Wahlberg*: Advertisers Probe Brains, at Q1, cited by *Tushnet*: Gone in Sixty Milliseconds, p. 513, fn. 16.

Children "preferred the taste of foods and drinks if they thought they were from McDonald's."[1449]

(ii) Trademarks & Market Power

In both the U.S.[1450] and the EU,[1451] courts and competition authorities have generally held that mere ownership of intellectual property rights will *not* automatically amount to a dominant position or market power. Gauging market power *with respect to* trademark rights is, however, particularly challenging.

In the U.S., there have been numerous cases dealing with market power of patents and copyrights (and, in fact, prior to the 2006 Supreme Court *Illinois Tool Works*[1452] decision, there was a presumption that the mere possession of a

---

1449 *Robinson/Borzekowski/Matheson/Kraemer*: Effects of Fast Food Branding, p. 792. "By the early age of 3 to 5 years, low-income preschool children preferred the tastes of foods and drinks if they thought they were from McDonald's, demonstrating that brand identity can influence young children's taste perceptions. This was true even for carrots, a food that was not marketed by or available from McDonald's. These taste preferences emerged despite the fact that 3 of the foods were from McDonald's and only the branding was changed, indicating that the effects were not due to familiarity with the taste or smell of McDonald's food … [but instead] indicating they preferred more of the branded foods." *Id.* at 794; cited by *Tushnet*: Gone in Sixty Milliseconds, p. 514, fn. 23.

1450 On the U.S. side, see *United States v. E. I. du Pont de Nemours & Co.*, 351 U.S. 377 (1956); and *United States v. Loew's, Inc.*, 371 U.S. 38 (1962). In their 1995 IP Licensing Guidelines, the DOJ and FTC stated that "The Agencies will not presume that a patent, copyright, or trade secret necessarily confers market power upon its owner. Although the intellectual property right confers the power to exclude with respect to the specific product, process, or work in question, there will often be sufficient actual or potential close substitutes for such product, process, or work to prevent the exercise of market power. If a patent or other form of intellectual property does confer market power, that market power does not by itself offend the antitrust laws." *DOJ/FTC*: 1995 IP Licensing Guidelines, § 2.2 and reiterated at § 5.3. It should be noted, however,

1451 On the EU side, see Case 24/67, *Parke, Davis and Co. v Probel, Reese, Beintema-Interpharm and Centrafarm*, 29 February 1968 [1968] ECR 55; Case 78-70, *Deutsche Grammophon Gesellschaft mbH v Metro-SB-Großmärkte GmbH & Co. KG*, 8 June 1971 [1971] ECR 487, para 16; and as reaffirmed in Joined cases C-241/91 P and C-242/91 P, *Radio Telefis Eireann (RTE) and Independent Television Publications Ltd (ITP) v Commission* (Magill), 6 April 1995 [1995] ECR I-743.

1452 *Illinois Tool Works, Inc. v. Independent Ink, Inc.* 547 U.S. 28 (2006). For a discussion of the *Illinois Tool Works* case, see *Katz*: Making Sense of Nonsense.

patent or copyright was sufficient to establish market power and that such was sufficient to warrant antitrust condemnation).[1453]

No U.S. *Supreme Court* case has extended the presumption of market power to trademarks.[1454] Most U.S. courts find that no inference of market power can be drawn from a trademark, trade name, or brand name, even if such is prestigious.[1455]

(iii) Trademarks as Barriers to Entry

Although mere ownership of a trademark will not amount to a dominant position or market power on either side of the Atlantic, ownership of powerful trademarks, when combined with other factors, may result in market power – either through entry barriers or product differentiation. For competition purposes, a barrier to entry "is some factor in a market that deters or delays the entry of new rivals even as the firm or firms in the market are already charging supracompetitive prices."[1456]

Trademarks again pose a challenge: on the one hand, some have found that the exclusivity that inheres in a trademark will not restrain competition or serve as a barrier to entry in any meaningful way;[1457] others find famous marks can

1453 Prior to *Illinois Tool Works*, the Supreme Court viewed tying arrangements involving patented or copyrighted products with particular mistrust, believing patents and copyrights to have the potential to create legally sanctioned monopolies in particular markets. See, for example, *Int'l Salt Co. v. United States*, 332 U.S. 392, 396 (1947) (applying market power presumption to patents); *United States v. Paramount Pictures, Inc.*, 334 U.S. 131, 157-58 (1948) (applying market power presumption to copyrights). For an excellent review of the history of the Supreme Court's cases involving tying and market power presumptions, see *Feldman/Alaily/Farrell*: At the Intersection of Antitrust and Intellectual Property Law.

1454 *Hovenkamp/Janis/Lemley/Leslie*: IP and Antitrust, § 4.2e7(A), fn. 216, pp. 4–56 (2011 Supplement), citing *Photovest Corp. V. Fotomat Corp.*, 606 F.2d 704 (7th Cir. 1979) and *Siegel v. Chicken Delight*, 448 F.2d 43 (9th Cir. 1971).

1455 As noted by the Ninth Circuit, "unlike a patent or copyright, which is designed to protect the uniqueness of the product itself, a trademark protects only the name or symbol of the product. Market power, if any, is derived from the product, not from the name or symbol as such." *Mozart Co. v. Mercedes-Benz of North America, Inc.*, 833 F.2d 1342, 1346 (9th Cir. 1987).

1456 *Hovenkamp/Janis/Lemley/Leslie*: IP and Antitrust, § 4.3a2, p. 4–67.

1457 *VMG Enter. V. F. Quesada & Franco*, 788 F. Supp. 648, 658 (D.P.R. 1992).

be so powerful that they insulate themselves from price competition and create "nearly insurmountable barriers to entry".[1458]

In the EU, the cases against *Der Grüne Punkt - Duales System Deutschland GmbH*[1459] are a case in point. In both cases, the General Court dismissed an appeal by Duales System Deutschland AG (DSD) regarding the European Commission's two 2001 decisions concerning abuse of a dominant position by DSD in the market for systems for the collection and recycling of packaging waste. DSD's "Green Dot" (*Der Grüne Punkt*) trademark became the symbol of the service which collected and recovered packaging waste as required under the German Packaging Ordinance.

In 2001, the European Commission published two judgments which found DSD to have abused its dominant position in the market for systems for the collection and recycling of packaging waste in Germany and the payment system for the collection of fees for packaging. The Commission found that the Green Dot trademark prevented entry of competitors on the market in how it used and licensed its trademark in its collection and recycling systems. Much of the case and the hearings centered on whether "*Der Grüne Punkt*" was a trademark.[1460] Competitors had challenged DSD's "*de facto* monopoly" in use of the Green Dot logo.[1461]

1458 *McClure*: Trademarks and Unfair Competition, pp. 307 and 345. "The primary value of the modern trademark lies in the conditioned reflex developed in the buyer... To the extent that advertising of this type succeeds,... economically irrational elements are introduced into consumer choices; and the trademark owner is insulated from the normal pressures of price and quality competition. In consequence... the economically irrelevant appeal of highly publicized trademarks is thought to constitute a barrier to the entry of new competition into the market... In some markets this barrier to entry may be insuperable." *Smith v. Chanel, Inc.*, 402 F.2d 562, 567 (9th Cir. Cal. 1968) (footnotes and citations omitted).

1459 Case T-151/01, *Der Grüne Punkt - Duales System Deutschland GmbH v Commission*, 24 May 2007 [2007] ECR II-1607 (Appeal Case before the Court of Justice C-385/07 P); and Case T-289/01, *Der Grüne Punkt - Duales System Deutschland GmbH v Commission*, 24 May 2007 [2007] ECR II-1691.

1460 *European Commission*: Press Release IP/01/584; and *European Commission*: Press Release MEMO/07/205. For a summary of the judgments, see *Natur-Pack*: Green Dot.

1461 *Gremminger/Miersch*: The Court of First Instance confirms Duales System Deutschland's abuse of dominance.

(iv) *Trademarks & Abuse of Power*

The problem with trademarks is that, even if a brand has *de facto* monopoly power (as was the case with *Der Grüne Punkt*), it is difficult to determine whether there is an abuse of such power by the trademark owner. Under competition laws, mere possession or even acquisition of a monopoly is not illegal; an offense of the competition laws is only triggered when anti-competitive conduct interferes with competition. Hence, certain anti-competitive behaviors – such as unilateral refusals to deal, tying, insistence on exclusive rights, excessive or predatory pricing (e.g., drastic price cutting), acquisitions of intellectual property rights, and even the filing of baseless infringements claims – raise little concern from competition authorities *unless* the actor has relevant market power.

Most intellectual property-competition law issues involve patents. Courts and competition authorities have developed – and continue to develop[1462] – principles and remedies to address these cases.[1463] Courts and competition authorities do not seem to know what to do with trademarks. They can distinguish why trademarks are different from other intellectual property rights (that is easy), but are consistently bad at recognizing the market power of trademarks or determining how to address the anti-competitive effects of trademark ownership.

1462 For example, the behavior of so-called non-practicing entities (NPEs) (more derogatorily known as "patent trolls") has increasingly interested competition authorities. According to complaints in the industry, NPEs buy portfolios of patents from multiple sources, aggregate them into a bundle, and then file "nuisance lawsuits" against smaller companies. These smaller companies are forced to license the patents, since they don't generally have the resources or sophistication to defend themselves. A growing trend has been for companies – e.g., mobile device makers – to move their portfolio of patents to NPEs with the goal of positioning themselves to commence litigation (because they don't manufacture anything, NPEs cannot be countersued for infringement, so the mobile device manufacturers who have sold the patents can use such NPE patents by proxy against rivals without fear of retribution – driving up costs and harming competition in the process). At a joint workshop held by the U.S. Federal Trade Commission and U.S. Department of Justice last year, FTC Chairman Jon Leibowitz described such deals between patent owners and NPEs as "unsavoury". See *Knox*: Global Competition Review.

1463 For example, antitrust limitations on patent licensing practices and patent misuse have been codified at 35 U.S.C. § 271(d).

(g) Lack of Applicable Remedies

As is clear in the *Der Grüne Punkt* – or as may be the case with many trademarks – a famous, commercially significant trademark can restrict new market entrants. If *Der Grüne Punkt* had been a patent, the European Commission may have applied compulsory licensing principles and required DSD to license its "technology". Such practices allow multiple market players access to technology or resources which have become standard in the industry.[1464]

Applying compulsory licensing requirements to a trademark holder, however, would not be practical (nor solve the issue): a trademark used by multiple market players would be in a contradiction of the very principle of trademarks – i.e., to distinguish one company's goods from that of another. Furthermore, as a remedy, it would in essence grant a third party a legal right to free ride on the reputation of the famous trademark owner, which is also in direct contradiction of the other principle of trademarks – i.e., to prohibit free riding.

8.4 Chapter Observations

(a) Trademarks & Commerce

As long ago articulated by the U.S. Supreme Court, trademarks are essential "as aids to the exchange of commodities in the great markets of the world … and they are considered … vitally important to the protection of commerce".[1465] The Court continued:

> "Trade-marks are important instrumentalities, aids, or appliances by which trade, especially in modern times, is conducted. They are the means by which manufacturers and

1464 In the famous line-up of EU compulsory license cases – *Volvo v Veng, CICRA v. Renault, Magill, Ladbroke, Bronner* and *IMS Health*, culminating in the more recent *Microsoft* decision – the CJEU has held that under "exceptional circumstances" a dominant party's refusal to license intellectual property could violate Article 102, thereby requiring such dominant party to grant its rivals access to its intellectual property. Case 238/87, *Volvo v Veng*, 5 October 1988 [1988] ECR 6211; Case C-53/87, *CICRA v Renault*, 5 October 1988 [1988] ECR 6039; Joined cases C-241/91 P and C-242/91 P, *Magill*, 6 April 1995 [1995] ECR I-743; Case C-353/95 P, *Ladbroke v Commission*, 9 December 1997 [1997] ECR I-7007; Case C-7/97, *Oscar Bronner*, 26 November 1998 [1998] ECR I-7791; Case C-418/01, *IMS Health*, 29 April 2004; and COMP/C—3/37.792—Microsoft, March 2004, Decision of 24 May 2007, OJ L 32/23; upheld by Case T-201/04, *Microsoft Corp. v Commission*, 17 September 2007 [2007] ECR II-3601.

1465 *Trade-Mark Cases*, 100 U.S. 82 (1879), Syllabus at 10.

merchants identify their manufactures and merchandise. They are the symbols by which men engaged in trade and manufactures become known in the marts of commerce, by which their reputation and that of their goods are extended and published; and as they become better known, the profits of their business are enhanced."[1466]

Trademarks influence consumer decisions every day. A strong trademark creates an identity, builds trust, distinguishes one company from its competition, and makes communication between seller and buyer simpler.[1467] Trademarks save time for consumers (who can rely on distinctive marks as proxies for quality[1468] and assess the goods and services they desire without repeatedly undertaking independent research and investigation[1469]).

Trademarks are used in more expansive ways than ever imagined, functioning as psychological symbols of persuasion. Consumers today are far more likely to make purchases to satisfy both physical and psychological needs than simply to make purchases based on quality or sources.[1470] Nowhere is this shift more apparent than in the ever-growing marketplace of celebrity placements[1471] in particular with sports merchandising.[1472]

1466 *Trade-Mark Cases*, 100 U.S. 82 (1879).

1467 *Ealy*: The Common Law, the States, and Historical Perspective, p. 15.

1468 The "essential function of the trade-mark... is to guarantee the identity of the origin of the trade-marked product to the consumer or ultimate user, by enabling him without any possibility of confusion to distinguish that product from products which have another origin." Case 102/77, *Hoffmann-La Roche & Co. AG v Centrafarm Vertriebsgesellschaft Pharmazeutischer Erzeugnisse mbH*, 23 May 1978 [1978] ECR 1139, summary para. 2, grounds para. 7.

1469 Trademarks "facilitate consumers' choice among [previously] experienced goods and transmit quality signals." *Economides*: The Economics of Trademarks, p. 523. See also *Folsom/Teply*, Trademarked Generic Words, pp. 1335–36 (1980).

1470 In fact, consumers "are often more concerned with identifying *themselves* than with identifying the *source* of the goods they buy." *Katyal*: Trademark Intersectionality, pp. 1619–1620 (emphasis mine), citing *Swann/Aaker/Reback*: Trademarks and Marketing, p. 796.

1471 *Böhler*: Celebrity Placement.

1472 For example, Nike built its early success on a special relationship with runners. Phil Knight, the company's founder, and legendary track coach Bill Bowerman understood athletes' preferences in running shoes. Knight and Bowerman used this advantage to build a unique rapport with sport stars such as Steve Prefontaine, Jon Anderson, and Ilie Nastase. Nike's association with these star athletes increased its customers' willingness to pay for the company's products. Nike's association with these star athletes increased its customers' willingness to pay for the company's products. See generally *Christensen/Rikert*: Nike, describing the history of Nike

(b) Trademarks & Competition

In our quest to "protect commerce" by protecting trademarks, we have supplemented and – more dangerously – *supplanted* protection grounded in unfair competition principles with protection based on proprietary, quasi-property right principles. The expanding scope and categories of signs protected, along with the plethora of claims and causes of action available, illustrates the "unbounded nature of trademarks within the judicial consciousness".[1473] In so doing, we deplete the creative "library" of signs, narrowing the scope of words, marks, and signs available for productive, legitimate use. The rationale behind such expanded protection is questionable, in particular in cases where there is no consumer confusion or dilution. Our society is complex and ever-changing: by narrowing the scope of available signs we diminish the types of complex communication available.

Competition laws protect competition and the competitive process, by preventing certain types of conduct that threaten a free market.[1474] Application of competition laws to certain anti-competitive behaviour has been successful; application of competition laws to the expanding "commercial magnetism" (and economic power) of trademarks has been less successful. There are strong arguments that the promotion of trademarks by influential advertising may lessen competition by insulating a differentiated product from price competition and making rational consumer spending more difficult. Product differentiation can produce nearly insurmountable barriers to entry into an industry, causing greater industrial concentration and preserving existing monopolies and oligopolies.[1475] By not addressing the anti-competitive effects of expanded trademark protection, we have permitted protectionist barriers which stifle competition. By not acknowledging the fundamental differences between the protection of intellectual property rights – and in particular between patents, copyrights, and trade secrets on the one hand and trademarks on the other – we lose sight of the *effects* such expanded protection have on commerce.

---

and its economic strategy. For the Knight-Bowerman story, see *Nike*: History & Heritage: "Before there was the Swoosh, before there was Nike, there were two visionary men who pioneered a revolution in athletic footwear that redefined the industry." Further star athletes who promoted the brand include Michael Jordan, Bo Jackson, and the "vastly talented but as-yet-unproven young golfer named Eldrick "Tiger" Woods". *Nike*: History & Heritage.

1473 *Bartow*: The True Colors of Trademark Law, p. 263.

1474 *Hovenkamp/Janis/Lemley/Leslie*: IP and Antitrust, § 1.2, pp. 1–5.

1475 *McClure*: Trademarks and Unfair Competition (citations omitted).

Trademarks today have all the benefits of traditional intellectual property rights (exclusive rights, broad protection) *without* the inherent boundaries (limited duration, limited scope, statutory exceptions): "In simplest terms, we are in a world where the law fosters *cradle to grave* protection for companies' branded goods and services."[1476]

(c) Chapter Summary

The ever-increasing legal rights afforded trademark owners – coupled with the aggressive commercial and litigation strategies used by such trademark owners to benefit from such rights – allow trademark owners to erect highly effective competitive barriers to other market entrants, unduly distorting the underlying "pro-competitive" nature of trademarks. What was once a means to ensure fair competition has evolved into a means to restrict competition. Neither the trademark rules nor the competition rules adequately address this conflict. However, to protect trademarks and robust competition, courts, legislatures, and regulatory authorities need to find a balance between the pro-competitive functions of trademarks and the anti-competitive effects of their protection.

1476 *Desai/Waller*: Brands, Competition, and the Law, pp. 1494–1495 (emphasis mine).

"Ours is a mixed system of government and private enterprise and it is also *a mixed system of monopoly and competition*....

The challenge is to work out laws and customs that help to improve the working of our less-than-perfect competitive system.

The ... relevant choice for policy is not a decision between ... extremes, but rather the degree to which public policy should do *less or more* to modify the operation of particular private economic activities."[1477]

Paul Samuelson

9. Solutions: Striking a Balance

9.1 Interim Summary

(a) Trademarks: "You've Come a Long Way, Baby"[1478]

Trademarks play a fundamental role in our every day lives as consumers: they help us distinguish the products we like (and avoid those that we don't); they signal a short-hand catalogue of quality distinctions that allow us to make choices quickly and efficiently; they give us information about a source or company. For producers, this ability for consumers to distinguish products and producers and make choices accordingly is key, incentivizing companies to build brand value and brand loyalty.

Although it would be difficult to imagine a world without trademarks, the function of trademarks in our society has evolved significantly: trademarks today are used (and useful) in far more expansive ways than their original means of origin, source, or quality identification. Today, the "psychological function"

1477 *Samuelson*: Problems of Economic Organization, p. 70 (emphasis in the original).

1478 The slogan comes from Virginia Slims, a brand of cigarettes manufactured by Altria Group (formerly Phillip Morris Companies). The brand was introduced in 1968 and marketed to young professional women. *Toll/Ling*: The Virginia Slims identity crisis. For a history of the slogan – from inception to commercial campaign launch, see *Weinstein*: How an Agency Builds a Brand – the Virginia Slims Story. For an overview of the campaign as launched in 1968, see *Minnesota Historical Society*: The 1968 Exhibit. For an archive of Virginia Slims TV commercials, see the *Internet Archive*: Legacy Tobacco Documents Library.

of trademarks as symbols[1479] has in many cases elevated trademarks above both physical assets and other forms of intellectual property as the most valuable assets of many companies.[1480] We live in a branded world and the power of trademarks lies in their ability to establish brand loyalty:

> "In the marketing cycle of [*x*],
> without a consumer-related identity, there is no brand loyalty
> and *without brand loyalty there is no market*."[1481]

(b) The Competitive and Non-Competitive Effects of Trademarks

Trademarks are pro-competitive, essential to fair and efficient competition.[1482] Trademark protection provides incentives for investment "by securing to the producer the benefit of the good reputation which excellence creates."[1483] Trademark laws promulgate stable standards of commercial practices[1484] by preventing competitors from unfairly appropriating another's goodwill through passing-off

1479 As Justice Felix Frankfurter in *Mishawaka Rubber* noted: "The protection of trademarks is the law's recognition of the psychological function of symbols. If it is true that we live by symbols, it is no less true that we purchase goods by them.... The owner of a mark exploits this human propensity by making every effort to impregnate the atmosphere of the market with the drawing power of a congenial symbol.... Once this is attained, the trade-mark owner has something of value." *Mishawaka Rubber & Woolen Mfg. Co. v. S. S. Kresge Co.*, 316 U.S. 203, 205 (1942).

1480 *Klieger*: Trademark Dilution, pp. 790–91.

1481 *Weinstein*: How an Agency Builds a Brand – the Virginia Slims Story, cover page (emphasis mine). In the original, the "[x]" was "cigarettes". The statement was made in relation to the importance of establishing a new brand personality for Virginia Slims as a cigarette created for women only. *Weinstein*: How an Agency Builds a Brand – the Virginia Slims Story, cover page (emphasis mine).

1482 Trademarks "enable one seller to compete more effectively with another [and are] congruous with and even necessary to competition." *Chamberlin*: The Theory of Monopolistic Competition, p. 60, cited by *Klieger*: Trademark Dilution, p. 856, fn. 386. "Trade-marks are not... restraints of competition. They are the essence of competition. Their purpose and effect is to distinguish competitive goods." *Taggart*: Trade-Marks: Monopoly or Competition?, p. 668.

1483 S. Rep. No. 1333, 79th Cong., 2d Sess. 4 (1946), reprinted in 1946 U.S.C.C.A.N. 1274, 1275, cited by *Klieger*: Trademark Dilution, p. 856, fn. 387.

1484 McClure called this "commercial morality. *McClure*: Trademarks and Unfair Competition, p. 308, fn. 16, citing *Nims*: The Law of Unfair Competition and Trade-Marks, §§ 6–9a.

(i.e., free riding).[1485] Trademark laws protect the public from deception and reduce consumer search costs and confusion.

> "To protect trade-marks, therefore, is to protect the public from deceit, to foster fair competition, and to secure to the business community the advantages of reputation and good will by preventing their diversion from those who have created them to those who have not."[1486]

In fact, trademarks are the very *symbol* of competition, as without competition, no need would arise to distinguish the goods of one producer from those of another.[1487]

The same characteristics which make trademarks so vital to fair and robust competition, however, can also produce anti-competitive effects and imbue trademarks with the power to stifle and even "swallow up all competition".[1488] Those who maintain that trademark protection is anti-competitive resort mainly to two arguments. The first is that product differentiation by trademark through persuasive advertising creates a monopoly: trademarks create product differentiation that – especially when it is "artificial" differentiation on the basis of brand for essentially fungible products – stifles competition by subdividing larger markets into little ones in which price, demand, output, etc., can be manipulated.[1489]

1485 *Ridgway*: Revitalizing the Doctrine of Trademark Misuse, p. 1560, discussing *Nw. Corp. v. Gabriel Mfg. Co.*, 48 U.S.P.Q. 2d 1902, 1908 (N.D. Ill. 1998): "Congress expressed its intention to protect both the consumer and the trademark owner.... In protecting the consumer, "[the public] may be confident that, in purchasing a product bearing a particular trademark..., it will get the product which it asks for and wants to get." In addition,... the trademark owner's expenditure of "energy, time, and money in presenting to the public the product" should be protected from "misappropriation by pirates and cheats"." (citations omitted).

1486 S. Rep. No. 1333, 79th Cong., 2d Sess. 4 (1946), reprinted in 1946 U.S.C.C.A.N. 1274, 1275, cited by *Nesvold/Pollard*: Half a Century of Federal Trademark Protection, p. 50, fn. 3.

1487 Economides posits that trademark protection actually stimulates an additional form of competition – that of "perception advertising" or competition in advertisements. *Economides*: The Economics of Trademarks, pp. 532–33.

1488 "Until [the anti-dilution] statute is interpreted more fully by a California court, we feel constrained not to give it overly broad application lest it swallow up all competition in the claim of protection against trade name infringement." *Coffee Dan's, Inc. v. Coffee Don's Charcoal Broiler*, 305 F. Supp. 1210, 1217 at n. 13 (N.D. Cal. 1969).

1489 *McClure*: Trademarks and Unfair Competition, pp. 328–32. "Trademark promotion may in some markets be the sole cause of high barriers to entry which preserve

The second is that protecting trademarks allows producers to insulate their products' market share from price competition by creating consumer allegiances based on brand loyalty[1490] – a price-insensitive loyalty that may be based "purely on superior advertising techniques" – which can prove difficult, and sometimes near impossible, for future market entrants to break.[1491] "The link between persuasive advertising, consumer allegiance, and trademarks … lead some to argue that a trademark, once established, can serve as a barrier to entry more powerful even than a patent or copyright."[1492]

Although market power will not be inferred from the mere ownership of a trademark,[1493] an established position in the market as exemplified by a famous

---

the monopoly power of one maker. New brands of equal or higher quality may be unable to compete solely because of the strength of the established trademark whose power is sustained by persuasive advertising. Consumers end up paying higher prices for a better-known but lower-quality brand." *Id.* at 351.

1490 "Consumer allegiances built over the years with intensive advertising, trademarks, trade names, copyrights and so forth extend substantial protection to firms already in the market. In some markets this barrier to entry may be insuperable." *Papandreou*: The Economic Effect of Trademarks, pp. 508–09.

1491 "Economically irrational elements are introduced into consumer choices; and the trademark owner is insulated from the normal pressures of price and quality competition. In consequence the competitive system fails to perform its function of allocating available resources efficiently." *Klieger*: Trademark Dilution, p. 856–58. "A differentiated brand, like a patent, a secret process, control over distribution channels, or control of raw materials, is a safeguard against the risks of competition." *Smith v. Chanel, Inc.*, 402 F.2d 562, 567 (9th Cir. 1968). The "promotion of trademarks by noninformative, influential advertising may lessen competition by insulating a differentiated product from price competition and making rational consumer spending more difficult. Product differentiation can also produce nearly insurmountable barriers to entry into an industry, causing greater industrial concentration and preserving existing monopolies and oligopolies." *Brown*: Advertising and the Public Interest, p. 1177.

1492 *Aaker*: Managing Brand Equity, p. 187, cited by *Klieger*: Trademark Dilution, p. 860, fn. 421. See also *McClure*: Trademarks and Unfair Competition, p. 345; and *Ealy*: The Common Law, the States, and Historical Perspective, pp. 18–19.

1493 See *DOJ/FTC*: 1995 IP Licensing Guidelines, § 2.2 (albeit referring to "intellectual property rights" in general). Commission Notice: TTBE Guidelines (OJ C 89/3, 28.03.2014), paras. 2, 16–17. *European Commission*: DG Competition discussion paper, para. 40.

trademark can create significant barriers to entry into or expansion of such a market.[1494]

(c) Private Rights v. Public Interests

Trademark protection recognizes rights *only insofar as necessary* to prevent consumer confusion. The balance is thus between protecting free trade and fair trade. At all times, the benefits of granting private, proprietary rights (i.e., protecting trademarks) to prevent consumer confusion and free-riding is balanced with the public interest in free market competition. Since the traditional balance inherent in the protection of intellectual property is absent (statutory protection of patents, copyrights, and trade secrets is justified by the balancing of *short-term* exclusive rights with *long-term* contributions of inventions and writings to the public domain), seeking a balance for trademark rights, which can be protected indefinitely, is more challenging. The goals of promoting competition by protecting producers (from free riding by competitors) and protecting consumers (from confusion, deceit, or unfair business practices) are compelling economic and social justifications for the protection of trademarks. So too are the goals of ensuring a robust, competitive market distinguished by few barriers to expansion or market entry. Trademark law is thus "a compromise between promoting [goodwill, business, consumer, and commercial] principles and furthering the competitive ideal with which trademark protection is in conflict."[1495]

The expanding legal protection and commercial deference afforded trademarks and trademark owners, coupled with the aggressive litigation strategies used by trademark owners – made under the guise of *protecting* competition – has imbalanced this "compromise". We have allowed trademark protection even in cases where there is no confusion, no market failure, no economic rivalry, and

1494 The European Commission defines barriers to expansion and entry as "factors that make entry impossible or unprofitable while permitting established undertakings to charge prices above the competitive level. *European Commission*: DG Competition discussion paper, Public consultation, para. 38. For barriers specifically related to intellectual property rights, including legal barriers, absolute cost advantages, privileged access to supply, a highly developed sales and distribution network, and an established position in the market, see *Id.*, para. 38; for additional barriers to entry not necessarily related to intellectual property rights, see *Id.*, para. 40.

1495 *McClure*: Trademarks and Unfair Competition, p. 308. McClure notes further that: "This historical conflict, long recognized as present in unfair competition and trademark law, *has never been satisfactorily resolved* at any level." *Id.*

no deceit. By widening the scope of protection,[1496] and permitting more causes of action and lower standards of liability, trademark protection has broadened considerably from its original protection of the public against deception (through unfair business practices) and of producers (against free riding from competitors) to shielding trademark owners from competition in general.[1497]

The expanding standards of liability and causes of action beg the question: what is the ultimate role of trademark protection? Do trademark infringement and unfair competition actions serve primarily to protect consumers and producers *from unfair trade practices* or do the actions primarily serve to protect the business of individual trademark holders without regard to the best interests of consumers and the workings of a competitive market?

Taken one-by-one, the legislative trend of expanding rights, the expanded justifications for protection, the significance given to the fame of a trademark, and the increased trademark bullying and trademark turf wars which are now common, have changed our perception of trademarks from identification, source, and quality signifiers to quasi-sovereign symbols. Taken together, they have allowed the competitive market mandate to give way to protectionist rights.

(d) The Trademark Paradox

The paradox lies in how we have dealt with this situation: the protection of trademarks – including the protection of famous trademarks – is a vital component in our complex, competitive market. However, in light of the legal system's failure to adequately balance the private, protectionist forces with the public interest, these anti-competitive effects threaten to diminish competition. We have allowed trademark rights to expand significantly without building in any corresponding internal limits to such rights. This sort of protection is more akin

---

1496 A "trademark need no longer identify any particular commodity (other than itself) in order to receive protection.... In many cases, the trademark referent is now little more than a legal fiction. The modern trademark is dyadic in structure." *Beebe*: The Semiotic Analysis of Trademark Law, p. 625.

1497 The increased scope of dilution law has weathered the most criticism: "Dilution theory is a wholly new legal basis of trademark exclusivity that has nothing to do with protecting consumers from being confused or deceived." *McCarthy*: Proving a Trademark Has Been Diluted, p. 727. "Unlike traditional infringement law, the prohibitions against trademark dilution are not the product of common-law development, and are not motivated by an interest in protecting consumers." *Moseley v. V Secret Catalogue, Inc.*, 537 U.S. 418, 429 (2003).

to the protection afforded patents and copyrights.[1498] It borders on protecting a trademark – and the nebulous idea of a brand personality associated with such trademarks – as property[1499] or rights "in gross"[1500] sometimes only based on the

---

1498 Patent and copyright protection offer commercial incentives (or rewards) to inventors and authors in the form of exclusive rights; these rights, however, expire at some point and the public is rewarded with the release of such achievements into the public domain. Trademark rationales have traditionally been about "the delicate balance" of (i) protecting the goodwill of the tradesperson and (ii) protecting the consumer from being deceived. *Doellinger*: A New Theory of Trademarks, p. 826. As Justice Clifford noted in 1880, "courts in all civilized countries have for centuries afforded protection to trade-marks, the object of such protection being not only to secure to the individual the fruits of his skill, industry, and enterprise, but also to protect the public against fraud." *Mfg. Co. v. Trainer*, 101 U.S. 51, at 57 (U.S. 1880) (Clifford, J., dissenting). See also *Lastowka*: Trademark's Daemons.

1499 Sonia Katyal has noted that "trademark law permits one party to propertize terms". *Katyal*: Trademark Intersectionality, p. 1604. Katyal further observed: "The law governing trademarks presumes that a mark is a type of economic property – it has a fixed presumption of meaning as a brand, and as an identity, in the marketplace of goods.... Trademarks are owned properties, brand owners may argue, rather than simply ideas. Yet while trademarks are commodities in one sense, they are also expressions in another, to both the markholder that owns them and to the public that perceives them, and the law inherits the responsibility of navigating a trademark's potential contradiction between its status as corporate property and as cultural icon." *Id.* at 1605 and 1612.

1500 A number of scholars (and even some courts) have noted that the expanded scope of trademark infringement claims – and in particular anti-dilution statutes – have worked to "whittle away the traditional basis of trademark protection until trademark rights in gross displace the consumer protection model as the talisman of most trademark actions." *Klieger*: Trademark Dilution, p. 835. "It may just be a matter of time before dilution eclipses confusion as the gravamen of most federal trademark actions and trademark rights in gross displace consumer protection as the defining feature of United States trademark law." *Id.* at 847–848. "Because the dilution statute has no clear threshold of fame, it has the capacity to transform much or all of trademark law into a system of in gross property rights." *Moskin*: Dilution Act, p. 1, cited by *Klieger*: Trademark Dilution, p. 825, fn. 201. "Protection of trademarks against dilution comes very close to recognition of an 'in gross' property right in the mark". *Winner*: Right of Identity: Right of Publicity and Protection, p. 206. "Until [the anti-dilution] statute is interpreted more fully by a California court, we feel constrained not to give it overly broad application lest it *swallow up all competition* in the claim of protection against trade name infringement." *Coffee Dan's, Inc. v. Coffee Don's Charcoal Broiler*, 305 F. Supp. 1210, 1217 at n. 13 (N.D. Cal. 1969) (emphasis mine). "The asserted doctrine is based upon the *fundamental* "commercial magnetism" imbued in marks. However, unlike the protection of patents and copyrights, which remain narrow and limited in duration, trademark protection has ballooned out of proportion and is no longer "constant and limited".[1501]

Recalling Justice Holmes' opinion in *International News Service*, Holmes made the observation that property rights are creations of law: they do *not* arise automatically from value, even if that value is exchangeable.[1502] Instead, they depend on a legal judgment that recognizing a right to exclude is *needed* to protect against unwarranted interferences. As the commercial significance of brands in the market has increased, we have allowed special interests (in particular famous trademark owners) to unduly shape such expanding protection without determining whether there is a need to protect such value. Although developments and changes in law are *vital* to adapt our laws to a mature and modern society, what is problematic is our failure to establish (and "wisely" guard, in Justice Brandeis' words) the boundaries of such developments or to address the anticompetitive effects of such changes.

In so doing, we have allowed trademark owners to use their trademarks strategically within the market in order to erect highly effective competitive barriers through brand identification and brand loyalty. What was once a means to ensure fair competition has evolved into a means to restrict competition. The expanded rights and causes of action are *imprudent* in that they pose anti-competitive threats to market competition. The result is clear: "Infinitely expanding trademark owner's rights in the name of consumer protection is a mistake and will ultimately harm consumers by hampering competition."[1503]

---

error of supposing that a trade-mark right is a right in gross or at large, like a statutory copyright or a patent for an invention, to either of which, in truth, it has little or no analogy." *United Drug Co. V. Theodore Rectanus Co.*, 248 U.S. 90, 97 (1918) (emphasis mine).

1501 "Throughout the development of trademark law, the purpose of trademarks remained constant and limited: Identification of the manufacturer or sponsor of a good or the provider of a service (in economic terms, trademarks reduce consumer search costs by informing people that trademarked products come from the same source). And the wrong protected against was traditionally equally limited: Preventing producers from free-riding on their rivals' marks." *New Kids on the Block v. News America Pub., Inc.*, 971 F.2d 302, 305 (9th Cir. 1992).

1502 *International News Service v. Associated Press*, 248 U.S. 215, 246 (1918) (Holmes, J., separate opinion, with McKenna, J., concurring).

1503 *Tushnet*: Gone in Sixty Milliseconds, p. 565.

(e) Establishing a Balanced Trade-Off

Recognizing the anti-competitive effects of trademarks (through the power of brands) and trademark law (through expanded protection) is one thing; determining what, if anything, can be done about such effects is quite another. The challenge in granting any sort of exclusive rights is ensuring that the trade-off is correctly balanced:[1504] for copyrights and patents, this arises primarily in determining how long the duration of protection should be as well as the scope of subject matter to be protected. For trademarks, the issue is more complicated, since trademarks can theoretically be protected indefinitely. For trademarks, the issue centers primarily on the *scope* of protectable subject matter and the ability to exclude others from using similar trademarks. The search for a balance implicitly raises the debate regarding "the trend towards judicial protection of trademarks against uses that do not affect consumers adversely".[1505] Paul Samuelson sagely observed that:

> "Ours is a mixed system of government and private enterprise and it is also *a mixed system of monopoly and competition…*"[1506]

Samuelson's observations are key: our market is a mixed set of monopoly and competition. It is also a mixed set of private investment interests and public market interests. Trademark protection grants certain exclusive rights to the trademark owner. This can lead to restrictions on commerce as well as efficiencies for commerce. By accepting this dual nature of private proprietary rights and public interest competition, we can approach the paradox and navigate a sensible and pragmatic solution that balances free and fair competition. Samuelson's advice is thus prescient:

> "The challenge is to work out laws and customs that help to improve the working of *our less-than-perfect competitive system*…. [T]he relevant choice for policy is *not a decision between … extremes*, but rather the degree to which public policy should do *less or more* to *modify the operation of particular private economic activities*."[1507]

1504 As the European Commission stated in promoting its "Blueprint" for intellectual property rights: "Getting this balance right will make a real difference to businesses. … This will benefit the EU's growth and competitiveness which is delivered through the single market." *European Commission*: Press Release IP/11/630.

1505 *Barnes*: A New Economics of Trademarks.

1506 *Samuelson*: Problems of Economic Organization, p. 70 (emphasis in the original).

1507 *Id.* (emphasis mine).

Extreme positions applied to any challenge are imprudent. For example, solutions calling for the elimination of trademark laws altogether is certainly not the solution; nor are recommendations of implementing durational limits (akin to the restriction on patents and copyrights) pragmatic.[1508] Any solution needs to navigate a sensible middle-ground between *balancing* the pro-competitive functions of trademarks with the anti-competitive effects of their protection.[1509] Hence, the goal would be a framework which achieved "reasonable effective 'workable competition'".[1510] The private property rights of trademark owners need to be protected *only insofar as necessary* to protect the public and the public's interest in avoiding confusion, fraud, and unfair business practices (including protection of the trademark owner's investment against free riding by competitors).[1511] Such balance is inherent in – and thus can be found in – the underlying unfair competition principles governing trademarks and trademark law. We simply need to return to the basics, setting out pragmatic principles and establishing concrete guidelines and tools to implement those principles. Two pragmatic guidelines could be beneficial in helping to realign the public and private interests of trademarks and trademark law:

(i) Principle 1: Prune the Trademark Tree
(ii) Principle 2: Practice Regulatory & Statutory Humility

1508 Edward Chamberlin, a leading authority on product differentiation as a barrier to competition, proposed limiting trademarks, like patents and copyrights, to a specified number of years. See *Chamberlin*: The Theory of Monopolistic Competition, pp. 273–24, as cited by *Klieger*: Trademark Dilution, p. 861, fn. 422.

1509 With respect to copyright protection, Professor Lawrence Lessig has made a similar observation regarding the need to find a balance *between* extremes: "We live in a world governed by extremes. Two views about copyright dominate. There are those that believe that all rights must be controlled, and those who believe that no rights should be controlled. Call them the alls and the nones. But the world is divided not into two, but into three. There are those who believe in all rights reserved, those who believe in no rights at all, but there are also many who believe that some rights should be controlled but not all." *Lessig*: The Creative Commons, p. 10.

1510 *Samuelson*: Problems of Economic Organization, p. 74.

1511 Pratheepan Gulasekaram makes a similar argument with respect to trademarks and expressive works (i.e., with respect to artistic and expressive non-commercial speech). *Gulasekaram*: Policing the Border Between Trademarks and Free Speech, p. 891.

9.2 Prune the Trademark Tree[1512]

Pruning is a horticultural practice involving the *selective* removal of parts of a parts of a plant, such as branches, buds, or roots.[1513] Reasons to prune include the removal of deadwood, shaping (by controlling or directing growth), improving or maintaining health, reducing risk from falling branches, and increasing the yield or quality of flowers and fruits. The practice entails *targeted* removal of diseased, damaged, dead, non-productive, structurally unsound, or otherwise unwanted tissue.[1514] The result is a more robust, healthy plant.

The same language could be used to address the current state of trademark laws: trademark laws need pruning. Trademark laws need a mix of targeted "shaping" (to control and direct growth) and "nurturing" (to improve and maintain health) to rebalance the private and public interests in trademark protection. In so doing, the trademark laws and the trademark system could function more efficiently and effectively without the pendulum swings of imbalance due to over- and under-enforcement. Such a more balanced and mature system would be of benefit to consumers, producers, and competitors alike.

(a) Stop Analogizing: Let Trademarks be Trademarks

Patents, copyrights, and trademarks – as well as an increasing list of other rights – are all referred to as "intellectual property". However, the umbrella term is deceiving, as trademarks stand apart from their intellectual property brethren in a number of ways. These differences – although potentially immaterial on some levels – are material when it comes to understanding trademarks, when discussing the pros and cons of "intellectual property" rights, when making generalizations about the justifications for their protection, and – most importantly – when attempting to develop legal and policy strategies applicable to their use or restriction.

Furthermore, the analogy of intellectual property rights to real property is also problematic and not particularly well suited to trademarks (or any intellectual property right).[1515] Professor Mark Lemley has suggested that such analogies

1512 This principle was inspired by the title of Séverine Dusollier's article, "Pruning the European intellectual property tree: in search of common principles and roots". *Dusollier*: Pruning the European intellectual property tree.

1513 *French/Appleton*: A Guide to Successful Pruning.

1514 *Professional Tree and Garden Service*: Pruning Services.

1515 For an analysis of the trend, including examples of courts' and companies' treating intellectual property as absolute property, see *Carrier*: Cabining Intellectual

are faulty and are, in fact, the wrong approach when trying to understand intellectual property rights.[1516] In the end he concludes: "I don't know that we need an analogy at all. … The needs and characteristics of intellectual property are unique, and so are the laws that establish intellectual property rights."[1517]

Trademarks are a unique form of and aid to commerce. They are – with their focus on commerce – significantly different from their intellectual property brethren which focus on creation. Using the blanket "umbrella" term (intellectual property) to make broad statements regarding trademarks, as well as using real property rhetoric – or any rhetoric – for trademark rights, is not good policy. When we do so, we lose sight of the rationales underlying trademarks as well as the principles needed to monitor them. In essence, the lesson is to let trademarks be trademarks and let trademark law be governed by its own principles.[1518]

Property, in particular Part I, pp. 8–24; and *Singer*: The Reliance Interest in Property. For an example of the argument that trademarks are *not* property, see *Port*: The Illegitimacy of Trademark Incontestability.

1516 Lemley laments the application and influence of theories underlying real property to the theories of intellectual property: "As the term "intellectual property" settles over … bodies of law …, courts and scholars increasingly turn to the legal and economic literature of tangible property law to justify – or to modify – the rules of intellectual property. On the academic front, more and more scholars have expressly argued (or worse, assumed) that information is property in the traditional sense and that the rules that apply to one category of property ought presumptively to apply to the others as well." *Lemley*: Property, Intellectual Property, and Free Riding, pp. 1034–35. Lemley cites *Easterbrook*: Intellectual Property is Still Property, p. 112 (who maintained that a "right to exclude in intellectual property is no different in principle from the right to exclude in physical property"). See also *Carter*: Does It Matter Whether Intellectual Property Is Property?, and a list of additional sources at *Lemley*: Property, Intellectual Property, and Free Riding, fn. 8.

1517 *Lemley*: Property, Intellectual Property, and Free Riding, p. 1075 (footnotes omitted). Lemley carefully reviews how intellectual property rights might be considered in terms of real property, torts, government subsidies, or government regulations. Although he surmised that government-created subsidies might be the closest analogy to the intellectual property regime, none "is even close to perfect." Lemley argues that, if no analogy is needed, then a new term may be warranted, in particular to stop people thinking of intellectual property as simply another form of property: "So here's a modest suggestion: instead of intellectual property, let's start talking about "IP." Lots of people already use it as a shorthand anyway." *Id.*

1518 The tendency to equate intellectual property with property is also problematic in the context of competition law. Commissioner Rosch of the FTC has noted the inherent difficulties in applying antitrust policies to intellectual property rights as if they were another property right: "intellectual property is not comparable

(b) Prioritize Trademarks' "Information Role"

By "letting trademarks be trademarks", we can refocus on the functions trademarks have and perform in commerce today. We can distinguish their investment and brand communication functions from their information and commerce functions.

Trademarks have been used in commerce for centuries as means to distinguish products and producers long before any formal trademark laws existed.[1519] Trademarks are essential elements of commerce – allowing us to identify a manufacturer, know the source of a product, expect a known level of quality, and associate with the product we are purchasing. Originally, they were used primarily as a means of identification, source, or quality.

In today's society, trademark's fourth function – the advertising or investment function, resulting in the *goodwill essence* of the brand – has taken center stage. This goodwill factor – which is used primarily to benefit the private investment interests of the producer – *not the consumer* – has eclipsed the identification, origin, and source functions underlying trademark protection. Brand and firm goodwill are important to recognize and protect. Trademark laws have implemented laws to address these concerns well. However, the "supra" expansion of such protection – by protecting the so-called "inherent goodwill" factor – is more troubling: inherent goodwill, according to Robert Bone, "has nothing to do with safeguarding the quality of consumer information" and "assumes an extremely broad conception of goodwill".[1520]

We should not forget the identification, origin, and source functions – i.e., the fundamental role of trademarks as an informational aid to commerce. By placing more importance on the advertising and investment function, placing

---

to other forms of property for purposes of antitrust analysis. Patents, copyrights, trade secrets, know-how and trademarks, while they possess attributes of property in that they can be acquired and conveyed, do not always exhibit a clear and direct linkage to the goods markets that are the central focus of the antitrust laws." *Rosch*: Some Thoughts on the Role of Intellectual Property in Innovation Market Cases, p. 2.

1519 *Port*: The Illegitimacy of Trademark Incontestability, p. 522 (citations omitted). For additional reviews of uses in antiquity and after, see *Rogers*: Some Historical Matter Concerning Trade-Marks; *Schechter*: Historical Foundations; *Ruston*: On the Origin of Trademarks; *Paster*: Trademarks – Their Early History; *Diamond*: The Historical Development of Trademarks; *McClure*: Trademarks and Unfair Competition; and *Fezer*: Markenrecht.

1520 *Bone*: Hunting Goodwill, pp. 551–552.

more recognition on the merchandizing and branding rights, and placing more importance on the injury to the goodwill of the trademark owner over the public interests, we have eclipsed the underlying unfair competition and consumer welfare rationales.

(c) Reapply Unfair Competition Principles

From the start, the legal protection of trademarks – in both the U.S. and Europe – was based in principles of unfair competition and the deterrence of consumer confusion.[1521] Trademark's underlying rationales – preventing fraud and protecting the public – is what distinguishes it from other intellectual property rights.[1522]

Acts of unfair competition – i.e., unfair commercial practices which harm consumers or harmed the market – have traditionally framed trademark protection. Claims were based on: (i) acts likely to cause confusion (hurting consumers); (ii) acts that might mislead the public (hurting the market); and (iii) acts that discredit a competitor (hurting market participants). The underlying rationale was that protecting trademarks protected commerce and promoted a robust competitive market: trademark laws protected both producers and consumers against unfair trade practices *in commerce*. Modern unfair competition laws still cover these principles. For example, the German Act Against Unfair Competition (*Gesetz gegen den unlauteren Wettbewerb* or UWG) provides that "This Act shall serve the purpose of protecting competitors, consumers and other market participants against unfair commercial practices. At the same time, it shall protect the interests of the public in undistorted competition."[1523]

Trademark law today has expanded from these underlying principles of unfair competition to principles of private entitlement: trademark owners today (and in particular famous trademark owners) can claim rights to a mark or sign

---

1521 As has been noted by scholars and courts, "confusion to the public is the essence of both trademark infringement and unfair competition." *McCarthy*: McCarthy on Trademarks and Unfair Competition, § 2.12, at 2–59, quoting *Dart Drug Corp. v. Schering Corp.*, 320 F.2d 745, 748 n. 10 (D.C. Cir. 1963).

1522 For a list of cases and scholarly works confirming the underlying rationales of trademark law to protect the public, prevent fraud, promote fair competition, prohibit consumer deception, and protect the integrity of the marketplace, see *Lastowka*: Trademark's Daemons, p. 781, fn. 8.

1523 § 1 UWG. "Unfair commercial practices shall be illegal if they are suited to tangible impairment of the interests of competitors, consumers or other market participants." § 3(1) UWG.

that go beyond any reasonable protection of commerce.[1524] In large part, this is due to the application of the doctrine of dilution – whether inside the courtroom (where courts have been easily swayed by such arguments) or outside the courtroom (through bullying by senior trademark owners).

As a result, such expanded protection results in an anticompetitive threat to market efficiency and consumer welfare. *The law needs a <u>prudent</u> return to the consumer protection model of trademark rights.*

(d) Reign in Dilution: Apply Carefully (if at all)

As has been noted: "Dilution protects nothing but a trademark's persona – 'its identity, its quality of distinctiveness and uniqueness, quite apart from its function of identifying the source [or quality] of goods and services.'"[1525] Dilution protects the trademark owner's investment. In practice, dilution protection "encourages companies to invest more than they otherwise might in the creation of intangible associations that add no real value to the product and that deride economic efficiency."[1526]

Dilution protection does not protect consumers.[1527] In fact, there is little justification for the expanded dilution protection from the standpoint of consumer welfare. While a new competitor should certainly not be able to benefit from the success of a senior mark (the classic free-riding concern) nor deceive the public (by falsely suggesting a connection or association), a new competitor should have rights to enter a market by using *existing* marks, colors, and shapes in a new manner to create it own associations and product differentiation.

By allowing a trademark owner to prohibit *any* connection to the "broad imagery" of an established mark, the trademark owner obtains rights in a word or sign that extends to situations even absent consumer confusion. These

1524 Protection of brand and personality "does nothing to reveal the value many referential and customary users place on search information so does little to ensure that the optimal amount of search information is provided." *Barnes*: A New Economics of Trademarks, p. 65.

1525 *Winner*: Right of Identity: Right of Publicity and Protection, p. 193, cited by *Klieger*: Trademark Dilution, p. 862.

1526 *Klieger*: Trademark Dilution, p. 862.

1527 "The lack of a compelling consumer interest requires the dilution doctrine to rest entirely upon the sense of inequity aroused by specific takings, leaving it vulnerable to attacks premised on an overriding public interest in unrestrained competition." *Denicola*: Trademarks as Speech: Constitutional Implications, p. 183. See also *Klieger*: Trademark Dilution, pp. 864–866.

expanded rights to exclude *non-competing* uses diminish market competition without any long-term benefit. Dilution laws have upset the balance of interests between trademark protection for the benefit of the market and trademark protection for the benefit of trademark owners. Furthermore, because a trademark, unlike a patent or copyright, can last forever, anti-dilution statutes create rights that extend well beyond the limited terms of protection of patent and copyright law

Finally, dilution protection does not enhance competition. In fact, it allows famous trademark owners overly broad rights to restrain other market players, creating, in some cases, insurmountable barriers to entry for new competition in a market and sometimes even in an *unrelated* market. In legal terms, it has eclipsed competition by eliminating a trademark owner's burden of proof to show consumer confusion. It has also removed the requirement that the marks at issue are related to products that "compete". Instead, a trademark owner only has to show that the mark is "famous". What this term means is nebulous.[1528]

(e) Implement a Meaningful Use Requirement

Trademark *use* defines the scope, contours, and limits of trademark protection. By allowing trademark registrations without genuine use (or without a bona fide intent to use), the law grants an exclusive right without the requisite balanced return: a holder receives a right, but neither consumers nor the market see the benefit, since no origin, source, quality, or goodwill functions are exercised or shared with the public.

Trademark rights "are said to flow from its use, not from its existence".[1529] Only use – and association of use with a product – permits distinction between sources and thus defines the limits of trademark protection. Use requirements can assist in implementing a proper trade-off between private rights and public interest. If there is no use, there is no consumer confusion, there can be no deceit, and there can be no goodwill (which is associated with such use). Hence, without use, there is little need for protection.

1528 In the EU, dilution protection is extended to marks that are only famous in a "niche" market". For a review of the U.S. and EU position on dilution law (and the notion of niche markets), see *Luepke*: Taking Unfair Advantage or Diluting a Famous Mark, pp. 819–824.

1529 *Carter*: Does It Matter Whether Intellectual Property is Property?, p. 720 (citations omitted).

(f) Balance Injury v. Harms

Trademark owners regularly rely on claims of free riding, dilution of their mark's reputation, or consumer confusion to justify expanded sovereignty of their trademarks (i.e., their unmitigated ability to prohibit another's use of a mark they feel is too closely associated with their own). When faced with such claims, courts should assess whether these claims are based on legitimate examples of injury of the type trademark laws were intended to prevent (i.e., confusion, fraud, deception, unfair practices) or whether these claims are merely based in a desire to capture *more* market share (i.e., proprietary, private rights). This means that court should carefully assess the ways in which an alleged infringer's conduct does or does not affect competition, requiring the *plaintiff* to demonstrate that their injury results from consumer confusion, free-riding, or fraud.

With respect to consumer confusion, trademark laws should focus on actual consumer confusion, not merely – or solely – the likelihood of confusion. As Advocate General Jacobs wisely noted in *SABEL*, the fact that the junior mark "serves merely to call to mind the senior mark" is not sufficient to establish a likelihood of confusion of association.[1530] The same has been recognized in the U.S., where the Court of Customs and Patent Appeals noted that "The very fact of calling to mind may indicate that the mind is *distinguishing*, rather than being *confused* by, two marks."[1531]

Intellectual scholars Ridgway and Lemley/McKenna have all made strong arguments for implementing a trademark injury doctrine, akin to the U.S. antitrust injury doctrine, that deals with overly broad rights.[1532] Under the antitrust injury doctrine, the plaintiff (or a defendant asserting an antitrust counterclaim) must

---

1530 Case C-251/95, *SABEL BV v Puma AG, Rudolf Dassler Sport*, [1997] ECR I-6191, Opinion of AG Jacobs, 29 April 1997, para. 56.

1531 *In re Ferrero*, 479 F.2d 1395, 1397 (C.C.P.A. 1973) (emphasis mine).

1532 *Ridgway*: Revitalizing the Doctrine of Trademark Misuse. Lemley/McKenna: Owning Mark(et)s. This trademark *injury* doctrine needs to be distinguished from a trademark *misuse* doctrine. Under a *misuse* doctrine, the defendant need not prove individual harm from the misuse at all, and is protected if she can prove that the plaintiff misused the trademark, even if the defendant was *unaffected* by the misuse. See *Lemley*: The Economic Irrationality of the Patent Misuse Doctrine, pp. 1612–1613. Many scholars have derided the intellectual property misuse doctrine. See, for example, *Carter*: Does It Matter Whether Intellectual Property Is Property?, p. 718, finding the patent misuse defense "one of the most embarrassing aspects of current patent doctrine". See also *Carter*: Doctrine of Patent Misuse Misused, finding copyright misuse a equally bad theory.

prove injury "of the type the antitrust laws were intended to prevent and that flows from that which makes the defendants' acts unlawful." For a trademark injury, a plaintiff would have to demonstrate not simply that their mark was "diluted" by association, but that the dilution resulted from consumer confusion. If there is no consumer confusion, there is less need to protect the trademark more than it already is. To date, special interest groups have a particularly persuasive presence. This adds to the "burden on the courts to be more mindful of the competitive interest in IP law".[1533] Famous trademark owners have used claims of "dilution" to claim expansive rights,[1534] without necessarily demonstrating any injury to consumers or the market.

By refocusing on the balance of injury versus harm, courts can watch for behaviour that harms the competitive ideal versus claims that merely add to the trademark holder's rights. By establishing limits to the expansion of private rights, this will encourage a robust, competitive market, which balances the need to protect private rights and investment with the public's interest in fair competition.

9.3 Practice Statutory & Regulatory Humility[1535]

It is (largely) undisputed that the protection of trademarks promotes competition, yet at a basic level conflicts with the competitive ideal: trademark law

1533 *Hovenkamp*: Empire: Innovation and the Domain of Competition Policy, p. 128.

1534 Judges and lawyers should identify the specific type of goodwill involved in a case – whether it is brand goodwill, firm goodwill, or the inherent goodwill associated with a mark's popularity – and explain how protecting that type of goodwill protects competition. As Robert Bone has suggested "judges should avoid goodwill misappropriation as a distinct policy rationale. That approach only misdirects trademark law away from what should be its core mission: to ensure the efficient and honest communication of product quality information to consumers." *Bone*: Hunting Goodwill.

1535 This term was borrowed from Maureen K. Ohlhausen, Commissioner, Federal Trade Commission, who regularly uses it to explain one of her priorities when analyzing the intervention of competition authorities in high-technology fields: "I believe dynamic markets need a lighter touch to allow them the flexibility to develop. Government bureaucrats... are not business people. The danger of hindering dynamic efficiently with government intrusion is especially high in technology business... I am therefore generally circumspect about injecting the government into these markets. This is a principle I have referred to as "regulatory humility." *Ohlhausen*: A Pragmatist's Approach to Navigating the Intersection of IP and Antitrust, p. 6. Commissioner Ohlhausen introduced this term in 2012, in her dissent

protects private entitlements which by their very nature excludes others thereby conflicting with the ideal of free competition. The challenge for the legislative and judicial branches is how to address this "not perfect competition"[1536] effectively. As Justice Brandeis admonished in 1918 in *International News Service v. Associated Press*:

> "...the creation or recognition by courts of a new private right may work serious injury to the general public, unless the boundaries of the right are definitely established and wisely guarded."[1537]

To date, authorities have had the tendency to allow over-protectionist claims – in effect granting "new" or expanded rights without definitely establishing "the boundaries" of such rights. Rights have been granted without a sufficient determination of whether such rights (i) improve competition, (ii) result in an enhanced benefit to the public (e.g., decreased confusion), or (iii) reasonably protect the investment trademark owners have made (by prohibiting free riding by competitors). Below a few pragmatic steps that legislatures, courts, and regulatory authorities can keep in mind for approaching the trademark conflict in order to "salvage the economic utility of trademark law."[1538]

(a) Implementation of "*sui generis*" Laws: Be prudent

Legislative, judicial, and regulatory authorities need to temper their tendency to develop and implement *sui generis* laws whenever a new claim, technology, or issue arises. When new laws are needed, then they need to address the private-public balance and consider both (i) the short-term solution (in granting new or expanded exclusive rights, which may restrain trade) and (ii) the long-term public interest (ensuring efficient and dynamic market commerce). Any new or

---

statement regarding the FTC's allegations that Bosch's acquisition of SPX, as originally proposed, would have been anticompetitive. Bosch and the FTC entered into a settlement agreement resolving anticompetitive conduct that occurred prior to the announcement of the acquisition. Commissioner Ohlhausen suggested that the FTC should show a little more "regulatory humility" with respect to its intervention regarding standard essential patents (SEPs) and the activities of SEP holders. *Ohlhausen*: Statement In the Matter of Robert Bosch GmbH, p. 2.

1536 *Samuelson*: Problems of Economic Organization, p. 72.

1537 *International News Service v. Associated Press*, 248 U.S. 215, 262–63 (1918) (Brandeis, J., dissenting).

1538 *Travis*: The Battle for Mindshare, para. 145.

expanded rights need to have well-defined boundaries. The lesson: if intervention is necessary, do so prudently.[1539]

Trademarks are important and should be protected. However, sensible limits to their contours are equally important: "the recognition that trademarks can be the valuable property of their owners does not require disregarding sensible limits on the contours of their property rights."[1540]

(b) Reconsider Competition's Role

The intersection of intellectual property rights with competition laws has a long history. Competition rules promote and maintain fair market competition by regulating anti-competitive conduct. Application of competition restrictions on intellectual property rights can play an important role in restraining market power.[1541] To date, competition laws have done a good job of regulating anti-competitive behaviours with respect to trademark licensing – including prohibitions on excessive or predatory pricing, tying ("bundling"), horizontal price fixing, resale price maintenance, or the territorial division of customers or markets. However, competition laws have not been so successful dealing with the anti-competitive effects of trademark ownership – including arguments that the promotion of trademarks and their "influential advertising may lessen competition by insulating a differentiated product from price competition and making rational consumer spending more difficult".[1542] Powerful brand personas and other non-rational elements of product differentiation can produce nearly insurmountable barriers to entry into an industry, "causing greater industrial concentration and preserving existing monopolies and oligopolies."[1543] However, applying competition policies to such

1539 The result should be prudent but effective intervention. To use the words of Renata Hesse, Deputy Assistant Attorney General Antitrust Division U.S. Department of Justice:"We took action, but we did so prudently. When we identified an anticompetitive transaction or conduct we challenged it. But we also were quick to clear deals that did not threaten competition." *Hesse*: IP, Antitrust and Looking Back on the Last Four Years.

1540 *Travis*: The Battle for Mindshare, para. 100.

1541 *Miller*: This Bitter Has Some Sweet, pp. 881–82. *Miller*: Patent Ships Sail an Antitrust Sea, pp. 403–405.

1542 *McClure*: Trademarks and Unfair Competition, p. 345 (citations omitted).

1543 *Id*, p. 345.

anti-competitive effects have been extremely difficult.[1544] They may also be the wrong policies to apply.[1545]

The increasing tendency to apply competition laws to a host of intellectual property issues has tended to "reduce the pressure to seek more rational solutions within intellectual property law."[1546] As Vice-President and Commissioner for Competition Joaquín Almuñia noted in a speech in December 2013: "it is important to realize that competition-law tools have their limits. They cannot be a panacea for issues that relate solely to the nature of IP protection."[1547] Finding the correct balance – avoiding both over and under enforcement[1548] – is key, but challenging.[1549] Competition authorities on both sides of the Atlantic have struggled to "determine the correct balance between the rightful exercise of … rights and a [right] holder's incentive and ability to harm competition through

---

1544 "The courts have found numerous violations of the antitrust laws where a trademark is used in tying arrangements, division of territorial markets by cartels, resale price maintenance agreements, or other well-recognized antitrust offenses. But the use of a trademark to preserve monopolistic or oligopolistic market power has not been considered a violation of the antitrust laws... The aggressive promotion of a trademark and defending a trademark by numerous infringement suits, even where an exercise of monopoly power is threatened, have been held not to be a violation of Section 2. Such acts "merely represent fair and aggressive competition which does not constitute a violation of the antitrust laws." One Court has stated: "There is not now, nor has there ever been, a conflict between the antitrust laws and trademark laws or the law of unfair competition." *Id.* (citations omitted; emphasis mine).

1545 Hewitt Pate, in his role as assistant attorney general for the Antitrust Division of the DOJ remarked that "reforms decided upon by the IP community are in my view likely to be better vehicles to address any problems in the system than proposals to "ratchet up" antitrust enforcement in order to limit IP rights. … Antitrust's tools of factual and economic analysis of specific transactions are not very well suited to this task." *Pate*: Antitrust and Intellectual Property, § IV (Concluding Observations).

1546 *Mylly*: Intellectual property and competition law in the information society, pp. 116–117.

1547 Joaquín Almuñia, regarding Google's concessions to the Commission in the search case, comments made at the IP Summit, Premier Cercle, Paris, 9–11 December 2013. *Newman/Crofts*: Publishers can't rely on antitrust rules.

1548 *Katz*: Making Sense of Nonsense.

1549 See *Hovenkamp*: Post-Chicago Antitrust: A Review and Critique; and *Pitofsky*: Past, Present, and Future of Antitrust Enforcement, cited by *Czapracka*: Intellectual Property and the Limits of Antitrust, p. 57, fn. 56.

the anti-competitive use of those rights".[1550] Ultimately, the goal is a simple one: to protect consumer welfare and a competitive market by using all the tools available – but by using them wisely, judiciously, and properly.[1551]

(c) Proceedings: Act Timely

At the heart of most trademark disputes is whether there is a likelihood of confusion among consumers regarding use of a trademark, typically arising in situations when a (junior) trademark user goes to register their mark and a (senior) trademark owner objects. The courts have let such questions sit and fester as legal issues – when instead they could (and should) be expected to be answered more quickly.

In the case of *Environmental Manufacturing LLP v OHIM*,[1552] the junior trademark owner (the predecessor of Environmental Manufacturing) filed an application for registration of a CTM in March 2006 of a figurative sign representing a wolf's head for "machines for professional and industrial processing of wood and green waste; professional and industrial wood chippers and shredders". Following publication of the application in Community Trade Marks Bulletin No 38/2006 in September 2006, the senior trademark owner (Société Elmar Wolf) filed a notice of opposition against the registration, based on a number of earlier French and international word and figurative trademarks. In January 2010, the Opposition Division of OHIM dismissed the opposition on the ground that there was no likelihood of confusion between the marks at issue.[1553] Already here, both the junior and senior trademark owners had to wait *more than* 3 years for an *initial* determination.

In March 2010, Elmar Wolf filed a notice of appeal against that decision, which was then annulled. The Second Board of Appeal found that the earlier marks *were* highly reputed in three Member States and found that there *was some* similarity between the marks at issue and that the relevant public *might* establish a link between the signs, having regard to the distinctiveness and reputation of the

---

1550 *DOJ*: Statement on its Decision to Close Investigations. See also *FTC*: The Evolving IP Marketplace: Aligning Patent Notice and Remedies with Competition.

1551 Mark Lemley argues that "The goal of the IP and antitrust laws should be to seek a robust balance between competition and monopoly in the service of dynamic efficiency. When IP laws are strong, antitrust laws should also be strong, and vice versa." *Lemley*: A New Balance Between IP and Antitrust.

1552 Case C-383/12 P, *Environmental Manufacturing LLP v OHIM, Société Elmar Wolf*, 14 November 2013, 2014/C 9/16.

1553 *Id.*, paras. 5–9.

earlier marks, and to the similarity of the goods covered by the marks at issue. Finally, the Board of Appeal concluded, referring to the arguments put forward by Elmar Wolf, that the mark applied for might dilute the unique image of the earlier marks and take unfair advantage of their distinctive character or their reputation.

Regardless of whether or not the outcome was correct ("some similarity" that "might establish a link"), the decision on whether there was confusion took six years – "which means that investment in the branding, marketing and sale of good has so far been suspended for six year for the sake of a question that can be determined empirically".[1554] Such lengthy proceedings are not good for "commerce" or competition from any perspective.

(d) Articulate Confusion

Identifying precisely who the average consumer is – much less what they think – can be difficult. Courts have not been particularly adept at analyzing or determining such issues nor what form such evidence should take to satisfy judicial inquiry. The CJEU has held that any claims regarding likelihood of confusion between competing marks must be substantiated by evidence,[1555] in order to demonstrate that the average consumer makes or would make a link between

---

1554 *Phillips*: Assessing risks, p. 11. Phillips further discusses the ongoing dispute over the registration of the word mark "DIESEL" which has been in the court system for over a decade, "with the prospect of two rounds of domestic appeal and maybe reference to the CJEU" – is far from over. *Id.* In 1994, Diesel SpA applied to register four trademarks for the word 'Diesel'. On advertisement, the applications were opposed by Montex Holdings Limited. A number of the oppositions were dismissed by the hearing officer finding that Diesel's registration to a number of classes demonstrated "'typical brand extension classes' for clothing companies who often produce printed materials, bags and textile products bearing their marks". The hearing officer noted that the opponent had not produced any evidence or even claimed that it had used its DIESEL marks on any goods other than clothing. *DFMG Solicitors*: Diesel fails to register marks. However, the status of the registration of the word mark in a number of other classes still remains in dispute. Case C-281/05, *Montex Holdings Ltd v Diesel SpA*, 9 November 2006 [2006] ECR I-10881.

1555 Case C-425/98, *Marca Mode CV v Adidas AG and Adidas Benelux*, 22 June 2000 [2000] ECR 1-4861, para. 39, which emphasised that national courts must assess the evidence ("the assessment of evidence which the national court must undertake in each case pending before it").

the contested marks.[1556] The CJEU has confirmed that "the perception of marks in the mind of the average consumer of the type of goods or services in question plays a decisive role in the global appreciation of the likelihood of confusion."[1557] It is unclear, however, how is evidence of "consumer confusion" is to be demonstrated and analyzed.

One traditional method of documenting the perception of the "average consumer" has been to produce market surveys. Such surveys are costly and have many weaknesses. Although a well-executed survey can be instructive, they are often found by courts and tribunals to be poorly designed (based on the wrong questions or drafted to extract the answer the questioner is seeking), asked of a strategically (incorrect) selected proportion of the public, lacking in objectively or probative value (thus producing irrelevant or unhelpful responses), and not necessarily scrutinized for their content or need.[1558] Based on these weaknesses, they are generally given little weight and rendered useless as evidence.[1559]

In England, for example, even though "the critical issue of confusion of any kind is to be assessed from the viewpoint of the average consumer",[1560] public surveys have been rejected as unreliable: in one case, the judge found that survey evidence of members of the public could not stand proxy for the "average consumer" because "no one individual is such a consumer or end-user and the issue

1556 Case C-408/01, *Adidas-Salomon AG and Adidas Benelux BV v Fitnessworld Trading Ltd.*, 23 October 2003 [2003] ECR I-12537, in particular paras. 31–38.

1557 Case C-251/95, *SABEL BV v Puma AG, Rudolf Dassler Sport*, 11 November 1997 [1997] ECR I-6191, para. 23.

1558 To address some of these issues, the Courts & Tribunals Subcommittee of INTA's Enforcement Committee compiled a Report which considers guidelines and best practices from dozens of countries regarding survey content, implementation, and use. *INTA*: Report on Best Practices in Conducting Surveys in Trademark Matters.

1559 Marques posted the results of a panel asking UK judges on the merits of surveys in trademark cases: "Are surveys in trade mark cases (including surveys to demonstrate reputation) dead?". The answer: "Surveys are perhaps not dead, but certainly resting ("pining for the fjords" as some might say)." *Marques*: The Identity of Brand Owners, Ask the TM Judges. In *ZEE Entertainment Enterprises Ltd & Ors v Zeebox Ltd*, 7 June 2013 [2013] EWHC 1644 (Ch), para. 54, the Hon Mr Justice Birss refused submission of a survey, holding that "..I think the survey is not likely to be of real value. It will be of some value, but I am not satisfied that the value justifies the substantial cost of carrying it out and the increase in the length of the trial which it will inevitably cause."

1560 *esure Insurance Ltd v Direct Line*, 23 July 2008 [2008] EWCA Civ 842, para. 62.

cannot be resolved by counting heads".[1561] As recently as 2012, Judge Arnold in *Marks and Spencer* severely criticized survey evidence put before him.[1562] Judge Arnold suggested that, should a survey be justified, and should permission to produce such a survey be granted (for example, in active case management), then compliance with the "Whitford guidelines", as set out by Judge Whitford in his 1984 decision in *Imperial Tobacco Group*[1563] would be recommended.

Since finding the "average consumer" or accurately knowing what she may perceive is difficult, the CJEU has suggested that it is the *court* who determines what factors the "average consumer" would take into account (as opposed to hearing evidence directly from such average consumers):

> "in order to determine whether the description, trade mark or promotional description or statement in question was liable to mislead the purchaser, the Court took into account the presumed expectations of an average consumer who is reasonably well-informed and reasonably observant and circumspect, without ordering an expert's report or commissioning a consumer research poll."[1564]

Without further guidance regarding the understanding of the "average consumer" and the framework for providing evidence of "consumer confusion", a number of key dangers arise. First, courts and judges taking into account the public making a connection between the marks without being confused (the danger of dilution run amok). As noted in the Whitford guidelines, a key aspect is determining the relevant "average consumer": they must be representative of the market for the goods or services concerned, and in sufficient numbers to render any evidence statistically significant. For example, if two brands of tennis balls are at play, then the "average consumer" should not simply be someone who plays sports, but someone who actually buys tennis balls or plays tennis. Such consumer will likely be in the best position to determine whether she is

1561 *Healing Herbs Ltd vs. Bach Flower Remedies Ltd*, 21 October 1999 [2000] RPC 513, para. 35.

1562 *Marks And Spencer Plc v Interflora Inc & Anor*, 20 November 2012 [2012] EWCA Civ 1501. For more on this case, see *Smith/Montagnon*: Master of all you survey?

1563 *Imperial Group plc v Philip Morris Ltd*, 1 January 1984 [1984] RPC 293. For a summary of the Whitford guidelines, see *Marks And Spencer Plc v Interflora Inc & Anor*, 20 November 2012 [2012] EWCA Civ 1501, para. 61. For further analysis of the guidelines, as well as practical advice on developing surveys, see *Willoughby/Smith/Bravin*: Trade mark surveys.

1564 Case C- 210/96, *Gut Springenheide and Tusky*, 16 July 1998 [1998] ECR I-4657, para. 31; confirmed in Case C-299/99, *Koninklijke Philips Electronics NV v. Remington Consumer Products Ltd*, 18 June 2002 [2002] ECR I-5475, para. 63.

confused regarding two competing marks. In contrast, she may be less likely to be able to differentiate between subtle differences in marks where she has no experience, for example between two brands of hockey pucks, where similarities may be confusing to her, but not to someone else who regularly buys them. Second, in the absence of evidence from consumers, judges are using their own common sense and experience in the world to make determinations of what the average consumer may perceive. This is fine, so long as the benchmark "an average consumer who is reasonable well-informed" is met.

In general, more rigorous application of "consumer confusion" is needed and would strengthen the economic utility of trademark law. It would also help to deter meritless claims based on nebulous perceptions of consumer confusion.

(e) Deter Meritless Litigation

Courts should monitor and caution against litigation based on nebulous claims. These cases, often brought by trademark bullies, do not help clarify the "consumer confusion" issues. Some countries already have such protection in place. Several common law jurisdictions (e.g., Ireland, England, and Wales) have specific statutory threat provisions dealing with patents, trademarks, and design rights. In England, for example, the law provides victims of trademark infringement claims with the ability to mount a legal attack on the sender of the threat where the threat is "groundless".[1565] As a defense, the bully must prove that "the acts in respect of which proceedings were threatened constitute (or if done would constitute) an infringement of the registered trade mark concerned." If the defendant cannot establish such proof, then the plaintiff may be entitled to a judicial declaration that the threats are unjustified, an injunction against the threats, and possibly monetary damages.[1566]

By contrast, most civil law countries (e.g., Germany, the Netherlands, and France) deal with the problem of groundless threats as an aspect of the general law of tort or through unfair competition law.[1567] The policy rationales for such

1565 Trade Marks Act, c. 26, § 21(2) (Eng. & Wales), cited by *Grinvald*: Shaming Trademark Bullies, p. 685, fn. 370.

1566 For an analysis questioning whether the Trade Mark Act § 21 is useful, see *Poulter/Cassidy*: Unjustifiable Threats in UK Trade Mark Actions. For a review of the law by the UK Law Commission, see *UK Law Commission*: Patents, Trade Marks and Design Rights.

1567 In Germany, the key provisions are found in the Act Against Unfair Competition (*Gesetz gegen den unlauteren Wettbewerb* or UWG), published on 3 March 2010 (Federal Law Gazette [BGBl.]) Part I p. 254. Section 3 deals with unfair

laws are good: unfair competition laws are an integral part of the enforcement of intellectual property rights and play an important role in balancing the protection of existing rights and stimulating new ideas and products (and encouraging new market entrants) to promote economic growth and encourage robust competition.

(f) Be Governed by *Sic Utere Tuo*

One final recommendation would be worth keeping in mind: the principle of *Sic utere tuo ut alienum non laedas.*[1568] Although the maxim today is used with increased importance for establishing liability in cross-border misuse of resources (including such varied issues as the environment, nuclear weapons, pollution of outer space, access to the internet, and integrity of electronic information),[1569] the maxim is an established principle in both the common law[1570]

---

commercial practices and Section 4 provides examples of practices that would be unfair. The UWG only applies to acts done in the course of commerce. Wider protection is provided by the more general tort set out in § 823 of the German Civil Code (*Bürgerliches Gesetzbuch* or BGB).

1568 In English, it is translated as: "Use your own property, or exercise your own rights, in such a manner as not to injure that of another." Black's Law Dictionary, p. 1380 (6th ed. 1990). It is often shortened to simply *sic utere* ("use it thus"). In German, it is translated as „Gehe mit deinen Dingen so um, dass du einen anderen nicht schädigst." *Vitzthum*: Völkerrecht, para. 95, p. 452.

1569 See, for example *Hickey*: Custom and Land-Based Pollution; *Hickey/Walker*: Refining the Precautionary Principle; *Sands*: Principles of International Environmental Law, p. 461; *Tanaka*: Regulation of Land-Based Marine Pollution, pp. 537–538; *Hinds*: Das Prinzip „sic utere tuo", pp. 298–325; *Viikari*: The Environmental Element in Space Law, § 4.2.2, pp. 150–157; *Kettemann*: Das Internet als internationales Schutzgut, p. 478; and *Stein/Marauhn*: Völkerrechtliche Aspekte von Informationsoperationen, p. 21.

1570 The earliest English case known to have cited it is the 1610 case called "William Aldred's Case". *William Aldred's Case*, (1610), Mich. 8 Jacobi Regis, 9 C9 Rep 57b, 59, as cited in The reports of Sir Edward Coke, pp. 102–108. *Shepherd*: Selected Writings of Sir Edward Coke. *Vaughan v Menlove* (1837) 132 ER 490 (CP) is the seminal English tort law case that then introduced and developed the concept of the reasonable person in law to the common law tradition. The court viewed the "reasonable man" standard as supported by the long-settled principle that persons must use their property so as not to harm that of others. In the U.S., the doctrine was also well known. In 1876, the Supreme Court noted that the doctrine "is the rule by which every member of society must possess and enjoy his property". *Munn v. Illinois*, 94 U.S. 113, 145 (1876). Aldred's case, and the doctrine, was noted in *Sophia Booth v. The Rome, Watertown and Ogdensburg Terminal Railroad Company*,

and civil law[1571] traditions. Traced back to Justinian's *Digest*,[1572] the maxim is deeply imbedded in legal principles regarding the *reasonable* responsibilities between citizens to *co-exist*.

For centuries in both England and the U.S., this maxim exemplified the core legal structure defining the contours of private property rights[1573] and tort law.[1574] The maxim stood for adopting a balance of interests – reciprocity and justice – between private property owners and the public interest.[1575] As described by Chief Justice Andrews in the NY Court of Appeals case *Booth*:

> "The general rule that no one has absolute freedom in the use of his property, but is restrained by the *co-existence of equal rights* in his neighbor to the use of his property, so that each in exercising his right must do no act which causes injury to his neighbor, is so well understood, is so universally recognized, and stands so impregnably in the necessities of the social state, that its vindication by argument would be superfluous."[1576]

Although the maxim has been scathingly dismissed by legal scholars,[1577] the idea of the "co-existence" of resources – which balance private and public interest – is

---

140 N.Y. 267 (Court of Appeals of New York, 1893), at 274–275. In *Scribner v. Summers (K. Douglas Scribner and Laurie B. Scribner v. John M. Summers, Stephen A. Summers and Jasco-Sun Steel Treating, Inc.)*, 84 F.3d 554, 556–557 (2d Cir. 1996), the Second Circuit Court of Appeals noted that the maxim is "axiomatic to generations of common lawyers" (citations omitted).

1571 In German law, the concept has been present in the civil code since the 19th century, evident in §§ 906, 823, 1004, and 903 of the German Civil Code (*Bürgerliches Gesetzbuch* or *BGB*); see *Vitzthum*: Völkerrecht, p. 452, fn. 289.

1572 The court in *Scribner v. Summers*, 84 F.3d 554, 556–557 (2d Cir. 1996), referred to the maxim and cited The Digest of Justinian, "*De Cloacis*," at 601. Attribution to Justinian is also made by Sir William Blackstone (The Commentaries on the Laws of England, 1 Bl. Com. 306); Herbert Broom (A Selection of Legal Maxims, Classified and Illustrated, Broom's max. 160); and John Bouvier (Institutes of American Law, 2 Bouv. Inst. n. 2379).

1573 *Guth*: Law for the Ecological Age, p. 447.

1574 "Use thine own so that thou dost no harm to another." *Prosser*: Handbook of the Law of Torts, p. 616, n. 55.

1575 *Guth*: Law for the Ecological Age, pp. 448–49.

1576 *Sophia Booth v. The Rome*, Watertown and Ogdensburg Terminal Railroad Company, 140 N.Y. 267 (Court of Appeals of New York, 1893) (emphasis mine).

1577 International environmental legal scholar Dr. Alfred Rest argues that the principle is not specific enough to be useable. *Rest*: Neue Tendenzen im internationalen Umwelthaftungsrecht, p. 2155. U.S. Supreme Court Justice Oliver W. Holmes called it an "empty general proposition" that leads to "hollow deductions". *Holmes*: Privilege, Malice, and Intent, p. 120. English jurist Sir Frederick Pollock, held it to be

an engaging one and particularly suitable to the conflicting private and public aspects of trademarks. Maintaining trademark rights is vital. However, all rights are subject to reasonable limitations necessary to preserve the common good. Trademark owners should have the right to protect their trademarks, but such rights need sensible limits.

9.4 Chapter Observations

(a) Intellectual Property Protection

Patents, copyrights, and trademarks are central to our modern society and competitive business strategies.[1578] Courts, legislatures, and regulatory authorities have emphasized the need to protect intellectual property rights in order to encourage innovation and protect investment.[1579] Strategy papers increasingly focus on the importance of intellectual property rights for a competitive economy.[1580] The underlying goal is to balance the economic incentives for creation as a means of "promoting creation and innovation",[1581] which will "improve competitiveness".[1582] The short-run "exclusionary" rights which benefit rights' holders will turn into long-run contributions to the public domain.

"One of the tritest of maxims in the law of England." In 1854, a New York court of appeals court described it as "vague and undefined" and found it "utterly useless as a legal maxim," *Auburn & Cato Plank Road Co. v. Douglass*, 9 N.Y. 444, 445 and 446 (1854).

1578 A recent WIPO study finds that intellectual property rights are key elements of business strategies by innovation firms worldwide. *WIPO*: The Changing Face of Innovation.

1579 *European Commission*: Europe 2020, pp. 10 and 15. See also *European Commission*: Single Market Act – Twelve levers to boost growth and strengthen confidence, § 2.2, p. 12; and *European Commission*: A Single Market for Intellectual Property Rights, § 1, p. 3.

1580 *Beiter/Fischer/Früh/Jaeger/Kordic/Postl*: Lessons from "Lisbon"; cited by *Geiger*: The construction of intellectual property in the European Union, p. 14, fn. 41.

1581 *European Commission*: A Single Market for Intellectual Property Rights, p. 6. See also *European Commission*: Press Release IP/11/630.

1582 "To create a genuine Single Market in Europe, restrictions on freedom of movement and anti-competitive practices must be eliminated or reduced as much as possible, while creating an environment favourable to innovation and investment. In this context, the protection of intellectual property is an essential element for the success of the Single Market....[The] protection of intellectual property is important not only for promoting innovation and creativity, but also for developing

The challenge is ensuring that the trade-off is correctly balanced. Trademarks involve an economic trade-off that has different implications for the market and market competition than patents or copyrights. The economic purpose of trademark law is not in general to encourage innovation and creativity, but instead to reduce consumer search costs by identifying the source of goods or to encourage quality by protecting reputation.

(b) Trademarks & the Global Economy

Our society today is global, with unprecedented and diverse public access: the internet gives us access to almost every location, every event, and every creation in the world. Many of the historical barriers or natural boundaries that once defined our lives have long disappeared. This is particularly true for trademarks, where the inherently "national" characteristics of trademarks have morphed into a single, global, public sphere. Geographical boundaries, language differences and – for the most part – differences in access to information are no longer substantial considerations or barriers for consumers who demand access to goods or services or the companies who supply such goods and services. Technological change has "completely changed the world in which [such rights] operate",[1583] allowing us to receive, communicate, and disseminate unlimited amounts of information.[1584]

Social changes reflect how trademarks influence our lives: companies strategically invest in their brand image – including their brand representatives[1585] – very

employment and improving competitiveness." *European Commission*: The EU Single Market: Intellectual Property.

1583 *European Commission*: Press Release IP/11/630.

1584 For a historical (and historically significant) review of how we communicate using the internet, see the first 48 numbered paragraphs of the "Findings of Fact" in *American Civil Liberties Union (ACLU) v. Janet Reno*, 929 F. Supp. 824 (E.D. PA. 1996), pp. 830–38.

1585 Celebrities are frequently used for product endorsement. Consider how Nike used celebrity ad campaigns to re-invent and re-charge its image. Although Nike had been the industry leader into the early 1980s, by mid-1980 it had slipped from that position. In 1985, Nike debuted a new signature shoe for an NBA rookie by the name of Michael Jordan. In 1987, Nike launched a major marketing campaign around Air Max, designed to regain the industry lead and differentiate Nike from its competitors. The campaign was supported by a memorable TV ad using the tagline "Revolution in Motion" whose soundtrack was the original Beatles' recording of "Revolution". A year later, Nike built on the "Revolution" campaign by launching a series of ads with the tagline "Just do it." The series included three ads with a young two-sport athlete named Bo Jackson, who espoused the benefits

carefully and for good reason. A consumer's section of Coke over Pepsi[1586] has more to do with a consumer's brand "association" or social "identification" than with a trademark's traditional function as a source identifier or symbol of quality.[1587]

---

of a new cross-training shoe. By 1989, thanks in part to the incredibly popular "Bo Knows" ad campaign, Nike had regained its position as the industry leader. *Nike*: History & Heritage. Celebrities are also routinely – depending on their public image – dropped from such ad campaigns. Consider Tiger Woods. The former Nr. 1 golfer was a prominent celebrity in many ad campaigns. In 2009, amid the growing public outrage concerning his personal life (including allegations of infidelity), Proctor & Gamble removed him from the Gillette ads. *Associated Press*: Gillette phasing Tiger Woods out of ad campaigns. Tag Heuer followed suit days thereafter. *Associated Press*: Swiss Watch Maker Tag Heuer Drops Tiger Woods From Advertising Campaigns. In 2010, Nike tried to positively spin Tiger Wood's fall from grace in a few advertising campaigns. In April 2010, Nike distributed an ad featuring Tiger Woods looking forlorn and dejected, with a voice-over from his father Earl Woods asking "Did you learn anything?" *Vary*: Tiger Woods' new Nike ad. The ad appeared to do more damage than good. *Pomerantz*: Don't Hire Tiger Woods or Lance Armstrong. The fate of Lance Armstrong, once amongst the most sought-after product endorsers, is similar. Nike, along with Anheuser-Busch, Oakley, Trek, 24-Hour Fitness, and other sponsors, quickly dropped Lance Armstrong after the U.S. Anti-Doping Agency banned him for life for running what it called the most "sophisticated" doping operation the sport had ever seen. *McCarthy*: Lance Armstrong Blew His Last Chance; and *Schultz*: Rewind: When Lance Armstrong Rode in the Super Bowl.

1586 Consumers prefer the *taste* of diet Pepsi over diet Coke in blind taste tests, but prefer diet Coke over diet Pepsi when choosing the *brand* to drink. *Ghose/Lowengart*: Taste Tests: Impacts of Consumer Perceptions and Preferences on Brand Positioning Strategies, p. 30. Choices of products can also have a "social meaning": In 1999, the Street.com (a business-oriented website) named Nike's "Revolution in Motion" ads, featuring the soundtrack from the original Beatles' recording of "Revolution" as one the top 100 business events that shaped the 20th century. The Street.com claimed that Nike's 1987 Revolution ads "commodify dissent": "It's not the first time the ideals of the 1960s – freedom, individuality, antimaterialism, dissent – are called upon to push product. … Nike uses The Beatles song to sell sneakers. Now it's almost impossible to escape ads that sell not just products but *breaking the rules, dude*." *TSC Staff*: Countdown – The Basics of Business History. The use of The Beatles' song was a revolution in itself, since this was the first time an original Beatles' recording was licensed for use in a television commercial. *Old School*: Back to the 80s. For the litigation that followed, see *Pareles*: Nike Calls Beatles Suit Groundless; and *Doyle*: Nike & The Beatles.

1587 "When trademarks are used in this way, they acquire certain functional characteristics that are different from – and sometimes inconsistent with – their traditional

(c) Fundamental Changes to Trademark Protection

Trademark law has "come unhinged from its traditional consumer protection moorings."[1588] Trademark protection was – and still often is – justified by its protection of the *consumer* for the benefit of *commerce* and a *competitive market.* Trademark protection also protected the producer (from free riding or other illegitimate or unfair trade practices), which similarly protected *commerce* and a *competitive market.* Trademark law's traditional focus, however, has fundamentally shifted from a *market*-focus to a *mark*-focus. That is, trademark protection today does more to protect the owner's rights to its mark than to protect the competitive market. Today, trademark owners are permitted to suppress other's use of marks based on claims that have nothing to do with source identification and do not benefit the functioning of the market. This proprietary focus is inconsistent with the traditional role of trademarks as source identifiers and inconsistent with the principles of trademark law.

(d) Achieving Reasonable (and Effective) Competition

Competition laws protect the market – in terms of protecting competition and the competitive process – by prohibiting certain behaviors that threaten "free competition" and a "free market". The underlying principle of modern competition law is that competition is generally desirable in order to achieve "economic efficiency"[1589] and maintain "effective competition on the market."[1590]

These principles are good ones to remember when considering trademarks. Trademarks are vital to a dynamic, modern marketplace. Trademark protection reduces consumer confusion and consumer search costs, prohibits competitors from free-riding, protects trade dress and product designs,[1591] and increases goods of consistent (and, in many cases, high) quality.[1592] Trademark rights,

---

role as identifiers of source.... This trend raises questions about whether – and to what extent – the law should protect trademarks when they are pressed into service as separate products." *Kozinski*: Trademarks Unplugged, pp. 962–63.

1588 *McKenna*: The Normative Foundations of Trademark Law, p. 1841.

1589 *Landes/Posner*: Trademark Law: An Economic Perspective.

1590 "The Community competition rules protect competition on the market as a means of enhancing consumer welfare and of ensuring an efficient allocation of resources." *European Commission*: DG Competition discussion paper, Public consultation, para. 88, p. 27.

1591 *Lemley*: The Modern Lanham Act; and *Chiappetta*: Trademarks: More Than Meets the Eye.

1592 *Perlman*: Taking the Protection-Access Tradeoff Seriously.

however, need “sensible limits”, since by preventing overreaching by trademark owners we “will salvage the economic utility of trademark law.”[1593] The goal should be to ensure that trademark protection encourages private investment “up to the optimal level, but no further”, since “overly strong IP laws unduly interfere with competition and therefore reduce welfare unnecessarily”.[1594]

1593 *Travis*: The Battle for Mindshare, para. 145.
1594 *Lemley*: A New Balance Between IP and Antitrust, p. 254.

10. Summary in the Form of 10 Theses

This paper had the goal of examining the legal and commercial boundaries of trademark ownership and use, in order to better understand the competitive and anti-competitive effects of such rights. Alongside this goal, the intention was to set out whether and in what manner courts, legislatures, and regulatory authorities have approached the conflict between private and public interest rights inherent in trademark protection. This final section summarizes the issues and the lessons learned in a few key theses.

1. Trademarks play a fundamental role in our everyday lives as consumers: they help us distinguish the products we like (and avoid those that we don't); they signal a short-hand catalogue of quality distinctions that allow us to make choices quickly and efficiently (and give us certainty of what we have chosen); they give us information about the source or manufacturer of goods. For producers, this ability for consumers to distinguish products and producers and make choices accordingly is key, incentivizing companies to invest in the quality of their products (and their brand) in order to differentiate their goods from those of their competitors and to build brand (i.e., customer) loyalty. Producers are certain their brand value is protected, as they are able to prohibit others from free-riding on their efforts. To protect trademarks is therefore to protect the public from deceit, to enable consumers effective and efficient ways to purchase, and to secure to businesses the advantages of investment in reputation and quality.
2. Trademarks today are useful in more expansive ways than in their earliest incarnations. What began primarily as a means of ownership, source, and quality identification intended to prevent consumer confusion, minimize consumer search costs, and prohibit unfair practices has now become a commercial tool of "compelling, distinctive, and desirable" psychological "magnetism". In our modern, global market economy, trademarks perform multiple, overlapping functions as identifying symbols, source indicators, quality signifiers, and advertising agents. Well-known (and well-managed) trademarks are symbols of brand loyalty (and, as we know, without brand loyalty there is no market). Trademarks today are big money, big business, competitive assets, reflecting the changing dynamics of our economy and lifestyles.
3. Trademark protection has kept pace with these changing functions, ensuring protection across borders and in light of new technologies and changing business and social needs. Trademarks owners have sought protection for

their commercial investments and the business value of their trademark as assets and have gained significantly expanded rights – in terms of the scope of categories protected and the types of claims available to thwart third-party users who might infringe on their rights. Trademark owners have also engaged in a variety of strategies *outside* of the courtroom to ensure protection of their proprietary rights (including engaging in bullying tactics and other predatory behaviour intended to thwart competitors).

4. With any exercise (and certainly with any expansion) of rights, concerns regarding the anti-competitive effects of such rights are raised. Even if expanded rights are granted under the rationale of *protecting* competition, such expanded rights can serve to *restrict* competition. Although trademarks act as important aids to competition (by prohibiting free-riding) and benefit consumers (by decreasing confusion and preventing fraudulent trade practices), they can restrict competition by maintaining barriers to entry, permitting trademark owners to carve out niche markets through "artificial" product differentiation (i.e., based on brand loyalty and advertising, not on quality). Trademarks have been strategically used to erect significant (and at times insurmountable) barriers to trade – against competitors, foreign market participants, and other trademark owners. Trademark law (and particularly modern trademark law) provides for the protection of private entitlements – protection which by its very nature excludes others. This protection inevitably clashes with a strong public interest policy in our society in favor of free competition. The recognition of this conflict is not new or startling. However, given the expanding legal protections, coupled with the commercial significance and dominance of well-known trademarks and the global economy in which they operate, the full extent of the conflict is more striking and troublesome than ever before.
5. With any set of rights, it is the task of the legal system – through the legislatures, courts, and regulatory authorities – to take into account the competing private and public interest claims. To date, trademark laws have not effectively dealt with the anti-competitive effects of such expanded rights: they have allowed trademark rights to become "untethered" from their "traditional moorings" by failing to build in reasonable limitations or clearly defined boundaries to the increased protection. The paradox lies in how we have dealt with this conflict. We have set aside the key principles underlying trademark protection, expanding trademark laws to protect rights not related to competition or the prevention of unfair competition. We have allowed special interests (in particular famous trademark owners) to unduly shape such expanding protection.

6. Competition laws seek to minimize or prohibit anti-competitive effects which arise from the acquisition, exploitation, or enforcement of power in the market. Competition authorities regulate businesses, agreements, and activities with the aim of preserving and ensuring open and competitive markets. Although competition laws are suitable to address a broad range of exclusive or monopolist practices which have the effect of restraining trade, they have side-stepped the problems of powerful trademarks stifling competition. In the end, competition laws may not be the most suitable mechanism to align or "fix" the expanding legal and commercial boundaries of trademark ownership and use.
7. Recognizing the growing anti-competitive effects of trademarks (through the strong brand personalities they exude) and trademark law (through the expanded legal protection trademarks have been afforded) is one thing; determining what, if anything, can be done about such effects is quite another. Any solution needs to *balance* the pro-competitive *functions* of trademarks with the anti-competitive *effects* of their protection in order to achieve some reasonable measure of "workable competition". A balanced approach – in the words of Samuelson – "is *not a decision between ... extremes*". Instead, solutions can be found in "the degree to which public policy should do *less or more* to *modify the operation of particular private economic activities*."
8. Two pragmatic principles can be applied to "do less or more". The first principle relates to the nature and functions of trademark and trademark laws: the goal would be to realign the functions and rationales of trademark protection in order to prohibit "unfair competition". Although courts and policy makers have allowed imprudent expansion of private trademark rights, trademark laws are essentially good; they simply need some healthy "gardening" – i.e., pruning. By doing so, we can more effectively balance the competing public and private interests in inherent in trademark protection, resulting in a more measured and consistent approach to trademark use, protection, and exploitation, benefiting businesses, consumers, and the market.
9. The second principle relates to the legislative and judicial framework which governs and protects trademarks. We need to encourage courts and authorities to engage in a more thoughtful, mature application of trademark law, ensuring an effective "administrative machinery" that recognizes and balances the competing private and public interests – whether from the perspectives of consumers, trademark owners, competitors, competition authorities, or legislatures). Courts and authorities need to ensure enforcement and protection of proprietary trademark rights, but at the same time establish clearly defined and enforceable boundaries of such rights to ensure protection of

the public and the competitive market. The tools to protect both proprietary trademark rights and competitive market public interests need to reviewed – and applied – with a rigorous attitude that acknowledges the conflict between private and public interests.

10. Trademarks are vital to a dynamic, modern marketplace. Trademark laws protect commerce and the functionality of the market, by balancing society's interest in *free* competition against its interest in *fair* competition. Trademark rights, however, just like any other private right, need "sensible limits". Armed with principles of balance, and a mature recognition of the conflicting private and public interests inherent in trademark protection, we can ensure the continued "economic utility" of trademarks and trademark protection. This will allow us to continue to adapt trademark laws to meet future challenges, protecting private interests and investments "up to the optimal level, but no further", to ensure they do not unnecessarily interfere with our modern, robust competitive market.

Bibliography

***Aaker**, David A.*: Managing Brand Equity: Capitalizing on the Value of a Brand Name, New York: The Free Press (1991).

ABA, American Bar Association:

— ABA Section of Antitrust Law, Antitrust Law Developments, (6th edition, 2007).

— American Bar Association: ABA Section of Antitrust Law, Antitrust Federalism: the Role of State Law, Monograph No. 15 (1988).

— American Bar Association: ABA Section of Antitrust Law, State Antitrust Enforcement Handbook (2nd edition, 2008).

— American Bar Association: ABA Section of Antitrust Law, The Federal Antitrust Guidelines for the Licensing of Intellectual Property: Origins and Applications (3rd edition, 2010).

— American Bar Association: Criminal Justice Section, ABA Standards for Criminal Justice, (2nd edition, 1980).

— American Bar Association: Division for Public Education, Dialogue on the Separation of Powers, Part III: Mending Wall and the Separation of Powers.

About.com - Inventors: Points To Ponder – Trademarks: Fingerprints of Commerce, available at http://inventors.about.com.

***Abramowicz**, Michael/**Stearn**, Maxwell*: Defining Dicta, 57 Stan. L. Rev. 953 (2005) (Stanford Law Review).

Agile IP LLP: ipad trade mark settlement in china, available at http://www.agile-ip.co.uk.

***Ainsworth**, Lesley/**Capel**, Tim*: United Kingdom, Pharmaceutical Antitrust (2012).

***Aldisert**, Ruggero J.*: Precedent: What it is and What it Isn't; When Do We Kiss it and When Do We Kill it?, 17 Pepp. L. Rev. 605, 607 (1990) (Pepperdine Law Review).

***Alexander**, Larry*: Constrained by Precedent, 63 S. Cal. L. Rev. 1 (1989) (Southern California Law Review).

***Alfonso**, Shylah R./**Foster**, Susan E./**Reingold**, Barry J.*: US: IP and Antitrust, The Antitrust Review of the Americas, Global Competition Review (2013).

***Almunia**, Joaquín*: Competition Policy Issues in Financial Markets, Vice President of the European Commission responsible for Competition Policy, SPEECH/11/337, CASS Business School London, 16 May 2011.

Alpha Delta Pi: Heritage: Learn About ADPi, available at http://www.alphadeltapi.org.

ALWD Citation Manual: A Professional System of Citation, compiled by the Association of Legal Writing Directors, Coleen Barger (ed.) (5th edition, 2014).

American Law: Averill Chemical Paint Co. v. National Mixed Paint Co. and others, Circuit Court, S. D. New York, 29 October 1881, available at http://bulk.resource.org.

***Anderman**, Steven D.*:

— EC Competition Law and Intellectual Property Rights: The Regulation of Innovation, Oxford University Press (1998).

— The competition law/IP 'interface': an introductory note, in Anderman: The Interface between Intellectual Property Rights and Competition Policy.

***Anderman**, Steven D. (ed.)*: The Interface between Intellectual Property Rights and Competition Policy, Cambridge: Cambridge University Press (2007).

***Anderman**, Steven D./**Schmidt**, Hedvig*: EC competition policy and IPRs, in Anderman: The Interface between Intellectual Property Rights and Competition Policy.

***Anderson**, Mae*: iPad prompts the question: What's in a brand name?, News Tribune, 9 April 2012.

***Anthon**, Charles*: A Classical Dictionary: Containing An Account Of The Principal Proper Names Mentioned in Ancient Authors, Harper & Bros (1841).

Apfelkind: die apfelkind idee, available at http://apfel-kind.de.

***Apostolopoulos**, Haris*: Anti-Competitive Abuse of IP Rights and Compulsory Licensing Through the International Dimension of the TRIPS Agreement and the Stockholm Proposal for its Amendment, 6 Rich. J. Global L. & Bus. 265 (2007) (Richmond Journal of Global Law and Business).

Apple Computer Inc.: Form 10-K for the fiscal year ended 24 September 2004.

Apple Inc.:

— Apple Inc. and The Beatles' Apple Corps Ltd. Enter into New Agreement, Press Release, 5 February 2007.

— Apple Introduces iTunes – World's Best and Easiest To Use Jukebox Software, Press Release, 9 January 2001.

— Apple Introduces New iMacs in Stunning New Colors, Press Release, 19 July 2000.

— Apple Launches iPad: Magical & Revolutionary Device at an Unbelievable Price, Press Release, 27 January 2010.

— Apple Presents iPod, Press Release, 23 October 2001.

— Apple Reinvents the Phone with iPhone, Press Release, 9 January 2007.

— Form 10-K, for the fiscal year ended 29 September 2012.

— Form 8-K, 9 January 2007.

— Guidelines for Using Apple Trademarks and Copyrights.

— iPad Available in Nine More Countries on May 28: Pre-Orders Begin May 10, Press Release, 7 May 2010.

— PC Data Ranks iBook Number One Portable in U.S., Press Release, 25 January 2000.

***Areeda**, Philiip*:

— Antitrust Analysis, Boston: Little Brown (2nd edition, 1974).

— Essential Facilities: An Epithet in Need of Limiting Principles, 58 Antitrust L.J. 841 (1989/1990) (Antitrust Law Journal).

***Areeda**, Phillip/**Hovenkamp**, Herbert*: Antitrust Law: An Analysis of Antitrust Principles and Their Application, Aspen Publishers (2nd edition and Supplement, 2001).

***Arena**, Amedeo*: The Doctrine of Union Preemption in the E.U. Internal Market: Between Sein and Sollen, 17 Colum. J. Eur. L. 477 (2011) (Columbia Journal of European Law).

***Arnold**, Hon Mr Justice Richard*: Initial Interest Confusion in European Trade Mark Law, remarks at the 19th Fordham IP Law & Policy Conference, New York, NY, 28 April 2011.

Associated Press:

— Gillette phasing Tiger Woods out of ad campaigns, CBS Sports.com Canada, 12 December 2009.

— Swiss Watch Maker Tag Heuer Drops Tiger Woods From Advertising Campaigns, ESPN Sports, 18 December 2009.

— Wegmans, Walgreens Settle Suit Over 'W' logos, The Wall Street Journal, WSJ Blogs: In Charge, 26 April 2011.

Atkins, *Michael*: Are Anti-Genericism Ads Effective?, Seattle Trademark Lawyer, 26 October 2007.

Baches Opi, *Sergio*:

— The Application of the Essential Facilities Doctrine to Intellectual Property Licensing in the European Union and the United States: Are Intellectual Property Rights Still Sacrosanct? 11 Fordham Intell. Prop. Media & Ent. L.J. 409 (2001) (Fordham Intellectual Property, Media and Entertainment Law Journal).

— The Approaches of the European Commission and the U.S. Antitrust Agencies Towards Exclusivity Clauses in Licensing Agreements, 24 B.C. Int'l & Comp. L. Rev. (2000) (Boston College International & Comparative Law Review).

Backhaus, *Jürgen G (ed.)*.: Historische Schulen, Wirtschaft, Forschung und Wissenschaft, Vol. 11, Münster: LIT Verlag (2005).

Baker, *J.H.*/***Milsom***, *S.F.C.*:

— Sources of English Legal History – Private law to 1750, London: Butterworth Legal Publishers (1986).

— Introduction to English History, London: Butterworth Legal Publishers (2nd edition, 1979).

Baker, *Tyler A.*: Antitrust Alert – Everything Must End Eventually: The Fifth Circuit Buries Leegin; Epic Vertical Price Fixing Case is Over, 18 August 2010.

Bank, *David*: Why Software and Antitrust make an Uneasy Mix, Wall Street Journal, 22 October 1997.

Banner, *Brian Edward*: U.S. Trademark Law: Part I, Hershkovitz & Associates, LLC, slide 25 (2011).

Bannon, *Elizabeth C.*:

— Revisiting "The Rational Basis of Trademark Protection": Control of Quality and Dilution – Estranged Bedfellows?, 24 J. Marshall L. Rev. 65 (1990) (John Marshall Law Review).

— The Growing Risk of Self-Dilution, 82 TMR. 570 (1992) (Trademark Reporter).

Barnard, *Catherine*: The Substantive Law of the EU: The Four Freedoms, Oxford: Oxford University Press (3rd edition, 2010).

***Barnes**, David W.*:

— A New Economics of Trademarks, 5 Nw. J. Tech. & Intell. Prop. 22 (2006) (Northwestern Journal of Technology and Intellectual Property).

— Trademark Externalities, 10 Yale J.L. & Tech. 1 (2007) (Yale Journal of Law & Technology).

***Barrett**, Margreth*: Finding Trademark Use: The Historical Foundation for Limiting Infringement Liability to Uses "in the manner of the mark", 43 Wake Forest L. Rev. 893 (Winter 2008) (Wake Forest Law Review).

***Barron**, Timothy J./**Luk**, Olivia T.*: The Patent Misuse Defense after Princo, American Bar Association, Intellectual Property Litigation, Volume 22, Number 2 (Winter 2011).

***Bartenbach**, Kurt*: Patentlizenz- und Know-how-Vertrag, Cologne: Verlag Dr. Otto Schmidt (6th edition, 2006).

***Bartholomew**, Mark*: Advertising and the Transformation of Trademark Law, 38 N.M. L. Rev. 1 (2008) (New Mexico Law Review).

***Bartow**, Ann*:

— The True Colors of Trademark Law: Greenlighting a Red Tide of Anti Competition Blues, 97 Ky. L.J. 263 (2008/2009) (Kentucky Law Journal).

— When Bias is Bipartisan: Teaching About the Democratic Process in an Intellectual Property Law Republic, 52 St. Louis L.J. 715 (2008) (St. Louis University Law Journal).

***Baudenbacher**, Carl*: Trademark Law and Parallel Imports in a Globalized World - Recent Developments in Europe with Special Regard to the Legal Situation in the United States, 22 Fordham Int'l L.J. 645 (1999) (Fordham International Law Journal).

***Bauer**, Joseph P.*: The Foreign Trade Antitrust Improvements Act: Do We Really Want to Return to American Banana?, Notre Dame Legal Studies Paper No. 12–77, 65 Me. L. Rev. 3–26 (2012–2013) (Maine Law Review).

BBC News:

— Mackintosh opens first fashion store in London, 21 January 2011.

— On This Day 1950–2005.

***Beckerman-Rodau**, Andrew*: The Problem with Intellectual Property Rights: Subject Matter Expansion, 13 Yale J.L. & Tech. 35 (2010) (Yale Journal of Law & Technology).

***Beebe**, Barton*:

— A Defense of the New Federal Trademark Antidilution Law, 16 Fordham Intell. Prop. Media & Ent. L.J. 1143 (2006) (Fordham Intellectual Property, Media and Entertainment Law Journal).

— Search and Persuasion in Trademark Law, 103 Mich. L. Rev. 2020 (2005) (Michigan Law Review).

— The Semiotic Analysis of Trademark Law, 51 UCLA L. REV. 621 (2004) (UCLA Law Review).

***Behr**, Lauren*: Trademarks for the Cure: Why Nonprofits Need Their Own Set of Trademark Rules, 54 B.C. L. Rev 243 (January 2013) (Boston College Law Review).

***Beier**, Friedrich-Karl*:

— Grenzen der Erschöpfungslehre im Markenrecht: Zur Beurteilung des Vertriebs umgepackter und neu gekennzeichneter Originalware in den Ländern der Europäischen Wirtschaftsgemeinschaft, GRUR Int. 1978/263.

— Industrial Property and the Free Movement of Goods in the Internal European Market, IIC 1990/131.

— Territoriality of Trademark Law and International Trade, IIC 1970/48.

— Ziele und Leitgedanken des europäischen Markenrechts, GRUR Int. 1976/36.

***Beiter**, Klaus-Dieter/**Fischer**, Oliver/**Früh**, Alfred/**Jaeger**, Thomas/**Kordic**, Robert/**Postl**, Manuela*: Lessons from "Lisbon": The Potential, Necessity and Pitfalls of a Primary Law Reform - An Assessment in the Light of Intellectual Property Law, The European legal forum (2009).

***Bellis**, Mary*:

— Linoleum - The History of Linoleum, available at http://inventors.about.com.

— The History of the YoYo (Or What Goes Up Must Go Down), available at http://inventors.about.com.

— This History of the Zipper, available at http://inventors.about.com.

***Bently**, Lionel/**Davis**, Jennifer/**Ginsburg**, Jane C. (eds.)*: Trade Marks and Brands: An Interdisciplinary Critique, Cambridge Intellectual Property and Information Law, Cambridge: Cambridge University Press (2008).

***Bently**, Lionel/**Kretschmer**, Martin (eds.)*: Primary Sources on Copyright (1450–1900) (2008), available at http://www.copyrighthistory.org.

***Bently**, Lionel/**Suthersanen**, Uma/**Torremans**, Paul (eds.)*: Global Copyright: Three hundred years since the Statute of Anne, from 1709 to Cyberspace, Cheltenham: Edward Elgar Publishing (2010).

***Bently**, Lionel*: The Making of Modern Trade Marks Law: The Construction of the Legal Concept of Trade Mark (1860–80), available at http://www.cipil.law.cam.ac.uk.

***Bently**, Sherman/**Bently**, Lionel*: The Making of Modern Intellectual Property Law (1999).

***Bernier**, Roland*: Avoiding an E-Discovery Odyssey, 36 N. Ky. L. Rev. 491 (2009) (Northern Kentucky Law Review).

***Bernstein**, David Allen*: A Case for Mediating Trademark Disputes in the Age of Expanding Brands, 7 Cardozo J. Conflict Resol. 139 (2005) (Cardozo Journal of Conflict Resolution).

***Bettig**, Ronald V.*: Copyrighting Culture: The Political Economy of Intellectual Property, Boulder: Westview Press (1996).

***Bhatti**, Jabeen*: German Court Adopts Wide Application of ECJ Composite Mark Confusion Doctrine, The Bureau of National Affairs, Inc. (BNA), 4 December 2013.

Bird & Bird: Budějovický Budvar National Corporation v Rudolf Ammersin GmbH, Case C-478/07, case summary, 8 September 2009.

***Bitttinger**, Cyndy*: The Business of America is Business?, available at http://www.calvin-coolidge.org.

Black's Law Dictionary, West Publishing (6th edition, 1990).

***Blackstone**, Sir William*: The Commentaries on the Laws of England, originally published by the Clarendon Press, Oxford (1765–1769) (1 Bl. Com. 306).

***Blake**, N.F.: Caxton*: England's First Publisher, New York: Barnes & Noble (1975).

***Blakeney**, Michael*: The International Protection of Industrial Property: From the Paris Convention to the Agreement on Trade-Related Aspect of Intellectual Property Rights (The TRIPs Agreement), WIPO National Seminar on Intellectual Property Rights, Ajman, 5–6 May 2004, WIPO/IP/UNI/DUB/04/1, April 2004.

***Blanke**, Jordan M.*: Vincent Van Gogh, "Sweat of the Brow", and Database Protection, 39 Am. Bus. L.J. 645 (2002) (American Business Law Journal).

***Blumenthal**, William*: Merger Analysis under the U.S. Antitrust Laws, 18 January 2001, available at http://www.kslaw.com.

Bodenhausen, *G. H. C.*: Guide to the Application of the Paris Convention for the Protection of Industrial Property as revised at Stockholm in 1967, United International Bureaux for the Protection of Intellectual Property (BIRPI), WIPO Publication N°611 (E) (1969).

Bogatz, *Jana*:

— EuGH: Rechtserhaltende Benutzung einer Marke in der EU unabhängig von Ländergrenzen - „ONEL/OMEL", GRUR-Prax 2013, 8.

— Sparkassen-Rot, Nivea-Blau, Langenscheid-Gelb: Quo vadis konturlose Farbmarke?, GRUR, 22/2013, 481–483.

Böhler, *Dirk*: Celebrity Placement, MarkenR 03/2013, 89–93 (MarkenRecht).

Bone, *Robert G.*:

— Hunting Goodwill: A History of the Concept of Goodwill in Trademark Law, 86 B.U.L. Rev. 547 (2006) (Boston University Law Review).

— Taking the Confusion out of "Likelihood of Confusion": Toward a More Sensible Approach to Trademark Infringement, 106 Nw. U.L. Rev. 1307 (Summer 2012) (Northwestern University Law Review).

Borchardt, *Professor Klaus-Dieter*: The ABC of European Union law, Publications Office of the European Union (2010).

Bork, *Robert H.*: The Antitrust Paradox: A Policy at War with Itself, New York: Basic Books (1978).

Borzcik, *Joni*: Trademark Rights and Their Implementation: Cancellation of Generic Incontestable Marks, 19 J. Contemp. Legal Issues 185 (2010) (The Journal of Contemporary Legal Issues).

Boston University School of Law: Trademark Law Research Guide, Pappas Library, available at http://lawlibraryguides.bu.edu.

Bouckaert, *Boudewijn*/***De Geest***, *Gerrit (eds.)*: Encyclopedia of Law and Economics, Volume I: The History and Methodology of Law and Economics, Cheltenham: Edward Elgar Publishing (2000).

Bouvier, *John*: Institutes of American Law, Philadelphia (1860) (2 Bouv. Inst. n. 2379).

Bowman, *Jr., Ward S.*: Patent and Antitrust Law: A Legal and Economic Appraisal, Chicago: The University of Chicago Press (1973).

Bradsher, *Keith*: Apple Settles an iPad Dispute in China, The New York Times, 2 July 2012.

Bragdon, *C.R.*/***Renfrew***, *M.M.*: Paint, Varnish, and Plastics Chemistry: Out of white lead paint, furniture varnish and billiard balls, grew a multi-billion dollar industry, Industrial & Engineering Chemistry, Vol. 43, Nr. 6, 1272–1282, June 1951.

Brand Finance Plc:

— About Us, available at http://www.brandfinance.com.

— League Tables, available at http://brandirectory.com. A (free) subscription is required for access.

Brankin, *Sean-Paul*: European Commission Enforcement in the Pharmaceutical Sector: Less Than Expected? The Boehringer Case Closure Suggests As Much, CPI Antitrust Chronicle, July 2012.

Brennan, *Timothy J.*: Essential Facilities and Trinko: Should Antitrust and Regulation Be Combined?, 61 Fed. Comm. L.J. 133 (2008–2009) (Federal Communications Law Journal).

Bretthauer, *Stefan Christian*: Die Beurteilung von Markenlizenzverträgen nach deutschem und europäischem Kartellrecht, Baden-Baden: Nomos Verlagsgesellschaft (2003).

Breyer, *Stephen G.*:

— The Uneasy Case for Copyright: A Look Back Across Four Decades, Keynote address delivered at The George Washington University Law School symposium entitled “Celebrating the Fortieth Anniversary of Justice Breyer’s Article The Uneasy Case for Copyright,” on 4 November 2010, 79 Geo. Wash. L. Rev. 1635 (2011) (George Washington Law Review).

— The Uneasy Case for Copyright: A Study of Copyright in Books, Photocopies, and Computer Programs, 84 Harv. L. Rev. 281 (1970) (Harvard Law Review).

Brinkmann, *Bastian*: Café Apfelkind besiegt Apple, Süddeutsche Zeitung GmbH, 1 October 2013.

Briton, *Isabel*/***Karet***, *Ian*: Parallel Imports Continue: The Patent Exhaustion Principle Upheld, 19(4) EIPR 207 (1997) (European Intellectual Property Review).

Broom, *Herbert*: A Selection of Legal Maxims, Classified and Illustrated, T&JW Johnson, Philadelphia (1854).

Brown, *Jr., Ralph S.*: Advertising and the Public Interest: Legal Protection of Trade Symbols, 57 Yale L.J. 1165 (1948) (Yale Law Journal).

Bundesgerichtshof:

— Press Release Nr. 136/2013, Bundesgerichtshof entscheidet im Streit zwischen der weltweit tätigen Hard Rock-Gruppe und dem "Hard Rock Cafe Heidelberg", 15 August 2013.

— Press Release Nr. 150/2010, Schutz des "Goldhasen" muss neu bestimmt werden, 16 July 2010.

Bundesgesetzblatt des Norddeutschen Bundes, Nr. 19 (1870), available at http://de.wikisource.org/wiki.

Bundeskartellamt:

— Act Against Restraints of Competition (English translation), available at http://www.gesetze-im-internet.de.

— German legal provisions and notices, available at http://www.bundeskartel lamt.de.

— Rechtsgrundlagen, available at http://www.bundeskartellamt.de.

Bundesministerium für Wirtschaft und Energie, Nationales Kartell- und Wettbewerbsrecht: Wettbewerbsrecht, available at http://www.bmwi.de.

Bundeszentrale für politische Bildung (BPB): Geschichte des Urheberrechts, available at http://www.bpb.de.

***Burger**, Harald/**Dobrovol'skij**, Dmitrij/**Kuhn**, Peter/**Norrick**, Neal R. (eds.)*: Phraseologie: Ein Internationales Handbuch zeitgenössischer Forschung // Phraseology: An International Handbook of Contemporary Research, Volume 1, Berlin: Walter de Gruyter GmbH & Co., KG (2007).

***Burrill**, Alexander Mansfield*: A Law Dictionary and Glossary: Containing Full Definitions of the Principal Terms of the Common and Civil Law, New York: Baker, Voorhis & Company, Vol. I (2nd edition, 1867).

***Buxbaum**, Hannah L.*:

— German Legal Culture and the Globalization of Competition Law: A Historical Perspective on the Expansion of Private Antitrust Enforcement, 23 Berkeley J. Int'l L. 474 (2005) (Berkeley Journal of International Law).

— Territory, Territoriality, and the Resolution of Jurisdictional Conflict, 57 Am. J. Comp. L. 631 (2009) (American Journal of Comparative Law).

***Byford**, Sam*: California judge dismisses Proview's iPad trademark case, The Verge, 9 May 2012.

***Calboli**, Irene*: Trademark Exhaustion in the European Union: Community-Wide or International? The Saga Continues, 6 Marq. Intell. Prop. L. Rev. 47 (2002) (Marquette Intellectual Property Law Review).

***Calkins**, Richard*: Patent Law: The Impact of the 1988 Patent Misuse Reform Act and Noerr–Pennington Doctrine on Misuse Defenses and Antitrust Counterclaims, 38 Drake L. Rev. 175 (1989) (Drake Law Review).

***Campbell**, Mikey*: Apple accuses Proview of 'misleading Chinese courts' over iPad name, AppleInsider, 13 March 2012.

Canadian Geographic: Canadian food firsts, January/February 2001.

Canadian Intellectual Property Office: Registration Nr. TMA232145, available at http://www.cipo.ic.gc.ca.

***Cappelletti**, M./**Seccombe**, M./**Weiler**, J.H.H (eds.)*:

— Integration Through Law, Berlin: De Gruyter (1986).

— Europe and the Federal American Experience, Vol. I, Book I, 3–68, in **Cappelletti/Seccombe/Weiler**: Integration Through Law.

***Carboni**, Anna*: Zino Davidoff SA v A&G Imports Ltd.: A Way Around Silhouette, 21(10) EIPR 524 (1999) (European Intellectual Property Review).

***Carr**, George*: Copyright Misuse: An Overview, American Bar Association, Intellectual Property Litigation Committee, Intellectual Property Litigation (Summer 2010).

***Carrier**, Michael A.*:

— Cabining Intellectual Property Through a Property Paradigm, 54 Duke L. J. 1 (2004) (Duke Law Journal).

— Unraveling the Patent-Antitrust Paradox, 150 U. Pa. L. Rev. 761 (2002) (University of Pennsylvania Law Review).

***Carter**, Stephen L.*:

— Doctrine of Patent Misuse Misused, Legal Times, 26 October 1992.

— Does It Matter Whether Intellectual Property is Property?, 68 Chi.-Kent L. Rev. 715 (1993) (Chicago-Kent Law Review).

— The Trouble with Trademark, 99 Yale L.J. 759 (1990) (Yale Law Journal).

***Castillo de la Torre**, Fernando*: Trade Marks and Free Movement of Pharmaceuticals in the European Community: To Partition or Not to Partition the Market, 19(6) EIPR 304 (1997) (European Intellectual Property Review).

CBC News: No apple for Vancouver Island school, says computer corporation, 6 October 2008.

CCIA, Computer & Communications Industry Association: Changed Antitrust Rules Could Curb Tech Mergers, 18 May 2009.

***Chaffin**, Bryan*: Apple Objects to Chinese Food Company's Logo, the Mac Observer, 6 September 2011.

***Chamberlin**, Edward Hastings*: The Theory of Monopolistic Competition: A Re-Orientation of the Theory of Value, Cambridge: Harvard University Press (7th edition, 1958).

***Chan**, Casey*: Why Is Apple Suing a Chinese Food Company for Stealing LG's Logo?, GizModo, 7 September 2011.

***Cheng**, Jacqui*: Kindle Fire dragged into Apple's "app store" suit against Amazon: Amazon began dropping "for Android" from its "Amazon Appstore for Android", Ars Technica, 18 November 2011.

***Chiappetta**, Vincent*: Trademarks: More Than Meets the Eye, 2003 U. Ill. J.L. Tech. & Pol'y 35 (2003) (University of Illinois Journal of Law, Technology & Policy).

Chilling Effects Clearinghouse: Frequently Asked Questions (and Answers) about Trademark: What to Expect When You're Expecting to Be Sued for Trademark Infringement, maintained by the Berkman Center for Internet & Society, Harvard University.

Chiu**, Alan C. W./**Wong, Kenny K.S.: iPads Being Taken off Shelves in China, Mayer Brown JSM Legal Update, 14 February 2012.

***Choney**, Suzanne*: Kindle Fire added to Apple app store suit against Amazon, NBC News.com, 18 November 2011.

***Christensen**, C. Roland/**Rikert**, David C.*: Nike: Case Study, HBS No. 9-391–238, Harvard Business School, 16 October 1984.

***Clark**, Cynthia L. (ed.)*: The American Economy: A Historical Encyclopedia, Vol. 1, ABC-CLIO, LLC (2011).

***Cleaver**, Hannah*: Bonn café stands up to Apple over trademark, The Local: Germany's News in English, 26 October 2011.

CNN: Coke CEO Roberto C. Goizueta dies at 65, CNN Interactive, 18 October 1997.

***Cody**, Jason Allen*: Initial Interest Confusion: What Ever Happened to Traditional Likelihood of Confusion Analysis? 12 Fed. Cir. B.J. 643 (2003) (The Federal Circuit Bar Journal).

Colston, *Catherine*/***Galloway***, *Jonathan*: Modern Intellectual Property Law, Oxon: Routledge (3rd edition, 2010).

Columbia University: Asia for Educators website, Technical Advances during the Song, available at http://afe.easia.columbia.edu.

Commission of the European Communities: Amended proposal for a Council Regulation on the Community trade mark, COM (84) 470 final, Brussels, 31 July 1984, available from the University of Pittsburgh, Archive of European Integration (AEI) at http://aei.pitt.edu.

Commission of the European Communities: New trade-mark system for the Community: Proposed Directive and Regulation, Bulletin of the European Communities, Supplement 5/80, COM (80) 635, 19 November 1980, available from the University of Pittsburgh, Archive of European Integration (AEI) at http://aei.pitt.edu.

Cone, *John M.*: Evaluating Trade Dress Functionality After The Supreme Court's "TrafFix Devices" Ruling, The Intellectual Property Strategist, Volume 10, Number 1, January 2003.

Cook, *Trevor*: Exhaustion – a casualty of the borderless digital era, in **Bently/ Suthersanen/Torremans**: Global Copyright.

Cooley, *Amanda Harmon*: Trade Dress Protection of Business Décor: What is this Tertium Quid?, Southern Law Journal, Vol. 18, 19–44 (2008).

Cornell University Law School, Legal Information Institute:

— Antitrust, available at http://topics.law.cornell.edu.

— Commerce Clause, available at http://www.law.cornell.edu.

— Dilution (Trademark), available at http://www.law.cornell.edu.

— Federal Question Jurisdiction, available at http://www.law.cornell.edu.

— Supreme Court Bulletin, available at http://www.law.cornell.edu.

— Trademark, http://topics.law.cornell.edu.

Cornish, *William R.*/***Llewelyn***, *David*/***Aplin***, *Tanya*: Intellectual Property: Patents, Copyright, Trade Marks and Allied Rights, London: Sweet & Maxwell (7th edition, 2010).

Cortada, *James W.*: Rise of the knowledge worker, Volume 8, Resources for the knowledge-based economy, Knowledge Reader Series, Oxford: Butterworth-Heinemann (1998).

Cotter, *Thomas F.*: Fair Use and Copyright Overenforcement, 93 Iowa L. Rev. 1271 (2008) (Iowa Law Review).

Council of Europe: Committee of Ministers, Declaration by the Committee of Ministers on Internet governance principles (Adopted by the Committee of Ministers on 21 September 2011 at the 1121st meeting of the Ministers' Deputies.

Council of the European Union:

— Agreement on a Unified Patent Court, Council Register 16351/12, 11 January 2013.

— Conclusions on the future revision of the Trade Mark system in the EU, 3016th Competitiveness Council meeting, Brussels, 25 May 2010.

— EU unitary patent: a big boost for innovation, 17 December 2012.

— Fact Sheet: The long road to unitary patent protection in Europe, 17 December 2012.

— General Secretariat, 16218/13, PI 165 CODEC 2573, Progress Report, 15 November 2013.

— Press Release 10123/10, 3016th Council meeting, Competitiveness (Internal Market, Industry and Research), Presse 136, 25 and 26 May 2010.

— Statement by the Participating Member States concerning the share of distribution of renewal fees for European Patents with unitary effect, Interinstitutional File: 2011/0093 (COD), 17503/12 ADD 1 REV 1, CODEC 2983 PI 171, OC 733, 14 December 2012.

— Transport, Telecommunications and Energy Council meeting, Press Release 7847/12, Presse 116, PR CO 17, 22 March 2012.

Cox, *Rowland:*

— A Manual of Trade-Mark Cases: Comprising Sebastian's Digest of Trade-Mark Cases, Covering All the Cases Reported Prior to the Year 1879, Boston: Houghton, Mifflin & Co. (2nd edition, 1892).

— American Trade Mark Cases, Boston: Houghton, Mifflin & Co. (1871).

CTV: Will Apple's suit against B.C. school bear fruit?, The Globe & Mail, 6 October 2008.

Curia, Court of Justice of the European Union:

— Civil Service Tribunal, April 2011.

— General Court, February 2011, available at http://curia.europa.eu.

— General Presentation, available at http://curia.europa.eu.

— Judgment in Case C-96/09 P, Anheuser-Busch Inc. v Budějovický Budvar, Press Release No°25/11, 29 March 2011.

— Judgment of the Court of First Instance in Joined Cases T-225/06, T-255/06, T-257/06 and T-309/06, Budějovický Budvar v OHIM, Press Release No°95/08, 16 December 2008.

— The Court of Justice: Composition, jurisdiction and procedures, December 2010.

— Your Questions on the Court of Justice of the European Union, September 2010.

Currie, *David P.*: The Constitution in the Supreme Court: State and Congressional Powers, 1801–1835, 49 U. Chi. L. Rev. 887 (1982) (University of Chicago Law Review).

Curtin, *Rebecca Schoff*: The "Capricious Privilege": Rethinking the Origins of Copyright Under the Tudor Regime, 59 J. Copyright Soc'y 391 (2012) (Journal of the Copyright Society U.S.A).

Czapracka, *Katarzyna:*

— Intellectual Property and the Limits of Antitrust: A Comparative Study of US and EU Approaches, Cheltenham: Edward Elgar Publishing Limited (2009).

— Where Antitrust Ends and IP Begins – On the Roots of the Transatlantic Clashes, 9 Yale J. Law & Tech. (2007).

D'Agostino, *Giuseppina*: Copyright Treatment of Freelance Work in the Digital Era, 19 Santa Clara Computer & High Tech. L.J. 37 (2002) (Santa Clara Computer and High Technology Law Journal).

Dallon, *Craig W.*: The Problem with Congress and Copyright Law: Forgetting the Past and Ignoring the Public Interest, 44 Santa Clara L. Rev. 365 (2004) (Santa Clara Law Review).

Danish Patent & Trademark Office: International IP Policy, available at http://www.dkpto.org.

Daunt, *Jacqueline A.*: Entering the U.S. Market for High Technology Companies, Fenwick & West LLP (2002).

Davidson, *Benjamin*: Lost in Translation: Distinguishing Between French and Anglo-American Natural Rights in Literary Property, and How Dastar Proves that the Difference Still Matters, 38 Cornell Int'l L.J. 583 (2005) (Cornell International Law Journal).

Davies, *Karen*: Understanding European Union Law, Oxon: Routledge (4th edition, 2011).

Davis, *Paula K./**Caltrider***, *Steven P.*: Timing (of Invention) Is Everything: The Essential Role of the Written Description Requirement in Determining Conception, 15 Fed. Cir. B.J. 39 (2005) (Federal Circuit Bar Journal).

Dawson, *Mark*: Soft Law and the Rule of Law in the European Union: Revision or Redundancy?, European University Institute, Robert Schuman Centre for Advanced Studies, EUI Working Paper RSCAS 2009/24 (2009).

De Micco, *Pasquale*: Does ACTA still matter? Protecting intellectual property rights in international trade, European Parliament, Policy Briefing, EXPO/B/INTA/2013/26, PE 491.469 EN, 14 January 2013.

de Sola Pool, *Ithiel*: On Free Speech in an Electronic Age: Technologies of Freedom, Belknap Press, Harvard University Press (1983).

Dehousse, *R./**Weiler***, *J.*: The Legal Dimension, in Wallace: The Dynamics of European Integration.

Delrahim, *Makan*: The Long and Winding Road: Convergence in the Application of Antitrust to Intellectual Property, Deputy Assistant Attorney General, Antitrust Division, U.S. Department of Justice, Remarks presented at The George Mason Law Review Symposium, 6 October 2004.

Demand Media: Who was the first U.S. citizen to have a trademark, Answerbag.co, available at http://www.answerbag.com.

Demetriades, *Christina/**Holmes***, *Steve*: The Copyright Directive: the path to harmonisation?, Practical Law Company, 21 June 2004.

Demsetz, *Harold*: Industry Structure, Market Rivalry, and Public Policy, 16 J. L. & Econ 1 (April 1973) (Journal of Law & Economics).

Denicola, *Robert C.*:

— Institutional Publicity Rights: An Analysis of the Merchandising of Famous Trade Symbols, 62 N.C. L. Rev. 603 (1984) (North Carolina Law Review).

— Trademarks as Speech: Constitutional Implications of the Emerging Rationales for the Protection of Trade Symbols, 1982 Wis. L. Rev. 158 (1982) (Wisconsin Law Review).

Derambure, *Christian*: The IP Guide to ... France, New Legal Review, CPA Global, 24 October 2006.

Derclaye, *Estelle*/***Leistner***, *Matthias*: Intellectual Property Overlaps: A European Perspective, Oxford: Hart Publishing Ltd. (2011).

Derclaye, *Estelle*: The IMS Health decision: a triple victory, World Competition, Vol. 27, January 2004.

Derenberg, *Walter J.*: Trade-Mark Protection and Unfair Trading, Albany: Matthew Bender & Co. (1936).

Desai, *Deven R.*/***Rierson***, *Sandra L.*: Confronting the Genericism Conundrum, 28 Cardozo L. Rev. 1789 (2007) (Cardozo Law Review).

Desai, *Deven R.*/***Waller***, *Spencer*: Brands, Competition, and the Law, 2010 B.Y.U.L. Rev. 1425 (2010) (Brigham Young University Law Review).

DFMG Solicitors: Diesel fails to register marks in Class 25, World Trademark Review, 30 September 2013.

Diamond, *Sidney A.*:

— The Historical Development of Trademarks, 65 TMR 265 (1975) (Trademark Reporter).

— The Public Interest and the Trademark System, 62 J. Pat. Off. Soc'y 528, 544 (1980) (Journal of the Patent and Trademark Office Society).

Die Welt: Goldhase von Lindt muss Konkurrenz dulden: Schweizer Schokoladenhersteller verliert Dauerstreit endgültig, 28 March 2013.

Dilbary, *Shahar J.*: Famous Trademarks and the Rational Basis for Protecting "Irrational Beliefs", 14 Geo. Mason L. Rev. 605 (2007) (George Mason Law Review).

Dinwoodie, *Graeme B.*/***Janis***, *Mark D:*

— Trademarks and Unfair Competition: Law and Policy (2nd edition, 2007).

— Confusion over Use: Contextualism in Trademark Law, 92 Iowa L. Rev. 1597 (2007) (Iowa Law Review).

Djelic, *Marie-Laure*: Exporting the American Model: The Postwar Transformation of European Business, Oxford: Oxford University Press (1998).

Dobni, *Dawn*/***Zinkhan***, *George M.*: In Search of Brand Image: a Foundation Analysis, Advances in Consumer Research, Vol. 17, 110–119 (1990).

DocumentArchiv.de: Verfassung des Norddeutschen Bundes (16.04.1867), Verfassung des Norddeutschen Bundes: 16 April 1867, Bundes-Gesetzblatt des Norddeutschen Bundes 1867, 1–23, available at http://www.documentarchiv.de.

Doellinger, *Chad J.*: A New Theory of Trademarks, 111 Penn St. L. Rev. 823 (2007) (Penn State Law Review).

Dogan, *Stacey L./**Lemley***, *Mark A.*: The Merchandising Right: Fragile Theory or Fait Accompli?, 54 Emory L.J. 461 (2005) (Emory Law Journal).

DOJ/FTC, U.S. Department of Justice and the Federal Trade Commission:

— Antitrust Enforcement and Intellectual Property Rights: Promoting Innovation and Competition: A Report Issued By the U.S. Department of Justice and the Federal Trade Commission, April 2007.

— Antitrust Guidelines for the Licensing of Intellectual Property, 6 April 1995 (1995 IP Licensing Guidelines).

— Antitrust Enforcement Guidelines for International Operations, 5 April 1995.

— Statement Accompanying Release of Revised Merger Guidelines, 2 April 1992.

— Horizontal Merger Guidelines, 19 August 2010.

DOJ/USPTO, U.S. Department of Justice/U.S. Patent & Trademark Office: Policy Statement on Remedies for Standards-Essential Patents Subject to Voluntary F/RAND Commitments, 8 January 2013.

DOJ, Department of Justice:

— Antitrust Division Manual, Chapter II. Statutory Provisions and Guidelines of the Antitrust Division, July 2013.

— Antitrust Division, About the Division: Enforcing Antitrust Laws, available at http://www.justice.gov.

— Antitrust Division, International Competition Policy Advisory Committee, available at http://www.justice.gov.

— Antitrust Enforcement and the Consumer, available at http://www.justice.gov.

— Competition and Monopoly: Single Firm Conduct Under Section 2 of the Sherman Act (September 2008), withdrawn pursuant to DOJ Press Release 09-459.

— Press Release 09-459, Justice Department Withdraws Report on Antitrust Monopoly Law: Antitrust Division to Apply More Rigorous Standard With Focus on the Impact of Exclusionary Conduct on Consumers, 11 May 2009.

— Press Release 10-776, Office of Public Affairs, Citing Conflict with Federal Law, Department of Justice Challenges Arizona Immigration Law, 6 July 2010.

— Press Release 11-1364, United States and European Union Antitrust Agencies Issue Revised Best Practices for Coordinating Merger Reviews: Agencies Celebrate 20th Anniversary of Cooperation Agreement, 14 October 2011.

— Press Release 12-210, Statement of the Department of Justice's Antitrust Division on its Decision to Close Investigations of Google Inc.'s Acquisition of Motorola Mobility Holdings Inc. and the Acquisitions of Certain Patents by Apple, Inc., Microsoft Corp. and Research in Motion Ltd., 13 February 2012.

— United States Attorneys' Office, United States Attorneys' Manual, Title 9, Criminal Resource Manual, Section 1701 "Trademark Counterfeiting - Introduction".

Donnelly, *Darren E.*: Parallel Trade and International Harmonization of the Exhaustion of Rights Doctrine, 13 Santa Clara Computer & High Tech. L.J. 445 (1997) (Santa Clara Computer & High Technology Law Journal).

Doyle, *Jack*: Nike & The Beatles, 1987–1989, PopHistoryDig.com, 27 September 2008, available at http://www.pophistorydig.com.

DPMA, Deutsches Patent- und Markenamt:

— Benutzer-Information, No. 71, January 2004, available at http://www.dpma.de.

— Jahresbericht 2008, available at http://www.dpma.de.

— Registernummer 36433, available at https://register.dpma.de.

— The German Patent and Trade Mark Office, available at http://www.dpma.de.

— Trademarks: Trade mark protection for your products and services, available at http://www.dpma.de.

Dratler, *Jr., Jay*: Intellectual Property Law: Commercial, Creative, and Industrial Property, with Stephen McJohn, New York: Law Journal Press (Supplement 2003).

Drescher, *Thomas D.*: The Transformation and Evolution of Trademarks - From Signals to Symbols to Myth, 82 TMR 301 (1992) (Trademark Reporter).

Dreyfuss, *Rochelle Cooper*:

— Are Business Method Patents Bad for Business?, 16 Santa Clara Computer & High Tech. L.J. 263, 274 (2000) (Santa Clara Computer & High Technology Law Journal).

— Does IP Need IP? Accommodating Intellectual Production Outside the Intellectual Property Paradigm, 31 Cardozo L. Rev. 1437 (2010) (Cardozo Law Review).

— Expressive Genericity: Trademarks as Language in the Pepsi Generation, 65 Notre Dame L. Rev. 397 (1990) (Notre Dame Law Review).

Dubois, *Pierre-André*: Trademark Law Evolves in Europe's Highest Courts, IP Europe, April 2003.

Duguid, *Paul:*

— Developing the Brand: The Case of Alcohol, 1800–1880, Enterprise & Society, Vol. 4, No. 3 (September 2003).

— French Connections: The International Propagation of Trademarks in the Nineteenth Century, Enterprise & Society, Vol. 10, No. 3 (March 2009).

Dusollier, *Séverin*: Pruning the European intellectual property tree: in search of common principles and roots, in Geiger: Constructing European Intellectual Property.

EAGCP: Report by the EAGCP – An economic approach to Article 82, July 2005.

Ealy, *Jill Ann*: The Common Law, the States, and Historical Perspective: Utilitarianism and Trademark Protection, 19 J. Contemp. Legal Issues 14 (2010) (The Journal of Contemporary Legal Issues).

Easterbrook, *Frank H.*: Intellectual Property is Still Property, 13 Harv. J.L. & Pub. Pol'y 108, (1990) (Harvard Journal of Law & Public Policy).

Eccles, *Richard*: CJEU dismisses appeals by AstraZeneca and upholds General Court judgement, Bird & Bird, 18 December 2012.

Economides, *Nicholas S.*: The Economics of Trademarks, 78 TMR 523 (1988) (Trademark Reporter).

ECTA, European Communities Trade Mark Association: Position Paper on the revision of the OHIM Manual of the Trade Mark Practice with regard to the protection of non-registered trade marks and other signs used in the course of trade of more than mere local significance under Article 8 (4) of the Council Regulation (EC) N° 207/2009 of 26 /02/2009, 1 December 2012.

Ehrlich, *David*: When Should Post-Sale Confusion Prevent Use or Registration of Marks?, 81 TMR 267 (1991) (Trademark Reporter).

Elhauge, *Einer*: Defining Better Monopolization Standards, 56 Stan. L. Rev. 253 (November 2003) (Stanford Law Review).

EUR-Lex:

— Founding treaties, available at http://eur-lex.europa.eu.

— Official Journal of the European Union, available at http://eur-lex.europa.eu.

— Treaties – Chronological Overview, available at http://eur-lex.europa.eu.

— Treaties Currently in Force, available at http://eur-lex.europa.eu.

Eurobrand: Eurobrand Study 2009, Country Review, cited in European Commission: Intellectual Property Strategy – Frequently Asked Questions, available at http://study.eurobrand.cc.

Eurofound: Soft law, European industrial relations dictionary, available at http://www.eurofound.europa.eu.

Europa.eu:

— Application of Articles 101 and 102 TFEU (formerly Articles 81 and 82 of the EC Treaty), available at http://europa.eu.

— EU Law, EU Treaties, available at http://europa.eu.

— EU Law, Regulations, Directives and other acts, available at http://europa.eu.

— EU Treaties, available at http://europa.eu.

— European Union, Countries, available at http://europa.eu.

— European Union, Institutions and Bodies, European Commission, available at http://europa.eu.

— European Union, The history of the European Union, 1945–1959: A peaceful Europe – the beginnings of cooperation, available at http://europa.eu.

— Publications Office, Official Journal of the European Union, available at http://publications.europa.eu.

— Summaries of EU Legislation, available at http://europa.eu.

— Summaries of EU Legislation, ECSC Treaty, available at http://europa.eu.

— Summaries of EU Legislation, EEC Treaty, available at http://europa.eu.

— Summaries of EU Legislation, Glossary: Community acquis, available at http://europa.eu.

— Summaries of EU Legislation, Glossary: European Commission, available at http://europa.eu.

— Summaries of EU Legislation, Single European Act, available at http://europa.eu.

— Technology transfer agreements, summary of legislation, available at http://europa.eu.

— The history of the European Union, 2000–2009: Further expansion, available at http://europa.eu.

— Treaty of Lisbon: The Treaty at a glance, available at http://europa.eu.

European Commission:

— 2012 roadmaps, available at http://ec.europa.eu.

— A Single Market for Intellectual Property Rights: Boosting creativity and innovation to provide economic grow, high quality jobs and first class products and services in Europe, Communication from the Commission to the European Parliament, the Council, the European Economic and Social Committee and the Committee of the Regions, COM(2011) 287 final, 24 May 2011, available at http://ec.europa.eu.

— About the European Commission: Departments (Directorates-General) and services, available at http://ec.europa.eu.

— Actions for Damages – Key documents, available at http://ec.europa.eu.

— Antitrust Legislation, available at http://ec.europa.eu.

— Antitrust Manual of Procedures: Internal DG Competition working documents on procedures for the application of Articles 101 and 102 TFEU (March 2012).

— Application of EU Law, available at http://ec.europa.eu.

— Article 102 legislation, available at http://ec.europa.eu.

— Commission consults on review of current regime for technology transfer agreements, Press release, 6 December 2011, available at http://ec.europa.eu.

— Commission warns AstraZeneca of preliminary findings in Losec antitrust investigation, Press Release IP/03/1136, 31 July 2003.

— Communication from the Commission: A Single Market for Intellectual Property Rights: Boosting creativity and innovation to provide economic growth, high quality jobs and first class products and services in Europe, Brussels, COM(2011) 287, 24 May 2011.

— Communication from the Commission: Europe 2020: A strategy for smart, sustainable and inclusive growth, Brussels, COM(2010) 2020, 3 March 2010.

— Communication from the Commission: Single Market Act – Twelve levers to boost growth and strengthen confidence, Brussels, COM(2011) 206, 13 April 2011.

— Communication from the Commission: Single Market Act II – Together for new growth, Brussels, COM(2012) 573, 3 October 2012.

— COMP/C-3/39.985 – Apple/Motorola, case description, available at http://ec.europa.eu.

— COMP/C-3/39.986 – Microsoft/Motorola, case description, available at http://ec.europa.eu.

— Competition policy and the exercise of intellectual property rights, Intergovernmental Group of Experts on Competition Law and Policy, presented in Geneva, during the Eighth Session, 17–19 July 2007, Round Table on Competition Policy and the exercise of intellectual property rights, available at http://www.unctad.org.

— DG Competition discussion paper on the application of Article 82 of the Treaty to exclusionary abuses, Public consultation, Brussels, December 2005.

— DG Competition Discussion Paper on the Application of Article 82 of the Treaty to Exclusionary Abuses, December 2005.

— Directorate-General for Competition website, available at http://ec.europa.eu.

— Directorate-General for Competition, Competition Policy in the European Union, available at http://ec.europa.eu.

— Draft Commission Regulation EU (No) .../.. of XXX on the application of Article 101(3) of the Treaty on the Functioning of the European Union to categories of technology transfer agreements, C(2013) 921 draft.

— Draft Communication, Guidelines on the application of Article 101 of the Treaty on the Functioning of the European Union to technology transfer agreements, C(2013) 924 draft.

— Draft proposal for a revised block exemption for technology transfer agreements and for revised guidelines, DG Competition consultation page, Public consultations, available at http://ec.europa.eu.

— Enlargement, available at http://ec.europa.eu.

— EU Competition Law: Rules Applicable to Antitrust Enforcement, Volume I: General Rules, Situation as at 1 July 2013, Luxembourg 2013.

— EU Competition Law: Rules Applicable to Merger Control, Situation as at 1 April 2010, Brussels 2010.

— European Commission at Work: Decision Making, available at http://ec.europa.eu.

— European Competition Network: Commission Authorities, available at http://ec.europa.eu.

— European Competition Network: Frequently Asked Questions, available at http://ec.europa.eu.

— European External Action Service, European Economic Area (EEA), available at http://eeas.europa.eu.

— Eurostat, European Patent Convention (Munich Convention), available at http://epp.eurostat.ec.europa.eu.

— Free movement of goods – Guide to the application of Treaty provisions governing the free movement of goods, publication prepared by Directorate C, Regulatory Policy, of the Enterprise and Industry DG (2010).

— Intellectual Property Strategy – Frequently Asked Questions, MEMO/11/332, Brussels, 24 May 2011.

— Internal Market and Services DG, Letter of Invitation to Tender, MARKT/A1/Bud/BF/fm (2009) 204180, 22 July 2009.

— Internal Market, Trade Marks including Community Trade Mark, available at http://ec.europa.eu.

— Legislation, available at http://ec.europa.eu.

— Making Markets Work Better, part of The European Union Explained series, July 2013.

— National Competition Authorities, available at http://ec.europa.eu.

— Official Languages, available at http://ec.europa.eu.

— Press Release 17824/12, Unitary patent protection: a big leap towards innovation for EU companies, PRESSE 534, 17 December 2012.

— Press Release AGENDA/13/10, Top News from the European Commission 16 March – 12 April 2013, 15 March 2013.

— Press Release IP/01/584, Commission acts against Duales System Deutschland AG (Green Dot) for the abuse of a dominant position, 20 April 2001.

— Press Release IP/04/382, Commission concludes on Microsoft investigation, imposes conduct remedies and a fine, 24 March 2004.

— Press Release IP/05/1626, Commission publishes discussion paper on abuse of dominance, 19 December 2005.

— Press Release IP/05/1634, Commission launches consultations on facilitating damages claims for breaches of EU competition law, 20 December 2005.

— Press Release IP/05/737, Commission fines AstraZeneca €60 million for misusing patent system to delay market entry of competing generic drugs, 15 June 2005.

— Press Release IP/06/804, 2005 Annual Report on Competition Policy, 20 June 2006.

— Press Release IP/08/22, European Commission welcomes Apple's announcement to equalise prices for music downloads from iTunes in Europe, 9 January 2008.

— Press Release IP/09/683, Commission adopts report on functioning of key antitrust Regulation, 30 April 2009.

— Press Release IP/10/870, Patents: Commission proposes translation arrangements for future EU Patent, 1 July 2010.

— Press Release IP/11/470, Commission proposes unitary patent protection to boost research and innovation, 13 April 2011.

— Press Release IP/11/630, Commission sets out "blueprint" for Intellectual Property Rights to boost creativity and innovation, 24 May 2011.

— Press Release IP/11/842, Commission welcomes improved market entry for lung disease treatments, 6 July 2011.

— Press Release IP/12/129, Mergers: Commission approves acquisition of Motorola Mobility by Google, 13 February 2012.

— Press Release IP/12/1448, Commission sends Statement of Objections to Samsung on potential misuse of mobile phone standard-essential patents, 21 December 2012.

— Press Release IP/12/345, Commission opens proceedings against Motorola, 3 April 2012.

— Press Release IP/12/89, Commission opens proceedings against Samsung, 31 January 2012.

— Press release IP/13/120, Commission consults on proposal for revised competition regime for technology transfer agreements, 20 February 2013.

— Press Release IP/13/196, Antitrust: Commission fines Microsoft for non-compliance with browser choice commitments, 6 March 2013.

— Press Release IP/13/287, Trade marks: Commission proposes easier access and more effective protection, 27 March 2013.

— Press Release IP/14/299, Commission adopts revised competition regime for technology transfer agreements, 21 March 2014.

— Press Release IP/II/1194, EU and US celebrate 20 years of cooperation; agree to advance cooperation further, 14 October 2011.

— Press Release IP10/74, Patents: Commission opens the way for some Member States to move forward on a unitary patent, 14 December 2010.

— Press Release MEMO/07/126, European Commission confirms sending a Statement of Objections against alleged territorial restrictions in on-line music sales to major record companies and Apple, 3 April 2007.

— Press Release MEMO/07/205, Commission welcomes Court of First Instance judgments in German recycling cases, 24 May 2007.

— Press Release MEMO/07/330, Commission confirms sending a Statement of Objections to Rambus, 23 August 2007.

— Press Release MEMO/12/1021, Samsung - Enforcement of ETSI standards essential patents (SEPs), 21 December 2012.

— Press Release MEMO/13/120, Commission consults on proposal for revised competition regime for technology transfer agreements - frequently asked questions, 20 February 2013.

— Report on Competition Policy 2004.

— Report on Competition Policy 2005.

— Revision of the rules for the assessment of licensing agreements for the transfer of technology under EU competition law, available at http://ec.europa.eu.

— Roundtable Discussion on Techniques and Evidentiary Issues in Proving Dominance/Monopoly Power, Statement by the European Commission Before the OECD Competition Committee, Working Party No. 3 on Co-operation and Enforcement, DAF/COMP/WP3/WD(2006)30, 24 May 2006.

— Summary of Commission Decision of 16 December 2009 relating to a proceeding under Article 102 of the Treaty on the Functioning of the European Union and Article 54 of the EEA Agreement (Case COMP/39.530 - Microsoft (Tying)) (OJ C 36, 13.2.2010).

— Technology transfer agreements, available at http://europa.eu.

— The EU Single Market - The European Observatory, available at http://ec.europa.eu.

— The EU Single Market: Intellectual Property, available at http://ec.europa.eu.

— The EU Single Market: Patents, available at http://ec.europa.eu.

European Council:

— Records of the Luxembourg Conference on the Community patent 1975, Office for Official Publications of the European Communities, Luxembourg

1982, available from the University of Pittsburgh, Archive of European Integration (AEI), http://aei.pitt.edu.

— Presidency Conclusions, 29 October 1993, Annex II, Article 1(h), Nr. SN288/93, available from http://www.ab.gov.tr.

European Court of Human Rights (ECHR): The Court in Brief, available at http://www.echr.coe.int.

European Economic and Social Committee: Opinion of the European Economic and Social Committee on the Proposal for a Directive of the European Parliament and of the Council to approximate the laws of the Member States relating to trade marks, COM(2013) 162 final – 2013/0089 (COD), INT/697, 11 July 2013.

European Organisation for the Safety of Air Navigation (EUROCONTROL): Member States, available at https://www.eurocontrol.int.

European Parliament:

— Legislating more efficiently: questions & answers on new delegated acts, available at http://www.europarl.europa.eu.

— Task Force on Economic and Monetary Union, Briefing 26, Second revision, PE166.626/rev.2, briefing prepared by the Directorate-General for Research Economic Affairs Division, Luxembourg (18 March 1998).

European Patent Lawyers Association: NL - Philips v. SK Kasetten/FRAND, case summary, EPLaw Patent Blog, available at http://www.eplawpatentblog.com.

European Patent Office:

— History, available at http://www.epo.org.

— Member States of the European Patent Organisation, available at http://www.epo.org.

— National law relating to the EPC, 15th edition (May 2011), available at http://documents.epo.org.

European Union: EU-28 and candidate countries – Countries, languages and currencies: names, codes and listing order, Development project for point 7 of the Interinstitutional style guide, Rev. 16, 1 July 2013.

Evangelista, *Benny*: Monster Fiercely Protects Its Name: Cable Products Company Sues Those Who Use M-Word, San Francisco Chronicle, 8 November 2004.

Fahran: Another Lawsuit? Sichuan Fangguo Infringes On Apple's Logo, Maypalo, 6 September 2011.

***Fairhurst**, John*: Law of the European Union, Harlow: Pearson Education Limited (8th edition, 2010).

***Feather**, John*: Publishing, Piracy and Politics: An Historical Study of Copyright in Britain, Mansell (1994).

Federal Bar Association: About U.S. Federal Courts, available at http://www.fedbar.org.

Federal Circuit Historical Society: History of the United States Court of Appeals for the Federal Circuit, available at http://federalcircuithistoricalsociety.org.

Federal Judicial Center: The U.S. District Courts and the Federal Judiciary, available at http://www.fjc.gov.

***Feil**, Markus*: Lizenzkartellrecht: US-amerikanische und europäische Entwicklungen, Inaugural-Dissertation zur Erlangung der Doktorwürde einer Hohen Juristischen Fakultät der Ludwig-Maximilians-Universität zu München (2008).

***Feldman**, Leonard J./**Alaily**, Rima J.,/**Farrell**,* Chad D.: At the Intersection of Antitrust and Intellectual Property Law: Looking Both Ways to Avoid a Collision, Independent Ink at the Crossroads of Antitrust and Intellectual Property Law: The Court's Holding Regarding Market Power in Cases Involving Patents and Implications in Cases Involving Copyrights, 30 Seattle Univ. L. R. 407 (2007) (Seattle University Law Review).

***Feng**, Samuel*: Trademark: Its history, influence and issues, available at http://cnx.org.

Fenwick & West LLP: 2004 Update: International Legal Protection for Software – Trademarks, available at http://www.softwareprotection.com.

***Fezer**, Karl-Heinz*:

— Das Markenrecht im Aufwind des Europäischen Binnenmarktes – Überlegungen zum Markenschutz in Europa nach dem Urteil des Europäischen Gerichtshofs vom 17. Oktober 1990 – "Hag II", in: Wild/Schulte-Franzheim/Lorenz-Wolf: Festschrift für Alfred-Carl Gaedertz.

— Der Wettbewerb der Markensysteme: Chancen und Risiken der Änderungsvorschläge der EU-Kommission zur Markenrichtlinie und Gemeinschaftsmarkenverordnung, GRUR 2013, 1185–1195.

— Die Kollision komplexer Kennzeichen im Markenverletzungsrecht, GRUR 2013, 209–320.

— Markenrecht: Kommentar zum Markengesetz, C.H. Beck, Munich (4th edition, 1999).

Fina, *Prof. Dr. Siegfried (ed.)*: European Union Intellectual Property Law - Trademarks, available at http://www.law.stanford.edu.

Finnegan, Henderson, Farabow, Garrett & Dunner, LLP:

— Internet Trademark Case Summaries, available at http://www.finnegan.com.

— Overview of TTAB Oppositions, available at http://www.finnegan.com.

Finnegan, *William*: Sheriff Joe: Joe Arpaio is tough on prisoners and undocumented immigrants. What about crime?, Profiles, The New Yorker, 20 July 2009.

Fisher *III, William W.*: The Growth of Intellectual Property: A History of the Ownership of Ideas in the United States, originally published in German as "Geistiges Eigentum - ein ausufernder Rechtsbereich: Die Geschichte des Ideenschutzes in den Vereinigten Staaten," in Eigentum im internationalen Vergleich, Vandenhoeck & Ruprecht (1999).

Fitzpatrick, *Simon A.*: Prospects of Further Copyright Harmonisation?, EIPR (2003) (European Intellectual Property Review).

Fleischer, *Holger*: Comparative Approaches to the Use of Legislative History in Statutory Interpretation, 60 Am. J. Comp. L. 401 (2012) (American Journal of Comparative Law).

Floyd, *Tori*: Apple threatens to sue small German cafe for logo, The Right Click, Yahoo! News 26 October 2011.

Flynn, *John J.*: Antitrust and the Suppression of the Technology in the United States and Europe: Is there a Remedy? Antitrust Policy, Innovation Efficiencies, and the Suppression of Technology, 66 Antitrust L.J. 487 (1998) (Antitrust Law Journal).

Foer, *Albert A.*: United States of America, AAI Working Paper 06-04, American Antitrust Institute, August 2005.

Folsom, *Ralph H./**Teply**, Larry L.*: Trademarked Generic Words, 89 Yale L.J. 1323 (1980) (Yale Law Journal).

Fontaine, *Pascal*: Europe in 12 Lessons, European Commission Directorate-General for Communication (July 2010), available for download at ec.europa.eu/publications.

Forstner, *Barbara*: Osterhase legt Hauswirth bittere Niederlage ins Nest, WirtschaftsBlatt, 25 March 2012.

Foster, *Sharon E.*: Invitation to a Discourse Regarding the History, Philosophy and Social Psychology of a Property Right in Copyright, 21 Fla. J. Int'l L. 171 (2009) (Florida Journal of International Law).

Fox, *Eleanor M.*:

— Monopolization and Dominance in the United States and the European Community - Efficiency, Opportunity, and Fairness, 61 Notre Dame L. Rev. 981 (1986) (Notre Dame Law Review).

— US and EU Competition Law: A Comparison, Chapter 10 in **Richardson/ Graham**: Global Competition Policy.

— What is the Harm to Competition? Exclusionary Practices and Anticompetitive Effect, 70 Antitrust L.J. 371 (2002), Issue 2 (Antitrust Law Journal).

Frankel, *Miri*: gTLDs and anticompetitive behaviour: is there a monopolistic trend on the web?, posted on the IPKat blog, 15 March 2013, available at http://ipkitten.blogspot.de.

Franklin, *Magnus*: EU single market trumps treaty rights in copyright, top court says, MLex EU, 13 February 2014.

French, *Susan C.*/***Appleton***, *Bonnie Lee*: A Guide to Successful Pruning: Pruning Basics and Tools, Virginia Cooperative Extension, Virginia Tech, and Virginia State University, 1 May 2009, Publication 430–455.

Friedel, *Robert D.*: Zipper: An Exploration in Novelty, New York: Norton & Company (1994).

Frischmann, *Brett M.*/***Lemley,*** *Mark A.*: Spillovers, 107 Colum. L. Rev. 257 (2007) (Columbia Law Review).

Fritch, *David M.*: Searching for Initial Interest Confusion and Trademark Protection in Cyberspace, 6 PGH. J. Tech. L. & Pol'y 1 (2005) (University of Pittsburgh Journal of Technology Law & Policy).

Fromer, *Jeanne C.*:

— A Psychology of Intellectual Property, 104 Nw. U. L. Rev. 1441 (2010) (Northwestern University Law Review).

— Claiming Intellectual Property, 76 U. Chi. L. Rev. 719 (2009) (University of Chicago Law Review).

— Creativity and the Law: The Role of Creativity in Trademark Law, 86 Notre Dame L. Rev. 1885 (September 2011) (Notre Dame Law Review).

Frotscher, *Werner*/***Pieroth***, *Bodo*: Verfassungsgeschichte, Munich: C.H. Beck (8th edition 2009).

Frumkin, *M.*: The Origin of Patents, Journal of the Patent Office Society, Vol. XXVII, No. 3, March 1945.

FTC/DOJ, Federal Trade Commission and the U.S. Department of Justice: Antitrust Guidelines for Collaborations Among Competitors, April 2000 (Collaboration Guidelines).

FTC, Federal Trade Commission:

— A Brief Overview of the Federal Trade Commission's Investigative and Law Enforcement Authority, Office of the General Counsel, July 2008.

— Anticipating the 21st Century: Competition and Consumer Protection Policy in the New High-Tech, Global Marketplace, Office of Policy Planning, May 1996.

— Competition and IP Law and Policy in the Knowledge-Based Economy Hearings, 2 February 2002.

— Competition Guidance: The Antitrust Laws, available at http://www.ftc.gov.

— Federal Trade Commission and Department of Justice Issue Report on Antitrust and Intellectual Property, Press Release, 17 April 2007.

— FTC Policy Statement on Unfairness, 17 December 1980, Appended to International Harvester Co., 104 F.T.C. 949, 1070 (1984).

— The Enforcers, available at http://www.ftc.gov.

— The Evolving IP Marketplace, Conference, 26 May 2010.

— The Evolving IP Marketplace: Aligning Patent Notice and Remedies With Competition, March 2011.

— To Promote Innovation: The Proper Balance of Competition and Patent Law and Policy, October 2003.

Funderburg, *Anne Cooper*: Paint Without Pain, American Heritage, Invention & Technology Magazine, Vol. 17, Issue 4, Spring 2002, available at http://www.americanheritage.com.

Funding Universe:

— Interbrand Corporation History, available at http://www.fundinguniverse.com.

— The Sherwin-Williams Company, available at http://www.fundinguniverse.com.

Gallacher, *Ian*: Cite Unseen: How Neutral Citation and America's Law Schools Can Cure Our Strange Devotion to Bibliographical Orthodoxy and the Constriction of Open and Equal Access to the Law, 70 Alb. L. Rev. 491 (2007) (Albany Law Review).

Gallagher, *William T.*: Trademark and Copyright Enforcement in the Shadow of IP Law, 28 Santa Clara Computer & High Tech. L.J. 453 (2011–2012) (Santa Clara Computer & High Technology Law Journal).

Gambrell, *James B.*: Patents and Antitrust: An Integrated Approach in the European Economic Community, 6 B.C.L. Rev. 541 (1965) (Boston College Law Review).

Gamm *Frhr. v., Otto-Friedrich*: Warenzeichengesetz, Einführungskommentar Nr. 6, 18 (1965).

Geiger, *Christophe (ed.)*: Constructing European Intellectual Property: Achievements and New Perspectives, European Intellectual Property Institutes Network series, Cheltenham: Edward Elgar Publishing Limited (2013).

Geiger, *Christophe*: The construction of intellectual property in the European Union: searching for coherence, in Geiger: Constructing European Intellectual Property.

Geiss, *Karlmann*/***Gerstenmaier***, *Klaus-A.*/***Mailander***, *Peter (eds.)*: Festschrift für Karl Peter Mailänder zum 70 Geburtstag am 23 Oktober 2006 (2006).

Geller, *Paul Edward*:

— Must Copyright Be For Ever Caught Between Marketplace and Authorship Norms?, in **Sherman/Strowel**: Of Authors and Origins.

— Toward an Overriding Norm in Copyright, based on a longer essay, "Must Copyright Be For Ever Caught Between Marketplace and Authorship Norms?," in **Sherman/Strowel**: Of Authors and Origins.

— Toward an Overriding Norm in Copyright: Sign Wealth, Revue Internationale du Droit d'Auteur (RIDA), No. 159, January 1994.

General Court of the European Union: Judgment in Joined Cases T-225/06 RENV, T-255/06 RENV, T-257/06 RENV and T-309/08 RENV Budějovický Budvar, národní podnik v OHIM, Press Release No 6/13, Luxembourg, 22 January 2013.

Geradin, *Damien*/***Petit***, *Nicolas*/***Walker***, *Mike*/***Hofer***, *Paul*/***Louis***, *Frédéric*: The Concept of Dominance, GCLC Research Papers on Article 82, July 2005.

Gerber, *David J.*:

— Constitutionalizing the Economy: German Neo-liberalism, Competition Law and the "New" Europe, 42 Am. J. Comp. L. 25 (1994) (The American Journal of Comparative Law).

— Law and Competition in Twentieth Century Europe: Protecting Prometheus, Oxford: Oxford University Press (1998).

— The Extraterritorial Application of the German Antitrust Laws, 77 Am. J. Int'l L. 756 (1983) (American Journal of International Law).

— The Future of Article 82: Dissecting the Conflict, paper presented at the 12th Annual Competition Law and Policy Workshop, Robert Schuman Centre EUI, Florence (2007).

Ghalamkarizadeh, *Anthonia*: Hard Fight for the Hard Rock Cafe – Germany, Marques, 6 September 2013.

Ghose, *Sanjoy*/***Lowengart***, *Oded*: Taste Tests: Impacts of Consumer Perceptions and Preferences on Brand Positioning Strategies, 10 Journal of Targeting, Measurement & Analysis for Marketing 26 (2001).

Gibson, *James*: Risk Aversion and Rights Accretion in Intellectual Property Law, 116 Yale L.J. 882 (2007) (Yale Law Journal).

Gilbert, *Richard*/***Shapiro***, *Carl:* Antitrust Issues in the Licensing of Intellectual Property: The Nine No-No's Meet the Nineties, in **Winston/Baily/Reiss**: Microeconomics.

Gilbert, *Richard J.:*

— Converging Doctrines? US and EU Antitrust Policy for the Licensing of Intellectual Property, Deputy Assistant Attorney General, Antitrust Division, U.S. Department of Justice, Remarks prepared for the Antitrust Section Spring Meeting, 16 February 2004, University of California, Berkeley, Competition Policy Center, Working Paper No. CPC04-44.

— Antitrust Policy for the Licensing of Intellectual Property: An International Comparison, International Journal of Technology Management, Vol. 19, No. 1/2 (2000).

Ginsburg, *Jane C.*/***Goldberg***, *David*/***Greenbaum***, *Arthur J.*: Trademark and Unfair Competition Law: Cases and Materials (3rd edition, 2001).

Giocoli, *Nicola*: Competition Versus Property Rights: American Antitrust Law, the Freiburg School, and the Early Years of European Competition Policy, 5 J. Comp. L. & Econ. 747 (2009) (Journal of Competition Law & Economics).

Glazer, *Daniel C.*/***Dhamija***, *Dev R.*: Revisiting Initial Interest Confusion on the Internet, 95 TMR 952 (2005) (Trademark Reporter).

Global Competition Law Centre:

— GCLC Research Papers on Article 82 EC, Global Competition Law Centre, College of Europe, Bruges, Belgium, July 2005.

— Intellectual Property Protection and Enforcement Manual: A Practical and Legal Guide for Protecting Your Intellectual Property Rights, Case Studies: Johnson & Johnson & Co., Inc.

GMA News: Apple lawyers hit Chinese food maker over logo, GMA News, 8 September 2011.

Govaere, *Inge*: Abuses of dominant position, intellectual property rights and monopolization in EU competition law: some thoughts on a possible course of action, in **Mateus/Moreira**: Competition Law and Economics.

Granstrand, *Ove (ed.)*: Economics, Law and Intellectual Property: Seeking Strategies for Research and Teaching in a Developing Field, Dordrecht: Springer Science & Business Media (2003).

Greek Pages: History of College Fraternities, Locals Online, available at http://www.greekpages.com.

Greenberg, *Abraham S.*: The Ancient Lineage of Trade-Marks, 33 J. Pat. & Trademark Off. Soc'y 876 (1951) (Journal of the Patent and Trademark Office Society).

Greene, *K.J.*:

— Abusive Trademark Litigation and the Incredible Shrinking Confusion Doctrine - Trademark Abuse in the Context of Entertainment Media and Cyberspace, 27 Harv. J.L. & Pub. Pol'y 609 (2004) (Harvard Journal of Law & Public Policy).

— Intellectual Property Expansion: The Good, the Bad, and the Right of Publicity, 11 Chap. L. Rev. 521 (2008) (Chapman Law Review).

Gremminger, *Michael*/***Miersch***, *Gerald*: The Court of First Instance confirms Duales System Deutschland's abuse of dominance in the packaging recycling system, Competition Policy Newsletter, Number 3 (2007).

Griffin, *Joseph P.*: The Demise of the "Nine No-No's" and Other Significant Changes in U.S. Antitrust Policies Concerning Transnational Technology Licensing, 15 Swiss Review of International Competition Law 39 (1982).

Grinvald, *Leah Chan*: Shaming Trademark Bullies, 2011 Wis. L. Rev. 625 (2011) (Wisconsin Law Review).

Grubisich, *T.*: Washington's Flour, Chicago Sun-Times, 23 April 1976.

Grynberg, *Michaela* The Road Not Taken: Initial Interest Confusion, Consumer Search Costs, and the Challenge of the Internet, 28 Seattle U. L. Rev. 97 (2004) (Seattle University Law Review).

Gulasekaram, *Pratheepan*: Policing the Border Between Trademarks and Free Speech: Protecting Unauthorized Trademark Use in Expressive Works, 80 Wash. L. Rev. 887 (2005) (Washington Law Review).

Guth, *Joseph H.*:

— Cumulative Impacts: Death-Knell for Cost-Benefit Analysis in Environmental Decisions, 11 Barry L. Rev. 23 (Fall 2008) (Barry Law Review).

— Law for the Ecological Age, 9 Vt. J. Envtl. L. 431 (Spring 2008) (Vermont Journal of Environmental Law).

Hackbarth, *Ralf*: Weiter Schutzbereich berühmter Marken ("Volkswagen"), BGH 11.04.2013 - I ZR 214/11, GRUR 21/2013, 466.

Hamilton, *Melissa*: Software Tying Arrangement under the Antitrust Laws: A More Flexible Approach, 71 Denv. U. L. Rev. 607 (1994) (Denver University Law Review).

Hamilton, *Walton H.*: Patents and Free Enterprise, Investigation of Concentration of Economic Power, Washington: U.S. Government Printing Office (1941).

Hammer, *Peter J.*: Antitrust Beyond Competition: Market Failures, Total Welfare, and the Challenge of Intramarket Second-Best Tradeoffs, 98 Mich. L. Rev. 849 (2000) (Michigan Law Review).

Handler, *Milton*/***Pickett***, *Charles*: Trade-Marks and Trade Names - An Analysis and Synthesis: I, 30 Colum. L. Rev. 168 (1930) (Columbia Law Review).

Hard Rock Cafe International:

— Berlin, available at http://www.hardrock.com.

— London, available at http://www.hardrock.com.

— Milestone Victory In Trademark And Unfair Competition Dispute With Unauthorized Hard Rock Cafe In Heidelberg, Germany, 15 August 2013.

Hardacre, *Dr. Alan*/***Kaeding***, *Dr. Michael*: Delegated and Implementing Acts: the New Worlds of Comitology - Implications for European and National Public Administrations, European Institute of Public Administration (EIPA), EIPAscope, Bulletin 01/2011.

Hardy, *I. Trotter*: Not So Different: Tangible, Intangible, Digital, and Analog Works and Their Comparison for Copyright Purposes, 26 U. Dayton L. Rev. 211 (2001) (University of Dayton Law Review).

Hartman, *Stephen H.*: Subliminal Confusion: The Misappropriation of Advertising Value, 78 TMR 506 (1988) (Trademark Reporter).

***Hay**, Peter/**Oldekop**, Dieter*: EMI/CBS and the Rest of the World: Trademark Rights and the European Communities, 25 Am. J. Comp. L. 120 (1977) (American Journal of Comparative Law).

***Hays**, Thomas*: Silhouette is not the Proper Case on which to decide the Parallel Importation Question, 20(7) EIPR 277 (1998) (European Intellectual Property Review).

***Heath**, Christopher/**Sanders**, Anselm Kamperman (eds.)*: Landmark Intellectual Property Cases and Their Legacy: IEEM International Intellectual Property Conferences, Alphen aan den Rijn: Kluwer Law International BV Kluwer Law International (2011).

***Heibert**, Aaron*: Apple Sues Canadian School for Similar Logo, Tom's Hardware: The Authority on Tech, 7 October 2008.

Heinisch**, Oliver/**Woodgate, Tony: EU Intellectual property transactions, PLC Practice Note, Practical Law Company, Thomas Reuters (2014).

***Heise**, Alexandra/**Ebert-Weidenfeller**, Andreas/**Nordemann-Schiffel**, Anke/ **Kefferpütz**, Martin/**Hackbarth**, Ralf*: Relevant public for determining the degree of recognition of famous marks, well-known marks and marks with reputation (Q234), GRUR Int 2013.

***Hesse**, Renata B.*: IP, Antitrust and Looking Back on the Last Four Years, Deputy Assistant Attorney General Antitrust Division, U.S. Department of Justice, Presented at Global Competition Review, 2nd Annual Antitrust Law Leaders Forum, Miami, Florida, 8 February 2013.

***Hickey**, Jr., James E./**Walker**, Vern R.*: Refining the Precautionary Principle in International Environmental Law, 14 Va. Envtl. L.J. 423 (1995) (Virginia Environmental Law Journal).

***Hickey**, Jr., James E.*: Custom and Land-Based Pollution of the High Seas, 15 San Diego L. Rev. 409 (1978) (San Diego Law Review).

***Higgins**, David*: The Making of Modern Trade Mark Law: The UK, 1860–1914, in **Bently/Davis/Ginsburg**: Trademarks and Brands: An Interdisciplinary Critique.

***Hildebrandt**, Dr. Ulrich*: Harmonised Trade Mark Law in Europe: Case-Law of the European Court of Justice, Cologne: Carl Heymanns Verlag (2005).

***Hille**, Kathrin*:

— Apple faces new fight in China IP dispute, Financial Times, 7 March 2012.

— Proview drags Apple through a legal hailstorm, Financial Times, 28 February 2012.

Hinds, *Caroline*: Das Prinzip „sic utere tuo ut alienum non laedas" und seine Bedeutung im internationalen Umweltrecht, Archiv des Völkerrechts, Vol. 30. Nr. 3, H. Mohr Siebeck GmbH & Co. KG (1992).

Holah, *Mark*: United Kingdom – Unconventional marks in Europe since SIECKMANN, LIBERTEL and SHIELD MARK, Field Fisher Waterhouse, 9 March 2005.

Holmes, *Oliver W.*: Privilege, Malice, and Intent, in Collected Legal Papers (1920).

Honan, *Mathew*: Apple drops 'Computer' from name, PCWorld, 9 January 2007.

Hooghoff, *Kai*/***Lange***, *Markus*: ICN – Unilateral practices – dominance analysis – recommended practices: The ICN recommends practices on dominance analysis in unilateral, Concurrences – Revue des droits de la concurrence, Politique internationale, Chroniques, Concurrences N° 1, 205–209, 2010.

Hopwood, *Shon R.*: Matters of Practice: Citations and Quotations in U.S. Supreme Court Briefs, 8 June 2011, available at http://www.thecocklebur.com.

Horns, *Axel H.*: A Unified European Patent System – The Historical Perspective, 18 February 2010.

Horwitz, *Ethan*/***Levi***, *Benjamin*: Fifty Years of the Lanham Act: A Retrospective of Section 43(a), 7 Fordham Intell. Prop. Media & Ent. L.J. 59 (1996) (Fordham Intellectual Property, Media and Entertainment Law Journal).

Hovenkamp, *Herbert*/***Janis***, *Mark D.*/***Lemley***, *Mark A*/***Leslie***, *Christopher R.*: IP and Antitrust: An Analysis of Antitrust Principles Applied to Intellectual Property Law (2nd edition, 2011).

Hovenkamp, *Herbert*:

— Empire: Innovation and the Domain of Competition Policy, 60 Ala. L. Rev. 103 (2008) (Alabama Law Review).

— Innovation and Competition Policy, Cases and Materials, Chapter 7 Intellectual Property Misuse, 25 November 2012 (2nd edition).

— Post-Chicago Antitrust: A Review and Critique 2001, Colum. Bus. L. Rev. 257 (2001) (Columbia Business Law Review).

Hubbard, *Bradley G.*/***Meehan***, *Taylor A.R.*/***Young***, *Kenneth A. (eds.)*: Vol. 80 (2013).

Huber, *Ernst Rudolf*: Dokumente zur Deutschen Verfassungsgeschichte, Vol. II: Deutsche Verfassungsdokumente 1851–1900, Stuttgart: Kohlhammer (3rd edition, 1986).

***Hughes**, Mark*: Logos that became legends: Icons from the world of advertising, The Independent, 4 January 2008.

***Hull**, David/**Geradin**, Damien/**Bogaert**, Peter/**Clancy**, Michael*: The Advocate General's Opinion in AstraZeneca v. Commission, E-Alert, Life Sciences, Covington & Burling LLP, 17 May 2012.

***Hulme**, E. Wyndham*:

— The History of the Patent System under the Prerogative and at Common Law, Law Quarterly Review, Vol. 46 (1896).

— The History of the Patent System Under the Prerogative and at Common Law, A Sequel, 16 Law Q. Rev. 44 (1900).

***Humpe**, Christophe/**Ritter**, Cyril*: Refusal to Deal, in GCLC Research Papers on Article 82 EC, Global Competition Law Centre, College of Europe, Bruges, Belgium, July 2005.

***Hutchens**, Beth*: Apple and Microsoft Fight Over "APP STORE" Trademark App, IPWatchDog, 17 January 2011.

***Hutton**, Susan M. (ed.)*: Intellectual Property & Antitrust 2009, Global Competition Review (GCR), Getting the Deal Through series.

***Ibbetson**, David J.*: A Historical Introduction to the Law of Obligations, Oxford: Oxford University Press (1999).

Instituut voor Informatierecht (Institute for Information Law): Study on the Implementation and Effect in Member States' Laws of Directive 2001/29/EC on the Harmonisation of Certain Aspects of Copyright and Related Rights in the Information Society, Executive Summary, February 2007, University of Amsterdam.

INTA, International Trademark Association:

— About, available at http://www.inta.org.

— Courts & Tribunals Subcommittee, Report on Best Practices in Conducting Surveys in Trademark Matters, available at http://www.inta.org.

— History, available at http://www.inta.org.

— Request for Action by the INTA Board of Directors, Initial Interest Confusion, 18 September 2006, and Report of the Online Use Subcommittee Concerning the Proposed Resolution on Initial Interest Confusion.

— Trademark Basics, Fact Sheets: Assignments, Licenses and Valuation, available at http://www.inta.org.

— Trademark Basics: A Guide for Business, available at http://www.inta.org.

Interbrand:

— About Us, available at http://www.interbrand.com.

— Best Global Brands – Previous Years, reports for 2000–2012, available from the drop-down menu at http://www.interbrand.com.

— Best Global Brands 2011, report available at http://interbrand.com.

— Best Global Brands 2012 – Apple, available at http://www.interbrand.com.

— Best Global Brands 2013, report available at http://www.interbrand.com.

— Best Global Brands 2014, report available at http://www.interbrand.com and http://www.bestglobalbrands.com.

— Best Global Brands: Our Methodology, available at http://www.interbrand.com.

— Brand Value by Region/Country, available at http://interbrand.com.

— Branding in the Post-digital World (2012), available at http://www.interbrand.com.

— Interbrand Released 14th Annual Best Global Brands Report, Press Release, 30 September 2013.

— Interbrand's Methodology Becomes the World's First ISO Certified Approach for Valuing Brands, Press Release, 1 December 2010.

— Methodology: Interbrand's method looks at the ongoing investment and management of the brand as a business asset, available at http://interbrand.com.

International Competition Network: History, available at http://www.internationalcompetitionnetwork.org.

International Court of Justice:

— Legality of the Threat or Use of Nuclear Weapons, Advisory Opinion of 8 July 1996, ICJ Reports (1996).

— The Court, available at http://www.icj-cij.org.

International Organization for Standardization: ISO 10668:2010 (Brand valuation – Requirements for monetary brand valuation).

Internet Archive: Legacy Tobacco Documents Library, hosted by the University of California San Francisco, available at https://archive.org.

Invention Geek: Beginning of US Trademark Laws, Patent Plaques, 2 September 2011, available at http://www.patentplaques.com/blog.

IP Australia (Australian PTO):

— Trade Mark History 1258288, 18 April 2011, available at http://pericles.ipaustralia.gov.au.

— Trade Mark History 1258288, 6 April 2011, available at http://pericles.ipaustralia.gov.au.

IPDL, Industrial Property Digital Library of the Japanese Patent Office:

— Trademarks, available at http://www.jpo.go.jp.

— Thermos, search results available at http://www3.ipdl.inpit.go.jp.

IPKat:

— Apps: do we regard them as a protected species?, 19 February 2013, available at http://ipkitten.blogspot.de.

— Get-up and go! Protecting interior features of stores, 28 March 2013, available at http://ipkitten.blogspot.de.

— Monday Miscellany, 24 December 2013, available at http://ipkitten.blogspot.de.

— Some additional thoughts on the BGH's landmark decision in Hard Rock Café, 10 February 2014, available at http://ipkitten.blogspot.de.

Italianer, *Alexander*: The new economic climate: driving competition in key sectors, Directorate General for Competition, Speech at the Annual Competition Policy Conference 2011, Chatham House, London, 24 June 2011.

Ivits, *Ellen*: Café Apfelkind gewinnt gegen Apple, Stern.de, 2 October 2013.

Jack In the Box: History, available at http://www.jackintheboxinc.com.

Jacob, *Ayla*: Apfelkind in der Südstadt: Apple bedrängt das Apfelkind, General-Anzieger, 21 October 2011.

Jane: Apple tells Chinese food company to change its logo, GoChengdoo, 6 September 2011.

Japan Patent Office: An international trend: 20th Annual Trilateral Conference, available at http://www.jpo.go.jp.

Jasinski, *Douglas M.*/***Kanter***, *Daniel*: DOJ Report on Section 2 of The Sherman Act: Skirmish or Schism?, White & Case publication DG0221, March 2009.

Jefferson, *Thomas*: Report on the policy of securing particular marks to Manufacturers, by Law, in Lipscomb, Andrew A. (ed.): The Writings of Thomas Jefferson (1905).

Jeffery, *Charlie*/***Lees***, *Charles (eds.)*: Issues in German Politics, Manchester: Manchester University Press (2003).

Jehoram, *Tobias Cohen*/***van Nispen***, *Constant*/***Huydecoper***, *Tony (eds.)*: European Trademark Law: Community Trademark Law and Harmonized National Trademark Law, AH Alphen aan den Rijn: Kluwer Law International BV (2010).

Joliet, *Rene*: Trademark Licensing agreements Under the EEC Law of Competition, 5 NW. J. Int'l L. & Bus. 755 (1983–84) (Northwestern Journal of International Law & Business).

Joyce, *Craig*: The ©©© Conference: Celebrating Copyright's Tri-Centennial Institute for Intellectual Property and Information Law Symposium: Prologue, Symposium, 47 Hous. L. Rev. 779 (2010) (Houston Law Review).

Justia: U.S. Law, Copyrights and Patents, available at http://law.justia.com.

Kaczorowska, *Alina*: European Union Law, Oxon: Routledge (2nd edition, 2011).

Kahney, *Leander*: Apple Doin' the Logo-Motion, Wired News, 26 September 2003.

Kamina, *Pascal*: Towards new forms of neighbouring rights within the European Union?, in **Vaver/Bently**: Intellectual Property in the New Millennium.

Kaplow, *Louis*: The Patent Antitrust Intersection: A Reappraisal, 97 Harv. L. Rev. 1813 (1984) (Harvard Law Review).

Kappa Alpha Theta: Theta Roots, available at http://www.kappaalphatheta.org.

Katyal, *Sonia K.*: Trademark Intersectionality, 57 UCLA L. Rev. 1601 (2010) (UCLA Law Review).

Katz, *Ariel*: Making Sense of Nonsense: Intellectual Property, Antitrust, and Market Power, 49 Ariz. L. Rev. 837 (2007) (Arizona Law Review).

Kavilanz, *Parija*: Trademark wars heat up. Be ready., CNNMoney, 1 December 2011.

Kawohl, *Friedemann*: Commentary on the German Imperial Copyright Act (1870), in **Bently/Kretschmer** (eds.): Primary Sources on Copyright.

Kaysen, *C.*/***Turner***, *D.*: Antitrust Policy, Cambridge: Harvard University Press (1959).

Keeling, *David T.*: Intellectual Property Rights in EU Law, Vol. I: Free Movement and Competition Law, Oxford: Oxford University Press (2003).

Kertcher, *Zack*/***Margalit***, *Ainat N.*: Challenges to Authority, Burden of Legitimisation: The Printing Press and the Internet, 10 Int'l J. Comm. L. & Pol'y 3 (2005) (International Journal of Communications Law and Policy).

***Kettemann**, Matthias C.*: Das Internet als internationales Schutzgut: Entwicklungsperspektiven des Internetvölkerrechts anlässlich des Arabischen Frühlings, ZaöRV 2012, 469 (Zeitschrift für ausländisches öffentliches Recht und Völkerrecht).

***Kim**, Minjeong*: The Representation of Two Competing Visions on the Fundamentals of Copyright: A Content Analysis of Associated Press News Coverage on Copyright, 2004–2009, 16 Comm. L. & Pol'y 49 (2011) (Communication Law & Policy).

***Kitch**, Edmund W.*: The Nature and Function of the Patent System, 20 J.L. & Econ. 265 (1977) (Journal of Law & Economics).

***Klein**, David M./**Glazer**, Daniel C.*: Reconsidering Initial Interest Confusion on the Internet, 93 TMR 1035 (2003) (Trademark Reporter).

***Klett**, Dr. Alexander R./**Schlüter**, Kathrin*: ONEL/OMEL-decision of the CJEU regarding genuine use – territorial borders are not relevant, Reed Smith LLP, 25 March 2013.

***Klett**, Dr. Alexander R./**Sonntag**, Dr. Matthias/**Wilske**, Dr. Stephan*: Intellectual Property Law in Germany: Protection, Enforcement and Dispute Resolution, C.H. Beck, Lexis/Nexis (2008).

***Klieger**, Robert N.*: Trademark Dilution: The Whittling Away of the Rational Basis for Trademark Protection, 58 U. Pitt. L. Rev. 789 (1997) (University of Pittsburgh Law Review).

***Knox**, Ron*: Global Competition Review, European Edition, 22 February 2013.

***Kohler**, Dr. Joseph:*

— Lehrbuch des Patentrechts in rechtsvergliechender Darstellung (Mannheim and Leipzig, 1908), available from the Max-Planck-Institut für europäische Rechtsgeschichte, Digitale Bibliothek, at http://dlib-pr.mpier.mpg.de.

— Die Idee des geistigen Eigenthums (1893).

— Lehrbuch des Patentrechts, Mannheim and Leipzig (1908).

— Handbuch des Deutschen Patentrechts in rechtsvergliechender Darstellung, Mannheim (1900), available from the Max-Planck-Institut für europäische Rechtsgeschichte, Digitale Bibliothek, at http://dlib-pr.mpier.mpg.de.

Kölner Stadt-Anzeiger: Lindt verliert im Teddy-Streit, 18 December 2012.

***Korah**, Valentine:*

— Intellectual property law in the context of competition law: "Consent" in relation to curbs of parallel trade in Europe, 25 Fordham Int'l L.J. 972 (2002) (Fordham International Law Journal).

— Intellectual Property Rights and the EC Competition Rules, Portland: Hart Publishing (2006).

Kotler, *Philip*: Marketing Insights from A to Z: 80 Concepts Every Manager Needs to Know, John Wiley & Sons, Inc. (2003).

Kozinski, *Alex*: Trademarks Unplugged, 68 N.Y.U. L. Rev. 960 (1993) (New York University Law Review).

Kraßer, *Rudolf*: Patentrecht: Ein Lehr- und Handbuch zum deutschen Patent- und Gebrauchsmuterrecht, Europäischen und Internationalen Patentrecht, Munich (6th edition, 2009).

Krattenmaker, *Thomas G.*/***Lande***, *Robert H.*/***Salop***, *Steven C.*: Monopoly Power and Market Power in Antitrust Law, Airlie House Conference on the Antitrust Alternative, 76 Geo. LJ 241 (1987) (Georgetown Law Journal).

Kreutzman, *Dr. Alix*: Neues Kartellrecht und geistiges Eigentum, Wettbewerb in Recht und Praxis (WRP), April 2006, 453–460.

Kühn, *Kai-Uwe S.*: Germany, Chapter 4, 115–150, in **Richardson/Graham**: Global Competition Policy, available at http://www.piie.com.

Kutzim, *Julian*: Markenrechtsstreit: Apple macht Zugeständnisse an Apfelkind, SpiegelOnline: Wirtschaft, 28 February 2013.

Kwall, *Roberta R.*: Copyright and the Moral Right: Is an American Marriage Possible?, 38 Vand. L. Rev. 1 (1985) (Vanderbilt Law Review).

Ladas, *Stephen P.*:

— Trademark Licensing and the Antitrust Law, 63 TMR 245 (1973) (Trademark Reporter).

— Patents, Trademarks, and Related Rights: National and international Protection, Cambridge: Harvard University Press (1975).

— The Community Trademark, available at http://www.ladas.com.

Lampert, *Michael A.*: Antitrust in IP Licensing: Selected Concerns and Considerations, ALI-ABA Course of Study Materials, Cross-Border Transactions: Intellectual Property and Related Issues, October 2007.

Landes, *William M.*/***Posner***, *Richard A.*:

— The Economics of Trademark Law, 78 TMR 267 (1988) (Trademark Reporter).

— Trademark Law: An Economic Perspective, 30 J.L. & Econ. 265 (1987) (Journal of Law & Economics).

Landschaftsverband Westfalen-Lippe: Westfälische Geschichte, available at http://www.lwl.org.

Lane, *Denise C.*: The Antico.unterfeiting Consumer Protection Act of 1995, 3 B.U. J. Sci & Tech. L. 14 (1997) (Boston University Journal of Science and Technology Law).

Lang, *John Temple*: Defining Legitimate Competition: Companies' Duties to Supply Competitors and Access to Essential Facilities, 18 Fordham Int'l L.J. 437 (1994) (Fordham International Law Journal).

Larkin, *Thomas Ardell*: Harmony in Disarray: The European Community Trademark System, 82 TMR 634 (1992) (Trademark Reporter).

Larrick, *Andrew*: Resource Guide for Researching Intellectual Property Law in an International Context, Arthur W. Diamond Law Library Research Guides, Columbia University Law School, June 2008.

Larson, *Erik*: Apple sues New York over logo, Los Angeles Times, 4 April 2008.

Lastowka, *Greg*:

— Google's Law, 73 Brook. L. Rev. 1327 (2008) (Brooklyn Law Review).

— Trademark's Daemons, Trademark: Today and Tomorrow, Institute for Intellectual Property & Information Law Symposium, 48 Hous. L. Rev. 779 (2011) (Houston Law Review).

Lavenue, *Lionel Marks*: Patent Infringement Against the United States and Government Contractors Under 28 U.S.C. § 1498 in the United States Court of Federal Claims, 2 J. Intell. Prop. L. 389 (1995) (Journal of Intellectual Property Law).

Lee, *Julian*:

— Apple bites over Woolworths logo, The Age: Business Day, 5 October 2009.

— Apple claims Woolies is getting fresh with new logo, The Sydney Morning Herald, Technology Section, 5 October 2009.

Lee, *Kirby W.*: Permitted Use of Patented Inventions in the United States: Why Prescription Drugs Do Not Merit Compulsory Licensing; 36 Ind. L. Rev. 175 (2003) (Indiana Law Review).

Lemley, *Mark A.*/***McKenna***, *Mark P.*:

— Is Pepsi Really a Substitute for Coke? Market Definition in Antitrust and IP, 100 Geo. L.J. 2055 (August 2010) (Georgetown Law Journal).

— Owning Mark(et)s, 109 Mich. L. Rev. 137 (2010) (Michigan Law Review).

Lemley, *Mark A.*:

— A New Balance Between IP and Antitrust, Antitrust and Intellectual Property in Global Context: A Symposium in Celebration of the Work of Lawrence A. Sullivan, 13 Sw. J.L. & Trade Am. 237 (2007) (Southwestern Journal of Law and Trade in the Americas).

— An Empirical Study of the Twenty-Year Patent Term, 22 AIPLA Q.J. 369 (1994) (American Intellectual Property Law Association Quarterly Journal).

— Beyond Preemption: The Law and Policy of Intellectual Property Licensing, 87 Calif. L. Rev. 111 (1999) (California Law Review).

— Ex Ante Versus Ex Post Justifications for Intellectual Property, 71 U. Chi. L. Rev. 129 (2004) (University of Chicago Law Review).

— Property, Intellectual Property, and Free Riding, 83 Tex. L. Rev. 1031 (2005) (Texas Law Review).

— Romantic Authorship and the Rhetoric of Property, 75 Tex. L. Rev. 873, (1996) (Texas Law Review).

— The Economic Irrationality of the Patent Misuse Doctrine, 78 Calif. L. Rev. 1599 (1990) (California Law Review).

— The Modern Lanham Act and the Death of Common Sense, 108 Yale L.J. 1687 (1999) (Yale Law Journal).

— The Surprising Virtues of Treating Trade Secrets as IP Rights, 61 Stan. L. Rev. 311 (2008) (Stanford Law Review).

Lepore, *Jill*: Benched, The New Yorker, 77–82, 18 June 2012.

Lessig, *Lawrence*:

— The Creative Commons, 65 Mont. L. Rev. 1 (2004) (Montana Law Review).

— Copyright's First Amendment, 48 UCLA L. Rev. 1057 (2001) (UCLA Law Review).

— Free Culture: The Nature and Future of Creativity, New York: Penguin Press (2004).

— The Creative Commons, 65 Mont. L. Rev. 1 (2004) (Montana Law Review).

Lévêque, *François/****Shelanski****, Howard (eds.)*: Antitrust, Patents and Copyright: EU and US Perspectives, Edward Elgar Publishing, Inc. (2005).

Leymore, *Varda L.*: Hidden Myth: Structure & Symbolism in Advertising, New York: Basic Books, Inc. (1975).

Library of Congress:

— A Century of Lawmaking for a New Nation: U.S. Congressional Documents and Debates, 1774–1875, available at http://memory.loc.gov.

— Primary Documents in American History: Judiciary Act of 1789, at http://www.loc.gov.

— U.S. States and Territories, available at http://www.loc.gov.

Lienhard, *John H.*: Engines of Our Ingenuity – No. 663: Zippers and Design, available at http://www.uh.edu.

Lim, *Daryl*: Misconduct in Standard Setting: The Case for Patent Misuse, IDEA: The Intellectual Property Law Review, Franklin Pierce Law Center (2011).

Lind, *Robert C.*/***Kleymenova***, *Anya V.*/***Miauton***, *Marie*/***Muysert***, *Paul*: Report on Multiparty Licensing, Charles River Associates, Ltd., 22 April 2003.

Lindbeck, *Assar (ed.)*: Nobel Lectures, Economics 1969–1980, Singapore: World Scientific Publishing Co. (1992).

Lindberg, *Van*: Intellectual Property and Open Source: A Practical Guide to Protecting Code, O'Reilly Media, Inc. (2008).

Lipscomb, *Ernest B. III*: Lipscomb's Walker on Patents (3rd edition, 1989).

Lipsky, *Abbott B. Jr.*/***Kory*** *Wilmot*: The Foreign Trade Antitrust Improvements Act: Did Arbaugh Erase Decades of Consensus Building?, The Antitrust Source, August 2013.

Lipsky, *Abbott B.*: Current Antitrust Division Views on Patent Licensing Practices, Deputy Assistant Attorney General Antitrust Division, 50 Antitrust L.J. 515 (1981) (Antitrust Law Journal).

Lipstein, *Robert*/***Blumenfeld***, *Jeffrey*/***Antoine***, *Olivier*/***Carson***, *Ty*: United States, in Hutton (ed.): Intellectual Property & Antitrust.

Lisby, *Gregory C.*: No Place in the Law: The Ignominy of Criminal Libel in American Jurisprudence, 9 Comm. L. & Pol'y 433 (Autumn 2004) (Communication Law and Policy).

Litman, *Jessica*: Breakfast with Batman: The Public Interest in the Advertising Age, 108 Yale L.J. 1717 (1999) (Yale Law Journal).

Little, *Trevor*: European Union: OHIM gets green light to expand activities, World Trademark Review Blog, 26 March 2012.

Liu, *Joe*: Overview of Trademark Law, Berkman Center for Internet and Society, Harvard Law School, Spring 1998, available at http://cyber.law.harvard.edu.

Lizerbram, *David*: Tiffany Setting – A Generic Term?, Navigating Business and Branding, 24 April 2013.

Lockhart, *Timothy J.*: Did you know … There's a Trademark Graveyard?, INTA Bulletin, Vol. 63, No. 923, 15 December 2008.

Loewenheim, *Ulrich (ed.)*: Handbuch des Urheberrechts, C.H. Beck (2nd edition, 2010).

Loewenheim, *Ulrich*: Warenzeichen und Wettbewerbsbeschränkung, Eine rechtsvergleichende Untersuchung über das Verhältnis des Warenzeichenrechts zum deutschen und europäischen Kartellrecht, Bad Homburg: Athenäum (1970).

Long, *Clarisa*: Dilution, 106 Colum. L. Rev. 1029 (2006) (Columbia Law Review).

Louw, *Andre M.*: Ambush Marketing & the Mega-Event Monopoly: How Laws are Abused to Protect Commercial Rights to Major Sporting Events, ASSER International Sports Law Series, 2012.

Lowe, *Philip*:

— Current Issues of EU Competition Law: The New Competition Enforcement Regime, 24 NW. J. Int'l L. & Bus 567 (2004) (Northwestern Journal of International Law & Business).

— How different is EU anti-trust? A route map for advisors: An overview of EU competition law and policy on commercial practices, Director General DG Competition, Remarks made at the American Bar Association meeting, Brussels, 16 October 2003.

Lowe, *Roger*: An Apple A Decade, Keeps The Lawyers At Work, The London Times, 7 September 2004.

Luepke, *Marcus H.H.*: Taking Unfair Advantage or Diluting a Famous Mark – A 20/20 Perspective on the Blurred Differences Between U.S. and E.U Dilution Law, 98 TMR 789 (2008) (Trademark Reporter).

Lunney, *Glynn S.*: Trademark Monopolies, 48 Emory L.J. 367 (1999) (Emory Law Journal).

Mackaay, *Ejan*: Schools and Approaches (0500), in **Bouckaert**/**De Geest**: Encyclopedia of Law and Economics.

MacLeod, *Christine*: Inventing the Industrial Revolution: The English Patent System, 1660–1800, Cambridge: Cambridge University Press (2002).

MacQueen, *Hector*/***Waelde***, *Charlotte*/***Laurie***, *Graham*: Contemporary Intellectual Property: Law and Policy, Oxford: Oxford University Press (2nd edition, 2010).

Madow, *Michael*: Private Ownership of Public Image: Popular Culture and Publicity Rights, 81 Calif. L. Rev. 127 (1993) (California Law Review).

Maetschke, *Matthias*: Ursprünge der Zwangskartellgesetzgebung: Der Entwurf eines Gesetzes über den Absatz von Kalisalzen vom 12. Dezember 1909, Baden-Baden: Nomos (2008).

Maggiolino, *Mariateresa*: Intellectual Property and Antitrust: A Comparative Economic Analysis of US and EU Law, Cheltenham: Edward Elgar Publishing (2011).

Magid, *Julie Manning*/***Cox***, *Anthony D.*/***Cox***, *Dena S.*: Quantifying Brand Image: Empirical Evidence of Trademark Dilution, 43 Am. Bus. L.J. 1 (2006) (American Business Law Journal).

Maier, *Paul*: OHIM's Role in European Trademark Harmonization: Past, Present and Future, 23 Fordham Intell. Prop. Media & Ent. L.J. 687 (2013) (Fordham Intellectual Property, Media & Entertainment Law Journal).

Marques: The Identity of Brand Owners, Ask the TM Judges: a report from the UK, 11 November 2013.

Martino, *Tony*: Trademark Dilution, Oxford: Oxford University Press (1996).

Mateus, *Abel M.*/***Moreira***, *Teresa (eds.)*: Competition Law and Economics: Advances in Competition Policy Enforcement in the EU and North America, in association with the Portuguese Competition Authority, Cheltenham: Edward Elgar Publishing Limited (2010).

Matyszczyk, *Chris*: Apple objects to Chinese food maker's logo, report says: A maker of flour and noodles reportedly receives a letter from Apple, asking it to change its logo, which might seem, to objective eyes, to resemble LG's more than Apple's, CNET News, 6 September 2011.

Maxeiner, *James*: Policy and Methods in German and American Antitrust Law, New York: Praeger (1986).

Max-Planck-Institut für europäische Rechtsgeschichte: Digitale Bibliothek, available at http://dlib-pr.mpier.mpg.de/.

McAffee, *Thomas B.*: The Dilemma of American Federalism: Power to the People, the States, or the Federal Government?: Federalism and the Protection of Rights: The Modern Ninth Amendment's Spreading Confusion, 1996 B.Y.U.L. Rev. 351 (1996) (Brigham Young University Law Review).

McCarthy, *J. Thomas*:

— Dilution of a Trademark: European and United States Law Compared, 94 TMR 1163 (November-December 2004) (Trademark Reporter).

— Lanham Act 43(a): The Sleeping Giant is Now Wide Awake, 59 Law & Contemp. Probs. 45 (1996) (Law & Contemporary Problems).

— McCarthy on Trademarks and Unfair Competition, Eagen: West Publishing (4th edition, 1996).

— Proving a Trademark Has Been Diluted: Theories or Facts?, 41 Hous. L. Rev. 713 (2004) (Houston Law Review).

McCarthy, *Michael*: Lance Armstrong Blew His Last Chance, Experts Say – Other Disgraced Athletes Have Made Comebacks, So How Marketable Is the Former Champion Cyclist? Not at all, Ad Age Media News, 11 January 2013.

McClure, *Daniel M.*: Trademarks and Unfair Competition: A Critical History of Legal Thought. 69 TMR 305 (1979) (Trademark Reporter).

McClure, *Samuel M./**Li**, Jian/**Tomlin**, Damon/**Cypert**, Kim S./**Montague**, Latané M./**Montague**, P. Read*: Neural Correlates of Behavioral Preference for Culturally Familiar Drinks, Neuron, Vol. 44, 379–387, 14 October 2004.

McDaniel, *Katherine L.*:

— Slammed! How Trademark Laws Hurt the Little Guy, New Matter, The State Bar of California, Intellectual Property Section, Vol. 35, Nr. 3, 35–36 (2010).

— The Madrid Protocol/Section 44: More Bad Trade Policy?, New Matter, The State Bar of California, Intellectual Property Section, Vol. 36, Nr. 4, 33–35 (2011).

McDonald, *J. Bruce*: Antitrust Division Update: Trinko and Microsoft, Deputy Assistant Attorney General, Antitrust Division, U.S. Department of Justice, Remarks before the Houston Bar Association, Antitrust and Trade Regulation Section, 8 April 2004.

McGrew, *Anthony G./**Wilson**, M. J. (eds.)*: Decision Making: Approaches and Analysis, The Open University, Manchester: Manchester University Press (1982).

McKenna, *Mark P.*:

— The Normative Foundations of Trademark Law, 82 Notre Dame L. Rev. 1839 (2007) (Notre Dame Law Review).

— Trademark Use and the Problem of Source, 2009 U. Ill. L. Rev. 773 (2009) (University of Illinois Law Review).

Meisenheimer, *Lucky*: Lucky's History of the Yo-Yo, available at http://www.yoyos.net.

Meredith, *Sandra*/***Nolan***, *Donal (eds.)*: Oxford University Standard for the Citation of Legal Authorities (OSCOLA), Faculty of Law, University of Oxford (4th edition, 2012).

Mergers, *Robert Patrick*/***Duffy***, *John Fitzgerald*: Patent Law & Policy: Cases and Materials 1–13 (3rd edition, 2002).

Metzler, *Falk*: Will the Unified EU Patent Court be Situated in Munich, or rather Warsaw?, Visae Patentes, 21 October 2011.

Meurer, *Michael J.*:

— Controlling Opportunistic and Anti-Competitive Intellectual Property Litigation, 44 B.C. L. Rev. 509 (2003) (Boston College Law Review).

— The Settlement of Patent Litigation, 20 RAND J. Econ. 77 (1989) (RAND Journal of Economics).

Miller, *Joseph Scott*:

— This Bitter Has Some Sweet: Potential Antitrust Enforcement Benefits from Patent Law's Procedural Rules, 70 Antitrust L.J. 875 (2003) (Antitrust Law Journal).

— Patent Ships Sail an Antitrust Sea, Symposium: At the Intersection of Antitrust and Intellectual Property Law: Looking Both Ways to Avoid a Collision, 30 Seattle Univ. L. R. 395 (Winter 2007) (Seattle University Law Review).

Minnesota Historical Society: The 1968 Exhibit, in partnership with the Atlanta History Center, the Chicago History Museum and the Oakland Museum of California, available at http://the1968exhibit.org.

Monti, *Mario*: Market definition as a cornerstone of EU Competition Policy, European Commissioner for Competition Policy, SPEECH/01/439, Workshop on Market Definition, Helsinki Fair Centre, Helsinki, 5 October 2001.

Moore, *Mattthew*: Apple demands Woolworths drops new logo, The Telegraph, 5 October 2009.

Morano, *Michael F.*: Legislating in the Face of New Technology: Copyright Laws for the Digital Age, 20 Fordham Int'l L.J. 1374 (1997) (Fordham International Law Journal).

Moskin, *Jonathan E.*: Dilution Act: Patent Medicine for Trademark Ailment?, New York Law Journal, 8 March 1996.

Mueller, *Charles E.*: Source of Monopoly Power: A Phenomenon Called "Product Differentiation", 18 Am. U. L. Rev. 1 (1968) (The American University Law Review).

Müller, *Felix*: The New Council Regulation (EC) No. 1/2003 on the Implementation of the Rules on Competition, 5 German Law Journal 722 (2004).

Murphy Bed Company: The History of Murphy Bed, available at http://www.murphybedcompany.com.

Murray, *Peter L.*/***Sturner***, *Rolf*: German Civil Justice, Carolina Academic Press (2004).

Myers, *Gary*: Litigation as a Predatory Practice, 80 Ky. L.J. 565 (1992) (Kentucky Law Journal).

Mylly, *Tuomas*: Intellectual property and competition law in the information society, in Geiger (ed.): Constructing European Intellectual Property.

Nadel, *Mark S.*: Questioning the Economic Justification for Copyrights, draft manuscript, 14 February 2003.

Nathenson, *Ira S.*: Civil Procedures for a World of Shared and User-Generated Content, 48 U. Louisville L. Rev. 911 (2010) (University of Louisville Law Review).

Natur-Pack: GREEN DOT - European Court judgement, available at http://www.naturpack.sk.

Nesvold, *H. Peter*/***Pollard***, *Lisa M*: Half a Century of Federal Trademark Protection: The Lanham Act Turns Fifty, 7 Fordham Intell. Prop. Media & Ent. L.J. 49 (1996) (Fordham Intellectual Property, Media and Entertainment Law Journal).

Newman, *Daniel E.*: Portraying a Branded World, 2008 U. Ill. J.L. Tech. & Pol'y 357 (2008) (University of Illinois Journal of Law, Technology & Policy).

Newman, *Matthew*/***Crofts***, *Lewis*: Publishers can't rely on antitrust rules to resolve alleged IP problems with Google, Almunia says, 9 December 2013, MLex.

Nike, Inc., History & Heritage, available at http://nikeinc.com.

Nims, *Harry D.*: The Law of Unfair Competition and Trade-Marks, New York: Baker, Voorhis & Co. (4th edition, 1947).

Nobel Foundation: Paul A. Samuelson – Biography, available at http://www.nobelprize.org.

Nörr, *Knut Wolfgang*: Die Leiden des Privatrechts: Kartelle in Deutschland von der Holzstoffkartellentscheidung zum Gesetz gegen Wettbewerbsbeschrankungen, Tübingen: J.C.B. Mohr (Paul Siebeck) (1994).

NYSE, New York Stock Exchange: Walgreens (WAG), available at http://www.nyse.com.

O'Callaghan, *Kieron*/***Hutt***, *Giles*: Harmonisation of EU contract law: a step closer?, Practical Law Company, 15 November 2010.

O'Melinn, *Liam Séamus*: The Recording Industry v. James Madison, aka "Publius": The Inversion of Culture and Copyright, 35 Seattle Univ. L. R. 75 (2001) (Seattle University Law Review).

O'Rourke, *Kenneth R*/***McIntyre***, *Stephen*: United States, in Hutton (ed.): Intellectual Property & Antitrust.

Office of Fair Trading (OFT):

— Article 101(3) – A discussion of narrow versus broad definition of benefits, Summary note for OFT breakfast roundtable (2010).

— Assessment of market power: Understanding competition law, December 2004.

Office of the Secretary of the Senate:

— Constitution of the United States, available at http://www.senate.gov.

— U.S. Senate, available at http://www.senate.gov.

Official Journal of the European Union (OJEC): what is the OJEC, available at http://www.ojec.com.

OHIM, Office for Harmonization in the Internal Market:

— Decisions of the Office, available at http://oami.europa.eu.

— Examination Guidelines, available at https://oami.europa.eu.

— Gemeinschaftsmarkengerichte, available at http://oami.europa.eu.

— List of Community trade mark courts, available at http://oami.europa.eu.

— National Law Relating to the Community Trade Mark and the Community Design, Information Brochure of the Office for Harmonization in the Internal Market (Trade Marks and Designs) (3rd edition, December 2006).

— Observatory transfer agreed by European Parliament, Press Release, 14 February 2012.

— Regulations and related texts, available at http://oami.europa.eu.

— Seat Agreement between the Kingdom of Spain and the Office for Harmonization in the Internal Market – Trade Marks and Designs – (OHIM), Press Release (20 September 2011).

— What is a Community Trade Mark?, available at http://oami.europa.eu.

Ohlgart, *Dr. Dietrich C.*: Gebrauch der Marke eines Dritten ohne Verwechslungsgefahr (95) – Bericht für die Deutsche Landesgruppe erstattet, GRUR Int. 1989, 211.

Ohlhausen, *Maureen K.*:

— A Pragmatist's Approach to Navigating the Intersection of IP and Antitrust, Commissioner, Federal Trade Commission, Special Address at the 2013 Standards and Patents Conference, London, United Kingdom, 4 December 2013.

— Statement In the Matter of Robert Bosch GmbH, Case Nr. 121–0081, 26 November 2012.

Ohly, *Ansgar*/***Klippel***, *Diethelm (eds.)*: Geistiges Eigentum und Gemeinfreiheit, Tübingen: Mohr Siebeck (2007).

Ohly, *Ansgar*: Geistiges Eigentum und Wettbewerbsrecht: Konflikt oder Symbiose?, in **Ohly/Klippel**: Geistiges Eigentum und Gemeinfreiheit.

Old School: Back to the 80s: Nike Air 'Revolution' Commercial from 1987 – Kickin' it Old School, 18 March 2012.

Olins, *Wally*: Corporate Identity, Harvard Business School Press (1990).

Olivarez-Giles, *Nathan*: Judge Says No One Is Confusing Apple's App Store and Amazon's Appstore, Wired, 2 January 2013.

Oliver, *Valerie*: History of the Yo-Yo (1996), available at http://www.spintastics.com.

Oltermann, *Philip*: Apfelkind cafe owner wins trademark battle with Apple: US firm withdraws objection to Bonn cafe's trademark application in Germany after two-year legal correspondence; The Guardian, 7 October 2013.

Omega Psi Phi: About Omega, available at http://www.omegapsiphifraternity.org.

Omega: Omega: A Journey Through Time, Omega Literature, available at http://www.omegawatches.com.

Ong, *Josh*: iCloud Communications drops trademark suit; Apple in dispute over Chinese logo, Apple Insider, 6 September 2011.

Otis Elevator Company: Otis: A Visual Time Line, 1895: A New Word is Coined, available at http://www.otisworldwide.com.

Oxford University Press: Citing of Legal Materials (Including Legal Tables), available at http://global.oup.com.

Oxford University, Faculty of Law & Bodleian Law Library: Legal Research & Mooting Skills Programme (LRMSP), available at http://www.law.ox.ac.uk.

Papandreou, *A.G.*: The Economic Effect of Trademarks, 44 Cal. L. Rev. 503 (1956) (California Law Review).

Pareles, *Jon*: Nike Calls Beatles Suit Groundless, The New York Times, Arts, 5 August 1987.

Parsons, *Ralph Linoleum*: A Chiswick Invention, Brentford & Chiswick Local History Journal No 5 (1996).

Paster, *Benjamin G.*: Trademarks – Their Early History, 59 TMR 551 (1969) (Trademark Reporter).

Pate, *R. Hewitt*:

— Antitrust and Intellectual Property, Acting Assistant Attorney General, Antitrust Division, U.S. Department of Justice, Address before the American Intellectual Property Law Association, Marco Island, Florida, 24 January 2003.

— Refusals to Deal and Essential Facilities, Testimony Submitted On Behalf of the United States Telecom Association, DOJ/FTC Hearings on Single-Firm Conduct, Washington, DC, 18 July 2006.

Patterson, *L. Ray*: The DMCA: A Modern Version of the Licensing Act of 1662, 10 J. Intell. Prop. L. 33 (2002) (Journal of Intellectual Property Law).

Pattishall, *Beverly W.*: Two Hundred Years of American Trademark Law, 68 TMR 121 (March, 1978 – April, 1978) (Trademark Reporter); originally published as "Two Hundred Years of English and American Patent, Trademark and Copyright Law", published by the ABA, American Bar Association, Section of Patent, Trademark and Copyright Law (1977).

Pearce, *Kerry A.*/***Hoover***, *Kevin D.*: After the Revolution: Paul Samuelson and the Textbook Keynesian Model, History of Political Economy, Vol. 27, Issue 5, 183–216 (1995).

Peritz, *Rudolf J.*:

— A Genealogy of Vertical Restraints Doctrine, 40 Hastings L.J. 511 (1989) (Hastings Law Journal).

— Frontiers of Legal Thought I: A Counter-History of Antitrust Law, 1990 Duke L.J. 263 (1990) (Duke Law Journal).

— The "Rule of Reason" in Antitrust Law: Property Logic in Restraint of Competition, 40 Hastings L.J. 285 (1989) (Hastings Law Journal).

— Competition policy and its implications for intellectual property rights in the United States, in Anderman, Steven D. (ed.): The Interface between

Intellectual Property Rights and Competition Policy, Cambridge: Cambridge University Press (2007).

Perkins, *David*: The Apple Computer vs Apple Corps Trademark Litigation, Arnold & Porter (UK) LLP (December 2011).

Perlman, *Harvey S.*: Taking the Protection-Access Tradeoff Seriously, 53 Vand. L. Rev. 1831 (2000) (Vanderbilt Law Review).

Perschbacher, *Rex R.*/***Bassett***, *Debra Lyn*: The End of Law, 84 B.U. L. Rev. 1 (2004) (Boston University Law Review).

Perzanowski, *Aaron*/***Schultz***, *Jason*: Digital Exhaustion, 58 UCLA L. Rev. 889 (2001) (UCLA Law Review).

Phillips, *Jeremy (IPKat)*: Assessing risks – Tea-time reflections by the IPKat and Merpel, Assessing risk 2: the trouble with trade marks, GRUR Newsletter 02/2013, 11.

Phillips, *Jeremy*/***Stanes***, *Simon*: Losing its fizz: the end of the Euro-Bud dispute?, The IP Kat, 22 January 2013, available at http://ipkitten.blogspot.de.

Pierce, *Kenneth R.*: The Trademark Law Revision Act: Origins of the Use Requirement and an Overview of the New Federal Trademark Law, Florida Bar Journal, Nr. 64, May 1990.

Pitofsky, *Robert*:

— Antitrust and Intellectual Property: Unresolved Issues at the Heart of the New Economy, Remarks Before the Antitrust, Technology and Intellectual Property Conference, Berkeley Center for Law and Technology, University of California, Berkeley, 2 March 2001.

— Challenges of the New Economy: Issues at the Intersection of Antitrust and Intellectual Property, Remarks Before the American Antitrust Institute Conference: An Agenda for Antitrust in the 21st Century, 15 June 2000.

— Past, Present, and Future of Antitrust Enforcement at the Federal Trade Commission, 72 U. Chi. L. Rev. 209 (2005) (University of Chicago Law Review).

Ploman, *Edward W.*/***Hamilton***; *L. Clark*: Copyright: Intellectual Property in the Information Age, London: Routledge & Kegan Paul (1980).

Pollock, *Earl E.*: Alternative Distributor Methods after Schwinn, 63 Nevada University Law Review 595 (1968) (Nevada University Law Review).

Pomerantz, *Dorothy*: Don't Hire Tiger Woods or Lance Armstrong For Your Ad Campaign, Forbes.com, 13 January 2011.

Popple, *Louise*/***Rendle***, *Adam*/***Suchopar***, *Anna*: Trade marks: Appellations of origin defeat CTM application for BUD, Journal of Intellectual Property Law & Practice (2009) 4 (6): 390–392.

Porcelli, *Frank*: Bowman v. Monsanto and an Introduction to the Patent Exhaustion/First Sale Doctrine in the United States, 1/2013 GRUR Int. 27–32.

Port, *Kenneth L.*:

— The "Unnatural" Expansion of Trademark Rights: Is a Federal Dilution Statute Necessary?, 18 Seton Hall Legis. J. 433 (1994) (Seton Hall Legislative Journal).

— The Congressional Expansion of American Trademark Law: A Civil Law System in the making, 35 Wake Forest L. Rev. 827 (2000) (Wake Forest Law Review).

— The Illegitimacy of Trademark Incontestability, 26 Ind. L. Rev. 519 (1993) (Indiana Law Review).

— Trademark Extortion: The End of Trademark Law, 65 Wash. & Lee L. Rev. 585 (2008) (Washington & Lee Law Review).

Posner, *Richard A.*:

— Antitrust in the new Economy, 68 Antitrust L.J. 925 (2001) (Antitrust Law Journal).

— Goodbye to the Bluebook, 53 U. Chi. L. Rev. 1343 (1986) (University of Chicago Law Review).

— The BlueBook Blues, 120 Yale L.J. 850 (2011) (Yale Law Journal).

Potere, *Michael*: Who Will Watch the Watchmen?: Citizens Recording Police Conduct, 106 Nw. U.L. Rev. 273 (2012) (Northwestern University Law Review).

Poulter, *Allan*/***Cassidy***, *Leighton*: Unjustifiable Threats in UK Trade Mark Actions: should the Unjustifiable Threats Provisions be maintained?, Field Fisher Waterhouse, 13 March 2007.

Powell, *Mark*/***Czapracka***, *Katarzyna*: CPI Antitrust Chronicle: Recent EU Antitrust Investigations into Financial Services – What Is the Scope for Antitrust Intervention?, White & Case, July 2011.

Practical Law Company:

— Overview: EU competition law, published by Practical Law Publishing Limited (2011).

— Trade marks: Registration and portfolio management, IPIT & Communications, Practice Note, published by Practical Law Publishing Limited.

Preserving History: Trademark Timeline, 82 TMR 1021 (1992) (Trademark Reporter).

Professional Tree and Garden Service, Pruning Services Cornwall, available at http://falmouthtreesurgery.co.uk.

Prosser, *William L.*: Handbook of the Law of Torts (3rd edition, 1964).

Purcher, *Jack*:

— Fujitsu Assigns their Entire Interest in iPad to Apple, Patently Apple, 27 March 2010.

— The Beatles' Apple Corps Logo is now a Registered TM of Apple, Patently Apple, 26 October 2012.

Purvis, *Sue A.*: What Every Small and Medium Sized Business Should Know About Intellectual Property, U.S. Patent and Trademark Office, Department of Commerce, 25 February 2013.

Q College:

— Apples and Oranges: The VSBT vs. Apple Inc. Logo Dispute, Q College, Victoria's School for Business Technology, available at http://www.qcollege.ca.

— Victoria's School for Business Technology, available at http://www.qcollege.ca.

Qinghu, *An*: Well-Known Marks & China's System of Well-Known Mark Protection, Director General of the Trademark Office, SAIC, Vol 95, Nr. 3, Trademark Reporter 705, May-June 2005.

Radin, *Margaret Jane*: Information Tangibility, Chapter 17, 395–418, in Granstrand, Ove: Economics, Law and Intellectual Property.

Ramsey, *Lisa P.*: Free Speech and International Obligations to Protect Trademarks, 35 Yale J. Int'l L. 405 (2010) (Yale Journal of International Law).

Randag, *Sarah*: Xerox Enlisting Hollywood in Fight Against "Genericide" with Ad, ABAJournal.com, 11 March 2010.

Raphael, *JR*: Apple's Logo Lunacy: 5 Previous Trademark Tiffs, PCWorld, 5 October 2009.

Raszl, *Ivan*: Interview with Rob Janoff, designer of the Apple logo, Creative Bits, 3 August 2009.

Rayle, *Rudolf*: The Trend Towards Enhancing Trademark Owners' Rights – A Comparative Study of U.S. and German Trademark Law, 7 J. Intell. Prop. L. 227 (2000) (Journal of Intellectual Property Law).

Regibeau, *Pierre*/***Rockett***, *Katharine*: European Commission, Assessment of Potential Anticompetitive Conduct in the Field of Intellectual Property Rights and Assessment of the Interplay Between Competition Policy and IPR Protection, European Commission contract COMP/2010/16, November 2011.

Reichman, *J.H.*:

— Charting the Collapse of the Patent-Copyright Dichotomy: Premises for a Restructured International Intellectual Property System, 13 Cardozo Arts & Ent. L.J. 475 (1993) (Cardozo Arts & Entertainment Law Journal).

— The TRIPS Component of the GATT's Uruguay Round: Competitive Prospects for Intellectual Property Owners in an Integrated World Market, 4 Fordham Intell. Prop. Media & Ent. L.J. 171 (1993) (Fordham Intellectual Property, Media and Entertainment Law Journal).

Reindl, *Andreas*: Intellectual Property and Intra-Community Trade, 20 Fordham Int'l L.J. 819 (1997) (Fordham International Law Journal).

Rest, *Dr. Alfred*: Köln, Neue Tendenzen im internationalen Umwelthaftungsrecht - Völkerrechtliche und international-privatrechtliche Aspekte, NJW 1989, 2153 (Neue Juristische Wochenschrift).

Rich, *Hon. Giles S.*: Are Letters Patent Grants of Monopoly?, 15 W. New Eng. L. Rev. 239 (1993) (Western New England Law Review).

Richardson, *J. David*/***Graham***, *Edward M. (eds.)*: Global Competition Policy, Washington, D.C.: Institute for International Economics (1997).

Richardson, *Megan*: Trade Marks and Language, 26 Sydney L. Rev. 193 (2004) (Sydney Law Review).

Ricker, *Thomas*: Apple drops "Computer" from name, Engadget, AOL Inc., 9 January 2007.

Ridgway, *William E.*: Revitalizing the Doctrine of Trademark Misuse, 21 Berkeley Tech. L.J. 1547 (2006) (Berkeley Technology Law Journal).

Riehle, *Gerhard*: Immaterialgüterschutz in Sekundärmärkten, 175–194, in **Geiss/Gerstenmaier/Mailander**: Festschrift für Karl Peter Mailänder.

Rill, *James F.*: Remarks presented to Federal Trade Commission and Department of Justice Hearings on Section 2 of the Sherman Act: Single-Firm Conduct as Related to Competition, Session on International Issues (12 September 2006).

Roberts, *Jr., John G.*: Lecture: What Makes the D.C. Circuit Different? A Historical View, 92 Va. L. Rev. 375 (Virginia Law Review) (2006).

Robinson, *Thomas N./****Borzekowski***, *Dina L. G./****Matheson***, *Donna M./****Kraemer***, *Helena C.*: Effects of Fast Food Branding on Young Children's Taste Preferences, Archives of Pediatrics & Adolescent Medicine (now JAMA Pediatrics), Vol. 161, No. 8, 792–797, August 2007.

Robinson, *William C.*: The Law of Patents for Useful Inventions, Boston: Little, Brown, and Co. (1890).

Rodbard, *Matt*: I Invented … the Apple Logo, first published in Sync Magazine, republished 29 March 2009.

Rodgers, *Paul*: United States Constitutional Law: An Introduction, Jefferson: McFarland & Company, Inc. (2011).

Rogers, *Edward S.*:

— Good Will, Trade-Marks and Unfair Trading, Chicago: A.W. Shaw Company (1919).

— Some Historical Matter Concerning Trade-Marks, 62 TMR 239 (1972) (Trademark Reporter).

Rohnke, *Christian/****Thiering***, *Frederik*: Die Rechtsprechung des EuGH und des BGH zum Markenrecht seit dem Jahr 2012, GRUR 20131073-1086.

Rosch, *J. Thomas*: Some Thoughts on the Role of Intellectual Property in Innovation Market Cases and Refusals to License, Commissioner, Federal Trade Commission, Remarks before the Conference on Antitrust and Digital Enforcement in the Technology Sector, Menlo Park, California, 31 January 2011.

Rose, *Simone A./****Jessup***, *Debra R.*: Whose Rules Rule? Resolving Ethical Conflicts During the Simultaneous Representation of Clients in Patent Prosecution, 12 Fed. Cir. B.J. 571 (2003) (Federal Circuit Bar Journal).

Rosen, *Zvi S.*: In Search of the Trade-Mark Cases: The Nascent Treaty Power and the Turbulent Origins of Federal Trademark Law, 83 St. John's L. Rev. 827 (2010) (St. John's Law Review).

Ruess, *Peter/Obex*, Hannes: Rechtserhaltende Benutzung einer Gemeinschaftsmarke nach der Entscheidung ONEL./. OMEL – von rechtlichen und wirtschaftlichen Realitäten, Markenrecht 03/2013, 101-105.

Rule, *Charles F.*: The Antitrust Implications of International Licensing: After the Nine No-Nos; Remarks to the Legal Conference sponsored by the World Trade Association and The Cincinnati Patent Law Association, 21 October 1986.

Ruston, *Gerald*: On the Origin of Trademarks, 45 TMR 127 (1955) (Trademark Reporter).

Ryan, *Patrick S.*: DoubleMint: Case C-191/01, Office for Harmonisation in the Internal Market (Trade Marks and Designs) v WM. Wrigley Jr. Company (ECJ October 23, 2003), 10 Colum. J. Eur. L. 393 (2004) (Columbia Journal of European Law).

Sack, *Rolf*: Die abstrakte Verwechslungsgefahr im Markenrecht, GRUR 2013.

Samson, *Ted*: Apple fights NYC over green apple logo, InfoWorld, 7 April 2008.

Samuelson, *Pamela*:

— Information as Property: Do Ruckelshaus and Carpenter Signal a Changing Direction in Intellectual Property Law?, 38 Cath. U.L. Rev. 365(1989) (Catholic University Law Review.

— The Uneasy Case for Software Copyrights Revisited, 79 Geo. Wash. L. Rev. 1746 (2010) (George Washington Law Review).

Samuelson, *Paul A.*:

— Economics, New York: McGraw-Hill Inc. (1976).

— "Economics" at Fifty: Remarks on the Occasion of the Anniversary of Publication, The Journal of Economic Education, Vol. 30, No. 4, 352–363 (Autumn, 1999).

— Problems of Economic Organization; originally published in Samuelson, Paul: Economics; reprinted in **McGrew/Wilson**: Decision Making: Approaches and Analysis, 67–86.

Sanders, *Anselm Kamperman*: Odol: The Introduction of a Watery Concept with Steeled Resilience, Chapter 4, 51-61, in **Heath/Sanders**: Landmark Intellectual Property Cases and Their Legacy.

Sanford, *Glen*: Apple History – iMac, available at http://apple-history.com.

Schechter, *Frank I.*:

— The Historical Foundations of the Law Relating to Trade-Marks, New York: Columbia University Press (1925).

— The Rational Basis of Trademark Protection, 40 Harv. L. Rev. 813 (1927) (Harvard Law Review).

Schechter, *Roger E.*/***Thomas***, *John R.*: Intellectual Property: The Law of Copyrights, Patents, and Trademarks, West Publishing Company (2003).

Schlickeysen, *C.*: Die Anerkennung des Geistigen Eigenthums, eine soziale Frage, Berlin: Verlag von F. Berggold (1871).

Schlosser, *Sarah Mayhew*: The High Price of (Criticizing) Coffee: The Chilling Effect of the Federal Trademark Dilution Act on Corporate Parody, 43 Ariz. L. Rev. 931 (2001) (Arizona Law Review).

Schricker, *Gerhard*/***Loewenheim***, *Ulrich*: Urheberrecht, Kommentar, C.H.Beck (3rd edition, 2006).

Schultz, *E.J.*: Rewind: When Lance Armstrong Rode in the Super Bowl – Back in 2010, Michelob Said Athlete Was Model For 'Beer Drinkers Who Lead Active Lifestyles', Ad Age Agency News, 28 January 2013.

Schwartz, *Arthur*/***Morfesi***, *David*: Dilution Comes of Age: The United States, Europe and South Africa, 87 TMR 436 (1997) (Trademark Reporter).

Schwartz, *Ivo E.*: Antitrust Legislation and Policy in Germany – A Comparative Study, 105 U. Pa. L. Rev. 617 (1957) (University of Pennsylvania Law Review).

Science on the Streets: Charles Macintosh, available at http://scienceonstreets.phys.strath.ac.uk.

Segall, *Karin*: United States, in World Trademark Review, Yearbook 2008: A global guide for practitioners, London: Globe Business Publishing Ltd. (2008).

Seifert, *Fedor*: Über Bücher, Verleger und Autoren – Episoden aus der Geschichte des Urheberrechts, in NJW 1992, 1270–1276 (Neue Juristische Wochenschrift).

Sekicho: An Outline of US Copyright, Patent and Trademark Law, Edition 1.0, Wikibooks, 5 March 2006.

Seville, *Catherine*: Intellectual Property, Intellectual Property, 50 Int'l & Comp. L.Q. 714 (2001) (International and Comparative Law Quarterly).

Shankland, *Stephen*: Apple bumps Coca-Cola to become world's top brand, CNET, 30 September 2013.

Shannon, *Matthew A.*: The Increasing Polarization of the Antitrust Law and Trademark Licensing, 62 TMR 548 (1972) (Trademark Law Reporter).

Shapiro, *Stephen M.*/***Geller***, *Kenneth S.*/***Bishop***, *Timothy S.*/***Hartnett***, *Edward A.*/***Himmelfarb***, *Dan*: Supreme Court Practice, Bureau of National Affairs (BNA) (10th edition, 2014).

Shaughnessy, *Robert J.*: Note: Trademark Parody: A Fair Use and First Amendment Analysis, 72 Va. L. Rev. 1079 (1986) (Virginia Law Review).

Shaw, *Katerina*: Likelihood of Coexistence: A Comparative Analysis of the Interplay between European Trademark Law and Free Competition, 18 U. Balt.

Intell. Prop. L.J. 51 (2009) (University of Baltimore Intellectual Property Law Journal).

Shelton, *Dinah*: Normative Hierarchy in International Law, 100 A.J.I.L. 291 (2006) (American Journal of International Law).

Shepherd, *Steve (ed.)*: Selected Writings of Sir Edward Coke, Vol. I (1600), available through the Online Library of Liberty, at http://oll.libertyfund.org.

Sherman, *Brad*/***Strowel***, *Alain (eds.)*: Of Authors and Origins: Essays on Copyright Law, Oxford: Clarendon Press (1994).

Singer, *Joseph William*: The Reliance Interest in Property, 40 Stan. L. Rev. 611 (1988) (Stanford Law Review).

Skousen, *Mark*: The Perseverance of Paul Samuelson's Economics, Journal of Economic Perspectives, Vol. 11, No. 2 (Spring 1997).

Smith, *Joel*/***Montagnon***, *Rachel*: Master of all you survey?, IP News Flash, Herbert Smith Freehills LLP, 23 November 2012.

Snyder, *Frances*: The Effectiveness of European Community Law: Institutions, Processes, Tools and Techniques, The Modern Law Review, Vol. 56, Issue 1, 19-54 (January 1993).

Somorjai, *John E.*: The Evolution of a Common Market: Limits Imposed on the Protection of National Intellectual Property Rights in the European Economic Community, 9 Intl. Tax & Bus. Law 431 (1992) (International Tax & Business Lawyer) renamed Berkeley J. Int'l L. (Berkeley Journal of International Law) (1992).

Sosnitza, *Prof. Dr. Olaf*: Auslegung des Begriffs "ernsthafte Benutzung", GRUR 2/2013, 185-186.

Sottek, *T.C.*: Proview sues Apple in US over iPad trademark, The Verge, 23 February 2012.

Spiegel & Utrera, P.A.: A Brief History of Trademark Law in the USA, available at http://www.amerilawyer.com.

Sports Career Consulting, LLC: Lesson 8.4 – Ambush Marketing (2011).

Stanford University Libraries: Copyright and Fair Use, resources available at http://fairuse.stanford.edu.

Stefan, *Oana*: Relying on EU Soft Law Before National Competition Authorities: Hope for the Best, Expect the Worst, Competition Policy International, Summer 2013, Volume 7 Number 1, 15 July 2013.

Stein, *Torsten*/***Marauhn***, *Thilo*: Völkerrechtliche Aspekte von Informationsoperationen, ZaöRV 60 (2000) 1-40 (Zeitschrift für ausländisches öffentliches Recht und Völkerrecht).

Stern, *Klaus*: Das Staatsrecht der Bundesrepublik Deutschland, Vol. V: Die geschichtlichen Grundlagen des deutschen Staatsrechts, Die Verfassungsentwicklung vom Alten Deutschen Reich bis zur wiedervereinigten Bundesrepublik Deutschland, Munich: C. H. Beck Verlag (2000).

Stieger, *Werner*: „Kodak" – Eine Momentaufnahme des Schnittbereichs von Immaterialgüter- und Kartellrecht aus Helvetischer Sicht, 10 March 2006.

Stinson, *Judith M.*: Why Dicta Becomes Holding and Why it Matters, 76 Brook. L. Rev. 219 (2010) (Brooklyn Law Review).

Stolte, *Keith M.*: How Early Did Anglo-American Trademark Law Begin? An Answer to Schechter's Conundrum, 8 Fordham Intell. Prop. Media & Ent. L.J. 505 (1997) (Fordham Intellectual Property, Media and Entertainment Law Journal).

Stone, *David*/***Domingo***, *Laura Alonso*/***Groebl***, *Marc*/***du Sorbier***, *Denis Monégier*: European Union, in World Trademark Review, Yearbook 2008: A global guide for practitioners, London: Globe Business Publishing Ltd. (2008).

Stone, *Terri*: Logo Smackdown! Apple vs. NYC: Apple delivered a backhand chop to New York; the city fought back with a crossbody block. Who will win this match of the graphic design titans?, CreativePro.com, 4 April 2008.

Stothers, *Christopher*: Patent Exhaustion: the UK perspective, paper presented at the 16th Annual Conference on Intellectual Property Law and Policy Fordham University School of Law (27–28 March 2008).

Strasser, *Mathias*: The Rational Basis of Trademark Protection Revisited: Putting the Dilution Doctrine into Context, 10 Fordham Intell. Propr. Media & Ent. L.J. 375 (2000) (Fordham Intellectual Property, Media and Entertainment Law Journal).

Straus, *Joseph*: Patent Application: Obstacle for Innovation and Abuse of Dominant Position under Article 102 TFEU?, J. Eur. Competition L. & Prac. (2010) (Journal of European Competition Law & Practice).

Subrin, *Stephen N.*: On Thinking About a Description of a County's Civil Procedure, 7 Tul. J. Int'l & Comp. L. 139 (1999) (Tulane Journal of International and Comparative Law).

Sullivan, *Lawrence A.*/***Fikentscher***, *Wolfgang*: On the Growth of the Antitrust Idea, 16 Berkeley J. Int'l L. 197 (1998) (Berkeley Journal of International Law).

Swann**, Jerre B.*/**Aaker**, *David A.*/Reback**, Matt*: Trademarks and Marketing, 91 TMR 787 (2001) (Trademark Reporter).

***Swartz**, Teresa A.*: Brand Symbols and Message Differentiation: Viable Tools for Product Differentiation?, Journal of Advertising Research, 59-64 (October/ November 1983).

***Swift**, Hester*: European Union, Foreign and International Law Librarian, Institute for Advanced Legal Studies, August 2007 (updated May 2010).

***Taggart**, Leslie D.*: Trade-Marks: Monopoly or Competition? 43 Michigan L. Rev. 659 (1945) (Michigan Law Review).

Taladay**, John M.*/Carlin**, Jr., James N.*: Compulsory Licensing of Intellectual Property under the Competition Laws of the United States and European Community, 10 Geo. Mason L. Rev. 443 (2001–2002) (George Mason Law Review).

***Tanaka**, Yoshifumi*: Regulation of Land-Based Marine Pollution in International Law: A Comparative Analysis Between Global and Regional Legal Frameworks, ZaöRV 66 (2006) 535-574 (Zeitschrift für ausländisches öffentliches Recht und Völkerrecht).

***Tart**, Alana*: Competition: Apple to Equalise iTunes Music Downloads Across Europe, Brussels Brief, McDermott Will & Emery, 18 January 2008.

The Beatles Wiki: Apple Corps, available at http://beatles.wikia.com.

The Bluebook: A Uniform System of Citation, compiled and edited by The Columbia Law Review Association, Inc., The Harvard Law Review Association, the University of Pennsylvania Law Review, and The Yale Law Journal Company, Inc. (19th edition, 2010).

The Coca-Cola Company: Coke Lore: Trademark Chronology, 1 January 2012, available at http://www.coca-colacompany.com.

The Economist: Economics focus – Paul Samuelson: The last of the great general economists died on December 13th, aged 94, 17 December 2009.

The Macintosh: Contact, available at http://www.themacintoshcharleston.com.

The New York Times: Joe Arpaio, Times Topics, 8 November 2012.

The Wall Street Journal: Wegmans, Walgreens Settle Suit Over 'W' logos, WSJ Blogs: In Charge, 26 April 2011.

The White House: About the White House: Presidents – 30. Calvin Coolidge (1923–1929).

Thermos: Our History, available at http://www.thermos.com.

***Thill**, Russell George*: The 1988 Trademark Law Revision Act: Damage Awards for False Advertising and Consumer Standing under Section 43(A) – Congress Drops the Ball Twice, 6 DePaul Bus. L.J. 361 (1994) (DePaul Business Law Journal).

***Thornhill**, Ted*: German cafe owner sued by Apple after computer firm says her logo is too similar to theirs, Daily Mail: MailOnline, 31 October 2011.

***Thumma**, Samuel A./**Kirchmeier**, Jeffrey L.*: The Lexicon Has Become a Fortress: The United States Supreme Court's Use of Dictionaries, 47 Buffalo L. Rev. 227 (1999) (Buffalo Law Review).

***Thurmon**, Mark A.*: Confusion Codified: Why Trademark Remedies Make No Sense, 17 J. Intell. Prop. L. 245 (2010) (Georgia Journal of Intellectual Property Law).

Tiffany & Co.: Apple Paperweight, available at http://www.tiffany.com.

***Timberg**, Sigmund*: The Impact of Antitrust Laws on Multinational Licensing and Franchising Arrangements, 13 Antitrust Bulletin 39 (1968).

Times Colonist: Business school drops use of Apple's forbidden fruit, 1 April 2011, archived at http://archive.is/yEePI.

***Toll**, B.A./**Ling**, P.M.*: The Virginia Slims identity crisis: an inside look at tobacco industry marketing to women, Tobacco Control 2005;14:172–180. doi: 10.1136/tc.2004.008953, available at http://www.ncbi.nlm.nih.gov.

***Travis**, Hannibal*: The Battle for Mindshare: The Emerging Consensus that the First Amendement Protects Corproate Criticism and Parody on the Internet, 10 Va. J.L. & Tech 3 (2005) (Virginia Journal of Law and Technology).

Trends Gadget: Apple Ipad Logo Font From First Production to Recent, 4 December 2013.

Trilateral Offices: Trilateral Harmonization Working Group, U.S. Patent and Trademark Office (USPTO), European Patent Office (EPO) and Japan Patent Office (JPO), available at http://www.trilateral.net.

TSC Staff: Countdown – The Basics of Business History: Nos. 100 to 81, The Street, 19 May 1999.

***Turek**, Morris E.*:

— Ridiculous Trademark Opposition of the Week – 12/06/09, 6 December 2009.

— Ridiculous Trademark Opposition of the Week – Walgreens v. Wegmans, 21 November 2010.

Turner, *Donald F.*: Basic Principles in Formulating Antitrust and Misuse Constraints on the Exploitation of Intellectual Property Rights, 53 Antitrust L.J. 485 (1984) (Antitrust Law Journal).

Tushnet, *Rebecca*: Gone in Sixty Milliseconds: Trademark Law and Cognitive Science, Georgetown University Law Center, 86 Tex. L. Rev. 507 (2008) (Texas Law Review).

Tuten, *Nancy Lewis*/***Zubizarreta***, *John (eds)*: The Robert Frost Encyclopedia, Greenwood Publishing Group (2001).

Twyman, *Michael*: The British Library Guide to Printing: History and Techniques, Toronto: University of Toronto Press (1999).

U.K. Intellectual Property Office: Trademark UK00000341636, available at http://www.ipo.gov.uk.

U.S. Administrative Office of the U.S. Courts:

— Comparing Federal and State Courts, available at http://www.uscourts.gov.

— Court Locator, available at http://www.uscourts.gov.

— Courts of Appeal, available at http://www.uscourts.gov.

— District Courts, available at http://www.uscourts.gov.

— Precedents, available at http://www.uscourts.gov.

— Understanding Federal and State Courts, available at http://www.uscourts.gov.

— United States Courts – Circuit Map, available at http://www.uscourts.gov.

U.S. Copyright Office:

— A Brief Introduction and History, available at http://www.copyright.gov.

— Circular 1: Copyright Basics, available at http://www.copyright.gov.

— Copyright: Fair Use, available at http://www.copyright.gov.

— International Copyright Relations of the United States, 2010, available at http://www.copyright.gov.

— What does Copyright Protect?, available at http://www.copyright.gov.

U.S. Court of Appeals for the Federal Circuit:

— An Act To establish a United States Court of Appeals for the Federal Circuit, to establish a United States Claims Court, and for other purposes, available at http://www.fjc.gov.

— Jurisdiction, available at http://www.cafc.uscourts.gov.

U.S. Court of Appeals: District of Columbia Circuit, available at http://www.cadc.uscourts.gov.

U.S. Government Printing Office:

— About Public and Private Laws, available at http://www.gpo.gov.

— About United States Code, available at http://www.gpo.gov.

U.S. House of Representatives:

— Legislative Activity, available at http://www.house.gov.

— Office of the Law Revision Counsel, United States Code: Popular Names, available at http://uscode.house.gov.

— Office of the Law Revision Counsel, About the Office and the United States Code, available at http://uscode.house.gov.

U.S. National Archives and Records Administration:

— A More Perfect Union: The Creation of the U.S. Constitution, available at http://www.archives.gov.

— Charters of Freedom, available at http://www.archives.gov.

— Declaration of Independence, transcript available at http://www.archives.gov.

— Hawaii Statehood, August 21, 1959, The Center for Legislative Archives, available at http://www.archives.gov.

— The Charters of Freedom: Bill of Rights, available at http://www.archives.gov.

— The Constitutional Convention - Creating the Constitution, available at http://www.archives.gov.

— The First Constitution - The Articles of Confederation, available at http://www.archives.gov.

— U.S. Constitution, transcript available at http://www.archives.gov.

— Visitor Information, available at http://www.archives.gov.

U.S. Senate: Constitution of the United States, available at http://www.senate.gov.

U.S. Supreme Court:

— A Brief Overview of the Supreme Court, available at http://www.supremecourt.gov.

— Biographies of Current Justices of the Supreme Court, available at http://www.supremecourt.gov.

— Members of the Supreme Court, available at http://www.supremecourt.gov.

— Visitor's Guide to Oral Argument, available at http://www.supremecourt.gov.

Uhle, *Dr. Arnd*, in: **Maunz/Dürig**, Kommentar zum Grundgesetz, established by Theodor Maunz and Günther Dürig, current editors Roman Herzog, Rupert Scholz et al, Supplement (loose sheets) (69th edition, 2013).

UK Intellectual Property Office:

— Patents: Essential Reading, rev. July 2011, available at http://www.ipo.gov.uk.

— Trademark UK00001469513, filing date 29 June 1991, register entry date 14 July 1995, available at http://www.ipo.gov.uk.

UK Law Commission: Patents, Trade Marks and Design Rights: Groundless Threats, Consultation Paper No 212, July 2013.

Ungerer, *Herbert*: The Current Competitive Issues, Speech made at the Telecommunications and EC Competition Law IBC Conference, Brussels, 19 September 1996.

Unilateral Conduct Working Group: Int'l Competition Network, Dominance/ Substantial Market Power Analysis Pursuant to Unilateral Conduct Laws 1 (2007).

Unisource Design: The Apple Logo Story – Part I: Isaac Newton and William Wordsworth: Who's really behind the Apple logo design?, Unisource Canada, Inc., 22 March 2004.

United Nations General Assembly: Rio Declaration on Environment and Development, Report of the United Nations Conference on Environment and Development, A/CONF.151/26, Vol. I, 12 August 1992.

United Nations Secretariat: Survey of International Law in Relation to the Working Codification of the International Law Commission, at 34, U.N. Doc. A/CN. 4/1/Rev. 1 (1949).

United Nations:

— Declaration of the United Nations Conference on the Human Environment, Stockholm, 5–16 June 1972, available from the United Nations Environment Programme.

— Office for Outer Space Affairs, Treaty on Principles Governing the Activities of States in the Exploration and Use of Outer Space, including the Moon and Other Celestial Bodies, signed by the Russian Federation, the United

Kingdom and the United States of America in January 1967, and entered into force in October 1967.

University of Chicago Law Review: The MaroonBook: The University of Chicago Manual of Legal Citation.

University of Texas Libraries: U.S. Trademark History Timeline, McKinney Engineering Library, available at http://www.lib.utexas.edu.

University of Washington: United States Federal Government Resources, available at http://guides.lib.washington.edu.

Upton, *Francis H.*: A Treatise on the Law of Trade Marks: with a digest and review of the English and American authorities, Albany (1860). A pdf scan is available at: http://www.ipmall.info.

USPTO, U.S. Patent & Trademark Office:

— Geographical Indications (GI) Protection, Office of the Administrator for Policy and External Affairs, available at http://www.uspto.gov.

— Types of Patents, available at http://www.uspto.gov.

— U.S. Trademark Law, Rules of Practice & Federal Statutes, 6 January 2012.

— Careers: Trademark Positions, available at http://www.uspto.gov.

— The USPTO: Who We Are, available at http://www.uspto.gov.

— About the USPTO, available at http://careers.uspto.gov.

— Examination Guide 2-03, Guide to Implementation of Madrid Protocol in the United States, 28 October 2003.

— Frequently Asked Questions about Trademarks, available at http://www.uspto.gov.

— Manual of Patent Examining Procedure (MPEP), 8th edition August 2011 (revised August 2012).

— Nr. 157, Questions and Answers: New Trademark Application Filing Requirements, available at http://www.uspto.gov.

— Patent Law Harmonization, Office of the Administrator for Policy and External Affairs, available at http://www.uspto.gov.

— Patent Trade Secrets, Office of the Administrator for Policy and External Affairs, available at http://www.uspto.gov.

— serial nr. 70025036, registration nr. 0025036, registered 24 July 1894, available at http://tess2.uspto.gov.

— serial nr. 73120444, registration nr. 1078312, international registration nr. 0870749, registered 29 November 1977, available at http://tess2.uspto.gov.

— serial nr. 73162799, registration nr. 1114431, registered 6 March 1979, available at http://tess2.uspto.gov.

— serial nr. 73193803, registration nr. 1130288, registered 5 February 1980, available at http://tess2.uspto.gov.

— serial nr. 73303406, registration nr. 1225776, registered 1 February 1983, available at http://tess2.uspto.gov.

— serial nr. 73307818, registration nr. 1191895, registered 9 March 1982, available at http://tmsearch.uspto.gov.

— serial nr. 76497338, registration nr. 3776575, filing date 7 March 2003, registration change dated 20 April 2010, available at http://tmsearch.uspto.gov.

— serial nr. 85036986, registration nr. 4277913, registered 22 January 2013, available at http://tmsearch.uspto.gov.

— serial nr. 85036990, registration nr. 4277914, registered 22 January 2013, available at http://tmsearch.uspto.gov.

— Trademark Basics, available at http://www.uspto.gov.

— Trademark Electronic Search System (TESS).

— Trademark Status & Document Retrieval (TSDR) listing for US Serial Number 77179942, available at http://tsdr.uspto.gov.

— Trademark Trial and Appeal Board (TTAB) Manual of Procedure, Third Edition, Revision 1, June 2012.

— What is a trademark or service mark?, available at http://www.uspto.gov.

Vaidhyanathan, *Siva*: Copyrights and Copywrongs: The Rise of Intellectual Property and How It Threatens Creativity, New York: New York University Press (2001).

Valentine, *Debra A.*:

— Abuse of Dominance in Relation to Intellectual Property: U.S. Perspectives and the Intel cases, Federal Trade Commission, Prepared Remarks before The Israel International Antitrust Conference, Sheraton Hotel & Towers, Tel Aviv, Israel, 15 November 1999.

— The Evolution of U.S. Merger Law, prepared remarks before INDECOPI Conference, Assistant Director for International Antitrust, Federal Trade Commission, 13 August 1996.

Van Dan Elzen, *Tom*: History of the Yo-Yo, available at http://www.yoyomuseum.com.

Vary, *Adam B.*: Tiger Woods' new Nike ad features late father asking 'Did you learn anything?' Okay, you got our attention, Entertainment Weekly, 7 April 2010.

Vaver, *David/**Bently**, Lionel (eds.)*: Intellectual Property in the New Millennium, Essays in Honour of William R. Cornish, Cambridge: Cambridge University Press (2004).

Viikari, *Lotta*: The Environmental Element in Space Law: Assessing the Present and Charting the Future, Studies in Space Law, Vol. 3, Koninklijke Brill NV (2008).

Vogelaar, *Floris O.W./**Stuyck**, Jules/**van Reeken**, B. L. P. (eds.)*: Competition law in the EU and the Netherlands: a practical guide, Kluwer Law International (2000).

Vogl, *Dr. Roland (ed.)*:

— US Antitrust Laws, Program in Law, Science and Technology, Stanford Law School, available at http://www.law.stanford.edu.

— US Intellectual Property Law: Trademarks, Program in Law, Science and Technology, Stanford Law School, available at http://www.law.stanford.edu.

Von Ziegler, *Alexander/**Burckhardt**, Thomas (eds.)*: Internationales Recht auf See und Binnengewässern, Festschrift für Walter Müller, Schulthess Juristische Medien (1993).

Vosberg-Rekow: Max Der schutz des industriellen und geistigen eigenthums in den handelsverträgen, J. Guttentag (1902).

Wadlow, *Christopher*: The Law of Passing-Off: Unfair Competition by Misrepresentation, Sweet & Maxwell (2011).

Wahlberg, *David*: Advertisers Probe Brains, Raise Fears, Atlanta Journal Constitution, 1 February 2004.

Walgreens: Company Information, Walgreens Historical Highlights, available at http://www.walgreens.com.

Wallace, *William (ed.)*: The Dynamics of European Integration, London: Pinter (1990).

Waller, *Spencer Weber*:

— Antitrust and American Business Abroad, West Group (3rd edition, 1997).

— Neo-Realism and the International Harmonization of Law: Lessons from Antitrust, 42 U. Kan. L. Rev. 557 (1994) (Kansas Law Review).

— Oliver Wendell Holmes, Jr.: The Judging Years: The Antitrust Philosophy of Justice Holmes, 18 S. Ill. U. L.J. 283 (1994) (Southern Illinois University Law Journal).

— Understanding and Appreciating EC Competition Law, 61 Antitrust L.J. 55 (1992) (Antitrust Law Journal).

Walterscheid, *Edward C.*:

— Defining the Patent & Copyright Term: Term Limits and the Intellectual Property Clause, 7 J. Intell. Prop. L. 315 (Spring 2000) (Journal of Intellectual Property Law).

— Novelty & the Hotchkiss Standard, 20 Fed. Cir. B.J. 219 (2010) (Federal Circuit Bar Journal).

Ward, *Annsley Merelle*: Letter from AmeriKat: James Bond's gun, pre-1972 recordings, ITC patent fun, and Walgreens' "Flying W", The IP Kat, 7 November 2010.

Warren, *Dr. John W.*: Historical Information, Prelude to the New Millennium: Promoting Honor for Seventy-Five Years, Association of College Honor Societies (2000), available at http://www.achsnatl.org.

Watt, *Peggy*: Apple Has No Monopoly on Fruit Trademark, PCWorld, 5 October 2009.

Weatherill, *Stephen*/***Beaumont***, *Paul*: EU Law: The Essential Guide to the Legal Workings of the European Union, London: Penguin Books (3rd edition, 1999).

Wegmans:

— Company Overview, available at http://www.wegmans.com.

— History, available at http://www.wegmans.com.

— Wegmans Logos: Looking Back and Moving Forward, available at http://www.wegmans.com.

Weinstein, *Hal*: How an Agency Builds a Brand – the Virginia Slims Story, Vice President and Creative Director Leo Burnett Company, Papers from the 1969 American Association of Advertising Agencies (A.A.A.A.) Region Conventions, AAAA Eastern Annual Conference, Biltmore Hotel, New York, 28–29 October 1969 (© 1970), available from the University of California San Francisco, Legacy Tobacco Documents Library, Bates Nr. 1002430029/0059.

Weinstein, *Michael M.*: Paul A. Samuelson, Economist, Dies at 94, The New York Times, New York edition, 14 December 2009.

Werden, *Gregory J.*:

— Assigning Market Shares, 70 Antitrust L.J. 67 (2002) (Antitrust Law Journal).

— Initial Thoughts on the American Needle Decision, American Bar Association Section of Antitrust Law, The Antitrust Source, August 2010.

West's Encyclopedia of American Law, West Publishing Company (1998).

Westkamp, *Guido*: The Implementation of Directive 2001/29/EC in the Member States, February 2007.

Wikipedia: Apple First Logo, available at http://en.wikipedia.org.

Wild, *G./**Schulte-Franzheim***, I.-M./***Lorenz**-Wolf, M. (eds.)*: Festschrift für Alfred-Carl Gaedertz, Munich (1992).

Wilkof, *Neil/**Basheer**, Shamnad (eds.)*: Overlapping Intellectual Property Rights, Oxford: Oxford University Press (2012).

Williams, *Gregg*: The Apple Macintosh Computer, BYTE: The Small Systems Journal, Vol 9, Nr. 2 (February 1984).

Willoughby, *Tony/**Smith**, Catriona/**Bravin**, Andrew*: Trade mark surveys: what in-house lawyers need to know, The In House Lawyer, 1 June 2011.

Wilson, *Bruce B.*: Patent and Know-How License Agreements: Field of Use, Territorial, Price and Quantity Restrictions, Address Before the Fourth New England Antitrust Conference, Boston, MA, 6 November 1970.

Wilson, *Susan*: Is Apfelkind's apple a ripped off Apple logo?, Tech.Blorge: Top Technology News, 22 October 2011.

Winner, *Ellen P.*: Right of Identity: Right of Publicity and Protection for a Trademark's "Persona", 71 TMR 193 (1981) (Trademark Reporter).

Winston, *Clifford/**Baily**, Martin N./**Reiss**, Peter C. (eds.)*: Brookings Papers on Economic Activity, Microeconomics, Brookings Institution Press (1997).

WIPO, World Intellectual Property Organization:

— Article 6bis Marks: Well-Known Marks, available at http://www.wipo.int.

— Berne Convention for the Protection of Literary and Artistic Works, available at http://www.wipo.int.

— Berne Convention, Contracting Parties, available at http://www.wipo.int.

— Berne Convention, available at http://www.wipo.int.

— Copyright Treaty, Contracting Parties, available at http://www.wipo.int.

— Intellectual Property Handbook: Policy, Law and Use, Chapter 5 – International Treaties and Conventions on Intellectual Property, WIPO PUBLICATION NO. 489 (E), Geneva (2nd edition, 2004).

— Intellectual Property Handbook: Policy, Law and Use, Chapter 2 – Fields of Intellectual Property Protection, WIPO PUBLICATION NO. 489 (E), Geneva (2nd edition, 2004).

— International Exhaustion and Parallel Importation, available at http://www.wipo.int.

— International Treaties and Conventions on Intellectual Property, available at http://www.wipo.int.

— Madrid Agreement (Marks) (1891) and Madrid Protocol (1989), available at http://www.wipo.int.

— Member Information: United States of America, available at http://www.wto.org.

— Paris Convention for the Protection of Industrial Property, Article 10bis, available at http://www.wipo.int.

— Paris Convention, Contracting Parties, available at http://www.wipo.int.

— Paris Convention, Summary, available at http://www.wipo.int.

— Patent Law Harmonization: What Happened?, June 2006.

— Resources, available at http://www.wipo.int.

— Sekretariat, Interface Between Exhaustion of Intellectual Property Rights and Competition Law, CDIP/4/4 REV./STUDY/INF/2, 1 June 2011.

— State member status (Madrid), available at http://www.wipo.int.

— The Changing Face of Innovation, World Intellectual Property Report 2011, WIPO Economics & Statistics Series, Geneva, November 2011.

— What is Intellectual Property?, available at http://www.wipo.int.

— WIPO Treaties – General Information, available at http://www.wipo.int.

Wittmann, *Reinhard*: Geschichte des deutschen Buchhandels, Munich: C.H. Beck (1999).

Wong, *Kenny*: The IPAD Saga Continues and Rolls Bigger, Mayer Brown JSM Legal Update, 27 February 2012.

Wong, *Tzen*: Exceptions to the Free Movement of Parallel Imports: Does art. 30 of the Treaty of Rome Protect Trade Mark Rights Beyond their Specific Subject Matter, 22(12) EIPR 585 (2000) (European Intellectual Property Review).

Wood, *Zoe*: Gummy bear wins court battle: Haribo victorious as rival confectioner Lindt banned from selling ursine chocolate due to overly similar packaging, The Guardian, 18 December 2012.

World Trade Organization:

— Members & Observers, available at http://www.wto.org.

— TRIPS: Agreement on Trade-Related Aspects of Intellectual Property Rights, PART II – Standards concerning the availability, scope and use of Intellectual Property Rights.

Woyke, *Elizabeth*: Identifying The Tech Leaders In LTE Wireless Patents, Forbes Media LLC, 21 September 2011.

Yo-Yo: History, available at https://www.yo-yo.com.

Zimmerman, *Diane Leenheer*: Who Put the Right in the Right of Publicity?, 9 DePaul-LCA J. Art & Ent. L. 35 (1998) (DePaul University Journal of Art and Entertainment Law).

Zimmerman, *Gordon J./**Zimmerman***, *Colleen Spring*: Canada, in World Trademark Review, Yearbook 2008: A global guide for practitioners, London: Globe Business Publishing Ltd. (2008).

Schedule 1 – 2014 Ranking of the Top 100 Brands*

*Chart courtesy of *Interbrand*: Best Global Brands 2014 report. Please refer to www.bestglobalbrands.com for more information.

21	H&M	+16%	21,083 $m
22		+16%	19,875 $m
23	AMERICAN EXPRESS	+11%	19,510 $m
24	pepsi	+7%	19,119 $m
25	SAP	+4%	17,340 $m
26	IKEA	+15%	15,885 $m
27	ups	+5%	14,470 $m
28	ebay	+9%	14,358 $m
29	f	+86%	14,349 $m
30	Pampers	+8%	14,078 $m
31		+23%	13,716 $m
32	Kellogg's	+4%	13,442 $m
33	HSBC	+8%	13,142 $m
34	Budweiser	+3%	13,024 $m
35	J.P.Morgan	+9%	12,456 $m
36	ZARA	+12%	12,126 $m
37	Canon	+6%	11,702 $m
38	NESCAFÉ	+7%	11,406 $m
39	Ford	+18%	10,876 $m
40	HYUNDAI	+16%	10,409 $m

41 GUCCI +2% 10,385 $m	42 PHILIPS +5% 10,264 $m	43 L'ORÉAL PARIS +3% 10,162 $m	44 accenture +4% 9,882 $m
45 Audi +27% 9,831 $m	46 HERMÈS PARIS +18% 8,977 $m	47 Goldman Sachs +3% 8,758 $m	48 citi +10% 8,737 $m
49 SIEMENS +2% 8,672 $m	50 Colgate +5% 8,215 $m	51 DANONE +3% 8,205 $m	52 SONY -3% 8,133 $m
53 AXA +14% 8,120 $m	54 Nestlé +6% 8,000 $m	55 Allianz +15% 7,702 $m	56 NISSAN +23% 7,623 $m
57 THOMSON REUTERS -8% 7,472 $m	58 Cartier +8% 7,449 $m	59 adidas -2% 7,378 $m	60 PORSCHE +11% 7,171 $m

Rank	Brand	Change	Value
61	CATERPILLAR	-4%	6,812 $m
62	xerox	-2%	6,641 $m
63	Morgan Stanley	+11%	6,334 $m
64	Panasonic	+8%	6,303 $m
65		+14%	6,288 $m
66	3M	+14%	6,177 $m
67		+7%	6,143 $m
68	KFC	-2%	6,059 $m
69	VISA	+10%	5,998 $m
70	PRADA	+7%	5,977 $m
71	TIFFANY & CO.	+9%	5,936 $m
72	Sprite	-3%	5,646 $m
73	BURBERRY	+8%	5,594 $m
74	KIA	+15%	5,396 $m
75	Santander	+16%	5,382 $m
76		+22%	5,382 $m
77	Adobe	+9%	5,333 $m
78	Johnson & Johnson	+9%	5,194 $m
79	JOHN DEERE	+5%	5,124 $m
80	MTV	+2%	5,102 $m

Rank	Brand	Change	Value
81	DHL	New	5,084 $m
82	CHEVROLET	+10%	5,036 $m
83	RALPH LAUREN	+9%	4,979 $m
84	DURACELL	+6%	4,935 $m
85	Jack Daniel's	+5%	4,884 $m
86	Johnnie Walker	+2%	4,842 $m
87	Harley-Davidson	+13%	4,772 $m
88	MasterCard	+13%	4,758 $m
89	Kleenex	+5%	4,643 $m
90	SMIRNOFF	+8%	4,609 $m
91	LAND ROVER	New	4,473 $m
92	FedEx	New	4,414 $m
93	Corona Extra	+3%	4,387 $m
94	HUAWEI	New	4,313 $m
95	Heineken	-3%	4,221 $m
96	Pizza Hut	-2%	4,196 $m
97	BOSS HUGO BOSS	New	4,143 $m
98	NOKIA	-44%	4,138 $m
99	GAP	+5%	4,122 $m
100	Nintendo	-33%	4,103 $m

Schedule 2 – U.S. Circuit Court Map*

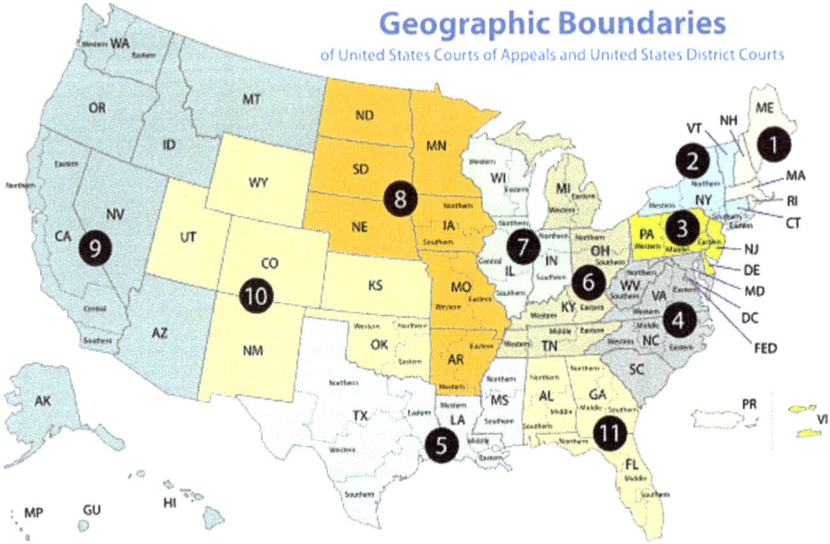

*Map courtesy of U.S. Administrative Office of the U.S. Courts: United States Courts – Circuit Map. Please see http://www.uscourts.gov for more information.

Federal Circuit (Washington, D.C.)	
D.C. Circuit (Washington, D.C.)	District of Columbia
1st Circuit (Boston)	Maine; Massachusetts; New Hampshire; Rhode Island Puerto Rico
2nd Circuit (New York)	Connecticut; New York; Vermont
3rd Circuit (Philadelphia)	Delaware; New Jersey; Pennsylvania U.S. Virgin Islands
4th Circuit (Richmond)	Maryland; North Carolina; South Carolina; Virginia; West Virginia
5th Circuit (New Orleans)	Louisiana; Mississippi; Texas
6th Circuit (Cincinnati)	Kentucky; Michigan; Ohio; Tennessee
7th Circuit (Chicago)	Illinois; Indiana; Wisconsin
8th Circuit (St. Louis)	Arkansas; Iowa; Minnesota; Missouri; Nebraska; North Dakota; South Dakota

9th Circuit (San Francisco)	Alaska; Arizona; California; Hawaii; Idaho; Montana; Nevada; Oregon; Washington Guam; Northern Mariana Islands
10th Circuit (Denver)	Colorado; Kansas; New Mexico; Oklahoma; Utah; Wyoming
11th Circuit (Atlanta)	Alabama; Florida; Georgia

Schedule 3 – Generic Trademarks

Brassiere	The word "brassiere" is a familiar French word, found in all the dictionaries. Quite simply it means "brace", but it also includes the idea of "restraint". In 1905, the Chancery Court in New Jersey found that simply using a well-known French word for the first time in the U.S. would not be sufficient to grant a manufacturer an exclusive appropriation of the word as a trademark.[1595] The court noted that the word had been used in France "for a long time" to describe an article of women's apparel, namely a corset cover and bust supporter.
Cola	In 1886 in Atlanta, Georgia, the name Coca-Cola was adopted by John S. Pemberton for his beverage.[1596] The product was sold under a label registered in the Patent Office, which advertised Coca-Cola syrup as an extract for carbonated beverages possessing a peculiar flavor and the tonic and nerve stimulant qualities of the coca plant and cola nuts.[1597] In litigation, the Coca-Cola company argued that no one should be able to use the "cola" in a trademark, even in connection with a prefix that prevents all confusion with the name Coca-Cola. The reason given was that the word was so closely associated with Coca-Cola in the public mind that any drink, bearing the word as part of its name, will be thought to proceed from the same source. The court disagreed, holding that "the word 'cola' is a descriptive and generic term, open to all the world, which may be lawfully used as part of a trade-mark by competitors so long as the whole trade-mark is not confusingly similar to Coca-Cola."[1598]

1595 *Charles R. De Bevoise Co. v. H&W. Co.*, 60 A. 407 (1905).

1596 *The Coca-Cola Company*: Coke Lore.

1597 *Dixi-Cola Labs., Inc. v. Coca-Cola Co.*, 117 F.2d 352, 355 (4th Cir. 1941).

1598 *Id.*

Escalator	In 1895, Charles D. Seeberger coined the word Escalator (probably derived from the Latin word "scala" or ladder) for application to his moving stairway. He sent it in with his 1895 patent, but the term was rejected by the patent office.[1599] The trademark "Escalator" was registered to Seeberger in 1900. Seeberger was working with the Otis Elevator Company at the time.[1600] The first moving stairway was set up in 1898 at Otis' Yonkers Works in New York. When the unit was moved to France to be exhibited at the Paris Exhibition of 1900, it was labeled Escalator.[1601] In 1900, the Otis Elevator Company took an assignment of Charles Seeberger's federal registration of the trademark.[1602] Otis renewed the registration in 1930. In 1950, the Commissioner of Patents cancelled the registration, noting that the term had become "a generic descriptive term". Although the name originally may have been fanciful (or a least suggestive), the Commissioner found that it had become generic in part because even the trademark owner used the mark "Escalator" to refer to the product generally, rather than only to refer to the specific brand of the product.[1603]
Linoleum	In April 1863 in England, Frederick Walton applied for the patent linoleum for his floor-cloth.[1604] Originally called "Kampticon", Walton changed the name to 'Linoleum' based upon the latin *linum*, flax or linseed, and *oleum*, oil. However, when the patent expired, it was held that the word linoleum "directly or primarily means solidified oil [, and] only secondarily means the manufacture of the plaintiffs, and has that meaning only so long as the plaintiffs are the sole manufacturers."[1605]
Murphy Bed	William L. Murphy lived in a one-room apartment in San Francisco that had a standard bed taking up most of the floor space. Because he wanted to entertain, he began experimenting with a folding bed, and applied for his first patent around 1900.[1606]

1599 *Otis Elevator Company*: A Visual Time Line.

1600 *Borzcik*: Trademark Rights and Their Implementation, p. 185 and n. 1.

1601 *Otis Elevator Company*: A Visual Time Line.

1602 *Borzcik*: Trademark Rights and Their Implementation, p. 185 and n. 1.

1603 *Haughton Elevator Co. v. Seeberger*, 85 U.S.P.Q. 80, 81 (Comm'r Pat. 1950).

1604 *Parsons*: Linoleum: A Chiswick Invention. See also *Bellis*: Linoleum – The History of Linoleum.

1605 *Linoleum Mfg. Co. v. Nairn*, LR 7 Ch.D. 834 (1878).

1606 *Murphy Bed Company*: The History of Murphy Bed.

	The corresponding trademark he used – "The Murphy in-a-Dor Bed Full Size Bed Through Ordinary Closet Door" – was first used in commerce in 1913.[1607] The "Murphy Wall Bed Company" of California came into being that year; in 1918, Murphy invented the pivot bed that pivoted on a doorjamb of a dressing closet, and then lowered into a sleeping position.[1608] In 1989, the Second Circuit held that the term "Murphy bed" described a kind of bed that could fold into the wall and was thus a generic term which could no longer be protected.[1609]
Yo-Yo	The yo-yo is considered the second oldest toy in history (the oldest being the doll). In ancient Greece, the toy was made of wood, metal, and terra cotta and the two yoyo halves were decorated with pictures of Greek gods.[1610] The British called the yoyo the bandalore, quiz, or the Prince of Wales toy. The French used the name incroyable or l'emigrette. However, the name is a Tagalog word (the native language of the Philippines) and means "come-come" (i.e., "come back").[1611] It was not until the 1920s that Americans first heard the word yoyo. Pedro Flores, a Philippine immigrant, had begun manufacturing a toy labeled with that name. Donald Duncan saw the Flores toy, liked it, bought the rights from Flores in 1929, and then trademarked the name "Yo-Yo".[1612] In Canada, the yo-yo trademark is valid, currently owned by Papa's Toy Co. Ltd., for "Bandalore tops, return tops, paddle balls and parts therefor." The registration materials claim use in Canada since at least as early as 1931.[1613] In the U.S., it was declared generic by the Seventh Circuit in 1965.[1614]

1607 *USPTO*: serial nr. 73047062.

1608 *Murphy Bed Company*: The History of Murphy Bed.

1609 *Murphy Door Bed Co. v. Interior Sleep Systems, Inc.*, 874 F.2d 95, 95-96 (2d Cir. 1989).

1610 See *Yo-Yo*: History; *Bellis*: The History of the YoYo; *Van Dan Elzen*: History of the Yo-Yo; and *Meisenheimer*: Lucky's History of the Yo-Yo.

1611 *Id.*

1612 *Id.*

1613 *Canadian Intellectual Property Office*: Registration Nr. TMA232145.

1614 *Donald F. Duncan, Inc. v. Royal Tops Mfg. Co.*, 343 F.2d 655 (7th Cir. 1965).

Zipper	The "slide fastener" was originally a patented invention.[1615] In April 1925, the B.F. Goodrich company originally obtained the trademark for the word "zipper", as a trademark for "boots made of rubber fabric". It had been used as a trademark for "boots made of rubber and fabric, and more especially overshoes made of rubber and fabric," from about 13 June 1923.[1616] In 1930, the Court of Customs and Patent Appeals[1617] court confirmed the Commissioner of Patents registration by Closgard of the word "zipper" as a trademark for wardrobe bags, holding that the "only physical element common to the goods is the type of slide-fastener, and we should be unwilling to hold that this element served to render them 'of the same descriptive properties', they being in all other respects wholly dissimilar."[1618]

Schedule 4 – Treaty of Lisbon: New Terminology & Numbering

The Treaty of Lisbon[1619] *amended* (but did not replace) both the Treaty establishing the European Community (the TFEU, previously known as the EC Treaty or the Treaty of Rome) and the Treaty on the European Union (the TEU or the Maastricht Treaty).[1620] In its restructuring of the TFEU (formerly the EC Treaty), the Treaty of Lisbon introduced some terminology and numbering changes. The primary terminology changes are as follows:

EC Treaty (Old Terminology)	TFEU (New Terminology)
Community/ies	European Union
European Community	European Union
EC Treaty	Treaty on the Functioning of the European Union

1615 For an entertaining history of the zipper patent, see *Bellis*: This History of the Zipper; and *Lienhard*: Engines of Our Ingenuity. For a more scholarly review, see *Friedel*: Zipper: An Exploration in Novelty.

1616 *B. F. Goodrich Co. v. Closgard Wardrobe Co.*, 17 C.C.P.A. 823 (C.C.P.A. 1930).

1617 CCPA is a former United States federal court which existed from 1909 to 1982.

1618 *B. F. Goodrich Co. v. Closgard Wardrobe Co.*, 17 C.C.P.A. 823 (C.C.P.A. 1930).

1619 Treaty of Lisbon amending the Treaty on European Union and the Treaty establishing the European Community, signed at Lisbon, 13 December 2007 (OJ 2007, C 306/1).

1620 For a text of the treaties as consolidated following the Treaty of Lisbon, see OJ 2010 C83.

EC Treaty (Old Terminology)	TFEU (New Terminology)
Council meeting in the heads of state or government	European Council
Common market	Internal market
Ecu[77]	Euro
Court of Justice of the European Communities (often abbreviated as ECJ)	Court of Justice of the European Union
Court of First Instance (often abbreviated as CFI)	General Court

In addition, a number of provisions (of particular relevance to this paper) were renumbered. Throughout this paper, the new terminology and the current (post-Treaty of Lisbon) numbering have been used.[1622]

EC Treaty (old numbering)	TFEU (new numbering)	Topic
Article 23	Article 28	Free movement of goods
Article 39	Article 45	Free movement of workers
Article 43	Article 49	Freedom of establishment
Article 49	Article 56	Freedom to provide services
Article 56	Article 63	Free movement of capital
Article 81	Article 101	Competition: Restrictive agreements
Article 82	Article 102	Competition: Abuse of dominance
Article 86	Article 106	Public undertakings / special exclusive rights

1621 Although the term "euro" had already long been introduced into and adopted by the EU beforehand, the EC Treaty (Art. 109g) still referred to the older "ECU" (the European currency unit) as a generic term. Council Regulation (EC) No 1103/97 of 17 June 1997 on certain provisions relating to the introduction of the euro (OJ L 162/1, 19.06.1997), preamble paras 2, 6 and 7. Regulation 1103/97, Art. 2(1) and (3), ensured that every reference in a legal instrument to the ECU would be replaced by a reference to the euro at a rate of one euro to one ECU. The EC Treaty's use of ECU, however, remained. For more background on the definition and valuation of the euro, see *European Parliament*: Task Force on Economic and Monetary Union, and Council Regulation (EC) No 974/98 of 3 May 1998 on the introduction of the euro (OJ L 139/1, 11.05.1998).

1622 For a full table of equivalents setting out the new numbering, see Tables of Equivalences (OJ 2010 C 83/361, 30.03.2010).

EC Treaty (old numbering)	TFEU (new numbering)	Topic
Article 87	Article 107	State aid
Article 88	Article 108	State aid
Articles 174-176	Articles 191-193	Environment
Article 226	Article 258	Failure to fulfill Treaty obligations
Article 230	Article 263	Review of legality of acts of an EU institution
Article 232	Article 265	Failure to act
Article 234	Article 267	Preliminary reference
Article 295	Article 345	Property Ownership

German Summary
(*Deutsche Zusammenfassung*)

1. Einführung in das Thema

1.1 Das Markenparodoxon

Eine Welt ohne Marken ist nicht mehr vorstellbar. Vom morgendlichen Aufstehen (geweckt von einem Sony-Wecker, Duschen mit Hansgrohe, im BMW zur Arbeit, davor ein Kaffee bei Starbucks, im Büro den Dell-Computer hochfahren, eine Google-Suche durchführen, mit dem Samsung-Smartphone telefonieren, prüfen, ob auf dem Blackberry E-Mails angekommen sind) bis zum Ende des Tages (wenn wir uns mit Freunden bei einem Glas Veuve Cliquot erholen): Wir sind ständig, ob bewusst oder unbewusst, von einer Vielzahl von Marken umgeben, die alle um unsere Aufmerksamkeit werben und von uns ausgewählt werden wollen.

Marken helfen uns, Produkte, die wir mögen, von jenen zu unterscheiden, die wir nicht mögen und deshalb meiden. Sie dienen als Erkennungsmerkmal, das uns die nötige Sicherheit gibt, die richtige Kaufentscheidung getroffen zu haben. Marken übermitteln uns Informationen über Herkunft, Hersteller oder Qualität der Produkte und versetzen uns in die Lage, entsprechende Auswahlentscheidungen rasch und effizient zu treffen. Sie geben Unternehmen die Möglichkeit, ihre Produkte von denen ihrer Mitbewerber abzugrenzen und in Marken- und damit Kundentreue zu investieren, ohne dass Mitbewerber als Trittbrettfahrer auftreten.

Marken sind somit das Kernstück des Wettbewerbs. Sie sind ein Wettbewerbssignal, denn ohne Wettbewerb bestünde keine Notwendigkeit, die Waren eines Unternehmens von denen eines anderen abzuheben. Ein belastbares Markenrecht fördert folglich den Wettbewerb, weil dadurch Verwechslungen oder Enttäuschungen verringert, Suchkosten gesenkt, unlautere Handelspraktiken wie Trittbrettfahren, Ähnlichkeitsstrategien oder Windschatten-Marketing unterbunden und Qualitätswettbewerb ermöglicht wird. Marken vereinfachen damit auch die Kommunikation zwischen Verkäufer und Käufer. Sie sind „ein wesentlicher Bestandteil des Systems eines unverfälschten Wettbewerbs".[1623] Sie dienen

1623 C-10/89, *SA CNL-SUCAL NV v HAG GF AG*, 17. Oktober 1990 [1990] ECR I-3711 (*HAG II*), para. 13.

als „Hilfsmittel beim Austausch von Waren“ und werden „für den Schutz von Handel und Gewerbe als unverzichtbar angesehen“.[1624]

Dem entsprechend hat die Bedeutung von Marken rasch zugenommen, während zugleich ein Markenparadoxon entstanden ist: Unter dem Vorwand, den Wettbewerb durch Abbau von Verwechslungsgefahren bei Verbrauchern und durch Bekämpfung des Trittbrettfahrens zu ***fördern***, ist der Markenschutz durch Gesetze in Verbindung mit aggressiven Geschäftsstrategien von Markeninhabern erheblich ausgeweitet worden. Das wiederum hat zur Folge, dass übertrieben protektionistische und häufig auch unüberwindliche Marktzutrittsschranken errichtet wurden, die zu einer ***Beschränkung*** des Wettbewerbs führen.

In unserem Streben, den Wettbewerb zu fördern, haben wir Markeninhabern neue Individualrechte gewährt und ihre Ansprüche ausgeweitet und tun dies auch weiterhin, ohne für diese Rechte geeignete Grenzen zu setzen. Dies hat paradoxerweise zu einer Unterdrückung von Wettbewerb geführt. Es ist uns nicht gelungen, einen tragfähigen Kompromiss zwischen den persönlichen Interessen (größerer Schutz von Investitionen in den Geschäftswert einer Marke) und dem öffentlichen Interesse (Gewährleistung eines belastbaren Wettbewerbs am Markt ohne Beschränkungen oder Handelsschranken) zu finden.

Schon vor einem knappen Jahrhundert hat der US-Richter Brandeis in dem Verfahren *International News Service v. Associated Press* folgende Ermahnung ausgesprochen:

> „... mit der zunehmenden Komplexität der Gesellschaft wird das öffentliche Interesse nach und nach zu einer allgegenwärtigen Erscheinung. Und die Probleme, die durch neue Forderungen nach Gerechtigkeit aufgeworfen werden, sind nicht mehr einfach zu lösen. In diesem Zusammenhang kann die Schaffung oder Anerkennung eines neuen Individualrechts durch die Gerichte der Allgemeinheit ernsthaft schaden, *es sei denn, die Grenzen für dieses Recht werden klar gezogen und ihre Einhaltung weise gewahrt.*“[1625]

1624 In den sog. *Markenverfahren* („Trade-Mark Cases“) verwies das oberste US-Gericht darauf, dass die Verwendung von Marken „als Hilfsmittel beim Austausch von Waren an den großen Märkten der Welt allgemein anerkannt ist und diese (...) für den Schutz von Handel und Gewerbe als unverzichtbar angesehen werden.“ *United States v. Steffens, United States v. Wittemann*, and *United States v. Johnson* (gesammelt als die *Trade-Mark Cases*) 100 U.S. 82 (17 November 1879).

1625 *International News Service v. Associated Press*, 248 U.S. 215, 262-263 (1918). Richter Brandeis in seiner von der Mehrheitsauffassung abweichenden Stellungnahme (Hervorhebung durch die Verfasserin).

Die vorliegende Dissertation über das Markenparadoxon liefert einen – auch historischen – Überblick über die Entwicklung des Markenrechts in den USA und in Europa. Die Arbeit befasst sich dann auf dieser Grundlage mit den Herausforderungen, die sich aus einer unkontrollierten Ausdehnung der rechtlichen und wirtschaftlichen Grenzen von Marken ergeben. Sie stellt schließlich in ihrem zentralen Ergebnis mehrere pragmatische Grundsätze zur Diskussion, die es ermöglichen können, die widerstreitenden persönlichen und öffentlichen Interessen im Zusammenhang mit dem Markenschutz wieder in ein Gleichgewicht zu bringen.

1.2 Das Problem: Wo stehen wir?

In unseren globalisierten Märkten dienen Marken längst nicht mehr nur als bloße Hinweise auf den Eigentümer, die Herkunft oder als Qualitätssiegel. Sie gehören im heutigen Wettbewerb zu den wichtigsten Vermögensgegenständen, die ein Unternehmen besitzen kann.[1626] Sie sind überaus wertvolle „Assets", die mit Nachdruck geschützt werden, weil Unternehmen damit Kundentreue aufbauen, Marktanteile erobern und sichere Gewinne erzielen können.

Marken werden verwendet, um die „Persönlichkeit" eines Unternehmens an die Verbraucher auf der ganzen Welt zu kommunizieren. Sie gelten als unverzichtbarer Bestandteil einer umfassenden, globalen Unternehmensstrategie.[1627] Marken sind vor allem Informationsträger, Investitionssignale und Instrumente, mit denen man Einfluss erlangen, seine Identität begründen und Vertrauen erwerben kann.

Mit der Zunahme der wirtschaftlichen und finanziellen Bedeutung von Marken haben jedoch auch Fälle von Markenmissbrauch zugenommen. Zu nennen ist hier zunächst der traditionelle Missbrauch durch Wettbewerber, die „unentgeltlich" vom Erfolg einer bekannten Marke profitieren wollen. Sie bewegen sich im Windschatten einer Marke, indem sie ihre eigenen Waren als Ware dieser Marke ausgeben. Damit wollen sie von deren Anziehungskraft profitieren, ohne dafür einen

---

1626 Sie werden als „unverzichtbare Vermögensgegenstände eines Unternehmens" bezeichnet. *Klieger*, Robert N.: Trademark Dilution: The Whittling Away of the Rational Basis for Trademark Protection, 58 U. Pitt. L. Rev. 789 (1997) (University of Pittsburgh Law Review), S. 790. *Drescher*, Thomas D.: The Transformation and Evolution of Trademarks – From Signals to Symbols to Myth, 82 TMR 301 (1992) (Trademark Reporter).

1627 *Klett*, Alexander R. / *Sonntag*, Matthias / *Wilske*, Stephan: Intellectual Property Law in Germany: Protection, Enforcement and Dispute Resolution, C.H. Beck, Lexis/Nexis (2008), S. XXVIII.

finanziellen Ausgleich zu zahlen. Das Bestreben, dieses Trittbrettfahrerproblem zu lösen, hat maßgeblich zur Ausweitung des modernen Markenrechts beigetragen. Insgesamt haben die Inhaber von Marken im Zeitverlauf ihre Anstrengungen verstärkt, um auf aggressive Weise den Rechtsschutz einzufordern, der ihrer Meinung nach zur Aufrechterhaltung des Marktwerts ihrer Marken notwendig ist.

Diese Anstrengungen, die auf einer behaupteten Verwässerung oder missbräuchlichen Nutzung von Goodwill beruhen, finden ihren Ausdruck in wirkungsvollen Einschüchterungsmaßnahmen, die sowohl in als auch außerhalb von Gerichtssälen zu beobachten sind. Auch dies kann eine Art von Missbrauch sein, der zu weitreichenden und vielleicht sogar überzogenen Rechten führen mag. Dominant auftretende Markeninhaber besitzen heute umfangreiche Rechte. Sie stellen sicher, dass ihre Marken – zusammen mit einem großen Teil des Goodwills, der mit diesen Marken und dem dahinterstehenden Unternehmen verbunden ist – nicht beeinträchtigt werden oder dass auch nur am Rande darauf Bezug genommen wird.

Die breite Ausdehnung von Rechten und wirtschaftlicher Macht ist nicht einhergegangen mit einer entsprechenden Festlegung von Grenzlinien – weder im Rahmen des Markenrechts noch durch konsequente Anwendung von Grundsätzen des Wettbewerbs oder der Bekämpfung von unlauteren Handelspraktiken. Bislang hat sich weder im Marken- noch im Kartellrecht ein ausgereiftes und zusammenhängendes Regelwerk herausgebildet, das die Verwendung von Marken in unserer modernen Wirtschaft steuern kann.

Einerseits hat man sich im Markenrecht von den traditionellen Argumenten entfernt, die bisher den Markenschutz begründet haben und die sich gegen unlauteren Wettbewerb und eine Verwechslungsgefahr beim Verbraucher richten. Stattdessen ist man dazu übergegangen, die „Geschäftspersönlichkeit" einer Marke durch ein Quasi-Eigentumsrecht zu schützen, sodass sich Markenrechte aus ihrer „traditionellen Verankerung gelöst" haben.[1628]

Obwohl das Kartellrecht geeignet ist, gegen bestimmte Praktiken vorzugehen oder rechtswidrige, unlautere oder betrügerische Geschäftspraktiken zu unterbinden, macht es einen Bogen um die wettbewerbsbeschränkenden Wirkungen, die sich aus der Verwendung und dem Schutz starker Marken ergeben. Das Kartellrecht ist möglicherweise nicht das am besten geeignete Mittel, um das Markenparadoxon zu korrigieren oder zu „beheben".

1628 *Travis*, Hannibal: The Battle for Mindshare: The Emerging Consensus that the First Amendement Protects Corproate Criticism and Parody on the Internet, 10 Va. J.L. & Tech 3 (2005) (Virginia Journal of Law and Technology), para. 7.

Als Folge hiervon fungieren Marken nicht mehr als Herkunfts- oder Qualitätssiegel *zum Schutz der Verbraucher*, um damit einen gerechten und effizienten Markt zu gewährleisten. Sie werden vielmehr von ihren Inhabern strategisch eingesetzt, *um Marktzutrittsschranken zu errichten*, die Mitbewerber, ausländische Marktteilnehmer und andere Inhaber von geistigem Eigentum abhalten sollen.

1.3 Die Gründe: Wie sind wir an diesem Punkt angelangt?

Diese Konstellation mit neuen, aber nicht vorausschauend gewährten Rechten ist mit der Problematik vergleichbar, mit der sich die Richter im Fall *International News Service* konfrontiert sahen. In diesem Verfahren vertraten die Richter mehrheitlich die Auffassung, dass Gerichte „jedes Bürgerrecht mit monetärem Charakter als ein Eigentumsrecht" behandeln dürfen und dass „das Recht, Eigentum durch ehrliche Arbeit oder das Führen eines rechtmäßigen Geschäftsbetriebs zu erwerben, genauso schutzwürdig ist wie das Recht, bereits erworbenes Eigentum zu bewahren."[1629]

An den Anfang seiner gesonderten Stellungnahme[1630] stellte Richter Holmes die Anmerkung, dass Eigentumsrechte durch Gesetz geschaffen werden. Sie entstehen nicht automatisch aus einem Wert – selbst wenn dieser Wert austauschbar ist. Vielmehr hängen sie von einer rechtlichen Einschätzung ab, dass die Anerkennung eines Ausschlussrechts *erforderlich* ist, um Schutz vor ungerechtfertigten Eingriffen zu bieten. Nach Auffassung von Richter Holmes war es nicht richtig, dass die Mehrheit seiner Kollegen ein neues Recht zum Schutz von Interessen schuf. Wenn ein Schutz *ohne* Gewährung eines Ausschlussrechts erreicht werden kann – *und insbesondere wenn gegen unlauteren Wettbewerb gerichtete Grundsätze angewandt werden können, um das Problem zu lösen* –, war es Richter Holmes zufolge unnötig, zu diesem Zweck neue Eigentumsrechte zu schaffen.[1631]

Dasselbe gilt für Marken. Indem wir eine Ausweitung des Markenschutzes zugelassen haben – auch durch die Einführung „neuer" Rechte, um den Problemen

1629 *International News Service v. Associated Press*, 248 U.S. 215, 236 (1918). Siehe auch *Samuelson*, Pamela: Information as Property: Do *Ruckelshaus* and *Carpenter* Signal a Changing Direction in Intellectual Property Law?, 38 Cath. U.L. Rev. 365 (1989) (Catholic University Law Review), S. 389.

1630 *International News Service v. Associated Press*, 248 U.S. 215, 246 (1918). Gesonderte Stellungnahme von Richter Holmes. Richter McKenna teilte seine Auffassung.

1631 *Samuelson*: Information as Property, S. 392.

des Trittbrettfahrens und Windschatten-Marketings zu begegnen –, haben wir der „Geschäftspersönlichkeit", von der die Marke erfüllt ist, Quasi-Eigentumsrechte zugestanden. Dabei haben wir die Gründe für eine solche Ausweitung nicht ausreichend berücksichtigt und nicht bedacht, ob es bereits Grundsätze für die Lösung dieser Probleme gibt oder wie sich eine solche Ausweitung auf den Wettbewerb und den Markt auswirken wird.

Bei Betrachtung aus einer rechtlichen Perspektive sollte der Markenschutz nie dazu dienen, die *Inhaber* für eine Erfindung oder ein künstlerisches Werk zu belohnen[1632], was traditionell als Grund angeführt wird, um die Patent- oder Urheberrechtsinhabern gewährten Ausschließlichkeitsreche zu rechtfertigen. Statt dessen beruhte und beruht das Markenrecht auf Grundsätzen, die gegen unlauteren Wettbewerb gerichtet sind.[1633] Das heißt, es wurde entwickelt, um *Verbraucher* vor Verwechslungen zu schützen. Durch Patente und Urheberrechte werden Erfindungen und Schriftstücke geschützt, so dass die Patent- und Urheberrechtsinhaber andere daran hindern können, die betreffende Erfindung oder das betreffende Schriftstück herzustellen, zu verkaufen, zu verwenden oder auszunutzen.

Eine Marke gestattet es ihrem Inhaber lediglich, anderen die Verwendung derselben zu untersagen. Sie erlaubt es ihm jedoch nicht, anderen die Herstellung eines ähnlichen Produkts zu verbieten. Die zentrale Frage in jedem Verfahren, in dem es um die Verletzung von Markenrechten (oder um unlauteren Wettbewerb) geht, lautet, ob davon auszugehen ist, dass die Marke des Beklagten beim Verbraucher zu Verwechslungen, Irrtum oder Täuschung führen wird. Ursprünglich war der Bereich, in dem es Verwechslungen seitens des Verbrauchers geben konnte, eng definiert: Das Gesetz und die Gerichte ließen nur eine Verletzung von Markenrechten zwischen direkten Wettbewerben innerhalb einer Branche zu. Heute sind die Standards für eine solche Verletzung viel weiter gefasst und erstrecken sich nicht nur auf „tatsächliche" Verwechslungen, sondern auch auf die Wahrscheinlichkeit von Verwechslungen – ob in einem konkurrierenden Markt oder *sogar in bisher noch nicht betretenen Märkten.*

1632 Obwohl die Rechte, die Markeninhabern gewährt werden, im Wesentlichen jene „belohnen", die in die Herstellung eines Qualitätsprodukts investieren, zielt der Schutz im Grunde darauf ab, eine Verwechslung seitens des Verbrauchers zu verhindern, indem Herkunft und Qualität der Güter garantiert werden.

1633 „Das Markenrecht ist lediglich ein Teil des weiter gefassten Rechts zur Verhinderung von unlauterem Wettbewerb." *United Drug Co. v. Theodore Rectanus Co.*, 248 U.S. 90, 97 (1918).

Da Marken außerdem theoretisch auf unbestimmte Zeit geschützt werden können, ist der traditionelle Kompromiss, der dem Patent- und Urheberschutz zugrunde liegt – die kurzzeitige Gewährung von Ausschließlichkeitsrechten als Gegenleistung für langfristige Beiträge zum Wohl der Allgemeinheit –, auf Marken nicht übertragbar. Die erweiterten Rechte für Marken haben deshalb eine viel stärker spürbare und länger anhaltende Wirkung.

Und schließlich sind Markenrechte – ähnlich wie geistige Eigentumsrechte – von Hause aus territorialer und nationaler Natur.[1634] Durch die weltweite Verwendung von Marken über Ländergrenzen hinweg, jenseits derer andere Gesetze gelten mögen, hat sich die Komplexität des Sachverhalts noch einmal deutlich erhöht. Heutzutage sind die global führenden Marken vor allem eines: global. Ihr Name oder Logo ist auf der ganzen Welt bekannt. Sie fungieren über sprachliche, kulturelle und rechtliche Grenzen hinweg als internationale „Botschafter". Unterschiedliche nationale Rechte geraten zunehmend in Konflikt miteinander und stellen die Fähigkeit nationaler Rechtssysteme und Unternehmen auf die Probe, mit widerstreitenden Gesetzen, Richtlinien und Trends zu Recht zu kommen. Vor allem in der EU wird die *per se* ausschließliche und territorial begrenzte Beschaffenheit von Marken als Hindernis für die Schaffung des gemeinsamen Marktes angesehen.

Wegen dieser elementaren Unterschiede hinsichtlich Begründung, Umfang und Dauer wie auch wegen des Widerstreits zwischen Gebietsschutz und internationaler Verwendung und Reputation bleibt es schwierig, allgemeine Überlegungen zum geistigen Eigentum (die hauptsächlich mit dem Gedanken an Patente und Urheberrechte entwickelt wurden) oder Grundsätze und Beschränkungen des Kartellrechts auf die Verwendung von Marken anzuwenden. Diese Unterschiede machen auch die unterschiedlichen Interessen (aus Sicht der Markeninhaber) und Herausforderungen (aus Sicht der Gesetzgeber) deutlich, mit denen wir in Bezug auf Marken konfrontiert sind.

1.4 Die Folgen: Wohin bewegen wir uns?

Obwohl die Gerichte heutzutage den Wert von Marken verstehen und anerkennen,[1635] gibt es bisher keine systematische oder einheitliche Anwendung

1634 „Der Schutz von geistigem Eigentum ist nach wie vor weitgehend durch nationale Besonderheiten geprägt." *Klett/Sonntag/Wilske*: Intellectual Property Law in Germany, S. XXVIII.

1635 "Was das Warenzeichenrecht angeht, ist festzustellen, daß dieses Recht ein wesentlicher Bestandteil des Systems eines unverfälschten Wettbewerbs ist, das der

rechtlicher Beschränkungen auf Marken. Bis heute ist weder in den Gesetzen zu geistigem Eigentum noch in Wettbewerbsbestimmungen ein ausgereiftes oder zusammenhängendes Rechtssystem entwickelt worden, um die Verwendung von Marken in unserer modernen und globalen Wirtschaft zu steuern. In Abhängigkeit von der aktuellen politischen Situation, der Wirtschaftslage und sogar von dem jeweiligen Land, in dem eine Marke eingetragen ist, schlägt das Pendel bei den Gesetzen und Regelungen zur Verwendung und zum Schutz von Marken mal in Richtung uneingeschränkter Rechte, mal in Richtung einer übermäßigen Kontrolle aus.

Zurzeit klammern die Wettbewerbsbestimmungen und rechtlichen Grundsätze Marken aus der Diskussion von geistigem Eigentum aus – z. B. sind Marken in den USA und der EU ausdrücklich von den Wettbewerbsrichtlinien zur Vergabe von Nutzungsrechten für geistiges Eigentum ausgenommen. Oder betrachten diese von einem irrelevanten oder nicht praktikablen Standpunkt aus – z. B. verweisen die EU-Richtlinien auf die „nebensächliche" Beziehung zu anderen geistigen Eigentumsrechten.

Vor allem dominate Markeninhaber haben diese Unausgewogenheit ausgenutzt und mit aggressiven rechtlichen Schritten nach und nach die Grenzen des Markenschutzes ausgedehnt und in einigen Fällen *neue* Rechte geschaffen, um den Geltungsbereich von Markenrechten zu erweitern. Diese erweiterten Rechte werden die Macht starker Marken noch weiter vergrößern und den Markteintritt für neue Mitbewerber immer schwieriger machen. Allerdings haben wir es im Hinblick auf diese erweiterten Individualrechte versäumt – wie Richter Brandeis es formuliert hat –, „für den Gebrauch dieser Rechte Grenzen zu setzen und Regeln festzulegen und einen Verwaltungsapparat für die Durchsetzung der Regeln aufzubauen."[1636]

Vertrag schaffen und erhalten will. In einem solchen System müssen die Unternehmen in der Lage sein, die Kundschaft durch die Qualität ihrer Erzeugnisse oder ihrer Dienstleistungen an sich zu binden, was nur möglich ist, wenn es Kennzeichen gibt, mit deren Hilfe sich diese Erzeugnisse und Dienstleistungen identifizieren lassen. Damit das Warenzeichen diese Aufgabe erfuellen kann, muß es die Gewähr bieten, daß alle Erzeugnisse, die mit ihm versehen sind, unter der Kontrolle eines einzigen Unternehmens hergestellt worden sind, das für ihre Qualität verantwortlich gemacht werden kann." C-10/89, *SA CNL-SUCAL NV v HAG GF AG*, 17. Oktober 1990 [1990] ECR I-3711, para. 13 (*HAG II*).

1636 *International News Service v. Associated Press*, 248 U.S. 215, 262-263 (1918). Richter Brandeis in seiner von der Mehrheitsauffassung abweichenden Stellungnahme.

2. Die Kapitel im Überblick

2.1 Kapitel 1–3: Marken und die Gesellschaft

Die Kapitel 1–3 befassen sich vor allem mit Marken und ihren Aufgaben in der Gesellschaft.

In Kapitel 1 werden die Grundlagen für das Verständnis der wirtschaftlichen Bedeutung und Funktion von Marken gelegt. Kapitel 1 beginnt mit einer Betrachtung von Marken in unserer modernen Gesellschaft und gibt einige Beispiele für aktuelle „Grabenkämpfe" wie z. B. die Auseinandersetzung um die iPad-Marke in China, um die Präsenz und wirtschaftliche Bedeutung von Marken in unserer heutigen Gesellschaft herauszustreichen. Das Kapitel befasst sich dann mit der historischen Funktion und den Grundlagen von Marken. Dabei wird untersucht, wie sich die Ausgestaltung des Markenrechts weiter verändert, um geschäftlichen und gesellschaftlichen Anforderungen Rechnung zu tragen.

Am Ende von Kapitel 1 steht die Aussage, dass sich die Funktion von Marken in unserer Gesellschaft erheblich verändert hat: Was ursprünglich als Eigentums-, Herkunfts- oder Qualitätssiegel gedacht war, mit dem Hersteller und Verbraucher geschützt werden sollten, hat sich zu einem profitablen und in wirtschaftlicher Hinsicht mächtigen Instrument entwickelt, mit dem Unternehmen eine Fülle von Informationen über ihre Geschäftstätigkeit weitergeben, was manchmal völlig getrennt von den verkauften Produkten geschieht. Diese grundlegende Veränderung der Funktion von Marken, um geschäftlichen, politischen und gesellschaftlichen Anforderungen Rechnung zu tragen, hat konsequenterweise die Grenzen des modernen Markenrechts weit über dessen eng gefasste praktische Ursprünge hinaus ausgedehnt. Marken sind heute im Wettbewerb wichtige Vermögensgegenstände, mit denen viel Geld verdient wird und die zum Big Business gehören.

Kapitel 2 beschäftigt sich mit den rechtlichen Rahmenkonzepten, innerhalb derer sich die Markenrechte in den USA entwickelt haben, und erörtert grundlegende Aspekte, die für diese Rechte heute bestimmend sind. Der *Lanham Trademark Act of 1946*[1637] soll im Wirt-schaftsleben Verwechslungen bei Verbrauchern verhindern, indem es Unternehmen anhält, ihre Erzeugnisse mit unterscheidbaren Kennzeichen zu versehen, damit Verbraucher die Erzeugnisse einer Firma von denen ihrer Wettbewerber unterscheiden können.

Kapitel 2 enthält ferner die Feststellung, dass US-Gesetzgeber und -Gerichte mit der Umsetzung, Novellierung und Auslegung des *Lanham Act* den

1637 15 U.S.C. § 1127.

Geltungsbereich des Markenschutzes drastisch ausgeweitet haben. Manche Experten beurteilen diese Ausweitung sehr skeptisch: „Das Markenrecht, das früher einmal darauf begrenzt war, den Verbraucher vor Verwechslungen zu schützen, nimmt zunehmend die Eigenschaften eines Eigentumsrechts an mit dem Ergebnis, dass ‚Inhaber' von Marken jetzt die Macht haben, verschiedene Verwendungen ihrer Marken zu verhindern – unabhängig davon, ob es bei den Verbrauchern zu Verwechslungen kommt."[1638]

Die Schlussfolgerung legt nahe, dass dieser erweiterte Schutz Einschränkungen hinsichtlich Markteffizienz und Verbraucherwohlfahrt mit sich bringt. Insbesondere enthält Kapitel 2 Beispiele für die zunehmende Verwendung und den wachsenden Geltungsbereich des Markenverwässerungsrechts in den USA, das als „radikale und wenig durchdachte Alternative zum Verbraucherschutzmodell von Markenrechten"[1639] angesehen wird.

Als Pendant zu Kapitel 2 befasst sich Kapitel 3 mit den rechtlichen Rahmenkonzepten, innerhalb derer das Markenrecht in der EU entwickelt wurde, wobei ebenfalls die grundlegenden Aspekte untersucht werden, die für diese Rechte heute bestimmend sind. Nationales geistiges Eigentumsrecht (und insbesondere das nationale Markenrecht) steht in zweierlei Hinsicht im Widerstreit mit den Grundsätzen, auf denen der gemeinsame europäische Markt aufbaut.

Erstens steht das Geflecht aus nationalem Markenrecht und nationalen Markenregistrierungssystemen, das sich in ganz Europa entwickelt hat, im Widerspruch zum Grundsatz eines einheitlichen Marktes. Zweitens gibt es Diskrepanzen zwischen den Rechten, die durch die eigenständigen nationalen Systeme gewährt werden. In dem Kapitel wird weiter untersucht, wie der Vertrag über die Arbeitsweise der Europäischen Union (AEUV) ausdrücklich auf den Schutz von geistigen Eigentumsrechten eingeht (z. B. in Artikel 36 und 345 AEUV), und es befasst sich mit dem Fallrecht, das versucht, die nationalen (und von Hause aus territorialen) Rechte, die Inhabern von geistigem Eigentum gewährt werden, mit den elementaren Grundsätzen des gemeinsamen europäischen Markts in Einklang zu bringen.

Wie die Europäische Kommission festgestellt hat, sind die Förderung, Schaffung, Gewährung, Durchsetzung und der Schutz von geistigen Eigentumsrechten innerhalb Europas und an Europas Grenzen nach wie vor unvollkommen.

1638 *Lemley*, Mark A.: The Modern Lanham Act and the Death of Common Sense, 108 Yale L.J. 1687 (1999) (Yale Law Journal).

1639 *Klieger*: Trademark Dilution, S. 795.

Die EU-Markenrichtlinie[1640] und die EU-Markenverordnung[1641] wurden zu dem Zweck ausgearbeitet, eine „Annäherung“ zwischen dem Markenrecht der Mitgliedstaaten zu erreichen und diejenigen Unterschiede in der nationalen Gesetzgebung der einzelnen Mitgliedstaaten zu beseitigen, welche die Funktionsweise des gemeinsamen Marktes besonders unmittelbar beschränken (oder beeinträchtigen). Somit bilden die Richtlinie und die Verordnung ein „supranationales“ Regelwerk im Bereich Markenrechte und -politik. Mit der Richtlinie und der Verordnung wurden zweierlei Ziele verfolgt: Zum einen sollte ein einheitlicher Schutz im Rahmen der verschiedenen Rechtssysteme gewährleistet werden. Zum anderen sollten Barrieren beseitigt werden, die den freien Warenverkehr behindern.

In Kapitel 3 wird ausgeführt, dass die EU anders als die USA (mit ihrem auf Bundesebene integrierten Markenrecht) weiter nach Wegen sucht, das in den einzelnen Mitgliedstaaten geltende Markenrecht zu vereinheitlichen. Geistige Eigentumsrechte im Allgemeinen und Marken im Besonderen werfen in Bezug auf den in der EU geltenden Grundsatz des freien Warenverkehrs und des Verbots von Handelshemmnissen ein besonderes Problem auf.

2.2 Kapitel 4–6: Marken und Wettbewerb

Bei jeder Ausübung – und sicherlich auch bei jeder Ausweitung – von Rechten ergeben sich Bedenken im Hinblick auf die wettbewerbsbeschränkenden Wirkungen dieser Rechte. Auch wenn zusätzliche Rechte mit der Zielsetzung gewährt werden, dass dadurch der Wettbewerb *gefördert* wird, können solche erweiterten Rechte in Wirklichkeit zu einer *Beschränkung* des Wettbewerbs führen.

Ziel des Kartellrechts ist es, einen fairen und wirksamen Wettbewerb an den Märkten zu fördern, zu schützen und aufrechtzuerhalten und Handelsschranken abzubauen. Dies geschieht durch eine Minimierung oder ein Verbot von wettbewerbsbeschränkenden Wirkungen, die sich aus dem Erwerb, der Ausnutzung oder Durchsetzung von Marktmacht ergeben. Die Ausübung von geistigen

---

1640 Erste Richtlinie 89/104/EWG des Rates vom 21. Dezember 1988 zur Angleichung der Rechtsvorschriften der Mitgliedstaaten über die Marken (ABl. Nr. L 40, 11.2.1989); kodifizierte Fassung Richtlinie 2008/95/EG (ABl. Nr. L 299/25, 8.11.2008).

1641 Verordnung (EG) Nr. 40/94 des Rates vom 20. Dezember 1993 über die Gemeinschaftsmarke (ABl. EG Nr. L 11/1, 14.1.1994), kodifizierte Fassung Verordnung (EG) Nr. 207/2009 (ABl. Nr. 78/1, 24.3.2009).

Eigentumsrechten – einschließlich Marken – entzieht sich sicherlich nicht einer kritischen Würdigung durch das Kartellrecht.

In Kapitel 4–6 wird deshalb die Kollision der Gesetze zu geistigem Eigentum mit dem Kartellrecht im Hinblick darauf untersucht, wie die Gewährung von Ausschließlichkeitsrechten für geistiges Eigentum in unmittelbarem oder mittelbarem Widerstreit mit den Wettbewerbsbestimmungen zugrunde liegenden Einschränkungen in Bezug auf Monopole und monopolistisches Verhalten steht.

Kapitel 4 beschreibt die Konfliktbereiche zwischen Markenrechten und Grundsätzen des Kartellrechts. Stark vereinfacht ausgedrückt gewähren die Gesetze zu geistigem Eigentum bestimmte Ausschließlichkeitsrechte, um andere zurückzuhalten – d. h. *auszuschließen* –, wohingegen das Kartellrecht eine Behinderung des Handels und wettbewerbsbeschränkende Praktiken verbietet.

Grundsätzlich begründet ein Verhalten, das nach den einschlägigen Gesetzen zu geistigem Eigentum zulässig ist, keine Haftung nach dem Kartellrecht. Allerdings sind geistige Eigentumsrechte nicht von einer kritischen Würdigung unter Wettbewerbsgesichtspunkten ausgenommen und können mit den dem Kartellrecht zugrunde liegenden Grundsätzen in Konflikt geraten. Wie im genannten Kapitel ausgeführt, ist es für die Gerichte eine schwierige Aufgabe, zwischen den allgemeinen Zielen der Gewährleistung eines freien Wettbewerbs und der Förderung von Investitionen in geistiges Eigentum eine geeignete Trennlinie zu ziehen. Darüber hinaus wirft die territoriale Geltung geistiger Eigentumsrechte in der EU weitere Probleme auf, da nationale Rechte durch die Errichtung von Han-delsschranken zu einer Aufspaltung des gemeinsamen europäischen Markts führen können.

Kapitel 4 enthält zwei wesentliche Beobachtungen. Erstens besteht sowohl in den USA als auch in der EU ein breiter Konsens, dass geistige Eigentumsrechte (i) nicht zur Errichtung von Monopolen führen; (ii) das gemeinsame Ziel verfolgen, Innovation und Wirtschaftswachstum zu fördern; und (iii) mit Achtung zu behandeln sind, damit durch die Durchsetzung des Wettbewerbs nicht die Zielsetzungen der in Bezug auf geistiges Eigentum verfolgten Politik untergraben werden. Bei der Auseinandersetzung mit Fragen, die geistiges Eigentum betreffen, verfolgen die Wettbewerbsbehörden auf beiden Seiten des Atlantiks allerdings unterschiedliche Ansätze: Die US-Behörden praktizieren bei der Anwendung kartellrechtlicher Beschränkungen auf Unzulänglichkeiten im Bereich geistiges Eigentum einen eher „distanzierten" Ansatz, während die EU-Behörden eher bereit sind einzugreifen und Grundsätze der Wettbewerbspolitik auf Fragen des geistigen Eigentums zu übertragen.

Zweitens gibt es eine Reihe von Faktoren, die das Zusammenspiel zwischen der Gesetzgebung zu geistigem Eigentum und dem Kartellrecht und die

Vereinbarkeit beider Rechtsgebiete erschweren. Beispiele hierfür sind: die Ausgestaltung der Gesetzgebung zu geistigem Eigentum verändert sich; es gibt Zuständigkeitskonflikte zwischen Gerichten und Ländern und hinsichtlich der Art von Forderungen; die rechtlichen Grenzen zwischen verschiedenen Arten von geistigen Eigentumsrechten verschwimmen; und die EU stellt die Integration des Marktes über nationale Rechte.

Kapitel 5 beschäftigt sich mit einschlägigen US-Bundesgesetzen, nämlich dem *Sherman Antitrust Act of 1890*, dem *Federal Trade Commission Act of 1914* und dem *Clayton Act of 1914*,[1642] welche die Anwendung kartellrechtlicher Bestimmungen auf geistiges Eigentum im Allgemeinen betreffende Vorgänge regeln. Ferner wird in diesem Kapitel untersucht, wie Gerichte und Wettbewerbsbehörden kartellrechtliche Grundsätze auf die Ausübung geistiger Eigentumsrechte angewandt haben, und erörtert, welche Praktiken eines Markeninhabers als Verstoß gegen US-Kartellrecht angesehen würden.

Weiter wird in Kapitel 5 festgestellt, dass die USA eher zu einer an der *Verbraucherwohlfahrt* orientierten Sichtweise neigen: Ziel ist es dabei, „die *Öffentlichkeit* vor einem Versagen des Marktes zu schützen". Im Allgemeinen haben die Kartellbehörden in den USA bisher wenig Bereitschaft gezeigt, auf dem Gebiet der geistigen Eigentumsrechte tätig zu werden. Nach der in den USA vorherrschenden Auffassung dient das Antitrust-Recht dazu, *Exzesse* privater Eigentümer zu verhindern, um für einen effektiven Wettbewerb an den Märkten zu sorgen und den Zugang zu diesen offen zu halten.

Die Grundsätze, auf denen das Kartellrecht beruht, sollten allerdings flexibel genug sein, um den besonderen Eigenschaften und der besonderen Dynamik geistiger Eigentumsrechte Rechnung zu tragen. Im Schlussteil des Kapitels werden Aussagen der *Federal Trade Commission* (die auf die Schwierigkeiten bei der Übertragung kartellrechtlicher Grundsätze auf geistige Eigentumsrechte hingewiesen hat) und anderer Kommentatoren erörtert (die darauf hinweisen, dass Fälle im Zusammenhang mit geistigem Eigentum und Antitrust-Fälle sehr schwierige fachliche und wirtschaftliche Fragen aufwerfen, die von Richtern ohne spezielles Fachwissen nicht beantwortet werden können, und dass die Märkte besser mit Wettbewerbsfragen umgehen können als für Kartellrecht zuständige Aufsichtsbehörden).

Kapitel 6 beschäftigt sich mit dem EU-Gesetzesrahmen, der die Anwendung kartellrecht-licher Bestimmungen auf Geschäfte mit geistigem Eigentum im

1642 15 U.S.C. §§ 1–7 (*Sherman Antitrust Act*); 15 U.S.C. §§ 12–27, 29, 52–53 (*Clayton Antitrust Act*); und 15 U.S.C. §§ 41–58 (*Federal Trade Commission Act*).

Allgemeinen regelt. Ferner wird untersucht, wie Gerichte und Wettbewerbsbehörden kartellrechtliche Grundsätze auf die Ausübung geistiger Eigentumsrechte angewandt haben. Es wird gefragt, welche Praktiken eines Markeninhabers als Verstoß gegen EU-Recht angesehen würden. Das übergeordnete Ziel der AEUV ist nach wie vor der Abbau von „Schranken, die Europa spalten".

Das Kapitel befasst sich weiter mit der zweidimensionalen Herausforderung, vor der die EU mit ihrem in Bezug auf wettbewerbsbeschränkendes Verhalten verfolgten Ansatz steht: erstens die Anwendung von Kartellrecht, um den Wettbewerb am Markt zu fördern; und zweitens die Anwendung der Gesetze als einer Art von *supranationalem* Recht, um eine integrierte und in wirtschaftlicher Hinsicht wettbewerbsfähige Gemeinschaft zu schaffen. Im genannten Kapitel wird untersucht, welche Herausforderungen die Gewährung und Durchsetzung nationaler geistiger Eigentumsrechte – und die Bedingungen, unter denen diese Rechte ausgeübt oder ausgenutzt werden können – mit sich bringen, da nationale Rechte die Schaffung eines gemeinsamen Binnenmarkts durch Handelsbeschränkungen selbst innerhalb eines Mitgliedstaates behindern können.

Kapitel 6 enthält die Schlussfolgerung, dass eine konsequente Anwendung und Durchsetzung von Wettbewerbsgrundsätzen in der EU als ein Mittel zur Erreichung eines übergeordneten Ziels angesehen wird, nämlich die Integration des Marktes. Deshalb verfolgt die EU häufig einen Ansatz, der stärker auf Intervention setzt, um die Funktionsweise des Marktes zu überwachen, zu schützen und zu beeinflussen und so einen einheitlichen und integrierten Wirtschaftsraum zu schaffen.

Betrachtet man Kapitel 5 und 6 zusammen, wird deutlich, dass die USA und die EU vor unterschiedlichen Herausforderungen stehen, wenn sie mit Situationen konfrontiert werden, in denen sich geistiges Eigentum und Wettbewerb im Widerstreit miteinander befinden. Wegen ihrer integrierten Wirtschaft neigen die USA in Situationen, in denen der Wettbewerb durch das Vorhandensein bzw. die Ausübung geistiger Eigentumsrechte beschränkt wird, zu einem eher „distanzierten" Ansatz. Dagegen ist die EU eher bereit, in Situationen, in denen geistiges Eigentum und Wettbewerb aufeinandertreffen, einzugreifen, und sieht breiteren Spielraum für Interventionen.

2.3 Kapitel 7–8: Wirtschaftliche und rechtliche Grenzen von Marken und ihre Konflikte

Ausgehend von diesem Hintergrund über Marken, Wettbewerb und den Widerstreit zwischen geistigen Eigentumsrechten und Kartellrecht werden in Kapitel 7 und 8 die Schwierigkeiten behandelt, vor denen Gerichte, Gesetzgeber und

Aufsichtsbehörden bei der Beurteilung der wettbewerbsfördernden und wettbewerbsbeschränkenden Wirkungen der Verwendung, des Schutzes und der Ausnutzung von Marken stehen. Marken sind wettbewerbsfördernd und für einen fairen und effizienten Wettbewerb unverzichtbar. In Kapitel 7 und 8 wird allerdings festgestellt, dass der breit angelegte rechtliche Markenschutz in Verbindung mit den aggressiven Geschäftsstrategien von Markeninhabern (unter dem Deckmantel der Wettbewerbs*förderung*) zu einer *Beschränkung* des Wettbewerbs führt.

Kapitel 7 befasst sich mit dem besonders heiklen Problem der wettbewerbsbeschränkenden Wirkungen von Marken infolge ihrer sich ausweitenden *wirtschaftlichen* Grenzen. Die Art und Weise, wie Marken heute verwendet werden und wie Markeninhaber aggressive Geschäftsstrategien und rechtliche Maßnahmen zum Schutz ihrer Marken verfolgen, bringt erhebliche Konsequenzen und Herausforderungen für die Rechtssysteme mit sich. Der Aufstieg der auf Englisch als „trademark bullies" bezeichneten Unternehmen, die ihre Markenrechte aggressiv durchsetzen, führt zu erheblichen Veränderungen der Wettbewerbsbedingungen, soweit diese sich außerhalb des Einflussbereichs der Gerichte und Behörden befinden.

In dem Kapitel wird untersucht, wie Markeninhaber – vor allem bekannte Unternehmen, die über beträchtliche finanzielle Ressourcen verfügen – mit aggressiven rechtlichen und geschäftlichen Maßnahmen versuchen, den wirtschaftlichen Wert ihrer Marken zu wahren. Dazu gehören u. a. (i) eine penible Durchsetzung von Rechten, verbunden mit einer großen Bereitschaft, Gerichtsverfahren anzustrengen; (ii) die Einleitung rechtlicher Schritte, die keine Aussicht auf Erfolg haben; und (iii) Einschüchterungen außerhalb des Gerichtssaals.

In Kapitel 8 wird die Auffassung vertreten, dass weder die Marken noch den Wettbewerb betreffende Bestimmungen hierfür eine angemessene Antwort bieten. Obwohl die Weiterentwicklung und Novellierung von Gesetzen unverzichtbar ist, um diese an die Bedürfnisse einer hochentwickelten und modernen Gesellschaft anzupassen, ist das eigentliche Problem unser Unvermögen, die Grenzen für eine solche Weiterentwicklung festzulegen (und – mit den Worten von Richter Brandeis – „weise zu wahren") oder gegen die wettbewerbsbeschränkenden Wirkungen solcher Veränderungen vorzugehen.

Es wird postuliert, dass sowohl die Gesetze zum Schutz geistigen Eigentums als auch das Kartellrecht die Stellung von Marken anerkennen und diese Probleme entsprechend bewältigen müssen, dabei aber keiner der beiden Bereiche dem jeweils anderen „die Arbeit abnehmen" kann. Tatsächlich stehen andere bewährte Mechanismen zur Verfügung, die möglicherweise eher als das

Kartellrecht geeignet sind, die wettbewerbsbeschränkenden Wirkungen von Marken zu steuern. Diese Beobachtung ist der Ausgangspunkt für Kapitel 9.

2.4 Kapitel 9: Der richtige Mittelweg

Die zunehmenden wettbewerbsbeschränkenden Wirkungen von Marken und des Markenrechts zu erkennen, ist eine Sache. Zu überlegen, ob und was man dagegen tun kann, eine andere. Bei jeder Lösung müssen die wettbewerbsfördernden *Funktionen* von Marken den wettbewerbsbeschränkenden *Wirkungen* des Markenschutzes gegenübergestellt werden, damit das richtige Maß von „funktionierendem Wettbewerb" gefunden wird.

Ein ausgewogener Ansatz ist – um es mit den Worten von Samuelson zu sagen – „nicht eine Entscheidung zwischen (…) Extremen". Vielmehr können Lösungen darin gefunden werden, „inwieweit im Rahmen der öffentlichen Ordnung *weniger oder mehr* getan werden sollte, um die Ausführung bestimmter wirtschaftlicher Aktivitäten zu modifizieren."[1643]

Im letzten Kapitel geht es um pragmatische Grundsätze, die man bei der Lösung des Konflikts zwischen individuellen Eigentumsrechten und dem öffentlichen Interesse an fairem Wettbewerb beachten sollte, um einen vernünftigen und *funktionsfähigen* Wettbewerb zu gewährleisten. Ein solches ausgewogeneres und ausgereifteres System wäre für Verbraucher, Hersteller und Wettbewerber gleichermaßen von Vorteil.

Im Wesentlichen sind für das Markenrecht und dessen Anwendung durch Gerichte, Gesetzgeber und Aufsichtsbehörden sinnvolle und praktikable Grenzen erforderlich; das heisst, das Markenrecht muss „zurechtgestutzt" werden.

Außerdem müssen die Rahmenkonzepte für Marken in der Gesetzgebung und in der Rechtsprechung weiter optimiert werden, um Gerichte und Behörden zu einer durchdach-teren und ausgewogeneren Anwendung des Markenrechts anzuhalten und so den „wirt-schaftlichen Nutzen" von Marken und des Markenschutzes auch weiterhin sicherzustellen.

3. Ergebnisse

Zielsetzung der vorliegenden Arbeit war es, die rechtlichen und wirtschaftlichen Grenzen der Inhaberschaft und Verwendung von Marken zu beleuchten, um

1643 *Samuelson*, Paul A.: Problems of Economic Organization, S. 70, in *McGrew*, Anthony G. / *Wilson*, M. J. (Hrsg.): Decision Making: Approaches and Analysis (Manchester: 1982), S. 67-86.

Lösungsmöglichkeiten aufzuzeigen, welche die wettbewerbsfördernden *Funktionen* von Marken und die wettbewerbsbeschränkenden *Wirkungen* des Markenschutzes ins richtige Gleichgewicht bringen.

Weiter sollte dargelegt werden, ob und wie sich Gerichte, Gesetzgeber und Aufsichtsbehörden dem zwangsläufig mit dem Markenschutz verbundenen Konflikt zwischen Individualrechten und dem öffentlichem Interesse gestellt haben.

Das Thema der vorliegenden Arbeit wird abschließend in zehn Thesen zusammengefasst:

1. Marken haben eine grundlegende Rolle in der Wirtschaft und dienen dem Wohl des Verbrauchers wie auch der Unternehmen.
2. Marken erfüllen mehrere, sich überlappende Funktionen in unserer modernen globalisierten Wirtschaft.
3. Der Schutz der Marke hat sich deutlich erweitert, um mit den sich ändernden geschäftlichen und gesellschaftlichen Bedürfnissen Schritt halten zu können.
4. Die Spannungen zwischen den wachsenden privaten Ansprüchen nach Markenschutz und der öffentlichen Politik zugunsten eines freien Wettbewerbs nehmen zu.
5. Das Markenrecht hat sich von seinen traditionellen Grundprinzipien entfernt. Vor allem prominenten Markeninhabern wurde erlaubt, den Schutz ihrer Markenrechte in unzulässiger Weise auszudehnen.
6. Das Kartellrecht ist nicht in der Lage (oder ungeeignet), dieser wachsenden rechtlichen und wirtschaftlichen Ausdehnung der Grenzen von Markeninhabern bzw. der Verwendung von Marken entgegenzutreten.
7. Herausfordernd bleibt, die wettbewerbsbeschränkenden Auswirkungen von Marken mit den wettbewerbsfördernden Wirkungen von Marken so in Einklang zu bringen, dass ein richtiges Maß an "funktionierendem Wettbewerb" erreicht wird.
8. Um eine ausgewogene Lösung zu finden, sollten zwei pragmatische Grundsätze berücksichtigt werden: Es sollten erstens einige "gesunde Beschneidungen" bei Markenrechten vorgenommen werden, um miteinander konkurrierende öffentliche und private Interessen effektiver in Einklang zu bringen.
9. Der zweite Grundsatz umfasst die Straffung und Neuausrichtung des exekutiven und judikativen Rahmens, der die Marken regelt. Gerichte und Behörden sollten ermutigt werden, das Markenrecht umsichtiger und mündiger anzuwenden, um einen vernünftigen und effektiven "Verwaltungsapparat" sicherzustellen.

10. Schließlich benötigen Markenrechte wie jede anderen privaten Rechte "sensible Grenzen", obwohl Marken lebenswichtig für einen dynamischen modernen Handel sind. Gerüstet mit Prinzipien der Balance und einer mündigen Sicht auf konkurrierende private und öffentliche Interessen, die dem Markenschutz innewohnen, können wir sicherstellen, dass der "wirtschaftliche Nutzen" von Marken und Markenschutz gewährleistet bleibt.

Schriften zum Medien-, Urheber- und Wirtschaftsrecht

Herausgegeben von Prof. Dr. Georgios Gounalakis

Band 1 Thomas Lang: Immaterialgüterrechtliche Lizenzierung und kartellrechtliche Verhaltenskontrolle. Eine Untersuchung der Reichweite gemeinschaftskartellrechtlicher Eingriffsbefugnisse in Immaterialgüterrechtspositionen vor dem Hintergrund der schutzrechtsspezifischen wettbewerblichen Ausschließlichkeit. 2009.

Band 2 Anna-Karina Bonacker: Der Widerruf von Fernabsatzverträgen am Beispiel der Internetauktion eBay. 2009.

Band 3 Rainer Jürgen Scharf: Der unbefristete Widerruf internetbasierter Verträge. Zugleich ein Beitrag zur Dogmatik des § 355 BGB. 2009.

Band 4 Sebastian Gorski: Effizienz, Wahlfreiheit und Gleichbehandlung? Eine Untersuchung der Einführung von Wettbewerb zwischen musikalischen Verwertungsgesellschaften durch die Europäische Kommission. 2009.

Band 5 Daniel Walter: Die rechtliche Behandlung der Erbringung unbestellter Leistungen nach § 241a BGB. 2009.

Band 6 Richard Helwig: Die Kompetenz der Europäischen Gemeinschaft zur Schaffung eines europäischen Medienkonzentrationsrechts. Notwendigkeit, Voraussetzungen und Reichweite einer möglichen Regulierung zur Sicherung von Medien- und Meinungsvielfalt in Europa. 2009.

Band 7 Bettina Yunis: Alternative Streitbeilegung über elektronische Datennetze. 2011.

Band 8 Andreas Walter: Störerhaftung bei Handeln Dritter. 2011.

Band 9 Andreas Zenner: Die zivilrechtliche Verantwortlichkeit des Abschlussprüfers für den Bestätigungsvermerk. 2011.

Band 10 Kristine Wagner: Die Privatkopie als urheberrechtliche Schrankenregelung. 2011.

Band 11 Ina Lutz: Testierfreiheit und Pflichtteilsrecht im spanischen *Código Civil* im Vergleich mit dem deutschen Bürgerlichen Gesetzbuch. Unter besonderer Berücksichtigung von Immobilienerbschaften. 2011.

Band 12 Heiko Drebes: „Datenschutz“ für Unternehmen im B2B? Schutz der Daten des geschäftlichen E-Business im Spannungsfeld zwischen technisch-organisatorischer und rechtlicher Regulierung. 2012.

Band 13 Heiko Zimmer: Zugriff auf Internetzugangsdaten. Unter besonderer Berücksichtigung der Verhältnismäßigkeit einer verdachtsunabhängigen Vorratsdatenspeicherung. Eine Interessenabwägung zwischen Datenschutz, Strafverfolgung und Urheberrecht im Internet. 2012.

Band 14 Ricarda Leffler: Der strafrechtliche Schutz des Rechts am eigenen Bild vor dem neuen Phänomen des Cyber-Bullying. Eine Untersuchung der Normanwendungs- und Auslegungsprobleme der strafrechtlichen Bildnisschutzvorschriften bei deren Verletzung im Rahmen von Internetdelikten. 2012.

Band 15 Nadine Kristin Keil: Verdachtsberichterstattung. Medienberichterstattung über Straftatverdächtige. 2013.

Band 16 Alexandra Sommerhoff: Meinungsvielfalt und Medienkonvergenz. Die Sicherung der Meinungsvielfalt in Deutschland und Großbritannien. 2013.

Band 17 Christoph Wege: Roman und Persönlichkeitsrecht. Ein partikulardogmatischer Entwurf. 2013.

Band 18 Florian Jäkel: Netzneutralität im Internet. Verfassungsrechtliche Aspekte und Sicherungsmechanismen. Zugleich ein Beitrag zu Kommunikations- und Medienfreiheiten im Internet. 2013.

Band 19 Lars Querndt: Selektivvertrieb und eBay-Versteigerungen. Die kartellrechtliche Zulässigkeit des eBay-Ausschlusses aus dem Selektivvertrieb in Vertragshändlerverträgen und Markenlizenzen unter besonderer Berücksichtigung des Markenrechts. 2014.

Band 20 Catherine M. Manley: The Trademark Paradox. Trademarks and Their Conflicting Legal and Commercial Boundaries. 2015.

Band 21 Arne Neubauer: Internetvertrieb im Kartellrecht. Eine kritische Auseinandersetzung mit herstellerseitigen Vertriebsbeschränkungen. 2015.

www.peterlang.com

www.ingramcontent.com/pod-product-compliance
Ingram Content Group UK Ltd.
Pitfield, Milton Keynes, MK11 3LW, UK
UKHW021828100926
8556IPUK00004B/229

9 783631 656433